Texas Politics and Government

Ideas, Institutions, and Policies

STEFAN D. HAAG
Austin Community College

GARY A. KEITH
Tarleton State University

REX C. PEEBLES
Austin Community College

SECOND EDITION

Longman

New York   San Francisco   Boston
London   Toronto   Sydney   Tokyo   Singapore   Madrid
Mexico City   Munich   Paris   Cape Town   Hong Kong   Montreal

Publisher: Priscilla McGeehon
Senior Acquisitions Editor: Eric Stano
Marketing Manager: Megan Galvin-Fak
Supplements Editor: Kristinn Muller
Production Manager: Joseph Vella
Project Coordination, Text Design, and Electronic Page Makeup: Shepherd, Inc.
Cover Design Manager: John Callahan
Cover Designer: Maria Ilardi
Cover Photo: Copyright © PhotoDisc, Inc.
Manufacturing Buyer: Roy Pickering
Printer and Binder: R. R. Donnelley & Sons—Harrisonburg
Cover Printer: Coral Graphics Services

For permission to use copyrighted material, grateful acknowledgment is made to the copyright holders on p. 506, which are hereby made part of this copyright page.

Library of Congress Cataloging-in-Publication Data

Haag, Stefan D.
    Texas politics and government : ideas, institutions, and policies / Stefan D. Haag, Gary A. Keith, Rex C. Peebles.—2nd ed.
        p. cm.
    Includes bibliographical references and index.
    ISBN 0-321-05274-9 (alk. paper)
        1. Texas—Politics and government. 2. Local government—Texas. I. Keith, Gary. II. Peebles, Rex C. III. Title

JK4816 .H3 2000
320.4764—dc21

                                                                00-040177

Copyright © 2001 by Addison Wesley Longman, Inc.

Please visit our website at http://www.awl.com/haag

ISBN 0-321-05274-9

1 2 3 4 5 6 7 8 9 10—DOH—03 02 01 00

Contents

PART THREE   *Political Institutions*

CHAPTER 8   TEXAS LEGISLATIVE POLITICS   221

PART FOUR   *Public Policies in Texas*

Preface

We have been teaching and participating in politics and government for a quarter of a century. In that time we have witnessed many changes, not only in politics and government, but also in how the subject has been taught. We wrote this textbook because we feel that college students need to learn more than some interesting, but soon forgotten, facts; they need to understand Texas politics and government. We feel that the most productive method of explaining the ideas, institutions, and policies of Texas in this textbook is to provide a framework for understanding Texas politics and government that will help students process new knowledge long after the semester ends. The framework makes the factual material more interesting and relevant for students and gives them the tools that they need to understand changes and trends in Texas politics and government. The framework also helps college and university professors explain and bring to life the excitement of Texas politics and government that we feel in our own teaching.

WHAT'S CHANGED

We appreciate the support, the readership, and the comments we received on the first edition of the textbook. In this second edition (which is also available electronically on the web through http://www.awl.com), we have tried to make changes that will assist both students and faculty in using the book. First, of course, we have updated the book to reflect the many changes in Texas politics and government in the late 1990s. Second, we have modified the framework. While it is still a comprehensive framework, we have tried to simplify some features of it to make it more accessible. Third, we have shortened the book to make it more "user friendly" within the confines of a semester. It still provides a thorough coverage of Texas politics and government, but we have tried to accomplish that coverage with fewer words! We also combined two chapters on state finance and economic and social policies into one chapter—and shortened it. Finally, we have provided more and better photos and graphics to guide the reader's attention to the material.

THE FRAMEWORK

The framework gives students the ability to understand the forces behind Texas politics, government, and political change. We have found that students are receptive to a framework that explains politics, government, and political change in terms of five ideas: individualism, liberty, equality, democracy, and constitutionalism. These ideas constitute a Texan Creed—a core set of beliefs and values that are important to all Texans. Students recognize the importance of these ideas today, and understanding the history of their development helps them make the connection between the past and the present in Texas politics and government. Because politics, government, and political change are distinct concepts, we use different elements of the Texan Creed to explain each aspect of the Texas political system.

Understanding Politics: Individualism, Liberty, and Equality

Individualism, liberty, and equality are central to understanding politics because they provide the goals for government and the bases for the ideological conflicts and struggles that characterize politics.

- *Politics involves a choice between equality and individualism on one hand and between individualism and an ordered liberty on the other hand.* Students recognize that when government promotes greater equality for some people, the individual liberties of other people may be threatened. They also understand that governmental efforts to maintain social order limit individual freedom. The framework presents these choices clearly and relates them to contemporary and historical issues in Texas politics.
- *Politics is explained in terms of four ideologies.* Liberalism, conservatism, populism, and libertarianism are presented in Chapter 2 and are reinforced throughout the text in a way that even students who are unfamiliar with the concept of political ideologies can understand. For example, Chapter 4 uses the ideologies to explain intraparty and interparty conflict in Texas.
- *The framework does not promote a particular ideology.* The authors of this textbook hold quite different views about politics, yet we agree that the framework provides the conceptual tools necessary to enrich and magnify an understanding of Texas politics. Students will benefit from the flexibility in our use of ideology.

Understanding Government: Constitutionalism and Democracy

Constitutionalism and democracy are central to understanding government because they indicate how political goals should be achieved.

- *Our treatment of constitutionalism gives students a perspective on the functions and development of constitutions.* From our treatment of Texas's constitutions in Chapter 3, students will realize that constitutions are a product of politics, that they reflect the changing political values and beliefs of the times, and that they change to accommodate changing political values and beliefs. The presentation enlivens a normally dull topic, giving students an appreciation for the continuing influence of a century-old document and its predecessors.

- *The sophisticated treatment of democracy facilitates the students' assessment of democracy in Texas.* Democracy is defined in terms of the conditions that are essential to its existence: political equality, nontyranny, participation, and deliberation. In Chapter 1, we describe three forms of democracy—classical, majoritarian, and pluralist—that meet these conditions. Elitism, a nondemocratic alternative, is also described. Students are encouraged to assess whether Texas government is really democratic and which form, if any, of democracy is prevalent. In each chapter we discuss how democracy is promoted or inhibited in Texas. For example, in Chapter 8, we indicate how the legislature promotes democracy in Texas, encouraging students to think critically about the processes, institutions, and policies of government.

Understanding Political Change: The Ideal–Reality Gap

The framework describes political change in terms of the gap that exists between the ideal of what people want politics and government to be (equal, democratic, constitutional, libertarian, and individualistic) and the reality of the institutions and processes by which political decisions are made.

- *Political change is explained in terms of four responses to the ideal-reality gap: moralism, cynicism, complacency, and hypocrisy.* In Chapter 1 we explain the factors that produce the four responses. From our experience in the classroom, we find that students quickly grasp the meaning of the four responses and apply them almost intuitively to recent events. Students realize that although political change occurs continuously, the pace and magnitude of political change is different during each response. For example, in Chapter 8, we explain how the Sharpstown scandal sparked a period of moralism and the politics of creedal passion during the 1970s that led to dramatic changes in the power of the Texas speaker of the House and the operation of that chamber.
- *Students are encouraged to assess the effect of the processes, institutions, and policies of Texas government on political change.* Political change is an integral part of each chapter of the textbook. For example, in Chapter 10 we explain the role of the bureaucracy in promoting or inhibiting political change.

We have endeavored to ensure that the factual material is current and accurate, but we have also included historical material about Texas politics and government. To understand contemporary Texas politics and government, students need a perspective on how and why Texas government and politics has developed as it has. For example, in Chapter 14, we describe the 1960s origins of today's school finance policies, and in Chapter 4, we describe the nineteenth century origins of modern party politics.

Our hope is that students who read our textbook will learn not only the "what" and the "who" of Texas politics and government, but also the "why."

More important, we hope that the knowledge that students acquire during their study of Texas government and politics will equip them to understand Texas politics and government throughout their lives.

FEATURES

We have incorporated several pedagogical features in this textbook to make it more readable, entertaining, and informative:

- Each chapter begins with a *chapter scenario,* which provides a compelling story about Texas politics that prepares students for the topics that are addressed in the chapter. The first scenario, for example, explains why college students in Texas are required to complete six semester hours of instruction in government. The interest generated by the scenarios makes the students want to read the chapters.
- Each chapter includes *critical thinking exercises* that ask the student to take the material presented in the chapter and apply policy, political, or ideological perspectives to it, given their own ideas and opinions.
- Each chapter includes a *TexasIndex,* which provides, in a series of brief statements, a perspective on how Texas compares with other states. The TexasIndex helps students realize that other states have different goals and values and pursue different public policies.
- Each chapter includes **key terms,** set in bold face in the text, and listed at the end of each chapter. The key terms are also defined in the *Glossary* at the end of the book.

ANCILLARIES

The ancillary package for the second edition has been expanded to assist both instructors and students.

- The Instructors Manual/Test Bank contains learning objectives, chapter outlines, detailed lecture outlines, teaching suggestions, Web sites, and ideas for classroom activities. The Test Bank contains hundreds of student-tested multiple-choice, true-false, short-answer, and essay questions and answer keys.
- TestGen-EQ 3.0 is a computerized testing system that allows instructors to view, edit, add questions, transfer questions to tests, and print tests in a variety of fonts and forms. The system also allows instructors to locate questions quickly and arrange them according to their preference. Several question formats are available, including true-false, multiple-choice, essay, matching, and short-answer.
- The Student Study Guide, prepared by Albert Rambo of Blinn College, facilitates study learning by reinforcing key concepts and themes in the text-

book. It includes learning objectives, critical thinking exercises, suggested learning activities involving application problems, and review questions.
- The Companion Web site provides additional learning resources for instructors and students. The site, located at www.awl.com/haag, includes practice test questions, a syllabus builder, links to Internet sites, and more!

ACKNOWLEDGMENTS

Of course, we could not have written this textbook without the assistance of many people. Eric Stano, political science editor at Addison Wesley Longman, provided insights, encouragement, and support at every stage of the book's development. To our wives—Pat, Jacqueline, and Sandra—we are eternally indebted for your understanding, counsel, comfort, and encouragement. To the librarians at the Legislative Reference Library, we appreciate your help in securing so many good materials in one place and in directing us to them. To Tom Whatley at the House Research Organization, thanks for sharing your wealth of knowledge about Texas politics and government. There were also many colleagues at other universities and colleges in Texas who reviewed the manuscript at various stages of its development and whose comments and suggestions were instrumental in improving the final manuscript. We are especially grateful to: Valentine J. Belfiglio, Texas Woman's University; Nancy Bond, Ranger College; J. Terry Booker, Kilgore College; James Brown, Southern Methodist University; Jim Carter, Sam Houston State University; Jeremy Curtoys, Tarleton State University; Joel Franke, Blinn College; Ernest Wayne Frederickson, Del Mar College; William Hoffman, Del Mar College; David Ligon, Tyler Junior College; Gary Lipscomb, Texas A&M; Thomas R. Myers, Baylor University; Mary Alice Nye, University of North Texas; Patricia Parent, Southwest Texas State University; James Perkins, San Antonio College; Gregory Powell, Kilgore College; James W. Riddlesperger, Texas Christian University; Frank J. Rohmer, Austin College; Arturo Vega, University of Texas–San Antonio; and Neal Wise, St. Edward's University. For the second edition, we gratefully acknowledge the assistance of: Jeremy Curtoys, Ranger College; Gary E. Lipscomb, Texas A&M University—Kingsville; and Arturo Vega, University of Texas—San Antonio.

Of course, we assume full responsibility for any errors of omission or commission that remain.

Stefan D. Haag, Gary A. Keith, Rex C. Peebles, Spring 2000

Studying Texas Politics and Government

★ Scenario: The Government Requirement for College Students

Some of you, we hope, are taking a course in Texas politics and government because you find politics fascinating. Most of you, however, are really taking this course because the Texas legislature requires every student enrolled in a public institution of higher education in Texas to complete six semester hours of instruction in government or political science as a graduation requirement. How did this requirement come about? Who was responsible for the legislation? What was the legislature's intent?

The current requirement that you are obliged to follow was created in fits and starts and has evolved a great deal since the late 1920s. In 1929, the 41st Texas Legislature passed a bill that established sixth-and seventh-grade history and civil-government courses on patriotism and the duties of citizenship. Also, the bill required courses in the United States Constitution and the current Texas Constitution for high school and college students and exams on both constitutions.

In its final version—the one that actually passed the legislature—the requirement for studying "patriotism and the duties of a citizen" was deleted.

The law must have created a storm of controversy because the legislature revisited the issue three times during the next year. Each change in the legislation involved the effective date of the requirement so that students who had already started their college educations were not prevented from graduating on schedule.

For several years, there were no more changes or amendments, and the issue seemed resolved. However, in 1937, the legislature passed another bill, sponsored by Representative A. P. Cagle, who was also chair of the Baylor University Political Science Department, which specified that *any* six semester hours of study in American government—not just studying the U.S. and Texas Constitutions—would fulfill the college requirement. However, the bill was amended so that no student could graduate without a total of six semester hours in Texas and American government. Again, the law resulted in problems for many students, forcing the legislature to adopt a measure ensuring that the bill would not apply to students who had enrolled prior to September 1, 1937.

More changes followed. In 1939, students were allowed to substitute Reserve Officer Training Corps (ROTC) for one of the two required courses. In 1955, the legislature added a new requirement for six semester hours of history, supposedly because of a "disturbing lack of knowledge" by students. In 1995, students were allowed to meet the requirement by passing an examination rather than taking government classes.

Thus, an initial attempt to provide citizenship training in the public schools was expanded numerous times over many years to include six semester hours of government and six semester hours of history in college. Almost certainly, the law will be amended again in the future.

Not surprisingly, this requirement still creates concerns for some students. Although the law as written may seem straightforward or obvious, it has been interpreted historically in two different ways, both of which meet the obligations of the law. At about half of the state's universities and colleges, the requirement is met by offering students one three-hour course in Texas state and local government and a second three-hour course in United States government—a format commonly called the "Texas A&M method." The other half of the universities and colleges offer six semester hours of instruction, usually in two courses, that covers United States government and Texas state and local government in both classes—a format called the "University of Texas method." Unfortunately, some students run into problems because of these two interpretations.

For many students, the government requirement is met during the first two years of college. Increasingly, students in Texas and other states are beginning their college careers in community or junior colleges and then transferring to four-year institutions. Thus, if you take one government course at one institution, transfer to a different institution, and then take a second government course, you may find, when applying for graduation, that you haven't met the legislative requirement and can't graduate because the second school interpreted the law differently than did the first. You're then stuck fulfilling the second school's requirement.

The legislative requirement for six semester hours of instruction in government affects Texas college and university students such as these students at the University of Texas at Austin.

This example, which affects each of you enrolled in a public college or university, demonstrates in one small way the complexity, effects, and evolution of government actions. Your awareness of government and politics will increase whenever you secure a job, purchase a home, have children, or settle in a community, and governmental and political decisions will certainly change over your lifetime. Therefore, it is important for you to learn not only what decisions governments have made but also how and why they have made those decisions, how and why politics and government change, and how you can influence those decisions. ★

INTRODUCTION

This chapter provides a framework for understanding and analyzing Texas politics and government. Without a framework, a person's knowledge of politics and government is limited to a set of unrelated specific facts, which cannot provide a real understanding of government and politics. For example, a person may know that Texas was a one-party Democratic state for the nineteenth and much of the twentieth centuries and that only since the mid-1980s has the Republican Party posed a real challenge to Democratic Party dominance. Without a framework, however, a person will not understand how that one-party system and the rise of the Republican challenge has affected Texas politics; political processes, such as campaigns and elections; government institutions, such as the legislative and executive branches; and the extent and direction of political change. A good framework, on the other hand, pulls together those facts and places them in a meaningful context. Therefore, it is important to have a framework for analyzing the political system in Texas, the United States, or any state or nation.

The framework that we use throughout this textbook explains (a) the history of Texas politics and government, (b) how current Texas politics and government differ from their historical antecedents, and (c) the reasons that Texas politics and government changed. The use of our framework allows a person to gain an appreciation for Texas's political past, to comprehend contemporary Texas politics, and to understand how and why Texas politics and government developed as they did.

In this chapter, we first define and contrast the concepts of politics and government. After we explain the distinction between these two concepts, we introduce a core set of five ideas, which constitutes the foundation for our framework and which we use to analyze and explain politics, government, and political change in Texas. The different meanings that people give to these core ideas and the relative importance that people attach to these ideas are the sources for changes in politics and government. The extent and speed of political change depends on how closely the society's institutions mirror the core set of ideas.

POLITICS AND GOVERNMENT

It makes sense to say that if you want to understand how and why governments make decisions, you should study the nature and processes of politics and government. What do those words mean? There is an important distinction between politics and government. **Politics** is "the authoritative allocation of values for a society," which just means that politics involves the distribution of important things in a society.[1] In other words, in every society, there are things, both material (e.g., food, clothing, cars, and money) and nonmaterial (e.g., influence, respect, and power), that are valued, and because these things are scarce, they are not available to everyone in the society. Thus, politics involves the distribution of these valued things to members of the society, and it includes private as well as public, or government, decisions.

For example, when General Motors executives decided to close an automobile assembly plant that produced large automobiles, they had to choose between a

Te★as*Index*

Measures of Democracy in the States

Precentage of Voting-Age Population Registered (1990s)
Texas—69.2
California—66.7
New York—69.2
Florida—65.6
Average Voter Turnout (1992, 1996, 1998)
Texas—38.8
California—42.8
New York—45.0
Florida—44.4
Index of Party Competition (1990s)
Texas—53.2
California—55.4
New York—50.7
Florida—49.3

plant in Michigan and one in Texas. This was surely politics, even though the decision was made by a private corporation, not a government body. On the other hand, the decision by Governor Ann Richards to use the resources of government to persuade General Motors to keep the Texas plant open is also politics, but this decision involves government.

Although government obviously does not make all of the political decisions in our society, given its ability to force compliance with its decisions, government does make many of those allocation decisions. **Government** consists of those institutions and processes that make public policy for a society. **Public policy** is any government decision. The **institutions** of government consist of the structures (legislature, courts, and executive agencies) that make those decisions. Of course, in passing laws, such as the requirement for six hours of instruction in government, the legislature is making public policy. However, the interpretation of the law by colleges and universities is also public policy. **Processes** include the ways that these decisions are made, as well as the procedures whereby you and other Texans can influence those decisions. The method of selecting trustees for a college or university, for instance, constitutes a political process.

Politics and government are essential concepts in our framework. In the next section, we identify the five ideas that we use to explain politics and government in Texas.

Critical Thinking Exercise: Think about the difference between politics and government. Politics, because it involves the distribution of important things, is a struggle. Conflict characterizes politics. What characterizes government? Is conflict also the norm, or is it consensus?

THE CENTRAL ROLE OF IDEAS: THE AMERICAN CREED

Of course, there are many ways to study politics and government. The method we have chosen emphasizes the central role of ideas. Political ideas, especially when they are elevated to ideals, as they are in America, exert a dominant influence on politics and government. We realize that politics and government are complex, and their study can be confusing. One of our goals, though, is to present the complexity of Texas politics and government in a manner that allows you to make sense of it (Figure 1.1). As you read subsequent chapters and learn how Texas politics and government work, you may find it helpful to refer to Figure 1.1. The remainder of this chapter is devoted to describing the approach we use throughout this textbook.

America is unique among nations because it was built on a set of ideas. Foreign visitors to America, from the eighteenth century to the present, have acknowledged that fact. As one political scientist has explained, "Americans worried and wondered about their basic ideas and institutions . . . , and they do so today in a somewhat different but nonetheless intense fashion, because the American nation has no substantial existence apart from these ideas and institutions. The United States isn't, as most countries are, based on a particular ethnicity: rather it is one erected upon and around a political philosophy."[2]

America was built on the ideas of **individualism, liberty, equality, constitutionalism,** and **democracy.** These five ideas make up the **American Creed** and have received strong and consistent support from Americans since the late eighteenth or early nineteenth century.[3] As we discuss in Chapter 2, these ideas were carried to Texas by early settlers. While other ideas that have been important can be identified, these five ideas have endured because they have consistently performed important functions for Americans, both providing a national identity and limiting government's authority. Americans, immigrating from many nations and bringing with them diverse cultures, created a set of ideas to forge a common bond, to define themselves to the world, and to limit government's authority, and these same ideas can be used to understand politics, government, and political change. Three of these ideas (individualism, liberty, and equality) are used to analyze politics, and two of the ideas (democracy and constitutionalism) are used to analyze government.

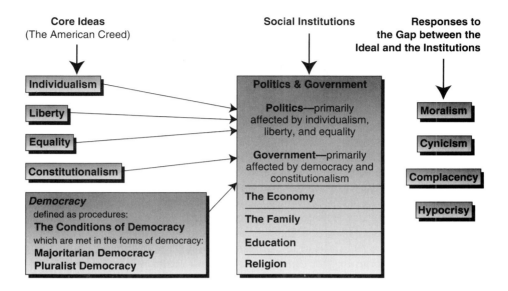

Figure 1.1   Studying Texas Politics and Government: A Framework for Analysis
The framework identifies the concepts that are necessary to analyze politics, government, and political change. The core ideas of the American political culture (individualism, liberty, equality, constitutionalism, and democracy) are the bases for politics and government. Americans attempt to incorporate all five ideas in their social institutions (politics and government, economy, family, education, and religion). Politics primarily involves the ideas of individualism, liberty, and equality. Government primarily involves the ideas of democracy and constitutionalism. The source for political change is the gap between what America should be (the ideal of a full incorporation of the five ideas) and what America is (the failure of American institutions to incorporate all five ideas). The four responses to the ideal-reality gap determine the rate (fast or slow) and extent (comprehensive or piecemeal) of political change.

> **Critical Thinking Exercise:**   The ideas of the American Creed provide a national identity—a basis for nationalism. Are these ideas as important as they once were or is the American national identity based on other characteristics now? How would you justify your answer?

ANALYZING POLITICS

The ideas of individualism, liberty, and equality are most relevant to an analysis of politics because they provide the goals for government. In America as a whole and Texas in particular, there is strong support for limited government, and people must often be convinced that government authority is being used to accomplish important ends before they will accept it.[4] That is, authority must be used to preserve individualism, ensure liberty, or promote equality. However, these terms have different connotations for Americans in general and for Texans in particular, so using them to understand and analyze politics requires an understanding of each idea.

Individualism

Individualism is the most important value for Texans and other Americans and is the source for the other political values of liberty and equality. As a component of the American Creed, individualism confirms the worth of each human being, regardless of social status, income, or heritage. As a political value, individualism grants each person the right to pursue life, liberty, and property, free from the limits of social institutions. Carried to the extreme, individualism accepts no authority over the individual, promoting complete individual freedom. Of course, most Texans and other Americans recognize that a society could not be created and maintained without some limits on individualism. However, at the core of the idea of individualism is the belief that individual concerns and actions are central and much more valuable than group or community concerns. Thus, when Texas passed a law called the "open shop" law, which allows each employee to decide individually whether to join a labor union, that expressed the high priority that Texans place on individualism.

Liberty

Like individualism, liberty relates to individual freedom in that liberty exists when people are permitted by government, as much as possible, to make their own choices. Whereas individualism calls for complete freedom from any restraints, liberty places limits on government. Accepting the need for some restrictions in order to create and maintain a society, liberty allows some government interference. People disagree about the amount of liberty that is acceptable. Some people maintain that government should place only those restrictions on individual liberty that are absolutely necessary to maintain the public order. Others, however, view the protection of social order, in the broad sense of maintaining traditional social values, as so important that they will allow much greater restrictions on individual liberties to protect those values.

When Gregory Lee Johnson burned a United States flag in Dallas, Texas, during the 1984 Republican Convention, he was arrested and convicted under a Texas law that prohibited flag burning as an imminent threat to public safety. Johnson argued that his action was an expression of political speech, protected by the United States and Texas Constitutions. The Texas Court of Criminal Appeals and the United States Supreme Court overturned Johnson's conviction, stating that a person should be free to express political viewpoints unless the expression of these views poses a serious threat to the safety of others. The appeals courts found no such threat in Johnson's action. Public opinion polls, however, indicated that a majority of Texans disagreed with the Supreme Court's decision and would allow greater restrictions on political expression (see Chapter 6). As this example indicates, the protection of individual liberties from government infringement is an important part of the United States and Texas Constitutions (see Chapters 3 and 13).

Equality

As the most recent component of the American Creed, equality has posed the greatest problem for Texans and other Americans. Equality has at least three different meanings. For some Americans, equality means political equality—each person's vote should count equally, or "one person, one vote." Efforts to extend the right to vote to women and ethnic minorities during the nineteenth and twentieth centuries promoted political equality. For others, however, equality means economic equality—each person should have approximately the same wealth. Supporters of an economic definition of equality maintain that political equality is impossible without greater economic equality, and they support changes in the tax structure that would more equitably distribute the tax burden in Texas (see Chapter 14). A final definition advocates social equality, so that each person is accorded the same status or position in society, as reflected in efforts to end "hate crimes" against certain ethnic minorities or against homosexuals.

How people view the government's actions in promoting the ideas of individualism, liberty, and equality depends on the relative importance of the ideas. In Chapter 2, we describe four ideologies based on the relative importance of the ideas when they are in conflict. Throughout the remaining chapters of the textbook, we describe and analyze Texas politics in terms of a Texan Creed and the four political ideologies we describe in Chapter 2. First, however, we explain how we plan to analyze Texas government.

> **Critical Thinking Exercise:**   The analysis of politics requires an understanding of the relative importance of three ideas: individualism, liberty, and equality. Why can't all three ideas be achieved? Which idea is most important to you?

ANALYZING GOVERNMENT

Of the five ideas of the American Creed, two ideas—constitutionalism and democracy—are especially relevant in analyzing Texas and United States government. Both ideas place limits on the scope of political authority by defining how government can achieve its goals. Nonetheless, democracy and constitutionalism are complex concepts that have meant different things at different times in history.

Democracy

Democracy, as a theory and form of government, dates from the ancient Greek city-states. Most simply, it means that the people rule. However, in its theoretical and practical evolution, democracy has come to assume a variety of forms, principles, and values, not all of which are consistent with each other.

By the mid-twentieth century, debates over the meaning of democracy had been resolved in favor of a definition of democracy in terms of the procedures for constituting government.[5] Consequently, we adopt a procedural definition of democracy that focuses on how government decisions are made, who participates in those decisions, and how much weight is assigned to each participant. The degree of democracy in Texas will be determined by how open and inclusive the methods of governmental decision making are, how many or few participants are involved in those decisions, and how equal or unequal the participants are. In other words, democracy requires certain conditions.

Conditions of Democracy   Democracy requires that the institutions of government meet four conditions: *political equality, nontyranny, participation,* and *deliberation.*[6] Each of these **conditions of democracy** requires some explanation.

- **Political equality** requires that each citizen's preferences count equally. In a formal sense, this means that each person has the same number of votes. For example, each person's vote in an election of public officials or in a referendum must count the same. A voting procedure that violates this principle would be undemocratic.

- **Nontyranny** requires that government policy not infringe on the fundamental rights of any member of the society. For example, freedom of religion—a fundamental right—must extend to all Texans. To satisfy this condition, every member of the society must be provided the same protections, regardless of socioeconomic status, ethnicity, or religion. The institutional protections, of course, must prevent tyranny by majorities, as well as by minorities. Institutional protections are usually provided in a constitution (discussed later).

- **Participation** requires that a significant percentage of the adult population is engaged in politics and government. Of course, there are many forms of political participation (see Chapter 7), ranging from voting to organizing social movements. For a government to be democratic, however, means that the forms are not only available, but that the citizens use them to influence public policies and political procedures. Because of the precipitous decline in voter turnout rates in Texas between the late 1890s and 1910, Texans became less participatory and, consequently, less democratic.

- **Deliberation** requires a discussion of the issues or candidates so that alternatives can be considered before a decision is reached. Thinking seriously and fully about public issues or candidates for public office is a requirement for meeting this condition. As political scientist James S. Fishkin notes, "Political equality without deliberation is not of much use, for it amounts to nothing more than power without opportunity to think about how that power ought to be exercised."[7] Issue forums and candidate debates constitute efforts to meet this condition.

Forms of Democracy: Classical, Majoritarian, and Pluralist Ideally, all four conditions—political equality, nontyranny, participation, and deliberation—should be met in a democracy. However, the reality of government institutions usually involves a trade-off so that all four conditions may not be either met or met equally well. For example, institutional processes that promote political equality and participation may reduce the opportunity for deliberation by providing for direct votes without allowing or requiring a full discussion of the issues or candidates. The use of primary elections to nominate candidates for public office, which promotes political equality by expanding the opportunity for participation in the nomination process and by counting each participant's vote equally, has been criticized on this count.[8] Nevertheless, the goal is to form a democratic government that satisfies all four conditions. Historically, there have been several forms created in an attempt to achieve these conditions.

Classical democracy promotes individual, direct participation in those decisions that affect one's life. Participation is valued both because it develops the individual and because it builds a commitment to the political system and its decisions. Also, classical democratic theory expands the scope of democratic decision making to include social, economic, and family decisions.[9] In contemporary Texas, with more than 20 million residents, making political decisions according to the principles of direct democracy would seem impossible. Consider even the feasibility of direct democracy in any large metropolitan area in Texas. In a direct democracy, every citizen would be allowed to debate and vote on every issue that came before the city's government. If only 10 percent of the citizens in a fairly large city wished to debate an issue, city council meetings would become incredibly long, bringing the policy process to a standstill. Consequently, in populous societies, two forms of democracy are considered more plausible: majoritarian democracy and pluralist democracy.

Majoritarian democracy refers to a form of democracy in which the majority rules. It is probably the form of democracy that most people think of when asked to define democracy. Majoritarian democracy emphasizes the formation and adoption of government policy by a majority of its citizens, either through a direct vote or through elected representatives. Whether policy is made through a direct vote or through elected officials, the majoritarian principle requires that public policy reflect the wishes of a majority of the people. Without some protections for minorities, however, the majoritarian principle poses a major problem. What if the majority desires a public policy that is detrimental to a minority, or in an extreme case, subjects the minority to persecution? Should the policy be allowed in a democracy? For example, is slavery justifiable in a democracy?

Another fundamental value in majoritarian democracy is political equality. Formal political equality means that each person's vote on issues or candidates counts equally. At least in the voting booth and in the tally of those votes, everyone is equal, regardless of how rich or poor one is, how famous or unknown, how educated or ignorant. Also, majoritarian democracy's commitment to political equality prevents the majority from stripping a minority of its fundamental political rights, such as the right to engage in political activity and to attempt to become or to influence the majority.

The institutional implications of majoritarian democracy include the centralization of authority and of political processes. The centralization of authority is favored because majorities should, according to this form of democracy, be based on the widest possible constituency. To represent the broadest constituency, political authority needs to be unified in one office or, if that is not acceptable, in as few offices as possible. Thus, a majoritarian democracy would feature a single executive, such as the presidency in the U.S. political system, rather than a plural executive, such as now exists in Texas. The same is true of political processes. Thus, government decisions need to be based on as broad a consensus as possible because the more centralized the political process, the broader the political consensus, and the more majoritarian the result. For example, in Texas, if the decision-making process is centralized at the state level, public policy is more likely to reflect the desires of a majority of the people of the state. This would mean that decisions on public education, for example, would be made by one state agency rather than by the more than 1000 school districts in the state.

Pluralist democracy, in contrast to majoritarian democracy, places a higher priority on protecting minority rights and ensuring representative government in a diverse society. According to political scientist David Everson, "Pluralism is often seen as a solution to problems inherent in democracy, or the presumed excesses of democracy. . . . The solution to the problem [of majority factions] is implied in the term 'pluralist': namely, the political system disperses power in such a way that individual liberty and the interests of minorities are protected."[10] Consequently, pluralists favor institutional arrangements that decentralize authority and political processes that divide decision making among several levels and branches of government. The greater the decentralization, the greater the number of decision makers who can be influenced. If a group is unsuccessful at one level of government (the city) or with one branch of government (the legislature), the group can switch its efforts to another level of government (the state) or to another branch of government (the executive or the judiciary). This decentralization may slow the decision-making process and thwart efforts to achieve a definitive solution; however, the importance of government efficiency in decision making is secondary to the ability of groups to express their views and gain access to decision makers.

The major institutional and procedural characteristics of majoritarian and pluralist democracy are summarized in Table 1.1. Which model is more descriptive of the United States as a whole or of Texas in particular?

Most students of American politics consider its institutions pluralistic rather than majoritarian. Most political decisions are made by representatives rather than directly by the people; the U.S. Congress and the presidency are both representative institutions. There is no provision for national initiatives and/or referenda. Although the U.S. Constitution provides for majority rule on some issues, many decisions require an extraordinary majority, such as a two-thirds U.S.

Table 1.1 MAJOR CHARACTERISTICS OF MAJORITARIAN AND PLURALIST DEMOCRACY

Characteristics	Majoritarian democracy	Pluralist democracy
Major values	Majority rule; formal political equality	Protection of minority rights; representative government in diverse societies; deliberation
Institutional implications	Unification of authority; centralization of political units	Separation of authority; decentralization of political processes
More representative institution	Executive	Legislature
Executive	Single	Plural
Selection of chief executive	Direct election	Indirect election
Selection of other executives	Appointed	Elected
Preferred process for representing demands to government	Political parties	Interest groups
Constitutional amending process	Easy	Difficult
Separation of powers	Undesirable	Desirable
Judicial review	Undesirable	Necessary
Major reforms	Responsible parties; initiative and referenda	None advocated

Source: Adapted from David H. Everson, *Public Opinion and Interest Groups in American Politics* (New York: Franklin Watts, 1982), pp. 7, 9, and 16.

Senate vote to ratify a treaty, which provides a minority veto. Furthermore, the U.S. Constitution limits government authority, chiefly through the Bill of Rights, to protect minorities against majorities. The U.S. Supreme Court also acts as a check on the legislative and executive branches to ensure that the more popular branches do not restrict minority rights.

Texas is similar to the United States in its institutional design. Texas also incorporates constitutional guarantees of civil liberties through a bill of rights, more extensive even than the rights found in the U.S. Constitution. Also, a study of the Texas legislature would reveal that there are numerous ways to prevent the passage of legislation, but basically only one way to pass legislation. Furthermore,

Texas is governed by representative institutions, such as the *bicameral* (two-chambered) legislature, independently elected executive leaders, and numerous county, local, and special district public officials.

For some political scientists, neither majoritarian nor pluralist democracy adequately describes government in Texas or the United States. They maintain that **elitism** is a more accurate description.

The Elitist Challenge   The elitist challenge to majoritarian and pluralist democracy is based on the answer to a central question in political science: Who is actually governing? The majoritarian and pluralist answer is that the people govern, either through individual, majoritarian decisions or through membership in groups that represent the interests of their members. The elitist response is that a small group of privileged people, an elite, rule. Of course, neither majoritarian nor pluralist democracy denies the fact that some people possess greater talents and skills than other people, but both theories maintain that these differences are not magnified through institutional arrangements that provide greater influence to some people than to others. Elitists, by contrast, maintain that the most important cleavage in societies is between the few who constitute the society's elite and the many who make up the society's masses. The basis for the distinction between elites and masses varies among elite theories; however, the most common difference is economic. In other words, the elite control the economic base of society, and they use that economic control to accumulate and hold political power. Elitists would argue that political campaigns, for example, are financed by an economic elite that gains political influence through their campaign contributions. For elitists, the cohesion among the elite produced by their shared economic status overcomes any differences among the elite in ethnicity, gender, or other social characteristics. Most elite theorists also maintain, either explicitly or implicitly, that elite values and preferences are different from mass values and preferences. Elite theorists argue that the elite oppose campaign finance reforms that are favored by a substantial majority of the population because the reforms would decrease the elite's influence on public officials.

Among elite theorists, there are some who consider elite rule to be democratic. For example, Dye and Ziegler argue that "all societies are governed by elites, even democratic societies. The elitist theory of democracy is not an attack on democracy, but rather an aid in understanding the realities of democratic politics. . . . [I]t is a realistic explanation of how democracy works, how democratic values are both preserved and threatened, how elites and masses interact, how public policy is actually determined, and whose interests generally prevail."[11] We disagree with Dye and Ziegler and view elitism as incompatible with democracy because elitism is unable to meet the conditions of political equality, participation, nontyranny, and deliberation. Nevertheless, we also acknowledge the influence that elites have on Texas politics and government.

As we describe and analyze Texas politics and government in the remaining chapters, you will frequently be asked to reconsider the structure and processes of Texas politics and government. You should consider proposals for reform in Texas in relation to your values or goals for Texas government. Do you value more or less direct participation in decision making? Do you value more or less protection for minority viewpoints? These and other similar questions should frame your participation in Texas politics and government. Texas government is dynamic and changing, not static and fixed. The direction of those changes depends on you and others who reside in Texas now and who will do so in the future.

> **Critical Thinking Exercise:**   Which form of democracy—classical, majoritarian, or pluralist—do you favor? What changes in Texas's political institutions and processes would be necessary to more fully achieve that form? What would you add to Table 1.1?

Constitutionalism

As our discussion in the previous section demonstrates, constitutions play a pivotal role in the government and politics of a society. In Chapter 3, we examine the various constitutions of Texas in detail. In this chapter, we are interested only in demonstrating how the idea of constitutionalism affects those institutions of government that have developed in Texas.

Constitutionalism affirms that the supreme or fundamental law of the land, the constitution, is neither a product of, nor capable of being altered by, the whims of the legislature, the executive, or the judiciary. Because constitutions represent a compact or contract among the members of the political community, they provide the legitimacy for government. To be legitimate, however, the constitution must have been created democratically. Remember that the essence of a democratic system is the consent of the governed. This consent is created with the formal ratification or approval of the constitution by the people.

Constitutions also provide the structure and distribute the powers of government. However, as you will discover in later chapters, if you are not already aware, the Texas Constitution establishes much more than the basic structure, powers, and context of government. To a great extent, a constitution will determine whether a government is democratic. In establishing the political institutions, a constitution will set the limits for political participation. Lengthy residency requirements and difficult registration requirements for voting inhibit participation in elections. Likewise, a constitution will establish the formal decision rules to be used in making public policy, and a constitution may even encourage or inhibit deliberation.

ANALYZING POLITICAL CHANGE

Simply expressing a belief in the American Creed is not sufficient for most Americans. If the five ideas that make up the American Creed constitute a cultural ideal, then the society's institutions—the structures and processes for making decisions—must embody those ideas. However, the five ideas of the American Creed are frequently in conflict, especially when one of the ideas is pushed to its limits. Perhaps the most important conflicts in post–World War II American and Texas politics have involved issues of equality, as the following examples illustrate.

In 1946, Heman Sweatt, a Houston postal worker, applied for admission to the University of Texas School of Law. Because he was an African American and the law school was only for whites, Sweatt was denied admission. When Sweatt sued the state, the judge ordered the state to establish a separate "Negro" law school. At that time, the U.S. Supreme Court's interpretation of the Fourteenth Amendment's equal protection clause allowed racial segregation if substantially equal facilities were provided.

Rather than attend the school that Texas created for him, Sweatt continued his lawsuit against the university. When he lost in the Texas state courts, Sweatt, with help from the National Association for the Advancement of Colored People (NAACP), appealed to the U.S. Supreme Court. In 1950, the U.S. Supreme Court ordered the University of Texas to admit Sweatt, citing the inequities that existed between the "Negro" law school and the University of Texas.

Nearly five decades later, four whites sued the University of Texas law school, claiming that the school's affirmative-action program had denied them admission while admitting minorities who had lower Law School Aptitude Test (LSAT) scores and grade point averages. By excluding African Americans from the law school in 1946, the university had denied them equality of opportunity. However, by establishing different requirements in considering the applications of African Americans and Mexican Americans, the university was attempting to ensure an "equality of results" (a certain percentage of minorities). When U. S. District Court Judge Sam Sparks did not order the law school to admit the four students, they appealed his decision. On March 18, 1996, a three-judge panel of the U.S. Fifth Circuit Court of Appeals reversed Judge Sparks's District Court ruling in *Hopwood v. State of Texas,* declaring that the University of Texas Law School's use of race in its admissions policy violated the U.S. Constitution's Fourteenth Amendment. The court ordered the law school to cease considering an applicant's race in making its admissions decisions. Texas Attorney General Dan Morales appealed the appeals court's decision to the U.S. Supreme Court on April 30, 1996. When the U.S. Supreme Court refused to hear Morales's appeal, the appeals court's decision stood. When Judge Sparks reconsidered the students' case in 1997, as the Court of Appeals had ordered, he again found that the students should not be admitted, but he did order the University of Texas to pay more than $700,000 in legal fees. The University of Texas appealed that decision in 1999. Furthermore, in September 1999, Texas Attorney General John Cornyn revoked former Attorney General Morales's 1997 opinion that Texas colleges and universities could not consider race in admissions or granting scholarships. However, Cornyn also cautioned universities not to take any actions regarding affirmative-action programs until the courts resolved the issue. Though a great deal of support exists for equality of opportunity in Texas and the rest of the United States, many people feel that ensuring equality of results goes too far.

When such conflicts occur (and they are frequent), there is rarely a consensus on which idea should have priority.

Despite these conflicts, the American Creed does provide goals for the society and its institutions, and government does have a hand in achieving those goals by attempting to assure that these ideas exist in all of society's institutions. Every institution in America should incorporate, to the greatest degree possible, the five ideas of the American Creed.

The Ideal-Reality Gap

The discrepancy or gap between the American ideal (what America should be) and the institutions (what America is)—**the ideal-reality gap**—is both the dilemma in American politics and the impetus for political change. Because the ideas are inconsistent and there is no consensus on the relative importance of the components of the creed, the institutions can never achieve the ideal for everyone. No institution will ever be sufficiently constitutional, individualistic, equal, democratic, or libertarian to satisfy all Americans. Consequently, Americans suffer from a collective **cognitive dissonance,** a discrepancy between what the society is (the reality of America's institutions) and what the society should be (the ideal of the American Creed). According to the psychologist who developed the theory of cognitive dissonance, to resolve the dissonance, a person must change either his or her beliefs (ideals) or his or her behavior (institutions) to relieve the tension or anxiety caused by the discrepancy.[12] For Americans, altering the ideal is impossible. The ideal is, of course, what differentiates America from other nations and makes it America. The only route to consonance—to harmonizing the dissonance—is to change the institutions. But are Americans constantly questioning and reforming their institutions? No, of course not. So what determines how America responds to the gap between the ideal and reality?

Responses to the Ideal-Reality Gap

Americans' **response to the ideal-reality gap** depends on the relationship between two variables: (1) how clearly Americans perceive the gap, and (2) how strongly they believe in the ideal or creed (Figure 1.2). Undoubtedly, the gap is always present, and Americans always believe and have believed in the ideal. However, the clarity with which Americans perceive the gap and the strength of their belief in the ideal are not constant over time. Political scientist Samuel Huntington identifies four responses to the gap:

1. **Moralism.** If Americans intensely believe in their ideals and clearly perceive the gap, they moralistically attempt to eliminate the gap through reforms that will bring the practice and institutions into accord with principles and beliefs.

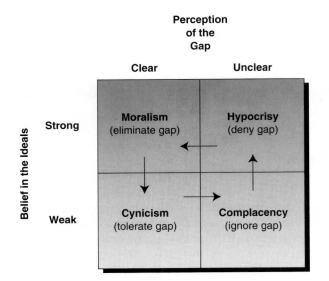

Figure 1.2   Responses to the Ideal-Reality Gap

The gap between the American ideal (what America should be) and the American reality (what America is) is both the dilemma in American politics and the impetus for political change. Professor Samuel P. Huntington of Harvard University visualizes America's responses to the gap as a result of two factors: (1) the clarity of the perceived gap, and (2) the strength of Americans' belief in the ideal. Logically, the responses, which are temporary because no response adequately resolves the dilemma, follow a counterclockwise progression (depicted by arrows). For example, from the mid-1960s to the mid-1970s, a strong belief in the ideals and a clear perception of the gap produced a moralistic response. Efforts to reduce the gap by reforming the institutions were evident in the Civil Rights movement, protests against the Vietnam War, and protests against the abuse of presidential powers in Watergate. By the mid-1970s, however, the failure of the moralistic response to produce the changes sought by protestors led Americans to a rejection of politics and political movements as their belief in the ideal waned during a period of cynicism.

Source: Adapted by permission of the publisher from *American Politics: The Promise of Disharmony* by Samuel P. Huntington, Cambridge, MA: Harvard University Press. Copyright © 1981 by Samuel P. Huntington.

2. **Cynicism.** If intensity of belief is low and perception of the gap is clear, Americans will resort to a cynical willingness to *tolerate* the gap's existence.
3. **Complacency.** If intensity of belief is low and their perception of the gap is unclear, Americans can attempt to *ignore* the existence of the gap by in effect reducing its cognitive importance to themselves through complacent indifference.
4. **Hypocrisy.** If they are intensely committed to the American ideals and yet *deny* the existence of a gap between ideals and reality, they can[not] alter . . . reality, [so they alter] . . . their perceptions of reality through an immense effort at "patriotic" hypocrisy.[13]

At any given time, all four responses will be exhibited by some Americans. However, the collective response—the one shared by most Americans—generally occurs in a particular cycle or sequence: moralism, cynicism, complacency, and then hypocrisy. Attempting to deal with the national dilemma and to achieve consonance, Americans experiment with one response for a while and then abandon it to try the next. Since the mid-1960s, Americans have experimented with each of these responses.

The Moralistic Response   The **politics of creedal passion** (periods of **moralism**) are rare but memorable epochs in American history. Between the mid-1960s and mid-1970s, many Americans, especially young people, fervently promoted the values of the American Creed. They became obsessed with the lack of freedom and equality and with the arbitrary use of power in American society. In the Civil Rights movement for African Americans, as well as the demonstrations against America's involvement in the Vietnam War, the politics of creedal passion created a passion for politics and a commitment to institutional reform, which had been absent in America for some time. As they dramatized those facts with demonstrations and protests, such as the one at the 1968 Democratic National Convention in Chicago, public officials and politically active citizens found that they could not ignore the contradiction between American beliefs and American reality. As the perception spread, the public became outraged, and America's confidence in its institutions plummeted. The result was a politics of protest and outrage, of verbal and physical attacks on the symbols of power and authority in America.

This moralistic response occurs when the commitment to the American ideal is intense and the perception of the gap between the ideal and the institutions is clear. It results in an attempt to restructure the institutions to conform to the ideal. It is this combination of intensity and perception that provides the motivation for reform.[14]

The Cynical Response   Following the moral rush that accompanies periods of creedal passion, **cynicism** often sets in. The moral outrage, unleashed by the attacks on America's institutions, cannot be sustained for long periods and soon succumbs to cynicism. Typically, periods of creedal passion begin with the assumption that America can achieve the ideal if only the evil people in power are removed. However, when the removal of leaders does not achieve the desired effect, the institutions are targeted for reform, and extensive restructuring is considered necessary to achieve the ideal. Finally, the efforts to achieve the ideal generally end with a sense that neither action will be sufficient. In 1968, opponents of American involvement in Vietnam forced President Johnson to forgo seeking another term, but the war and America's involvement continued. Similarly, Watergate revelations forced President Nixon to resign his presidency, but presidential power was not permanently limited. Also, the Civil Rights Act of 1964 and the Voting Rights Act of 1965 did not end the discrimination and inequities experienced by minorities.

Although a clear perception of the gap remains, the hope that the gap can be closed is dashed for the time being. Moral outrage yields to moral helplessness. America lapses into cynicism—a temporary toleration of the gap.[15]

The Complacent Response   Unable to sustain their toleration of the gap, people escape to **complacency** by ignoring the existence of the gap. Their passions are shifted from politics to other pursuits, and they cope with the gap by removing it from their list of concerns. In the 1980s, as complacency settled widely across America, many college students avoided majoring in the social sciences and humanities and instead chose majors in fields, such as business, that offered greater opportunities for employment and substantial incomes. Interest in politics on college campuses declined. Protests were infrequent, and those that did occur were devoid of political content.

Of course, if reminded of the existence of the gap, people still acknowledge it, but they refuse to allow it to mobilize them to change it. The American ideal engenders no enthusiasm, nor does the discrepancy between reality and the ideal.

The Hypocritical Response   There is, however, a limit to the complacency that seems to characterize America's response for long periods of time. The national identity requires a periodic reaffirmation of the American Creed—the commitment to individualism, equality, liberty, democracy, and constitutionalism. In promoting those values, though, Americans may still not acknowledge the existence of the gap. During these periods of **hypocrisy,** Americans alter their perceptions to exclude any recognition of the gap between the facts of America's institutions and the values of the American Creed: "The United States not only should be the land of liberty, equality, and justice for all; it actually is."[16] In the early 1960s, America was called on to remake the world in its image. In his inaugural address, President Kennedy announced that America would "bear any burden, pay any price" to promote freedom throughout the world. An entire generation of Americans celebrated the American ideal, joined the Peace Corps, and committed themselves to achieving the democratic ideal in other lands. The ideal had been achieved in America; now it would be achieved everywhere.

However, the politics of denial also proves unsatisfactory. After a while, the intense proclamation of the American ideal leads to a renewed perception of the gap. Groups that do not share in America's perceived achievement of the ideal counter the glorification of America with the exposure of America. During the early 1960s, for African Americans, Hispanics, and American women, the gap between the ideas of the American Creed and the reality of their social and economic inequality was clear and convincing proof that America had not achieved the ideal. Waiting in the wings for a reappearance is the politics of creedal passion, which sooner or later takes center stage.

The Responses and Political Change in Texas   Political change in Texas is analyzed in this textbook using the responses to the gap as an important part of our framework. In many respects, Texas is the quintessential American state. It was administered by a European nation; its population included Native Americans, European Americans of almost every European nationality, *Tejanos*, African Americans, and Asian Americans; it won its independence in an armed rebellion; and it was an independent nation for nine years before joining the union of states in 1845. Furthermore, the five ideas of the American Creed are important to Texans, and the gap between those ideas and the institutions in Texas has resulted in the responses of moralism, cynicism, complacency, and hypocrisy. Periods of moralism are evident in Texas history. Perhaps the most obvious was Texas's revolution against Mexico in the mid-1830s (Chapter 2). Less obvious, but dramatic nevertheless, was the farmers' revolt of the late nineteenth century (Chapter 4). More recently, the period from the late 1960s to the mid-1970s was a period of institutional reform in Texas government, especially in the legislature (Chapter 8) and in civil rights and liberties (Chapter 13), and it even involved attempts to revise Texas's fundamental law—its constitution (Chapter 3).

Texas politics and government are always changing. As you learn the facts about Texas politics and government in subsequent chapters, you will be encouraged to consider the changes in Texas politics and government. How and why have Texas politics and government changed? Were the changes the result of the politics of creedal passion, or were they the result of competition among groups in the governmental institutions? As you begin to think analytically about politics, government, and political change, they will become less confusing and more comprehensible.

> **Critical Thinking Exercise:** Rapid and comprehensive political change is associated with periods of creedal passion. What conditions do you think would ignite a period of creedal passion in contemporary Texas?

THE REST OF THE STORY

In each chapter, we employ the framework to explain and analyze Texas politics, government, and political change. In the next two chapters, we present the ideas and values and some of the history and geography that form the foundation for political decisions in Texas. Chapter 2 introduces the Texan Creed, explains how each generation of Texans acquires and organizes those ideas, and describes how the changing population and economy of Texas have affected those ideas. Chapter 3 provides the legal context for contemporary Texas politics and government by describing the legacies of Texas's constitutions and by explaining the effects of federalism on Texas politics and government.

Part 2, a set of four chapters, is devoted to the political processes that allow the public to influence politics and government. Chapter 4 describes the functions of political parties in Texas. Chapter 5 identifies how interest groups represent their members in government. Chapter 6 considers the roles that the media and public opinion play in the formation of public policy. The final chapter, Chapter 7, describes political participation, campaigns, and elections in Texas.

Part 3, consisting of four chapters, describes the institutions that make public policy in Texas, explains their role in the political system, and explores their place in our framework. Chapter 8 describes the legislature in Texas, indicating how it traditionally maintains the balance of power in Texas and how it has sometimes been affected by periods of creedal passion. The governor is described in Chapter 9, and the rest of the executive branch is described in Chapter 10, highlighting its role not only in implementing public policy but also in actively participating in policy making. Chapter 11 describes the structure and operation of the Texas judiciary. The final chapter, Chapter 12, describes the various local governments in Texas.

Part 4, constituting two chapters, describes public policy in Texas. Chapter 13 describes the protections of civil liberties and civil rights that we have in Texas. Chapter 14 considers economic and social policies, including taxing and spending policies and the role they play in politics, and an examination of education and other social policies.

In each chapter, the final sections provide an assessment of how the subject of the chapter—for example, political parties in Chapter 4—affects democracy and political change in Texas.

SUMMARY

In this chapter, we introduced you to a framework for describing and analyzing Texas government and politics, based on the importance of ideas. Texas politics and government, like government and politics in the United States, is greatly influenced by a political creed, a set of ideas that establish the goals for politics and the methods of government. We indicated that politics are analyzed using three of the five ideas—individualism, liberty, and equality. In analyzing government, constitutionalism and democracy guide our framework. We provided a set of conditions that must be met for a government to be considered democratic, and we offered two contemporary democratic models—majoritarian and pluralist democracy—and one nondemocratic alternative—elitism.

In the next chapter, we begin the application of our framework by describing the development of the five ideas in Texas, indicating how individuals acquire their political beliefs and attitudes, describing the peoples of Texas, and providing an overview of the Texas economy.

KEY TERMS

politics
government
public policy
institutions
processes
individualism
liberty
equality
constitutionalism
democracy
American Creed
conditions of democracy
political equality
nontyranny

participation
deliberation
classical democratic theory
majoritarian democracy
pluralist democracy
elitism
ideal-reality gap
cognitive dissonance
response to the ideal-reality gap
politics of creedal passion
moralism
cynicism
complacency
hypocrisy

SUGGESTED READINGS

Domhoff, William. *The Power Elite and the State: How Policy Is Made in America.* New York: Aldine de Gruyter, 1990.

Fishkin, James S. *Democracy and Deliberation: New Directions for Democratic Reform.* New Haven, Conn.: Yale University Press, 1991.

———. *The Voice of the People: Public Opinion and Democracy.* New Haven, Conn.: Yale University Press, 1995.

Hill, Kim Quaile. *Democracy in the Fifty States.* Lincoln, Nebr.: University of Nebraska Press, 1994.

Huntington, Samuel P. *American Politics: The Promise of Disharmony.* Cambridge, Mass.: Harvard University Press, 1981.

———. *The Third Wave: Democratization in the Late Twentieth Century.* Norman, Okla.: University of Oklahoma Press, 1991.

Ladd, Everett Carll. *The American Ideology: An Exploration of the Origins, Meaning, and Role of American Political Ideas.* Occasional Papers and Monographs Series, no. 1. Storrs, Conn.: The Roper Center for Public Opinion Research, 1994.

Yankelovich, Daniel. *Coming to Public Judgment: Making Democracy Work in a Computer World.* Syracuse, N.Y.: Syracuse University Press, 1991.

NOTES

1. David Easton, *A Framework for Political Analysis* (Englewood Cliffs, N.J.: Prentice Hall, 1965), 50.
2. Everett Carll Ladd, *The American Ideology: An Exploration of the Origins, Meaning, and Role of American Political Ideas,* Occasional Papers and Monographs Series, no. 1 (Storrs, Conn.: The Roper Center, 1994), 30.
3. Samuel P. Huntington, *American Politics: The Promise of Disharmony* (Cambridge, Mass.: Harvard University Press), 1981.
4. This is an expansion of our distinction between politics and government: politics concerns what is to be accomplished (ends), and government relates to processes for achieving them (means). Chapters 2 and 3 further explain this distinction.
5. Samuel P. Huntington, *The Third Wave: Democratization in the Late Twentieth Century* (Norman, Okla.: University of Oklahoma Press, 1991), 6.
6. James S. Fishkin, *The Voice of the People: Public Opinion and Democracy* (New Haven, Conn.: Yale University Press, 1995), 34.
7. James S. Fishkin, *Democracy and Deliberation: New Directions for Democratic Reform* (New Haven, Conn.: Yale University Press, 1991), 36.
8. See Nelson W. Polsby, *The Consequences of Party Reform* (New York: Oxford University Press, 1983), 171–172.
9. David H. Everson, *Public Opinion and Interest Groups in American Politics* (New York: Franklin Watts, 1982), 8–9.
10. Ibid., 5.
11. Thomas Dye and Harmon Ziegler, *The Irony of Democracy: An Uncommon Introduction to American Politics,* 9th ed. (Belmont, Calif.: Wadsworth, 1993), 19.
12. Leon Festinger, *A Theory of Cognitive Dissonance* (Evanston, Ill.: Row, Peterson and Company, 1957), 3.
13. Huntington, *America Politics,* 64.
14. Ibid., 68.
15. Ibid., 69.
16. Ibid., 70.

2 The Ideological and Socioeconomic Context for Texas Politics and Government

Scenario: The Professor and Affirmative Action

- Introduction
- Texas Index: The Socioeconomic Context in the States
- The Ideological Context
- The Peoples of Texas
- The Economy of Texas

★ Scenario: The Professor and Affirmative Action

Law School Professor Lino Graglia is no stranger to controversy. In his more than 30 years at the University of Texas, Graglia has spoken out frequently on race-related issues. He has written articles and a book, *Disaster by Decree: The Supreme Court Decisions on Race and the Schools,* in opposition to busing to achieve desegregation. In 1986, his outspoken opposition to busing in Austin, Texas, allegedly cost him a nomination to the U.S. Court of Appeals for the Fifth Circuit, as well as a chance to head the Civil Rights Division of the Justice Department. More recently, he has written extensively in opposition to affirmative-action programs. Nevertheless, he probably did not anticipate the storm of controversy created by his statements on affirmative-action programs and the *Hopwood* decision in 1997.

At a press conference called by Students for Equal Opportunity, a group of University of Texas students formed to oppose affirmative action, Graglia, an honorary cochair of the group, stated that African-American and Mexican-American students are "not academically competitive" with white students at the more prestigious universities. He ascribed the differences primarily to ". . . cultural effects. They [African Americans and Mexican Americans] have a culture that seems not to encourage achievement. Failure is not looked upon with dis-grace." Graglia also suggested that ". . . racially preferred students would be better served if encouraged to enroll in the best institutions for which they meet the ordinary admissions criteria." Graglia subsequently issued a statement, ex-plaining that his remarks in support of the *Hopwood* decision and in opposition to racial preferences had led to misunderstandings and inaccurate statements.

Nevertheless, University of Texas officials, law school professors, Texas legislators, minority-group leaders, and students condemned Graglia's re-marks. Speakers at a rally at the University of Texas, attended by about 5000 people, condemned Graglia's remarks. Reverend Jesse Jackson, speaking to the rally, encouraged students to boycott Graglia's classes. After the rally, mem-bers of a student group, Students for Access and Opportunity, staged a sit-in at the law school until the university's Board of Regents agreed to meet with them.

The *Hopwood* decision had an immediate impact on minority enrollments at the University of Texas Law School. In 1996, the first-year class included 31 African Americans and 42 Hispanics. In 1997, the first-year class included only four African Americans and 26 Hispanics. Although the number of minorities in the University of Texas Law School has increased in subsequent years, the num-bers have not achieved the pre-*Hopwood* numbers of 1996.

Professor Graglia's remarks and the ensuing reactions demonstrate the conflict between two ideas in the American and Texan Creed. For Professor

Law Professor Lino Graglia created a controversy when he stated that minority students couldn't compete academically at prestigious universities.

Graglia, any government attempt to promote equality by providing compensation for past discrimination and promoting diversity violates the idea of individualism and equality of opportunity. For Graglia's opponents, equality of opportunity is a sham, used by whites to deny minorities access to prestigious universities and law schools. Relegating minorities to less prestigious institutions is a form of racial segregation and limits the opportunities available to minorities.[1]★

INTRODUCTION

The politics and government of a state are shaped by its inhabitants' ideas about politics and government, by the social and ethnic composition of its population, by its history, and by its economy. These factors, along with its constitution and its relationship with the national government (see Chapter 3), constitute the context for politics and government. In this chapter, we describe the ideological, social, historical, and economic context for Texas politics and government. By placing Texas in context, we gain an appreciation for the unique and the common characteristics of Texas politics and government.

Our description of the ideological context focuses on the core set of ideas that motivate and shape Texas politics. We describe a Texan Creed, a set of political ideas that differentiates Texans from Oklahomans, Arkansans, New Yorkers, and Californians, just as the American Creed separates Americans from people of other nationalities. Because people are not born with a set of political ideas, we also describe how Texans acquire their political ideas. When we describe the people who have inhabited Texas, we indicate how each of these people has historically influenced and continues to influence Texas politics and government. Finally, we provide an overview of the Texas economy, revealing how changes in the Texas economy have influenced its politics and government.

Placing Texas government and politics in context is not an easy task. As even the most casual visitor to Texas can attest, there is something different about Texas and Texans. Of course, this difference is also reflected in Texas government and politics. The difference is more than the braggadocio of the stereotypical Texan. It is also more than an inexplicable, though infectious, optimism about life and the future of Texas. Perhaps John Steinbeck captured its essence best when he noted,

> But I think . . . that Texas is one thing. For all its enormous range of space, climate, and physical appearance, and for all the internal squabbles, contentions, and strivings, Texas has a cohesiveness perhaps stronger than any other section of America. Rich, poor, Panhandle, Gulf, city, country, Texas is the obsession, the proper study and the passionate possession of all Texans.[2]

Because of Texans' cohesiveness and passion for Texas, we begin our exploration of the context for Texas politics and government with more than a little trepidation.

Te★as*Index*

The Socioeconomic Context in the States

Total Population (1997)
Texas—19,439,000
California—32,268,000
New York—18,137,000
Florida—14,654,000

African-American Population (1997)
Texas—12.2%
California—7.4%
New York—17.7%
Florida—15.4%

Hispanic Population (1997)
Texas—29.4%
California—30.8 %
New York—14.2%
Florida—14.4%

Forbes 500 Companies (1997)
Texas—61
California—92
New York—81
Florida—16

THE IDEOLOGICAL CONTEXT

The ideological context for Texas politics and government centers around a **Texan Creed.** The Texan Creed incorporates the same five ideas that make up the American Creed—individualism, liberty, equality, constitutionalism, and democracy (see Chapter 1). The features that distinguish the Texan Creed from the American Creed arise from the unique historical experiences of Texas and Texans, especially between the 1820s and the 1880s. Although Texas has changed substantially since the late 1800s, the repetition of the prior historical experiences, whether mythical or not, keeps the creed alive and perpetuates it in each new generation. Consequently, we first explore how these experiences have shaped the five ideas of the Texan Creed.

Ideas and Texas Politics: The Texan Creed

For a majority of Texans, there is a consensus on the importance of the five ideas of the Texan Creed. Although contemporary Texas is more heterogeneous than nineteenth-century Texas, the ideas that were established during that century still prevail today. Among the five ideas, individualism holds a special place for most Texans.

Individualism   For most Americans, individualism, which stresses the primacy of the individual conscience as the basis for behavior, is the product of seventeenth-century Protestantism. For these early Anglo settlers, their reason for coming to America can be traced to individualism:

> The early Texans descended from clans and families, heavily Scotch Irish, who deserted the panoply of Europe, despising its hierarchies and social organism . . . , and who plunged into the wilderness. These folk sought land and opportunity, surely—but they were also consciously fleeing something: a vision of the world in which community and state transcended the individual family and its personal good.[3]

Coming to Texas in the late eighteenth century, these people created a society dedicated to individualism. According to the ideal, the individual is responsible for the benefits that she or he receives in life and in the hereafter. In reality, the feeling for the soil that these Texans developed created the society. For Texans, land possesses both a symbolic and a practical meaning. During the nineteenth century, Texans created a social environment in which every person, whether dirt farmer or rancher, could be a landowner, independent and supreme over his or her "country." The landowners' ethos remains in contemporary Texas, a legacy of early Texas individualism. For most Texans, the landowner remains the ideal and is accorded the highest social status.[4]

The individualism created in Texans' attachment to the land was nurtured by the frontier experience. For most Americans, the frontier era was short-lived, lasting usually no more than a decade. Civilization advanced rapidly. For Texans, however, the frontier era lasted four decades and involved three distinct challenges—a battle with Mexico for cultural and political dominance, a more dangerous conflict for survival with a Native-American population, and a struggle to conquer a difficult land. The duration of the **Texas frontier** era and its proximity to the present accentuates the frontier's effect on Texans.

For Texans, the most dangerous frontier was the western, Native-American frontier. By 1834, Texan colonists had placed themselves within range of the Comanches. Previous wars between Native Americans and Anglos followed a common pattern: Anglo encroachment engendered Native-American retaliation, which incited a military response that subdued the Native Americans. The Plains Indians were not stationary, agricultural peoples. They were nomads who followed the bison herds over the seemingly boundless prairie. They avoided contact with Anglo settlers, except for raids on established settlements. Thus, the conflict involved an Anglo farming population and powerful, warlike Native Americans who held a decided advantage. The Comanches were never numerous, but they were defending their territory from intruders, and their raids exacted a terrible toll: "Between 1836 and 1860, 200 men, women, and children were killed each year by Indians on the Texas border; between 1860 and 1875 at least 100 died or were carried off annually. The trek through central Texas cost seventeen white lives per mile."[5]

In order to survive on the frontier, Anglo farmers and ranchers had to adapt. They became true horsemen; they learned to survive in Native-American country; and they adapted their agriculture to raising stock. The most important adaptation, however, involved frontier defense—the creation of the **Texas Rangers.** Companies of Texas Rangers date from Austin's colony, having been formed as early as 1823. However, only after Texas independence was their presence significant. Although they have been characterized as an early state police, they were unique. The state authorized the rangers as a mounted militia, a paramilitary organization, which the state assisted when it could, which was not often. The rangers were composed of farmers and ranchers threatened by the native population; they were young, adventuresome, courageous volunteers. Though the rangers were less numerous than their enemies, they quickly found that the best defense was to attack, dominate, and subdue. Though moral and ethical questions surround their tactics, few have questioned their success in seeking out their enemies' weakness and then attacking it without mercy. These characteristics and the use of Samuel Colt's revolving pistol, which gave each ranger the firepower of six, enabled the rangers to subdue their enemies.[6] However, as one historian admits,

> The Rangers never halted all the lawlessness and violence, of course, and the Army, not they, waged all the final campaigns against the Indians. . . . But Texans applauded their efforts. . . . For Rangers, born of the frontier, embodied many of the bedrock values of the frontier. They were brutal to enemies, loyal to friends, courteous to women, kind to old ladies; they never gave up, claiming that no power on earth could stop the man in the right who kept "a-coming." These were male values, warrior values.[7]

The final contribution to individualism came from the cowboy, who experienced the closing of the frontier and its way of life. Similar to the ranger in many of his values, the cowhand adopted a semifeudal notion of loyalty to his boss and brand, taken from the Mexican cattle-ranching culture. To herd half-wild cattle over thousands of miles required physical courage, but not recklessness. However, no respectable cowboy backed away from a fight that was forced upon him.[8] In all its manifestations, individualism has produced in Texans "a hard pragmatism and absence of ideology, a worship of action and accomplishment, a disdain for weakness and incompetence, and a thread of belligerence—and finally, a natural mythology stemming from the Alamo."[9] Closely related to individualism and nearly as important to the Texas Creed is the idea of liberty.

Liberty   For most Americans, liberty is a product of the eighteenth century's Age of Enlightenment, with its emphasis on natural rights, the social contract, and a limited role for government. Liberty ensures that a person's inherent rights are free from government infringement, and it complements individualism. For Texans, a passion for liberty has additional sources—the reasons for Texas's revolt against Mexico and the battle for the Alamo.

The decision by Texans to declare their independence from Mexico in 1836 had many causes, but the most important causes involved Mexico's attempts to exert greater control over Texas and Texans. Perhaps the cultural differences between the Anglo settlers and their Mexican governors were such that conflict was inevitable. However, Stephen F. Austin's leadership had enabled the settlers to avoid involvement in domestic Mexican factional disputes for many years. Minor problems—religious requirements imposed on the settlers and Mexican opposition to slavery—offered potential areas of greater conflict, but a more serious concern involved the lack of an adequate local government through which the settlers could exercise a voice in the administration of their own affairs and the maintenance of order.[10] This grievance and Mexican suspicions of Anglo motives led the Mexicans to ban further immigration in 1830 and, two years later, to enforce the collection of tariff duties. In response to these Mexican actions, the colonists dispatched Stephen F. Austin to request separate statehood for Texas and other reforms. Until 1835, Texans considered themselves loyal Mexican citizens and were attempting to uphold the principles of the liberal, federal Mexican constitution of 1824. Only when the futility of such a position became evident were the "Texians," as they called themselves, willing to revolt against Mexico itself.[11]

In October 1835, Santa Anna replaced the federal constitution of 1824 with the *Siete Leyes*, a centralized government under the president's control. A summons to arms in 1835 appealed to the Texians:

> Fellow citizens, Your cause is a good one, none can be better; it is republicanism in opposition to despotism; in a word it is liberty in opposition to slavery. You will be fighting for your wives and children, your homes and firesides, for your country, for liberty.[12]

With the adoption of this declaration, Texas established the right to revolution and laid the foundation for its subsequent government.

More than any historic event, **the Alamo** exemplifies Texans' passion for liberty. In February and March of 1836, Lieutenant Colonel William Barret Travis and his band of a few more than 180 volunteers fought to their deaths against a Mexican army of more than 5000, and in the process, they "set the stage for ultimate Texas unification and victory"[13] and created a legacy that inspires and defines Texans more than a century and a half later. Over the years, fact and legend have intertwined so that the real story of the Alamo is impossible to discover. However, the true story is unimportant, for the power of the Alamo as a symbol of Texan independence and liberty transcends any measure of the truth. To a significant degree, the importance of the Alamo is embodied in the statements and the alleged actions of its heroes: Crockett, Bowie, and Travis.

Upon his arrival in Texas, David Crockett was administered the oath of allegiance by Judge John Forbes, who was forced to pause during his reading. Crockett had "noticed that he was required to uphold 'any future government' that might be established. That could mean a dictatorship. He refused to sign until the wording was changed to 'any future *republican* government.' "[14] Similarly, when he reached the Alamo, Crockett, noted for his verbal excesses, announced that "all the honor that I desire is that of defending as a high private, in common with my fellow citizens, the liberties of our common country."[15] For Crockett and others of his generation, the defining historical event was the American Revolution. To these men, the similarities between the American Revolution and the revolt by Texans were overpowering.

William Barret Travis, the youthful commander of the Alamo, probably best exemplifies the ideal of individual liberty and freedom. In his appeal for assistance, which was addressed "To The People of Texas & All Americans in the World," Travis pledged never to surrender or retreat and called on Americans everywhere "in the name of liberty, of patriotism & everything dear to the American character, to come to our aid."[16] In a subsequent letter to his friend, Jesse Grimes, Travis explained his stand at the Alamo: "he felt the spirit of the times—the conviction that liberty, freedom and independence were in themselves worth fighting for; the belief that a man should be willing to make any sacrifice to hold these prizes."[17]

Whether Travis ever drew the line in the dirt is disputed; nevertheless, his speech in which he gave his men three choices—surrender, escape, or fight to the end—is a cornerstone of the Alamo legacy. Although he urged his men to fight with him, he left the choice to each individual. Aware that no reinforcements were coming, all but one man crossed the line, choosing to fight and die with Travis. Jim Bowie, confined to a cot by typhoid-pneumonia, allegedly said, "Boys, I am not able to go to you, but I wish some of you would be so kind as to remove my cot over there."[18]

The symbolic power of the Alamo reaches all Anglo Texans, regardless of political ideology. To a conservative, the Alamo symbolizes rugged individualism on the frontier and the need to defend liberty. A liberal sees in the Alamo the struggle for a sense of community, justice, and civil liberties.[19] Both visions offer insight into Texas and its politics. For *Tejanos* (native Hispanic inhabitants of Texas), the Alamo is an ambiguous symbol. Although Texas independence was the result of an alliance between Anglos and *Tejanos*, who played a crucial role, the ambivalence that *Tejanos* feel "stems from . . . the long use of the Alamo as an everyday symbol of conquest over Mexicans, as a vindication for the repressive treatment of Mexicans."[20]

Constitutionalism and Democracy   Texans grant nearly equal status to the ideas of constitutionalism and democracy. Perhaps Texans give a slight edge to constitutionalism because of its greater harmony with the dominant values of individualism and liberty. Following a tradition established in the United States, Texas has, for each of its governments, adopted a formal, written constitution, that clearly and distinctly limits the authority of government. In fact, from their first constitution in 1836, Texans created a "state that did not and could not plan society—they saw this as an immoral intrusion upon personal liberty—and in fact had almost no control over society in general."[21] Further support for the connection between constitutionalism and liberty is seen in the inclusion, in all of Texas's constitutions, of an extensive bill of rights. We examine the constitutions of Texas and their provisions in detail in Chapter 3. Texans' desire for democracy was reflected in their commitment to creating an Athenian or Jeffersonian democracy—that is, a male, slave-owning democracy of property holders. Of the five ideas of the Texan Creed, democracy has probably experienced the greatest change.

Equality   The idea of equality that developed in Texas during the nineteenth century was a product of the social system. Although there were substantial differences in social and economic statuses of Anglo males, no rigid social or political hierarchy existed. The commitment to social and political equality reflected a society based on land ownership, a plentiful commodity. However, the equality accorded Anglo males did not extend to other members of the society. For non-Anglos, the nonegalitarianism was palpable and perverse. Slavery for African-American Texans was "a system of the entrepreneurial exploitation of labor for profit, based on a law and society that was explicitly racist, in that the servitude of black people was justified by their racial inequality with whites."[22] The end of slavery was followed by the legal segregation of African Americans. Though no longer supported by law, there are still, in many areas of contemporary Texas, two societies—one Anglo and one African American, separate and unequal. The Anglo response to Hispanics has been similar, and Mexican Americans have been subjected to segregation and discrimination also.

Like the American Creed, the Texan Creed provides the ideas that are the foundation for politics and government. Though similar to the American Creed, the Texan Creed has been shaped by historical events to place more emphasis on individualism and liberty than does the American Creed. If the Texan Creed is to endure, it must be transmitted from generation to generation. This is accomplished through political socialization.

The Acquisition of Political Ideas

In spite of one bumper sticker's assertion, Texans are made, not born. The essential point is that political ideas, like other ideas, are learned. Texans consider the inculcation of the Texas ideal important, and they take considerable care to guarantee the indoctrination of its residents, whether native born or naturalized. The process whereby a person learns the political values and beliefs of his or her culture is **political socialization.** The process involves several **agents of socialization:** families, schools, and the media.

Families shape basic political attachments and loyalties. These include an identity with the nation and state and with basic political symbols and arrangements. For example, the family is usually responsible for a person's initial understanding of being an American and a Texan. Other significant identifications, such as ethnicity, race, religion, social class, and region, as well as a partisan affiliation, result from socialization in the family. These basic political notions, acquired early in life, are persistent but not unchangeable.

The family can successfully transmit political attitudes when the attitudes are articulated consistently by the parents, understood by the children, and deemed important to understanding political life. Thus, we can expect native Texans to develop an early attachment to their state and its fundamental political values. They should be aware of their ethnic identities as well. Partisan attachments, in an era of weakening partisan attachments among adults, might also be acquired. Native Texans will probably also gain some appreciation for the major historical events in nineteenth-century Texas history.

When each child enters an elementary school, a new world of political education and indoctrination awaits him or her. The school's socialization process is direct, unlike the family's indirect socialization; schools are expected to teach directly a broad range of attitudes about the political system. Also, during the course of the child's elementary and secondary education, the school introduces the child to many authority figures who may acquaint the child with different, and possibly contradictory, attitudes. These contradictions may reduce the impact of the school in the socialization process; nevertheless, the school is situated to influence significantly the child's political attitudes.

In Texas, the public or private school's impact is enhanced by the pride and patriotism that characterizes the state. According to one historian, "the state's history and legends are taught to its children with far greater intensity than a Boston child is taught about the battle of Bunker Hill. . . . Texas history is treated in the state's public schools as if it were about as important as United States history; state law even allows college students to substitute . . . Texas history for one-half of the required six hours of American history."[23] In fact, the required Texas history course is taught in the seventh grade, where the students are more receptive; United States history is reserved for high school juniors or seniors.

The curriculum is a major instrument of political socialization in the schools. Because textbooks provide a method for standardizing the curriculum throughout Texas, they offer an insight into which topics and events are most important in Texas history. Two studies of Texas history textbooks, conducted a decade apart, demonstrate a continuity in focus and emphasis. In both periods, the textbooks devoted most of their coverage, consistent with Texas Education Agency (TEA) guidelines, to events before the twentieth century. Events of the twentieth century warranted between 11 and 17 percent of the total pages. As one of the studies stated,

> The bias is understandable. The events of early Anglo settlement, revolution, independence, Civil War, Reconstruction, Indian warfare, cattle ranching, and border disturbances are exciting and interesting. This history gives to Texas a unique character. It is the foundation of myth and Texas patriotism and should be recognized. *The overemphasis, however, glorifies the early period, perpetuates the myths, and leaves the impression that more recent developments are less significant.* [emphasis added][24]

The treatment of nineteenth-century events heightens their emphasis. For example, one of the leading textbooks currently used in the required Texas history course teaches the following lesson about the Alamo: "It [the Alamo] represents the high price people sometimes have to pay for freedom."[25] Presentations covering other events of pre-twentieth-century Texas further the establishment of the core values of liberty and individualism. For Texas schoolchildren, Texas history is the story of prominent individuals, fighting for liberty and survival in a hostile environment, not of the creation of social institutions.

For adults, the principal agent of socialization is the mass media. Of course, the mass media include print media (books, magazines, and newspapers), broadcast media (radio and television), and increasingly computer-based on-line services. However, television now so clearly dominates in its pervasiveness and use as a source of political information that we restrict our discussion of the media's influence on socialization to that medium. A *Texas Poll Report* indicated that 73 percent of Texans acknowledge receiving most of their political information about national events from television; a majority, 53 percent, indicated that television was the source of most of their information about local events.[26]

Early studies of media influence on socialization indicated a limited impact. Recent studies, however, confirm that the media can have considerable influence on people's political attitudes and behaviors.[27] There is also a consensus among political scientists and politicians that the media shape the political agenda.[28] That is, the media may not directly affect what the public thinks concerning a particular event or issue (e.g., attitudes concerning civil liberties for gays), but they do affect what events or issues the public thinks about (e.g., the relative importance of gay rights as an issue). Thus, although early socialization may immunize people from media influence or manipulation, people do use the media as a cue to the relative importance of events or issues. This reliance on the media leads to other effects on adults, which we consider more fully in Chapter 6.

Throughout the socialization process, as people acquire additional knowledge about politics and government, there is a growing need to organize that information and make it meaningful. For those who are most involved and active in politics, it means the development of a political ideology. A **political ideology** is a consistent set of beliefs and attitudes concerning the scope and purpose of government. People who have an ideology are called **ideologues.**

The Texan Creed and Political Ideology

We noted in the previous chapter that politics involves the authoritative allocation of values for a society. If everyone agreed on how the important things in society (its values) should be allocated, there would be no need for politics. However, there is disagreement, and politics involves conflict and battles over that allocation. In this chapter, we stated that Texans have a Texan Creed, which involves several values that frequently are in conflict. Some people may want the government to regulate individual behavior so that greater liberty is enjoyed by all; others may claim that the individual's right should be supreme and absolute. For example, for some Texans, the law that required motorcyclists to wear protective helmets infringed upon individualism in the interest of the general welfare. Furthermore, some people may wish government to extend equality to those people who have been subjected to discrimination in the past, whereas others may wish to allow individuals the freedom to decide how to interact with other people, free from government interference.

Figure 2.1 depicts the kinds of conflicts that occur over the allocation of values in Texas. One axis represents the conflict between individualism and various degrees of social order. This conflict involves an individual's conception of the extent of government regulation in matters of morality and conscience. For example, some Texans feel that government should limit a woman's freedom to seek an

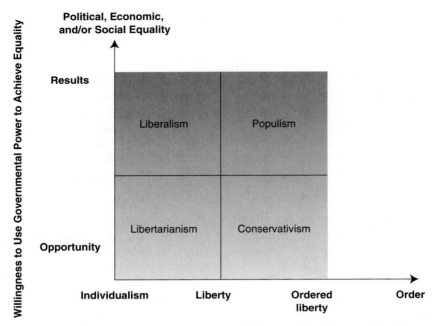

Figure 2.1   The Four Ideologies

The axes represent people's attitudes concerning the use of government to achieve certain goals. The horizontal axis represents a person's willingness to use government power to limit personal freedoms in order to maintain order. The vertical axis represents a person's willingness to use government power to achieve equality. Each ideology reflects a choice between conflicting values. For example, liberals oppose the use of government power to limit personal freedoms in order to maintain order, but liberals support the use of government power to promote equality over protecting personal freedoms. On the other hand, conservatives support the use of government power to maintain order over protecting personal freedoms, but conservatives support the protection of personal freedom over the use of government power to promote equality. Libertarians support the protection of personal freedom over the use of government power either to promote equality or to maintain order. Populists support the use of government power to maintain order and to promote equality over the protection of personal freedom.

abortion, while other Texans feel that the abortion decision is a matter of personal choice or conscience. The other axis pits a preference for individualism against a desire for greater political, economic, and/or social equality. This conflict includes an individual's conception of the extent of government involvement in economic affairs. The choices that a person makes on these issues indicate both his or her idea of the scope of government (how much should government do) and the purpose of government (what goals are legitimate for government). Those choices also determine the person's political ideology: libertarian, liberal, conservative, or populist.[29]

Libertarians   Starting with the origin, where the axes converge, **libertarians** make individualism the highest value, opposing government actions both to promote equality and to promote an ordered liberty. Libertarianism is "a highly individualistic extension of classical liberalism. . . . Libertarians emphasize very strongly the autonomy of the individual and the minimal role required of government."[30] Compared to conservatives, who view government as a necessary evil, libertarians see government as an evil, limiting the ability of individuals to make choices and achieve their own destinies. In Texas, libertarians have managed to place Libertarian Party candidates on the ballot for statewide and local offices since 1980. In most contests, however, their candidates receive only 3 to 5 percent of the vote. The party has never elected a member to state office, and most voters, even if they share the libertarian ideology, consider the Libertarian Party either too extreme or unable to win against a major party candidate. However, this lack of support for the Libertarian Party's candidates is not a valid measure of the support for the ideology.

Populists   Opposite the libertarians in Figure 2.1 are the **populists,** who favor government intervention both to promote equality and to establish or maintain an ordered liberty. Populists support the greatest scope of government action. Texas has a strong populist tradition. Started in Comanche County by Thomas Gaines in 1886 as a protest against the Democratic Party's leaders of that county, the People's Party led the political struggle for the ideas promoted by the Farmers' Alliance. The fundamental value championed by the People's Party was the equality of humankind. The view was incorporated in the Farmers' Alliance slogan: "Equal rights to all, special privileges to none." Despite the supposed equality of humans, the People's Party noted that certain economic inequalities existed in America, which placed a burden on all working people and most especially on the agricultural classes. These inequities had to be eliminated, and this could only be accomplished with the assistance of the government's power. Thus, the People's Party sought government intervention in the economy to regulate or, if necessary, to control the economy. The economic issues of greatest concern to the populists involved land, transportation, and money.[31]

Concerning the conflict between individualism and an ordered liberty, the People's Party showed less tolerance for diversity and individual choice in matters of morality. The People's Party had a strong Protestant religious flavor and drew few converts in counties where African Americans, Mexican Americans, and foreign-born residents were numerous. The populist movement was essentially a native Anglo movement, which was unsuccessful with foreign-born Texans and ignored Mexican Americans. For example, Germans, who were courted by the populists, viewed the movement as antialien, anti-Catholic, antiliberal, and Prohibitionist.[32] Although the political party eventually ceased to contest elections, populism persists as an ideology in Texas.

Conservatives **Conservatives** believe that government should not promote equality, but they support government regulation of individual behavior in order to ensure an ordered liberty. The contradiction that conservatives exhibit in terms of the scope of government action can be explained by American conservatism's view of human nature. According to this view of human nature, humans are selfish, flawed by original sin, and in need of moral guidance. Thus, American conservatism believes in the necessity for moral principles to guide human behavior and allows government, through legislation and other devices, to apply those principles. Similarly, doubts about the capabilities of humans lead to a reluctance to allow government tampering with natural economic and social laws. Despite their opposition to government intervention in the economy, contemporary conservatives recognize the value of some forms of economic promotion and regulation. This concession to government involvement in our capitalist economy by contemporary conservatives has forced some traditional conservatives to abandon conservatism in favor of libertarianism.

In contemporary Texas, self-identified conservatives are prominent in both of the major political parties and both state and local government, as well as the population generally.[33] Economic issues have provided the basis for Texas conservatism, viewing government programs to provide public services as unnecessary and anticapitalist. However, some of Texas's most intense confrontations historically have involved the use of government authority to protect traditional values—for example, the prohibition of alcohol in the early 1900s. Increasingly, in Texas as well as in other states, conservatives are joined by libertarians in battles that involve government's regulation of the economy.

Liberals   The final ideology, liberalism, favors a government that uses its authority to promote equality but that leaves an individual free to make moral or personal decisions. Modern liberalism in Texas is traceable to the effects of industrialization and the economic and social dislocations associated with it. The events that define modern American liberalism are the Great Depression, which promoted the use of government authority to limit the economic effects of dramatic swings in the business cycle, and the Civil Rights movement, which promoted the use of government authority to ensure equality for all elements of society. While favoring government's promotion of economic, political, and social equality, modern **liberals** oppose government infringement on each individual's freedom to make personal choices on moral issues, such as the decision by a woman to terminate a pregnancy. In Texas, liberals have always constituted a minority of the population.

We revisit the ideologies frequently in subsequent chapters. For now, understanding the ideologies is important for two reasons. *First, most issues in Texas politics are expressed in terms of a preference either for individualism or for an ordered liberty or in terms of a preference either for equality or for individualism.* Almost every political issue in Texas politics can be viewed as a conflict over ideas in the Texan Creed. As Figure 2.1 illustrates, the choices are usually between individualism and equality or between individualism and social order. Furthermore, although only a small fraction of Texans are ideologues, they are the ones who frame the political debates over issues. They are the most sophisticated and active people politically. Understanding the bases for their views helps you understand political discussions and the positions of the participants and, if you are so inclined, allows you to join in.

Second, most people in Texas have ideological tendencies. Although not ideologues, most Texans do hold consistent attitudes in a general policy area, such as social policy or economic policy. Most political debates play to these tendencies because political activists realize that this is how most people organize their political information.

> **Critical Thinking Exercise:**   Consider your own political socialization and how it has affected your political beliefs, attitudes, and behaviors. What role has the Texan Creed played, if any? Which agents of socialization had the most influence on your political views? Which ideals—equality, individualism, liberty—are most important to you? Which ideology most accurately reflects your political ideals?

THE PEOPLES OF TEXAS

Currently, Texas, with more than 20 million residents, is the second largest state in population and in territory.[34] With an area of 267,339 square miles, Texas is larger than most nations and contains every major landform: mountains, plains, plateaus, and hills. West of the Pecos River, in far West Texas, are the Chisos and Davis Mountains, a part of the Rocky Mountain chain. Plains constitute the major landform in Texas, covering much of West Texas, North Texas, the Gulf Coast, and northwestern Texas. The Edwards Plateau, in west central Texas, is the major plateau, or tableland, in Texas. Hills are found in many parts of Texas, but they are especially prominent in the German Hill Country, located northwest of San Antonio. The variety of landforms and the geographical size of Texas has an effect on its inhabitants. As a geographer told one of the authors when he first moved to Texas, if you show a Texan a picture of the Grand Canyon, he or she will ask, "What part of Texas is that?" The geographic size of Texas makes its inhabitants feel that almost any natural wonder must be within its borders.

Texas's population is almost as diverse as its geography. Whereas the United States in 1998 was nearly 72 percent Anglo, 12 percent African American, and 11 percent Hispanic, Texas, in the same year, was 56 percent Anglo, 29 percent Hispanic, and 12 percent African American. The Institute of Texan Cultures identifies 27 ethnic groups in contemporary Texas (see the box titled, "The Institute of Texan Cultures"). Its past held even more diversity. At first, of course, there were the American Indians, or Native Americans.

BOX *The Institute of Texan Cultures*

Located next to the Tower of the Americas in Hemisfair Park in downtown San Antonio, The University of Texas's Institute of Texan Cultures offers insights into the diversity of Texas peoples. Visitors to the institute are greeted by 27 exhibits that celebrate different ethnic groups whose culture is represented in contemporary Texas. Each exhibit provides information about notable Texans who represent that particular ethnic group. Also, there is a display indicating when members of the ethnic group came to Texas and significant events in the history of that group's experience in Texas. Did you know, for example, that Scott Joplin, the "King of Ragtime," was born in Texas? Also, did you know that one of the first men to shed his blood in the Texas Revolution was Samuel McCollough, Jr., an African American? These are just a few of the many interesting people that the visitor to the institute encounters.

The Institute of Texan Cultures currently has exhibits for the following cultures:

Spanish	French	Lebanese
Belgian	Greek	Dutch
Italian	Japanese	Chinese
Polish	Czech	Wendish
German	Swiss	African American
Norwegian	Swedish	Danish
Irish	Scottish	Anglo American
Native American	English	Mexican
Jewish	Filipino	*Tejano*

One of the more interesting exhibits depicts the Wends, who were Slavs that inhabited a part of Saxony and Prussia in Europe, called Lusatia. They came to Texas in the mid-1800s seeking freedom. Unlike most Slavs, the Wends were Protestant and were subjected to persecution by the Catholic majority. The first Wends settled at Rabb's Creek in Lee County. The Wendish culture is still evident in contemporary Texas in Serbin, Giddings, Fedor, Warda, Manheim, McDade, Loebau, Lincoln, Winchester, LaGrange, and Walburg. As described in the exhibit, "Wherever found they [Wends] are gregarious and convivial people, still very much in the habit of turning work into social occasions." Texas Wends convene at McDade the second Saturday of July for an annual Watermelon Festival and barbecue, with music and the crowning of a festival queen.

continued

Native Americans

There are few Native-American tribes in contemporary Texas. However, from prehistoric times, **Native Americans** representing four different cultural traditions established permanent residence in Texas, and members of many more tribes and nations, some of whom are still present in Texas, were brief inhabitants.

BOX *The Institute of Texan Cultures—Continued*

Other Texas ethnic groups hold similar festivals to celebrate their heritage. Wurstfest, a German festival in New Braunfels, began in 1961, when the mayor proclaimed that a Saturday in November should be set aside to celebrate German food and tradition brought to the Texas Hill Country in the 1840s. Today, Wurstfest is a ten-day event that draws over 150,000 celebrants. Also, the Easter celebration in Fredericksburg follows a unique tradition from the Texas frontier. An annual Easter Fires Pageant commemorates John O. Meusebach's treaty with the Comanches. During the negotiations, the Comanches posted guards around the village and periodically lighted signal fires in the nearby hills. Frightened children were calmed, it is said, by a kindly woman who assured them that the fires were the Easter rabbit boiling eggs and dyeing them with flowers. At West, Texas, about ten miles north of Waco, Czechs hold Westfest over the Labor Day weekend, featuring Czech fun (a Taroky Tournament), food (a Kolache Baking Contest), and dance (the polka and the waltz). In Castroville, settled by French immigrants in the mid-1800s, thousands congregate to honor the patron saint of the century-old St. Louis Catholic Church in late August. Alsatian sausage and Texas barbecue are served during the celebration of St. Louis Day Homecoming. Rather than traveling to these various festivals, one could attend the Institute of Texan Culture's annual Texas Folklife Festival in early August and experience the many cultures that make up Texas.

Although the ethnic festivals are interesting and enjoyable, there is a more important point. As one of the displays at the Institute of Texan Cultures states:

> People of different cultures came from around the world to settle in Texas. These diverse people contributed to the growth and development of Texas. Their accomplishments are many, but achievements have not come without conflict—and change. By being aware of the past and taking time to learn how people live and think today, we can celebrate accomplishments, understand conflict and change, and appreciate the society around us.

Sources: Institute of Texan Cultures. *Texas Highways* (September 1993) devoted a special issue to Texans and their cultures, including a comprehensive list of displays, festivals, landmarks, and events for each ethnic group.

In the coastal areas of the state and extending into all of south Texas, the Coahuiltecan and Karankawan tribes maintained an imperiled existence in a harsh environment by hunting and gathering. In central Texas, scattered bands of Native Americans, known contemporarily as Tonkawas, established themselves during the opening of the historical period. By the eighteenth century, they had become a buffalo-hunting, tepee-using, horse-riding Plains people. To the north of the Tonkawas were the ancestors of the Lipan Apache. "The other Plains tribes vitally associated with Texas in those early days were Kiowa Apaches, Kiowas, and especially Comanches."[35] The Jumano, related to the Puebloan culture of the

These dancers celebrate their heritage during the Texas Folklife Festival at the Institute of Texan Cultures in San Antonio, Texas.

American Southwest, were present from historical times, especially in the Rio Grande Valley from El Paso to the confluence of the Rio Grande and Mexican Rio Conchos. Spanish Fort on the Red River was the headquarters for a group of semi-sedentary tribes, known today as the Wichitas, who extended to Waco in central Texas. The Wichitas had much in common with the Caddoes, but after their adoption of horses in the eighteenth century, their culture became more Plains-like. In east and northeast Texas, tribes of Caddoes, joined together in confederacies, possessed a complex culture built around intensive farming and agriculture.

The Native-American legacy in Texas is substantial. The Caddoes established economic and cultural patterns on which subsequent inhabitants of Texas expanded. The Caddoes also greeted early Spanish explorers as *Tayshas*, meaning "friends." The term was subsequently Hispanicized to *Tejas*, and then Anglicized to *Texas*. Similarly, the most feared and respected Native Americans in Texas, the Comanches, displayed many of the characteristics of individualism that Anglo Texans on the frontier most admired.[36] Also, as noted earlier, their resistance to Anglo expansion forced the farmers and ranchers to become horsemen and to adapt to the challenges of existence on the frontier.

Currently, there are only three Native-American tribes on reservations in Texas: the Alabama-Coushattas in Polk County, the Kickapoos near Eagle Pass, and the Tiguas near El Paso. The Tiguas became embroiled in Texas politics when they opened their Speaking Rock Casino in 1993. In 1987, Congress recognized the Tiguas, and in exchange, the tribe agreed to prohibit gambling in all forms and to obey Texas laws. Nevertheless, the tribe filed a lawsuit, which they lost, attempting to force the state to negotiate a casino compact with the tribe under the 1988 Indian Gaming Regulatory Act. In 1999, Attorney General John Cornyn sought an injunction to halt gambling on tribal property. Entering electoral politics in 1998, the Tiguas contributed heavily to Democratic gubernatorial candidate Garry Mauro, who supported the Tiguas's right to maintain the casino. In 1999, the Alabama-Coushatta tribe voted to bring gambling to its Texas reservation.

Hispanics

Although the Spaniards had explored Texas previously, only in the early eighteenth century did they establish permanent settlements in Texas. An early colony in Nacogdoches was followed by a *presidio,* San Antonio de Bexar, and a mission, San Antonio de Valero, along the San Antonio River. A colony in La Bahia (Goliad) followed. Only in the 1740s and 1750s did the Spaniards colonize the Rio Grande, although these were some of their most successful settlements.

The mainstays of Spanish colonization included four institutions: (1) the mission, which performed civilian as well as religious functions; (2) the *presidio,* which provided frontier defense; (3) the *rancho,* which sustained civilian life; and (4) towns or civilian settlements. By the end of the eighteenth century, only about 5000 *pobladores* (settlers) inhabited Texas.[37] Nonetheless, their legacy far exceeds what their numbers suggest. They created a culture that valued "egalitarianism, a sense of duty, and a respect for physical prowess and gallantry in the face of adversity."[38] They also provided cultural norms for ranchers, sheep herders, and goat raisers. Also, Spanish legal traditions, such as those pertaining to women's property rights, endured, as did customs protecting debtors.[39]

After Mexico's independence from Spain in 1821, the colonialization of Texas was no more successful. In 1836, when Texas became an independent republic, no more than 7000 or 8000 Spaniards, Christianized Native Americans, and *mestizos* resided in Texas. In 1850, the United States census reveals a **Hispanic** population of only 14,000—less than 7 percent of Texas's population. As late as 1887, the state census counted only 83,000 Hispanics, only 4 percent of the Texas population. Concentrated in the border counties along the Rio Grande, Hispanics were outnumbered even by German Americans. However, between 1890 and 1910, a major influx of Mexicans occurred, resulting in a doubling of the Hispanic population of 1877. Between 1910 and the present, the Hispanic population in Texas has grown tenfold, caused largely by an explosive birth rate in Mexico and the steady industrialization of Texas. Some time during the late 1940s, Hispanics displaced African Americans as the largest ethnic minority in Texas.[40]

By the late 1990s, Hispanics had achieved considerable political clout in Texas. In 1999, there were approximately 1800 Hispanic elected public officials in Texas, more than in any other state. Although only two Hispanics (Railroad Commissioner Tony Garza and Supreme Court Justice Alberto R. Gonzales, both Republicans) hold statewide elective offices, 35 Hispanics serve in the Texas Legislature, 204 are county officials, 531 are municipal officers, 312 hold judicial posts, and 609 serve on elected school boards. Democratic Representative Rene Oliveira, Chairman of the Mexican American Legislative Caucus, was selected chair of the powerful House Ways and Means Committee in 1999. Currently, most Hispanic elected officials are Democrats; however, the Republican Party made a concerted effort to attract Hispanic voters in 1998, appealing to Hispanic's desires for educational advancement, personal responsibility, and economic opportunity.[41]

African Americans

Although **African Americans** have inhabited Texas since Spanish rule, few African Americans, probably no more than 12 percent of the population, lived in Texas prior to 1836, primarily because the Mexican government opposed slavery, and most early settlers in Texas came from the southern mountain states, where slavery was less common. In the late 1830s, however, an influx of African Americans accompanied Anglo planters from coastal southern states. With slavery legalized in the Republic of Texas, the number of African Americans increased rapidly, composing 20 percent of the population by 1840. The growth of the African-American population in Texas was effectively halted by the Civil War. Between 1865 and 1880, only 6 percent of immigrants were African American, and the percentage of African Americans has continued to decline since 1865, the year in which nearly one-third of Texas's population was African American.[42]

The bulk of the settlement by African Americans in Texas occurred between 1836 and 1865. The states that contributed the largest number of slaves were Alabama, Virginia, Georgia, and Mississippi, and the area of greatest settlement for African Americans lay east of a line connecting Texarkana and San Antonio. This was also the area dominated by Anglos from the lower South. By 1860, 13 Texas counties had African-American majorities. All of these counties were located along the major rivers of eastern and southeastern Texas, especially the lower Brazos, Colorado, and Trinity Rivers. After emancipation, African-American freedpersons remained in that area; consequently, as recently as 1887, 12 counties had African-American majorities. However, with the decline and fall of the sharecropper system, African Americans abandoned the rural areas of east Texas for the urban centers that were closest to the old plantation districts— Houston and Dallas. In 1930, only four counties had African-American majorities, and by 1980, there were none.[43]

African Americans in Texas held fewer elective offices in 1997 than they did in 1993. In 1997, 448 African Americans held elective office, 24 fewer than in 1993, which dropped Texas from fifth to sixth among the states in number of African-

American elected officials. Among the elected officials, 2 African Americans were state senators, 14 were representatives, 15 were county officials, 279 were municipal officials, 45 were judicial or law enforcement officials, and 92 were elected to school boards and other elected education positions.[44] In 1999, only one African American, Republican Railroad Commissioner Michael L. Williams, held a statewide elective office. Williams was appointed to the Railroad Commission in 1998 to fill the position vacated by Carole Keeton Rylander, who was elected Comptroller in 1998. In September 1999, Williams was elected chair of the Railroad Commission. He then announced plans to campaign for the remainder of Rylander's term in the 2000 general election. Among the prominent African-American politicians in Texas are Mayors Ron Kirk of Dallas and Lee Brown of Houston (see Chapter 12). Kirk was elected in 1995 and reelected in 1999, and Brown, who faced stiff opposition from Robert Mosbacher in his first election in 1997, was easily reelected in 1999.

Asian Americans

The first permanent resident Asian Americans in Texas were probably Chinese immigrants who arrived in Houston in 1869 to clear land for the Houston and Texas Central Railway. Chinese laborers also worked for the Southern Pacific Railroad and the Texas and Pacific line during the 1870s and 1880s. In the early 1900s, a distinguished Japanese businessman, Seito Saibara, was invited to the United States to help develop the rice industry on the Gulf coast. In 1903, Harris County officials invited him to start a colony in Webster, just south of Houston. Saibara bought 304 acres and began bringing families from Japan. Several Japanese colonies were subsequently established in the Rio Grande Valley and in Orange County. During the 1970s, thousands of Vietnamese immigrants came to Texas when the South Vietnamese government neared collapse and ultimately fell to North Vietnam.

In 1997, there were 523,972 **Asian Americans** in Texas, primarily Vietnamese, Chinese, Indians, Filipinos, Koreans, and Japanese residents. In the larger cities in Texas, there are Asian neighborhoods. In Houston, which has the largest Asian-American population, there are two Chinatowns—a historic district near the George R. Brown Convention Center and a newer area on Bellaire Boulevard. In fact, a number of small malls, many along Bellaire, have signs in Chinese, Japanese, Vietnamese, and other Asian languages.

In 1999, few Asian Americans held elective political office in Texas. At that time, all of the Asian Americans held county or municipal offices.[45] Martha Wong, long time community activist, served on the Houston city council from 1993 until 1999, when term limits prohibited her reelection.

Anglos

As the term is used in Texas, **Anglos** are non-Hispanic whites. During the early period of Anglo settlement in Texas, 1815 to 1836, most of the Anglo immigrants to Texas were natives of the upper South. From their initial movement into Texas, the pioneers were predominantly upper southerners from Tennessee, Kentucky, Arkansas, and North Carolina. By 1820, these people had firmly established themselves in northeast Texas.

During the 1820s, the *empresario* program of the Mexican government drew additional upper southerners to the Austin, DeWitt, and Robertson colonies in south central Texas. Missouri, Kentucky, Tennessee, and Arkansas provided most of these settlers.

In the southeastern border area of Texas, known as the Atascosita District, Anglos began drifting in after 1819. These settlers were lower southerners, mostly poor whites from Louisiana, Mississippi, and Alabama.

North of the Big Thicket, between the Trinity and Sabine Rivers, a few small Anglo settlements developed. Most of these settlers were upper southerners, although many slave-owning planters were attracted by the fertile Redlands area. Thus, by 1836, more than 60 percent of Anglos in Texas were from the upper South, about 25 percent were from the lower South, and about 10 percent were New Englanders.[46]

From Texas's independence to the Civil War, Anglo immigration increased, drawing more heavily from the lower South. The legalization of slavery in the Texas Republic resulted in the first major wave of lower southerners, primarily from Alabama, Georgia, Mississippi, and Louisiana. According to the 1850 census, lower southerners had become almost as numerous as the upper southerners. The two groups did, however, occupy different areas of Texas. Most of eastern and southeastern Texas was successfully settled by lower southern planters, and the continuing waves of upper southerners were directed to the western interior of Texas (Figure 2.2).

In the post–Civil War period, upper and lower southern immigration continued in roughly equal proportions. The western expansion to the New Mexico border by 1880 was primarily an achievement of upper southerners, who settled most of West Texas, and lower midwesterners (Illinois, Kansas, and Iowa), who dominated the upper Panhandle.

The patterns of settlement established by Texas's first residents are still evident today; however, new patterns have been imposed on the old pattern. Consequently, contemporary Texas is more heavily populated, more urbanized, and more Hispanicized.

The Contemporary Population of Texas

Population estimates indicate that Texas will exceed 20.3 million inhabitants by the time the 2000 census is completed. The previous census, in 1990, revealed that Texas's population had grown faster than the population of the United States, although slower than its growth during the 1970s. Also, whereas more than half of Texas's growth during the 1970s was the result of net in-migration, over two-thirds of Texas's growth during the 1980s was due to natural increase (internal population growth). Furthermore, the migration of the 1980s was primarily from

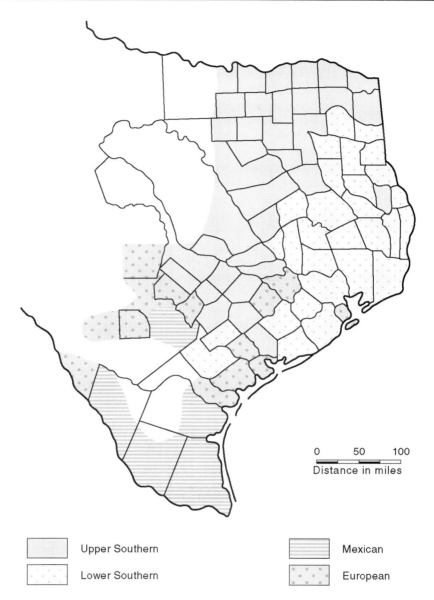

Figure 2.2 Cultural/Ethnic Regions in Texas, 1850

In the first census after Texas joined the United States, the prevalence of Texans from the lower South had expanded westward. The Mexican population was concentrated around San Antonio and along the Rio Grande River, which formed the border between Mexico and Texas. Texans from the upper South had also pushed westward.

Source: Terry G. Jordon with John L. Bean, Jr., and William M. Holmes, *Texas: A Geography;* Boulder, CO: Westview Press, 1984, p. 75. By permission.

other nations, not from other states in the United States. By 1994, Texas's population size had surpassed New York's population, making Texas's population the second largest in the nation. Since the 1990 census, Texas has added nearly 2.8 million people to its population. Texas's population growth between 1990 and 1998 was the result of natural increase (57 percent), immigration from other states (20 percent), and immigration from other nations (24 percent). This balance among the components of population growth combined with a relatively constant rate of growth through natural increase makes continued population growth in Texas likely.[47]

The urbanization of Texas also continued during the 1990s, and the rural population of Texas fell below 16 percent. Despite the rural image frequently associated with Texas, a majority of Texans have lived in urban areas since the 1940s. In 1997, Texas had 27 metropolitan areas, ranging in size from Victoria, with 82,580 people, to Dallas-Ft. Worth, with 4,683,991 people. During the 1990s, the 27 metropolitan areas accounted for more than 90 percent of Texas's population growth. The fastest growing metropolitan areas are in Texas's central core—Dallas-Ft. Worth, Houston-Galveston-Brazoria, San Antonio, Austin-San Marcos—or are located along the border with Mexico—El Paso, McAllen-Edinburg-Mission, Brownsville-Harlingen-San Benito, and Laredo. One of the fastest growing regions is the Lower Rio Grande Valley.[48] Three Texas cities (Dallas, Houston, and San Antonio) are among the ten most populous cities in the United States.

Probably the most important demographic change in Texas between 1990 and 2000 involves the ethnic composition of the population. Texas's minority populations are expected to increase much more rapidly than the Anglo population. Hispanics, the largest minority group, are expected to make up 31 percent of the population, increasing by 45 percent during the decade. African Americans, who will compose about 11.4 percent of the population, are projected to increase by 17 percent. In 2000, Anglos, who will still constitute a majority with 54.5 percent of the population, will have increased by only 8 percent.[49] However, population projections for Texas anticipate that Anglos will cease to be the majority sometime during the first decade of the twenty-first century, and early in the third decade, Hispanics will probably outnumber Anglos in Texas (Table 2.1). In this book, we return frequently to the topic of Texas's people; however, we now shift our focus to the economy of Texas.

Table 2.1   PROJECTED TEXAS POPULATION BY ETHNICITY

Year	Anglo	Hispanic	African American	Other
1990	60.7	25.5	11.7	2.1
2000	54.5	31.0	11.4	3.1
2010	48.4	36.3	10.9	4.4
2020	42.3	41.4	10.3	6.0
2030	36.4	46.2	9.5	7.9

Source: Texas Almanac, 2000–2001 (Dallas: Dallas Morning News, 1999), p. 288.

AUSTIN COMMUNITY COLLEGE

Student Test Request and Grade Form

All Items Must Be Completed Clearly and Correctly – Please Print Firmly

NAME ___Veronica Getz___   PHONE # ___494-1074___   DATE ___12-11-00___

Section # ___03188___   Course Abbreviation ___GOVT___   Course # ___2306___   Test Number ___4___

Circle the item(s) which apply: ON CAMPUS COURSES   (OPC – OPEN CAMPUS COURSES)   *RETEST

RETESTING ALLOWED ONLY WITH YELLOW RECEIPT FROM INITIAL TEST (IF RETESTING IS PERMITTED)

INSTRUCTOR'S NAME ___S. Haag___   INSTRUCTOR'S CAMPUS ___RVS___

I have read and understand the "Guide to the Student Use of the Testing Center." I further understand that once I begin a test, I must stay until I am ready to turn in the test for grading. Students may not take any materials to testing carrel unless approved by instructor and listed on upper right hand corner of exam. I also understand that cheating, including using unauthorized materials while testing, is subject to disciplinary action which may include scholastic suspension and/or dismissal.

Student's Signature ___Veronica Getz___   Social Security # ___466 - 73 - 9509___

FOR OFFICE USE ONLY:

FORM GIVEN ___A___   Staff Initials ___

SCORE ___45/50 = 90___   Staff Initials ___

[ ] SCRATCH PAPER   [ ] LINED PAPER   [ ] GRAPH PAPER   [ ] OTHER ___

[ ] THIS STUDENT'S ANSWER SHEET IS BEING HELD WHILE THE STUDENT DEVELOPMENT OFFICES INVESTIGATE AN INCIDENT REPORT REGARDING THIS TEST.

TESTING CAMPUS

Austin Community College

DEC 1 1 2000

RGC Testing Center

Critical Thinking Exercise: Think about the changes that have occurred in the population of Texas since the early 1800s. How have politics
and government in Texas been affected by those changes? What do the projected changes in the Texas population over the next 30 years portend for
Texas politics and government?

THE ECONOMY OF TEXAS

Until quite recently, the Texas economy was land-based and colonial in structure.
Texas produced, processed, and shipped its agricultural and mineral products to
outside markets. Thus, the Texas economy was dependent on external demand
and the prices paid for its cotton, cattle, or petroleum.

Cotton

The first real economy in Texas was created by southern planters and resembled
the southern seaboard of the United States in prior centuries. The economy was
based on large slave plantations. The money crop, cotton, was barged down Texas
rivers to the Gulf of Mexico because reefs prevented the development of ports at
the mouths of Texas rivers. The cotton was then shipped to Europe or the United
States, mostly through New Orleans. Later, Galveston was developed as a port,
and it was the commercial center of Texas from the 1840s to the 1880s. During
Texas's experience as a republic and during its early statehood, cotton was the
economic heart. Consequently, the region flourished during the cotton boom that
preceded the Civil War. Although cotton survived the Civil War, the plantation
system did not, and it was replaced by sharecropping. Nevertheless, even in the
late 1990s, Texas's annual cotton harvest accounted for a fourth of the total cotton
production in the United States, providing $1.18 billion in receipts in 1998.[50]

Cattle

The cattle kingdom, inherited from the Mexicans, spread across the entire
American West, capturing the fancy of Texas and the world in the late nineteenth
century. Initially, the cattle business involved rounding up stray cattle and driving
them to the Kansas railheads. The demand for beef created a link between the
western frontier and the industrial marketplace. Like King Cotton, the cattle kingdom drew people and money from afar and involved agricultural products
shipped to distant markets. For example, the largest ranch in Texas, the XIT, involved a Chicago syndicate, which was given 3,050,000 acres in return for con-
structing the state capitol in 1881. Covering parts of nine counties in the
Panhandle, the XIT ranch, which operated until the early 1900s, featured more
than 1500 miles of fence.[51]

Cattle and cowboys roamed the Texas plains during the late nineteenth and early twentieth centuries when ranching was a major economic activity in Texas.

Petroleum

For much of the twentieth century, petroleum was the basis for the Texas economy. From the first major oil discovery at Spindletop, near Beaumont, by mining engineer Captain A. F. Lucas in 1901, Texas and the production of crude oil have been synonymous. Between 1900 and 1901, Texas oil production increased fourfold. In 1902, Spindletop alone produced 17 million barrels, 94 percent of the state's production. In 1923, the success of Santa Rita No. 1 ushered in the West Texas oil industry. The largest Texas oil field, the East Texas field, was discovered by C. M. "Dad" Joiner in 1930. However, the discovery of the East Texas field created a surplus of petroleum in a depressed economy. After World War II, the United States market sought cheaper oil in the Middle East. However, the oil embargo by the Organization of Petroleum Exporting Countries (OPEC) in 1973, a year after Texas reached its peak in oil production, caused an economic boom during the 1970s as prices were driven upward. This boom, of course, was followed by the bust of the 1980s when, in 1986, the price for West Texas crude fell below ten dollars a barrel. In 1981, the petroleum industry contributed 27 percent of the state's gross state product (GSP). Eighteen years later, in 1999, the industry contributed only 7.5 percent to the GSP.[52]

The Contemporary Economy

Since the 1980s, the Texas economy, which produced a GSP of $632 billion in 1998, has become more diverse, more nationalized, and more globalized than in the past. The diversity was thrust upon the Texas economy by the decline of the petroleum industry in the early 1980s. Furthermore, the economic regions of Texas that were most dependent on oil and natural gas—the Gulf Coast, West Texas, and portions of South Texas—have substantially altered their economies. The larger regions of Texas are the most diverse, with the metroplex area of Dallas-Ft. Worth being the most diverse. The importance of increased economic diversity is that it allows regions to withstand economic setbacks in one or more industries.[53] Currently, the greatest economic growth is occurring in a core area anchored by Houston, Dallas-Ft. Worth, and San Antonio. According to the Comptroller,

> This core triangle of high-growth industries and population tends to dominate the business sections of newspapers and to draw the most attention in plans for future development. Power is shared in a variety of ways by the three largest urban centers. Each is a distinct market and supply center, defining not only itself and the surrounding areas, but serving as a business link to the rest of the world, too.
>   . . . With just 10 percent of the state's land mass, the core is home to 60 percent of Texans, less than two-thirds of whom were born in Texas. . . .
>   Economic characteristics draw the most vivid distinctions. With the obvious exceptions of agriculture, forestry, and fisheries, jobs are more plentiful in the central triangle, higher education more readily available and the growth of future industries more assured. The triangle cities are particularly strong in the financial, insurance and real estate sectors, in business and repair services, and in microelectronics, computer technology and biotechnology.[54]

The Texas economy more closely resembles the national economy, although the Texas economy grew faster than the United States economy during the 1990s. During the 1990s, Texas led all states in net job creation. In 1998, Texas created 268,000 new jobs, producing a 3.1 percent growth in jobs and ranking second in the nation in total jobs added. The growth in jobs occurred in most sectors of the economy. Construction jobs increased by 5.8 percent, bolstered by low interest rates and increasing demand for residential and nonresidential construction. Growing by 30 percent between 1993 and 1998, manufacturing jobs in Texas are concentrated in high-technology areas, primarily computers and electronics. The service-producing sectors of the economy accounted for 84 percent of the growth in jobs in 1998. Leading the service-producing sectors were communications, transportation, and business services. Meanwhile, employment in public utilities and in government decreased. In late 1999, the unemployment rate in Texas was 4.5 percent and ranged from a low of 1.7 percent in Bryan-College Station to a high of 13.1 percent in McAllen-Edinburg-Mission. In the early 2000s, job growth is expected to slow in the construction industry; manufacturing in durable goods

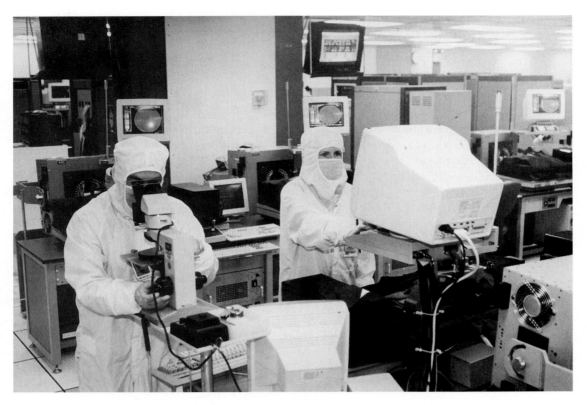

Workers in a Texas Instruments wafer-fabrication clean room demonstrate the effects of modern technology on jobs in the contemporary Texas economy.

will remain strong, especially in semiconductor and other electronic component manufacturing; communications jobs will continue to expand, and government jobs, except at the local level, will continue to shrink. Overall, Texas economic growth in 2000 will remain strong and comparable to the 1990s.[55]

The Texas economy has also become globalized. Competition for Texas business takes place throughout the world. The North American Free Trade Agreement (NAFTA), approved by Congress in 1993, benefited the Texas economy. In 1998, Texas exports reached $86.9 billion, growing by 66 percent since 1993. Electronics, industrial machinery (which includes both computers and oil and gas field machinery), and chemicals accounted for a majority of Texas's exports in 1998.[56] However, for long-term, sustained economic growth, competition in the global marketplace requires a commitment to developing a highly skilled, high-wage workforce supported by advanced technology, efficient telecommunications, strong research and development, and innovative marketing systems.[57] This is the economic challenge to Texas in the twenty-first century. If and how Texas meets the challenge will be interesting, to say the least.

> **Critical Thinking Exercises:** As the Texas economy evolved from a colonial economy to a mature, industrial, and service-oriented economy, the politics of Texas changed. How have Texas politics and government changed? How has power shifted? How has the political agenda been affected by the economic changes?

SUMMARY

In this chapter, we have described the context for Texas politics. The Texan Creed includes five ideas that are the product of the state's historical development and the continuing process of political socialization. Also, we identified three agents of political socialization—the family, the schools, and the media—and indicated how each contributes to the acquisition of political beliefs, attitudes, and values. We indicated the bases for ideologies in Texas and explained four ideological types—liberals, conservatives, populists, and libertarians. The chapter also identified the major peoples of Texas, historically and contemporarily. Finally, we provided a sketch of the Texas economy, indicating how the Texas economy has evolved from a colonial base to a diverse, modern, service and manufacturing economy.

KEY TERMS

Texan Creed
Texas frontier
Texas Rangers
the Alamo
political socialization
agents of socialization
political ideology
ideologues
libertarians

populists
conservatives
liberals
Native Americans
Hispanics
African Americans
Asian Americans
Anglos

SUGGESTED READINGS

Barkdull, John. "Globalization and Texas," *Texas Journal of Political Studies* 20, no. 2 (1998): 1–24.

Barr, Alwyn. *Black Texans: A History of Negroes in Texas, 1528–1995.* 2d edition. Norman, Okla.: University of Oklahoma Press, 1996.

Fehrenbach, T. R. *Seven Keys to Texas.* Rev. edition. El Paso: Texas Western Press, 1986.

Himmel, Kelly. *Conquest of the Karankawas and the Tonkawas, 1821–1859.* College Station, Tex.: Texas A&M University Press, 1999.

Maddox, William S., and Stuart A. Lilie, *Beyond Liberal and Conservative: Reassessing the Political Spectrum*. Washington, D.C.: Cato Institute, 1984.

Newcomb, W. W., Jr. *The Indians of Texas: From Prehistoric to Modern Times*. Austin, Tex.: University of Texas Press, 1961.

Tijerina, Andres. *Tejanos & Texas Under the Mexican Flag, 1821–1836*. College Station, Tex.: Texas A & M University Press, 1994.

Whisenhunt, Donald. *Five States of Texas: An Immodest Proposal*. Austin, Tex.: Eakin Press, 1987

NOTES

1. Mary Ann Rosser, "UT Group Praises Hopwood Ruling," *Austin American-Statesman*, 11 September 1997; Mary Ann Rosser, "UT Professor Stands Firm on Race," *Austin American-Statesman*, 12 September 1997; Mary Ann Rosser, "UT Cools Off, but Fight Over Graglia Still Simmers, *Austin American Statesman*, 18 September 1997; James E. Garcia, "Hostile Words in Texas," *Black Issues in Higher Education* 14 (October 2, 1997): 13–15; Nat Hentoff, "Should This Professor Be Fired?" *Village Voice*, 42 (November 18, 1997): 22; Lydia Lum, "Minority Rolls Cut by Hopwood," *Houston Chronicle*, 15 September 1997.

2. John Steinbeck, *Travels with Charlie: In Search of America* (New York: Viking Press, 1962), 203.

3. T. R. Fehrenbach, *Seven Keys to Texas*, rev. ed. (El Paso: Texas Western Press, 1986), 3–4.

4. T. R. Fehrenbach, "Seven Keys to Understanding Texas," *The Atlantic*, March 1975, 123–124.

5. Fehrenbach, *Seven Keys to Texas*, 22.

6. T. R. Fehrenbach, *Lone Star: A History of Texas and the Texans* (New York: Macmillan, 1968), 472–476.

7. Fehrenbach, *Seven Keys to Texas*, 29.

8. Ibid., 24–25.

9. Ibid., 76.

10. Alwyn Barr, *Texans in Revolt: The Battle for San Antonio, 1835* (Austin, Tex.: University of Texas Press, 1990), 1–4.

11. William C. Brinkley, *The Texas Revolution* (Austin, Tex.: Texas State Historical Association, 1952).

12. Quoted in Mark E. Nackman, *A Nation Within a Nation* (Port Washington, N.Y.: Kennikat Press, 1975), 27.

13. Joe B. Frantz, *Texas: A Bicentennial History* (New York: Norton, 1976), 69.

14. Walter Lord, *A Time to Stand: The Epic of the Alamo* (Lincoln: University of Nebraska Press, 1961), 54.

15. Ibid., 82.

16. Paul Andrew Hutton, "The Alamo: An American Epic," *American History Illustrated*, March 1986, 24.

17. Lord, *A Time to Stand*, 142.

18. Lon Tinkle, *The Alamo* (New York: McGraw-Hill, 1958), 118.

19. Gilbert M. Cuthbertson, "Individual Freedom: The Evolution of a Political Ideal," in *Texas Myths*, ed. Robert F. O'Connor (College Station, Tex.: Texas A&M University Press, 1986), 179.

20. David Montejano, *Anglos and Mexicans in the Making of Texas, 1836–1986* (Austin, Tex.: University of Texas Press, 1987), 305.

21. Fehrenbach, *Seven Keys to Texas*, 95.

22. Ibid., 128.
23. George Norris Green, *The Establishment in Texas Politics: The Primitive Years, 1938–1957* (Westport, Conn.: Greenwood Press, 1979), 3–4.
24. Margaret Swett Henson, "Texas History in the Public Schools: An Appraisal," *Southwestern Historical Quarterly* 82 (April 1979): 403–422; David G. McComb, "Texas History Textbooks in Texas Schools," *Southwestern Historical Quarterly* 93 (October 1989): 191–196.
25. Larry Willoughby, *Texas, Our Texas* (Austin, Tex.: Holt, Rinehart, & Winston, 1993), 250.
26. *Texas Poll Report* (Summer 1986): 7.
27. Doris Graber, *Mass Media and American Politics,* 2d ed. (Washington, D.C.: Congressional Quarterly Press, 1984), 138–140.
28. See Shanto Iyengar and Donald Kinder, *News That Matters: Television and American Opinion* (Chicago: University of Chicago Press, 1987), passim.
29. William S. Maddox and Stuart A. Lilie, *Beyond Liberal and Conservative: Reassessing the Political Spectrum* (Washington, D.C.: Cato Institute, 1984), 7–21.
30. Ibid., 14–15.
31. Roscoe Martin, *The People's Party in Texas* (Austin, Tex.: University of Texas Press, 1970), 31–52.
32. Ibid., 82–112.
33. *Texas Poll Report* (January–March 1994): 6.
34. During 1994, Texas passed New York in population, replacing it as the second largest state in population. California, with more than 33 million residents, is still the largest state.
35. W. W. Newcomb, Jr., *The Indians of Texas: From Prehistoric to Modern Times* (Austin, Tex.: University of Texas Press, 1961), 22.
36. Ibid., 182.
37. Arnoldo De Leon, *Mexican Americans in Texas: A Brief History* (Arlington Heights, Ill.: Harlan Davidson, 1993), 7–19.
38. Ibid., 20.
39. Donald E. Chipman, *Spanish Texas, 1519–1821* (Austin, Tex.: University of Texas Press, 1992), 242–260.
40. Terry G. Jordan, "A Century and a Half of Ethnic Change in Texas, 1836–1986," *Southwestern Historical Quarterly* 89 (April 1986): 392–394.
41. "Hispanics Key in '98 Vote, Both Parties Say," *Corpus Christi Caller-Times Interactive,* 22 September 1998. Accessed 19 October 1999, http://corpuschristionline.com/texas98/texas20612.html; A. Phillips Brooks, "Hispanics Wield New Clout at Capitol," *Austin American-Statesman,* 31 January 1999, pp. A1, A10.
42. Jordan "A Century and a Half of Ethnic Change," 400–401; Terry G. Jordan, John L. Bean, Jr., and William M. Holmes, *Texas: A Geography* (Boulder, Col.: Westview Press, 1984) 77, 79.
43. Jordan, "A Century and a Half of Ethnic Change," 402, 404; Jordan, Bean, and Holmes, *Texas,* 79.
44. David A. Bositis, "Black Elected Officials, 1994–1997," *Focus Magazine,* September 1998, Joint Center for Political and Economic Studies web site. Accessed 29 October 1999, http://www.jointctr.org/focus/issues/sep98.htm.
45. Comptroller of Public Accounts, "Lone Star Asians," *Fiscal Notes,* November 1997, 3–5; *1998–99 National Asian Pacific American Political Almanac,* (Los Angeles: UCLA Asian American Studies Center, 1999), 300–302.
46. Jordan et al., *Texas,* 71, 73.
47. Steve H. Murdock, "Trends in Texas Population Growth," in *Texas Almanac, 1996–1997* (Dallas: Dallas Morning News, 1995) 284; Steve H. Murdock, Md. Nazrul Hoque, and Beverly Pecotte, "Twenty Million Texans and Growing," in *Texas Almanac, 2000–2001* (Dallas: Dallas Morning News, 1999), 285.

48. "The Texas Economy Online," Texas Department of Economic Development web site, 26 October 1999. Accessed 29 October 1999, http://www.bidc.state.tx.us/overview/2-2te.htm.

49. Steve H. Murdock, Md. Nazrul Hoque, and Beverly A. Pecotte, "Texas Population: Historical Patterns and Future Trends," in *Texas Almanac, 1994–1995* (Dallas: Dallas Morning News, 1993), 303–304; Texas State Data Center, *Population Projections for Texas,* February 1998.

50. Fehrenbach, *Seven Keys to Texas,* 50–52; "Agriculture in Texas," in *Texas Almanac, 2000–2001,* 567–568.

51. Fehrenbach, *Seven Keys to Texas,* 52–54; Mike Kingston, "A Concise History of Texas," in *Texas Almanac, 1986–1987* (Dallas: Dallas Morning News, 1985), 212.

52. Fehrenbach, *Seven Keys to Texas,* 58–60; Donald A. Hicks, "Advanced Industrial Development," in eds. Anthony Campagne and Edward J. Harpham (College Station: Texas A&M University Press, 1987), 49–50; *Texas at the Crossroads: People, Politics, and Policy Texas Almanac, 1994–1995,* 608; Comptroller of Public Accounts, "10 Forces of Change," *Fiscal Notes,* January 1994, 1, 14; "A History of Oil in Texas" "The Texas Economy Online," Texas Department of Economic Development web site, 26 October 1999. Accessed 29 October 1999, http://www.bidc.state.tx.us/overview/2–2te.htm.

53. Comptroller of Public Accounts, "The Texas Economies: What Makes Them Tick," *Fiscal Notes,* December 1993, 7–10.

54. Comptroller of Public Accounts, "10 Forces of Change," *Fiscal Notes,* January 1994, 16–17.

55. Comptroller Public Accounts "Texas Economy: Employment Growth and Low Inflation," *Texas Almanac, 2000–2001* (Dallas: Dallas Morning News, 1999), 577–579; Comptroller of Public Accounts, *Fiscal Notes,* July 1999, 10–11.

56. "The Texas Economy Online," Department of Economic Development web site, 26 October 1999. Accessed 29 October 1999, http://www.bidc.state.texas.us/overview/2–2te.htm.

57. Comptroller of Public Accounts, "10 Forces of Change," *Fiscal Notes,* January 1994, 12–13.

3

The Legal Context: The Constitution and Federalism

★ Scenario: A New Constitution for Texas

The constitution of the state of Texas is often criticized, and calls for a comprehensive revision of the document are often heard. One such attempt occurred in 1999 during the 76th legislative session. House Joint Resolution (HJR) 1, sponsored by House Appropriations Chairman Robert Junell, D-San Angelo, and Senate Joint Resolution (SJR) 1, introduced by Senator Bill Ratliff, R-Mount Pleasant, would have created a new constitution for the State of Texas. The origin of the proposal was rather unique, to say the least.

Under the direction of Angelo State University Professors Edward C. Olson (Government Department Head), Jack Barbour (Head of the Public Administration Master's Program), and Jerry W. Perry, students in a combined undergraduate and graduate government class rewrote the Texas Constitution as a class project. Conducted during the spring semester of 1998, the class comprised eight undergraduate students, five graduate students, and three area public school teachers, who audited the course. Meeting once a week for 16 weeks, the students were divided into four-member groups to study the Texas and other state constitutions and to present their proposals for a portion of a new constitution for Texas. The members of each group were carefully selected to ensure that there would be different opinions represented in the group, promoting lively discussions and vigorous debates during the weekly class meetings when the students presented their proposals. After each group's presentation had been discussed, the class voted on the constitution's provision with 9 of the 14 regular participants in the class required for the adoption of a provision. During the last few weeks of the semester, the class held longer sessions to draft the final document. Representative Junell attended all of the class sessions, offering his expertise and recruiting additional experts to speak to the class, including 3rd Court of Appeals Chief Justice Marilyn Aboussie, attorney Tom Luce, Texas Tech University Chancellor John Montford, and Senator Bill Ratliff.

The Angelo State University proposal would have preserved many essential features of the current constitution, such as the Bill of Rights, but it would have also made several substantial changes. The structure and powers of the three branches would have been extensively revised. The governor's office would have been strengthened considerably by allowing the governor to do such things as appoint a cabinet of the heads of departments and granting the governor direct authority over them. The proposed constitution would have also consolidated the two supreme courts of Texas into a single, 15-member Supreme Court, with a chief justice and two divisions (criminal and civil) consisting of 7 justices each. In the proposed judicial article, the governor would appoint appellate court judges from a list submitted by a nominating committee, subject to Senate confirmation and retention elections. District Court judges would be elected from districts in nonpartisan elections. The proposal also would have changed the terms of office

Dr. Edward Olson's Government 6391 class at Anglo State University drafted a new Constitution for Texas that was introduced by Representative Rob Junell (Democrat-San Angelo) in 1999.

of senators and representatives to six years and four years, respectively, and increased the size of the Senate to 50 members.

According to Professor Olson, the most significant changes proposed by the students included:

- *The elimination of the "deadwood" in the current constitution.* Many sections of the current constitution have been made obsolete by amendments to the United States Constitution, federal laws, or state laws. These provisions and many statutory provisions in the current constitution were eliminated in the students' proposal.
- *The elimination of most partisan elections of judges.* Only county-level judges would be elected in partisan elections in the students' proposal. A form of the Missouri Plan or nonpartisan elections would be used to select other judges.
- *The streamlining of the plural executive.* The governor's authority over the executive branch would be increased, providing greater accountability of the executive agencies to the chief executive (the governor) and of the governor to the people. The governor would have a cabinet and appoint many of the officials who are currently elected, including the attorney general, comptroller, and land commissioner.
- *The consolidation and simplification of the local government provisions.* The article on local governments (counties, municipalities, and special districts) would consolidate the provisions that currently are spread throughout the constitution and grant additional powers to the counties. The county's governmental structure would be retained.[1]

Overall, the new constitution would have reduced the Texas constitution from 376 sections and approximately 81,000 words to 150 sections and 19,000 words. Despite a public opinion poll that showed that 49 percent of the population thought that constitutional revision was a "very important" or "somewhat important" issue, the proposed new constitution never left the Select House Committee on Constitutional Revision, which was created by Speaker Pete Laney to consider HJR 1. Nevertheless, the students in Government 6391 at Angelo State University gained a greater appreciation for the Texas Constitution and its weaknesses and learned important lessons in the politics of constitution-building. Also, Representative Junell and Senator Ratliff still believe that the Texas Constitution needs a comprehensive revision. As Senator Ratliff told the *Austin American-Statesman*, "[Voters know] . . . that any document that you have to amend 20 times every other year is broke. It's sort of a Texas tragedy, actually, that we can't seem to come to grips with the fact that we need a new, basic document going into the next century and the next millennium."[2] The students at Angelo State University provided just such a document. ★

INTRODUCTION

This chapter examines the legal context in which Texas government and politics operate, which is determined by two factors. The first factor is the relationship that Texas has with the government of the United States of America, the government

Te★as*Index*

Constitutions and Federalism in the States

Number of Constitutions Since Statehood
Texas—5
California—2
New York—4
Florida—6

Number of Words in Constitution (1998)
Texas—80,806
California—54,645
New York—51,700
Florida—38,000

Number of Amendments (1998)
Texas—submitted 547, ratified 377
California—submitted 826, ratified 493
New York—submitted 286, ratified 216
Florida—submitted 103, ratified 74

Initiative/Referendum
Texas—no
California—yes
New York—no
Florida—no

Total Number of States with Initiative/Referendum: 19
Grants to State and Local Governments in Millions of Dollars (1997)
Texas—13,184
California—27,014
New York—24,384
Florida—8,504

that is often referred to as the federal government. The system of government that a country adopts will govern the relationship between the national government and the separate state governments. The latter part of this chapter examines the place of Texas in a federal system of government.

The second factor that establishes the legal context for government and politics in the state of Texas involves the relationship between the state and its people. In the American tradition, that relationship has been determined by constitutionalism. As mentioned in Chapter 1, constitutionalism is the notion that people should be governed by the rule of law rather than by individual persons. In other words, the rules and regulations that govern a society should be the result of laws rather than the arbitrary whim of a particular person or a group of persons. Constitutions determine the type of government that a society has and may greatly affect its politics as well. The first part of this chapter studies the constitution of Texas.

THE TEXAS CONSTITUTION

Constitutions are an enduring part of both the national and the state governments in the United States. Prior to the establishment of the United States of America in 1789, the 13 colonies all had written constitutions or charters. Today, the national government and all 50 state governments have constitutions. The idea of a written charter has become so commonplace that local governments and corporations have charters. Even private organizations usually have bylaws that govern them. On one level, constitutions are simply basic, legal documents. On another level, they are complex embodiments of the ideals and fundamental premises of a political and governmental system. In this chapter, the constitution of the State of Texas is studied as the basis of the politics and government of Texas.

The Purposes of a Constitution

In the simplest terms, a constitution is merely a collection of words on paper. However, for people that conceive of themselves as living under the rule of law, constitutions provide the basis for that law. Constitutions provide a mechanism for establishing and maintaining order in a society without being subject to the arbitrary whims of a monarch or a dictator. In providing the framework for the rule of law, constitutions serve four purposes:

1. Provide government with legitimacy
2. Establish and organize government
3. Give government the necessary powers to operate
4. Limit government

Legitimacy   On one level, constitutions are merely collections of words on paper. Why do people tend to regard them so highly? The answer lies in the **legitimacy** of the constitution. If the constitution that establishes a government is perceived as being legitimate by the people who live under that government, then that government will in all likelihood be perceived as being legitimate. One of the components of the American Creed is constitutionalism. The legitimacy of any given constitution is closely linked to another part of the American Creed: democracy. Thus, legitimate constitutions, and hence legitimate governments, are obtained by democratic processes. In other words, legitimate governments are accomplished through the **consent** of the people, usually through some kind of ratification process.

The notion of legitimate governments having attained that status through ratification is problematic, however. Ratification processes usually call for some kind of vote to be taken. Under most circumstances, a simple majority of those voting is all that is needed to ratify, or legitimate, a constitution. Simple majority rule has a powerful appeal, and most people accept the results. Consider the current Texas constitution, however. It was ratified by a vote of the people of the state of Texas in 1876. At the time of that vote, the constitution's legitimacy was not seriously in doubt.

More than 100 years have passed since the ratification of the 1876 constitution. Is it still a legitimate constitution in light of the fact that the people who ratified it no longer exist? Is a document that has not been ratified by the people who currently live under it legitimate? Most political scientists would answer yes for at least two reasons. First, there is the concept of **tacit consent.** A popular way of explaining tacit consent would be to define it as "love it, or leave it." Tacit consent argues that because persons do not voluntarily leave a place, but choose to remain, they have indirectly, or tacitly, consented to abide by the laws, rules, and regulations of the place in which they live. Notice that tacit consent, to be truly effective as a ground for legitimacy, assumes that people can easily move from one state to another or from one country to another. As a practical matter, of course, that is not always easily accomplished.

The second reason for legitimacy is that the argument can be advanced that provisions can be made for ongoing consent by the people through such mechanisms as constitutional amendments and constitutional conventions. Constitutional amendments allow for change to be made to parts of a constitution. A constitutional amendment process in which the people are allowed to participate would be a mechanism by which those parts of the constitution that are deemed illegitimate by the people can be changed. Constitutional conventions would allow the entire constitution to be rewritten to reflect a call for fundamental change that might result from a period of creedal passion. The current constitution of Texas, the 1876 constitution, as just such an occurrence is discussed later in this chapter.

Establishment Constitutions also establish and organize government. The Texas constitution establishes the government of the State of Texas as the only legitimate government in the state. There is only one state government in Texas that people are compelled to obey. People are also compelled to obey local governments, but those governments derive their authority from the state. Constitutions establish at least the basic framework of government. Constitutions that set up the basic structure and establish the basic functions but allow the details of those structures and functions to be worked out by another entity, usually the legislature, are known as **ideal constitutions.**

The United States Constitution is often given as an example of the ideal type of constitution. It is a relatively short document that outlines the general structure of the national government without trying to say exactly what government can and cannot do in great detail. For example, the cabinet and hence the vast bureaucratic structure under it that makes up a substantial portion of the modern executive branch at the national level is not mentioned in the constitution of the United States. On the other hand, the current Texas constitution goes to considerable length to specify what government can and cannot do. For example, the members of the plural executive in Texas are, with the exception of one, specified in the state constitution. The duties of the various offices are also specified to some extent. This type of constitution is known as a **statutory constitution.** Nonetheless, both ideal and statutory types of constitutions serve the basic purpose of establishing and organizing government. More is said later in this chapter and in subsequent chapters about the nature of that organization in Texas.

Operation   The third major purpose of constitutions is to give government the necessary powers to operate. Governments possess two basic powers that no other entity possesses: (1) police power, and (2) the power of taxation. The United States Constitution and the 50 state constitutions have been heavily influenced by social contract theory. A constitution is a compact among the people. A feature of that compact is that the power to enforce one's rights is given over to the state. The state may then authorize certain individuals or entities to act as its agent, but the ultimate authority for enforcing the law comes from the government. The police power is the right of the state to restrict individual freedom in the interest of the public health, welfare, safety, and morals.

Consider the following example. You arrive home from work one day to find that your home has been burglarized. You recognize the perpetrators as they drive away. You even know where they live. In a state of nature, before the establishment of the social contract, or government, you would have been responsible for your right to property. If robbed, you would have to retrieve the stolen property yourself. However, the social contract makes a crime against one individual a crime against all members of the society. As a result, the government has the sole responsibility to recover the stolen property and punish the perpetrators of the crime.

Government is an expensive proposition. In 1999, the average Texan paid 34 percent of his or her income in taxes to all levels of government. State and local governments took about 10 percent of the average Texan's income, with the remainder going to the national government. Although the United States compares favorably with other nations on the level of taxation, for the average American the single biggest investment made in a lifetime will be in government at all levels. The power to tax is essentially the power to confiscate. Even if a person explicitly votes against a particular tax, that person is still responsible for paying it. This may seem rather arbitrary at first glance. However, remember that one of the ideals is democracy. Few actions, if any, of a particular government will receive unanimous support. Nonetheless, in a democratic society, the wishes of the majority are supposed to be respected by the minority. If any given individual was obliged only to pay that part of taxes with which the person agreed, government might be impossible to operate.

Limitations   The last purpose of a constitution is to limit government. In addition to the purposes listed previously, constitutions are also used to say what government cannot do. The task of limiting government may come in the form of a bill of rights. Most, if not all, of you are familiar with the first ten amendments to the United States Constitution.

The first ten amendments to the United States Constitution were added as the result of a political compromise between those arguing for ratification of the new document, the Federalists, and those opposed to the new constitution, the anti-Federalists. Many of the anti-Federalists were worried about the lack of protection for the individual from the national government. The inclusion of the Bill of Rights afforded that protection. Many of the Federalists argued that a bill of rights was not necessary because state constitutions already had bills of rights in them. Texas would follow that tradition. Article 1 of the Texas Constitution is entitled "Bill of Rights" and contains 30 numbered sections. The fact that it is listed first is testament to the importance attached to limited government in the Texan and American traditions. Chapter 13 is devoted to a discussion of the provisions of the Texas Bill of Rights that grant its citizens greater protection than does the United States Constitution's Bill of Rights.

> **Critical Thinking Exercise:**   Ideal constitutions and statutory constitutions produce very different ways of governing. Given your ideological tendencies and beliefs about the proper role of government, which type of constitution do you think is best and why?

History of Texas Constitutions

Texas has had seven constitutions in its history. The first five were similar and are examined here only for their lasting contributions to Texas government and politics. The last two are examined in more depth. The last constitution of Texas deserves considerable attention for two basic reasons. First, it is the current constitution. Second, because it is statutory, it is more explicitly the basis of Texas government than the United States Constitution is of its government. The current Texas constitution's predecessor is studied in some detail because of its impact on the current constitution.

The First Five: 1827–1866[3]   Mexico declared its independence from Spain in 1821. What is now Texas was formerly a part of the Spanish Empire and then became a part of a state of Mexico, Coahuila y Tejas. The new republic of Mexico adopted a constitution similar to that of the United States in 1821. The state of Coahuila y Tejas adopted a similar constitution that reflected being a state of Mexico in 1827. In 1836, Texas declared its independence from Mexico. The constitution adopted by the Republic of Texas was also an ideal-type constitution and made several lasting contributions to Texas government and politics. The constitution established the county as the basic unit of local government. This constitution also made explicit the separation of powers: the division of the legislative, executive, and judicial functions of government into three independent branches. The separation of powers may or may not be accompanied by a system of checks and balances. In a system of checks and balances, the powers of the separate branches overlap, so that no one branch can become all powerful in its area.

Even before the declaration of independence from Mexico in 1836, many Texans wanted to become a part of the United States of America. In 1845, the Republic of Texas was annexed by the United States and became the state of Texas once again, albeit under a different national government. This move required a new constitution and, thus, the Texas Constitution of 1845. It was in many respects an ideal-type constitution and is considered by many to have been the best Texas constitution.

The 1845 constitution placed restrictions on the state's ability to incur indebtedness. Amendments in 1850 reflected what has come to be known as "Jacksonian democracy." Named after Andrew Jackson, Jacksonian democracy has two parts: (1) the election of as many people as possible and (2) the spoils system.

The first tenet of Jacksonian democracy manifests itself in Texas in the long ballot. Citizens in the state of Texas have a distinctive opportunity to elect public officials. One of the parts of the American Creed is democracy, generally requiring that public officials be accountable to the people they serve. The most direct method of achieving accountability in the democratic sense is to have those public officials directly elected by the people they serve. Hence, the citizenry should elect as many people as they can. As a result, Texas has one of the longest ballots in the country, making it, at least in one sense, one of the most democratic places in the world.

Not everyone that works for government can be elected. That is a practical impossibility. The term *spoils system* derives from the phrase, "to the victor belong the spoils." In the realm of democratic politics, there are, of course, winners and losers. Under the terms of Jacksonian democracy, the winner of an election should be allowed to appoint those people who will work for the victor. Until Andrew Jackson was elected President of the United States in 1828, the practice had been that presidents appointed individuals to work for the national government, but only if there was an opening. Once a person had been appointed to a job, in the absence of the person's death, resignation, malfeasance, or incompetence, the person kept the job. Jackson instituted the practice of new administrations replacing government workers with new employees attached to the new administration or to the new administration's political party.

The amendments to the 1845 constitution established a system in which numerous officials were elected, establishing the plural executive and the election of judges. The elected officials then appointed people to work for them. Two aspects of the system have drawn criticism. The first is that people are hired for particular jobs based on their connections to the officeholder or to people who have connections to those who have connections to the officeholder. Qualifications and merit may have little to do with getting a job. Second, individuals hired under the spoils system can be fired at will. Little job protection is given to employees under a spoils system.

The constitution of 1845 also provided for biennial sessions for the legislature, meaning that the legislature was to meet once every two years. The 1845 constitution also provided for the establishment of a permanent school fund, the distribution of which has provided controversy right up to the present. It also adopted elements of Mexican law that are reflected in the current constitution and were later adopted by other states. One of those elements is the establishment of homestead protection. A homestead is a person's permanent place of residence. A homestead can only be seized for the nonpayment of taxes and the nonpayment of a lien against the property. A lien may be a mortgage, money borrowed to purchase the homestead, or a mechanic's lien, money borrowed or owed for repairs or improvements to the homestead, or money borrowed on the equity in a home. A homestead cannot be sold for the settlement of other debts regardless of the size of that other debt. A second element borrowed from Mexican law is a provision that forbids the sale of the homestead by one spouse without the permission of the other spouse. Last, the constitution contained a community property provision that was also borrowed from Mexican law. Community property is the notion that any property gained by one spouse during a marriage is equally the property of the other spouse.

Texas joined the Confederate States of America in 1861, necessitating a change in constitutions. The 1861 constitution was basically the 1845 constitution, with changes made to reflect membership in the Confederacy. It also made slavery explicitly constitutional by including a provision allowing for it. A new constitution was then needed in 1866 to reflect the defeat of the South and Texas's subsequent reentry into the United States of America. Like the 1861 constitution, the 1866 constitution was basically the 1845 constitution, with changes made to reflect the changed circumstances of the state of Texas. Readmittance to the Union required that Texas reflect three things in its new constitution: (1) the abolition of slavery; (2) the repudiation of secession from the Union; and (3) the cancellation of debts and obligations incurred as a Confederate state. One lasting legacy of the constitution of 1866 was the introduction of the line-item veto. The line-item veto provides for the veto by the governor of separate budget lines in any appropriations bill (see Chapter 9).

The Constitution of 1869   Just three years after the adoption of the 1866 constitution, the state of Texas acquired another one. The 1869 constitution was adopted to meet the demands of Reconstruction.[4] To some extent, it could be argued that the constitution of 1866 reflected Abraham Lincoln's position regarding the South. His was an attitude of reconciliation. Having defeated the Confederacy, abolished slavery, and restored the Union, Lincoln seemed to want to let the South return to as normal a life as possible as quickly as possible. However, Lincoln was assassinated in 1865.

The assassination of Lincoln elevated Andrew Johnson to the Presidency. Johnson was a southern Democrat who enjoys the distinction of being the first of two presidents in United States history to have been impeached.[5] Although he was not removed from office, Johnson lost most, if not all, of his political power and influence as president. The power vacuum was filled by the Radical Republicans. The Radical Republicans, who formed a faction of the Republican Party, were more interested in retaliation than in reconciliation. In other words, they wanted to punish the former Confederate states for their transgressions in the Civil War.

Lest one get the impression that the Radical Republicans were solely out for revenge, it should be pointed out that many Southern states bear at least some culpability for their plight. Many ex-Confederates acted as though the "South would rise again" or even that it had never really been defeated. From the

Union's point of view, the South was not a very "good loser." More important, many southern states were reluctant to include ex-slaves in the social, political, and economic milieu. For example, the constitution of 1866 called for a segregated school system, and even though African Americans were granted equality before the law in many respects, they were not allowed to testify in cases involving Anglos. The 1861 and 1866 constitutions were largely continuations of the 1845 constitution, with minimal changes made to reflect changed circumstances. In many ways, efforts were made to approximate the status quo that had existed prior to the Civil War.

The constitution of 1869 was the result of the Reconstruction Act of 1867, which demanded that southern states draw up new constitutions meeting three basic requirements: (1) granting suffrage, the right to vote, to African Americans; (2) ratification of the Fourteenth Amendment; and (3) other provisions acceptable to the U.S. Congress. The constitutional convention that met to draw up the constitution used much of the time available to them debating issues over which they had no control. The convention adjourned without a finished document. (There is much confusion surrounding the 1869 constitution. Forty-five of the 90 delegates signed the collection of documents that existed and left. Obviously, nothing had been passed by a majority.) The military governor then gathered up those documents, arranged them into a coherent whole and presented the results for ratification.

The constitution of 1869 was destined for trouble from the beginning. In many respects, it was an ideal-type constitution not remarkably different from its predecessors. However, in many other respects, the constitution was a major departure from the 1845 constitution. The 1869 constitution resulted in a centralized government, a large growth in government expenditures, an increase in taxation, and the rapid accumulation of a rather large debt.

The constitution of 1869 reduced Jacksonian democracy by making the attorney general and all state judges appointed offices. It also disenfranchised (prohibited from voting) former Confederate soldiers, officials, and individuals who had worked for the state during the Confederacy. The 1869 constitution also brought the Davis administration. Republican Edmund J. Davis was elected to office in 1870 and fully exploited various provisions of the constitution. In addition, Davis was given extraordinary powers under enabling acts adopted by the legislature.

Davis was given complete control over the registration of voters. The 1869 constitution also allowed the governor to appoint persons to a number of offices that had formerly been elective. The appointment power of the governor even extended to the governing bodies of towns and cities. A state police system was established, and the state militia were under the direct control of the governor. To exercise the power of the state police and the militia, the governor was given the ability to declare martial law in any district that he thought warranted it. As a result, the state police became the tool of the governor.

The constitutions of 1836, 1845, 1861, 1866, and 1869 were similar, ideal-type constitutions. The 1845 constitution had departed from the United States Constitution in establishing less frequent legislative sessions, the election of many public officials, shorter terms of office, and limitations on debt. The 1861 and 1866 constitutions were very similar to the 1845 constitution. The 1869 constitution was, then, in some respects a return to a constitution more like that of the United States. However, by 1872, the Democrats had regained control of the Texas legislature and then regained control of the governor's office in 1874. Calls for a constitutional convention went out immediately. The desire for change originated in the unique circumstances surrounding the adoption and implementation of the 1869 constitution.

First, recall that the 1869 constitution disenfranchised ex-Confederate soldiers and public officials of the Confederacy and of the state of Texas during the Confederacy. One component of the American Creed is that of democracy. For democracy to be fully functional, the state must allow all citizens to participate. The fact that individuals formerly allowed to participate were no longer allowed to do so undoubtedly raised questions concerning the legitimacy of the constitution and thereby created a certain degree of resentment. Second, the 1869 constitution was mandated by the national government. It was not a constitution that was called for by the people of the state. Many people in Texas, particularly Anglos, probably felt that the 1869 constitution did not have the consent of the people, further raising the question of its legitimacy. Last, the 1869 constitution was seen as being at least partly responsible for the expansion of governmental power during the Davis administration.

The Constitution of 1876   The constitution of 1876 is the seventh and current constitution of the state of Texas. Traditionally, it has often been interpreted in light of the two following premises:

1. The constitution of 1876 is almost wholly a reaction to the Reconstruction era and, therefore, fundamentally flawed.
2. The constitution of 1876 is a statutory constitution and, therefore, fundamentally flawed.

As a result of these assumptions, the constitution is considered by many to be badly in need of revision. This section of the chapter examines the 1876 constitution, its background and its provisions, identifying possible strengths and weaknesses. You will then be in a position to determine for yourself the viability of the constitution.

The Constitutional Convention of 1875[6] was called in the aftermath of Reconstruction. The Democratic Party had reasserted its dominance of Texas politics and had regained a majority of the legislature in 1872 and the governor's office in 1874. The momentum for a constitutional convention had been building for some time, although the idea was not universally accepted. In fact, the newly elected Democratic governor of Texas, Richard Coke, was initially opposed to a constitutional convention and argued that the 1869 constitution was basically a good document that only needed amending to fix a few flaws. Nonetheless, the forces seeking a new constitution were not to be denied, and a constitutional convention was called in 1875.

The convention originally consisted of 90 delegates: 75 Democrats and 15 Republicans. However, one of the Republicans served a short time and was replaced by a Democrat. In practice, then, the convention comprised 76 Democrats and 14 Republicans. Of the 90 delegates, 38 identified themselves as being members of the Grange. The Grange had started as a social club for farmers and eventually evolved into what would now be considered a special interest group (see Chapter 5). Only four of the delegates were native Texans. Seventy-two were originally from other southern states. Six African Americans, all Republicans, were originally elected as delegates. However, one of them resigned after the first day and was replaced in a special election by an Anglo man of the same county.

Then, as now, lawyers tended to dominate politics. Also then, as now, some of the lawyers owned land and claimed to be farmers when it was politically expedient to do so. Of those delegates for which an occupation has been identified, there were 33 lawyers, 28 farmers, 3 merchants, 3 physicians, 2 editors, 2 teachers, 2 mechanics, 1 minister, and 1 postmaster. At least 11 of the members had formerly served in a Texas constitutional convention. At least 30 members had served in the Texas legislature. Some of the delegates had served in the legislatures of other states, the United States Congress, and the Congress of the Confederate States. At least 8 had judicial experience, and 4 had executive and administrative experience. Of the delegates to the 1875 constitutional convention, J. E. Ericson has written,

> The convention of 1875 was composed, therefore of a much abler group of men on the basis of their previous experience and training than is generally conceded. Their background and training compares favorably with that of the delegates to any previous constitutional convention held in Texas. If their product is inferior, then the cause must lie elsewhere.[7]

The 1876 Constitution Explained What can account for the 1876 constitution, a constitution that is quite different from the United States Constitution? The United States Constitution has served as a model for many national and state constitutions. It is considered by many political scientists to be an ideal constitution. Texas's previous constitutions had been ideal-type constitutions. Why did the state of Texas, a state that had forsaken sovereignty for statehood, reject the United States model in 1876 and adopt a statutory constitution? The answer is threefold.

First, to some extent, the 1876 constitution is a reaction to the Reconstruction era. While that characterization does not completely explain the nature of the constitution, there is some truth to it. Certainly the imposition of the 1869 constitution on the state of Texas by the Union angered many people. To many, the 1869 constitution was an illegitimate constitution. However, recall that at least some Texans, including Governor Coke, supported retaining the 1869 constitution with certain amendments. The legislature in 1874 had even gone so far as to rewrite an amended 1869 constitution designed to ameliorate its worst features. A faction of the Democratic Party, led by Governor Coke, advocated its adoption, but it did not receive the necessary votes in the legislature for presentation to the voters for ratification.

Second, the 1869 constitution had engendered the regime of Governor Davis. The 1876 constitution is also then, in some of its provisions, a reaction to the Davis administration. Wanting to avoid another Governor Davis, the constitutional convention endeavored to prevent its recurrence.

A third factor is at work in the 1876 constitution, which is often overlooked. An agrarian movement swept through the United States in the 1870s. It called for greater democratic participation and a more limited government. Using the characterization of ideology employed in Chapter 2, the movement may be seen to have had both populist and libertarian elements. As a result of this movement, several states, both southern and northern, revised their constitutions.

The 1870s was clearly a period of creedal passion in the state of Texas. A period of creedal passion occurs when the gap between the political ideals and the behavior of the institutions that are supposed to act out the ideals becomes sufficiently large that people demand that the gap be closed, usually through government reform. In the 1875 constitutional convention, this passion took the form of "retrenchment and reform," the motto of the constitutional revision effort adopted by the members of the Grange and their allies. The constitution of 1869 had violated many of the ideals held by Texans. The 1869 constitution violated a belief in democratic government that served with the consent of the people. It also violated the principle of limited government by focusing extraordinary powers in the governor's office. The provisions of the 1876 constitution reflect a reaction both to the Reconstruction era and to the Davis regime, as well as a period of creedal passion aimed at restoring the ideals of a more democratic and limited government. In the sections that follow, various provisions of the 1876 constitution are examined.

Provisions of the 1876 Constitution   The current Texas constitution has 17 numbered articles (Table 3.1). Article 13, "Spanish and Mexican Land Titles," was deleted by amendment in 1969.[8] As a result, the constitution currently has 16 operable articles. Many of the provisions of the constitution are virtually identical to the way they were written when ratified in 1876, while others have been amended extensively. Like the United States Constitution, the Texas Constitution provides for a separation of powers, a system of checks and balances, and limitations on government. However, because the United States Constitution is an ideal type and the Texas Constitution is statutory, the two documents are also quite different.

Article 1 of the Texas Constitution is devoted to the Texas Bill of Rights. Many of its provisions are similar to the United States Constitution's Bill of Rights. The Texas Bill of Rights is both longer and in some respects more extensive than the United States Constitution's Bill of Rights (see Chapter 13).

Article 2 of the 1876 constitution establishes the separation of powers in Texas government. Articles 3, 4, and 5 deal with the legislative, executive, and judicial branches of the government of the state of Texas, respectively. It is in these three articles that many of the effects of the period of creedal passion can be detected, particularly with regard to the legislature. Regular legislative sessions are biennial (once every two years, in odd-numbered years) and currently limited to 140 days. Originally, no specific number of days was specified. However, the legislature could only receive full pay for the first 60 days of a session. One way of limiting government is to limit the legislature. One way to limit the legislature is to limit

Table 3.1   ARTICLES OF THE TEXAS CONSTITUTION

Preamble	
Article 1	Bill of Rights
Article 2	The Powers of Government
Article 3	Legislative Department
Article 4	Executive Department
Article 5	Judicial Department
Article 6	Suffrage
Article 7	Education
Article 8	Taxation and Revenue
Article 9	Counties
Article 10	Railroads
Article 11	Municipal Corporations
Article 12	Private Corporations
Article 13	Spanish and Mexican Land Titles (Repealed August 5, 1969)
Article 14	Public Lands and Land Office
Article 15	Impeachment
Article 16	General Provisions
Article 17	Mode of Amending the Constitution of this State

the amount of time that it can meet. If the legislature is not in session, then it cannot pass laws, thereby preventing the expansion of government authority.

Another way to limit the legislature is to limit its discretion over the expenditure of funds. The 1876 constitution does this in at least two ways. One is to mandate a balanced budget; the other is to dedicate funds. Debt incurred by the government of the state of Texas has been restricted since the 1845 constitution. The current constitution contains one of the most restrictive balanced-budget provisions in the United States (see Chapter 14). It is essentially a pay-as-you-go requirement. The state of Texas must not only start the biennium with a budget that has been certified as balanced, but it must also end with a budget that is balanced or in surplus. In other words, within very narrow parameters, the state may not spend more than it takes in. As a result, money for new programs must usually be taken from existing programs or from new or higher taxes. Both methods of funding are politically difficult.[9] Dedicated funds require that certain tax moneys be dedicated to—deposited into—particular funds. The money in that fund may then only be used for specified purposes. For example, 75 percent of the state portion of the gasoline tax is deposited into the Highway Trust Fund, which may then only be spent for the building and maintenance of roads and bridges in Texas. The other 25 percent is deposited into the Available School Fund, which may then only be spent on public education in Texas. The balanced-budget and dedicated-fund provisions of the Texas Constitution serve to limit the discretion of the legislature.

The salary of legislators was reduced, and the pay of legislators in Texas remains one of the lowest in the nation. Both the salary and the per diem pay (expenses) of legislators were specified by the constitution, requiring constitutional amendment to change either. Recent changes to the constitution allow the Texas Ethics Commission to set per diem pay and to recommend legislative salaries (but the commission has never exercised its power to recommend a salary change). However, a new salary is subject to approval by the voters. The legislature is limited in many other ways in the article on the legislature and other articles of the constitution. The constitutional convention of 1875 tried to specify what the legislature could and could not do. In keeping with the themes of democracy and limited government that characterized the agrarian movement of the 1870s, the state legislature must often ask the people of the state of Texas, through constitutional amendment, for permission to make major, and sometimes minor, changes in state government.

The executive branch of state government is indicative of the negative influence of the Davis administration and the agrarian movement's emphasis on democracy. When confronted with the legacy of what was considered by many Democrats of the day to be a corrupt gubernatorial administration, most, if not all, of the delegates to the 1875 constitutional convention strongly wished to prevent the recurrence of such an administration. The prevention of an abusive officeholder can be accomplished in two ways: (1) screen the candidates for a proclivity to corruption or (2) limit the office.

The writers of the 1876 constitution decided to design the office of governor in such a way that regardless of who was elected, the Davis administration could not be duplicated. This was accomplished by limiting the power of the governor severely. The governor of Texas today is considered one of the weakest in the nation (see Chapter 9). Executive power is divided among a plural executive. In addition to the governor and lieutenant governor, the attorney general, the comptroller of public accounts, the commissioner of the general land office, and the agriculture commissioner are elected statewide to four-year terms. Legally, all of the members of the plural executive are co-equals. The governor has no real control over their policies.

Currently, the 15-member State Board of Education and the 3-member Railroad Commission are elected to four-year, staggered terms and six-year, staggered terms, respectively. The executive branch in Texas is effectively made up of well over 200 state agencies and institutions of higher education over which the governor has traditionally had little or no control.[10] The power that would normally be vested in the governor's office is dispersed among many different agencies and individuals. Lord Acton is reputed to have said that "absolute power corrupts absolutely." The framers of the constitution evidently believed that they could create the opposite and equal reaction—that is, that little power would corrupt very little.

Jacksonian democracy is reflected not only in the proliferation of executive offices elected statewide, but also in the election of virtually every judge in the state of Texas. The 1876 constitution also strengthened local government. The county was reestablished as the basic unit of local government. Public services were also reduced dramatically.

Article 17 outlines the amendment process. The constitution of 1876 can only be amended in one way. There is only one method of proposal and one method of ratification. Amendments may be proposed by a two-thirds majority vote of both chambers of the legislature. Both the Texas Senate and the Texas House of Representatives must approve a proposed amendment by a two-thirds majority vote of their separate memberships. Ratification of a proposed amendment requires a simple majority of those who actually cast ballots in an election. The vote to ratify **constitutional amendments** may occur in a general election, which is conducted in even-numbered years in November, or in special elections, which are conducted at other times. In the 1980s, the legislature established a pattern of conducting constitutional amendment elections primarily in odd-numbered years in November. At this time, only constitutional amendments and local issues are on the ballot, which results in lower voter turnout and in a lower adoption rate for amendments (Table 3.2). Apparently, with the election limited to constitutional amendments and issues of local interest, the small percentage of voters who participate closely scrutinize the proposed amendments.

The statutory nature of the Texas constitution is reflective of both the democratic and the limited-government impulses of the 1870s agrarian movement. It reflects the democratic ideal, in that most major and many minor changes in Texas government require the permission of the people through the ratification process. This kind of process also limits the legislature and the executive by greatly reducing their discretion over legislation and rule making. However, the writers of the 1876 constitution did not wholly trust the democratic process. The citizens of Texas were not given the powers of initiative and referendum.[11] A little more than a century later, when Governor Clements asked the legislature to propose an amendment establishing initiative and referendum during his first legislative session in 1979, the legislature virtually ignored the idea.

Table 3.2 TYPE OF ELECTION, VOTER TURNOUT, AND CONSTITUTIONAL AMENDMENT ADOPTIONS

Decade	Type of election	Voter turnout*	Amendments considered	Amendments adopted	Percent adopted
1970s	General - Presidential	45.65	15	12	80.0
	General-Gubernatorial	25.47	16	12	75.0
	Special	5.42	26	16	61.5
1980s	General - Presidential	45.81	20	16	80.0
	General-Gubernatorial	29.44	10	10	100.0
	Special	10.23	77	65	84.4
1990s	General - Presidential	44.30	0	0	0.0
	General - Gubernatorial	30.41	1	1	100.0
	Special	9.47	91	63	69.2

*Voter turnout indicates the percentage of voting-age people who voted. Special election turnout figures are only for the 1977 and 1979 special elections (no figures were available for 1971, 1973, or 1975).

Source: Secretary of State, Election Results, 9 December 1999, *http://www.sos.state.tx.us/function/elec1/results/returns.html.* Texas Legislative Reference Library, Constitutional Amendments, 9 December 1999, *http://www.lrl.state.tx.us/legis/amendments/mainpage.html.*

The idea came before the legislature again in 1997. In 1996, Lieutenant Governor Bob Bullock appointed a Senate Interim Committee on Initiative and Referendum, charged with presenting a proposal to the 75th Legislature (1997). The committee recommended to the legislature that a constitutional amendment authorizing initiative and referendum be presented to the voters for ratification. Bullock and House Speaker Pete Laney, along with at least 14 senators and 58 representatives announced their support. The necessary legislation was drawn up, but the legislature waited to determine if there was any significant public support for the amendment. Hearing none, the legislature took no further action.

Having a statutory constitution that requires constitutional amendment to make major and even minor changes in government also means that the constitution has been amended many times. As of 1999, the Texas Constitution had been amended 390 times. The United States Constitution has survived since 1789 with only 27 amendments. One could plausibly argue that the first ten (the Bill of Rights) were necessary to achieve ratification and, therefore, are a part of the original document. The Twenty-First Amendment repeals the Eighteenth Amendment, leaving only 15 actual changes to the United States Constitution in 210 years. On the other hand, the Texas Constitution has been amended 390 times in only 123 years (Figure 3.1).

Criticisms of the 1876 Constitution   The constitution of 1876 has been heavily criticized on a number of grounds. It has been criticized by many for its excessive length and cumbersome organization. Texas has one of the longest constitutions (80,806 words) in the United States. Only Alabama (220,000 words) has a constitution that contains more words.[12] The constitution has also been accused of being disorganized. Sections that deal with local government, for example, can be found scattered throughout the constitution. They are not confined to Article 9, "Counties," where logically one might expect to find provisions on local government because that is the only article of the constitution directly related to local government.

Amendments have added numerous provisions to the constitution and have repealed numerous others. As a result, many have argued that the philosophy and substantive content of the constitution does not need to be changed, but it does need to be rewritten to make it a more coherent and readable document. In 1977, the Texas Advisory Commission on Intergovernmental Relations drafted a new constitution that retained the spirit and the meaning of the 1876 constitution, as amended to that point, but it simplified the numbering system and codified the separate provisions of the constitution that dealt with the same subject matter.[13]

The 1876 constitution has also been criticized on substantive grounds. The plural executive has been criticized because it weakens the power of the governor. Recall that the power normally given to a state's chief executive is divided among several officials elected statewide to four-year terms, just as is the governor. The constitution makes these officials the coequals of the governor. The governor's administrative authority over the agencies, boards, and commissions that make up a substantial portion of the executive branch of Texas government is also minimal. Consequently, governors in Texas are in a much weaker position to influence pub-

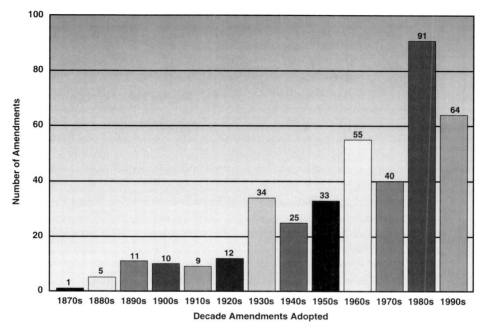

Figure 3.1 Amendments to the Texas Constitution

As the Texas Constitution aged, the rate at which amendments were added accelerated. Approximately 72 years were required to add the first 100 amendments, 22 years for the second 100, 17 years for the third 100, and only 12 years to add another 90 amendments.

lic policy than are most of their counterparts in the rest of the United States. For those who wish to see stronger executive authority in the state of Texas, those portions of the constitution that weaken the governor are a source of criticism.

The legislative branch also draws criticism for the duration of legislative sessions and the low pay of legislators. Regular legislative sessions are held every two years and last for 140 days. The constitution also provides for special sessions that may last up to 30 days each. It can be argued that such a short session is inadequate to the needs of a modern state. In particular, the ability of the state legislature to adequately budget for a two-year period is questioned. It can also be argued that legislative pay is too low. Legislators are paid $7,200 per year plus a per diem for expenses while the legislature is in session. The low pay can be criticized because it reduces the pool of legislative candidates to those who both can financially afford to serve and can afford the time needed to attend regular and special sessions (e.g., persons whose work permits them to take time off).

Dedicated funds have been a source of criticism because it is felt that they place undue restrictions on the legislature. The statutory nature of the Texas Constitution also reduces the power of the legislature. It can be argued that the legislature should be allowed more flexibility in its budgetary and law-making functions so that it can more easily and quickly respond to events and conditions in Texas.

The judicial branch of government in Texas is also the source of much criticism. An analysis of the structure of the court system in Texas reveals a rather unwieldy hodgepodge of overlapping jurisdictions that produce many different courts. The starting point of the system is the Texas Constitution, which calls for the creation of two supreme courts, the Texas Supreme Court (for civil cases) and the Texas Court of Criminal Appeals (for criminal cases). The selection of judges has also engendered much discussion. As a result of the strong attachment to Jacksonian democracy, virtually all judges in Texas are elected. Many political scientists and attorneys have wondered whether that is the best method of selection (see Chapter 11).

Local government is also criticized for being archaic. The structure of county governments is constitutionally determined. The smallest and the largest counties in Texas have basically the same structures. The county is greatly limited in its ability to raise revenue and to adapt to the changes that have occurred in Texas counties since the passage of the 1876 constitution, especially the urban counties. Changes to the structure of county government require constitutional amendment. Counties are left with little flexibility. The restrictions placed on county and city government in Texas have resulted in the creation of hundreds of special districts across Texas, which citizens are only sometimes vaguely aware of, at best (see Chapter 12).

> **Critical Thinking Exercise:**   The Constitution of 1876 has served the people of Texas for more than 120 years, in spite of widespread criticisms. Why do you think it has survived without a comprehensive revision? Is a comprehensive revision necessary? If so, how should it be accomplished?

Constitutional Revision

The Texas Constitution is obviously considered a flawed document. If the current constitution is so badly in need of reform, then why has there not been a comprehensive revision? In the paragraphs that follow, the attempts at comprehensive revision of the 1876 constitution are discussed.

Revision Efforts Prior to 1974   The last serious attempts at **constitutional revision** came in 1974 and 1975. Prior to 1974, constitutional revision had been discussed often, and several attempts were made to call a constitutional convention.[14] Indeed, almost immediately after ratification of the 1876 constitution, efforts were made to amend it, particularly the article on the judiciary. A single amendment was adopted in 1891 that revised the judiciary article. An attempt was made in 1877 to call a constitutional convention, which proved to be the first in a long series of such attempts. Finally, in 1917, both houses of the legislature passed a resolution calling for a constitutional convention. The governor was directed to issue a proclamation calling for the election of delegates, and the final document was to be submitted to the voters. However, the governor refused to issue the proclamation.

In 1919, the legislature passed a resolution that would submit the question of calling a constitutional convention to the voters in the form of a referendum. In November 1919, approximately 10 percent of the voters turned out and overwhelmingly defeated the proposition (23,549 for vs. 71,376 against). The defeat seemed to halt the movement for constitutional revision for a time, a pattern that was subsequently repeated. Between 1919 and 1949, several attempts were made in the legislature to revise the constitution. During that 30-year time span, four House Concurrent Resolutions, three Senate Concurrent Resolutions, eight Joint House Resolutions, and four Senate Joint Resolutions were introduced. Proposals calling for the creation of a constitutional revision commission were made in every legislative session from 1941 to 1949. None of the resolutions or proposals were approved by the legislature. Finally, in 1949, the governor formed a group of citizens into the Citizen's Committee on the Constitution. The committee recommended to the legislature that a commission be established to study the need for constitutional revision. A resolution following the recommendation of the committee and providing for funding for the study commission died in a House committee.

Perhaps exhausted by so many attempts and so little progress, no further action was taken regarding constitutional revision until 1957. A concurrent resolution was then passed directing the Legislative Council to begin a study of the 1876 constitution and to submit to the legislature its recommendations. At the same time, an 18-member Citizens' Advisory Committee was also established, with the governor, lieutenant governor, and speaker of the House each appointing six members to it. The Citizens' Advisory Committee submitted a report in 1959, indicating that at least some revision was necessary. However, in 1961, the Legislative Council submitted its report to the legislature, indicating that no revision was necessary.

Again, efforts at constitutional revision lay dormant for a time. In 1966, Governor John Connally announced his support for constitutional revision as a parting gesture before leaving office after serving for six years. Largely as a result of Connally's public support, the legislature passed a resolution creating a Constitutional Revision Commission in 1967. The governor appointed ten members, and the lieutenant governor, the speaker of the House, and the chief justice of the Texas Supreme Court appointed five members each. The lieutenant governor refused to make his appointments, so the already appointed members of the commission named the remaining five. The 1969 legislature was presented with a revised and simplified constitution by the commission. The legislature rejected the draft constitution but did submit an amendment to the constitution repealing 50 obsolete provisions of the 1876 constitution. The amendment was approved by the voters in November 1969.[15]

The 1974 Constitutional Convention   Interest in constitutional revision reached a peak in 1971. The legislature proposed a constitutional amendment that called for the

Texas legislature of 1973 to sit as a constitutional convention in 1974 and required the legislature to establish a study commission to draft a new constitution prior to the legislature meeting as a constitutional convention. The voters approved the amendment in November 1972, by almost a two-to-one margin (61 percent for vs. 39 percent against). The legislature, meeting as a constitutional convention, was authorized to submit to the voters of the state of Texas a new constitution or revisions to the old constitution. They could also present to the voters alternative sections or articles of either the old or the new constitution. The only real limitation placed on the legislature was a prohibition against revision of Article 1, the Bill of Rights. The constitutional convention was also limited in the amount of time it could meet. The convention would automatically end on May 31, 1974, unless the convention voted to adjourn earlier or to extend the session for not more than 60 days after the May deadline.

The 1972 amendment also called for the creation of a Constitutional Revision Commission. The commission consisted of 37 members. A six-member committee made up of the governor, lieutenant governor, speaker of the House, attorney general, chief justice of the Texas Supreme Court, and presiding judge of the Texas Court of Criminal Appeals appointed the members of the commission, who could not be public officials. The commission was appointed in February 1973 and started its work in March 1973. From April through June, the commission held 19 public hearings across the state. On November 1, 1973, the commission submitted to the members of the legislature a draft constitution.

The 181 members of the 1973 legislature (150 state representatives and 31 state senators) met as a constitutional convention on January 8, 1974. The convention started with great expectations. The amendment authorizing the process had been passed by the voters by a substantial margin. The Constitutional Revision Commission had prepared a draft constitution from which the convention could begin its work. The convention then only had to make whatever modifications it desired to the document and then submit it to the voters for ratification. Many fully expected that a new constitution would be presented to the voters of Texas on the November 1974 ballot. However, the convention adjourned on July 30, 1974, without producing a new constitution. The final vote was 118 for, 62 against, with one abstention. The final vote fell three short of the required two-thirds vote necessary to submit a new constitution to the voters.

Why did a process initiated with such high hopes fail? The reasons are both institutional and issue based. Institutional reasons for failure fall into two categories: (1) legislators as delegates and (2) the decision rules used. The entire revision effort bears the imprint of the legislature. The original resolution calling for a constitutional convention had been initiated by legislators. It did not come from a citizen's group or some type of grassroots-level organization. The constitutional amendment establishing the revision process designated the 1973 legislature as the constitutional convention. This, of course, meant that the legislators became convention delegates. The Texas experience was unique, in that the legislature met in a separate session devoted solely to revising the constitution. The 150 representatives and 31 senators met as a single body. The governor's role was minimal, at best.

The general practice among the states had been to have delegates to a constitutional convention elected by the people. In retrospect, the legislature as a consti-

Members of the 1973 legislature met as a constitutional convention in 1974. They adjourned without producing a new constitution for Texas.

tutional convention may have proved to be too politicized as a process. Being legislators, the convention delegates thought of constitutional revision as "politics as usual." The delegates were forced to consider reelection campaigns, future pieces of legislation that could be brought up to their colleagues, and their relationships with lobbyists. If the convention had been made up of citizen delegates whose political careers might have ended with the adjournment of the convention, the final result might have been different.

The second institutional reason for failure was the set of decision rules used in the convention. The convention delegates were divided into several substantive and procedural committees (Table 3.3). The substantive committees were responsible for conducting hearings, taking testimony, and drafting the articles or sections of the new constitution that they were assigned. Once the committee reported out a section, the section was then debated and voted on by the entire convention. For a particular article to be approved by the convention, a simple majority vote was required. However, the final document, made up of all previously approved sections and articles, required a two-thirds majority vote for submission to the voters. Articles passed by a simple majority of the convention may have given delegates a false sense of security about the prospects for final approval of a new constitution.

Table 3.3   COMMITTEES OF THE 1974 CONSTITUTIONAL CONVENTION

Substantive committees	Procedural committees
Finance	Rules
Local Government	Administration
Education	Submission and Transition
The Legislature	Style and Drafting
The Judiciary	Public Information
General Provisions	
The Executive	
Rights and Suffrage	

Issue conflicts also played a role in the failure to produce a new constitution for submission to the voters. The first article reported out of committee was the article on education. The delegates debated one sentence for two days, eventually spending three weeks on the entire article. The debate ensured a long, acrimonious convention.[16] The state's single largest expenditure is for public education. It has often been said that the single most important function any society serves is the education of its children. If this is even only partially true, then it is easy to see why it could be such a contentious issue, especially the financing of the public schools. The financing of public education remains mired in controversy and may never be settled to everyone's satisfaction. Although not fatal to the 1974 Constitutional Convention, the education issue proved to be a barometer for the rest of the convention (see Chapter 14).

The single most important issue that prevented presentation to the public of a new constitution was the right-to-work provision.[17] Texas has had a right-to-work provision since 1947. The Taft-Hartley Act of 1947 allowed interested states to establish a right-to-work provision, and the Texas legislature passed a **right-to-work law** in that year. Delegates representing business interests came to the 1974 constitutional convention determined to place a right-to-work provision in the Texas constitution, which would make it more difficult to repeal. Many of the delegates to the constitutional convention (i.e., legislators) had been elected with the strong support of labor unions. The labor unions decided to make the right-to-work provision an issue of the utmost importance and ultimately refused to support any constitutional revision that contained a right-to-work provision. Those in favor of the right-to-work provision were almost as intransigent, insisting that a right-to-work provision be ensconced in the constitution. At the very least, the issue had to be presented to the voters as a separate issue.[18]

The final vote on the proposed constitution reflected the right-to-work forces. The representatives of the labor unions made it clear that they would not support in future campaigns for office anyone who voted for the new constitution. Elections for all representatives and one-half of the senators were coming up in November, just a few months after the close of the convention. The failure of the convention over the right-to-work provision is somewhat incongruous. The state

THE TEXAS CONSTITUTION **81**

of Texas already had a right-to-work statute. For those opposed to the right-to-work provision, rejection of the new constitution did not change that. For those in favor of the right-to-work provision, the acceptance of a new constitution without the right-to-work provision would not have changed that fact either.

The 1975 Constitutional Amendments The 1974 Constitutional Convention ended without producing a new document to send to the voters. The legislature met in 1975 and decided to do in regular session what they could not do in the convention. The legislature divided the draft constitution from the 1974 convention into eight amendments and presented them to the voters. The effect of approving all eight of the amendments would have been a new constitution. Changes were made in the draft document to accommodate the event of passage of less than all eight of the amendments. Conventional wisdom suggested that the amendments would pass and that Texans would have a new constitution by the end of 1975.

When the final vote was taken, all eight amendments had lost by a two-to-one margin. In only two of Texas's 254 counties did all eight amendments pass. Why did the amendments fail so overwhelmingly? There are several possible answers. The constitutional revision efforts of 1974 and 1975 were preceded by the Sharpstown political scandal in Texas (see Chapter 8) and the Watergate scandal at the national level. Both scandals may well have engendered a loss of confidence in government. Many were concerned that the new constitution would make government more powerful. There was a particular concern that the new constitution would lead to a state income tax. The most visible politician in the state, the governor, did not support the new constitution, and Citizens to Preserve the Constitution actively campaigned against it. Possibly many voters just could not find a reason to change the old constitution. "If it ain't broke, don't fix it," goes the old saying. Perhaps many voters could not be persuaded that the old constitution was sufficiently flawed to warrant changing it.

Another explanation employs our theory of political change. Undoubtedly, the 1972 vote on the constitutional amendment showed strong support for the idea of a new constitution, and perhaps the creedal passion that surrounded Sharpstown, Watergate, and America's involvement in Vietnam fed that support. However, when the 1974 Constitutional Convention failed, Texans became disgusted and angry. The creedal passion that might have carried forward constitutional revision was dashed by the leaders themselves when they botched the attempt; the moment passed, and the forces of cynicism surged over the forces of moralism.

The Legacy of the Revision Effort The constitutional efforts of 1974 and 1975 were not entirely in vain. Even if no change results from an effort to produce change, the effort itself may be worthwhile. Governments, like individuals, need to be examined periodically for internal problems that are in need of correction. It may be that the examination reveals no problems. However, it is difficult to believe that thorough examination of either a human being or a government would reveal absolutely nothing that could not be changed for the better. Texas government is no exception. The revision effort revealed a number of problems with the operation of government. The draft constitution attempted to correct many of those. As a result, in the ensuing years, several proposals made in the draft constitution have since been adopted as amendments to the constitution.[19]

In both 1997 and 1999 the legislature proposed amendments to remove the "deadwood" from the constitution. Changes at the national level have rendered portions of the Texas constitution moot and/or unconstitutional, such as some of the provisions regarding voter registration. The amendments have also removed duplicative numbering in an effort to make the document more readable. Still other changes have simply removed provisions rendered obsolete by other constitutional amendments. Neither "clean up" amendment substantively changed the constitution. Consequently, voters overwhelmingly approved both.

The 1876 Constitution—Good or Bad?

The 1876 constitution has been maligned by many over the years. In spite of the criticism, it survives, albeit with 390 amendments. Perhaps the constitution is not as bad as perceived. A constitution, like beauty, is in the eye of the beholder. Whether a constitution is deemed bad or good depends on the point of view adopted. In discussions of politics and government, points of view are often determined by ideology. The particular ideology that a person holds will help determine whether that person believes the Texas Constitution is adequate.

Modern populists would tend to oppose a statutory constitution such as Texas's. Populists tend to favor more regulation of both the economic and the social realms. Regulation tends to be facilitated by an active legislature and a strong executive. Legislatures can be more active, passing more legislation, when allowed to meet often and to have few constitutional restrictions placed on them. The Texas system allows neither a strong executive nor an active legislature.

Liberals would also tend to be opposed to a statutory constitution. Like populists, liberals tend to favor regulation of the economy. Again, regulation of the economy requires an active legislature and a strong executive. Liberals face somewhat of a dilemma, however. While favoring regulation of the economy, they generally reject regulation of private and social behavior. Should liberals then favor a statutory or an ideal type of constitution? Liberals tend to be against a statutory constitution because a constitution can be used to limit government. By having a well developed bill of rights, for example, a constitution can be constructed in such a way that regulation of the social realm is difficult, but regulation of the economy is fairly easy. Given a strong bill of rights, an ideal-type of constitution would be favored by liberals.

Conservatives would tend to favor a statutory constitution. Conservatives are generally opposed to the regulation of the economy. The Texas Constitution is generally favorable to a strong business climate. Once a particular ideological stance is enshrined in a constitution, it is difficult to change. Conservatives face a dilemma, as well, however. While generally opposed to regulation of the economy, conservatives generally favor regulation of the social realm. Traditionally, however, conservatives have been more interested in keeping government spending under control, taxes at a minimum, and either minimal regulation of the economy or regulation favorable to business than in regulation of the social realm. As a result, conservatives tend to favor a statutory constitution.

Libertarians tend to favor a statutory constitution. The 1876 constitution is, at least partially, a response to the agrarian movement of the 1870s that called for less government and a more democratic one. However, the limited-government ideology of the 1870s agrarian movement would be labeled libertarian today. In terms of ideology, Texas remains a fairly conservative and libertarian state. Limited government, and hence limited government services, especially to the poor, are in keeping with a conservative-libertarian ideology. Low taxes and fiscal conservatism are also important elements of both libertarian and conservative thought.

Is the Texas constitution good or bad? Is it a document that, in spite of its shortcomings, continues to serve the basic needs and desires of the people it governs, or is it really badly in need of reform? The answer lies in the ideology of the person asking the question. If the person desires a very limited government that simply does not do much, then the Texas constitution is adequate. If a person desires a government that will be more involved in the life of its citizenry, then the Texas constitution is in need of reform.

The Constitution and Political Change

Political change may be pursued through constitutions in two ways: revision and amendment. Because a constitution is generally the fundamental law of a society, changing the constitution may result in a fundamental change in the law. This is true only if the constitution is an ideal type. If the constitution is statutory, as the Texas constitution is, then the changes may be relatively minor.

Constitutional revision may produce fundamental change. The 1869 constitution resulted in the disenfranchisement of ex-Confederates and in the regime of Governor Davis. The legacy of Reconstruction and the populist movement that swept the United States in the 1870s produced a period of creedal passion in Texas. The constitution of 1876 fundamentally changed the basic law of the state. Efforts to revise the constitution in the 1970s failed, due to the lack of a perceived need for change.

Constitutional amendments may also produce fundamental change. The passage of the Thirteenth, Fourteenth, and Fifteenth Amendments to the United States Constitution has profoundly changed the conduct of politics and government in the United States. Typically, in Texas, though, constitutional amendment does not radically alter the basic law of the state. The statutory nature of the Texas constitution dictates that most amendments are technical in nature. The revision experience of the 1970s was not a particularly pleasant one for the 1973 legislature, which served as the 1974 Constitutional Convention. No real effort has been made to revise the constitution since then. Without a period of creedal passion, the number of amendments to the current constitution will probably continue to grow.

The Constitution and Democracy

Constitutions help determine the form that democracy will take in a society. Constitutions help to determine the degree of majoritarian versus pluralist democracy in a society. Like most of the state constitutions throughout the United States, the Texas Constitution provides that laws must be passed by a simple majority in both houses of the legislature to be enacted into law. However, if vetoed by the governor, then the majority rises to two-thirds of both houses of the legislature. A minority of one, the governor, may require an extraordinary majority[20] of the legislature to pass laws. The constitution also requires that constitutional amendments be proposed by a two-thirds majority of both houses of the legislature. Then, however, a simple majority of those who vote may ratify the amendment. The Texas Constitution is a mixture of both majoritarian and pluralist principles. Article 1, the Bill of Rights, affords sometimes rather strong protections to individuals, the smallest minority of all.

Direct democracy is impossible in a state the size of Texas. Some form of representative government is mandatory. Several chapters in this textbook explore the issue of how representative that government is. The constitution of the state of Texas does allow the creation of home-rule cities and numerous special districts. For all of the faults of such a system, it does express a desire for government to be placed on as local a level as possible. In turn, the possibility of citizen involvement is enhanced, creating the possibility of at least a semidirect governmental system.

> **Critical Thinking Exercise:**   Which form of democracy—majoritarian or pluralist—does the Texas Constitution promote? Considering your answer and your ideological tendencies, should the Texas Constitution be revised? What changes would you support?

FEDERALISM

Federalism is one of the fundamental features of the American system of government. Over the years, federalism has been both lauded and lamented. Federalism is a way of organizing government that has many implications for the nature and scope of government. The implications for the state of Texas are explained in this section. The state of Texas operates within a federal system of government. This section of the chapter briefly examines the meaning of federalism, both in general and in terms of the implications of such a system for the citizens of the state of Texas. In order to understand the context of modern federalism, a short history of the evolution of federalism in the United States is provided. Given the meaning and evolution of federalism, the chapter ends with a brief discussion of the place of the state of Texas within the U.S. federal system.

Types of Government

The federal form of government can best be understood in the context of the three major forms of government. Government, as defined earlier, consists of the institutions and processes through which public policy is made (see Chapter 1). A society's governmental system describes how the offices of government are organized. In other words, government will dictate how political power is distributed among the various entities that make and execute the law. In terms of the distribution of powers among levels of government, there are three basic forms of government: a unitary government, a confederation, and a federation.

A **unitary government** is one in which the subdivisions of government (in the United States, these are the states) are allowed to do only what the national, or central, government allows them to do. This system is hierarchical; power flows from the top down. Political subdivisions, such as states, exist to carry out the will of the national government. If the United States operated as a unitary government, then the states would simply do what the people in Washington, D.C., told them to do. Most of the world's governments are unitary.

A **confederation** is the opposite of a unitary government. In a confederation, the national government is only allowed to do what the states allow it to do. In a confederation, the national government derives its power from the states. The United States has experimented with a confederation twice during its history. After declaring independence from Great Britain in 1776, the 13 original colonies lived under the Articles of Confederation until 1789. In 1861, 11 southern states formed the Confederate States of America, of which Texas was a member.

The founding fathers of the United States created a **federation.** The confederation under the Articles of Confederation had not worked well; so the consensus was to do something different. Nonetheless, the former colonies had fought a war of independence to rid themselves of a unitary government in Great Britain. The compromise between the two extremes is federalism. In a federation, a constitution divides power between the two levels of government—national and states—so that neither government derives its powers from the other.

A federation may provide states with a considerable amount of autonomy. This leads to the great advantage of having a federation in a country that is very diverse in terms of its economy, geography, social structures, and population. The independence provided by a federation may lead to a great deal of innovation and experimentation on the part of the states. It also allows government at a level that is closer to the people than a distant, centralized government. Of course, every system has its disadvantages, and federalism is no exception. A federal system may lead to a lack of uniformity in laws among the separate states. The ability of the states to provide services to their citizens also varies from one state to another, due to the differences in wealth among the states.

The Evolution of Federalism

Because the United States Constitution is vague about the powers of the national government and even vaguer about the states' powers, conflicts over the power of each level of government are unavoidable. When that happens, someone must settle the conflict. In the United States, the United States Supreme Court performs that task, exercising its right to interpret the Constitution. Consequently, federalism is not static. In the 210-year history of the United States, federalism has been given several interpretations. An analysis of the history of federalism in the United States reveals three distinctive types that will be briefly described.[21]

The concept of **dual federalism** was developed by the Supreme Court before the Civil War. After the war, it became the dominant interpretation, replacing the rivalry between nation-centered and state-centered federalism. Dual federalism implies that the national and state governments are equals. Functions and duties of government are divided between the two levels, and overlap (the sharing of functions) is rare and discouraged. The national government focuses on those things that it does best, and the state governments focus on the rest. Dual federalism implies a clear separation of duties between the state and national levels of government. Dual federalism enjoyed widespread support from the end of the Civil War to the 1930s.

In spite of the ascendancy of dual federalism, the national and state governments had always cooperated in a number of areas. With the Great Depression of the 1930s and the New Deal of Franklin Roosevelt, the United States entered the era of **cooperative federalism.** The concept was fully articulated in the 1950s. Cooperative federalism implies that instead of competing centers of power, government in the United States is actually made up of many centers that work together to solve the nation's problems. The national and state governments cooperate in efforts to address the needs and desires of the American people, both as a whole and as citizens of the separate states. Together, all the necessary functions of government are performed.

New federalism has been advanced since the 1970s, primarily by Presidents Nixon and Reagan. The national government was viewed as being too powerful, too big, and too unwieldy. New federalism returned much of the control over programs to the state and/or local governments, whereas government programs had tended to become centralized under cooperative federalism. New federalism sought to decentralize many programs. Centralization had caused many programs to lose touch with the people they were supposed to be serving. One of the central tenets of new federalism was the placement of control over a program at the level closest to the people that it served. That could be either the state or the local level.

Neither the new federalism of Nixon nor that of Reagan prevailed. During the Nixon administration, many categorical grants were consolidated into block grants. Other categorical grants and block grants were eliminated and replaced with revenue sharing. Revenue sharing gave state and local governments sums of money that could be spent by the state or local governments in any manner they thought appropriate. This did, of course, give a great deal of discretion to the state and local governments. Revenue sharing, however, was abolished in 1986. Block grants give money in sums that are designated for broad areas of public policy. For example, a block grant may be given for the area of education. The state and/or local government has discretion over the aspect of education that the money may be spent on, but the money must be spent on education. Categorical grants are designated for specific purposes and may only be spent for that specific purpose.

Federal grants to state and local governments are not as easy to get as they once were. In the era of cooperative federalism, the national government gave the state and local governments considerable sums of money. Much of that money came in the form of matching grants. The state and local governments were required to match money given by the national government. The match, however, was often less than equal. It was not unusual for the national government to match every dollar the state or local governments put up with two or three dollars from the national treasury. The interstate highway system was built with matching grants. The national government contributed nine dollars to the system for every one dollar contributed by the state governments.

The trend in recent years has been for the national government to require the states to provide more services and enforce more regulations, but to provide fewer funds for those activities. National-state relations since the advent of cooperative federalism have been characterized by the "carrot-and-stick" approach. The national government begins programs with the "carrot." In other words, the national government entices the states into doing something by offering to pay much of the cost of the program. When Medicaid was created in 1965, the national government paid virtually the entire cost of the program. Beginning in the 1980s and continuing into the 1990s, Medicaid has been expanded to cover more and more people. However, at the same time, the national government has not increased funding to cover the new recipients. That additional cost has been borne by the states. If the states refuse to pay for the expanded coverage, the national government will reduce funding for the rest of the program, if not eliminate it altogether—the "stick."

The national government has used the carrot-and-stick approach with such diverse policies as the raising of the legal drinking age from 18 to 19 years and then from 19 to 21 years; seat-belt laws; and civil-contempt proceedings for those in arrears on child-support payments. In the cases of drinking age and seat belts, the national government threatened to reduce the amount available to the states for highway projects. In the case of child-support payments, a reduction in the money granted the states for Aid to Families with Dependent Children (AFDC) was threatened. The carrot-and-stick approach can be used successfully in those programs where the national share of funding is predominant. However, as the share of funds given to a program by the national government becomes smaller, so too does the incentive on the part of the state or local government to maintain its share.

The stick results in the phenomenon of mandates. A **mandate** is simply something that a person or organization must do. As long as the national government was willing to pay for the goods and services that it mandated state and local governments to provide, the state and local governments did not complain too much. However, the growing budget constraints at the national level have meant that the national government has increasingly engaged in the passage of unfunded mandates.

Unfunded mandates have been the target of much criticism by mayors and governors across the nation, regardless of ideology or political party. Indeed, much of the impetus for the passage of Proposition 187 in California in 1994 was unfunded mandates. The national government had mandated that the state pay for medical care and public education for illegal immigrants. While it is true that illegal immigrants pay taxes in various forms, such as income taxes and Social Security taxes, and they rarely receive refunds or benefits, the moneys collected from them largely go to the national government's treasury. The states pay the costs of providing education and health care. In addition, a number of inmates in state prisons are illegal immigrants for which the state bears the cost. It is also true that illegal immigrants pay state income taxes, property taxes through rent, and sales taxes through purchases, which go to state and local governments. The perception remains, however, that the states bear a net cost.

The issue of illegal immigration is only a part of the story. Government regulations covering everything from the workplace to the environment have placed the costs of implementation and enforcement on state and local governments; hence, hostility on the part of mayors and governors toward the national government continues to grow. The cooperative federalism of the 1930s through the 1970s had turned into an era of uncooperative federalism.

The 1990s saw the further evolution of federalism. In 1995, the Republican-led United States House of Representatives introduced legislation that would reduce the ability of the national government to mandate new programs at the state or local level without appropriating the funds to implement them. After passage in the U.S. Senate, President Clinton signed the Unfunded Mandates Reform Act of 1995. The relationship between the national government and the states has also been altered in the 1990s by United States Supreme Court decisions:

- 1991: In *Gregory v. Ashcroft*, the Supreme Court upheld a Missouri law that requires state judges to retire at 70 years of age. Missouri justified its requirement with the Tenth Amendment, which reserves powers not delegated to the national government, nor denied to the states, to the states.
- 1992: In *New York v. United States*, the Supreme Court decided that Congress could not command the states to implement legislation enacted by Congress. According to the Court, Congress is limited by the Constitution in exercising its powers, noting that just as Congress is constrained by the First Amendment, it is also constrained by the Tenth Amendment. The Court concluded that the states possess "a residuary and inviolable sovereignty" that stems from the Tenth Amendment.
- 1995: In *United States v. Lopez*, the Supreme Court overturned the Gun-Free School Zone Act of 1990 because Congress had exceeded its authority under the interstate commerce clause of the Constitution.
- 1996: In *Seminole Tribe v. Florida*, the Supreme Court curtailed the authority of Congress to subject the states to lawsuits in federal courts. The decision affects the ability to force the states to abide by national laws.
- 1997: In *Printz v. United States*, the Supreme Court defined federalism as a system of dual sovereignty, indicating that the states are independent ex-

cept where the Constitution clearly states otherwise through the delegated powers of the national government or the supremacy clause. Also, the Supreme Court, in *City of Boerne v. Flores,* declared the Religious Freedom Restoration Act unconstitutional because Congress had exceeded its enforcement authority under the Fourteenth Amendment, which has been used frequently by Congress to extend the reach of national policy.[22]

How far the Supreme Court will go in curbing the power of the national government remains to be seen. However, the combination of a Republican-controlled Congress's predisposition to return power to the states and the Supreme Court's recent decisions may bring a return to something resembling dual federalism.

Federalism and Political Change

Federalism allows state governments discretion over public policy because the states are free to do what is not prohibited by the national government. The independence of the states means that they are free to pursue, within the boundaries set by the national government, their particular ideals. As described in Chapters 1 and 2, the state of Texas has a set of ideals similar to those of the rest of the nation, but they also differ in various respects. Federalism gives those differences in ideals among the states the opportunity to flourish.

The ability to pursue different ideals, and thereby to establish different institutions, also means that periods of creedal passion may occur at different times among the states. Periods of creedal passion may be experienced by the United States as a whole or in each of several states. States may then, on an individual basis, revise their own constitutions, amend them in a substantial way, or pass major pieces of legislation to close the gap between the ideals and the institutions.

Federalism and Democracy

Federalism has a rather strange relationship with democracy. In one sense, democracy and federalism may not seem connected to each other. However, the form of federalism can have a substantial impact on the way democracy is implemented in a society. Federalism allows for a devolution of government responsibility. Those things that society assigns to government to do may be done at one or more levels. As a result, democracy at different levels takes various forms.

Public policy can be made at the national, state, or local levels of government. Federalism allows for a wide variation in the degree of democracy that is practiced at those levels on a comparative basis. For example, recall that the state of Texas does not have initiative and referendum, as other states do. It could be claimed that Texas is less democratic than those states.

Federalism also allows for a mixture of pluralist and majoritarian democracies. While local governments may be majoritarian, for example, the state government could be pluralist. While the ability to experiment with different forms of democracy have been lauded, it has also been lamented. The very fact that one state may be more democratic than another may be cause to celebrate that state's position, but that means that some other state is less democratic, giving cause for regret.

Critical Thinking Exercise: Which type of federalism do you favor? Is the Supreme Court destined to return to dual federalism? What functions should each level of government be responsible for?

SUMMARY

This chapter has provided the last part of the context for studying Texas government and politics. The constitution of the state of Texas is a statutory type, making the study of it essential to an understanding of the Texas systems of government and politics. The current Texas Constitution is a product of both the Reconstruction era and the populist-libertarian movement of the 1870s. The result is a constitution that limits government and government officials, particularly the governor. Almost from the ratification of the constitution in 1876, it has been condemned by many. In spite of numerous attempts at revision, culminating in the 1974 Constitutional Convention and the 1975 amendments, the constitution still survives. However, it does not survive intact. It had been amended 390 times at the writing of this text. In spite of criticism and amendments, a period of creedal passion demanding constitutional revision does not appear likely in the near future.

Federalism is a form of government that defines the relationship between the national and state governments. Under federalism, a constitution divides power between the national government and the state governments. The relationship between the national and state governments has not been static. It has evolved over the 200-plus years of United States history and appears to be evolving again.

KEY TERMS

legitimacy

consent

tacit consent

ideal constitution

statutory constitution

constitutional amendment

constitutional revision

right-to-work law

unitary government

confederation

federation

dual federalism

cooperative federalism

new federalism

mandates

SUGGESTED READINGS

Angell, Robert H. *A Compilation and Analysis of the 1998 Texas Constitution and the Original 1876 Text.* Lewiston, N.Y.: E. Mellen Press, 1998.

May, Janice C. *The Texas Constitutional Revision Experience in the '70s.* Institute for Urban Studies, University of Houston, Austin, Tex.: Sterling Swift Publishing, 1975.

Peterson, Paul E. *The Price of Federalism.* Washington, D.C.: The Brookings Institution, 1995.

Posner, Paul L. *The Politics of Unfunded Mandates: Whither Federalism?* Washington, D.C.: Georgetown University Press, 1998.

Savage, David G. "A Watershed Term for Federalism." *State Legislatures* 25, no. 8 (1999): 18–22.

Tarr, G. Alan. *Understanding State Constitutions.* Princeton, N.J.: Princeton University Press, 1998.

NOTES

1. Personal Telephone Interview with Professor Edward C. Olson, Angelo State University, 8 December, 1999.
2. Juan B. Elizondo, Jr., "Ratliff: Time to Rewrite Constitution; Lawmaker Joined by Watchdog Group in Effort to Update State Document," *Austin American-Statesman,* 28 October 1999; Bill Ratliff and Rob Junell, "A New Constitution for the New Millennium," *Austin American-Statesman,* 9 December 1998; Osler McCarthy, "Poll Shows Support for New Constitution," *Austin American-Statesman,* 13 February 1999.
3. George D. Braden, *Citizen's Guide to the Texas Constitution* (Austin, Tex.: Texas Advisory Commission on Intergovernmental Affairs, 1972) 11–12; Fred Gantt, Jr., Irving O. Dawson, and Luther C. Hagard, Jr., eds., *Governing Texas: Documents and Readings,* 2 ed. (New York: Thomas Y. Crowell, 1970), 32–37; Nelson Wolff, *Challenge of Change* (San Antonio: Naylor Company, 1975), 30–35.
4. Braden, *Citizen's Guide,* 13–14; Seth McKay, *Seven Decades of the Texas Constitution of 1876* (Austin, Tex.: University of Texas Press, 1930), 9–46; and Wolff, *Challenge of Change,* 35–37.
5. Impeachment, which is like an indictment in a criminal case, requires a majority vote in the U.S. House of Representatives. Once impeached, a trial is conducted in the U.S. Senate. The House of Representatives sends managers to the Senate to act as prosecutors, and the senators act as the jury. The Senate may then vote to remove the president from office. Removal must be approved by a two-thirds majority vote. The vote to remove President Andrew Johnson fell one vote short. Bill Clinton is the other impeached president; the vote fell 17 short of the two-thirds vote necessary to remove him.
6. McKay, *Seven Decades,* 47–143.
7. J. E. Ericson, "The Delegates to the Convention of 1875: A Reappraisal," *Southwestern Historical Quarterly* 67 (1963/1964): 22–27. All of the information presented here on the delegates to the convention was taken from the Ericson article. However, as Ericson points out, there are at best incomplete records of the delegates' biographies. Nevertheless, the figures shown here represent the best available information.
8. Although the content of the section was deleted, the title remains to prevent confusion with the numbering of the remaining articles.
9. The state may borrow money by issuing bonds. However, the bonds are issued for specified purposes and require constitutional amendment to gain approval. Money has been borrowed by this method for such diverse purposes as the building of prisons and loans to Texas veterans who wish to buy rural land.

10. The Texas government has numerous agencies, boards, and commissions. During the 2000–2001 biennium, approximately 135 received funding.

11. Initiative allows citizens to place propositions on the ballot by obtaining a specified number of signatures of registered voters on a petition. Referendum would then allow the citizenry to vote for or against the proposition. It may not be entirely fair to disparage the constitutional convention for this oversight. The first state to allow initiative and referendum was South Dakota in 1898. However, the idea was not unheard of in the 1870s, and a constitution as committed to democracy, at least in some respects, as the 1876 constitution could have contained such a provision.

12. Council of State Governments, *Book of the States 1997–98,* vol. 32 (Lexington, Ky: Council of State Governments, 1998), 3.

13. Texas Advisory Commission on Intergovernmental Relations, *Reorganized Texas Constitution Without Substantive Changes* (Austin, Tex.: Texas Advisory Commission on Intergovernmental Relations, 1977).

14. For a discussion of these early attempts, see John E. Bebout and Janice C. May, *The Texas Constitution: Problems and Prospects for Revision* (Arlington, Tex.: The Texas Urban Development Commission, 1971), 9–15; *Informational Booklet on the Proposed 1976 Revision of the Texas Constitution,* 64th Legislature, 1975, 3–7; Janice C. May, *The Texas Constitutional Revision Experience in the 1970s* (Austin, Tex.: Sterling Swift, 1975), 25–30.

15. The amendment accounts for sections and articles of the current constitution that have only the title or section number appearing in the text. For example, Sec. 3a (repealed Aug. 5, 1969).

16. May, *The Texas Constitutional Revision Experience,* 11.

17. The essence of a right-to-work provision is given in Section 22a of the 1974 Constitutional Convention's draft document: "No person shall be denied employment on account of membership or non-membership in a labor organization or payment or non-payment of any dues, fees, or other sums of money or things of value to a labor organization." A right-to-work provision prevents the establishment of a closed shop, one in which a person must be a member of a labor union in order to get a job.

18. Recall that separate items could be presented to the voters, along with a constitution. The constitution could then be either rejected or accepted. Separate provisions could either be accepted or rejected on their individual merits to the voter. However, if the main constitution was not passed by the voters, then none of the separate provisions, regardless of acceptance or rejection, would be operable.

19. James Dickson, "Erratic Continuity: Some Patterns of Constitutional Change in Texas Since 1975," *Texas Journal of Political Studies* 14 (1991/1992): 41–56.

20. A majority is any number greater than one-half of the total votes cast. A simple majority is 50 percent plus one. An extraordinary (or super) majority is anything greater than a simple majority.

21. Richard H. Leach, *American Federalism* (New York: Norton, 1970), 10–17.

22. Charles R. Wise, "Judicial Federalism: The Resurgence of the Supreme Court's Role in the Protection of State Sovereignty," *Public Administration Review,* 58 (March/April 1998): 95–98. See Laura A. Jensen, "Federal Authority vs. State Autonomy: The Supreme Court's Role Revisited," *Public Administration Review* 59 (March 1999): 97–99, who notes that the national government can still dictate to the states through conditional spending, just as it has in the past.

4

Political Parties in Texas

★ **Scenario:** **The Challenge to Democratic Party Dominance in a Time of Transition**

Throughout most of its history, Texas has been a one-party, Democratic state. After the Civil War, most Anglo Texans perceived the Republican Party as representing carpetbaggers, African Americans, Reconstruction, and the Union. The Democratic Party, on the other hand, was viewed as representing states' rights and traditional Southern social and political values. However, being a one-party state did not mean that the Democratic Party's dominance went unchallenged. One of those challenges occurred during the late nineteenth century, in a period of creedal passion.

In the last quarter of the nineteenth century, as the United States began its transition from an agrarian to an urban society, Texas felt the dislocation acutely. In the 1870s, nearly 70 percent of Texans were employed in agricultural pursuits, but after 1873, a number of social and economic changes imperiled the small farm in Texas. As we noted in Chapter 2, the Texas economy during this period was based on cotton. In 1875, the price of cotton fell from about 15 cents to 11 cents a pound and remained close to that level until the end of the century. Because the cost of producing cotton was nearly 8 cents a pound, the farmers' situation was dire. Compounding the farmers' plight was the crop-lien system in which a merchant or landlord gave the farmer financial assistance in return for a lien on the farmer's crop. To make matters worse for the farmer, merchants often charged the farmer inflated rates of interest and inflated prices on goods and supplies. The effect of this system was to force most farmers into peonage, a condition of near slavery to merchants or landlords.[1]

Responding to these conditions, farmers in Texas initially formed an interest group, the Farmers' Alliance, and later a political party, the People's Party. In September 1877, a group of farmers met at the Lampasas County farm of J. R. Allen to form the "Knights of Reliance," which was later changed to the Farmers' Alliance. The group's initial efforts proved ineffective, despite increasing economic hardships for Texas farmers. In 1884, however, the alliance was transformed with the appointment of S. O. Daws as traveling lecturer. Daws's oratory skills were used to give voice to the alliance's strategies of economic cooperation in both purchasing and marketing. These strategies involved cooperative efforts by alliance members in purchasing what they needed to produce their crops and in marketing their crops. The alliance enjoyed only limited success because it failed to adequately address the fundamental problem—the crop-lien system. Nevertheless, the alliance's membership grew rapidly, primarily because the alliance identified the sources of the farmers' plight and proposed measures to correct these problems.[2] In these early efforts, the alliance was acting as a self-help organization for farmers and was not involved in politics.

In August 1886, at the state convention in Cleburne, the Farmers' Alliance discussed 16 "demands" authored by its political committee and addressed to the governments of Texas and the United States. The demands covered labor issues, the power of the railroads, financial problems, land policy, and commodity dealings in agricultural futures. The adoption of the demands by a narrow majority of the delegates reflected a split in the alliance between those delegates who wanted to remain a self-help organization, which continued its economic strategies, and the majority who favored an activist political organization, to augment its economic strategies. Despite the disruptive potential of the split, alliance president Charles W. Macune's leadership kept the alliance factions together and fostered the alliance's growth.[3]

With the adoption of the demands and the delegates' endorsement of political activism in 1886, the alliance was forced to choose between two political options: becoming an interest group or a political party. The alliance chose to enter politics as an interest group, focusing its efforts on influencing public officials. Initially, the alliance enjoyed some success, influencing the Democratic Party's platform in 1888 and its legislation to regulate monopolies in 1889. However, the alliance's greatest success came in 1890 when the Democratic Party nominated James Stephen Hogg, who had declared his support for railroad regulation, for governor. Hogg's election and the passage of legislation creating the Texas Railroad Commission gave the alliance great hope, despite the Democratic Party's refusal to adopt the alliance's scheme for government (rather than bank) loans to farmers. In only a matter of months, however, the alliance felt betrayed by the Democratic

This Lampasas County farmhouse was the site of the first meeting of the Farmers' Alliance in Texas. The house was later dismantled and reassembled at the Chicago Exposition of 1893.

Party and the governor when Governor Hogg failed to appoint an alliance member to the Railroad Commission.

The movement to form a political party began in the late 1880s, when some alliance members, most notably Thomas Gaines and W. R. Lamb, urged the creation of a new political party to advance the class interests of farmers and laborers. Subsequently, the alliance was again split, this time between those members who favored Governor Hogg and the Democratic Party and those members who favored the formation of a separate political party. Led by W. R. Lamb, the People's Party of Texas was created in August 1891. In subsequent meetings during that year, the party nominated candidates for state offices and created a party organization. In 1892, after being ostracized by the Democratic Party, Democrats who had favored the alliance's plan for government loans—called "Jeffersonian Democrats"—joined the People's Party. Thus, the People's Party was formed from two principal sources sympathetic to the program of the alliance—populist farmers and alienated Democrats.

The People's Party participated in seven general elections in Texas between 1892 and 1904, but only three of these elections were important. Between 1892 and

1896, the People's Party effectively challenged Democratic Party dominance in Texas. The policy of the People's Party was to nominate candidates for all statewide offices; however, the party never captured a statewide office, and the party's best showing was in 1896, when its gubernatorial candidate, Jerome Kearby, was supported by both populists and Republicans and received 44 percent of the vote. In the Texas legislature, the greatest representation by the People's Party occurred in 1894, when its members won 22 seats in the 128-member Texas House of Representatives and three seats in the 31-member Texas Senate. In congressional elections, the People's Party frequently ran strong races, but its candidates never defeated their Democratic opponents. In local elections, the party was much more successful, controlling entire counties or numerous offices. The party's success, however, was tempered by the lack of political experience of its candidates for public office and the ineffectiveness of their attempts to govern.[4]

Several factors led to the demise of the People's Party, but the most important factor involved national politics. When the national Democratic Party adopted populist positions in its platform and nominated William Jennings Bryan as its presidential candidate in 1896, the People's Party's principal issues had been taken over by one of the nation's two major parties. Because of the two-party tradition in the United States and the difficulty of sustaining a third-party effort, populism and the People's Party faded quickly after 1896. ★

INTRODUCTION

The evolution of the Farmers' Alliance from a self-help organization to an interest group to a political party illustrates the principal distinction between interest groups, which we discuss in Chapter 5, and political parties. Although both interest groups and political parties seek certain government policies, the activities of interest groups focus on influencing government; the activities of political parties focus on controlling government. For example, as an interest group, the Farmers' Alliance attempted to influence public policy through the Democratic Party and its public officials. As a political party, the People's Party formed a party organization, nominated candidates for public office, and attempted to get them elected. To control government, political parties must perform three functions: (1) electing their members to public office, (2) representing the groups that make up the party coalition, and (3) organizing the party's members and the government so that the policy preferences of the party's members can become public policy.

We describe political parties in Texas using political scientist V. O. Key's conception of a three-part party structure: (1) party leaders and officials, (2) people who identify with the party, and (3) the men and women elected to public office under the party label (Figure 4.1). As we describe and analyze the three components of the political parties, remember that these components, though separated for analysis, interact and often overlap as they perform the party's functions. We begin with the party as an organization, describing the party structure in Texas and assessing its performance. However, a party organization is meaningless

Te ★ as*Index*

Political Parties in the States

Rank among the 50 states in interparty competition, 1995–1998:
Texas: 1st (tied with Washington)
California: 6th
New York: 9th (tied with South Carolina)
Florida: 3rd

Party composition in the legislature, 1999–2000:
Texas House of Representatives: 78 Democrats, 72 Republicans
Texas Senate: 16 Republicans, 15 Democrats
California Assembly: 48 Democrats, 32 Republicans
California Senate: 25 Democrats, 15 Republicans
New York Assembly: 98 Democrats, 52 Republicans
New York Senate: 35 Republicans, 26 Democrats
Florida Senate: 25 Republicans, 15 Democrats
Florida House of Representatives: 73 Republicans, 47 Democrats

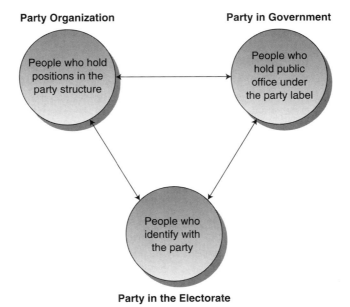

Figure 4.1   The Three-Part Structure of Political Parties

Source: Adapted from Paul Allen Beck and Frank J. Sorauf, *Party Politics in America,* 7th ed. (New York: HarperCollins, 1992), 11. By permission.

without party members. Consequently, we describe the party in the electorate, describing the historical and contemporary coalitions of the political parties in Texas. Next, we consider the party in government, through which the party attempts to transform its political promises into public policy. Finally, we consider the party's role in political change and the party's influence on the forms of democracy that we introduced in Chapter 1.

POLITICAL PARTY ORGANIZATION

The **party organization** consists of the structures that constitute the party organization and the party activists who occupy positions in the party structure. The party organization includes both a formal organization, established in state law, and a functional organization, which describes how the party actually operates. Our description and analysis of these organizations begins with the formal organization.

Formal Organization

In Texas, as in most states, state law establishes the formal organization for political parties. There is both a temporary and a permanent party organization for each political party.

The Temporary Organization The **temporary party organization** consists of conventions at the precinct, the county or state senatorial district, and the state levels. These conventions are held every two years, are attended by party activists, and last only a short period of time, ranging from a few hours to a few days. The conventions meet to select delegates to subsequent party conventions, choose party leaders, and establish party policies. They provide an opportunity for interested party members to select the party's leaders and influence its policies—an example of the representation function of political parties.

Every two years, the first party convention held in Texas occurs at the voting-precinct level. Election precincts are voting districts that usually contain fewer than 3000 registered voters. On the date of the primary election (currently the second Tuesday of March in even-numbered years) after the polls have closed, the parties hold their **precinct conventions.** The political parties conduct primary elections to select their nominees for elected public office—governor, state senator, state representative, and county judge, for example. A stamp, indicating which party's primary election the person voted in, is placed on the voter's registration card by the primary election official, and any person with such a stamp may participate in the party's precinct convention. Although participation is open, only about 1 percent of the voters in the party's primary election actually attend the precinct conventions. Even in presidential election years, when the precinct conventions in the Democratic Party have an effect on the selection of delegates to the party's national convention and the choice of the party's presidential nominee, attendance rarely exceeds 10 percent of the eligible participants.

The precinct convention's principal task is to select delegates to the party's **county convention** or, in those counties with more than one state senatorial district (such as El Paso, Harris, Tarrant, Dallas, Bexar, and Travis Counties), to the **state senatorial district convention.** In both the Democratic and the Republican Parties, each precinct in the county or senatorial district is allocated one delegate for each 25 votes cast in the precinct for the party's gubernatorial nominee in the most recent gubernatorial election. The allocation system is designed to reward those precincts that provided the greatest electoral support for the party's gubernatorial nominee by giving them a larger voice in selecting party officials and setting party policy. After delegates to the county or senatorial district convention have been chosen, the precinct convention debates and then either adopts or rejects resolutions; the resolutions that are adopted are forwarded to the county convention. Through this process, the party begins to build a party platform by discussing the concerns of party members on issues of public policy.

On the third Saturday after the primary election, each party holds its county and senatorial district conventions. The delegates and alternates who were selected in the precinct conventions attend the county and senatorial district conventions, which usually are all-day affairs.

The principal purpose of the county or senatorial district conventions is to select delegates to the party's state convention. Each county or senatorial district is allocated delegates based on its support for the party's gubernatorial nominee in the most recent general election (one delegate for each 300 votes). Also, the conventions consider resolutions adopted in the precinct conventions. Resolutions adopted at the county or senatorial district level are sent to the state convention for possible incorporation into the party's platform.

In June, on a date selected by the state executive committee of each party, the delegates assemble for the party's **state convention.** The state convention certifies the results of the party's primary, which nominates the party's candidates for public office, drafts and adopts the party's platform, and selects the party's state executive committee, including the state party chairperson and vice chairperson. In presidential election years, the state convention also selects the party's slate of presidential electors, nominates the state's members for the party's national committee, and selects the state's delegates to the party's national convention. The Republican Party allocates all of its national convention delegates based on the presidential primary results, and delegate selection committees, whose members are chosen by the presidential candidates, provide lists of delegates for the state convention to select. In the Democratic Party, delegates are allocated both on the basis of the presidential primary results (75 percent of the allotted delegates) and on the basis of support for the candidates at the precinct, county or state senatorial, and state conventions (25 percent of the allotted delegates).

The Permanent Organization   The parties' **permanent organization** consists of chairpersons and committees, which purportedly work throughout the year performing party-building and electoral functions. Because of their principal activities, the parties' permanent organizations are tied to electoral districts. Each electoral unit, from the smallest (the precinct) to the largest (the state) is represented

Susan Weddington (left) and Molly Beth Malcolm (right), who were elected in 1997, are state chairs of the Texas Republican Party and Democratic Party, respectively.

in the permanent organization. Although the political party appears hierarchical in structure, with power concentrated at the top, party organizations are more accurately described as stratarchies—organizations with power distributed in layers or strata.[5] Consequently, each level of party organization is relatively independent of the other levels and concentrates on electoral activities within its level or strata.

Each precinct in Texas has a **precinct chairperson** who represents the party in that electoral district. The chairperson is elected for a two-year term in the party's primary election. The chairperson is responsible for informing members of the party's activities and issue positions, getting party members to the polls on election days, and serving on the party's county executive committee.

Each county in Texas has a **county chairperson** and a **county executive committee.** The county chairperson is elected in the party's primary for a two-year term. The county executive committee, consisting of the county's precinct chairpersons, assists the county chairperson. At the county level, the party's duties, which are usually performed by the county chairperson, include conducting the party's primary elections, arranging for the county convention, raising funds for the county organization, campaigning for party candidates, and promoting precinct organization efforts.

In Texas state law, there is a provision for district executive committees, composed of county chairpersons from various electoral districts (senatorial, legisla-

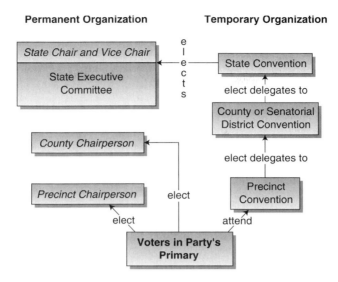

Figure 4.2   Party Organization in Texas

tive, congressional, and judicial); however, few of these organs are functional, leaving their duties to the county executive committees and chairpersons.

Formally, the supreme unit of the party's permanent organization is the **state executive committee,** composed of a chairperson and a vice chairperson (state law requires that the chairperson and vice chairperson not be of the same gender) and one man and one woman from each of the state's 31 senatorial districts. The representatives from the senatorial districts are elected at the state convention, based on nominations by the individual state senatorial districts, for two-year terms. Consequently, the selection is really made by the delegates from each of the state's senatorial districts. The **state party chairperson** and vice chairperson are chosen by the entire convention, but their selection may be influenced by the party's gubernatorial nominee. The state executive committee's duties include certifying the party's candidates for the general election, conducting the state convention, and promoting the party's candidates and issue positions. The formal party organization is depicted in Figure 4.2.

Functional Organization

As you probably know, the formal organization chart of any organization does not provide the real story of how well the organization functions and where decisions are made. That general statement is also true of the organization of political parties in Texas. For example, although the state chairperson formally heads the political party and is elected by the state executive committee, functional leadership may rest with the governor, who can be instrumental in selecting his or her party's state chairperson and shaping party policy. The formal organization provides a skeleton for the party organization, but its performance is determined by the effectiveness of the people who occupy those positions and who use those positions to further the party's political goals. Thus, in this section, we describe and assess the party organizations in Texas in terms of their unity and effectiveness in performing the party's functions.

Democratic Party Unity   In the Democratic Party in Texas, control of the party organization was, from the 1940s to the 1980s, the objective of an ideological conflict between liberals[6] and conservatives. After the populist challenge and until the 1940s, conservatives controlled the party structure, such as it was, in a period of one-party Democratic dominance, and the conservatives were rarely challenged. Also, the factions that existed in the party during that period were usually centered around personalities rather than ideologies.[7] The liberal-conservative split in the Democratic Party became public during the 1944 May convention[8] for selecting the party's presidential electors. Conservative Democrats, calling themselves the "Texas Regulars," selected a slate of independent electors who pledged not to vote for Franklin D. Roosevelt (FDR) in the electoral college. Before the September convention, pro-Roosevelt Democrats organized the precincts and, taking control of the state convention, purged the Texas Regular electors who refused to support FDR. They also gained control of the State Democratic Executive Committee (SDEC). This was the pivotal battle in the war that raged between liberals and conservatives for control of the Democratic Party's organization.[9]

Under liberal control, the SDEC attempted to build a strong state party organization that could raise money and promote progressive candidates and causes. In 1946, however, the liberals lost control of the SDEC when Homer Rainey, the liberal candidate for governor, was defeated in his bid for the nomination. Liberals briefly regained control of the SDEC, but they lost control for nearly three decades in 1950 when Democratic Governor Allan Shivers removed liberals from the SDEC and from party influence.[10]

Losing control of the party apparatus caused the liberals to redouble their efforts to regain control. During the 1950s and 1960s, liberal groups attempted to organize Democratic precincts, most effectively by the Harris County Democrats, the Bexar County Democratic Coalition, and the Nueces County Democratic Alliance. Also during this period, Frankie Randolph, the descendant of a prominent Texas lumber and banking family, created the Democrats of Texas (DOT) in her attempt to create a statewide liberal network.[11]

In 1976, liberal efforts and national party rule changes allowed the liberals to take control of the state Democratic Party organization for good. In that year, Billie Carr, a Houston Democratic precinct organizer and protégé of Frankie Randolph, led a coalition of liberals, which forced concessions from the conservatives at the September state convention and, although their candidate for state party chairperson, John Henry Tatum, lost to Calvin Guest, the liberals elected the vice chairperson, Eddie Bernice Johnson of Dallas, and more than half of the SDEC. In subsequent conventions, liberals consolidated their control over the state party organization, electing a series of moderate chairpersons. Billy Goldberg was elected in 1978. Bob Slagle defeated a more liberal candidate in

1980 but was seen as a moderate.[12] He was replaced in 1995 by Bill White, after Slagle was pushed out by statewide Democratic officeholders led by Lieutenant Governor Bob Bullock, who feared that Slagle could not lead the party against the growing Republican challenge. Two years later, White resigned as state party chair, and the SDEC elected Molly Beth Malcolm, a former Republican, to chair the party.

Legitimate questions include why the party organization was the locus of the liberal-conservative battle and whether the liberals' victory has really mattered. According to liberal activists in the 1960s, they sought control of the Democratic Party organization because it was the avenue to political power and control of public policy, given the difficulty of creating and sustaining a third-party effort in Texas. Furthermore, the functions performed by party organizations—contesting elections, organizing the government, and especially formulating policy positions—are performed in conventions in Texas. These conventions have the potential for creating grassroots power and serve as a training ground for political activists. Thus, not only was control of the party organization sought for political power, but it was also a means for training liberal activists in the processes of democratic politics.[13]

The effect of liberal control over the party organization can be measured by the increase in the number of liberals among Democratic candidates for statewide office, in the increase in their electoral success, and in the number of liberal positions incorporated in the party's platform (see the box titled, "The 1998 Democratic and Republican Platforms" on pages 106–107). During the 1950s and 1960s, the only liberal Democrat elected to statewide office in Texas was United States Senator Ralph Yarborough. However, in 1982, four liberal Democrats—Jim Mattox, Jim Hightower, Garry Mauro, and Ann Richards—were elected to statewide executive offices. All won reelection in 1986, and Ann Richards was elected governor in 1990. In recent elections, however, liberal Democrats have not fared as well. In 1990, Republican Rick Perry, a former conservative Democratic state representative who switched parties, defeated Jim Hightower for agriculture commissioner. Mattox, who unsuccessfully sought the Democratic gubernatorial nomination in 1990, was replaced as attorney general by moderate Democrat Dan Morales. In 1994, Ann Richards lost the governorship to George W. Bush. In 1998, Mattox lost his bid to become attorney general to Republican Supreme Court Justice John Cornyn. Mauro, who barely won reelection as land commissioner in 1994, lost his bid to become governor to George W. Bush in 1998. Consequently, Republicans replaced the liberal class of 1982 in statewide elective offices during the 1990s. The success of liberal Democrats in the 1980s and early 1990s also had an effect on the Republican Party, as conservative Democrats, having lost control of the Democratic Party, increasingly abandoned the Democratic Party for the Republican Party. By the 1990s, Democratic Party leaders were overwhelmingly liberal or moderate ideologically. As one study of Democratic Party leaders indicated, 43 percent were self-described liberals, 31 percent were moderates, and 26 percent were conservatives.[14]

Republican Party Unity   For the Republican Party in Texas, the problem was to create an organization and a following. After governing Texas from 1869 to 1874,

Republicans were unable to win statewide office for nearly a century. By 1920, the party was "a historical vestige, long past challenging the permanent [Democratic] majority party for control of the state."[15] During the 1920s, in fact, the Republican Party was dominated by four men: R. B. Creager, Henry F. McGregor, Frank E. Scobey, and Harry Wurzbach. Most of the party's activities were centered on distributing national patronage positions, such as postmasters and federal judgeships in Texas when the president was Republican.

However, the party did make efforts to contest statewide offices between 1922 and 1932. When R. B. Creager became the state party chair in 1921 and succeeded McGregor as national committeeman in 1923, he began organizing the Republican Party for electoral competition, creating a full-time, professional headquarters staff who supervised party operations. Creager opened a party headquarters in Dallas in 1921, secured a staff budget of $25,000 in nonelection years, and maintained a strong professional organization. Creager created a Republican Party from the top down rather than from the bottom up, appointing county chairs and strengthening his hold on the party organization. At that time, only one-fifth of the state's 254 counties returned sufficient Republican votes to warrant any formal party organization. Gillespie, Kendall, Bexar, Harris, Dallas, Tarrant, Nueces, Cameron, El Paso, and Jefferson counties accounted for a large majority of Republican votes in Texas.

With FDR's election to the presidency in 1932, the Republican Party lost its ability to distribute patronage. The party organization atrophied during the 1930s and 1940s, as rank-and-file membership reached an all-time low. During the 1950s, however, Jack Porter, by aligning himself with Eisenhower early in the 1952 presidential nomination battle, became national committeeman and gained control of the party, commencing a decade of organizational gains. Also in 1952, conservative Democratic Governor Allan Shivers endorsed Eisenhower rather than the Democratic presidential nominee, Adlai Stevenson, creating a group of voters known as "presidential Republicans" (Democrats who would vote for Democratic candidates in state and local contests but for Republicans for president). Porter's strategy was to create a substantial party organization, that emphasized electoral politics, selectively challenging Democratic candidates.[16]

Following John Tower's election to the U.S. Senate in 1961, the Texas Republican Party entered a new phase in party development. The party headquarters was moved from Houston to Austin, the state capital. The party hired a full-time executive director, Jim Leonard, who promoted the party through the state's political press. The party also took on grassroots party-building activities, candidate recruitment, public relations, and fund-raising activities. When Peter O'Donnell, the former Dallas County chair, was elected state chair, the party's organizational efforts expanded greatly. Known for his organizational skills, O'Donnell increased the state party's full-time staff (including an extensive field staff), developed new programs for fundraising and after 1964, devoted additional resources to public relations and advertising. By 1970, as a result of O'Donnell's efforts, the Republican Party was prepared to be competitive with the Democratic Party on a statewide basis.[17]

Though more cohesive ideologically than the Democratic Party, the Republican Party in Texas also has its intraparty conflicts. Republican Party leaders are overwhelmingly conservative (86 percent), with few moderates (12 percent) and even fewer liberals (3 percent).[18] In the Republican Party, the conflicts typically are over which of the party's three functions should be stressed—electing, representing, or governing—and policy emphasis. One group within the Republican Party, the pragmatists or economic conservatives, emphasizes the party's role in elections and governing and economic policies. More libertarian in political ideology, the pragmatists seek to expand the party's membership, reaching out to people who have not traditionally been members of the Republican coalition, and to pursue policies that advance the economic well being of its members. The other group, the ideologues or social conservatives, emphasizes the party's representation function, stressing the party's conservative political ideology over winning elections and controlling the government, and social conservatism. The ideologues are more interested in promoting conservative social policies, especially antiabortion, than electing Republican candidates to office.

The clash between the factions has been evident in every Republican state convention since 1994, when a coalition of religious conservatives and antiabortion activists dominated the party's state convention and elected its candidate, Tom Pauken, for state party chair, defeating U.S. Representative Joe Barton, who was endorsed by U.S. Senators Phil Gramm and Kay Bailey Hutchison and retiring state chair Fred Meyer. The Christian Coalition, a group that favors what it identifies as traditional social values, extended its control by electing the party vice chair, Susan Weddington, and a majority of the state executive committee.[19] In 1996, the issue that divided the convention was abortion. Although former governor William Clements urged the delegates to focus on the issues that united Republicans in the past, the social conservatives, who made up more than 80 percent of the delegates, attempted to exclude Senator Hutchison from the party's national convention delegation because her pro-life credentials were not staunch enough for them.[20] In 1997, when Susan Weddington was elected state chair, replacing Pauken, who resigned to seek the Republican nomination for attorney general, she pledged to unify the party's factions. She reached out to the party's moderates and economic conservatives, many of whom supported abortion rights. However, the election of David Barton, a social conservative like Weddington, as state vice chair raised concerns among some moderate Republicans. Nevertheless, Weddington declared a new leadership and focus for the state party.[21] In 1998, social conservatives proposed and adopted a provision that denied party funding and support to any candidates who refused to endorse a ban on the late-term abortion procedure, which social conservatives term *partial-birth abortion*. The social conservatives, who had lost every candidate for statewide office in the Republican Party primary election earlier in the year, defied the pleas of Governor Bush and other statewide elected officials not to restrict the party's growth in this manner.[22] The 1998 Republican Party platform reflects the extent of their control (see the box titled, "The 1998 Democratic and Republican Platforms").[23]

BOX *The 1998 Democratic and Republican Platforms*

Every two years, the Republican and Democratic Parties in Texas adopt their party platforms. The platform provides a statement of party principles or beliefs and provides information about the party's position on issues of public policy. In 1998, there were substantial differences between the parties' platforms on many issues.

Education

The Republican Party supports choice in education through the use of education vouchers, the transfer of education regulatory policy from the Texas Education Agency (TEA) to the State Board of Education (SBOE), regulation of the content of textbooks by the SBOE, character education curriculum and programs, termination of social promotion, the replacement of bilingual education with the immersion method, education in creation science in public schools, recitation of the Pledge of Allegiance and the Texas pledge, the Religious Freedom Amendment to the U.S. Constitution.

The Democratic Party supports smaller classes, increasing teacher pay, improved educational facilities, additional counselors, equal funding for public schools, diversity in teachers, and bilingual education. The party opposes the Hopwood decision and private school vouchers.

Criminal Justice

The Republican Party supports compensation for crime victims by criminals, prison reforms to ensure the goals of public safety, punishment, and "lastly rehabilitation"; determinant sentencing; capital punishment; only two appeals in capital cases; and vigorous enforcement of DUI laws.

The Democratic Party supports the punishment of criminals and the preservation of victims' rights; compensation to crime victims; more police officers; expansion of the prison system; stronger enforcement of DWI laws; punishment for hate crimes; juries that reflect the ethnic composition of the community; and improved pay and benefits for police officers.

continued

Party Effectiveness: What's at Stake?   Assessing party organizational effectiveness requires us to examine different factors, depending on the level of party organization being assessed. Consequently, we consider each level of party organization—state, county, and precinct—in turn.

At the state level, party effectiveness is related to the complexity of the party's organization and the capacity of the party's organization to perform its party-building functions. Indicators of organizational complexity include an accessible party headquarters, a complex division of labor, a substantial party budget, and professional leadership. In Texas, both parties maintain fairly complex organizations. A state party's ability to perform its party-building duties is calculated in

BOX *The 1998 Democratic and Republican Platforms—Continued*

Families

The Republican Party supports maintaining the traditional definition of marriage as a commitment only between a man and a woman, ending "partial-birth" abortions, reversing the Supreme Court's decision in Roe v. Wade, and adopting laws restricting and regulating abortions. The party opposes maintaining current no-fault divorce laws, granting benefits to domestic partners, granting rights to homosexuals, decriminalizing sodomy, cloning humans, and harvesting fetal tissue.

The Democratic Party supports strengthening social security, maintaining a woman's freedom to make personal choices in reproductive choices, providing secure and affordable housing, ensuring that medical choices are made by doctors and patients, protecting Medicare and Medicaid, expanding opportunities for people with disabilities, and ensuring education and services for people with HIV.

Civil Liberties/Civil Rights

The Republican Party supports English as the official language of Texas and the United States, criminal penalties for flag desecration, the right to keep and bear arms, the free exercise of religion, and private efforts to develop minority businesses. The party opposes race and gender-based preferences in education, hiring, employment, and contracting; multi-cultural courses in public schools and state-supported colleges; and sensitivity training courses.

The Democratic Party supports diversity in the workplace, the right to privacy, religious freedom and respect for the separation of church and state, and immigration policies that promote economic opportunities for all individuals and businesses. The party opposes discrimination based on race, gender, sexual orientation, ethnic or national origin, disability, socioeconomic status, color, creed or age; the imposition of religious beliefs on individuals; and limitations on the use of languages other than English.

Source: 1998 Democratic and Republican Party platforms.

two areas: (1) institutional support activities (fund-raising, electoral mobilization programs, public opinion polling, issue leadership, and publication of a newsletter) and (2) candidate-centered activities (contributions to candidates, recruitment of candidates, selection of convention delegates, and preprimary endorsements).

A national survey of state chairpersons in the mid-1980s revealed a Republican advantage in party resources and services to candidates.[24] A comparison of the contemporary Democratic and Republican parties in Texas reveals that an advantage in both measures of party-building is enjoyed by the Republican Party (Table 4.1).

At the county and precinct levels, the party organization's primary task is campaigning for the party's candidates and getting voters to the polls. County

Table 4.1 DEMOCRATIC AND REPUBLICAN STATE PARTY STRENGTH (1998)

Characteristic	Republican	Democratic
Organizational Complexity		
Party headquarters		
Location	Austin	Austin
Size	5,700 square feet	3,400 square feet
Division of labor		
complexity	Complex	Complex
number of full-time staff	34	8–12
Party budget (base operations)	$1,500,000+*	$660,000
Leadership		
Political (nonsalaried)	State chairperson	State chairperson
Professional (salaried)	Executive director	Executive director
Party-Building Ability		
Institutional support activities		
Fundraising	Yes	Yes
Electoral mobilization	Yes	Yes
Public opinion polling	Yes	Yes
Issue leadership	Yes	Yes
Newsletter	Biweekly	Yes
Web site	Yes	Yes
Candidate-centered activities		
Contributions	Yes	Yes
Recruitment	Yes	Yes
Preprimary endorsement	No	No

*The Republican Party of Texas does not make this information public. The figure is an estimate based on number of full-time staff and party activities.

Source: State Democratic and Republican Parties, Austin, Texas, November 1999.

and precinct chairpersons are most influential in determining the party's effectiveness at this level.[25] A national study of campaign activities, conducted in the mid-1980s, indicated that Democratic and Republican county chairpersons were involved in similar activities and at comparable levels of involvement.[26] A 1989 *Texas Poll Report*, however, indicated that Republicans were more likely than Democrats to have been contacted by the party to contribute money to a candidate (40 percent vs. 27 percent), to write to a local politician (32 percent vs. 25 percent), to work for the party (25 percent vs. 17 percent), and to vote in an election (60 percent vs. 55 percent).[27] These differences are evidence of the greater efforts by Republican Party activists to involve their members in party and political activities.

There is also a substantial difference between Republican chairpersons and Democratic chairpersons in their perceptions of changes in their parties' organizational strength and effectiveness. A large percentage of Republican county and precinct chairpersons (more than two-thirds on most measures) viewed their organizations as more effective in 1991 than they had been in 1981 or 1986. On the other hand, few Democratic chairpersons (about one-third or fewer on most measures) viewed their organizations as stronger during the same period.[28]

A study of Harris County (Houston) precinct chairpersons revealed interesting differences between the parties' chairpersons. The Republican precinct chairpersons were more committed to and active in the political campaign than were their Democratic counterparts, had nearly twice as many campaign workers per precinct, and assessed the organization's efforts more favorably than the Democratic chairpersons.[29]

How does the examination of the parties' functional organizations help us understand party politics in Texas? The lack of unity in both parties detracts from their effectiveness as organizations and from their ability to represent a majority of Texans. To become the majority party in Texas, Republicans must effectively deal with the differences between the ideologues and the pragmatists by becoming less interested in ideological purity and more interested in representing and governing. Although a majority of Texans consider themselves conservative politically, they are not as conservative as the Republican ideologues, and many Texans are probably less conservative than they think they are (see Chapter 6). The challenge for Democrats is to ensure that as conservative Democrats are drawn to the Republican Party, the Democratic Party does not become too liberal to represent a majority of Texans on most issues.

Critical Thinking Exercise: Given the challenges that each party faces and the factions within each party, what strategy would you employ to make the Democratic Party or the Republican Party a more effective organization? At what organizational level would you concentrate your efforts? Why?

PARTY IN THE ELECTORATE

The most important function for the party organization is winning elections, which means mobilizing interest in the party's goals and candidates among the voters—the electorate. The **party in the electorate** consists of those people who identify with a political party and consider themselves members (see Figure 4.1). In Texas, as in nearly half of the other states, voters do not register by political party. In the other half of the states, voters register as members of a political party or as independents.

Because Texans don't register by political party, the party identifications of Texans are revealed by polling the public.[30] Party identification is a psychological attachment formed early in life and is usually quite stable. Like an affiliation with a religious denomination, party affiliation has been viewed as almost an inherited attachment that influences a person's view of politics and politicians, rather than a rational attachment based on an agreement between a person's attitudes on important political issues and a party's views on the same issues.[31] For example, a Texan whose parents were Democrats will probably become a Democrat, regardless of his or her political views. More recently, this traditional conception of partisanship has been challenged by political scientists who view party identification as both more rational and more malleable.[32] Thus, a Texan whose parents are Democrats can become a Republican or Democrat, depending on which party's policy positions are closer to his or her own attitudes. Regardless of which view is correct, partisan attachments among the electorate are considered important in determining a party's chances for electoral victory and, consequently, its ability to control government.

Distribution of Party Attachments

Until the early 1950s, there were no surveys of party affiliations for Texans. Therefore, for the earlier period, we are forced to rely on voting in gubernatorial elections to estimate the distribution of partisans in Texans. Vote choice provides a poor estimate of party affiliations because party affiliation is not the only basis for the vote choice (see Chapter 7). From the 1920s to the 1940s, the Republican vote for governor rarely exceeded 20 percent of the vote and usually hovered around 10 percent. In 1952, when survey research began measuring party identification, only 6 percent of Texans identified themselves as Republicans, and 66 percent identified themselves as Democrats. Since 1952, however, the percentage of Democrats has steadily declined, and the percentage of Republicans has steadily increased. During the 1990s, the percentage of Republicans and Democrats were nearly identical. In a *Texas Poll* survey conducted in late 1999, there were more Republicans than Democrats in Texas. The Republican rise and Democratic decline is depicted in Figure 4.3.

The recent changes in party affiliation among Texans involve more than just a decrease in Democrats and an increase in Republicans. The percentage of independents—individuals who identify with neither major political party—has also increased in Texas. In fact, independents and people who identified with a party other than the two major parties constituted the most numerous category in 1999, as they have since 1986. Thus, whereas 72 percent of the population in Texas identified with one of the major political parties in 1952, only 57 percent did in 1999. Consequently, people with attachments to the Democratic or the Republican Party constitute a considerably smaller percentage of the electorate now than in 1952, and the percentage has been decreasing for the past four decades. This is not a good sign for supporters of strong political parties or for the view that strong parties are essential to democracy.

Party Coalitions: Social and Geographic Distribution

Political parties can also be viewed as coalitions, composed of members of social categories and groups that form the party in the electorate. Thus, each party is supported by certain groups or social categories who, because of historical cir-

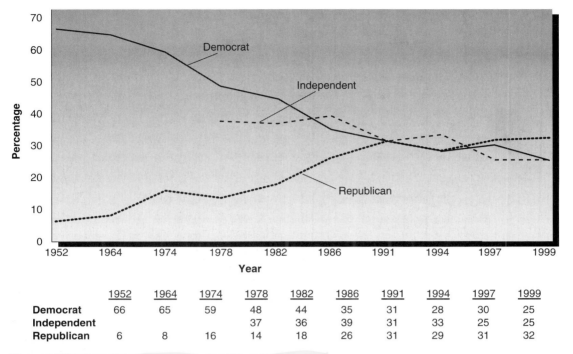

	1952	1964	1974	1978	1982	1986	1991	1994	1997	1999
Democrat	66	65	59	48	44	35	31	28	30	25
Independent				37	36	39	31	33	25	25
Republican	6	8	16	14	18	26	31	29	31	32

Figure 4.3 Party Identification among Texans, 1952–1999

Party identification in Texas has changed dramatically since 1952. The percentage of Texans identifying with the Democratic Party has declined, and the percentage of Texans identifying with the Republican Party has increased. Also, a large percentage of Texans identify with neither the Democratic Party nor the Republican Party.

Source: Texas Polls, various years.

cumstances and the party's position on issues important to those groups, develop an identification with the party. In describing the parties' coalitions, we indicate which groups or categories have belonged to the Democratic and Republican parties' coalitions and how those coalitions have changed.

For more than half of the twentieth century, the Democratic coalition incorporated two ideological factions, identified earlier as liberals and conservatives, formed during the New Deal. Throughout much of this period, candidates representing both factions competed in Democratic primary elections.

Liberal Democrats Support for liberal Democrats in contested primaries was concentrated in certain geographic areas and came from counties with certain characteristics. During the 1940s and 1950s, the liberal Democratic vote was concentrated east of a line from Ft. Worth through San Antonio to Laredo. Between 1944 and 1956, liberal candidates tended to do well in eastern and north central Texas but did less well in southwestern Texas. Much of this area was also the area of populist strength earlier, indicating again the sometimes-alliance of liberals and populists. However, between 1956 and 1972, liberals did less well in eastern and north central Texas but better in southwestern Texas. Also, antiliberal tendencies in the Texas Panhandle became more pronounced during the 1956–1972 period.[33] The counties that were most likely to support liberal Democrats were heavily populated, urbanized, and growing rapidly in population. They were also likely to contain poorer and less educated voters. Not surprisingly, given the liberal Democrats' relationship with organized labor, liberal Democratic counties were more likely to contain more factory workers and fewer independent farmers than conservative Democratic counties.

From the middle 1960s to the early 1990s, the liberal Democratic coalition has been heavily dependent on ethnic minorities. Mexican-American and African-American voters typically cast between 75 and 90 percent of their votes for liberal Democratic candidates.

Conservative Democrats   During the early years of factional intraparty Democratic conflict, the conservatives were dominant. Geographically, the conservative Democrats' voting support came from west of the line connecting Ft. Worth, San Antonio, and Laredo. The strongest support was generated in small, rural counties where most people were engaged in farming, ranching, and trade. Typically, conservative Democratic counties contained people who supported what may be called traditional social values, were almost entirely Anglo, and were suspicious of change. Perhaps they are best characterized as individualists who resented liberal schemes of economic intervention and redistribution of wealth, such as increased environmental regulations and more spending on social programs.

In urban areas, conservative Democrats tended to be upper income and well educated. Conservative Democratic counties were smaller than their liberal counterparts, experienced a slower rate of population growth, and had fewer Mexican Americans and African Americans. In economic terms, conservative Democratic counties were involved in wholesale and retail trade, personal services, and agriculture.

Republicans   During the period that the Democratic Party was split into two ideological factions, the Republican Party was attempting to build its support among the electorate. The geographic and demographic bases of Republican support are more distinctive and easier to describe than the more diffuse Democratic support. The Republican Party started with two traditional areas of support—the Texas Panhandle and the German Hill Country—and has expanded into areas of ideological and socioeconomic affinity for Republican values and ideas.

Economically and topographically, the Texas Panhandle is more characteristic of the Midwest than of either the South or the West. The ethnic composition of the population (primarily Protestant Anglo) in the Panhandle and the close cultural and social ties that its residents maintain with the neighboring states of Kansas and Oklahoma, from which many of its residents originally migrated, have produced a strong, conservative, midwestern Republicanism in the area.

The German Hill Country, which includes several counties north and northwest of San Antonio, was settled by German immigrants before the Civil War. Because of the economy of the area—mostly farming and ranching—and the native German ideology, the German immigrants took a Unionist position on the issue of slavery. These sentiments led them to oppose Texas's secession during the Civil War and to cast their lot with Republicans. Their descendants have continued the tradition of Republicanism.

Obviously, the Republican Party could not hope to govern Texas just with the support of these sparsely populated areas. Consequently, the Republican Party has sought supporters in Texas's expanding metropolitan suburban areas. The Republicans' party-building activities of the 1960s and 1970s were explicitly concentrated in these areas. Republican support has been developed in the Permian Basin counties of Midland and Ector counties, which include the cities of Midland and Odessa; the East Texas counties of Gregg, Rusk, and Smith, which include the cities of Tyler and Longview; and the Brazos River Valley counties of Brazos, Washington, and Austin, which include the cities of Bryan, College Station, and Brenham. Despite these efforts, Republican support was garnered primarily from the Houston metropolitan area, which includes Harris, Montgomery, and Ft. Bend counties, and from the Dallas-Ft. Worth metroplex, which includes Dallas, Tarrant, Rockwall, Denton, Collin, and Cooke counties. During the 1980s, these nine counties provided between 38 and 41 percent of the Republican gubernatorial candidate's total vote.

The demographic profile of Republican Party supporters and the counties in which they reside indicate that Republicans, to no one's surprise, tend to be highly educated and employed in high-income occupations. Republicans also tend to be younger than Democratic supporters, and many have moved to Texas from other states. The counties in which Republican supporters reside are more densely populated, faster growing, and more urbanized than Democratic counties. There are also fewer ethnic minorities in Republican counties. Generally, Republican counties are centers of manufacturing, mineral production, wholesale trade, or personal services.

The Contemporary Party Coalitions   During the 1990s, as more Texans identified with the Republican Party and fewer Texans identified with the Democratic Party, the coalitions changed. Republican and Democratic identifiers in Texas have become more like their national counterparts. Increasingly, people in the upper income categories identify with the Republican Party; people in the lower income categories identify with the Democratic Party. Also, the Democratic Party is the party of liberals and populists, African Americans and Hispanics, and women; the Republican Party is the party of conservatives and libertarians, Anglos, males, and the Christian Right. We discuss why the parties' coalitions have changed later in this chapter in the section on parties and political change.

If a political party mobilizes the electorate and wins elections, then it must govern. Governing effectively requires the third component of the party (see Figure 4.1)—the party in government.

Critical Thinking Exercise: Consider the distribution of partisan attachments displayed in Figure 4.3. Both parties have approximately the same share of the population. How would you appeal to the independents to make them identify with either the Republican or Democratic Party? What issues would you stress? Why?

THE PARTY IN GOVERNMENT

The **party in government** consists of the people who are elected or appointed to public office under a particular party label. The party in government is a political party's mechanism for establishing cooperation among the separate branches of government (executive, legislative, and judicial) in Texas. In theory, all public officials who are appointed or elected under the same party label work together to establish and implement public policies that represent the party's positions on issues. How strong is the party in government in Texas, and how well does it perform this unifying function?

In the Executive Branch

For members of the executive branch in Texas, the Texas Constitution establishes several impediments to cooperation. Foremost is the independent election of the most important executive officers in Texas. Even the governor and lieutenant governor do not run as a team on the ballot (see Chapter 9). Consequently, the relationship between the governor and lieutenant governor, even when they are members of the same party, may be strained. Also, because the Texas Attorney General's office has often been used as a stepping stone by politicians who aspire to be governor, the relationship between those two officials may not be the most cordial, even when they are members of the same political party. Other statewide elected officials in the executive branch may also harbor such ambitions. For example, shortly after Mark White was elected governor in 1982, Bob Bullock, a member of White's party and Comptroller of Public Accounts, announced his intention to seek the party's gubernatorial nomination in 1986.[34]

Because the executive officers are elected independently, candidates of the same political party have little incentive to campaign together or even to coordinate their campaigns for public office. Typically, each office seeker establishes his or her own campaign organization. This practice further reduces the likelihood of cooperation after the election. In 1982, faced for the first time with Republican opposition in all major executive races, the Democratic candidates showed a greater degree of cooperation than normal and even coordinated portions of their campaigns. However, efforts to continue the cooperation after the election were unsuccessful, as each official became involved in his or her own department or agency. Four years later, in 1986, most executive officials faced only token opposition, which provided little incentive for a repeat of the cooperation of 1982.

Consequently, each candidate for executive office staged his or her own campaign, and the difference between Governor Mark White's vote total and those of other Democrats seeking statewide executive offices was greater than in 1982. In 1990 and 1994, despite strong opposition in many executive contests, the Democrats again failed to coordinate their campaigns. In 1998, John Sharp and Paul Hobby, Democratic candidates for lieutenant governor and comptroller respectively, failed to endorse the Democratic gubernatorial nominee, Garry Mauro. In fact, Sharp ran television advertisements which pictured him with Republican Governor Bush, while the narrator stated that Sharp had worked well with Bush when he was comptroller, implying that the relationship would continue if Sharp were elected lieutenant governor. Republican candidates for statewide executive offices have usually demonstrated a similar tendency to run independent campaigns.

In the Legislative Branch

In the Texas legislature, as we show in Chapter 8, partisan considerations are usually minimized. Until recently, Texas was one of only five states that did not hold inclusive party caucuses, elect party leaders, or create party committees. Party caucuses and committees are formed to provide information to party members on policy issues and to formulate the party's position on issues. Party leaders are selected to provide leadership for a party's caucus and committees. In 1981, Jerry Benedict (D-Angleton) chaired a meeting attended by 30 of the 114 Democratic members of the Texas House of Representatives to form a Democratic caucus. In the 1983 session, the caucus increased to include 94 of the 114 Democrats in the House. By 1987, the caucus included all Democrats, including the speaker and all Democrats on his team, a practice that has continued in subsequent sessions. By 1989, the speaker's team and the caucus began to work together, reducing the tension that had characterized the earlier years.[35] Since 1993, when Pete Laney became speaker, the Democratic caucus has not been very active. However, Senate Democrats, faced with a Republican governor and lieutenant governor, decided to give the Senate Democratic Caucus a more prominent role in 1999. The caucus chair, Gonzalo Barrientos, called frequent meetings, discussed policy and strategy, and held press conferences to publicize the Democrats' positions on issues before the legislature.

Prior to 1989, the Republicans avoided party organization in the House, preferring to work with the speaker and conservative Democrats through the Texas Conservative Coalition. However, in 1989, the Republicans organized a caucus, "formed a policy committee to screen suggested legislation before it went to the full caucus for endorsement, and maintained a political arm called the Republican Campaign Legislative Committee."[36] Also, Governor Bill Clements, who had opposed a Republican organization in the House in 1979, now endorsed it during his second term (1987–1991), indicating the independence from the speaker and conservative Democrats, which Republicans felt as their number passed the one-third threshold. Breaking the one-third threshold allowed the Republicans to prevent

Legislative party caucuses are becoming more active. The Senate Democratic Caucus holds a news conference during the 1999 legislative session to propose an agenda of health, social service, and education legislation.

an override of a governor's veto, prevent a constitutional amendment from passing, keep a law from becoming effective immediately, and prevent a suspension of the rules (see Chapter 8). More important, it allowed the Republicans to create a working majority if they could maintain party unity and attract the votes of only one-fourth of the Democrats. During recent legislatures, the House Republican caucus has met, but it does not have much influence in the House.

Despite the predictions to the contrary, the Texas legislature continues to operate with strong institutional leaders, eschewing the opportunity to build strong party organizations.[37]

In the Judicial Branch

In Texas, all judges, except municipal court judges, are elected on a partisan ballot. Consequently, a reluctance to politicize the judiciary, which is evident in some states, is less pronounced in Texas. However, candidates for legislative and executive positions rarely team with members of their party seeking judgeships in a coordinated campaign. Thus, the elections are usually conducted independently.

The influence of party is often dominant in the appointment of judges when a vacancy occurs either through a judge's death, resignation, retirement, or removal. Because a large percentage of judges are initially appointed to their positions by the governor, he or she has many opportunities to reward party members with judicial appointments. A comparison of judicial appointments by Governor

Clements during his last term (1987–1991) and Governor Richards during her term (1991–1995) indicates that each appointed an overwhelming majority of judges who shared the governor's party affiliation.[38] Furthermore, when Republican Governor George W. Bush has been given the opportunity to fill vacancies on the Texas Supreme Court, he has chosen Republican judges. Apparently, governors consider judicial appointments as an opportunity to reward loyal party members.

Appointments of judges by governors could also be viewed as an attempt to fill the courts with judges who share the governor's political ideology. This assumes that judges, in interpreting the law, can exercise some discretion and that Republican judges and Democratic judges differ in how they interpret the law and decide cases. Evidence in certain kinds of cases indicates that this assumption is correct. Democratic judges are more likely to side with defendants in criminal cases, which involve offenses against society, such as murder and rape; Republican judges are more likely to support the government's position in criminal cases. Unlike criminal cases, civil suits involve disputes between individuals, such as a breach of contract or sexual harassment. In civil suits, Democratic judges are more likely to take the plaintiff's side. Republican judges, on the other hand, are more likely to support the defendant when businesses are being sued. For example, during the 1995 term, the Texas Supreme Court, on which Republicans held a majority, decided for the plaintiff in just 16 percent of its cases. In 1985, when Democrats controlled the Supreme Court, plaintiffs won 69 percent of the cases, and defendants won only 28 percent.[39] Recently, the Supreme Court has moderated its decisions. During the 1998–1999 term, defendants won 60 percent of the decisions in cases involving consumers, patients, and crime victims as plaintiffs against corporate, professional, or governmental defendants, far less frequently than the 70 percent averaged in the previous two years. There has also been a realignment of voting alliances among the justices. A contingent of four Republican justices originally appointed by Governor George W. Bush is apparently attempting to eliminate the excesses of the Republican justices elected between 1988 and 1994.[40]

> **Critical Thinking Exercise:** The party in government is weak in Texas. Would a strong party in government be an advantage or disadvantage? What changes would a strong party in government make? Why?

PARTIES AND POLITICAL CHANGE

Because of the functions performed by political parties (electing, representing, and organizing), political parties can play a central role in political change. Occasionally, a rapid change in party affiliations among the electorate translates into votes for a particular political party, which changes control of the branches of government and the public policies they enact. Periods of rapid and comprehensive political change, or periods of creedal passion in politics, are one example of political parties effecting political change.

The best-known theory linking parties with political change was first advanced more than four decades ago by Texas native V. O. Key, Jr. A **critical election** is an election "in which voters are . . . deeply concerned, in which the extent of electoral involvement is . . . quite high, and in which the decisive results of the voting reveal a sharp alteration of the . . . [partisan attachments] . . . within the electorate. Moreover, . . . the [partisan] realignment made manifest in the voting in such elections seems to persist for several succeeding elections."[41] According to most political scientists, the last **realignment** occurred in 1932, when the Democratic Party replaced the Republican Party as the majority party in the United States.

According to some political scientists, Texas has been experiencing an attenuated realignment for some time. To substantiate their claim, they offer the following evidence:

- Young voters are more likely to identify with the Republican Party than the Democratic Party. Among party identifiers, young people (age 18–39) are much more likely to identify with the Republican Party than older people (age 60–94). Consequently, generational replacement favors the Republicans.
- Some Democrats are switching to the Republican Party. These conversions are most likely among conservative, upper-socioeconomic status Democrats who are bringing their party identification into line with their political ideology and socioeconomic status.
- New residents of Texas are more likely to identify with the Republican Party than are native Texans or long-term residents. During the last three decades, when Texas experienced an influx of immigrants, most of the new residents brought identification with the Republican Party, which they kept.
- Party identification, especially among Republicans, is important in determining vote choices in elections. Between 80 and 90 percent of Republicans voted for Republican candidates in recent elections. Also, in the two largest counties of Texas, a majority of voters cast straight-ticket ballots, voting only for candidates of one party.
- Republican candidates win more counties (especially the most populous counties) than Democrats in presidential, gubernatorial, and other statewide elections. Indeed, a map illustrating voting trends in the 1970s (Figure 4.4) is dramatically different from a map showing voting trends in the 1990s (Figure 4.5).[42]

Another possible interpretation of the surveys on party identification in Texas would be that Texans are not realigning, they are dealigning. In a **dealignment,** party affiliations weaken, and the importance of party affiliation to the population's political attitudes and behavior also weakens. The dealignment interpretation concludes that although there are more Republican identifiers and fewer Democratic identifiers, the most important fact is the growth in independents— people who do not identify with either political party—and others—people who identify with a party other than the two major parties. As we noted earlier, there are currently more independents (and people who identify with other political parties or aren't sure about their partisan preference) than people who identify

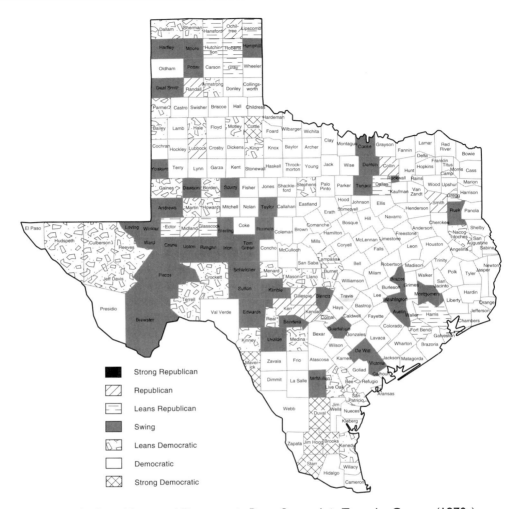

Figure 4.4   Republican and Democratic Party Strength in Texas by County (1970s)
The map reflects the strength of the Texas Republican and Democratic Parties based on votes for Republican and Democratic candidates in selected general election contests during the 1970s.

Source: Based on county election results in the following general elections: 1972 presidential, 1974 gubernatorial, 1976 presidential, 1978 gubernatorial, 1978 lieutenant governor, and 1978 attorney general. Mike Kingston, Sam Attlesey, and Mary G. Crawford, *The Texas Almanac's Political History of Texas* (Austin: Eakin Press, 1992); *1980–1981 Texas Almanac* (Dallas: A.H. Belo Corporation, 1979).

with either of the two major political parties (Table 4.2). According to this interpretation, Texas is not becoming a Republican state; it is becoming a no-party state. The increase in independents is cited as evidence that party identification is less important and that elections are not about parties but about candidates (see Chapter 7).

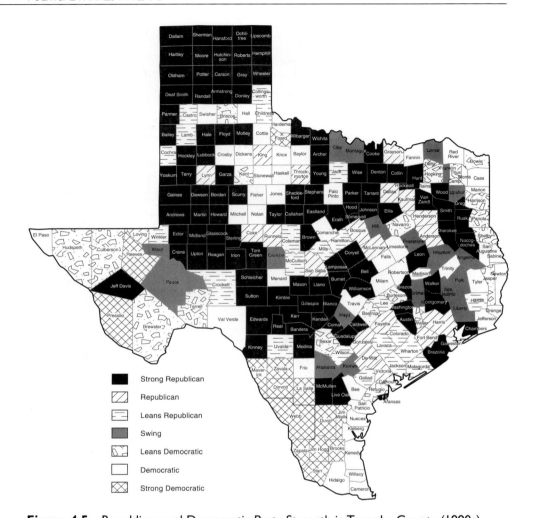

Figure 4.5   **Republican and Democratic Party Strength in Texas by County (1990s)**
The map reflects the strength of the Texas Republican and Democratic Parties based on votes for Republican and Democratic candidates in selected general election contests during the 1990s.

Source: Based on county election results in the following general elections: 1992 presidential, 1994 gubernatorial, 1996 presidential, 1998 gubernatorial, 1998 lieutenant governor, and 1978 comptroller. *1996–1997 Texas Almanac* (Dallas: The Dallas Morning News, Inc., 1995); *1998–1999 Texas Almanac* (Dallas: The Dallas Morning News, Inc., 1997); *2000–2001 Texas Almanac* (Dallas: The Dallas Morning News, L.P., 1999); Texas Secretary of State, Election Returns. Accessed 30 March 1999 http://www.sos.state.tx.us/function/elec1/results/returns.html.

Table 4.2   PARTY IDENTIFICATION IN TEXAS, 1999 (in percent)

	Republican	Democrat	Independent	Other	Don't Know
Total Percentage	32	25	25	9	9
Age					
18–29	27	24	25	13	11
30–39	40	18	22	9	11
40–49	39	24	23	9	5
50–59	27	25	32	9	7
60–94	29	31	25	9	6
Education					
Some high school	21	29	33	6	11
High school graduate	29	29	23	12	7
Some college	37	25	25	9	4
College graduate	38	19	30	9	4
Graduate work	43	27	21	6	3
Gender					
Male	32	24	27	10	7
Female	32	26	23	8	11
Income					
Less than $10,000	12	30	26	15	17
$10,001–$20,000	19	28	22	9	22
$20,001–$30,000	27	28	25	16	4
$30,001–$40,000	29	28	30	6	7
$40,001–$50,000	35	28	27	10	0
$50,001–$60,000	45	18	26	8	3
$60,001 and above	49	19	24	7	1
Race/Ethnicity					
Anglo	38	22	27	9	4
Hispanic	18	26	18	10	28
African American	7	52	23	12	6
Years in Texas					
10 or fewer years	29	22	22	9	18
11–20 years	34	19	27	9	11
More than 20 years	34	29	25	8	4

Methodology: The Fall 1999 Texas Poll was conducted October 13, 1999 to November 1, 1999 by The Scripps Howard Data Center. One thousand adult Texans were surveyed by telephone in a systematically random sample of active telephone exchanges statewide. Margin of error for the whole sample is ±3 percentage points; the error for subgroups is slightly larger. Responses are in percentages, rounded to the nearest whole number.

> **Critical Thinking Exercise:**   Study Table 4.2 to determine who iden-
> tifies with each major party in Texas. Then, consider the arguments that
> Texas has experienced a realignment. Has a realignment occurred? Are the
> policies favored by Republicans different from policies favored by conserva-
> tive Democrats? How?

PARTIES AND DEMOCRACY

The relationship between political parties and democracy can be analyzed on two
levels. On one level, political parties can promote either majoritarian or pluralist
democracy within the political system. Strong, centralized political parties promote majoritarian democracy. On the other hand, weak, decentralized parties are
associated with pluralist democracy. At another level, the parties can, in their internal operation, display or lack the conditions of democracy. It is possible for political parties to establish political equality among their members, provide participation opportunities for their members, ensure nontyranny for their members,
and promote deliberation among their members. We assess the internal operation
of the political parties in Texas first.

The conditions of democracy are evident in the internal operations of both political parties in Texas. The formal rules for party decisions meet the condition of
political equality. The parties' structures are open to any registered voters, and individuals who choose to participate are granted an equal voice in decisions made
by the parties' temporary and permanent organizations. The parties also meet the
condition of nontyranny by protecting minorities from discrimination. Finally, the
parties' temporary organizations promote deliberation in their conventions and
operations. Although the parties have failed to meet the conditions of democracy
in the recent past, they now can be considered democratic organizations.

In the political system, political parties can promote either majoritarian or
pluralist democracy. According to majoritarian democratic theory, the political
party is the institution that makes majoritarian democracy possible, in a political
system that features a separation of powers and a system of checks and balances.
Strong and cohesive parties are necessary for majoritarian democracy. Strong parties are hierarchically structured, produce a coherent party platform, control the
nomination of their candidates for public office, require their candidates for public office to support the party's platform positions, mobilize their rank-and-file
members to elect the party's candidates in the general election, and organize the
government to convert the party's platform promises into government policies. In
Texas, the political parties do not meet these requirements.

Political parties in Texas are more conducive to pluralist democracy. As coalitions of interests, the Democratic and Republican Parties in Texas compete with
other groups in Texas to influence public policy. Both parties represent a fairly narrow social, economic, and ideological spectrum in their membership, especially in
the Republican Party. Although both parties provide ample opportunities for participation and political involvement for their members, they ask little of their

members and demand nothing in return for those opportunities. In almost every respect, political parties in Texas act more like interest groups than like political parties, influencing the operation of the government, rather than controlling it.

> **Critical Thinking Exercises:** Many political scientists believe that democracy is impossible without political parties structuring the conflict and providing choices for people. Are political parties essential to democracy or could democracy exist without parties? Why?

SUMMARY

In this chapter, we have described the political parties in Texas as a social structure with three parts: (1) the party organization, (2) the party in the electorate, and (3) the party in government. In terms of their functions for the political system, we have described the political parties as electing party members to public office, representing the members of the party's coalition, and organizing the party's members and the government so that the party's preferences become public policy. We indicated that party organizations in Texas include a formal organization, consisting of a temporary and a permanent organization, and a functional organization, which describes how the parties really operate. In describing the Democratic Party, we emphasized the ideological split between liberals and conservatives and the battle for control of the party organization. In the Republican Party, we stressed the evolution of the party from a dispenser of patronage positions to a party that is competitive with the Democratic Party in most elections. We also assessed the strength of the Democratic and Republican Party organizations in Texas.

The party in the electorate was described in terms of its partisan attachments. We indicated how the electorate, since 1952, has become more Republican, less Democratic, and more independent in its party attachments. We also noted the social categories or groups that make up each party's identifiers in Texas and described the geographic distribution of each party's supporters.

Also, we described the party in government, indicating how each branch is organized or coordinated by political parties. Our description of the party in government in Texas provides considerable evidence that this component of the party is very weak.

Finally, we analyzed the political parties' role in political change and promoting democracy. We identified two perspectives on party change. Although some analysts view recent changes in Texas as evidence of a realignment or a dealignment, we believe that neither conclusion is justified. The parties are currently in a state of transition, attempting to adapt to new political realities. Also, the political parties act more like interest groups than like strong political parties in Texas; thus, we maintain that the parties promote pluralist rather than majoritarian democracy.

KEY TERMS

party organization
temporary party organization
precinct convention
county convention or state senatorial
   district convention
state convention
permanent party organization
precinct chairperson
county chairperson

county executive committee
state executive committee
state party chairperson
party in the electorate
party in government
critical election
realignment
dealignment

SUGGESTED READINGS

Davidson, Chandler. *Race and Class in Texas Politics.* Princeton, N.J.: Princeton University Press, 1990.

Dyer, James A., Jan E. Leighley, and Arnold Vedlitz. "Party Identification and Public Opinion in Texas, 1984–1994: Establishing a Competitive Two-Party System." In *Texas Politics: A Reader,* 2d ed. eds. Anthony Champagne and Edward J. Harpham, 108–122. New York: W.W. Norton and Company, 1998.

Green, George Norris. *The Establishment in Texas Politics: The Primitive Years, 1938–1957.* Westport, Conn.: Greenwood Press, 1979.

Hadley, Charles D., and Lewis Bowman, eds. *Southern State Party Organizations and Activists.* Westport, Conn.: Praeger, 1995.

Knaggs, John R. *Two Party Texas: The John Tower Era, 1961–1984.* Austin, Tex.: Eakin Press, 1986.

Martin, Roscoe. *The People's Party in Texas: A Study in Third-Party Politics.* Austin, Tex.: University of Texas Press, 1970.

Murray, Richard, and Sam Attlesey. "Texas: Republicans Gallop Ahead." In *Southern Politics in the 1990s,* ed. Alexander P. Lamis, 305–342. Baton Rouge, La.: Louisiana State University Press, 1999.

Nelson, Albert. *Democrats Under Seige in the Sunbelt Megastates: California, Florida, and Texas.* Westport, Conn.: Praeger, 1996.

NOTES

1. Donna A. Barnes, *Farmers in Rebellion: The Rise and Fall of the Southern Farmers Alliance and People's Party in Texas* (Austin, Tex.: University of Texas Press, 1984), 1–3.
2. Ibid., 6.
3. Lawrence Goodwyn, *The Populist Moment: A Short History of the Agrarian Revolt in America* (New York: Oxford University Press, 1978), 44–54.
4. Roscoe Martin, *The People's Party in Texas: A Study in Third-Party Politics* (Austin, Tex.: University of Texas Press, 1970), 209–229.
5. Samuel J. Eldersveld, *Political Parties in American Society* (New York: Basic Books, 1982), 99.

6. The liberals in Texas, during this conflict over control of the party, were assisted by populists who, according to the typology presented in Chapter 2, share liberalism's perspective on economic equality. Thus, many of the supporters of liberals would abandon their side when the issue became social equality rather than economic equality.

7. V. O. Key, Jr., *Southern Politics* (New York: Random House, 1949), 261–271.

8. Until 1988, the parties in Texas held two state conventions in presidential election years. The first, or presidential, convention selected the party's presidential electors; the second, or governor's, convention performed its state party functions.

9. Chandler Davidson, *Race and Class in Texas Politics* (Princeton, N.J.: Princeton University Press, 1990), 159.

10. Ibid., 159–166.

11. James R. Soukup, Clifton McCleskey, and Harry Holloway, *Party and Factional Division in Texas* (Austin, Tex.: University of Texas Press, 1964), 4–5; Davidson, *Race and Class in Texas Politics*, 180.

12. Davidson, *Race and Class in Texas Politics*, 180–197.

13. Ibid., 155–156.

14. Frank B. Feigert and Nancy L. Williams, "Texas: Yeller Dogs and Yuppies," in *Southern State Party Organizations and Activists*, eds. Charles D. Hadley and Lewis Bowman (Westport, Conn.: Praeger Publishers, 1995), 84–85.

15. Roger M. Olien, *From Token to Triumph: The Texas Republicans Since 1920* (Dallas: SMU Press, 1982), viii.

16. Ibid., 112–169.

17. Andrew M. Appleton and Daniel S. Ward, "Party Organizational Response to Electoral Change: Texas and Arkansas," *The American Review of Politics* 15 (Summer 1994): 191–212.

18. Feigert and Williams, "Texas: Yeller Dogs and Yuppies," 84–85.

19. Paul Lenchner, "The Party System in Texas," in *Texas Politics: A Reader*, 2d ed. eds. Anthony Champagne and Edward J. Harpham, (New York: W. W. Norton & Company, 1998), 165–167.

20. Louis Dubose, "Kay Bailey Finds Religion," *Texas Observer*, 12 July 1996, pp. 4–8.

21. A. Phillips Brooks, "GOP Lieutenant Gets Close Look," *Austin American-Statesman*, 9 August 1997, pp. B1, B7.

22. Nate Blakeslee, "Farewell to Barry G.," *Texas Observer*, 3 July 1998, 13–15; Sam Dealey, "Bush-Whipped: The Texas GOP Undergoes A Little Soul-Searching," *American Spectator*, August 1998, 58–59.

23. Thomas L. Whatley, ed., "A New Look for the Texas GOP," *Texas Government Newsletter*, 20 June 1994, 1.

24. Advisory Commission on Intergovernmental Relations, *The Transformation in American Politics* (Washington, D.C.: ACIR, 1986), 111–116.

25. Barbara Norrander, "Determinants of Local Party Campaign Activity," *Social Sciences Quarterly* 67 (September 1986): 567.

26. John P. Frendreis, James L. Gibson, and Laura Vertz, "The Electoral Relevance of Local Party Organizations," *American Political Science Review* 84 (March 1990): 227–228.

27. *Texas Poll Report* (Fall 1989): 2.

28. Feigert and Williams, "Texas: Yeller Dogs and Yuppies," 84–85.

29. Richard W. Murray and Kent L. Tedin, "The Emergence of Two-Party Competition in the Sunbelt: The Case of Houston," in *Political Parties in Local Areas*, ed. William Crotty (Knoxville, Tenn.: University of Tennessee Press, 1986), 47–51.

30. The Scripps Howard Texas Poll question is "Generally speaking, do you usually think of yourself as a Republican, a Democrat, an Independent or something else?" According to state law in Texas, a party member is anyone who participates in the party's primary election.

31. Angus Campbell, Philip Converse, Warren Miller, and Donald Stokes, *The American Voter* (Chicago: University of Chicago Press, 1960), 121.

32. Morris P. Fiorina, *Retrospective Voting in American National Elections* (New Haven, Conn.: Yale University Press, 1981), 86–89.

33. John R. Todd and Kay Dickerson Ellis, "Analyzing Factional Patterns in State Politics in Texas, 1944–1972," *Social Science Quarterly* 55 (December 1974): 718–731.

34. Thomas L. Whatley, ed., *Texas Government Newsletter,* 24 January 1983, 2.

35. Keith E. Hamm and Robert Harmel, "Legislative Party Development and the Speaker System: The Case of Texas," *The Journal of Politics* 55 (November 1993): 1145–1146.

36. Ibid., 1146.

37. See R. Bruce Anderson, "Party Caucus Development and the Insurgent Minority Party in Formerly One-Party State Legislatures," *The American Review of Politics* 19 (Fall 1998): 191–216.

38. *Texas Lawyer,* May 1994, 1, 28.

39. Paul Allen Beck and Frank J. Sorauf, *Party Politics in America,* 7th ed. (New York: HarperCollins, 1992), 420; Walt Borges, "The Court's Big Chill," *Texas Lawyer,* 4 September 1995, 1.

40. Walt Borges, "The Texas Supreme Court in 1998–1999: Moderating the Counter-Revolution," A Report of Court Watch, A Project of Texas Watch. Nd. Accessed 31 October 1999, http://www.texaswatch.org/cwreview.htm.

41. V. O. Key, Jr., "A Theory of Critical Elections," *Journal of Politics* 17 (February 1955): 4.

42. James A. Dryer, Arnold Vedlitz, and David B. Hill, "New Voters, Switchers, and Political Party Realignment in Texas," *Western Political Quarterly* 41(March 1988): 155–167; Kent L. Tedin, "The Transition of Electoral Politics in Texas: 1978–1990," in *Perspectives on American & Texas Politics: A Collection of Essays,* 3d ed., eds. Kent L. Tedin and Donald S. Lutz (Dubuque, Iowa: Kendall/Hunt Publishing Company, 1992), 129–151; James A. Dyer, Jan E. Leighley, and Arnold Vedlitz, "Party Identification and Public Opinion in Texas, 1984–1994: Establishing a Competitive Two-Party System," in *Texas Politics: A Reader,* 2d ed., eds. Anthony Champagne and Edward J. Harpham (New York: W. W. Norton and Company, 1998), 108–122.

5 *Interest Groups in Texas*

★ Scenario: Battle of the Titans

The challenge was hard to ignore. The lady in the clouds, wearing a denim shirt over a white turtle-neck sweater, khaki slacks and sitting on a stool, asked you to look at your next phone bill and "try and make sense out of the fact that it's more expensive to call within Texas than to call another state." Indignantly, she continued, "That's right. It costs more to call from Marfa to Midland than it does from Marfa to Honolulu." The commercial began airing in 1996, but the battle over telephone service wasn't decided by the Texas Legislature until the 76th Legislature in 1999. The ads provided the impetus for the legislature's action. According to Representative Sylvester Turner of Houston, "In the absence of the ads, it's questionable whether the Legislature would even be inclined to do anything on these issues."

The coalition that sponsored the commercial, Texas Partnership for Competition, included AT&T, Texas Citizen Action, Texas Consumer Association, and several small local and long-distance phone companies. Although the members

127

of the coalition joined for different reasons, the goal of forcing Southwestern Bell (SWB) to lower its long-distance access charges appealed to all. Texas Citizen Action, a consumer group, joined to champion more competition in local phone service. For small and midsized phone companies, the impetus for joining the coalition was ensuring that the Public Utility Commission (PUC) continued its regulation of SWB. The enemy was Southwestern Bell, the local phone company that operates in Texas and other states, is headquartered in San Antonio, provides nearly 98 percent of local residential phone service in Texas, employs about 37,000 people in Texas (including 25,000 members of the Communications Workers of America [CWA] labor union), and contributes generously to local charities and schools, libraries, and nonprofit health-care centers in Texas. For AT&T, the senior partner in the coalition, the larger issue was forcing SWB to open up local service to competition. With the acquisition of TCI Cable, AT&T has visions of being the sole provider of telecommunications services, comprising local phone, long distance, high-speed Internet, and cable TV.

In what could be considered a preemptive strike by Southwestern Bell, the battle began with House Bill 1701, which would have lowered Southwestern Bell's access charge by two cents a minute but would have given SWB complete control over setting the rates for most services, such as call forwarding, caller ID, as well as others. Also, Southwestern Bell would have been able to launch new services simply by giving the Public Utility Commission (PUC) just 24 hours' notice. Although the bill would have frozen the charge for basic residential service at its 1984 level, SWB would have been able to add surcharges and fees at will. Among the legislators, the bill was referred to as "Bell's bill." As one consumer advocate noted, "we call[ed] it the telecommunications wet dream for Southwestern Bell." However, House Bill 1701 got bottled up in committee, awaiting a hearing.

Across the rotunda from the House chamber, Senate Bill 560, the Senate's telecommunications bill suddenly began to move, allegedly at the urging of Lieutenant Governor Rick Perry. Senator David Sibley, the bill's sponsor, called SWB and AT&T to a meeting to negotiate a compromise. After getting an agreement from the two companies, Sibley quickly moved the bill through the legislative labyrinth, securing a unanimous vote on the Senate floor with no amendments. When the bill passed the Senate, it became the vehicle for House action.

After the Senate bill arrived at the House State Affairs Committee, however, a committee substitute bill that more closely resembled House Bill 1701 than the Senate's version replaced it. In fact, the House managers of the bill had to prepare 58 amendments to steer the substitute bill closer to the version that had passed in the Senate. Ultimately, House members sought another compromise involving SWB, AT&T, and other interested parties. The meeting confirmed that there would be no further compromises; Senate Bill 560 would be the telecommunications bill this session.[1]

Senate Bill 560 became the telecommunications law of 1999, revising the regulatory law that was adopted by the Texas Legislature in 1995. Its passage produced different interpretations of the bill's effects from supporters and opponents. According to supporters of Senate Bill 560, the telecommunications bill of 1999 moved Texas closer to competition in local phone service and protected consumers by capping rates on local services, reducing long-distance access rates, and requiring the rate reduction to benefit consumers. Opponents pointed out that the bill deregulated services, such as caller ID, before competition had been established in Texas so that consumers would have a choice among alternative local telephone providers. They also felt that the bill reduced the PUC's authority to prevent anticompetitive behavior and to review adequately any proposed rates.[2]

The activities of Southwestern Bell and of AT&T and its coalition illustrate the varied techniques used by interest groups to influence public policy. The "lady in the clouds" advertising campaign by Texas Partnership for Competition cost approximately $5 million, and SWB spent nearly the same amount countering the advertisement.[3] Both groups contributed heavily to candidates for public office through their respective political action committees (PACs). Both groups employed lobbyists to contact legislators and press their respective viewpoints. Texas Partnership for Competition established a web site, providing citizens with information and an opportunity to join the coalition opposing Southwestern Bell.[4] We revisit Texas Partnership for Competition's and Southwestern Bell's activities frequently in this chapter as we describe and analyze interest-group politics in Texas. ★

INTRODUCTION

Interest groups are organizations composed of people who share a common interest or concern and who attempt to influence public policy. In many ways, Southwestern Bell is typical of the most common type of interest groups in Texas

Te★as*Index*

Interest Groups in the States

Registered lobbyists in 1988
Texas—800
California—700
New York—1590
Florida—4000

Registered lobbyists in 1996
Texas—1200
California—1100
New York—2000
Florida—2000

Texas was ranked with 24 states (including California) where interest groups have considerable influence over public policy in late 1990s. Florida was ranked with 4 states where interest groups are the overwhelming and consistent influence on policy. New York was ranked with 15 states where interest groups are constrained in their influence.

and their political activities. The story of Southwestern Bell's battle with AT&T's coalition also raises several questions about interest groups, which we address in this chapter. For example, what causes people to form interest groups in the first place? What motivates individuals to join groups to achieve collective political goals? What kinds of goals do groups pursue? How can interest groups be classified or grouped? What makes interest groups influential? In what kinds of political activities do interest groups engage?

After answering these questions, we discuss how interest groups are involved in political change and whether interest groups promote or inhibit democracy. Although interest groups can provide an important opportunity for meaningful public participation in politics and government, they are often maligned by the media and viewed skeptically by the public. The media frequently refer to interest groups as "special" interest groups, indicating that the group's interests are distinct from the public's interest. Also, for many people, interest groups and their principal activity—lobbying—raise images of backroom deals, bribery, and corruption. We evaluate these popular images of interest groups later in the chapter.

THE CREATION OF INTEREST GROUPS

There are several theories or explanations regarding the formation of interest groups. We describe two of those theories—disturbance theory and entrepreneurial theory. How interest groups are created provides a clue to the effect of interest groups on democracy. If interest groups form easily in response to social and economic changes, then democracy is more likely.

Disturbance Theory

Probably the best-known theory explains interest-group formation through disturbances in society.[5] According to this explanation, there are two social disturbances that create interest groups. First, changes that affect the division of labor in the society, such as changes in the economy or in technology, are likely to create interest groups. For example, when the price of oil dropped during the 1980s, the Texas economy changed, forcing people to seek employment in new or different endeavors. The growth of new industries—such as the production of microprocessor chips for computers—creates new interests, which seek representation before government, hoping to gain benefits through public policy or to protect their position in the private sector of the economy, free from government regulation. The second disturbance occurs when a disruptive force—a war, a recession, or a newly formed interest group—upsets the existing relationships among groups in society. According to **disturbance theory,** groups are motivated to organize in order to reestablish an equilibrium among groups.

Central to disturbance theory is the concept of potential groups, which are defined as a large number of people who share common attitudes but who have not formally organized for political action. The existence of potential groups provides the basis for the formation of new groups.

The disturbance theory has been criticized for its failure to recognize the role of government itself in the creation of interest groups. Through its laws and rules, the government has promoted the formation of many interest groups and has sustained them once they were formed. For example, Southwestern Bell's independence and increased political clout was the result of a U.S. Justice Department lawsuit against AT&T that resulted in an end to AT&T's monopoly both on long-distance and local phone service and freed the "Baby Bells" to provide regional phone service. More important, however, disturbance theory maintains that groups occur more or less automatically in response to changing social conditions. The theory does not account for the numerous occasions when changes did not result in the creation of groups or when groups were created in the absence of a disturbance. In other words, the importance of individual leadership to the creation of interest groups is ignored.[6]

Entrepreneurial Theory

A second theory of interest-group formation recognizes the central role of leadership in the creation of interest groups. According to **entrepreneurial theory,** interest groups emerge through the efforts of individuals or entrepreneurs, who recognize the need for the groups' existence and provide the leadership necessary to form and sustain the groups. Entrepreneurs may be motivated by several desires—furthering a cause, promoting a career, or mingling with the powerful. Regardless of his or her motivation, the entrepreneur must have the energy, skills, and enthusiasm to recruit members and to provide them with reasons to maintain their membership in the organization.[7] However, this theory poses problems also. Leaders need followers, and without the existence of a number of people who share a perception that their interests need protection, leaders cannot create and sustain groups.

Consequently, neither theory alone adequately explains the rise of interest groups. Perhaps, the combination of social disturbances and the existence of an entrepreneur, plus a healthy dose of serendipity, account for the existence of interest groups. Regardless of the reason for their existence, once formed, groups must expand or at least sustain their membership. What motivates people to join groups?

> **Critical Thinking Exercise:** Consider the creation of Texas Partnership for Competition. Which theory of interest-group formation explains the group's existence? Was it a disturbance or an entrepreneur that created it?

MEMBERS OF GROUPS: JOINING AND STAYING

Interest groups vary greatly in size and resources. Some groups, such as the American Association of Retired Persons (AARP), have millions of members. Others are lucky to have hundreds. What attracts people to groups and sustains their membership?

Benefits of Group Membership

According to one scholar, interest groups attract and sustain their members through incentives. These incentives take various forms, but they can be differentiated by the type of reward or benefit that is offered. **Material benefits** are tangible rewards that result from group membership. Most labor groups, for example, work diligently to increase the pay and working conditions for their members. Joining the group can result in a job and, subsequently, increases in salary and improved working conditions. The Communication Workers of America, an affiliate of the AFL-CIO, strongly supported Southwestern Bell's efforts on behalf of House Bill 1701, feeling that it meant more jobs for its members. **Solidary benefits** refer to social contacts and interactions that result from group membership. The opportunity, for example, to meet others in a profession may motivate membership in an association of teachers or physicians. **Purposive benefits** accrue to members who join groups in order to advance a particular policy or political ideology. Christian Right groups and antiabortion groups, such as the Christian Coalition and Texans United for Life, draw members whose commitment is to creating a society that reflects their social philosophy.[8]

Obviously, the motivation for joining groups varies from person to person. Also, within any group, members have probably been drawn for a variety of reasons, regardless of the type of group or its political goals. In most cases, it is probably the package of benefits that attracts and holds group members.[9] However, if members are drawn to a group largely through material incentives and if those incentives are available to all members of a social category (such as all elderly people) whether they join the group or not, is there really any material benefit in joining the group? This is the dilemma noted by Mancur Olson, an economist, who questioned the rationality of collective action through interest groups.

Collective Benefits and the Free-Rider Problem

Olson's analysis of interest-group activities focused on the rationality of joining an interest group and incurring any real or potential costs involved in membership if an individual can receive the benefits of membership anyway. This dilemma is known as the **free-rider problem** and is most applicable to large groups that provide material, collective benefits. A **collective benefit** is any benefit that is available to one member of a social category or community and that cannot be denied to any other member, regardless of whether he or she helped acquire that benefit. For example, if the Texas Partnership for Competition were successful in lowering long-distance access rates and freezing rates for basic phone service, all Southwestern Bell consumers, whether they joined the coalition and contributed to its efforts or not, would benefit. Conversely, although some groups opposed the legislation, every Southwestern Bell customer shares in the cost of the legislation, in terms of future increases in the rates charged for services provided by Southwestern Bell, since the PUC's regulatory authority was reduced.

Olson explains the existence of many small groups and a few large groups in the interest-group system through the logic of collective benefits and the free-rider problem. Nevertheless, large groups have been created, and they are sustained. How is this possible? Olson argues that these groups offer their members **selective benefits**—benefits that are available only to members of the group.[10] These selective benefits may include information related to the industry, occupation, or profession that is represented, but they also may involve benefits that are primarily tailored to ensure the survival of the organization—discount travel, low-interest credit cards, health-care and life-insurance policies, and other valuable commodities.

After an interest group is created, the group must establish its goals, which may change as the group matures and its membership changes. In the next section, we consider the political goals sought by interest groups.

Critical Thinking Exercise: If a group of college students decided to form a group to present student interests and concerns to the college's governing board, what would make you join that group? Which benefit is most important to you? Would the group have a free-rider problem?

GOALS OF GROUPS: WHY GROUPS ARE INVOLVED IN POLITICS

An interest group's decision to attempt to achieve its goals through the political process is a calculated choice. The ultimate or primary goal of the group is to influence public policy by protecting an existing public policy or by effecting a new policy that promotes the group's objectives. However, accomplishing the group's primary goal may require the group to achieve some secondary goals first. Before a group can influence public policy, the group and its leaders may have to change the policy-making process and the contemporary social values, which are secondary goals.

Primary Goals

Most political scientists assume that affecting public policy is the goal of interest groups. Indeed, influencing public policy is usually the reason for the group's formation and is its ultimate goal. For example, interest groups representing teachers attempt to advance legislation that provides a more favorable work environment, such as smaller classes, less paperwork, and more classroom assistance. However, to achieve that ultimate goal may require a group to focus on other, secondary goals first. Before a group representing teachers can lobby for better working conditions, for example, it may have to change both the policy process, so that their views are heard, and the contemporary social values, so that the public sees its concerns as important. The achievement of these goals facilitates the group's ability to achieve its primary goal.

Texas Partnership for Competition describes its primary goal as the establishment of real competition in the local phone market in Texas. The benefits of real competition, they argue, will accrue to Texas consumers and businesses in the forms of lower rates and advanced technologies.[11]

Secondary Goals

Secondary goals fall into two categories, depending on the kind of change that is sought by the group. One secondary goal involves changing the policy process. For example, teachers' groups may seek greater local authority over working conditions, feeling that they are more likely to achieve their primary goals if the policy is made at that level rather than at the state level. As two political scientists note, changing the policy process leads to the acceptance of the group as legitimate and expands the consultation process that precedes the formulation of public policy.[12] Changes in the policy process may take several forms: the government may provide increased opportunities for input by groups and for the review of policy decisions, or it may decentralize political authority in the policy process. The willingness of political authorities to modify the policy process in response to group pressure may result from the authorities' desire to coopt the group, to diffuse responsibility for public policy, or to provide group assistance in monitoring the bureaucracy. Regardless of the reason for the change, access to the public-policy process enables the group to press its concerns and, possibly, to change social values.

Changing social values is a secondary goal that is often overlooked in the analysis of interest groups and their goals. In seeking to change social values, the group targets the society rather than the government. Thus, teachers' groups might focus their efforts on making parents and the general public aware of their working conditions and the need for change. The effect of changing social values is to extend the range of options, expanding what is possible in a particular policy area. Consequently, politics is affected because changing social values "changes perceptions of what the most important political problems are."[13] This redefines the political agenda. If an interest group representing teachers is successful in making the public view working conditions as the most important problem affecting public education, then the group is more likely to accomplish its primary goal.

The primary goal of the coalition of groups composing Texas Partnership for Competition was promoted by the achievement of some secondary goals. For some members, access to the legislators was an important secondary goal. Others, such as AT&T, sought public acceptance and support so that they could more easily achieve the coalition's primary goal in the future. Regardless, both primary and secondary goals influenced the activities of the participants.

TYPES OF INTEREST GROUPS

Usually, political scientists classify interest groups according to the type of interest that the group represents. We have adopted a classification scheme that focuses on the policy goals of the group: business groups and trade associations, professional associations, labor groups, racial and ethnic groups, and public interest groups.

Business Groups and Trade Associations

Although the interest groups representing businesses in Texas are diverse, business groups and trade associations generally agree that their primary goal is to maintain a favorable climate for businesses in Texas. More specifically, these groups attempt to ensure that business taxes remain low, that labor union influence is restricted, and that favorable business regulations exist. Some business interest groups (e.g., Texas Association of Business and Chambers of Commerce and Texas Association of Taxpayers) represent business interests generally. Others, known as trade associations, represent specific industries and their interests. Among the more influential trade associations are the Texas Automobile Dealers Association, the Texas Bankers Association, the Mid-Continent Oil and Gas Association, and the Texas Chemical Council. Many corporations (Southwestern Bell and AT&T), to increase their influence, also hire their own lobbyists when the legislature is considering a matter of particular importance to their interests.

Professional Associations

Some of the most influential interest groups in Texas represent professional associations, such as trial lawyers, physicians, teachers, and realtors. The Texas Trial Lawyers Association (TTLA) represents the interests of lawyers who make their living representing injured persons in personal injury lawsuits or product liability suits. The Texas Medical Association (TMA) represents physicians, and the Texas State Teachers Association (TSTA) and the Texas Federation of Teachers (TFT) compete to represent public school teachers. The Texas Association of Realtors (TAR) works for realtors in Texas. All of these groups attempt to influence regulations and public policies that affect their professions.

Labor Groups

Although labor groups have never been strong in Texas, their influence is greatest in the industrialized areas of Texas: Houston, Dallas, Ft. Worth, and especially in the Golden Triangle area of Beaumont, Port Arthur, and Orange. Labor unions attempt to establish rights for their members to collective bargaining, occupational safety, and increased wages. The membership of the American Federation of Labor-Congress of Industrial Organizations (AFL-CIO) has declined since the 1980s. Within the AFL-CIO, the more influential unions are the Texas Oil, Chemical, and Atomic Workers Union (OCAW), the American Federation of State, County, and Municipal Employees (AFSCME), and the Communication Workers of America (CWA).

Racial and Ethnic Groups

Racial and ethnic groups promote political, economic, and social equality for their members; freedom from discrimination; and representation in public offices. Because they are the largest minority groups in Texas, Hispanics and African Americans have the greatest number of groups representing their interests. The oldest and largest Hispanic group, the League of United Latin American Citizens (LULAC), is involved in efforts to change the method of selecting judges in Texas (see Chapter 11), and the Mexican American Legal Defense and Education Fund (MALDEF) was instrumental in the lawsuit that led to greater equality in funding for public education in Texas (see Chapter 14). The National Association for the Advancement of Colored People (NAACP) supported Lawrence Nixon's challenge to the Democratic Party's white primary, fought to end segregation in public education, and continues to fight for increased economic and social opportunities for African Americans (see Chapter 13).

Public Interest Groups

Public interest groups advocate public policies intended to benefit the public interest. Among the more active groups in Texas are the Baptist Christian Life Commission, Common Cause, Clean Water Action, the Sierra Club, Public Citizen, Consumers Union, Texans for Public Justice, Texas Alliance for Human Needs, Texas Citizen Action, the Gray Panthers, and Americans Disabled for Attendant Programs Today (ADAPT). These groups seek public policies that protect consumers, the environment, the poor, the elderly, the young, and the disabled.

In Figure 5.1, we have arranged several well-known interest groups, based on two dimensions of public policy: equality and ordered liberty. As we explained in Chapter 2, policy goals on the equality dimension can range from individualism, at one end of the spectrum, to equality, at the other end. Groups that seek governmental action to promote economic, social, and/or political equality are grouped in the upper half of Figure 5.1. Those groups that oppose governmental action to promote equality, feeling that individual freedom is more valuable than governmental promotion of equality, are located in the lower half of Figure 5.1. Similarly,

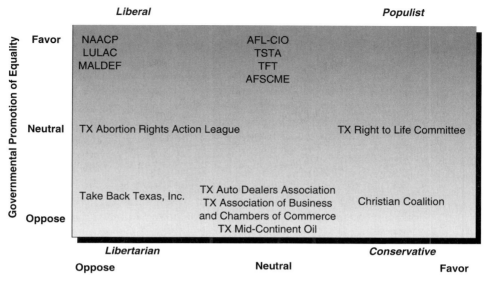

Figure 5.1   Classification of Interest Groups

Interest groups in Texas are classified by ideology using the four ideologies explained in Chapter 2. Groups, which support the use of government power to promote equality over the protection of personal freedoms but support the protection of personal freedoms over the use of government power to maintain order, are classified as liberal (e.g., the NAACP, LULAC). Groups, which support the use of government power to maintain order over the protection of personal freedoms but oppose the use of government power to promote equality over the protection of personal freedoms, are classified as conservative (e.g., the Christian Coalition). Groups, which support the protection of personal freedoms against the use of government power either to promote equality or to maintain order, are libertarian (e.g., Take Back Texas, Inc.).

groups that favor governmental action to create a more ordered liberty are located in the right half of Figure 5.1. On the other hand, groups that oppose governmental action, feeling that individual freedom is more important than order, are in the left half of Figure 5.1. Because most interest groups usually pursue a rather narrow set of policy objectives, they rarely involve themselves in both dimensions; thus, few groups are truly ideological. Nevertheless, some groups, most prominently those that are promoting governmental action in civil liberties and civil rights, are ideological. Other groups, representing conservative social preferences, also are ideological. Thus, our classification involves single-issue groups, which pursue narrow political goals, as well as broad-based groups, which have policy preferences that incorporate both policy dimensions. We have included examples of each category, including some of the more active and powerful groups in Texas politics.

INTEREST-GROUP INFLUENCE

The influence of interest groups largely depends on the resources of the group. In Texas, the most powerful groups possess several essential resources. The most important resource is *money*, because it can be used to obtain the other resources. For example, money can be used to hire professional lobbyists, to conduct research, and to perform other related tasks. The importance of money partially explains the number and power of business groups in the interest-group system.

The resource that is second in importance is the possession of information, expertise, and skills. In the contemporary Texas economy, several types of political, technical, and organizational skills are necessary for effective political influence. The interest group must employ people who understand the political situation in Texas, including the organization and authority of government institutions, the existing laws that affect the interest group's members, and the government rules and regulations that affect its members. Equally important is technical expertise, so that the interest group understands problems that affect the group and the policy area. The group must also possess the political skills to exert influence in the political system.

A third resource involves the group's members. Although the number of members in a group is important, the degree of cohesiveness among members of the group and the ability of the group to mobilize its members for political action is more important. A large but inert group usually has a limited impact on public policy. For example, the TMA and the TTLA are relatively small groups, but their members are very active and cohesive, making them more influential than some public interest groups, such as the Sierra Club.

Finally, the reputation of the interest group with politicians, public officials, and the public is important. For a group to influence public policy consistently, the group must have a reputation for power and for credibility and trustworthiness.[14] The Texas Automobile Dealers Association has had a reputation for power and influence for many years in Texas, primarily because of the reputation of its lobbyist, Gene Fondren.

Southwestern Bell is blessed with tremendous resources. First, it possesses the money necessary to influence politicians and public policy. SBC Communications, Inc. (SBC), the parent company of Southwestern Bell, is a San Antonio-based company with revenues of $45 billion annually. In addition to SWB, SBC now owns Pacific Bell and Ameritech Corp., expanding its operations and influence. With its resources, SBC and SWB hire lobbyists, conduct public relations campaigns, and contribute generously to Texas charities. Furthermore, with 37,000 employees in Texas, many of whom are members of the Communication Workers of America (a politically active labor union), SWB enjoys an advantage over other telecommunications companies.

POLITICAL ACTIVITIES OF GROUPS

Despite the large number of groups in the interest-group system, groups usually engage in three distinct, but related, types of political activities: lobbying, electioneering, and litigation. In this section, we identify and explain each of these activities.

Lobbying

When most people think of interest-group activities, lobbying is probably the first thing that comes to mind. Indeed, lobbying may be the universal activity of interest groups. Most groups practice both direct and indirect lobbying.

Direct Lobbying Attempting to influence public officials through direct contacts defines **direct lobbying.** Because public officials reside in all three branches of government (legislature, executive, and judiciary) and at all levels of government (national, state, and local), we would expect **lobbyists** (the people who lobby) to attempt to influence all of them. Indeed, lobbyists are evident wherever public policy and political decisions are made.

In 1987, there were approximately 800 lobbyists in Texas. In 1999, there were 1579 lobbyists registered with the Texas Ethics Commission. Those lobbyists were paid somewhere between $77 million and $180 million for their services.[15] Even so, those figures do not indicate the total number of interests represented in Austin. There were more than 4500 interest groups with lobbyists working in Austin during the regular legislative session in 1999. The discrepancy between registered lobbyists and the number of interest groups with lobbyists is partially due to the legal requirements for registration in Texas. However, much of the discrepancy arises because many lobbyists have more than one client. In 1987, 80 percent of the registered lobbyists represented only one client, but nearly 11 percent represented four or more clients.[16]

For the century following Reconstruction, Texas placed few restrictions on lobbying and lobbyists. In 1957, lobbyists were required by state law to register and to reveal some information about their activities. However, loopholes in the law made its reporting requirements easy to evade. In 1973, following the Sharpstown scandal (see Chapter 8), a more stringent reporting law was passed.[17] The law was amended in 1983 and again in 1991.

In some respects, the law is broad and encompassing. Lobbying is defined as efforts to influence the legislative and the executive branches, and the law applies even when the legislature is not in session. Furthermore, individuals who register as lobbyists must indicate their employer(s), provide information about their expenditures, and indicate the bills or regulations about which they are concerned. Individuals must register as lobbyists if they meet any of the following criteria: (1) they lobby as a regular part of their job (except government employees); (2) they receive more than $1,000 in any calendar quarter as payment for lobbying; or (3) they spend more than $500 in any calendar quarter for gifts, awards, or entertainment to influence legislation.[18] In 1991, the legislature limited the annual amount that a lobbyist could spend on a public official to $500. Pleasure trips and honoraria paid for by lobbyists were also prohibited.

In 1987, two trends were noted concerning the characteristics of lobbyists in Texas. First, since the 1970s, there has been an increase in the number of contract lobbyists ("hired guns"), who work for more than one client. Many of these contract lobbyists are former members of the legislative or executive branches. In the 1990s, that trend continued, as more former legislators and bureaucrats took positions representing interest groups (Table 5.1). The second trend involved greater

Table 5.1   TEN HIGHEST PAID LOBBYISTS WITH FORMER GOVERNMENT POSITIONS, 1999

Lobbyist	Former government position	Contracts	Major clients	Compensation	
				Minimum	Maximum
Neal T. "Buddy" Jones	Legislator	64	Holly Corporation; Pierce Ranch; Snap-on Corporation; Microsoft Corporation; Intel Corporation	$1,000,000	$2,254,949
Dan Pearson	TNRCC Executive Director	57	AT & T; Farmers Insurance, Inc,; Harcourt, Brace and Company; Houston Rockets, Inc,: Texas Bankers Association	$850,000	$1,929,957
Mack Wallace	Railroad Commissioner	19	Mitchell Energy and Development Corporation; Southern Union Gas; TXU Business Services Company; BAP Petroleum (Americas), Inc,; Texas Game Wardens Association	$870,000	$1,649,981
Kent Caperton	Senator	13	Winstead, Sechrest, and Minick, P.C.; Entre Corporation; Association of Electric Companies of Texas; Boys and Girls Club of Greater Ft. Worth; Credit Union Coalition of Texas; Southwestern Bell Telephone Company	$885,000	$1,326,989
Donald G. "Don" Adams	Senator	22	City of Austin; City of Austin Utility Department; Independent Bankers Association of Texas; Texas Association of Community Colleges; Mobil Oil Company	$690,000	$1,319,980
Hugo Berlanga	Representative	22	AT & T; City of Austin; Coalition of Nurses in Advanced Practice; DuPont Pharmaceuticals; Patton Boggs, LLP	$635,000	$1,294,985
Bill Messer	Representative	18	American Home Shield Corporation; Correctional Services Corporation; Texas Chemical Council; Texas Telephone Association; Texas Hospital Association	$595,000	$1,199,982
John "Cliff" Johnson, Jr.	Representative	13	Andrews County Industrial Foundation; City of Austin; City of Houston; GTECH Corporation; Southwestern Bell Telephone Company	$610,000	$1,174,987
A.W. Pogue	Insurance Commissioner	105	Highland Insurance Group, Inc.; AFLAC Incorporated; Hartford Life, Incorporated; Merrill Lynch Insurance Group, Incorporated; Mutual of Omaha Insurance Company	$10,000	$1,064,999
Thomas J. Bond	Insurance Commissioner	105	Prudential Insurance Company; SAFECO Insurance Company; Texas Hospital Insurance Network; Transamerica Life Insurance and Annuity Company; Viaticus, Incorporated	$0	$1,050,000

ethnic and gender diversity among lobbyists. In the late 1980s, there were more Hispanics, African Americans, and women representing group interests. In February 1987, 150 women and 39 Hispanics were registered as lobbyists.[19] By 1999, the number of women, Hispanics, and African Americans had increased significantly.[20] This trend reflects the changing ethnic and gender composition of government, as well as the tendency for interest groups to assemble a team of lob-

Texas lobbyists discuss strategy during a recess of a legislative hearing in the Capitol Office Complex in Austin.

byists who are individually assigned to specific legislators or bureaucrats, based on a number of shared characteristics.

According to lobbyists, their principal job involves access to public officials and presenting information about their issues. To present information to legislators or administrators though, lobbyists first need to gain access to public officials. Access comes from the lobbyist's reputation and from the interest group's

Kwame Walker, a Senate staff member for 13 years, became a "hired gun" in 1999, lobbying the Texas Legislature for his clients.

contributions to the legislator's campaign (a technique that we discuss more fully in the next section of this chapter). Consequently, many lobbyists are former public officials who have established personal relationships with the people to whom they now want access. Furthermore, their previous experience in public office increases their credibility with current legislators and bureaucrats. As Bill Messer, a lobbyist and former legislator states, "The real job is to articulate a position and to state a constituency. If you don't have a constituency, then you don't have any influence."[21]

The days when lobbyists could rely on the three B's (bourbon, beef, and broads) to influence public officials in Texas have passed. Nevertheless, Southwestern Bell's area vice president, Lisa Hughes, "spent $2,819 wining, dining, and entertaining legislators, their staffs, and their families during the first three months of 1999."[22] Currently, lobbyists must rely on their information and integrity. As Bill Clayton, a former Texas speaker of the House and a current lobbyist, stated, "Integrity is the one thing that counts more than anything. If you lie to one of the members, you won't ever get a job again."[23] Despite the personal friendships that many lobbyists have cultivated with legislators and administrators, lobbyists have to make their case on its merits. Currently, with increased personal and committee staffs, legislators are less dependent on lobbyists for information than they were 20 years ago; however, lobbyists still provide information that is useful to legislators because it is processed, interpreted, and packaged.

The information provided by lobbyists can be substantive (usually technical) or political. Substantive information provides details about the content of the legislation. Political information indicates how the legislation will affect the legislator's constituents and supporters. Furthermore, lobbyists can provide experts to testify at legislative hearings. Probably the most persuasive information provided by lobbyists involves what other states have done concerning a particular issue and the effects of those measures. For example, if the legislature is considering welfare reform, lobbyists can provide information on what other states have done and the effects of those efforts. Also, although the lobbyists represent particular interests, the case for or against a bill must be made in terms of good social policy, not the benefits to the particular interest.[24]

From legislative session to session, the interests that lobbyists represent vary according to the legislative agenda, but some interests are always present. Most prevalent are business interests. They include general business groups (e.g., Texas Association of Business and Chambers of Commerce) and various statewide associations (e.g., Texas Association of Builders and Texas Association of Realtors), but the largest group involves representation for single companies (e.g., Adolph Coors, Monsanto Company, Transamerica, and Foley's). The next largest category, noneconomic groups, includes a hodgepodge of interests, ranging from general ideological groups (e.g., Young Conservatives of Texas) and public-participation groups (e.g., Texas League of Women Voters) to specific single-issue groups (e.g., Texas Women for Pari-Mutuel Betting).[25] In 1999, the Texas industries that generated the most business were in finance, insurance, and real estate, establishing over 1700 contracts worth up to $34 million to the lobbyists that they employed. In second place was the energy and natural resources industry with 870 contracts worth up to $31 million, and third place belonged to the communications and electronics industry, which spent up to $22 million on 596 contracts.[26]

In 1999, Southwestern Bell led all interests in lobbying expenditures by employing 127 lobbyists through contracts worth between $2.6 and $5.1 million. EDS Corporation was a distant second, employing 32 lobbyists with contracts worth between $1.8 and $2.6 million.[27]

The individuals targeted by lobbyists vary. Some lobbyists pursue a "top-down" strategy, concentrating their efforts on the leadership. Because the Texas speaker of the House and president of the Senate (lieutenant governor) have considerable powers, lobbying the leadership can be productive. However, most lobbyists focus their efforts on the committees with jurisdiction over legislation that affects the interests of the group. Committee chairs receive more attention than committee members, but lobbyists cannot ignore committee members entirely because committee members' votes can be crucial to their success or failure. Legislative staff, as their numbers have increased, are also among the lobbyists' targets, particularly staff members who are considered influential with the legislator. Finally, in the legislature, lobbyists must cultivate members who will ultimately decide a bill's fate with their votes. Lobbyists tend to concentrate their efforts on those members who are undecided, rather than on members who have committed to vote for or against a given measure.[28]

Interactions between lobbyists and administrators of state agencies and departments are frequent in Texas. A 1982 study of executive agencies in Texas indicated that interest-group-initiated contacts with agencies occurred frequently or very frequently and that half of the contacts were administration initiated. These contacts usually involve an exchange of information or an attempt to influence policies. For example, an environmental group, such as the Sierra Club, might contact the TNRCC to relay information about water and air pollution in Texas or to lobby the commission for stronger environmental regulations. Administrative agencies contact interest groups to ascertain the effects of their programs on group members and to solicit input on proposed regulations. Interest groups, on the other hand, contact agencies to obtain information about their programs and to influence the agencies' rules and regulations.

Interest-group efforts to lobby state agencies are enhanced by group activities to influence appointments or elections of state executives. Although interest groups are rarely able to dictate appointments to state boards and commissions or to ensure the election of a favored candidate, they may hold a veto over appointees who are antipathetic to the group.[29] A study of gubernatorial appointments to vacancies on the Texas Railroad Commission in the 1960s and 1970s, for instance, indicated that "governors have never appointed a person to the Railroad Commission who was generally hostile to the industry, but neither have they picked individuals who were dictated by, or even suggested by, the industry."[30] In elections, groups use their advantage in fund-raising to assist their favored candidates. They give them an advantage in name recognition and visibility in low-visibility contests, such as a commissioner on the Railroad Commission. In 1994, incumbent Railroad Commissioner Jim Nugent received $630,743 in contributions during the year ending in June 1994. Of those contributions, $501,813 were contributions of more than $1,000. Seventy-three percent of those contributions ($366,323) came from individuals or from political action committees in the oil and gas, trucking, utilities, or pipeline business.[31] In 1999, Senator Gonzalo Barrientos, who represents Austin, invoked senatorial courtesy (see Chapter 9) to block the reappointment of Judy Walsh to the Public Utility Commission, citing Walsh's alleged hostility to labor unions. Barrientos stated that he sought the advice of many groups, but the most important may have been Joe Gunn, president of the Texas AFL-CIO and former head of the Communications Workers of America, and Southwestern Bell, which has not looked favorably on Walsh's voting record on the commission.[32]

Indirect Lobbying   In addition to direct lobbying, interest groups also engage in a form of lobbying called **indirect,** or **"grassroots," lobbying.** There are actually two forms of indirect lobbying. In the first form, interest groups attempt to activate their members, urging them to contact their representatives or executive officials to influence public policy. For example, the Texas Automobile Dealers Association (TADA) could encourage its members to write their representatives and senators about pending legislation and could even provide a sample letter. However, the second, increasingly common form attempts to change the climate of public opinion, largely through television advertising. As this form has become more popular, political activists have termed them "Astroturf" because although they look like grassroots political movements, they are actually campaigns that are manufactured by interest groups. Despite their artificial quality, they offer a semblance of popular support. The popularity of these television campaigns is attributable to the imputed success of the Harry and Louise campaign of 1994. In a series of television advertisements sponsored by the insurance industry, two actors portrayed Harry and Louise, a couple worried about the effects of President Clinton's health-care reform act. The advertisements were credited with turning public opinion against Clinton's plan.[33] In Texas, the commercials by the Texas Partnership for Competition, featured in this chapter's scenario, illustrate the effectiveness of these campaigns in getting an item on decision makers' agendas.

Grassroots public relations lobbying involves coalition building and strategic planning. These efforts are attempts by interest groups to make voting for a bill easier for legislators by building support for the bill in the legislators' districts. Obviously, the more districts that are affected by the policy that the coalition is attempting to effect, the greater the group's likelihood of success. Since Southwestern Bell's hold on local phone service is so pervasive, the coalition's ads were extremely effective. However, Southwestern Bell's counter-ads were also effective because the company pointed out that AT&T, a company headquartered in New Jersey, was behind the ads and blasted AT&T for its opposition to legislation that would "keep rates among the lowest in the nation." Although the ads may not have sparked much activity by legislators' constituents, the ads did put long-distance access charges on the agenda and forced the legislature to act.[34]

New technologies offer groups new methods of implementing grassroots campaigns. When Putting Children First, a coalition dedicated to establishing a pilot voucher program that would allow parents to use tax dollars to pay for tuition at private schools, wanted to reach what it calculated was its ideal member, a mother between 25 and 45 years of age who is also religious, it contacted Juno Online Services, the second largest provider of personal e-mail accounts. Juno identified 30,000 members among its 361,000 members in Texas who fit the profile, and in June 1998, those Texans were greeted with a colorful screen ad from Putting Children First. The cost of online issue ads is much less than direct mail, when the cost of producing, printing, and buying postage is considered. Although the effects of such ads are difficult to assess now, most students of politics feel that as the number of e-mail subscribers expands, the ads will become more prevalent.[35]

Until recently, most political scientists maintained that whether the number of people and/or interests affected by public policy were small or large, interest groups attempted to narrow the scope of conflict, reasoning that their chances of success were greater when the public was not informed or involved. However, a recent study demonstrates that interest groups now are more likely to broaden or socialize the conflict (see Chapter 8) by forming coalitions or providing the public with detailed narratives, explaining the problem and their solution to the problem.[36] Including more participants in policy discussions is now viewed as controllable by interest groups, and thus advantageous to the achievement of their particular interests. Controlling how the problem is defined by the public and influencing the solution to the problem that is favored by the public increases the interest group's influence with decision makers.

Electioneering

As an activity of interest groups, **electioneering** involves an interest group in the political campaigns of candidates for public office and has become a major political activity of interest groups since the mid-1970s. Interest groups maintain that their involvement in political campaigns is to ensure access to public officials. As one lobbyist notes, the price of access is a $1,000 contribution to a senator's campaign and a $250 contribution to a representative's campaign.[37] How do interest groups raise their money for political campaigns, and to whom do they contribute?

Like most states, Texas has experienced a recent boom in the activity of **political action committees (PACs),** which are groups formed to solicit funds and then to use those funds to help elect or defeat candidates for public office. In 1998, there were 891 general purpose PACs registered in Texas. Although there were 19 fewer PACs in 1998 than in 1996, PAC spending increased by 20 percent during the period, from $43 million in 1995–1996 to $52 million in 1997–1998. Of the 1997–1998 spending by PACs, business PACs spend $39.1 million (61 percent), ideological and single-issue PACs spent $17.7 million (35 percent), and labor PACs spent $2.3 million (4 percent).[38] Table 5.2 provides a list of the top 25 general PACs in 1998.

Contributions to PACs are largely the result of direct-mail solicitation. Corporate and labor PACs also use payroll deductions for their employees or members. Although the percentage of employees or members who contribute to the PAC usually does not exceed 20 percent, PACs are able to raise large amounts to contribute to candidates for public office, especially candidates for the legislature.

Although there has not been a comprehensive study of PAC contribution strategies in Texas, PACs probably follow the same strategies employed by PACs in other states.[39] Indeed, a study of two PACs in Texas—the Texas Medical Association PAC and the Texas Trial Lawyers Association PAC—indicate that PACs in Texas, like PACs in other states, concentrate their contributions on incumbents (those candidates who currently are in office) and committee chairs and members who are responsible for legislation affecting the PACs' interests. Although the study of these two PACs is more than a decade old, an analysis of the Texas Medical Association PAC's contributions in 1993–1994 and in 1997–1998 reveals an increasing preference for incumbents (Table 5.3).

Table 5.2   TWENTY-FIVE TOP GENERAL PURPOSE PACS, 1998

Rank 1998	Rank 1996	Political action committee	1998 spending	Interest category
1	1	Texas Democratic Party	$6,061,413	Democratic Party
2	2	Texas Republican Campaign Committee	$3,346,263	Republican Party
3	6	Associated Republicans of Texas	$1,432,945	Republican Party
4	5	Vinson and Elkins	$1,237,225	Profession
5	3	Texans for Lawsuit Reform	$1,207,261	Single-Issue
6	4	Texas Association of Realtors	$1,086,834	Business
7	7	Texas Trial Lawyers Association	$957,484	Profession
8	11*	Eight in Ninety Eight Committee	$824,433	Republican Party
9	26	Compass Bancshares	$821,750	Business
10	17	Fulbright and Jaworski Texas Committee	$773,445	Profession
11	9	Southwestern Bell Communications	$730,437	Business
12	16	Texas Medical Association	$661,652	Profession
13	12	Texas Automobile Dealers Association	$642,236	Business
14	49	Texas Partnership for Competition	$568,295	Single-Issue
15	15	Houston Industries	$563,296	Business
16	25	Texas Association of CPAs	$528,931	Profession
17	13	United Services Automobile Association	$496,350	Business
18	19	Texas Dental Association	$494,286	Business
19	20	Enron Corporation	$466,233	Business
20	23	Good Government Fund	$465,550	Business
21	7	Texas Manufactured Housing Association	$456,800	Business
22	28	Texas State Teachers Association	$432,004	Labor
23	29	Baker and Botts	$409,120	Profession
24	30	Farmers Employee and Agent PAC	$407,696	Business
25	18	American Airlines PAC	$396,405	Business

*Spending of predecessor PAC, "76 in '96;" Both PACs sought a GOP majority in the Texas House.

Source: Texans for Public Justice, "1999 Lobbyists, Data Tables." Available 28 November 1999, http://www.tpj.org/data/99lob/lobbyists_1.html; Texas Ethics Commission.

A study of campaign contributions by 22 Texas PACs that are interested in protecting businesses from civil lawsuits for personal injuries (torts) demonstrated how PACs target their contributions. The study concentrated on the two most influential PACS—Texans for Lawsuit Reform (TLR) and Texas Civil Justice League (TCJL)—and their contributions to members of the Texas Legislature during 1995 and 1996. Although the 22 PACs contributed to all but one of the 181 legislators in the House and Senate, the principal beneficiaries of the PACs's largess were House and Senate members who were involved in close elections, freshmen members of the legislature, Republicans, and the leadership in the chambers. In all, the 22 PACs contributed $3.1 million to winning legislative candidates between January 1995 and December 1996.[40] In 1998, TLRPAC contributed nearly

Table 5.3   TEXAS MEDICAL ASSOCIATION PAC (TMPAC) AND TEXANS FOR LAWSUIT REFORM PAC (TLRPAC) CONTRIBUTIONS TO STATE LEGISLATIVE CONTESTS

The contribution strategies of TMPAC indicate a trend of contributing a larger share to incumbents (state senators and representatives who were seeking reelection) in each period. Also, challengers (candidates who challenge incumbent state senators and representatives) were least likely to receive contributions from TMPAC. Candidates in open-seat contests (contests in which no incumbent state senator or representative was a candidate) were the principal recipients of TLRPAC's contributions during 1998, indicating a strategy that is different from TMPAC's.

Recipients in state legislative contests	TMPAC			TLRPAC
	1985–1986	**1993–1994**	**1997–1998**	**1998**
Total contributions	$630,668	$230,489	$261,443	$996,251
Incumbents	55%	75%	85%	25%
Challengers	1%	2%	0%	26%
Open seats	44%	23%	15%	49%

Sources: Keith E. Hamm and Charles W. Wiggins, "Texas: The Transformation from Personal to Informational Lobbying," in *Interest Group Politics in the Southern States* eds. Ronald J. Hrebenar and Clive S. Thomas (Tuscaloosa, Ala.: University of Alabama Press, 1993), 169. GPAC disclosure records, Texas Ethics Commission. Data on Texans for Lawsuit Reform PAC provided by Texans for Public Justice, Austin, Texas.

$1 million to legislative candidates, sending most of the money to candidates in open-seat contests (Table 5.3).

Litigation

The final interest-group strategy involves **litigation,** the use of the judicial system to advance the group's goals. Practiced extensively by civil rights and environmental groups in the 1950s and 1960s, litigation has become a more common weapon in the arsenal of interest-group activities recently. Much of the increased use of litigation can be attributed to the new judicial federalism, which has made state courts more likely to entertain such lawsuits (see Chapter 13). However, because litigation is expensive, the groups that are most likely to pursue litigation are those groups that are prosperous enough to afford the expense and that have been unsuccessful in lobbying and campaigning and, therefore, pursue the legal route as a last resort. The purpose of litigation is to effect changes or to prevent changes in public policy. Also, litigation can be used as a delaying tactic to slow change.[41]

> **Critical Thinking Exercise:** Consider the activities of Texas Partnership for Competition. Which activity was most effective for the coalition? Should they have used a different approach? What should they have done differently?

INTEREST GROUPS AND POLITICAL CHANGE

Interest groups and political change are connected in two ways. First, many interest groups are the product of political and economic changes in the society. Particular interest groups rise and fall as social changes spawn new groups and eradicate irrelevant groups. Although changes in the interest-group community are not always preceded by changes in the environment in which those groups operate, interest groups must adapt to those changes or face the possibility of their being deemed irrelevant. For example, an interest group that represented typewriter manufacturers would face extinction today unless it could expand its representation to manufacturers of word processors as well.

More important, interest groups are instrumental in changing political institutions and processes. Although some groups obviously are more interested in maintaining the status quo than in promoting change, a study of interest-group lobbying in 1983 indicated that most groups, regardless of the type of interest represented, supported rather than opposed change by significant ratios. As one might anticipate, given their dominant position among interest groups, business interests were least likely to support change.[42] However, when business groups do seek change, they try to ensure that the changes benefit their interests. For example, in 1989, business interests supported changes in Texas's workers' compensation law, which changed the process and established a new administrative agency.

INTEREST GROUPS AND DEMOCRACY

The relationship between interest groups and democracy has been debated for centuries. Supporters of interest groups maintain that groups effectively represent and promote the interests of their members, that no group or interest is able to dominate the political process and public policy, and that the compromises that policy makers reach to accommodate competing interests effectively reflect the general will or interest of society. In effect, interest groups promote pluralist democracy in Texas.

Critics of the pluralist position counter that interest groups do not represent all interests in Texas, that some groups are more powerful and influential than other groups, and that the groups that win most consistently in the competition among groups do not reflect the general will of society but their own, limited interests. In other words, interest groups, dominated by certain interests, promote elitism in Texas.

Which view is more accurate? Perhaps there is no answer, but we believe that the following six facts will help you reach your own conclusion. As you consider these facts, think about what you have read in the newspaper, seen on television, or read in magazines about interest groups and their influence in Texas.

First, there is no contesting the fact that business is the best represented interest in Texas. There are more business groups, they employ the greatest number of lobbyists, and they exhibit the greatest involvement in the three political activities of interest groups. Consequently, legislators tend to hold in high regard lobbyists for interest groups that are heavily involved in electioneering, and legislators are more likely to grant these lobbyists access. On the other hand, lobbyists for interest groups that are not as involved in electioneering, such as Public Citizen and Consumers Union, are less likely to be granted access to legislators.

Second, some interests in Texas have no interest group or lobbyists to represent them. Those members of Texas society who are least advantaged, such as the poor and homeless, are also the least likely to have their interest represented by lobbyists, PACs, or litigators. As one political scientist stated, "The flaw in the pluralist heaven is that the heavenly chorus sings with a strong upper-class accent. Probably about 90 percent of the people cannot get into the pressure system."[43]

Third, groups do not compete on many issues. A study of a sample of bills in the 1983 Texas legislature indicated that nearly half the bills (48.7 percent) featured either no interest group involvement or only one group taking a position on the bill.[44] In these situations, where is the competition among groups that purportedly characterizes pluralism?

Fourth, public policy making in administrative agencies in Texas is becoming more competitive and contentious. In the past, policy making has been described as a process featuring **iron triangles** (see Chapter 10) in which interest groups, government agencies, and legislative committees pursued their collective goals without regard for the public's preferences or interests. According to this description, policy making, especially regulatory policy making, was dominated by the interest groups that were being regulated. Thus, natural gas and oil interests, such as Mid-Continent Oil and Gas Association, were said to control the state agency that regulated the oil and natural gas industry, the Texas Railroad Commission.

More recently, the policy-making process has been described in terms of **issue networks,** which feature larger, more diverse, and more competitive interests confronting each other over procedures and regulations. For each policy area, these issue networks include academics, scientists, executives, legislators, interest groups, and others. The boundaries of issue networks are fluid, rather than fixed, and expand to include new participants, based on expertise and connection to the policy area around which the network is formed.[45] In many agencies in Texas, policy making has become more like an issue network than an iron triangle in the past decade. More participants are involved in agency policy making, and as one political scientist stated, "There is some reason to suspect that all is not sweetness and light as far as agency-interest group relations are concerned."[46]

Fifth, when a majority of the interest groups involved in a policy agree, the group's position wins approximately 55 percent of the time. In other words, when the interest groups are in agreement, they usually are successful; however, even when they do agree, they still are unsuccessful nearly half of the time.

Finally, when interest groups oppose the position taken by the governor and/or the legislative leaders (lieutenant governor in the Texas Senate and speaker in the Texas House of Representatives), the influence of interest groups on legislation decreases greatly. However, there are only a few of these cases that occur each legislative session. Also, the governor's opposition is less harmful to interest groups than opposition from the legislative leaders. Given the influence of the legislative leaders in their respective chambers, this is not surprising (see Chapter 8).

In the final analysis, do interest groups promote pluralist democracy in Texas or sustain an elitist oligarchy? Perhaps the perspective from which one views the interest-group system determines the answer. If one focuses on the processes or activities of interest groups, they appear to promote pluralist democracy (the growth in interests represented, in the number of lobbyists and PACs, and in expenditures to influence politics and government), but if one focuses on the results or outcomes (who wins and who loses), the answer is much less clear.

> **Critical Thinking Exercise:** Consider the arguments concerning interest groups and democracy. Which position seems more correct to you? Do interest groups promote pluralist democracy or elitism? What convinced you?

SUMMARY

In this chapter, we have discussed the reasons that interest groups are created, assessing two theories of interest-group formation—disturbance theory and entrepreneurial theory. We have also discussed the reasons that people join groups, providing several categories of benefits or incentives that groups offer to attract and maintain their members. Furthermore, the free-rider problem was discussed. We noted that although the ultimate goal of most groups is a change in public policy, groups also seek secondary or intermediate goals, that further the likelihood of their achieving a policy goal. Contending that the usual classification of groups does not further the analysis of groups, we offered a classification system for interest groups based on a group's policy preferences. Next, we described and analyzed the political activities in which interest groups participate—lobbying (direct and indirect), electioneering, and litigating. Finally, after assessing the role of interest groups in political change, we discussed whether interest groups promote pluralist democracy or elitist oligarchy.

KEY TERMS

interest groups
disturbance theory
entrepreneurial theory
material benefits
solidary benefits
purposive benefits
free-rider problem
collective benefits
selective benefits

direct lobbying
lobbyists
indirect (grassroots) lobbying
electioneering
political action committees (PACs)
litigation
iron triangles
issue networks

SUGGESTED READINGS

Berry, Jeffrey M. *The Interest Group Society,* 4th ed. New York: Addison, Wesley, Longman, 1997.

Goodwyn, Lawrence. *Texas Oil, American Dreams: A Study of the Texas Independent Producers and Royalty Owners Association.* Austin, Tex.: Texas State Historical Association, 1996.

Hrebenar, Ronald J., and Clive S. Thomas, eds. *Interest Group Politics in the Southern States.* Tuscaloosa, Ala.: University of Alabama Press, 1993.

Pittman, H. C. *Inside the Third House: A Veteran Lobbyist Takes a 50-Year Frolic Through Texas Politics.* Austin, Tex.: Eakin Press, 1992.

Rosenthal, Alan. *The Third House: Lobbyists and Lobbying in the States.* Washington, D.C.: Congressional Quarterly Press, 1993.

Thomas, Clive S., and Robert J. Hrebenar. "Interest Group Power in the Fifty States: Trends Since the Late 1970s," *Comparative State Politics* 20, no.4 (1999): 3–16.

West, Darrell M., and Burdett A. Loomis, *The Sound of Money: How Political Interests Get What They Want.* New York: W.W. Norton and Company, Inc., 1999.

NOTES

1. See Stuart Eskenazi, "Ring Ma Bell," *Dallas Observer Online,* 20–26 May 1999. Accessed 13 November 1999, http://www.dallasobserver.com/1998/052099/feature1-1.html.
2. House Research Organization, *Major Issues of the 76th Legislature,* no. 76–15, June 30, 1999. Accessed 13 November 1999, http://www.capitol.state.tx.us/ hrofr/frame4.htm.
3. Bruce Hight, "Bell, AT&T Toss $10 Million in Ad Battle," *Austin American-Statesman,* 12 May 1999, pp. D1, D9.
4. In late 1999, the web site was still operating. Visit it at http://www.competition.org/index.html.
5. David B. Truman, *The Government Process* (New York: Alfred Knopf, 1951), Chapters 3 and 4.
6. Kay Lehman Schlozman and John T. Tierney, *Organized Interests and American Democracy* (New York: Harper and Row, 1986), 122–123; Jeffrey M. Berry, *The Interest Group Society,* 2d ed. (New York: HarperCollins, 1989), 46.
7. Robert H. Salisbury, "An Exchange Theory of Interest Groups," *Midwest Journal of Political Science* 13 (1969): 1–31; Jack L. Walker, "The Origins and Maintenance of Interest Groups in America," *American Political Science Review* 77 (March 1983): 390–406.
8. James Q. Wilson, *Political Organizations* (New York: Basic Books, 1973), 30–55.
9. Berry, *The Interest Group Society,* 50–57.
10. Mancur Olson, *The Logic of Collective Action* (Cambridge, Mass.: Harvard University Press, 1965), 51–52, 132–133.
11. Texas Partnership for Competition Homepage, "About Us." Accessed 23 November 1999, http://www.competition.org/about/index.html.
12. Thomas R. Rochon and Daniel A. Mazmanian, "Social Movements and the Policy Process," *Annals* (July 1993): 77–80.
13. Ibid., 77.
14. Schlozman and Tierney, *Organized Interests and American Democracy,* 88–103.

15. Because lobbyists are only required to report their income to the Texas Ethics Commission in broad categories (e.g., $10,000–24,999), the exact amount paid to lobbyists for their services is unknown.

16. Keith E. Hamm and Charles W. Wiggins, "Texas: The Transformation from Personal to Informational Lobbying," in *Interest Group Politics in the Southern States*, eds. Ronald J. Hrebenar and Clive S. Thomas (Tuscaloosa, Ala.: University of Alabama Press, 1993), 163.

17. Ibid., 156.

18. Texas Ethics Commission, Rules, Rule 30.

19. Hamm and Wiggins, "Texas," 164–165.

20. See Osler McCarthy, "Minority Lobbyists Increase their Presence at Legislature," *Austin American-Statesman*, 12 April 1999, pp. A1, A12.

21. Quoted in Robert Bryce, "Access Through the Lobby," *Texas Observer*, 24 February 1995, 16.

22. Eskenazi, "Ring Ma Bell," *Dallas Observer Online*, 25 May 1999.

23. Quoted in Bryce, "Access Through the Lobby," 16.

24. Alan Rosenthal, *The Third House: Lobbyists and Lobbying in the States* (Washington, D.C.: Congressional Quarterly, 1993), 190–199.

25. Hamm and Wiggins, "Texas," 158–162.

26. Texans for Public Justice, "Austin's Oldest Profession: Texas' Top Lobby Clients & Those Who Service Them," Texans for Public Justice web site. Accessed 13 November 1999, http://www.tpj.org/reports/lobby/summary.html.

27. Texans for Public Justice, "1999 Texas Lobby Clients," Texans for Public Justice web site. Accessed 13 November 1999, http://www.tpj.org/data/99clients_1.thml.

28. Rosenthal, *The Third House*, 182–190.

29. Hamm and Wiggins, "Texas," 172–173.

30. David F. Prindle, *Petroleum Politics and the Texas Railroad Commission* (Austin: University of Texas Press, 1981), 158.

31. Ben Wear, "Regulated Donating Heavily to Regulators," *Austin American-Statesman*, 11 September 1994, p. B1.

32. Bruce Hight, "Senator Blocks Utility Official: Barrientos Tells Bush He Will Oppose Reappointment of PUC Commissioner Judy Walsh," *Austin American-Statesman*, 28 September 1999, pp. CI, C2.

33. Elizabeth Kolbert, "Labeled Astroturf, Grass-Root Campaigns Are Sown by Lobbyists," *Austin American-Statesman*, 26 March 1995, p. A4.

34. Bruce Hight, "Bell, AT&T Toss $10 Million in Ad Battle," p. D9.

35. Ken Foskett, "Advocacy Groups Go Stumping on the Web," *Austin American-Statesman*, 14 June 1998, pp. H1, H5.

36. Darrell M. West and Burdett A. Loomis, *The Sound of Money: How Political Interests Get What They Want* (New York: W.W. Norton and Company, Inc., 1999), 1–44, especially 42.

37. Bryce, "Access Through the Lobby," 16.

38. Texans for Public Justice, *Texas PACs: 1998 Election Cycle Spending* (Austin: Texans for Public Justice, 1999).

39. See Gregory S. Thielemann and Donald R. Dixon, "Explaining Contributions: Rational Contributors and the Elections of the 71st Texas House," *Legislative Studies Quarterly* 19 (November 1994): 495–506.

40. Lynn Tran and Andrew Wheat, *Tort Dodgers: Business Money Tips Scales of Justice* (Austin: Texans for Public Justice, 1997).

41. Berry, *The Interest Group Society,* 154–157.
42. Hamm and Wiggins, "Texas," 178–179.
43. E. E. Schattschneider, *The Semisovereign People* (New York: Holt, Rinehart, and Winston, 1960), 35.
44. Hamm and Wiggins, "Texas," 176.
45. Berry, *The Interest Group Society,* 172–187.
46. Richard C. Elling, "The Relationship Among Bureau Chiefs, Legislative Committees and Interest Groups: A Multistate Study," paper presented at the American Political Science Association Meeting, 1983, 12, quoted in Hamm and Wiggins, "Texas," 174.

6

Political Communications: The Media and Public Opinion

★ Scenario: Framing the Campaign—Does the Governor Really Want Her Job?

In providing the public with information about politics, the media frame issues and events. A newspaper or television story's theme takes several seemingly isolated events, places them in a context, and gives them meaning. In essence, the media interpret political events. An example of this framing by the media helps us understand the political roles and influence of the media.

For Paul Burka, a long-time political writer for *Texas Monthly,* the theme that framed an April 1994 article on Governor Ann Richards was her loss of faith in government and, by implication, of her desire to govern. After relating Richards's appearance at an elementary school dedication in the Lower Rio Grande Valley during late February 1994, in which he describes the governor as melancholy and unable to connect with a large and receptive crowd, Burka recounts a meeting that he had with the governor in the Texas Capitol near the end of the 1993 legislative session. Burka suggested to Richards that she did not seem to be enjoying

Ann Richards campaigns for reelection during the 1994 gubernatorial campaign.

herself as much as she had during the 1991 session. According to Burka, Richards answered, "If you mean, 'Am I sadder but wiser?' the answer is yes."

The bulk of Burka's article explains Ann Richards's disillusionment, recounting her numerous legislative successes but stressing her inability to transform the Texas bureaucracy as she had wished. According to Burka, Governor Richards's failure explains her disillusionment with government. The article concludes with Burka's assessment of Richards's dilemma in the gubernatorial contest with George W. Bush:

> The problem for Ann Richards is not so much Bush as it is herself. Who is she, really? What does she believe in anymore? What does she say to inspire the old Democratic constituency? It is an article of faith among liberal Democrats that moving to the center is a losing tactic. The only way to get the turnout necessary to beat a strong Republican, the argument goes, is to bring out the Democratic masses by promising to make their lives better. Ann Richards used to believe that—before she became sadder but wiser.[1]

As a panelist during the only televised debate between Bush and Richards, Burka posed the same question, in a slightly different form. He indicated that the governor's television campaign had included many attacks on Bush's business record but little about what the governor planned to do during her second term, if she were reelected. Pointedly, Burka asked Governor Richards whether she could "name a couple of things that you really do want to do in the next four years?" In response, Governor Richards thanked Burka for the opportunity to indicate her priorities for a second term and listed three goals: (1) In education, increase the pay for teachers, and expand the efforts to free local school districts from the rules of the Texas Education Agency; (2) ensure that the programs for ending the cycle of drug abuse and alcoholism in prisons are successful; and (3) build the infrastructure necessary to continue the expansion of Texas's economy.

Paul Burka's question during the debate created a self-fulfilling prophecy. Governor Richards's inability to build a commanding lead over George W. Bush in public opinion polls, despite a healthy economy and her own personal popularity, was due to her ambivalence about government's ability to effect change and her lack of a positive message. Burka's theme provided an explanation, but it also gave Governor Richards's potential supporters, especially those who were not deeply committed to her candidacy, a reason not to participate in the election. After all, if Governor Richards is not convinced that government can make a difference and doesn't have a plan, why should a potential supporter help reelect her? For undecideds, the dilemma was easily resolved: Vote for the candidate who obviously wanted the job and had a plan. ★

INTRODUCTION

In this chapter, we describe the media's roles as a provider of information, a channel for communication between the government and the public, and a protector of the public. Further, we describe the factors that shape the news provided by the media. We also provide an overview of the mass media in Texas and an analysis of news content. Because the media are the principal source of most people's information about politics and government, we devote a major portion of this chapter to assessing the political effects of the media.

Political communication also involves public opinion. Consequently, we also describe public opinion in this chapter, indicating how public opinion is measured. We also provide some results of public opinion surveys in Texas, to assess the policy preferences of Texans.

Finally, we assess the effects of the media and public opinion on political change and democracy. First, we consider the political roles of the media.

THE POLITICAL ROLES OF THE MEDIA

The conclusion from our scenario should not be that Paul Burka cost Ann Richards the election; he didn't. However, the media, whether print or broadcast, perform several roles in the political system, and in performing those roles, they do much more than simply provide us with facts about political events. Few Texans had the opportunity or the inclination to follow the gubernatorial

Te★as*Index*

Print and Broadcast Media in the States

Number of daily newspapers, 1998:
Texas—76
California—120
New York—74
Florida—46

Number of AM radio stations, 1998:
Texas—224
California—199
New York—145
Florida—151

Number of FM radio stations, 1998:
Texas—261
California—282
New York—232
Florida—171

Number of local television stations, 1998:
Texas—99
California—84
New York—49
Florida—65

Number of cable systems, 1998:
Texas—96
California—101
New York—44
Florida—32

Number of periodicals, 1998:
Texas—280
California—1,089
New York—2,065
Florida—254

Number of African-American publications, 1998:
Texas—9
California—42
New York—22
Florida—12

Number of Hispanic publications, 1998:
Texas—14
California—36
New York—14
Florida—28

candidates throughout the campaign in 1994, assessing their performance and their promises. The public depended on the media to observe the campaign, report the events, and provide the information necessary to reach an informed decision. The public's dependence on the media for information about politics and government is constant, and how the media perform their political roles has an impact on what we know and how we feel about politics and government.

In contemporary America, the media perform three political roles. First, and perhaps most important, the media provide the public with information about political events. The public depends on the media to observe events, select the important ones, and apprise the public about their significance. In performing this function, the media are considered gatekeepers, determining which events and people deserve our attention and consideration and which do not. From the thousands of daily events that are a part of Texas politics and government, the media are expected to select the most important and to inform the public of their significance.

Second, the media are expected to provide a channel of communication between the government and the public. Of course, the public, if it is going to assess the performance of government, must know what public officials are doing and their reasons for their actions. Also, public officials need to know what the public wants them to do and what the public thinks of their proposals and programs. In a majoritarian democracy especially, public opinion is supposed to guide public policy. The media provide public officials with information about the public's policy priorities and expectations of government action. Consequently, the media are expected to provide a two-way channel for communication.

Finally, in a democracy, where public officials and the government are supposed to be accountable to the people, the media should also perform a watchdog role, monitoring the branches of government and alerting the public to any misbehavior or mischief. When the media perform this role, the media and the government are viewed as adversaries.

The inherent tension between the media's communication role and its watchdog role shapes the relationship between public officials and the media. As the principal channel for government information to the public, the media are required to report the information provided by public officials. However, in their watchdog role, the media are expected to be skeptical of the motives of public officials and to be vigilant for attempts by public officials to mislead the public.

Neither government officials nor media reporters are entirely comfortable with this relationship. Obviously, the government, in pursuing a policy objective, does not want its every move analyzed and subjected to detailed investigations. Consequently, public officials may attempt to limit media access to information or to government personnel. However, the government also depends on the media to report the government's version of events to the public, which means that public officials cannot appear arbitrary in their decisions regarding media access. Similarly, the media depend on government officials for information about political events, and they cannot afford to alienate their primary sources. Consequently, neither the media nor the politicians, though admittedly wary of each other, perceive their relationship as truly antagonistic or adversarial. Rather, each views the other as necessary, and the relationship is more accurately described as **symbiotic**—mutually interdependent.

In Texas, the preference for a limited government role promotes an independent and critical media. This preference affects how the media perform their three roles in Texas, but there are also other, more generic factors that shape the media's conception of news and how the media report it.

> **Critical Thinking Exercise:** Considering the three political roles of the media, which role is most important? What is your impression of the media's performance of this role? Why?

FACTORS SHAPING THE NEWS

The factors that shape the content of the news and the media's presentation of the news include the media's definition of what constitutes news, the professional and personal values and ideologies of the people who work for the media, and the economic requirement that news organizations be profitable. We consider each of these factors in turn.

What Is News?

There is a remarkable consensus among professional news people about what constitutes news. Five criteria are used most often in choosing news stories. That is, from all of the events that could be included in the newspapers or television news on a particular day, the events that are most likely to be considered newsworthy contain these five elements:

1. News stories must involve events that have a strong impact on readers, listeners, or viewers. People want information that is relevant to their personal lives and with which they can identify.
2. News involves violence, conflict, disaster, or scandal. These kinds of events excite audiences and hold their attention.
3. News stories are about familiar people or about situations that concern many people.
4. An event must have proximity, meaning that the news story must relate an event that occurred close to the viewer's or reader's home.
5. The news should contain events that are timely and novel. The "news," by definition, is about "new" events, which have just occurred and which are not routine events.

Among the five criteria, the most important are timeliness, conflict, and proximity.[2]

News People and Their Values

According to a study of major news organizations, perhaps the most important effects of news people's values on their presentation of the news derive from their conceptions of how a democracy should operate, a distrust of partisan politics and bureaucracies, and a desire to be "above politics."[3] Thus, news people were apolitical and nonideological, emphasizing the media's watchdog role.

More recent studies have produced conflicting views of news people's values and ideologies; one of these views is probably more characteristic of how most people view journalists. Politically, a majority of journalists (54 percent) in a 1990 study described themselves as liberals, and only 17 percent considered themselves conservative. In voting behavior, the journalists were overwhelmingly Democratic. Furthermore, their attitudes on a broad range of economic and social issues supported their liberal self-identifications. As the authors of the study conclude, the media are "predominantly cosmopolitan and liberal. . . . Leading journalists criticize traditional social norms and establishment groups; they are very liberal on social issues such as abortion, homosexual rights, affirmative action, and environmental protection. Many endorse an expanded welfare state, but they also emerge as strong supporters of the free enterprise system."[4] A recent study of American journalists confirms the liberal and Democratic Party preferences of news people. According to Weaver and Wilhoit, 47 percent of journalists were liberal, 30 percent were moderates, and 22 percent were conservative.[5]

Other studies, however, raise doubts about the presumed liberal inclinations of journalists. A 1998 study of Washington-based journalists indicated that most journalists consider their political orientation "centrist" (moderate). As the author of the report states, "Of the minority who do not identify with the center, most have left leanings concerning social issues and right leanings concerning economic ones. This is consistent with a long history of research on profit-sector professionals in general. High levels of education tend to be associated with liberal views on social issues such as racial equality, gay rights, gun control and abortion rights. High levels of income tend to be associated with conservative views on economic issues such as tax policy and federal spending."[6] More important to our analysis are the results of a 1992 study of prominent journalists in the 50 states, which included journalists from every medium. According to that study, a majority of journalists in the South, which includes Texas, consider themselves Democrats (68 percent). Ideologically, the greatest percentage of journalists is moderate, with a small percentage of liberals and even fewer conservatives.[7]

Also guiding the selection and presentation of the news is the **journalists' creed,** whose main components are independence, objectivity, and balance. Independence requires that journalists remain free from political commitments and "outside" pressures, which include public officials, political activists, and the news organization, which has its own economic and political interests. Thus, reporters are expected not to become too friendly with politicians or others who have a stake in the results of the political process. Objectivity means that the journalist's role is to present the facts, free from judgment and opinion. Reporters should not allow their personal views or preferences on public policies to affect their reporting of an event. Finally, the news should provide impartial coverage of controversial topics, presenting the positions of all sides, without bias or favoritism.[8] Contemporary reporters and correspondents do not seek to interpret events and advocate specific public policies. In fact, to maintain the credibility of the news, journalists must promote the professional values of objectivity and detachment, the disregard of implications, and the rejection of ideology.

Journalists believe that they maintain objectivity in the news by focusing on gathering facts and by remaining detached from any personal concern for the effects of their story. They do not choose their coverage based on who gets hurt and who does not. Journalists maintain that their coverage of events is dictated by the criteria for news, especially timeliness, conflict, and proximity. Thus, a story about "welfare cheats" is reported because it is newsworthy, not because of the reporter's personal views about welfare recipients. When forced to admit that the decision to cover certain events and not others has consequences, journalists are comforted by their intentions of fairness. The value of fairness was supported by legal obligations placed on the broadcast media by the fairness doctrine (until 1987) and by news producers and editors. To protect themselves from charges of political or partisan bias, media personnel also tend to reject ideology, maintaining that they do not have a consistent set of attitudes or beliefs about politics and government (see Chapter 2).[9]

How can we reconcile the apparent contradiction between the tendency for journalists, in their personal views, to be Democrats and the requirement of the journalists' creed for objectivity? Journalists, like most people who occupy conflicting roles, separate their behaviors according to the different roles that they occupy. For example, a political scientist who is a conservative and a Republican separates her or his role as a private citizen who is active in politics from her or his role as a researcher and teacher. Likewise, journalists who possess political preferences separate their behavior as political participants from their behavior as professional journalists. To the extent that contemporary journalistic standards support the journalists' creed, the journalist will attempt to avoid slanting his or her reporting toward his or her political preferences. With the adoption of the game schema of politics, which we explain later in this chapter, journalists currently seem less likely to support the journalists' creed.

The Economics of the News

Finally, presenting the news is a business. The desire to make a profit requires a newspaper to expand its circulation and a television station to increase its ratings, thereby increasing its advertising revenues. As a private enterprise, the bottom line on the ledger sheet is important. This desire for greater circulation and higher ratings, according to many observers, drives the selection of news stories and the presentation of the news. To hold the viewer's or reader's interest, a news story must meet several criteria. First, it should be a "story," incorporating the attributes of drama. Thus, a news story, especially for television and to a lesser extent for newspapers, must "have structure and conflict, problem and denouement, rising action and falling action, a beginning, middle, and end."[10] For example, Paul Burka's story about Ann Richards constitutes a drama, showing how she became involved in politics to change government and how it operated but found that she was unable to make many of those changes. The conflict involved an internal struggle between Ann Richards the "idealist," who believed that government could change peoples' lives, and Ann Richards the "realist," who recognized that government was difficult to change.

Second, news is novel and current. News must, by definition, be "new" and "different." This requires that once a topic, such as candidates' positions on relevant issues, has been covered, the media should not revisit the topic unless something dramatic and different occurs, such as a candidate changing his or her position on an issue. A major consequence of this economic criterion is that the news, especially on television, lacks context. Events are reported as isolated and independent stories without background or a history. Critics of contemporary news find that this tendency in reporting produces disjointed and less meaningful news.

A third economic criterion involves "conflict, violence, disaster, and scandal; in sum, humans in circumstances or interactions that are dramatic and which involve trouble."[11] To hold the public's attention, the news must be sensational and entertaining, not dull and boring. This criterion also reflects the personal values of news personnel. Whether these criteria are valid is debatable; however, for the people who select the stories that make up the news, these criteria are important.

As we have seen, several factors shape the content and presentation of the news. Our next consideration is the kinds of news media available in Texas.

> **Critical Thinking Exercise:**   Which of the factors shaping the news has the greatest impact, in your opinion? Why is this factor the most important? What factor should be most important?

THE MEDIA IN TEXAS

Given its current geographic size, its historical experience, and its diverse population, Texas media could be expected to be large, independent, and diverse. Indeed, that appears to be the case. In fact, Texas newspapers may have adopted the modern journalistic practices of objectivity and fairness much earlier than most newspapers. During two nineteenth-century crises, Texas newspapers displayed an unusual, for the time, diversity and fairness in their presentation of events and issues.

During the 1830s, as Texas moved toward revolution against Mexico, Texas newspapers provided a fairly balanced coverage of issues during the revolutionary period. As the author of one study notes, "Some issues received more balanced treatment than others, and some newspapers may have been more balanced than others, but Texas journalism during the period did provide a measure of diversity."[12] Later in the century, as New York journalists advocated United

States military action against Spain after the sinking of the *Maine* in Havana harbor, Texas journalists initially counseled caution and attacked the "yellow journals" of New York. Later, as new evidence accumulated, Texas newspapers shifted to support United States intervention. However, the shift occurred only after the newspapers had received independent reports from sources they considered reliable.[13]

How big are the media? In 1998, the media in Texas comprised 607 newspapers, including 76 daily papers; 485 radio stations, with slightly more FM than AM stations; 99 television stations; and 96 cable systems.

According to a *Texas Poll Report* in 1986, a majority of Texans received most of their national news (73 percent) and local news (53 percent) from television. Newspapers, the second most popular source, were cited by about one-third of Texans for local news (34 percent) but only by about one in six Texans (18 percent) for national news.[14] Also, a 1994 *Texas Poll Report* indicated that television is the most trusted source for news, leading newspapers 73 percent to 68 percent.[15] We describe and analyze the media in Texas in terms of Texans' preferences for news sources.

Television

With nearly 100 television stations spanning 19 media markets, Texas provides more diverse viewing opportunities for its residents than do most states. However, what constitutes a good local news program, what does local news cover, and how can local news be improved? According to a group of television professionals, a quality local news program covers the community, selects significant events, provides important information, provides depth and context in its stories, relies on many authoritative sources, provides a balance of viewpoints, and has local relevance. How well does local television news generally and particularly in Texas meet these criteria?

In 1994, Rocky Mountain Media Watch (RMMW) began an annual evaluation of local TV newscasts in the United States on a particular date. The 1995 study revealed that 42 percent of the actual news component of local TV news broadcasts were stories about crime, disaster, and war. Also, the average time for actual news on local 30-minutes shows was approximately 12 minutes. The study also found that large cities covered more violence (47 percent) than medium-sized cities (45 percent) and much more than small cities (27 percent).[16] In 1998, the Project for Excellence in Journalism, which is affiliated with the Columbia University Graduate School of Journalism, began a three-year study of local news in selected cities throughout the United States. They discovered that most local newscasts are far from excellent. The typical local newscast is very local, covering the commonplace events and about equally divided between such everyday incidents as accidents and power outages (24 percent) and everyday crime (22 percent). The average story is short; nearly half (43 percent) were 30 seconds or shorter. Stories don't use a large number of sources, and many stories had no source at all. Also, in coverage of controversial topics, 43 percent of the stories gave only one side. In short, the study stated, " . . . local TV in general does not do basic things well: sourcing, getting both sides of the story, and thinking ahead."[17]

In the 1998 study by Rocky Mountain Media Watch, an Austin television station, KVUE, was selected as one of only four stations in the nation "whose newscasts stand out for quality, intelligence and creativity." According to RMMW, KVUE was noted because coverage of crime is restricted to incidents that have a significant impact on the community, a policy initiated in 1996 by then News Director Carole Kneeland. RMMW also praised KVUE for a story that reported residents' views on downtown growth and bond issues.[18] In the 1999 Project for Excellence in Journalism study, four Dallas local news stations were evaluated. Two of the stations received a rating of B (KTVT and KXAS), one a C (WFAA), and one a D (KDFW), with quality scores ranging from 315 to 377. According to most news directors, the biggest obstacle to quality is a lack of staff (cited by 77 percent). The lack of staffing is tied to profit expectations of local newscasts, which average around 40 percent.[19]

Cable systems have also entered the local news markets, attempting to gain a share of the lucrative business. Local news-on-cable stations provided more news, less advertising, and less violent content and triviality than most over-the-air local news stations. In 1999, Texas Cable News began a 24-hour state and local news station in Dallas, utilizing the news gathering capacity of A. H. Belo's Dallas Morning News and its affiliated television stations in Dallas, Houston, and San Antonio. A study by RMMW in 1999 indicated that a typical broadcast cycle contained approximately 40 percent news, 19 percent weather, and 19 percent commercials. The leading news topics were crime (37 percent) and government

Texas Cable News began a 24-hour state and local news-on-cable station in 1999.

(27 percent).[20] In 1999, News 8 Austin began local news, weather, and sports programming for Time-Warner Cable subscribers in the Austin area.

Newspapers

In 1998, of the 100 largest daily newspapers in circulation in the United States, Texas could claim five: the *Dallas Morning News* (eighth), the *Houston Chronicle* (ninth), the *San Antonio Express-News* (thirty-eighth), the *Fort Worth Star-Telegram* (fortieth), and the *Austin American-Statesman* (fifty-seventh). In a 1999 survey of newspaper editors, two Texas newspapers ranked among America's best newspapers: the *Dallas Morning News* ranked fifth, and the *Austin American-Statesman* was cited among five newspapers to watch.[21]

Despite the fact that Texas, among the 50 states, had the third largest number of newspapers among the top 100, the number of large Texas cities served by two daily newspapers shrank during the 1990s. In 1991, the *Dallas Times Herald* closed, followed in 1993 by the *San Antonio Light*. The *Houston Post*, citing mounting costs and decreasing circulation, closed its doors in 1995, and in 1997, the *El Paso Herald Post* ceased publication, leaving all major cities in Texas with just one newspaper each. These newspaper closings raise questions about diversity in news content and fairness in news coverage in large urban areas. Even before the trend toward one newspaper in large metropolitan cities, there was another trend of comparable importance—a decline in the number of locally owned newspapers. During the 1970s and 1980s, ownership of Texas newspapers, mirroring a national trend, shifted toward national media conglomerates. In 1970, the Times Mirror Corporation purchased the *Dallas Times Herald*. The ensuing competition between the *Dallas Times Herald* and the *Dallas Morning News* allegedly improved both newspapers. However, when the *Dallas Times Herald* was unable to sustain a profit during the economic recession of the early 1980s, Times Mirror sold the newspaper in 1986, and it eventually ceased publication. This concentration of newspaper ownership has raised questions about the quality and independence of decisions about the news. If profit is the newspaper's primary goal, do editors feel compelled to sacrifice journalistic ideals and judgments for corporate profits and increased circulation? Does the concentration of ownership homogenize the news and decrease diversity? In early 1995, two respected editors of the *Des Moines Register*, which was once considered one of the nation's best newspapers, resigned because they felt that the Gannett Company, the paper's owner, was more interested in profits than in the newspaper's quality.[22] In Texas, the Hearst Corporation owns six daily newspapers, including the *Houston Chronicle*, the *San Antonio Express-News*, the *Beaumont Enterprise*, the *Midland Reporter-Telegram*, the *Plainview Daily Herald*, and the *Laredo Morning Times*, which is the most extensive ownership of newspapers in Texas. These six newspapers have a combined circulation of over 1 million copies daily in almost every geographic area of the state. Cox Newspapers also owns six papers, but they are all located in East or Central Texas, and their combined circulation falls short of Hearst's six papers. With the demise of the *Houston Post*, the *Dallas Morning News* is the only newspaper in

Table 6.1   DAILY NEWSPAPER CIRCULATION IN TEXAS, 1985–1998

Newspaper	1985	1998	Change
Houston Chronicle	441,557	553,387	25.3 %
Houston Post	326,556	Closed	N/A
Dallas Morning News	360,347	521,162	44.6 %
Dallas Times Herald	270,622	Closed	N/A
Ft. Worth Star-Telegram	248,627	240,139	–3.4 %
San Antonio Express-News	174,558	218,661	25.3 %
San Antonio Light	140,116	Closed	N/A
Austin American-Statesman	160,526	187,593	16.7 %
El Paso Times	57,062	78,800	38.1 %
El Paso Herald Post	32,471	Closed	N/A
Total	**2,212,482**	**1,799,742**	**–18.7 %**

Source: Comptroller of Public Accounts, *Fiscal Notes* (September 1995): 12; *'99 Directory of Texas Daily Newspapers* (Austin, Tex.: Texas Daily Newspaper Association, 1999).

Texas's largest cities owned by a Texas-based corporation—the A. H. Belo Corporation, which also owns two other Texas newspapers.

The declining circulation among daily newspapers in Texas during the past decade constitutes a third significant trend. Between 1985 and 1995, daily circulation statewide in Texas fell from 3.6 million to 3.3 million. As Texas's population grew during that decade, the number of newspaper subscriptions fell from 220 to 178 subscriptions per 1000 residents.[23] Recent circulation reports show a continuation of the downward trend for newspapers (Table 6.1).

Radio

Less than 10 percent of Texans identify radio as their primary source of political news. However, given the size of the state and the limited use of mass transit in most Texas cities, most Texans spend a lot of time in their automobiles, frequently listening to their car's radio. Increasingly, radio stations have been adopting a talk radio format, allowing callers to comment on politics. Many of the hosts of talk radio—for example, Rush Limbaugh and former Texas Agriculture Commissioner Jim Hightower—have consistent ideological slants in their broadcasts.

Magazines

Although magazines are the principal source of news about politics for an extremely small percentage of Texans, they are still very influential. Magazines, because of the nature of the publication, are more likely to influence opinions and appeal to those people who are more interested in politics and public affairs. Because their articles are longer than newspaper articles and because they are published less frequently than newspapers, magazines tend to be more analytical and interpretative than newspapers. However, with analysis and interpretation comes the ability to persuade, either explicitly or implicitly. As we noted at the beginning of this chapter, magazine articles can have significant political effects.

Texas Monthly, which began publication in 1973 and enjoys a circulation of more than 300,000, is probably the premier Texas magazine containing political analysis and interpretation. Although *Texas Monthly* is probably best known for its biennial selection of Texas's 10 best and 10 worst legislators after each regular legislative session, it frequently contains major articles devoted to public affairs and politics.

Older than *Texas Monthly* but with a much smaller circulation, the *Texas Observer* has provided an independent voice for progressives since the mid-1950s. The *Texas Observer* is also more openly opinionated than the *Texas Monthly*. Over the years, the *Texas Observer* has featured many writers who have gained prominence nationally, as well as in Texas.

Internet

The Internet is a network of computers that offers a variety of services, such as World Wide Web (WWW) access, and e-mail through computer servers. In 1998, a survey of national, state, and local campaigns revealed that 63 percent used the Internet, primarily to provide information to potential voters about their candidacies and their positions on policy issues. Other uses included communicating with supporters, recruiting campaign volunteers, raising campaign contributions, and providing election information (polling places, election dates, voter registration, and absentee voting).[24] According to a 1995 report, Texas emerged as a leader in providing computer access to government information, providing more bulletin board systems and Internet sites than any other state government.[25]

There is little doubt that Texans are offered many diverse sources for political information. What kinds of political effects do these media have?

Critical Thinking Exercise: Considering the source of political information that is most important to you, are you satisfied with the information that you receive? How could the media provide more and better information?

THE POLITICAL EFFECTS OF THE MEDIA

In this section, we describe and analyze four kinds of media effects: (1) influencing which political events and issues people think about, (2) what people think about those events that receive media coverage, (3) how people organize their thinking about politics and political issues, and (4) what people feel about politics, politicians, and political participation. We begin with those effects that have the strongest research support and conclude with those effects that, though important, are less well substantiated by research. The effects that most political scientists currently attribute to the media have only been recognized within the past few decades. After World War II, as mass communications, and especially television, became a more pervasive component of political campaigns, scholars began to investigate the effects of attempts to use mass communication to persuade the public. These initial studies indicated minimal effects or consequences, leading political scientists to discount the effects of campaign messages on the public's views and electoral choices.[26] Most political scientists now believe that the media have very important effects on the public and the political process.[27]

What People Think About

The media effect that receives the greatest research support involves "setting the agenda" for politics. As Bernard Cohen, who originally developed the **agenda-setting hypothesis,** noted, "It [the press] may not be successful in telling its readers what to think, but it is stunningly successful in telling its readers what to think about."[28] Thus, the media can influence the public agenda (those issues and events that the public considers important) and the political agenda (those issues that government officials choose to address) through its coverage of events. If the media decide to cover an event, then it must be important. If a story receives front-page coverage and a banner headline, it signals a very important event or, at least, the most important event of that day. The lead story serves the same purpose for television news. Thus, the daily decisions of editors and news directors establish a set of political priorities for the public and for public officials.

The agenda-setting process is cogently described by Doris Graber: "We look at the front page of the newspaper and expect to find the most important stories there. We may watch the opening minutes of a telecast eagerly and then allow our attention to slacken. . . . When the media make events seem important, politicians are likely to comment about them and to take action. This enhances the perceived importance of these events and ensures even more public attention."[29] On the other hand, is it not possible, as some news people claim, that the media are, in their decisions to cover certain events and issues, merely responding to the public's *existing* agenda rather than *setting* the agenda? Studies of the causal relationship clearly indicate that the media set the agenda.[30] A classic example involved the famine in Ethiopia, which had been largely ignored by the media until late 1984, but which became a major issue in the United States after NBC News aired stories on three successive evenings, showing starving Ethiopians massed at government feeding stations.

Perhaps the most sophisticated study of television agenda-setting was conducted during the 1980s. Employing an experimental design, Shanto Iyengar and Donald Kinder manipulated the news coverage given to certain issues to ascertain their effects. The research confirmed that the amount of coverage that issues receive significantly affects the importance that people attach to the issues. However, people with certain characteristics are less susceptible to the media's agenda-setting effects. For example, greater media influence is exercised on those people who are least knowledgeable about and involved in politics. As Iyengar and Kinder note, "Those who rarely get caught up in the world of politics find the network news presentations particularly compelling. Partisans, activists, close observers of the political scene, on the other hand, are less apt to be swept away. The more removed the viewer is from the world of public affairs, the stronger the agenda-setting power of television news."[31]

The media do have competition in setting the agenda. Aware of the media's importance in agenda setting, public officials and candidates attempt to influence the news agenda. During election campaigns, candidates attempt to make the news agenda reflect the agenda of their campaigns, and sometimes they are successful. For example, a study of the 1990 gubernatorial campaign in Texas demonstrated that the candidates' campaigns influenced the news agenda: "To a considerable degree, the news agenda of the Austin newspaper and the three local television newscasts . . . reflected the issue priorities of the candidates."[32]

If the media can tell people what to think about, could they also tell people what to think?

What People Think

The media's influence on politics would be enormous if it spoke with one voice and could dictate our political attitudes and beliefs, but most political scientists doubt the ability of the media to do this. However, this is a question that sparks a great deal of controversy, especially between liberals and conservatives. Most political scientists feel that media influence on the public's judgments and preferences touches on three areas: priming, framing, and opinion change.

Priming **Priming** refers to "the capacity of the media to isolate particular issues, events, or themes in the news as criteria for evaluating politicians."[33] In their studies of priming and politicians, Iyengar and Kinder concluded that media coverage influences our judgments of politicians, especially when media coverage connects a politician's policies with particular policy results. For example, if media coverage focuses on crime in Texas and connects the policies of the incumbent governor with the level of crime in Texas, then crime will become a criterion on which the public will judge the governor's performance. Obviously, a politician can gain or lose support because of priming. If the crime rate has decreased, then the governor is evaluated positively; however, if the crime rate increases, the governor suffers. For Governor Mark White (1983–1987), the priming effect meant that his administration was evaluated on the basis of two issues: (1)educational reforms, which included "no pass, no play" and the testing of public school teachers, and (2) tax increases that were necessitated by the sudden drop in oil prices in 1983. In the 1986 gubernatorial election, White lost his reelection bid (see Chapter 7).

In essence, priming is an extension of the agenda-setting function of the media. However, studies of priming effects indicate that the agenda also affects what people think.[34]

Framing   **Framing** refers to "subtle alterations in the statement or presentation of judgment and choice problems, and 'framing effects' refers to changes in decision outcomes resulting from these alterations."[35] In other words, how a news story is told affects to whom or to what we attribute responsibility for social and political problems. For most news stories, the frame is either **episodic,** which involves a focus on particular events and provides concrete examples, or **thematic,** which places public issues in a general or abstract context and provides general outcomes or conditions. For example, an episodically framed story on public welfare might relate the personal, daily experiences of a welfare mother of three children, who is a high school dropout. In contrast, a thematically framed story on public welfare might report a decline in spending on government programs to educate welfare recipients so that they can qualify for well-paying jobs.

An important question in politics concerns responsibility: Why did something happen, and what can be done in the future, either to encourage (if the event was positive) or discourage (if negative) its repetition? The media's choice of a frame for a story affects the public's assignment of responsibility for events and social conditions. The public's assignment of responsibility involves both "causal responsibility" (why something happens) and "treatment responsibility" (who should do something about the problem). If the predominant frame for a story is episodic, then causal and treatment responsibility tends to be placed on the individual, such as the welfare recipient. Conversely, the thematic frame places responsibility on society and social conditions, such as inadequate opportunities for education and jobs.

Framing has several political implications. First, it has important policy implications. If the media's framing of crime and poverty issues is episodic, then policies that enhance personal and individual responsibility will be supported. On the other hand, the thematic framing of those issues would create support for policies that recognize the role of social conditions in causing and in reducing crime and poverty.

Second, framing affects the likelihood that the public will recognize the interconnections among issues. Television, a visual medium, tends to favor the episodic frame more than newspapers, a print medium. The use of the episodic frame leads the public to view issues and events as discrete and independent. Consequently, although such social problems as poverty, racial inequality, and crime are interrelated in cause and treatment, the public tends to compartmentalize these issues, discouraging the development of more abstract and general conceptualizations.

Third, framing reduces governmental accountability. When complex social and economic issues are presented in anecdotal form, the media lead the public to assign the responsibility for social conditions to individuals who are affected, thereby shielding government officials and society from causal and treatment responsibility.[36]

So far, we have indicated how the media affect the public through priming and framing, which are consequences of the news process. Next, we turn our attention to the effects of news people on our opinions.

Public Opinion Change   In their examination of **public opinion change** over 50 years, Benjamin Page and Robert Shapiro concluded that "the media themselves, and certain news sources whose statements and actions they report, have had strong effects on public opinion."[37] Although public opinion responds directly to events, for most people, those events are experienced through the news media. Thus, the authors wondered how public opinion responds to news sources and commentary reported in the media. In the study, 10 news sources were identified, and the effect that each source had on opinion change was calculated. News commentary (from news anchors, reporters, or special commentators) had the most dramatic impact on public opinion; a single commentary resulted in a four-percentage-point change in public opinion. Thus, a news commentary supporting a particular government policy, such as an increase in spending on education, increases the general public's support for that policy. Stories about experts or about research studies that favored a particular policy also had strong effects, increasing public support for the policy by approximately three percentage points.[38]

The direct persuasive effects of the media, such as those just described, depend on the characteristics of three factors: the source, the message, and the audience. The credibility or trustworthiness of the source affects its persuasive influence. In Texas, television is the most trusted source for news, making it more persuasive than newspapers, which are deemed less trustworthy.[39] Also, the properties of the message influence its persuasiveness, but the effects are complicated by the type of issue being presented and the characteristics of the audience. For example, argument-based messages are more effective on well-informed audiences; image-based messages are more effective on poorly informed audiences. The politically sophisticated are more likely to be influenced by substantive arguments relating to an issue than are the politically unsophisticated, who are more likely to be swayed by images. Finally, two audience characteristics have a significant impact on the effectiveness of direct persuasion—exposure to the message and acceptance of the message. Ironically, education, interest in politics, and partisanship—factors that make exposure to a persuasive message more likely—are also the factors that make acceptance of the message less likely. In other words, those people who are most likely to read an article about politics or government are also the people who are least likely to be persuaded by the article's presentation.[40]

Whether through priming, framing, or opinion change, there is convincing evidence that the media, in their presentation of the news, influence what people think. Nonetheless, there is a more subtle form of media influence on the public, which is important.

How People Think

According to social scientists, people employ schemas to process information about politics and government. A **schema** is a cognitive structure that people use to process new information and retrieve old information. Schemas help people cope with complexity by providing a framework for organizing and storing information.[41] Those schemas contain information that give people a notion of what is involved in politics and government: who are the participants; what are their goals; how do they accomplish those goals?

In 1993, a political scientist and media critic noted that the media have a dominant schema.[42] It is a product of the enduring values of the news media, which we described earlier in the chapter, and of the operational standards of professional journalism. According to this **journalistic schema** of politics:

> Politics is essentially a game played by individual politicians for personal advancement, gain, or power. The game is a competitive one, and the players' principal activities are those of calculating and pursuing strategies designed to defeat competitors and to achieve their goals. . . . Of course, the game takes place against a backdrop of governmental institutions, public problems, policy debates, and the like, but these are noteworthy only insofar as they affect, or are used by, the players in pursuit of the game's rewards. The game is played before an audience [the public] which controls most of the prizes, and players therefore constantly attempt to make a favorable impression. In consequence, there is an endemic tendency for players to exaggerate their good qualities and to minimize their bad ones, to be deceitful, to engage in hypocrisies, to manipulate appearances; though inevitable, these tendencies are bad tendencies according to the [schema] and should be exposed. They reduce the [public's] ability to make its own discriminating choices, and they hide players' infractions of the game's rules, such as those against corruption or lying.[43]

The public and politicians possess a schema of politics that differs from the game schema. The public's schema, termed the **governing schema,** focuses on politics not as a game, but as a morality play, with "good" pitted against "evil." The emphasis, therefore, is not on a strategy for winning, but on policy initiatives that will advance the common good, as defined by the politician or the public. According to one political scientist, the public, in thinking about politics, "actually do[es] reason about parties, candidates, and issues. They have premises, and they use those premises to make inferences from their observations of the world around them. They think about who and what political parties stand for; they think about the meaning of political endorsements; they think about what government can and should do. And the performance of government, parties, and candidates affects their assessments and preferences."[44] Unfortunately, what the public needs so that it can make choices among parties, candidates, and policy proposals either is not provided by the media or is provided in a format that does not mesh with the public's schema for processing information. The adoption of the game schema has also reduced the journalists' professional commitment to objectivity, making them less reluctant to interpret political events and politicians' behavior. The result is less descriptive reporting and more interpretive reporting by journalists. This transformation in reporting style makes it more difficult for candidates and politicians to present their views directly to the public, unhampered by media analysis and interpretation.[45]

The political effects of the journalistic or game schema include, at a minimum, making the public's search for information on which to make its assessments of government, parties, and candidates more difficult. Of greater consequence is the journalistic schema's tendency not only to divert attention away from policy issues and outcomes and toward strategies, but also to make policy questions less important and to increase the significance of the strategic moves. Because the media focus their attention on the strategies of groups or politicians to achieve policy goals, rather than on the policy goals themselves, the public is led to believe that political strategy is more important to politics than are political goals. Furthermore, the emphasis on strategy encourages the public to evaluate politicians in terms of the success of their strategies rather than on the worthiness of their policy goals. Perhaps the greatest consequence involves the possible replacement of the public's governing schema with the journalists' game schema, thereby changing not only how people think about politics but also how they feel about politics and politicians and how people react to them, thereby transforming people from political participants to political spectators and cynics.[46]

How People Feel

The public, in a democracy, is expected to possess an interest in politics. Although other subjects hold more interest and have a greater impact on their daily lives, people should be drawn to participate in politics and political controversy, even if only episodically. However, as we note in Chapter 7, few Texans are active in politics. To what extent are the media, especially television, responsible for this apathy?

In a 1994 book, a professor of communications and politics asserted that television's effect on politics reaches far beyond what we have discussed thus far in this chapter. Television, and our reliance on it for political information, has changed the way we *feel* about politics:

> Something larger and more subtle is happening to the American people because of their media habits. Television . . . now tells us how to feel about politics, producing in us a postmodern swagger: We tower above politics by making it seem beneath us. Television produces . . . a "structure of feeling" about politics, a complex of emotions that lies deeper than our individual attitudes about political parties or social issues or political referenda. During the last fifty years, this structure of feeling has made the burdens of citizenship increasingly taxing for us, and it is . . . responsible for much of the alienation we now feel.[47]

Politics, as experienced through television, offers viewers a trade-off. There are five feelings that make us, as humans, uncomfortable: detachment, ignorance, obsolescence, inertness, and impotence. Through our reliance on television, which promotes some emotions and inhibits others, we cut ourselves off from genuine political involvement. Television, through its emotional repertoire, offers us intimacy with politicians without offering us involvement; makes us feel informed while deflecting political involvement because we "know" everything; makes us feel clever about politics, thus immunizing us from participation; makes us feel busy, transforming the observation of politics into a perception of engaging in politics, thereby making real political participation superfluous; and finally, makes us feel important by creating a televised rhetorical establishment, which seems to act on our behalf, making participation unnecessary.[48]

A more recent study of the effects of reporters' use of the game schema concludes that an increase in public cynicism is the principal result. By focusing on the strategies of politicians rather than their substantive policies, the media activate public cynicism about politicians, political processes, and governance. A byproduct is increasing public cynicism about the media.[49] The important point is that all of these feelings of alienation and cynicism reduce the public's willingness to make a real connection to politics and to become better informed about politics and government. As we reveal in Chapter 7, a psychological connection to politics is important in explaining political participation, especially voting.

Having described and analyzed the effects of the media, we still need to consider in greater detail a related aspect of political communications: public opinion.

> **Critical Thinking Exercise:** Which media effect is most important? What are the consequences of this effect? Are these media effects exaggerated or understated?

PUBLIC OPINION

We have noted, in Chapter 2 and in the preceding section of this chapter, how people develop political opinions and attitudes during the socialization process. However, to make an impact on public policy, the public's concerns and preferences must come to the attention of public officials. The public's attitudes and opinions are communicated as **public opinion**—the evaluations of a large number of people on an issue of public policy. Before we describe and analyze public opinion in Texas, we describe how public opinion is measured.

The Measurement of Public Opinion

Sometime during your life, you have probably been asked your opinion about something for a public opinion poll. Your response was probably tabulated, combined with the responses of others, and analyzed to answer whatever questions were being raised in the opinion survey. Opinion surveys are conducted for a variety of reasons, including to determine how people feel about political issues. These public opinion polls are used to inform decision-makers and interested activists and can be used to make political decisions, as we show in our discussion of contemporary political campaigns in the next chapter. Now, however, our concern is with the methodology and evaluation of polls.

The Methodology of Polls   To discover the actual opinion of a public (a large group of people) on a particular issue of public policy, we would have to question everyone in the public. Because this is nearly impossible, both physically and economically, we estimate the public's opinion based on the opinions of a selected group, a **sample,** of those people in whose opinion we are interested. Statistical theory tells us the amount of **sampling error**—the chance-based difference between the

An interviewer collects data for a public-opinion poll, using an Apple Newton.

actual opinion of the total population and the opinion estimate based on the population sample—associated with a **random sample.** To be random, a sample must provide each member of the public that we are sampling an equal chance of being included in the sample. Generally, the larger the size of the sample, the smaller the sampling error. However, because the relationship is not linear, after a certain point, increasing the sample size has a modest effect on the size of the sampling error. Consequently, most samples for large publics are in the 1000 to 1500 range, establishing a sampling error of ±4 or ±3 percent. Selecting a random sample of 1000, consequently, ensures that the results of the sample will vary from the results of the public, if every member had been questioned, by no more than ±4 percent. This level of confidence is adequate for most public opinion surveys.

The Evaluation of Polls   Errors in public opinion polls can result from sources other than the size and selection of the sample, so questionnaires must be carefully constructed and administered. The order and the wording of questions in a poll can influence the results. Biased questions can lead to biased results. Therefore, the questions, as well as the results, should be studied in assessing opinion surveys. Furthermore, the administration of the poll, such as who is asking the questions and how, can influence the responses of the public. We know that certain characteristics of the person administering a questionnaire can influence a person's responses. Also, personal interviews are more likely than telephone interviews to elicit valid results. These problems should be considered when evaluating the results of public opinion polls.

Public Opinion in Texas

For nearly two decades (since 1984), the *Texas Poll* has been reporting the opinions of Texans on a variety of issues of public policy. What do these polls tell us about Texans and their policy preferences? For instance, is Texas really a conservative state politically?[50]

We have chosen several public policy issues—affirmative action, funding for public education, making English the official language, teaching creationism in public schools, flag burning, and abortion—that have been reported, some of them repeatedly, in the *Texas Poll* since 1984. We have chosen these issues because they relate to the two dimensions—individualism versus equality, and ordered liberty versus individualism—that are the bases for political ideologies in contemporary Texas (Chapter 2). In Figure 2.2, we demonstrated how an individual's policy preferences on these two dimensions resulted in four political ideologies: liberal, conservative, libertarian, and populist. What do the polls indicate about Texans' policy preferences?

Affirmative Action Affirmative action involves giving preferences in hiring and promotion decisions to certain categories of people, such as women and ethnic minorities, to redress the effects of past discrimination. In 1988, the *Texas Poll* indicated that 69 percent of Texans opposed emphasizing minority hiring in state agencies, and 72 percent opposed emphasizing it in private businesses.[51] In 1995, the *Texas Poll* reported that only 52 percent of Texans indicated that affirmative-action policies should be ended.[52] Although both polls indicate that Texans oppose government policies to ensure greater equality for minorities, the opposition has decreased significantly in the eight years between the polls.

Funding for Public Education In 1988, the *Texas Poll* indicated that a plurality of Texans (40 percent) considered the current system of funding for public education fair; 32 percent considered it unfair; and 28 percent stated that they did not know whether it was fair. Interestingly, in the same survey, a plurality of Texans (45 percent) indicated that the current system of funding was inadequate, and only 29 percent stated that they considered the current system adequate (see Chapter 14).[53]

English as an Official Language In 1987, the legislature considered a proposal to make English the official language of Texas. The *Texas Poll* reported that 74 percent of Texans favored the legislation.[54]

Religion in Public Schools   In 1987, the *Texas Poll* reported that 70 percent of Texans felt that the biblical account of creation should be taught, along with evolution, in public schools.[55] In 1999, the *Scripps Howard Texas Poll* reported that 76 percent of Texans favored allowing teachers to post the Ten Commandments in public school classrooms.[56]

Flag Burning   In 1989, the *Texas Poll* reported that 67 percent of Texans disagreed with the statement that a constitutional amendment that prohibited burning the American flag would limit a person's constitutional right to freedom of speech.[57]

Abortion   In 1989, the *Texas Poll* asked Texans whether government restrictions on access to abortions interfere with a woman's right to make a personal moral decision. Sixty-seven percent of Texans indicated that it would. Also, only 38 percent of Texans thought that the legislature should decide the circumstances, if any, under which an abortion should be legal.[58] Later in 1989, the *Texas Poll* asked Texans whether abortion should be legal under at least some conditions. Sixty-three percent indicated that it should, and only 16 percent would prohibit abortions. These results were nearly identical to the results reported in the Spring 1984 *Texas Poll*.[59] However, in 1997, 41 percent of Texans thought that abortion should be illegal.[60] Similarly, in 1999, 80 percent of Texans favored a state law requiring parental notification before minors could receive an abortion, and 72 percent favored a state law requiring parental consent before minors could receive an abortion. Furthermore, 77 percent of Texans favored a 72-hour waiting period for an abortion after a physician has provided a woman with information about possible medical complications.[61]

Interpretation of Polls   How should we interpret the results of these polls? First, do the responses indicate that most Texans are conservative? Two of the issues—affirmative action and funding for public education—indicate whether Texans want government to adopt policies that ensure greater equality. The results indicate that a majority of Texans feel that hiring decisions should be a matter of individual choice, rather than government policy. Also, funding for public education was considered fair by a majority of Texans who had an opinion on the issue. Consequently, at least on these issues, if given a choice between greater equality and individual freedom, most Texans would choose individual freedom. The remaining four issues—English language, religion in public schools, flag burning, and abortion—involve a conflict between social order and individual freedom. On all four issues, a substantial majority of Texans chose social order in the most recent polls.

   Although it is impossible, based on these polls, to determine with a great deal of certainty the ideological preferences of Texans, we believe that they do demonstrate Texans' preferences for less government and more individual freedom on questions that involve government's attempt to ensure greater social or economic equality. When the issue is preservation of traditional values (social order) or personal freedom, Texans favor government policies to maintain the social order. Thus, a majority of Texans have conservative ideological tendencies.

Critical Thinking Exercise: What effect should public opinion have on public policy? Are politicians reflecting public opinion in their choices of public policy or do politicians lead the public to adopt the opinions that support their public policy choices? What evidence supports your view?

THE MEDIA, PUBLIC OPINION, AND POLITICAL CHANGE

In a democracy, we assume that public preferences will influence public policy. If public opinion changes, the media and politicians should reflect those changes, both in terms of what the media report and in what politicians support. Although we do not expect the relationship to be perfect, the public should exercise considerable influence on the direction that public policy takes. Is that the case in Texas?

From our examination of issues of public policy, we can conclude that, at least on these issues and when Texas is not compelled by federal mandates (see Chapter 3), government policy fairly accurately reflects the preferences of most Texans. We are aware, of course, that many factors other than public opinion drive public policy, as we demonstrate in subsequent chapters.

In our analysis of political change, periods of creedal passion accompany a perceived gap between the political ideals and political institutions. This requires that the information received by the public indicates how the institutions of government are performing so that their achievement of the ideals can be assessed. As we have indicated, news coverage focuses more on personalities and concrete events than on institutions and abstract concepts. However, the values of the news do promote revelations of public corruption and institutional arrogance. In both the Sharpstown scandal (Chapter 8) and the populist revolt (Chapter 4), the news media played a substantial role in investigating and reporting dishonesty and inequities. However, the media's penchant for the dramatic, unusual, and sensational may also drive periods of cynicism and public withdrawal, making the development of democracy more difficult.

THE MEDIA, PUBLIC OPINION, AND DEMOCRACY

We have already implied that the media have effects that relate to democracy. In this section, we make those effects explicit. We also demonstrate the relationship between public opinion and the conditions and forms of democracy.

The conditions for democracy place several requirements on the mass media. First, political equality requires that access to information about issues of public policy and candidates for public office be available to everyone, regardless of social or economic status. Also, the sources of information must not either be controlled by any one group or promote only one side of an issue. Perhaps most important, deliberation requires a meaningful discussion of political issues. This necessitates that all relevant information concerning the candidates and issues be available and that the information be in a useful and relevant form. Do the media meet these requirements?

In Texas, as we have noted, plentiful and diverse media sources are available, regardless of a person's socioeconomic status. However, the news process does not provide information in a format that encourages or enhances deliberation. The journalistic or game schema portrays politics cynically, focusing on strategies of politicians and political activists, rather than on policies and their possible effects. Similarly, the media's penchant for personalities and human interest stories provides us with information about the personal lives of candidates and politicians, but not with information about their political experience and competence in governing. Furthermore, rather than promoting deliberation, the medium on which most Texans rely for the political information isolates people and inhibits the exchange of ideas. In addition, television gives people a false sense of political knowledge and involvement without the passion and dedication that real political involvement requires. Public opinion polls become less meaningful, therefore, because they represent an expression of preferences that gives equal value to thoughtful, meaningful opinions and to spontaneous, visceral responses.

The media also have consequences for the models of democracy. Majoritarian democracy depends on an educated, thoughtful, and involved citizenry. To the extent that the media provide irrelevant political information, discourage critical thought, and induce apathy, they inhibit rather than promote majoritarian democracy. There is little evidence to suggest that Texans are unable to process meaningful and substantive political information; however, the news product does little to facilitate the population's formulation of political preferences based on such information. Consequently, the media in Texas do not facilitate the development of majoritarian democracy.

Although the requirements for political information and individual political involvement in a pluralist democracy are less stringent, the media are still obliged to provide relevant and meaningful information. The media in Texas do not enhance pluralist democracy either; in fact, their focus on special interests and political corruption raises questions about the ability and desire of group leaders to adequately represent their members.

We are not, of course, advocating that the media become a cheerleader for the government and politicians. A healthy skepticism by individuals is essential to democracy. However, if a democratic government is the public's desire, then the media have an obligation both to provide the information that people need to participate in decisions and to do so in a format that facilitates its use. The media also have an obligation to encourage participation and political involvement.

Critical Thinking Exercise: Is the evaluation of the media's role in promoting democracy too harsh? Do the media deserve more credit for the quantity and quality of information that they provide? What would improve the media's evaluation?

SUMMARY

In this chapter, we have described the political role of the media, which is, in essence, to provide Texans with the information necessary to perform their responsibilities as citizens in a democracy. This means that the media should report events accurately and should provide the information about issues and politicians that is necessary for citizens to make decisions on issues of public policy and on choices among candidates for public office.

We have described the factors that influence the news process, indicating how media coverage of events is affected by personal characteristics of news people, the journalists' creed, and organizational goals.

We noted that the media in Texas are large, independent, and diverse. Also, we described how, in covering two important crises in the nineteenth century, newspapers in Texas displayed many characteristics of contemporary journalism. We also described Texans' preferences for news sources and the various media that blanket the state.

In analyzing the political effects of the media, we contended that the media influence what we think about, what we think, how we think, and how we feel. Thus, the media's influence extends beyond setting the agenda, producing more subtle effects.

We described public opinion, indicating the collection of public opinions through public opinion polls, and some ways that Texans can evaluate public opinion polls and their results. We also presented survey results from various Texas polls, in an attempt to ascertain Texans' ideological tendencies.

Finally, we noted how the media and public opinion affect political change and assessed the relationship between the media and public opinion and democracy in Texas.

KEY TERMS

symbiotic
journalists' creed
agenda-setting hypothesis
priming
framing
episodic frame
thematic frame
public opinion change

schema
journalistic schema
governing schema
public opinion
sample
sampling error
random sample

SUGGESTED READINGS

Ansolabehere, Stephen, Roy Behr, and Shanto Iyengar. *The Media Game: American Politics in the Television Age.* New York: Macmillan, 1993.
Beyle, Thad. "State News Media Structures," *Comparative State Politics* 19, no. 3 (1998): 1–44.

Capella, Joseph N., and Kathleen Hall Jamieson. *Spiral of Cynicism: The Press and the Public Good.* New York: Oxford University Press, 1997.

Graber, Doris A. *Mass Media and American Politics,* 4th ed. Washington, D.C.: Congressional Quarterly Press, 1993.

Harmon, Mark, and Bruce Pinkleton. "Broadcast News as a Source of Political Information: Shrinking Sound Bites Revisited," *Texas Journal of Political Studies* 20, no. 1 (1998): 1–16.

Hart, Roderick P. *Seducing America: How Television Charms the Modern Voter.* New York: Oxford University Press, 1994.

Iyengar, Shanto. *Is Anyone Responsible? How Television Frames Political Issues.* Chicago, Ill.: University of Chicago Press, 1991.

Niven, David. "Partisan Bias in the Media? A New Test," *Social Science Quarterly* 80 (December 1999): 847–857.

NOTES

1. Paul Burka, "Ann vs. Ann," *Texas Monthly,* April 1994, 141.
2. Doris A. Graber, *Mass Media and American Politics,* 4th ed. (Washington, D.C.: Congressional Quarterly Press, 1993), 118, 120.
3. Dean E. Alger, *The Media and Politics* (Englewood Cliffs, N.J.: Prentice Hall, 1989), 106.
4. S. Robert Lichter, Stanley Rothman, and Linda S. Lichter, *The Media Elite: America's New Powerbrokers* (New York: Hastings House, 1990), 20–32, quote at 32.
5. David H. Weaver and G. Cleveland Wilhoit, *The American Journalist in the 1990s: U.S. News People at the End of an Era* (Mahwah, N.J.: Lawrence Erlbaum, Publishers, 1996), 15–19.
6. David Croteau, "Examining the 'Liberal Media' Claim: Journalists' Views on Politics, Economic Policy, and Media Coverage," A FAIR Report. June 1998. Accessed 3 March 2000, http://www.fair.org/reports/journalists-survey.html.
7. Thad Beyle, Donald Ostdiek, and G. Patrick Lynch, "Is the State Press Corps Biased? The View from Political and Media Elites," *Spectrum* 70 (Fall 1996): 6–15.
8. Daniel C. Hallin, *The "Uncensored War": The Media and Vietnam* (New York: Oxford University Press, 1986), 68–69.
9. Herbert J. Gans, *Deciding What's News* (New York: Random House, 1980), 182–191.
10. Edward Jay Epstein, *News from Nowhere: Television and the News* (New York: Vintage Books, 1973), 4.
11. Alger, *The Media and Politics,* 111.
12. Michael Buchholz, "Social Responsibility of the Texas Revolutionary Press," *Journalism Quarterly* 65 (Spring 1988): 189.
13. Marvin Olasky, "Hawks or Doves? Texas Press and Spanish-American War," *Journalism Quarterly* 64 (Spring 1987): 205–208.
14. *Texas Poll Report* (Summer 1986): 7.
15. Cited in L. Tucker Gibson, Jr. and Clay Robison, *Government and Politics in the Lone Star State,* 3d ed. (Englewood Cliffs, N.J.: Prentice Hall, Inc., 1999), 140–141.
16. Paul Klite, Robert A. Bardwell, and Jason Salzman, "Pavlov's TV Dog: A Snapshot of Local TV News in America Taken on September 20, 1995," *Rocky Mountain Media Watch Content Analysis 7* (Denver, Colo.: Rocky Mountain Media Watch, 1995).
17. Tom Rosenstiel, Carl Gottlieb, and LeeAnn Brady, "Local TV: What Works, What Flops, and Why," *Columbia Journalism Review* (January/February 1999); Amy Mitchell, "The Big Picture: The Face of Local TV News Today," *Columbia Journalism Review* (January/February 1999).

18. Lee Nichols, "Channeling the News," *Austin Chronicle Online.* 21–27 August 1998. Accessed 19 December 1999, http://www.auschron.com/issues/vol17/issue50/pols.media.html; Diane Holloway, "Television Journalist Kneeland Dies at 49," *Austin American-Statesman,* 27 January 1998, pp. B1, B4.

19. Tom Rosenstiel, Carl Gottlieb, and Lee Ann Brady, "Quality Brings Higher Ratings, But Enterprise is Disappearing," *Columbia Journalism Review* (November/December 1999): 80–85.

20. Paul Klite, Robert A. Bardwell, and Jason Salzman, "Local News on Cable: 1999," *Rocky Mountain Media Watch Texts 7.* Accessed 18 December 1999, http://www.bigmedia.org/texts7.html.

21. "America's Best Newspapers," *Columbia Journalism Review* (November/December 1999): 14–16.

22. William Glaberson, "Departures at Paper Ignite Debate on Owners' Priorities," *New York Times,* 15 February 1995, pp. C1, C16.

23. Comptroller of Public Accounts, *Fiscal Notes,* September 1995, 12.

24. "63% of This Year's Political Campaigns Are Using the Internet, According to a Nationwide Survey," *Campaigns and Elections Online.* Accessed 29 September 1998, http://www.camelect.com/survey.html; Elaine Ciulla Kamarck, "Campaigning on the Internet in the Off Year Elections of 1998," John F. Kennedy School of Government Harvard University. Accessed 29 September 1998, http://www.ksg.harvard.edu/visions/kamarck.htm.

25. Gregory D. Cancelada and Jeff South, "Texas a Leader in Providing Access to Data," *Austin American-Statesman,* 15 January 1995, pp. D1, D7.

26. See Paul Lazarsfeld, Bernard Berelson, and Hazel Gaudet, *The People's Choice: How the Voter Makes Up His Mind in a Presidential Campaign* (New York: Columbia University Press, 1948); Bernard Berelson, Paul Lazarsfeld, and William McPhee, *Voting: A Study of Opinion Formation in a Presidential Campaign* (Chicago: University of Chicago Press, 1954); Angus Campbell, Philip Converse, Warren Miller, and Donald Stokes, *The American Voter* (Chicago: University of Chicago Press, 1960).

27. See, for example, Austin Ranney, *Channels of Power: The Impact of Television on American Politics* (New York: Basic Books, 1983), 8; Robert M. Entman, *Democracy Without Citizens: Media and the Decay of American Politics* (New York: Oxford University Press, 1989), 75–77.

28. Bernard Cohen, *The Press and Foreign Policy* (Princeton, N.J.: Princeton University Press, 1963), 13.

29. Graber, *Mass Media and American Politics,* 216.

30. Michael B. Mackuen and Steven L. Coombs, *More than News* (Beverly Hills, Calif.: Sage, 1981), 19–144.

31. Shanto Iyengar and Donald R. Kinder, *News That Matters: Television and American Opinion* (Chicago: University of Chicago Press, 1987), 60.

32. Marilyn Roberts and Maxwell McCombs, "Agenda Setting and Political Advertising: Origins of the News Agenda," *Political Communication* 11 (1994): 260.

33. Stephen Ansolabehere, Roy Behr, and Shanto Iyengar, *The Media Game: American Politics in the Television Age* (New York: Macmillan, 1993), 148.

34. Iyengar and Kinder, *News That Matters,* Chapters 7–11; Entman, *Democracy Without Citizens,* 34–46.

35. Shanto Iyengar, *Is Anyone Responsible? How Television Frames Political Issues* (Chicago: University of Chicago Press, 1991), 11.

36. Ibid., 136–140.

37. Benjamin I. Page and Robert Y. Shapiro, *The Rational Public: Fifty Years of Trends in Americans' Policy Preferences* (Chicago: University of Chicago Press, 1992), 322.

38. Ibid., 341–348.

39. Gibson, Jr. and Robison, *Government and Politics in the Lone Star State,* 140–141.

40. Ansolabehere, Behr, and Iyengar, *The Media Game,* 150–152.

41. Doris A. Graber, *Processing the News: How People Tame the Information Tide* (New York: Longman Inc., 1984), 22–25.

42. Thomas E. Patterson, *Out of Order* (New York: Random House, 1993), 134–175.

43. Paul H. Weaver, "Is Television News Biased?" *The Public Interest* 27 (1972): 69.

44. Samuel L. Popkin, *The Reasoning Voter: Communication and Persuasion in Presidential Campaigns* (Chicago: University of Chicago Press, 1991), 7.

45. Patterson, *Out of Order,* 78–84.

46. These effects are detailed in Patterson, *Out of Order,* 59–61, 63, and 91–93.

47. Roderick P. Hart, *Seducing America: How Television Charms the Modern Voter* (New York: Oxford University Press, 1994), 7–8.

48. Ibid., 153–159.

49. Joseph N. Capella and Kathleen Hall Jamieson, *Spiral of Cynicism: The Press and the Public Good* (New York: Oxford University Press, 1997), 139–246.

50. Chandler Davidson argues that Texas, like many states and the United States, contains people who are primarily moderate in their political ideology. His assessment is based on Texans' self-identification; that is, whether they consider themselves liberal, conservative, or moderate. The problems with self-labeling include misidentification (a person may not know what the labels mean) and a tendency for poll respondents, given two extreme choices and a middle choice, to choose the middle choice. Furthermore, self-labeling bears no relationship to the concept of ideology, which is a measure of the consistency in a person's political attitudes. See Chandler Davidson, *Race and Class in Texas Politics* (Princeton, N.J.: Princeton University Press, 1990), 36–39.

51. *Texas Poll Report* (Winter 1988): 4.

52. Lori Rodriguez, "Poll Shows Set-asides Split Texans," *Houston Chonicle,* 1 May 1995, pp. A1, A8.

53. *Texas Poll Report* (Summer 1988): 15.

54. *Texas Poll Report* (Spring 1987): 10.

55. *Texas Poll Report* (Fall 1987): 14.

56. *Scripps Howard Texas Poll Report* (Third Quarter 1999): 12.

57. *Texas Poll Report* (Summer 1989): 5.

58. Ibid.

59. *Texas Poll Report* (Winter 1989): 4.

60. *Scripps Howard Texas Poll Report* (First Quarter 1997): 9.

61. *Scripps Howard Texas Poll Report* (Second Quarter 1999): 14.

7

Political Participation, Campaigns, and Elections

★ Scenario: The Sharp-Perry Lieutenant Governor's Race of 1998

The event that triggered the most important electoral contest in 1998 occurred in 1997 when Lieutenant Governor Bob Bullock announced a press conference for June 5, 1997. At the bottom of the press release was an invitation for friends to stay after the conference for "cookies and coffee." The invitation sparked numerous rumors about Bullock's intentions: was he going to challenge Bush for the governorship? Would he switch parties, becoming a Republican? Or was it just Bullock's way of starting his campaign? Few were prepared for Bullock's announcement that he was not seeking reelection in 1998, citing his desire to spend more time with his family. In addition, growing speculation that George W. Bush would seek the Republican presidential nomination in 2000 made the lieutenant governor's contest even more important since the lieutenant governor would become governor if Bush were successful in winning the presidency.

With Bullock's announcement, Democratic Comptroller John Sharp immediately announced his intention to follow in Bullock's footsteps once again. Like Bullock, Sharp had served in the legislature and an executive office before being elected Comptroller in 1990, when Bullock sought and won the lieutenant governor's job. Republican Rick Perry had also served in the Texas House as a Democrat before switching political parties to challenge and defeat Democratic Agriculture Commissioner Jim Hightower in 1990. Interestingly, Perry and Sharp were classmates, squadron mates, and involved in campus activities (Perry as a yell leader and Sharp as student body president) at Texas A&M University in the late 1960s and early 1970s. Despite their similar backgrounds, the contest for lieutenant governor featured candidates with different political characteristics competing in a changed partisan environment.

Rick Perry's strength has always been his personality and gregariousness. As one political commentator noted, "Perry is blessed with as lively a face as you'll come across in politics. . . . These mannerisms aren't particularly dramatic in

Rick Perry, left, Republican candidate for lieutenant governor answers a reporter's question during a debate with his Democratic opponent, John Sharp, right.

person, but in a television close-up, they reach across a living room and connect with viewers. Rick Perry is the perfect candidate for the media age."[1] On the other hand, John Sharp's strength is his knowledge of government and his ability to turn a speech into a conversation. When the same audience hears Sharp and Perry, Sharp usually gets the better reviews. Of the two candidates, Sharp has the better credentials, though the agencies that each headed since 1991 explains some of Sharp's advantage. The comptroller's office is more powerful and visible to the public than the agriculture commissioner's office. But in contemporary Texas, record and experience do not ensure one's election to statewide office.

In contemporary Texas, Republican candidates are close to holding an advantage that Democrats held during the 1960s: when the voters don't know much about the candidates, they tend to pick the Republican. Thus, although Sharp led Perry by a large margin in name recognition, the polls indicated that the election would be very close. Given the tremendous lead in the governor's race that George W. Bush held over Garry Mauro in most polls, Sharp's strategy was to convince people who voted Republican for governor to vote for him for lieutenant governor. Consequently, his campaign refused to endorse Garry Mauro's campaign to unseat George W. Bush, and one of his campaign commercials pictured Sharp with Bush at an event outside the Blanco County courthouse, proclaiming: "Last year, Perry took the fat pay raise Governor Bush and Comptroller John Sharp turned down."[2] Perry's strategy was to match Sharp in expenditures, focus on a few issues, look great, and grab Bush's coattails. The partisan environment dictated different campaign strategies.

John Sharp, Democratic candidate for lieutenant governor, ran a television commercial that attempted to link him to Republican Governor George W. Bush in 1998.

To dislodge the Bush voters, Sharp needed either to give people a reason to vote for him or a reason to vote against Perry. Sharp's media adviser, David Axelrod, chose the latter route. The negative tactics involved several areas. One charged that Perry, while holding public office, had built a $3–4 million fortune through sweetheart business deals. The focus of the charges was Perry's relationship with a key campaign contributor, James Leininger, a San Antonio businessman who supports several conservative causes, especially tort reform and school vouchers. Another advertisement praised Sharp for his audits of public schools and his leadership on the Texas Tomorrow Fund (a program for prepaying college tuition) but then attacked Perry, stating that "Rick Perry would rob the public schools of hundreds of millions of dollars by shifting our tax money to private schools, a scheme backed by Perry's top contributors."[3] In another attempt to discredit Perry, Sharp criticized Perry for a 1987 vote in the House for the early release of state prisoners. The advertisement tried to link the vote with the rape and murder of a 15-year-old girl by released prisoner Gary Wayne Ethridge. Testimonial advertisements featured the victim's mother and a hero of law enforcement, Wise County Sheriff Phil Ryan.[4] The effectiveness of the negative campaign by Sharp was blunted by an infusion of money (nearly $7 million in the last six weeks of the campaign) to Perry which allowed him to increase his paid television advertisement by 50 percent during the stretch drive of the campaign.[5]

In the end, Perry won by a margin of two percentage points, trailing Governor Bush by 21 points. An analysis of voting patterns indicates that Sharp did well among Democratic Party identifiers, African Americans, Hispanics, and women. On the other hand, Perry secured majorities among Republican Party identifiers, Anglos, and men. Most importantly, Perry won 52 percent of the independent vote to Sharp's 43 percent. Nearly one-third of the Bush voters also voted for Sharp.[6] Clearly, if Bush had not been on the ballot, Perry probably would not be lieutenant governor today. The Perry-Sharp contest of 1998 demonstrates much about contemporary political campaigns in Texas. ★

INTRODUCTION

Political participation involves much more than the election of a lieutenant governor and other public officials. In this chapter, we describe the various forms of political participation in which Texans engage. Because voting in elections is the most common form of political participation, we describe and analyze several types of elections in Texas—primary, general, special, and local elections—and voting decisions relating to elections. Next, we describe and analyze how contemporary political campaigns are conducted in Texas, emphasizing the dominant influence of money, media, and marketing. Finally, we analyze three recent gubernatorial elections. After finishing this chapter, you will more fully understand how political participation, campaigns, and elections combine to influence political change and democracy in Texas. We begin with an overview of political participation in Texas.

Te★as*Index*

Voting and Elections in the States

Voting-age population, 1998:
Texas—14,299,000
California—23,665,000
New York—13,590,000
Florida—11,383,000

Percentage of the voting-age population designated as "active" registered voters, 1998:
Texas—67
California—63
New York—70
Florida—66

African-American voting-age population, 1998:
Texas—1,685,000
California—1,690,000
New York—2,278,000
Florida—1,530,000

Hispanic voting-age population, 1998:
Texas—3,799,000
California—6,653,000
New York—1,760,000
Florida—1,638,000

Number of African-American elected officials, 1997:
Texas—448
California—255
New York—311
Florida—216

Number of Hispanic elected officials, 1999:
Texas—1,724
California—762
New York—78
Florida—83

POLITICAL PARTICIPATION

Political participation is defined as "any attempt by an individual to influence or support government and politics."[7] Historically in Texas and the rest of the United States, political participation has taken two forms: conventional participation and unconventional participation. We examine both forms of participation and the factors that influence an individual's choice between the two forms.

Forms of Political Participation

The distinction between conventional and unconventional participation is based on the methods used in participating and the intention of the participant. On one hand, **conventional political participation** uses the routine, legitimate institutions provided by government and either shows support for government or attempts to influence public policy. Examples of conventional participation include such activities as flying the flag on Independence Day, campaigning for candidates, and voting. On the other hand, **unconventional political participation** involves the use of unusual, possibly illegal, forms of participation in order to challenge government or to oppose public policy. Examples of unconventional participation include some demonstrations and riots.

The choice that individuals make between conventional and unconventional participation is strongly related to two attitudes: internal political efficacy and political trust. Political efficacy is an individual's feeling about his or her political influence. **Internal political efficacy,** as opposed to external political efficacy, is an individual's feeling that he or she has the skills necessary to influence political decisions. External political efficacy, which we discuss later in the chapter, is an individual's feeling that the government is responsive to his or her efforts to influence it. Internal political efficacy is a product of political socialization, education, and prior political experience. For example, a woman who is raised in a politically active family, has received a college degree, and has been active in state and local politics probably feels that she has the ability to influence government and politics. **Political trust** is an individual's feeling that government decisions are made in the public interest and that public officials are honest and diligent public servants. For instance, a person who feels that a particular group of Texans exerts extraordinary influence on government decisions and that the government's decisions advance that group's interests rather than the general public's interests probably has little political trust.

These attitudes combine in four different ways to influence political participation. First, people who feel politically efficacious and trust public officials engage in conventional participation, attempting to influence public policy. For example, Texans who supported Rick Perry's campaign promises and felt that he would be able to accomplish his goals of creating vouchers for education and reducing crime probably voted for him because of his campaign promises. Second, people who feel inefficacious and distrust public officials will withdraw from politics. Texans who had little knowledge about the candidates for lieutenant governor in 1998 and who also felt that John Sharp and Rick Perry could not be trusted to keep their campaign promises anyway probably were among the nearly 75 percent of the population who did not vote in 1998. Third, the combination of efficacy and distrust of public officials results in unconventional participation, such as Gregory Lee Johnson's burning of an American flag during the 1984 Republican national convention in Dallas (see Chapter 1). Fourth, inefficacy coupled with trust of public officials leads to conventional participation that demonstrates support or allegiance to the government. For instance, many Texans probably voted in the 1998 election, not because they supported the candidates' policy goals but

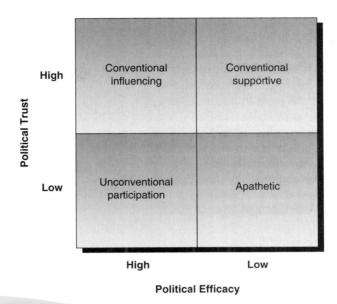

Figure 7.1 Political Efficacy, Political Trust, and Forms of Political Participation
The figure indicates the effects of two factors (political trust and political efficacy) on the forms of political participation. For example, a person who trusts politicians and who is internally efficacious will engage in conventional forms of political participation in order to influence public officials.
Source: Adapted from Lester W. Milbrath and M. L. Goel, *Political Participation: How and Why Do People Get Involved in Politics?* 2d ed (Chicago Ill.: Rand McNally, 1977), 70. By permission.

because they felt that they had an obligation, as citizens in a democracy, to vote and show their allegiance and support for democratic government. Figure 7.1 depicts the two attitudes and their influence on the forms of political participation.

Modes of Political Participation

Individuals who seek to influence or support government also adopt a particular "mode" or "style" of participation. These **modes of political participation** are distinguished by the effort required to participate, as well as by the method by which an individual relates to government and politics. National studies have discovered seven modes or styles of political participation.[8]

1. **Voters** do not need to make much effort to participate, and people vote for a variety of reasons. Some voters, of course, are attempting to elect people to public office in order to influence government policies. Others, however, are voting to express their support for democracy and the privilege of living in a democracy where people are allowed to express their preferences for public officials. The exact mix of voters' motivations is difficult, if

not impossible, to determine. Slightly fewer than 50 percent of the age-eligible population nationally voted in the 1996 presidential election, and even fewer voted in other types of elections.

2. **Contactors** participate by contacting public officials about personal problems related to government, such as a person who objects to a city's program that affects her or him personally. They make up about 4 percent of the population.

3. **Communicators** participate by discussing and criticizing government, performing a watchdog role. They also vote regularly.

4. **Campaigners,** about 15 percent of the population, routinely engage in campaign-related activities, either for candidates for public office or for political parties.

5. **Community activists,** approximately 20 percent of the population, join groups and attempt to influence public policy through pressure-group politics.

6. **Protesters** use unconventional methods to achieve their political goals, such as protesting public actions, civil disobedience, demonstrating, attending protest rallies, and rioting.

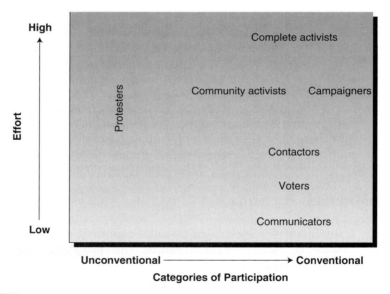

Figure 7.2   Modes of Political Participation

The figure illustrates a hierarchy of the modes of political participation based on the degree of effort required for each mode of participation. Thus, among conventional political activities, voting requires less effort than campaigning or community activities but more effort than talking about politics.

Source: Adapted from Lester W. Milbrath and M. L. Goel, *Political Participation: How and Why Do People Get Involved in Politics?* 2d ed. (Chicago Ill.: Rand McNally, 1977), 21. By permission.

Table 7.1   POLITICAL PARTICIPATION IN TEXAS AND THE UNITED STATES

Form of participation (U.S. respondents reporting)	1989	1995
Talked about politics often	18%	—
Voted in a local election (71%)	72%	—
Attended a political meeting (29%)	25%	22%
Displayed political bumper sticker or button	28%	12%
Worked for a political party or candidate (8%)	13%	13%
Contributed money to a candidate (24%)	26%	19%
Wrote a letter to a local politician (34%)	29%	24%
Worked with others to solve a community problem	41%	—
Joined a group to solve a community problem (17%)	—	26%
Contacted local school administrator	32%	—

Sources: Sidney Verba, Kay Schlozman, and Henry E. Brady, *Voice and Equality: Civic Volunteerism in American Politics* (Cambridge, Mass.: Harvard University Press, 1995), 50; *Texas Poll Report* (Fall 1989): 2, 12; *Texas Poll*, reported in *Austin American-Statesman*, 28 October 1995, pp. B3, B7.

7. **Complete activists,** about 11 percent of the population, engage in all modes of political participation, including both conventional and unconventional forms.[9]

The modes of participation are illustrated in Figure 7.2.

Surveys of political participation in Texas indicate only a slight variation from the national average in most kinds of political participation (Table 7.1). Given an appreciation for the various forms of political participation, we now describe the most common form of political participation—elections and voting.

Critical Thinking Exercise: Consider how you might participate in politics. Would you be more likely to engage in conventional or unconventional participation? Why? What could you expect to gain from your participation in politics?

ELECTIONS IN TEXAS

Texans are offered frequent opportunities to express their political preferences in elections. During the 1997–1998 election cycle, Texans were asked to vote in two special elections to approve 15 proposed amendments to the Texas Constitution; primary elections to nominate candidates for local, state, and national offices; runoff elections in those primary contests where no candidate received a majority of the vote; and a general election to select local, state, and national public officials. In addition, Texans who reside in special districts and cities (see Chapter 12) were asked to participate in even more elections. In Texas, elections are frequent, and the ballot tends to be longer than in other states. Before we discuss political campaigns and voting behavior, we describe the various types of elections that are conducted in Texas—primary elections, special elections, general elections, and local elections.

Primary Elections

Primary elections are intraparty contests to determine the party's nominees for local, state, and national offices. By Texas law, any party whose candidate for governor receives more than 20 percent of the vote must hold a primary election to nominate candidates. Parties whose gubernatorial candidate receives less than 20 percent of the vote can nominate their candidates in a primary or in party conventions. In Texas, the Democratic Party has held primary elections every two years since 1906. The Republican Party held primaries only five times between 1906 and 1962. Since 1962, the Republican Party has also held primaries every two years. Since 1988, primary elections have been held on the second Tuesday in March of even-numbered years.

Primaries were established in Texas in 1905 with the passage of the Terrell Election Law, which required a combination of the primary election and a state convention to determine the party's nominees. In 1907, the law was amended to establish a direct primary election, with a plurality vote necessary to secure the nomination. In 1918, in an attempt to thwart Jim Ferguson, the legislature adopted a majority vote requirement to win the primary and established a second, or runoff, primary between the first- and second-place vote getters if no candidate received a majority of the vote in the first primary.[10] In the 1990 Democratic primary, Jim Mattox, Ann Richards, and Mark White sought the nomination for governor. Because none of the three candidates received a majority of the vote in the primary, the top two vote getters in the first primary—Ann Richards and Jim Mattox—participated in the second primary.

Types of Primary Elections   Throughout the United States, the states employ four different types of primary elections. A majority of the states use a **closed primary,** which requires the voter to publicly state his or her party affiliation to participate in a party's primary election. Some states that use the closed primary require voters to register as a party member to participate in the party's primary election; other states, such as Texas, simply require a person to participate in only one party's primary. Most other states use an **open primary,** which allows the voter to participate in only one party's primary election but does not require the voter to identify his or her party affiliation. A voter participating in an open primary is issued a ballot for each party participating in the primary. Then, in the secrecy of the voting booth, the voter marks only one of the ballots. The voter then places that ballot in the ballot box and places the other parties' ballots in a discard box.

Three states—Alaska, California, and Washington—employ a **blanket primary,** which allows a voter to participate in any party's primary, as long as the voter only chooses one candidate for each office on the primary ballot. For example, a voter in a blanket primary could vote for a Democratic candidate for governor and for a Republican candidate for lieutenant governor, but she or he could not vote for both a Democratic and a Republican candidate for the same office (e.g., governor). Thus, the ballot resembles a general election ballot, containing the names of all the parties' candidates for each office that is contested in the primary.

Louisiana uses a unique system, termed the **unitary primary,** which combines features of the general election with the primary election. All candidates for a particular office are grouped together on the primary ballot, regardless of party affiliation. Thus, there are no separate Democratic and Republican primaries. If a candidate for an office receives a majority of the votes cast in the primary, he or she is elected to the office, and there is no general election for that office. However, for those offices in which no candidate receives a majority of the votes, the two candidates receiving the greatest number of votes, regardless of party affiliation, contest the office in the general election.

Although primary elections in Texas are supposedly closed elections, voters can still choose to participate in the opposition party's primary election, making them operate more like open primaries. For example, in the 1994 Democratic gubernatorial primary, incumbent Governor Ann Richards was challenged by Gary Espinosa, a political unknown who received 22 percent of the primary vote. Republicans contended that Espinosa's vote indicated that more than one-fifth of Richards's party members did not support her. However, a county-by-county analysis indicated that a large percentage of Espinosa's vote came from Republicans who "raided" the Democratic primary, attempting to discredit the popularity of the incumbent governor. In the 75 counties where few voters (5 percent or fewer) participated in the Republican primary, Espinosa received 27 percent of the vote. In the 36 counties where a majority of the voters participated in the Republican primary, Espinosa received only 13 percent of the vote.[11]

Participation in Primary Elections   Participation in primary elections is usually low in Texas. However, during the period of Democratic Party dominance, from 1906 until 1962, a larger percentage of Texas voters participated in the Democratic primary than participated in the general election. Participation in the Democratic primaries was high because they often included contests reflecting the ideological split in the party, making the results more important than the general elections, which were usually won by the Democratic candidates. In 1962, for the first time in Texas history, the number of voters in the general election in a nonpresidential election year exceeded the number of voters in the Democratic primary election. Since then, as participation in the general election has increased, participation in the Republican primary has increased, while participation in the Democratic primary has decreased. This change reflects the rise of the Republican Party in Texas and the resulting increase in the importance of the general election.[12] In 1998, 4.7 percent of the voting-age population voted in the Democratic primary, and 4.2 percent voted in the Republican primary.

Because primary elections are party elections, each party is responsible for administering its own primary election, which includes preparing the ballots, conducting the elections, tabulating and certifying the results, and financing the election. Candidates for statewide office file for positions on the ballot with the state party chairperson; candidates for county or precinct office file with the county party chairperson; and candidates for district office (e.g., court of appeals, state senator) file with each county party chairperson in the district.

Special Elections

Special elections are held in Texas to fill vacancies in state legislative and U.S. congressional offices, to approve local bond proposals, and if the legislature chooses, to approve amendments to the Texas Constitution. Executive and judicial vacancies are filled by gubernatorial appointment. The dates for special elections are set by the legislature, for amendments to the Texas Constitution; by the governor, to fill legislative and congressional vacancies; and by the local government, to approve bond proposals. The parties do not hold primaries to nominate candidates for special elections; thus, access to the ballot for legislative or congressional vacancies is through filing fees or signatures on petitions. Consequently, the number of candidates in special elections tends to be large. For example, the May 1993 special election for U.S. senator drew 24 candidates. Candidates who seek an office in special elections are identified by political party on the ballot, and they must receive a majority of the votes cast to win the office. If no candidate receives a majority of the vote, a runoff election between the top two vote getters is held one month after the first election.

Participation in special elections is usually extremely low but varies, depending on the issues involved in elections to approve constitutional amendments (see Chapter 3) or the competitiveness among candidates in elections to fill vacancies. Bond approval elections draw even fewer voters.

General Elections

General elections are interparty contests to determine which candidates will hold public office. In most states, the general election is held on the first Tuesday after the first Monday in November of even-numbered years. In Texas, state, district, and county officials are elected on that date. Since 1974, when Texas adopted a four-year gubernatorial term, the governor and other statewide elected executive officials who also serve four-year terms are elected in nonpresidential years. Other elected officials in Texas, because of the tenure of their offices, may be chosen in presidential or nonpresidential years. In elections for state, district, and county offices, the person who receives the most votes, a plurality, wins the election.

General elections are administered and funded by the state. The secretary of state, the state's chief election official, is responsible for certifying state and district candidates, ensuring that the county clerks certify local candidates, ensuring that the county commissioners court appoints the necessary officials to administer the election, and reporting and maintaining the election results.

Local Elections

Local elections are conducted to elect city councils, mayors, school board members, and special district boards. Cities and special districts may conduct their elections in odd-numbered years, and some cities require a majority vote to win, necessitating a runoff election if no candidate receives a majority. These elections are nonpartisan and are usually conducted in May. Although some local elections generate high voter interest and turnout, most local elections do not.

> **Critical Thinking Exercise:** Which type of primary election should Texas use? What would be the advantages and disadvantages of that type of election? How would you convince legislators to adopt that type of primary election?

POLITICAL CAMPAIGNS IN TEXAS

As we noted earlier, there are ample (some say too many) opportunities to vote in Texas. How do Texans find out about the candidates and the issues in all of these elections? **Political campaigns** are supposed to perform that function.

Ideally, election campaigns in a democracy should offer the electorate an opportunity to compare the candidates and their views on the major issues of public policy. Then, armed with this knowledge, voters should choose among the competing political views and, thereby, determine public policy. Unfortunately, many contemporary political campaigns are not really about issues of public policy. As W. Lance Bennett has noted, contemporary political campaigns are about money, media, and marketing.[13] We consider the influence of each of these factors in Texas campaigns before analyzing voting decisions and contemporary gubernatorial campaigns.

Money: The Mother's Milk of Politics

Everyone knows that contemporary political campaigns are expensive. In the 1998 gubernatorial campaign in Texas, incumbent Governor George W. Bush spent more than $17 million, and his challenger, Garry Mauro, spent $5 million in the general election. In 1994, the winning candidates in competitive campaigns for the Texas Senate spent an average of $347,626, while the losing candidates averaged $117,076.[14] In 1998, House candidates who won in contested House contests raised an average of $190,173 in campaign contributions to the losers average of $90,038.[15] Although **money** is not a guarantee of electoral success, winning candidates generally outspend their opponents. Why are election campaigns so expensive in Texas, compared to other states, and how do the candidates raise the money necessary to be competitive?

The High Cost of Texas Campaigns   The geographic size of Texas makes money important in electoral campaigns. As Kaye Northcott noted, "Money doesn't just talk in Texas elections: it does tap dances and sings the state anthem in three-part harmony."[16] In 1982, Peyton McKnight, a conservative Democratic state senator spent $1.5 million of his own fortune, estimated at over $30 million, attempting to win the Democratic nomination for governor. After loaning his campaign $500,000 in the fall of 1981, McKnight anteed up another loan of $1 million in January 1982. On the filing deadline for the primary election, Robert Squier, an influential media consultant for Democratic candidates, informed McKnight that another $1 million was necessary to raise his name recognition to a winnable percentage. Rather than ante up, McKnight folded.

McKnight was replaced by Buddy Temple, son of Arthur Temple, Jr., an East Texas timber magnate who merged his Eastex, Inc. with Time, Inc. in the 1970s. The key to name recognition, as Temple learned in an earlier statewide race for a seat on the Texas Railroad Commission, is television advertising. After spending nearly 10 months traveling the state meeting people and giving speeches, Temple had raised his name recognition from 5 to 12 percent. When his television advertising campaign started, two days yielded an increase from 12 to 24 percent. As Temple noted, "That made a believer out of me. If you don't have the money to make a good showing on television, you don't have a chance in Texas."[17]

In 1982, John Rogers, an Austin political consultant, estimated that each percentage point increase in name recognition between 15 and 75 percent costs a candidate $15,000 in advertising. After reaching 75 percent name recognition, the cost per percentage point increases to $25,000.[18] With the increase in cost for television advertising and inflation, these figures would be much higher today. In Texas, a personal fortune, though not a prerequisite for seeking statewide office, helps, but even that is not sufficient, as Peyton McKnight's experience demonstrates. In 1990, Clayton Williams used a portion of his fortune in seeking the Texas governorship, and in 1994, Richard Fisher used his fortune in attempting to defeat U.S. Senator Kay Bailey Hutchison. Neither candidate was successful. Those candidates who lack personal fortunes must seek campaign contributions. Where do they go to find them?

The Sources of Campaign Contributions   Individual contributions provide the majority of campaign contributions in Texas, but increasingly, contributions from groups, through their political action committees (PACs) (see Chapter 5), have become more important, especially to incumbents in state legislative contests. During the 1994 gubernatorial campaign in Texas, Ann Richards and George W. Bush both received most of their contributions from individuals, 77 percent and 94 percent, respectively. Also, both candidates received the greatest share of their contributions (about 40 percent) from contributions in amounts of $1,000–9,999. Contributions in amounts of $10,000 and greater made up between 20 and 30 percent of the total contributions for the candidates, with Richards being more dependent on large contributions than Bush.[19]

Limitations on Campaign Contributions   Not only is political money more important in Texas than in other states, but there are also fewer restrictions placed on its use in political campaigns. In Texas, campaign finance has usually come as a response to blatant excesses, both legal and illegal, by campaign contributors. A major reform was passed in 1973 in the wake of the Sharpstown scandal (see Chapter 8). However, even the politics of creedal passion associated with the scandal did not produce strong legislation. The law merely required candidates to designate a campaign treasurer and to report contributions and expenditures. There were numerous loopholes in the legislation, such as the requirement that only "opposed" candidates must report contributions and expenditures.[20] After Lonnie "Bo" Pilgrim passed out checks for $10,000 to Texas senators in an attempt to influence workers' compensation legislation in 1989, the legislature, at the urging of Governor Richards, attempted to strengthen the regulation of campaign finance in 1991. The legislature created an Ethics Commission, which now receives the contribution and expenditure reports for candidates for state office, and it did close some of the loopholes in the previous law. In 1999, the legislature adopted a law requiring candidates for statewide offices, the state legislature, and many district offices to file their contribution and expenditure reports electronically. Beginning with the 2000 elections, the information will be available on the Ethic Commission's web site. However, there are still no limits on contributions by individuals or PACs in Texas.

Media: Linking the Candidates and the Voters

Although politicians once felt that campaigning should be conducted personally and should involve face-to-face contacts with the voters at campaign rallies, technology has made personal contacts less effective. Campaign communications are now conducted through the **media.** This is especially true for statewide political campaigns, but it is also becoming more common in district and local campaigns. In a state the size of Texas, the only way to effectively reach potential voters is through the state's 19 media markets. As political consultant Mark McKinnon has noted, "It's impossible to effectively communicate with voters in Texas any other way but television. TV is the next best thing to being there. TV allows the candidate to be in everybody's living room, up close and personal."[21]

Among the media, television and newspapers seem to have the greatest impact. In 1986, although a majority of Texans in a survey after the gubernatorial election cited television as the source of most of their national and local news, a slight plurality indicated that they received most of their information about political candidates from newspapers, with television a close second.[22] How has this reliance on the media, especially television, changed political campaigns?

First, television has changed the way that candidates appeal to voters. As a visual medium, television is best at transmitting images. Thus, the appeal now emphasizes those personal characteristics the candidate possesses, which are considered important to voters. Furthermore, candidates appeal to demographic groups or categories by demonstrating that the candidate empathizes with the groups' problems, needs, goals, or viewpoints. Both the candidate's characteristics and concerns are demonstrated through "visuals" or pictures.

George W. Bush shoots marbles with children, demonstrating with a picture his concern for children of all ethnic backgrounds.

Thus, the candidate who wishes to appeal to African-American voters is pictured marching with African Americans on Juneteenth, a holiday celebrating the date in 1865 (June 19) that word of President Lincoln's Emancipation Proclamation reached Texas, and 250,000 slaves were freed. Conversely, because abstractions are difficult for a visual medium such as television, campaign appeals that emphasize the candidate's party affiliation or specific policy proposals are avoided.[23]

Second, the reliance on the media has spawned a new industry composed of experts adept at developing and producing political appeals for the media. As more people have become detached from their partisan affiliations, party leaders have lost the skills necessary to organize campaigns capable of electing candidates to public office. Thus, candidates have turned to political consultants, specialists in the modern campaign technology, to plan and organize their campaigns.[24] The specialized knowledge possessed by campaign consultants has led to the third component of contemporary campaigns—**marketing.**

Marketing: Selling the Candidate

The transition from party-centered to candidate-centered campaigns was facilitated by political consultants. At first, political consultants offered candidates only their technical expertise, probably gained from experience in commercial marketing or advertising. However, as candidates' dependence on media and the techniques of commercial advertising has increased, political consultants have expanded their influence in the campaign, as well as the specialization of their services to candidates. Increasingly, political consultants occupy a position that allows them to influence the basic strategy of the campaign and the selection of campaign issues.

Given the characteristics of political campaigns—the uncertainty of campaigning, the limited life of the campaign organization, and the win/lose final payoff—the candidates' reliance on experts should have been anticipated.[25] Also, the number of services provided by political consultants has increased dramatically since the 1970s. By the late 1980s, a directory of political consultants listed nearly two dozen types of services available to campaigns. For example, there are consultants who work only on television or radio commercials, others who only advise candidates on the best times to run campaign commercials, some who advise on fund-raising strategies for candidates seeking small contributions, and others who concentrate on fund-raising from big givers, the so-called fat cats.[26] Despite the proliferation of consultants and their specialization, the most important consultants operate in the area of opinion polling and media services.

Opinion Polling   Candidates use several techniques to assess the public's concerns and desires, but public-opinion polls have become the most commonly used technique. Candidates typically employ several kinds of surveys during their campaigns. The earliest and most comprehensive opinion survey is the **benchmark poll.** Conducted a year or more before the election, the benchmark poll is a planning document. The poll typically includes a large number of questions to assess the public's general mood and perception of the candidate's strengths and weaknesses, as well as the strengths and weaknesses of the candidate's likely opponent or opponents. The results of the benchmark poll are used to design the campaign's main themes and to establish the candidate's image.

In 1966, George H. W. Bush, a Republican businessman who would later become President of the United States, challenged Frank Briscoe, a Democratic district attorney, for a newly created congressional district in Houston. A benchmark poll conducted for Bush indicated that the candidate was not well-known, was not considered "warm" and "sincere," had little support from African Americans, and trailed his opponent badly in overall popularity. The poll also revealed that Briscoe was perceived as a competent district attorney, but he was perceived to be cold and aloof. The pollster recommended that Bush increase his visibility, appear moderate to attract African-American support, and project an image of warmth and dynamism. The Bush campaign theme, "Vote for Bush and Watch the Action," was created to increase his name recognition and to create a new image. Bush advertisements stressed "activity plus warmth," an image that, in contrast to Briscoe's cool and lackluster campaign, helped Bush defeat his better-known opponent.[27]

The benchmark poll can also reveal interesting information about voters' concerns. In 1978, William Russo of the Ringe-Russo agency discovered that the greatest concern of Texans in the gubernatorial election was not a political, economic, or social issue, but that the governor be a Texan. Because William P.

Clements *sounded* more Texan than other candidates, the advertising agency decided to make that a keystone of the advertising campaign, using Clements as the narrator for all of his campaign commercials. Postelection polls revealed that Clements's Texas drawl was appealing enough to be cited by 27 percent of his primary election supporters as the reason for their support.[28]

In 1994, a poll conducted for George W. Bush indicated that the primary concern of voters was crime. Micheline Blum, president of Blum and Weprin Associates, indicated that "We had done a poll early in the year about issues, and exactly what voters wanted done. . . . On crime, they needed to feel that once a criminal was put away for a really serious offense, he was going to stay away. There were certain safety issues people wanted to hear about and Bush addressed them."[29] Bush made crime and citizen safety a centerpiece of his gubernatorial campaign.

During the campaign, the most important polls are **tracking polls.** Conducted over a period of two or three weeks, the tracking polls are used to determine the effectiveness of the campaign's theme and advertising, to detect shifts in voters' preferences among various segments of the population, and to evaluate the changing image of the candidate. Because of the high cost of tracking polls, they are usually conducted near the end of the campaign; however, they must be conducted early enough to allow for adjustments in the campaign. Typically, tracking polls employ what are called "rolling samples." A typical tracking poll includes a random sample (see Chapter 6) of 450 to 900 people, collected in increments of 150 to 300 people interviewed over a three-day period. The initial sample is analyzed to provide a baseline for subsequent analyses. Daily, an additional increment of 150 to 300 people is added to the sample, while the oldest increment is deleted. The addition and deletion of portions of the overall sample, the "rolling" of the sample, ensures that the overall sample size remains large enough to prevent an enormous sampling error, but each increment is small enough to be collected in one evening. Campaign consultants compare the daily results to identify changes in the public's opinions and to adjust the campaign strategy accordingly.

To assess the emotional state of the electorate, pollsters employ **focus groups,** which include a small, not necessarily representative, sample of voters. The group members, led by a moderator who may be a pollster or a trained professional, engage in a discussion of issues. Typically, focus-group sessions last about two hours and include 12 to 20 participants. According to pollsters, these sessions are useful in finding the public's *hot-button issues,* which evoke the most emotional and intense responses. These groups are also employed to test campaign commercials before the ads are aired on television. Focus-group sessions are often conducted in rooms that feature a one-way mirror so that the candidate's political consultants and campaign staff can observe the participants' responses.[30]

For a statewide campaign in a state as large as Texas, polling is expensive. A typical benchmark poll, with a sample of 1000, will cost a candidate between $25,000 and $50,000, depending on the length of the questionnaire. Subsequent polls, which usually involve fewer questions, cost between $20,000 and $30,000. With each focus-group participant receiving between $25 and $50, a focus-group session can cost $3,000 or more. Public opinion polling during a major statewide campaign constitutes between 5 and 8 percent of the campaign budget.[31]

Media Services   Political scientists agree that the most important campaign consultants provide media services to their candidates. These media consultants furnish a number of campaign services—assistance in developing themes and strategies; writing, producing, and editing media advertisements; targeting and buying media time; and designing graphic materials for billboards, brochures, and news releases. Among these services, the consultant's most important activities are probably the creation of the media messages and the coordination of those messages with the campaign theme.

The goal of the media message varies during the campaign. In the campaign's early stages, the media message is designed to establish the candidate's name identification and to draw attention to the candidate. The message is meant to create an image and to evoke positive feelings about the candidate. As the campaign progresses, the goal shifts to identifying the candidate with certain campaign issues, but the appeal is still to the voters' emotions, tapping sentiments in the electorate and targeting key constituencies in the voting population. Also during this period, the candidate is linked with certain groups in the electorate. The efforts are designed both to activate old supporters and to entice new supporters. At each stage, however, the appeal is to image rather than substance because the voter is presumed to judge candidates more on feelings about personalities than on issues.[32]

The media consultant uses two methods to reach the voters: (1) commercial advertisements (paid media) and (2) news coverage (unpaid media). The relative

Mark McKinnon was George W. Bush's media consultant for his 1998 reelection campaign.

importance of these methods is determined by the media's interest in the campaign and the money available to the candidate. The advantage of news coverage, of course, is that the coverage is free, but it is not without cost to the candidate. Given the tendencies of news coverage, the coverage may not be positive. Thus, media consultants attempt to control the news coverage by facilitating access to the candidate when the access would be beneficial to the candidate and by influencing the coverage in the presentation of material. The attempt by media consultants to use news coverage to transmit the campaign's message to the voters is a constant struggle between the media and the consultants (see Chapter 6).

In commercial advertisements, there are two strategies available to media consultants: (1) **promotional spots,** which attempt to strengthen the candidate's personal image or to associate the candidate with popular policies and favorable outcomes or (2) **attack spots,** which attempt to undermine the opponent's personal image or to associate him or her with unpopular policies and failed outcomes. The positive ads attempt to ignite the spark of hope that resides in voters, that politicians should and can do something about the issues that most concern the voters. On the other hand, negative ads play on the inherent fears that people have about politicians, a distrust of their intentions and abilities. With negative perceptions of politicians common among the public, it is not surprising that people are more likely to believe negative information about a candidate than positive information. Consequently, attack advertisements have become more common and, many argue, more effective than promotional advertisements.[33] Attack spots were especially prominent in the 1990 gubernatorial campaign between Ann Richards and Clayton Williams and, as we noted in the chapter scenario, in the Rick Perry-John Sharp race of 1998.

The foundation for attack ads is **opposition research,** which probes the weakness of the opposition. Practitioners claim that opposition research and ads support democracy by concentrating on issues and providing more information to voters. Opponents contend that opposition research has brutalized politics by making it too personal and mean-spirited. The number of specialists offering this service has increased dramatically, and campaigns at all levels are likely to employ opposition research throughout the campaign.[34]

In addition to setting the campaign strategy, media services include recommendations on buying media time. Using both Nielsen ratings indicating which programs are watched and Arbitron ratings indicating the demographics—age, gender, race, ethnicity, and other variables—of viewers, media consultants select time slots for commercial advertisements for the campaign. According to Monica Davis of the Davis Group, a high-volume media buyer in Austin, "The first thing you'll see political consultants and buyers go for is the news adjacencies," which are the commercial periods before and after the 6:00 P.M. and 10:00 P.M. local newscasts. These times are popular because people who watch the news are likely to vote. During prime time, 7:00 P.M. to 10:00 P.M., the campaign targets its media buys by the audience it wishes to influence. For example, the Bush campaign in 1994 bought commercial time on *Murder, She Wrote* to air a commercial featuring Bush's proposal to revoke the licenses of individuals who fail to pay child support, knowing that women are more likely to watch that show than competition in the same time slot.[35] Similar decisions are made by other campaigns, depending on the targeted group and the program's audience.

With the number of services provided by media consultants, candidates spend a significant portion of their campaign expenditures on media consultants. In 1998, both George W. Bush and Garry Mauro employed consultants to conduct their media advertising. George W. Bush employed Mark McKinnon, principal in Maverick Media, and Garry Mauro retained Roy Spence, president of the Austin-based advertising agency GSD&M and a long-time Mauro friend. Media services typically consume 60 percent of a campaign's budget.

The ultimate goal in a political campaign is winning, which requires that eligible voters who support the candidate participate in the election and vote for the candidate in the election. Thus, our attention in the next section shifts to the factors that influence the voters' decisions during an election.

> **Critical Thinking Exercise:**   Consider the three Ms of contemporary political campaigns. If you were seeking political office, how would you organize your campaign? Which element is most important? Is it possible to seek and win political office without large amounts of money?

THE VOTERS' DECISIONS

In an election, the potential voter really faces two decisions. The first decision involves whether to participate. The second decision, which applies only if the person has chosen to participate in the election, involves which candidates to support. In Texas, fewer than half of those age-eligible (people 18 years of age and older) voters decide to participate in presidential elections, and fewer than one-third decide to participate in gubernatorial elections. Why is **voter turnout**—the percentage of voting-age people who vote—so low in Texas, ranking forty-eighth among the 50 states in 1996?

Voter Turnout

Like most decisions concerning political participation, the decision to vote is the result of a calculation that weighs the **costs of voting** against the **benefits of voting.** If the costs exceed the benefits, people do not vote. Only when people feel that the benefits are greater than the costs do they vote.

The Costs of Voting in Texas: 1900–1975   Although voting is generally perceived as a low-cost form of participation, voting does involve costs. For example, a voter must find out when the election is held and where the polling place is located, take the time to travel to the polling place, and most important, meet the legal requirements to vote. Until the mid-1970s, a number of legal restrictions in

DESPITE PRETENSIONS TO DEMOCRACY, TEXAS IS ACTUALLY GOVERNED BY A RULING CLASS OF FEW MEMBERS BUT VAST POWER.... THOUGH IMPERCEPTIBLY DISPERSED AMONG THE POPULACE, THIS ELITE MINORITY GATHERS FROM TIME TO TIME TO DICTATE PUBLIC POLICY AND TO PLACE PEOPLE OF THEIR OWN CHOOSING INTO PUBLIC OFFICE.... CURRENTLY, THIS TINY BUT POWERFUL GROUP IS THOUGHT TO COMPRISE NO MORE THAN 3 PER CENT OF THE STATE'S POPULATION.....

POLLING PLACE PRECINCT 119

Source: Copyright © 1979 Ben Sargent, *The Austin American-Statesman.* By permission.

Texas, including a poll tax and a white-only Democratic primary, made the costs of voting extremely high, especially for particular groups or categories of Texans. The legal restrictions fell most heavily on the poor, the uninformed, Mexican Americans, and African Americans (see Chapter 13).

The Contemporary Costs of Voting   In contemporary Texas, the costs of voting, in terms of legal requirements, are minimal. The nominal requirements include U.S. citizenship, being 18 years of age or older, residency in the state, and registration. The only people who are prohibited from voting are the "mentally incompetent" (as declared by a court of law) and convicted felons who have not had their civil rights restored through a pardon or by completion of two years since the end of their sentence. Thus, the only real legal barrier to voting is registration, which, in Texas, is a relatively low-cost requirement. A person who wishes to vote must register at least 30 days prior to the election. Once registered, a person is permanently registered and will receive a new registration certificate every two years unless he or she moves during that period, which necessitates completing a new registration form. However, forms are readily available and are printed in both Spanish and English on postage-free postcards. In 1991, the Texas legislature adopted a **motor-voter registration system,** which allows a person who is obtaining a driver's license or a Department of Public Safety (DPS) identification card to be registered to vote. Also, registration forms were made even more accessible by placing them in public buildings. The effect of the motor-voter registration system has been to increase significantly the percentage of the population that is registered to vote—from 65 percent before motor-voter in the 1980s to more than 81 percent in 1998.

Another reduction in the cost of voting in Texas involved the adoption and expansion of **early voting,** to replace absentee voting. In 1987, Texas modified the procedures for absentee voting, which required a person to certify that she or he was going to be absent from the county on election day or was incapacitated, to allow anyone to vote by absentee ballot without an excuse. In 1991, the law was modified to extend the period for early voting and to allow counties to establish several permanent and mobile sites for early voting. Presently, early voting extends over a two-week period, commencing 17 days before the election and continuing through the fourth day prior to the election. In most urban counties, there are numerous voting sites, publicized in local newspapers.

The effect of early voting on turnout has been negligible. Statewide in 1998, 28 percent of the votes were cast during the early voting period. Early voting has had an impact on the political parties' get-out-the-vote (GOTV) efforts, moving the start of activities to an earlier date and requiring an adjustment in organization and volunteer recruitment schedules.[36] However, an analysis of early voters and election-day voters indicated that early voters are more partisan, older, more conservative, and more likely to be male than election-day voters. Consequently, they require less mobilization than election-day voters. Candidates can allocate their resources to turn out their core supporters early and then concentrate their campaign efforts on those voters who require stronger issue and candidate appeals to secure their votes on election day.[37]

Although the costs of voting have been reduced significantly in Texas over the past 30 years, a large percentage of Texans still fail to vote. To complete our explanation of voter turnout, we need to consider the benefits of voting.

The Benefits of Voting   The most obvious benefit of voting involves election outcomes—the party and candidates that win the offices contested in the election. Although the results of elections have significant effects on people's lives, an individual person does not have to vote in an election to receive the benefits. The benefits, in terms of the election outcomes, are collective (remember our discussion of collective benefits in Chapter 5) and thus are available to nonvoters, as well as to voters. Consequently, the value of one's vote is not equal to the benefits derived from a given election outcome but to the probability that his or her individual vote will decide a given election. Therefore, the value of voting in most elections is quite small, and it raises questions about why anyone would bother to vote since there are some costs involved. Apparently, the answer lies in the fact that people derive benefits from voting that are not dependent on deciding the outcome of an election. In other words, there are selective benefits (see Chapter 5) associated with voting. According to Ruy Teixeira, the selective benefits are basically *expressive*, which means that the person must find his or her vote meaningful, and divide into two categories:[38]

1. Some people vote to express a general commitment to a political party, a group or social category (ethnicity, gender, or social class), or society in general. These benefits are largely symbolic because they are not directly connected to which candidate wins the election. For instance, an individual may find meaning in his or her commitment to the working class and may use the vote to express that commitment.

2. Other people vote to express a concern about that election and the election's effect on who is elected to public office and the public policies that are likely to be adopted. These benefits are instrumental because they express a desire to achieve certain results through the election of a particular candidate or political party. An individual who votes because he or she strongly supports the policy goals of a certain candidate would be an example.

What factors make a person's vote more meaningful? People with strong interpersonal, community, and general social ties—their **social connectedness**—are more likely to derive expressive benefits from voting. For example, married persons are more likely to vote than unmarried persons. Also, individuals who are members of community organizations are more likely to vote than are nonmembers.

However, **political connectedness** is more important than social connectedness in explaining voter turnout. Because voting is a political activity, a connection to politics—through an identification with or knowledge of a political party, through a psychological and media-based involvement in public affairs, and through a sense of a responsive link between individuals and government—affects how meaningful a person finds elections and influences his or her decision to vote. As we noted in Chapter 4, party identification is weak in Texas. Although the growing strength of the Republican Party in Texas and the resulting increase in electoral competition has probably increased political connectedness among some people, there are still many Texans who do not identify with either political party. Furthermore, feelings that the government is responsive to popular demands, which we defined earlier as **external political efficacy,** are low in Texas. Finally, involvement in public affairs—indicated by campaign interest, reading of campaign news stories, watching of campaign television, and following of government and public affairs—is low in Texas. How does this explanation of voter turnout help us understand changes in voter turnout in Texas over the past century?

Explaining Voter Turnout in Texas: 1890s–1990s   Voter turnout in gubernatorial elections in nonpresidential years over the past century has exhibited several trends. After reaching its zenith in the 1890s, when more than 75 percent of the eligible voters voted, voter turnout in Texas fell precipitously for the next decade, finally stabilizing at approximately 24 percent of the eligible voters by 1910. In the 1920s, voter turnout dipped again, falling into the low teens and remaining there for the next two decades. During the 1950s and 1960s, voter turnout rose to a high of 31 percent in 1970, before falling into the 20 percent range during the 1970s. Voter turnout increased during the 1980s, but it never exceeded 30 percent until the 1990s (Figure 7.3).

Several factors, involving both the costs and the benefits of voting, have contributed to the variation in voter turnout. The initial decline after the 1890s is partly due to the establishment of the poll tax in 1904; however, voter turnout had already declined to approximately 40 percent by the general election in 1902. In 1904, a presidential election year, voter turnout continued its decline to approximately 35 percent. Thus, the increased costs of voting are probably less important than a reduction in benefits in explaining the decline. After 1896, the Populist Party (Chapter 4) was no longer a threat to Democratic Party dominance. As Texas returned to a one-party Democratic state, general elections became less competitive, and voter turnout declined.

The changing composition of the electorate also affected voter turnout. The decline in voter turnout during the 1920s and the 1970s is associated with the enfranchisement of women and young people, respectively. With the ratification of the Nineteenth Amendment, extending suffrage to women, voter turnout decreased as the number of eligible voters nearly doubled. Similarly, when the minimum voting age was reduced from 21 to 18 years in 1972, a large number of former nonvoters were enfranchised, and voter turnout declined. However, when groups who have been disenfranchised have their right to vote restored, as when legal restrictions on voting are removed, voter turnout increases, as it did during the 1950s and 1960s, after the white primary and the poll tax were eliminated.

Undoubtedly, reducing the costs of voting increases voter turnout, but high rates of turnout cannot be achieved solely by lowering the costs of voting. People must be motivated by the benefits of voting. During the 1890s, political campaigns in Texas were party centered. Party workers and their supporters marched strong partisans to the polls. The parties were supported by a partisan press, and they distributed campaign literature to a politically active citizenry. Partisan politics occupied a central role in people's lives, both as a social activity and as a statement of personal identity. Obviously, one cannot recreate the society or the politics of the late nineteenth century, but efforts can be made to connect people with politics by providing the institutional means for people to find meaning in political participation. On the other hand, because of the efforts to reduce the cost of voting in Texas, the percentage of Texans who are registered to vote has increased from 65 percent in the 1980s and early 1990s to more than 81 percent of the voting-age population in 1998. However, early voting procedures have not increased turnout, as only 26.5 percent of the age-eligible voters voted in the most recent gubernatorial election.

The Vote Choice: Parties, Issues, and Candidates

During the entire nineteenth and first part of the twentieth century, the vote choice was party oriented. Most voters practiced **straight-ticket voting,** voting for the same party's candidates for all national, state, and local offices. Currently, the

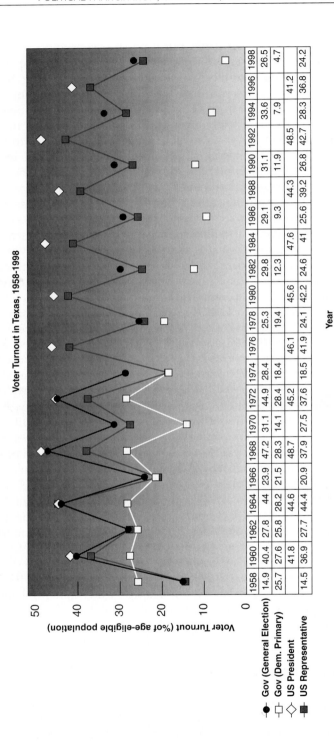

Voter Turnout in Texas, 1958-1998

	1958	1960	1962	1964	1966	1968	1970	1972	1974	1976	1978	1980	1982	1984	1986	1988	1990	1992	1994	1996	1998
Gov (General Election)	14.9	40.4	27.8	44	23.9	47.2	31.1	44.9	28.4		25.3		29.8		29.1		31.1		33.6		26.5
Gov (Dem. Primary)	25.7	27.6	25.8	28.2	21.5	28.3	14.1	28.4	18.4		19.4		12.3		9.3		11.9		7.9		4.7
US President		41.8		44.6		48.7		45.2		46.1		45.6		47.6		44.3		48.5		41.2	
US Representative	14.5	36.9	27.7	44.4	20.9	37.9	27.5	37.6	18.5	41.9	24.1	42.2	24.6	41	25.6	39.2	26.8	42.7	28.3	36.8	24.2

Year

Voter Turnout (% of age-eligible population)

Legend:
- ● Gov (General Election)
- □ Gov (Dem. Primary)
- ◇ US President
- ■ US Representative

Figure 7.3   Voter Turnout in Texas, 1958–1998

The figure depicts the changes in voter turnout in Texas between 1958 and 1998. Note that the percentage of age-eligible voters who voted in the general election for governor in nonpresidential election years until 1962. Also, note that the percentage of age-eligible voters who voted for governor, U.S. president, and U.S. representative varied greatly during the period; however, the general trend has been toward greater participation, with the exception of the most recent gubernatorial election.

Source: Statistical Abstract of the United States, various years; Secretary of State, "Election Turnout and Voter Registration, 1970–Present," Election Function. Accessed 9 January 2000, http://www.sos.state.tx.us/function/elec1/results/70-92.html.

vote choice is more office oriented and person oriented, meaning that the **basis for the vote choice** varies by political office and is more dependent on issues and candidates. Thus, more voters engage in **split-ticket voting,** voting for some Democrats and some Republicans.

Most explanations of the vote choice have focused on three psychological factors: party identification, issues, and candidate characteristics. **Party identification** provided stability in the voter's choice, and assessments of **candidate characteristics** were primarily responsible for the variation in the voter's choice. **Issues** were considered less important. Based on an analysis of voters' choices in presidential elections, the authors of *The American Voter* study implied that vote choices in other elections were motivated by the same factors. However, recent changes in electoral behavior indicate that partisanship is no longer able to structure the vote because of declining partisanship in the electorate and declining strength of partisanship among those members of the electorate who are partisan.[39] Because of the electorate's greater volatility, predicting and explaining the vote choice have become more difficult. Nonetheless, a comparison of the 1986, 1994, and 1998 gubernatorial elections in Texas helps clarify the relative importance of the factors.

The 1986 Gubernatorial Election   In 1986, an incumbent Democratic governor, Mark White, was seeking a second term as Texas's governor. In the Republican primary, three well-known candidates sought the party's gubernatorial nomination: Kent Hance, a former U.S. congressman who had barely lost the Democratic nomination for United States senator in a runoff with Lloyd Doggett in 1984 and who had switched parties in 1985; Tom Loeffler, a Republican U.S. congressman; and the front-runner, William P. Clements, who had become the first Republican governor in over a century in 1978 and who had lost his bid for reelection to Mark White. Despite facing a credible challenge, Clements won the first primary handily, avoiding a divisive and expensive runoff election. Meanwhile, in the Democratic primary, White faced five unknown and poorly financed opponents. Winning the first primary with only 53 percent of the vote, White barely escaped a runoff and was embarrassed.

In 1986, party identification favored the Democratic candidate. In a late 1986 survey, the *Texas Poll* reported that 35 percent of Texans identified with the Democratic Party, 26 percent identified with the Republican Party, and 32 percent were independent. However, among Democratic Party identifiers, White won only 82 percent of the vote, whereas Clements won 92 percent of the Republican vote. Also, among those demographic categories that traditionally support Democratic candidates (low- and moderate-income voters, African Americans, and Hispanics), voter turnout was lower, and support was less enthusiastic than in the gubernatorial election of 1982.[40] Finally, among reasons given for their vote, 20 percent of White's voters and a mere 4 percent of Clements's voters noted party loyalty.

Issues were important to a large number of voters in 1986. In giving reasons for their vote for Bill Clements, 23 percent of the voters mentioned his policies and campaign promises, and another 6 percent provided a specific policy, the economy. For Mark White voters, 27 percent voted for him because of his education reforms, and 16 percent cited his policies and record as governor to explain their vote.

The most important factor, however, to a large number of voters in 1986, involved the candidates. The largest percentage of Clements's voters (38 percent) indicated that they voted for Clements as a vote against Mark White. Almost one-fifth (19 percent) of White's voters indicated that they voted against William Clements.[41] As one study demonstrated, there are several dimensions to candidate characteristics: personal qualities, integrity, reliability, charisma, and competence. Of these factors, competence is the most important and was the basis for the vote against White.[42] Of course, the judgments of the candidates' competence made by the voters included some issue content, but the voters seemed less confident in Mark White's ability to deal with the fiscal situation, which included an estimated $5.3 billion revenue deficit for the next biennium, especially because he had presided over large tax and fee increases during his tenure. Also, the education reforms that White had championed, especially the "no pass, no play" requirements and the tests for public school teachers, and his inability to get the pay raises that he had promised educators hurt White in many areas of the state, especially in rural West Texas and the Texas Panhandle.

More than anything else, the 1986 election demonstrated that although party labels were still important to at least a portion of the electorate, "the better candidate with the better issues and the better campaign can win in most areas regardless of party label."[43]

The 1994 Gubernatorial Election   In 1994, a Democratic governor was also seeking reelection, but Ann Richards was an extremely popular governor and was presiding over what nearly two-thirds of the voters considered an excellent or good economy. Nevertheless, her reelection was not taken for granted when George W. Bush, eldest son of ex-President George H. W. Bush, announced in late 1993 that he would seek the Republican gubernatorial nomination in 1994. Both parties' nominees faced limited opposition in the March primaries, enabling them to save their money for the general election and to avoid a divisive intraparty battle.

In 1994, neither party enjoyed an advantage in party identification. As we noted in Chapter 4, Democratic and Republican identifiers had been approximately equal since 1991, and by early 1994, Republicans barely edged out Democrats in party identification. Fully one-third of the electorate were independents.[44] However, exit polls conducted during the 1994 election in Texas indicated a substantial shift to the Republican Party, with 40 percent of the voters identifying with the Republican Party and 34 percent identifying with the Democratic Party. This shift in party identification among voters is primarily attributed to young voters. In 1986, party identification among the two youngest age categories, 18–29 and 30–44, slightly favored the Democratic Party. In 1994, the Republican Party held an 8 percent lead among 30-to 44-year-old voters and a 22 percent lead among 18-to 29-year-old voters.[45] Among their respective party identifiers, both candidates did well; Richards received 90 percent of the Democratic identifiers' votes, and Bush received 87 percent of the Republican identifiers' votes. Among independents, Bush received 58 percent of the vote to Richards's 41 percent. Also, Richards drew support from those groups that traditionally support Democratic candidates, drawing 88 percent of the African-American vote, 71 percent of the Hispanic vote, 68 percent of low-income voters, and 84 percent of self-identified liberals.

The issues, especially those issues stressed by Bush during the campaign, were apparently important in the voters' choices. The top concerns of Bush voters were crime (39 percent) and education (31 percent). Richards voters indicated the candidates' experience (36 percent), education (31 percent), and crime (31 percent) as their top concerns. Of the two candidates, Bush was more aggressive in pursuit of issues that were considered important by the voters, continually criticizing Richards for her lack of leadership on crime, education, welfare, and tort reform. According to most analysts, Richards gave voters few reasons for giving her four more years as governor.[46]

In 1994, candidate characteristics were less important, although Richards attempted to plant doubts among voters in Bush's ability to be governor by emphasizing his business record. Approximately one-third of the voters thought that both candidates engaged in unfair attacks, but a substantially greater percentage (32 percent) attributed unfair attacks to Richards than to Bush (14 percent). Nevertheless, both candidates received high positive evaluations and low negative evaluations from the electorate throughout the campaign.[47]

Perhaps, the most important factors in the 1994 gubernatorial election were the increasing Republican identification among Texans who voted and a positive response to conservative proposals for dealing with their principal concerns—crime, education, and welfare. In addition, Bush took advantage of a national tide that swept many Republicans into public office. Surely, the election supported the contention that campaigns are important to the vote choice, and a candidate must provide the electorate with a reason to vote for him or her.

The 1998 Gubernatorial Election   In 1998, George W. Bush was expected to win reelection easily. He faced only token opposition in the Republican gubernatorial primary from R. C. Crawford, a Round Rock businessman and one-issue candidate upset with the doctrine of sovereign immunity, which prohibits citizens from suing the State of Texas. Crawford garnered only 3 percent of the primary vote. In the Democratic primary, Garry Mauro, land commissioner from 1983 to 1999, faced no opposition, primarily because John Sharp, who had contemplated seeking the party's gubernatorial nomination, decided to run for lieutenant governor.

In 1998, as in 1994, neither party held an advantage in party identification. Among their respective party identifiers, both candidates did well, but many more Democrats than Republicans defected to the opposition candidate. Mauro received 70 percent of the Democratic identifiers' votes, and Bush received 97 percent of the Republican identifiers' votes. Among independents, Bush received 70 percent of the vote to Mauro's 26 percent. Although Mauro won majorities from several groups that traditionally support Democratic candidates (72 percent of the African-American vote, 52 percent of the Hispanic vote, and 69 percent of self-identified liberals), Bush won a majority of the votes of women (62 percent).

Bush also drew the highest percent of Hispanic vote ever by a Republican gubernatorial candidate (47 percent).[48]

Bush and Mauro voters differed on the issues that were most important to
them, although both candidates' supporters considered education the most important issue. For Bush voters, the top concerns were education (35 percent), taxes
(15 percent), the economy/jobs (14 percent), and crime/drugs (13 percent). Mauro
voters rated education as the top concern (37 percent) followed by the economy/
jobs (21 percent), taxes (8 percent), and welfare (7 percent). Bush's campaign
promises included tax cuts, more money for schools, an end to the "social promotion" of public school students, and modest changes in the areas of juvenile crime
and welfare. During his campaign, Mauro tried several themes—giving a $6000
pay raise for teachers, eliminating the sales tax on automobiles, and giving Texans
in health-care plans the right to choose their doctor. Although Mauro's message
was popular according to public opinion polls, Bush was favored as a candidate.[49]

Analyzing the gubernatorial election in 1998 is more difficult than in 1994 because of the great disparity in campaign spending between Bush and Mauro.
Because of his enormous advantage in campaign contributions, Bush was able to
target his campaign to particular categories of voters, especially Hispanics.[50]
Perhaps the most important factors in the vote choice were Bush's high approval
ratings among Texans (74–75 percent favorable)[51] and Mauro's inability to raise
enough money to make his case effectively with the voters.

Critical Thinking Exercise: Voter turnout is lowest among young
people, age 18–24. Considering the costs and benefits of voting, how could
more young people be convinced to vote? What is your own experience
with voting?

CAMPAIGNS, ELECTIONS, AND POLITICAL CHANGE

Idealistically, elections and their attendant campaigns should provide a choice
between competing visions of government's role and of how to perform that
role—in other words, a governing vision. If these conditions are met, the voters
can choose between those visions and can affirm the status quo or effect political
change. When elections were party oriented, these conditions were more likely
to be met. However, in today's candidate-oriented and office-oriented elections,
the governing vision depends on the office and the candidate, breaking the link-
age that a party can provide between candidates and voters. Thus, the election
of George W. Bush as governor ratifies his governing vision, but it does not ensure that other public officials, elected at the same time, share his governing vision. In fact, because the vote is office and candidate oriented, it almost ensures
that they do not.

In the results of the 1994 election, there is some room for optimism. In Texas,
the 1986 gubernatorial election did not endorse William Clements's governing vision; it negated Mark White's governing vision.[52] In this sense, the election repre-

sented a **retrospective vote**,[53] an evaluation of the performance of the incumbent and a decision to approve or reject that performance. The election did not, consequently, provide any guidance for Governor Clements. On the other hand, there is evidence that the 1994 election was a **prospective vote,** a decision about the future and an indication of the direction that the voters would like Governor Bush to take. The 1998 election, however, provided evidence of both retrospective and prospective voting. Retrospectively, it affirmed George W. Bush's first term as governor, and prospectively, it provided support for his campaign proposals. At least on the issues that Bush addressed, the voters affirmed his vision. The problem of implementing and expanding that vision to include other issues remains. Beyond this problem, the greatest concern about contemporary campaigns and elections focuses on their impact on democracy.

CAMPAIGNS, ELECTIONS, AND DEMOCRACY

As political campaigns have become professionalized, political scientists have struggled with the democratic implications of those campaigns. Larry Sabato has summarized these concerns:

> Political professionals and their techniques have helped homogenize American politics, added significantly to campaign costs, lengthened campaigns, and narrowed the focus of elections. Consultants have emphasized personality and gimmickry over issues, often exploiting emotional and negative themes rather than encouraging rational discussion. They have sought candidates who fit their technologies more than the requirements of office and have given an extra boost to candidates who are more skilled at electioneering than governing. They have encouraged candidates' own worst instincts to blow with the prevailing winds of public opinion. Consultants have even consciously increased nonvoting on occasion.[54]

How realistic are these concerns, and how do they affect the conditions and forms of democracy?

Undoubtedly, the use of political consultants and the professionalization of political campaigns has increased the cost of elections. This increase has narrowed the candidate pool to people who have personal wealth or who have access to money from other sources. As campaign professionals have replaced volunteers, the cost of campaigns has risen dramatically. Also, as fewer volunteers are recruited for campaign-related activities, citizen involvement in political campaigns has decreased. In fact, because campaign consultants are more interested in winning than in promoting political participation, they target for mobilization only those segments of the population that are likely to support their candidate.

Thus, contemporary campaigns do not promote the democratic ideal of universal participation, which ensures political equality (see Chapter 1). Because the techniques employed in professional campaigns are more effective at mobilizing the more affluent segments of society, they increase the likelihood that the lower socioeconomic classes will be passive observers of politics. Also, if issues are a part of a contemporary campaign, they are most likely to be a selected set of issues, which are emotional and current. The full range of possible issues that the candidate, if elected, will have to face during his or her tenure in office is unlikely to be addressed. Finally, professional campaigns have promoted a new type of candidate, more adept in the use of the new technology of political campaigns than in the techniques of governing.

Given the characteristics of contemporary campaigns, elections do little to promote the majoritarian ideal of political equality. The importance of money in contemporary campaigns and the failure of campaigns to fully mobilize the potential electorate promotes political inequality and the interests of the higher socioeconomic classes over those of the lower socioeconomic classes. The exclusion of ethnic, racial, and gender categories through legal barriers to voting have been eliminated, and a form of tyranny has been removed from elections. However, contemporary campaigns do not meet the conditions of deliberation, as the discussion of issues is restricted and the explanation of candidates' positions is less than complete. Consequently, elections are more likely to conform to the pluralist democratic vision, where candidates appeal to and are supported by groups and their members.

Critical Thinking Exercise: Elections are a peaceful and legitimate method of political change in a democracy. However, political activists worry that contemporary campaigns do not address the concerns of most citizens. How could political campaigns be changed to ensure a stronger, more vibrant democracy in Texas? How did the Texan Creed influence your proposal?

SUMMARY

In this chapter, we identified and explained the principal forms of political participation—conventional and unconventional—and described the modes of political participation—voters, contactors, communicators, campaigners, community activists, protesters, and complete activists.

We have also described and analyzed elections, election campaigns, and the voter's decisions. We have noted the many opportunities for voting in Texas and described several kinds of elections—primary, special, general, and local. We described political campaigns in Texas and noted the increasing influence of money, media, and marketing on contemporary political campaigns. We explained the costs and benefits of voting and the effect of each on voter turnout. We explained the three bases for the vote choice—party, issues, and candidates—and compared the 1986, 1994, and 1998 gubernatorial elections in Texas.

Finally, we assessed the importance of political participation, campaigns, and elections to political change and democracy in Texas.

KEY TERMS

political participation
conventional political participation
unconventional political participation
internal political efficacy
political trust
modes of political participation
voters
contactors
communicators
campaigners
community activists
protesters
complete activists
primary elections
closed primary
open primary
blanket primary
unitary primary
special elections
general elections
local elections
political campaigns
money
media

marketing
benchmark poll
tracking polls
focus groups
promotional spots
attack spots
opposition research
voter turnout
costs of voting
benefits of voting
motor-voter registration system
early voting
social connectedness
political connectedness
external political efficacy
straight-ticket voting
bases of the vote choice
split-ticket voting
party identification
candidate characteristics
issues
retrospective vote
prospective vote

SUGGESTED READINGS

Ansolabehere, Stephen, Roy Behr, and Shanto Iyengar. *The Media Game: American Politics in the Television Age.* New York: Macmillan, 1993.

Bennett, W. Lance. *The Governing Crisis: Media, Money, and Marketing in American Elections,* 2d ed. New York: St. Martin's Press, 1996.

Bowler, Shaun, Todd Donovan, and Caroline Tolbert, eds. *Citizens as Legislators: Direct Democracy in the United States.* Columbus, Ohio: Ohio State University Press, 1998.

Hogan, Robert E. "Campaign and Contextual Influences on Voter Participation in State Legislative Elections," *American Politics Quarterly* 77 (October 1999): 403–433.

Rosentone, Steven J., and John Mark Hansen. *Mobilization, Participation, and Democracy in America.* New York: Macmillan, 1993.

Stein, Robert M. "Early Voting," *Public Opinion Quarterly* 62 (Spring 1998): 57–69.

Texans for Public Justice. *The Gated Community: How Texas Incumbents Locked Out Challengers in 1998.* Austin, Tex.: Texans for Public Justice, 1999.

Verba, Sidney, Kay Lehman Scholzman, and Henry E. Brady. *Voice and Equality: Civic Volutarism in American Politics.* Cambridge, Mass.: Harvard University Press, 1995.

NOTES

1. Paul Burka, "Two for Texas," *Texas Monthly,* October 1998, 124.
2. Juan B. Elizondo, Jr., "Opposing Bush Ads Heat Up Key Race," *Austin American-Statesman,* 10 October 1998.
3. Juan B. Elizondo, Jr., "Negative Ads Float on the Autumn Air," *Austin American-Statesman,* 8 October 1998, p. B6.
4. Juan B. Elizondo, Jr., "In Sharp-Perry Ad War, the Star Sheriff Wavers," *Austin American-Statesman,* 24 October 1998; Juan B. Elizondo, Jr., "Perry Aide: Ad Recalls Horton Jab," *Austin American-Statesman,* 19 October 1998, pp. B1, B7.
5. David Beiler, "The Eyes of America Were Upon Him," *Campaigns & Elections,* July 1999, 48–53.
6. "Looking Closer at the Texas Vote," *Dallas Morning News,* 4 November 1998, p. A28.
7. Lester W. Milbrath and M. I. Goel, *Political Participation in America: How and Why Do People Get Involved in Politics?,* 2d ed. (Chicago: Rand McNally, 1977), 2.
8. Ibid.; Sidney Verba and Norman H. Nie, *Participation in America: Political Democracy and Social Equality* (New York: Harper and Row, 1972).
9. Milbrath and Goel, *Political Participation in America,* 12–21.
10. Fred Gantt Jr., *The Chief Executive in Texas: A Study in Gubernatorial Leadership* (Austin, Tex.: University of Texas Press, 1964), 269–271.
11. Dave McNeely, "GOP Voters Switch to Fight Richards," *Austin American-Statesman,* 5 April 1994, p. A11.
12. Richard Murray, "The 1982 Texas Election in Perspective," *Texas Journal of Political Studies* 5 (Spring/Summer 1983): 49–50. Paul Burka, "Primary Lesson," *Texas Monthly,* July 1986, 104–105.
13. W. Lance Bennett, *The Governing Crisis: Media, Money, and Marketing in American Elections* (New York: St. Martin's Press, 1992), 84–111.
14. *Austin American-Statesman,* 18 February 1995, p. B3.
15. Texans for Public Justice, *The Gated Community: How Texas House Incumbents Locked Out Challengers in 1998* (Austin, Tex.: Texans for Public Justice, 1999).
16. Kaye Northcott, "Getting Elected," *Mother Jones,* November 1982, 18.
17. Quoted in Northcott, "Getting Elected," 19.
18. Northcott, "Getting Elected," 21.
19. *Austin American-Statesman,* 29 July 1994, p. B1; 3 November 1994, p. B1; and 6 November 1994, p. A15.
20. See Jon Ford, "Texas: Big Money," in *Campaign Money: Reform and Reality in the States,* ed. Herbert E. Alexander (New York: Free Press, 1976), 78–109.
21. Quoted in David Elliot, "Image Is Everything: How TV Has Reshaped Campaigning," *Austin American-Statesman,* 16 October 1994, pp. A1, A8.
22. *Texas Poll Report* (Fall 1986): 4.
23. Richard Joslyn, *Mass Media and Elections* (Reading, Mass.: Addison-Wesley, 1984), 35–47.
24. For an excellent article on Texas campaign consultants, see Juan B. Elizondo, Jr., "Political Consultants: How They Do It," *Austin American-Statesman,* 18 October 1998, pp. H1, H5.
25. Larry J. Sabato, *The Rise of Political Consultants: New Ways of Winning Elections* (New York: Basic Books, 1981), 36–37.
26. Harrison Donnelly, "The Business of Politics," *Editorial Research Reports,* 15 January 1988, 15–16.
27. Dan Nimmo, *The Political Persuaders: The Techniques of Modern Election Campaigns* (Englewood Cliffs, N.J.: Prentice-Hall, 1970), 90–91.
28. Sabato, *The Rise of Political Consultants,* 147.

29. Everett Carll, ed., *America at the Polls, 1994* (Storrs, Conn.: The Roper Center for Public Opinion Research, 1995), 78.

30. Jerry Hagstrom and Robert Guskind, "Calling the Races," *National Journal,* 30 July 1988, 1972–1975; Elliot, "Image Is Everything," p. A8.

31. Sabato, *The Rise of Political Consultants,* 79–80; Hagstrom and Guskind, "Calling the Races," 1975.

32. Sabato, *The Rise of Political Consultants,* 111–219.

33. Stephen Ansolabehere, Roy Behr, and Shanto Iyengar, *The Media Game: American Politics in the Television Age* (New York: Macmillan, 1993), 78–97.

34. John F. Persinos, "Gotcha," *Campaigns and Elections,* August 1994, 20–23, 56, 58.

35. Elliot, "Image Is Everything," p. A8.

36. Delbert A. Taebel, Nirmal Goswami, and Laurence Jones, "The Politics of Early Voting in Texas: Perspectives of County Party Chairs," *Texas Journal of Political Studies* 16 (Spring/Summer 1994): 43–44.

37. Robert M. Stein, "Early Voting," *Public Opinion Quarterly* 62 (Spring 1998): 57–69.

38. Ruy A. Teixeira, *The Disappearing American Voter* (Washington, D.C.: Brookings Institution, 1992), 12–13.

39. Morris P. Fiorina, "The Electorate at the Polls in the 1990s," in *The Parties Respond: Changes in American Parties and Campaigns,* 2d ed., ed. L. Sandy Maisel (Boulder, Colo. Westview Press, 1994), 124–125. Angus Campbell, Philip E. Converse, Warren E. Miller, and Donald E. Stokes, *The American Voter* (Chicago: University of Chicago Press, 1960), 523–531, provides the classic statement of the influence of these factors.

40. *Texas Poll Report* (Fall 1986): 4; Kent L. Tedin, "The 1982 Election for Governor of Texas," *Texas Journal of Political Studies* 5 (Spring/Summer 1983): 29.

41. John C. Henry, "Poll Shows Anti-White Sentiment," *Austin American-Statesman,* 5 December 1986, p. B2.

42. Arthur H. Miller, Martin P. Wattenberg, and Oksana Malanchuk, "Schematic Assessments of Presidential Candidates," *American Political Science Review,* 80 (June 1986): 521–540.

43. Thomas L. Whatley, *Texas Government Newsletter,* 17 November 1986, 2.

44. *Texas Poll Report* (January–March 1994): 6.

45. Ladd, *America at the Polls, 1994,* 90.

46. See, for example, Thomas L. Whatley, "Election '94—Post Mortem," *Texas Government Newsletter,* 14 November 1994, 2.

47. *The Dallas Morning News,* 9 November 1994, p. A17; *Texas Poll Report* (January–March 1994): 4.

48. "Looking Closer at the Texas Vote." *Dallas Morning News,* 4 November 1998, p. A28; Everett Carll Ladd, ed., *America at the Polls, 1998* (Storrs, Conn.: The Roper Center for Public Opinion Research, 1999), 97.

49. Wayne Slater and Terrace Stutz "Bush Wins Re-election, Boosts National Standing," *Dallas Morning News,* 4 November 1998, p. A28.

50. See Louis Dubose, "El Governador," The *American Prospect Online,* 23 November 1999, Accessed 27 November 1999, http://www.prospect.org/archives/V11-1/dubose.html.

51. *Scripps-Howard Texas Poll Report* (2d Quarter 1998): 7; *Scripps-Howard Texas Poll Report* (3d Quarter 1998): 7.

52. Jeanie R. Stanley, "Party Realignment and the 1986 Texas Elections," *Texas Journal of Political Studies* 9 (Spring/Summer 1987): 8–9.

53. Morris Fiorina, *Retrospective Voting in American National Elections* (New Haven, Conn.: Yale University Press, 1981).

54. Sabato, *The Rise of Political Consultants,* 7.

Texas Legislative Politics

★ Scenario: Sharpstown—How a Political Scandal Triggers Creedal Passion

The story of the **Sharpstown scandal** is a classic example of a public scandal in which public officials (a) took money to change public policy for the benefit of a few individuals; (b) covered up what had happened and intimidated and punished those who exposed it; (c) got caught in an embarrassing public exposé; (d) were convicted of violating the law; and (e) were thrown out of office.

In 1969, Houston banker and businessman Frank Sharp lobbied the Texas legislature to set up a new bank insurance system. The legislature authorized only a study of his idea.[1] Governor Preston Smith called a special session of the legislature to pass the state budget, and he also asked the legislature to consider "legislation providing for additional insurance on bank deposits." An ally of House Speaker Gus Mutscher introduced Sharp's proposals in two **bills,** legislative documents to create or amend a law. The bills' sponsor told his fellow legislators that

"These are the Speaker's bills," and they quickly passed. By the time the bills reached the governor's desk, bank lobbyists had persuaded Smith to veto them.

In 1970, Governor Smith, Lieutenant Governor Ben Barnes, and House Speaker Mutscher were reelected. During the 1971 inaugural festivities, newspapers reported allegations that Sharp had bribed state officials. Sharp allegedly loaned them money from his Sharpstown National Bank with which to buy stock in one of his companies, then manipulated the stock price, allowing them to make a profit—in exchange for approving his bills.

As the 1971 session got under way, legislators were nervous and embarrassed. Representative Frances Farenthold introduced a resolution to begin an investigation. Gus Mutscher was used to getting his way. A lobbyist later described him to one of your authors as a speaker who would "twist arms and break fingers" in ruling the House. Mutscher would not recognize Farenthold for a vote on the resolution, so Representative Lane Denton appealed the ruling of the chair to the House. This is a motion almost never made, because it is seen as a direct challenge of the speaker's authority.

Dirty Thirty leader Representative Frances (Sissy) Farenthold addresses the House from the front microphone. Speaker Gus Mutscher stands at the speaker's desk behind Representative Farenthold.

The House voted against the appeal, 30 to 118. By some accounts, business lobbyists in the gallery, supporters of Mutscher, exclaimed, "We're going to get those thirty dirty bastards who voted against us." Thus was born the "**Dirty Thirty**"—a group of liberal Democrats and conservative Republicans who over the next two years fought vigorously for reforms of the legislative process.

The 1971 session was tense and combative. The Dirty Thirty used speeches and parliamentary procedures to oppose the House leadership and to demonstrate to the public that Mutscher's ability to win passage of the bank bill was simply one embarrassing example of the closed nature of the legislative process. They referred to Mutscher as a dictator and to his chief allies as "Nazi pickpockets." A Mutscher ally called the Dirty Thirty "a bunch of playboy kids."[2] Fistfights broke out on the House floor, and armed police were sometimes on guard. Media coverage of the unfolding corruption scandal and the internal legislative battles fanned public support for reforms.

The Dirty Thirty had no success—for their bills, for legislative reform proposals, or for a legislative redistricting plan that would give them a fair chance of reelection. The Dirty Thirty decided "to take their reform program to the voters." In essence, they mounted a campaign for deliberative democracy, describing themselves as "independent, reform-minded" legislators "pressing for reform in the legislative rules to allow full and open debate on substantive issues." They ranked the legislators on key votes; recruited candidates to run against antireform **incumbents** (current officeholders) and endorsed 51 Democrats and 26 Republicans as reform candidates.[3] Newspapers carried articles on how their local legislators fared in the Dirty Thirty's rankings and reported a strong public reaction against the scandal-plagued legislature.

The Dirty Thirty toured the state to build support for their reform agenda and their candidates. In so doing, they exploited the perceived gap between the ideals of democracy and the reality of Texas political institutions. One said, "The problem must be solved by correcting the system itself. Democracy must be returned to the House."[4] At a banquet at Baylor University, 300 people heard that corrupt politicians were "the most dangerous type of criminals . . . They steal our confidence in our system of government. . . . It took a scandal to bring to light what is wrong in Austin." At the University of Houston, Dirty Thirty members said, "We're concerned with highhanded tactics which have made the deliberative process a farce."[5]

In early 1972, Speaker Mutscher and others were convicted on bribery charges. Mutscher received five years probation. When Governor Smith called a special session to consider election-financing measures, Mutscher resigned the speakership, and one of his allies won the speakership. Then came the astounding results of the 1972 elections. Seventeen of the 18 Dirty Thirty members who sought reelection won, and 2 of them won Texas Senate seats. Both former Speaker Mutscher and the replacement speaker were defeated for renomination, as were other supporters of Mutscher. Still others lost to Republicans in the general election.

The **turnover rate** for the 1973 legislature was the largest in recent history: Just over 50 percent of the House members were freshmen, compared to the usual turnover rate of about 20 percent. The reformers decided to run a candidate for speaker: Representative Price Daniel, Jr., a sometimes ally of the Dirty Thirty and son of former Governor and U.S. Senator Price Daniel. The younger Daniel ran on a reform platform. He campaigned around the state, rather than just inside the Texas legislature, and appealed to the public's perception of a gap between ideals and institutions. With the enlarged bloc of reform legislators, Daniel won the speakership. The 1973 session went down in history as the "Reform Session," passing Open Meetings, Open Records, Lobbyist Registration, and Campaign Finance Disclosure Acts.

The Sharpstown scandal triggered a period of creedal passion in Texas politics. The 1972 election results and the 1973 reforms would not have happened had the public not been aroused to bring public institutions more into line with their ideal of what they should be. The moral outrage at the dissonance between the core components of democracy—nontyranny, political equality, participation and deliberation—and the reality of legislative politics in the Mutscher era led to increased public participation and an attempt to realign the institution with those ideals. Twenty years went by before any significant demand for new reforms. Further, the reforms adopted in the 1993 session, occurring in a period of mild public anger (and cynicism) rather than intense creedal passion, were milder than the 1973 reforms. ★

INTRODUCTION

Sharpstown provides an entertaining backdrop for examining the Texas legislature. In addition, the events of Sharpstown are important to study because they encapsulate many of the issues of power, structure, and process that are critical to understanding the Texas legislature and its role in Texas democracy.

The Texas legislature serves the following functions: to represent the people in government; to legislate, budget, and tax; to perform constituent casework; to oversee the bureaucracy; to consider amendments (proposed changes) to the Texas and U.S. Constitutions; to confirm the governor's appointees; to **redistrict** (redraw election-district boundaries) itself and the U.S. congressional districts in Texas; and to **impeach** (accuse) and remove from office corrupt officials.

On Tuesday, January 12, 1999, the 76th Legislature convened in Austin.[6] The senators and representatives adopted rules, selected leaders, and set to work considering 5766 bills to change public policy, 142 resolutions to amend the Texas Constitution, and 3011 other resolutions. On May 31, 140 days later, the legislature adjourned, having passed 1622 of the bills, 17 of the constitutional amendments, and 2859 other resolutions. Governor Bush could call it back into special 30-day sessions later. This pattern of regular sessions and occasional special sessions of the legislature has been repeated for more than a century.

There is much to learn about the structure and process of the legislature, but were we to study it alone, we would not fully understand the place of the legislature in the political system. We must also look at external forces that influence its actions, such as elections, lobbyists, governors, the media, and, yes, periods of creedal passion.

Te★as*Index*

Legislatures in the United States

Number of legislatures with annual sessions: 43
Number of legislatures with biennial sessions: 7
Regular legislative sessions:
Texas—140 days, every other year
California—no limit on length
New York—no limit on length
Florida—60 days
Special legislative sessions:
Texas—30-day limit, called only by the governor
California—no limit, called by the governor
New York—no limit, may be called by the legislature
Florida—20-day limit
Size of the state house of representatives, 1999:
Texas—150 (8th)
California—80 (36th)
New York—150 (8th)
Florida—120 (16th)
Size of the state senate, 1999:
Texas—31 (40th)
California—40 (19th)
New York—61 (2nd)
Florida—40 (19th)
Number of states with legislative salaries set in the state constitution: 3
Annual legislative salaries, 1999:
U.S. Congress—$140,000
Texas state legislators—$7,200 (41st)
California—$78,624 (1st)
New York—$57,500 (2nd)
Florida—$24,912 (17th)
Women as a percentage of the legislature in 1999:
Texas—18%
California—25%
New York—20%
Florida—24%

In this chapter, we examine the structure and the membership of the legislature; the ways **legislative leadership** (the House speaker, Senate president, and committee chairpersons) and **legislative opposition** (those opposed to the leadership either on a bill or more generally) organize and operate; the legislative process; the role of legislative staff; and external influences on legislative behavior. We then return to Sharpstown as an example of the legislature and political change, especially in an era of creedal passion. We conclude with an examination of democracy in the legislature.

THE STRUCTURE OF THE TEXAS LEGISLATURE

The Texas legislature, like all state legislatures except Nebraska, is **bicameral**—it has two chambers. The Senate consists of 31 members, ranking fortieth in size among the states. The Texas House of Representatives consists of 150 members, ranking eighth.[7] The 1876 constitution set the size of the Senate but allowed the House to grow to a maximum of 150 seats, which it reached in 1923.

Both the House and the Senate must pass a bill for it to become law. Nonetheless, there are a few differences in the duties of the two chambers. The House has the responsibility of initiating action to raise state revenue. The Senate has the responsibility of confirming the governor's appointees to state offices. Article 15 of the constitution allows the House to impeach public officials and the Senate to try and, if convicted, to remove impeached officials from office.[8] It does not specify any breach of standards of conduct or any other reasons that must be given for the impeachment. **Impeachment** requires a majority vote in the House, and conviction requires a two-thirds vote in the Senate.

Sessions of the Legislature

Ours is a **biennial legislature**—it meets regularly once every two years. Biennial state legislatures were common in the nineteenth and into the twentieth century, out of the belief that "citizen" legislators could tend to the affairs of the state in a short period of time, then return to their jobs and families. Today, 43 states have annual sessions, and Texas is the only large, urban state that uses biennial sessions.[9]

The constitution calls the biennial session of the legislature a **regular session.** The original 1876 constitution did not say how long a regular session could last, but it did contain an economic incentive for short sessions. Legislators were paid more for the early part of the session than for the later weeks! In 1960, voters approved an amendment establishing a 140-day limit for regular sessions.

The constitution also allows for **special** or **called sessions** of the legislature. Only the governor may call the legislature into special session. This is a significant power of the governor because he or she may call one at any time for any purpose. The governor must specify what issues the legislature is being called to consider, although the governor can add subjects to the call of the session even after it has begun. Thus, the governor is in complete control of the agenda of a special session. A special session may last no longer than 30 days. However, there is no limit on how many sessions a governor may call, and they have been called back to back. Governor Ann Richards called four special sessions in the 1991–1992 biennium and none in the 1993–1994 biennium. Governor George W. Bush called none in his first five years in office.

> **Critical Thinking Exercise:** What are the implications of biennial sessions? What difference would it make if Texas had annual legislative sessions? If we were to change, how would you structure the sessions?

Leaders

The constitution declares that the lieutenant governor shall serve as **Senate president** and that the Senate shall elect a president **pro-tempore** (or **pro-tem**) to serve in the absence of the lieutenant governor.[10] The constitution states that the House of Representatives shall choose its leader, the **House speaker,** from among its

Outgoing Lieutenant Governor Bob Bullock Swears in Pete Laney for another term as Speaker of the House in 1999.

members. At the beginning of each regular session, the House elects a speaker for the biennium. The speaker appoints a speaker pro-tem.

Winning speaker candidates are usually veteran legislators. Lieutenant governors are typically older, experienced politicians, politically powerful enough to win a statewide election. In recent times, Ben Barnes has been the exception. He became the House speaker in 1965, at age 26, and lieutenant governor in 1969, at age 31.

The process of selecting the speaker is the most critical factor in how the House operates (see the section on organizing for power and influence). The concentration of power in the hands of the Senate president and the House speaker provides compelling evidence of a majoritarian rather than a pluralist form of democracy in the Texas legislature.

Committees

The legislature works through a system of committees. A **committee** is a subunit of the legislature appointed to work on designated subjects. Legislatures use committees because a full house or senate could not possibly do all the work as one large body. Committees also help legislators develop subject specialties and, presumably, to then make better-informed public policies. Table 8.1 defines the types of committees. Standing committees are the basic committees that do most of the work during legislative sessions. They can be either substantive, focusing on legislation, or procedural, focusing on legislative procedures. At the beginning of a regular session, the House and Senate create standing committees, and the chairs of those committees appoint ad hoc subcommittees for specific bills. Some Senate committees also have permanent subcommittees.

In most sessions, the standing committees from the previous legislature are simply re-created. However, when there is turnover in leadership, such as the election of a new speaker in 1993 and a new Senate president in 1999, the committee structure is changed. Table 8.2 lists the standing committees and the number of members of each one for the 1999–2000 biennium. House members typically serve on two or three committees. Senators serve on three or four standing committees and subcommittees.

Two of the most significant powers of the speaker and the lieutenant governor are the powers to appoint legislators to committees and to appoint the committee chairpersons. In the 1970s, the House created a weak seniority system for assignment to substantive committees. Each member selects one committee that he or she wants to serve on, but the speaker does not have to honor every seniority request—a maximum of one-half of a committee's members, excluding the chair and vice chair, may be determined by seniority, with the other half completely within the power of the speaker to name. House committee chairs appoint subcommittee members and chairs. In the Senate, the lieutenant governor appoints chairs of the standing subcommittees.

Committee meetings are perhaps the best and worst example of deliberative democracy. Committee work can be long, painstaking examination of policy mat-

Table 8.1 TYPES OF LEGISLATIVE COMMITTEES

Standing committees

A standing committee is created at the beginning of a legislative biennium and continues in existence throughout the biennium.

Substantive committees

A substantive committee considers legislation as its primary duty. Most substantive committees are standing committees.

Procedural committees

A procedural committee is a standing committee that has jurisdiction over such things as legislative rules and calendars and administration of the House or Senate.

Special (or ad hoc) committees

Sometimes the House or Senate will create a committee to study a specific problem or policy area. The committee is given a certain amount of time to complete its work, then it goes out of existence.

Interim committees

The speaker and lieutenant governor issue "charges" to the standing committees for what they are to study during the interim between sessions. For high-profile issues, sometimes a special interim committee (or a commission, including some nonlegislative members) will be appointed—for instance, the Select Committee on Teacher Health Insurance, created to report to the legislature in 2001.

Joint committees

A joint committee is one created by both the House and the Senate, with members from both chambers, for a specific duty. Examples include the Legislative Budget Board, the Legislative Council, and the Legislative Reference Library Board.

Conference committees

A conference committee is a joint committee appointed by the House and the Senate for one specific bill. When the House and the Senate both pass a bill, but with differing provisions, a conference committee is appointed to write a common version of the bill and to a report it back to the House and Senate.

ters, leading to mark-up, or redrafting and amending, of the bills. Public hearings can be educational for the committee members, who may not know much about the subject, but who must come to understand it enough to defend the committee's work. On the other hand, decisions are often made before the hearing, and public hearings can become what legislators derisively refer to as dog-and-pony shows, with no real chance to affect the outcome. (Table 8.3 presents a brief glossary of some legislative lingo.)

Table 8.2 LEGISLATIVE COMMITTEES OF THE 76TH LEGISLATURE, 1999–2000

House committees (number of members)	Senate committees (number of members)
Substantive committees	**Substantive committees**
Agriculture and Livestock (9)	Border Affairs (special) (7)
Appropriations (27)	Criminal Justice (7)
Business and Industry (9)	Economic Development (7)
Civil Practices (9)	Subcom. on Technology and Business Growth (5)
Constitutional Revision (9)*	Education (9)
Corrections (9)	Subcommittee on Higher Education (5)
County Affairs (9)	Electric Utility Restructuring (special) (7)
Criminal Jurisprudence (9)	Finance (11)
Economic Development (9)	Health Services (5)
Elections (9)	Human Services (5)
Energy Resources (9)	Intergovernmental Relations (5)
Environmental Regulation (9)	Jurisprudence (5)
Financial Institutions (9)	Natural Resources (7)
Higher Education (9)	Subcommittee on Agriculture (3)
Human Services (9)	State Affairs (9)
Insurance (9)	Subcommittee on Infrastructure (5)
Judicial Affairs (9)	Veterans Affairs and Military Installations (5)
Juvenile Justice and Family Issues (9)	
Land and Resource Management (9)	**Procedural committees**
Licensing and Administrative Procedures (9)	Administration (5)
Natural Resources (9)	Nominations (7)
Pensions and Investments (9)	
Public Education (9)	
Public Health (9)	
Public Safety (9)	
State Affairs (15)	
State, Federal, and International Relations (9)	
State Recreational Resources (9)	
Transportation (9)	
Urban Affairs (9)	
Ways and Means (11)	
Procedural committees	
Calendars (11)	
General Investigating (5)	
House Administration (11)	
Local and Consent Calendars (11)	
Redistricting (11)	
Rules and Resolutions (11)	

*Special committee

Table 8.3   A GLOSSARY OF LEGISLATIVE LINGO

Legislators often use colorful words and phrases in their debates. The following are some terms that may be unfamiliar or confusing to casual observers:

Backscratching
Helping another legislator with a vote, with the expectation that he or she will return the favor.

Carrying water
Sponsoring a bill or an amendment, at the request of a lobbyist.

Dog-and-pony show
Committee hearings that last for hours, featuring scores of witnesses who tell emotional and personal stories to persuade legislators to vote a bill out of committee or to kill it.

Gerrymandering
Drawing redistricting lines in a way that either helps or hurts either an incumbent or a group of voters, such as Democrats, Republicans, Anglos, or Mexican Americans.

Gutting
Amending a bill in committee or on the floor in such a way that it severely weakens the bill or changes its original purpose.

Keying
Watching another legislator to see which way he or she is voting before deciding how to vote. Floor leaders extend an arm with one finger held high to indicate that followers should vote "aye" or with two fingers held high to indicate that followers should vote "nay."

Logrolling
Supporting and voting for another member's bill, especially a "local" bill, affecting only the author's district, with the assumption that he or she will then support you when you have a bill coming up.

Pork barrel
Appropriations of money to a project in a single legislative district.

Taking a walk
Leaving a committee hearing or the floor to avoid having to take a vote on a controversial bill if such a vote would hurt the legislator with one group or another.

"That dog won't hunt"
A debating point suggesting that the legislator believes another member's argument to be weak.

LEGISLATIVE MEMBERSHIP—REPRESENTING THE PUBLIC

Members of the Texas legislature represent the public in government. Differences over the nature of **representation,** how to achieve representation, and equality of representation are never-ending battles for democracies.

Citizens authorize representation on their behalf by electing legislators to set terms of office, giving them the authority to represent. If legislators want to serve again, the reelection process provides a way for voters to evaluate their actions, judge how responsive they have been, and either reward them or turn them out of office. A key to the legitimacy of representation, then, must be the honesty and fairness of the electoral system. Questions arise about the adequacy and legitimacy of the representation if one group constantly wins representation and other groups constantly lose.

> **Critical Thinking Exercise:**   How would you judge the legitimacy of representation in Texas? What variables would you consider to make that judgment? How does Texas rate on those variables?

It is the members of the legislature who make the institution work, and thus it is important to examine qualifications and characteristics of the membership and what influences the selection of those members. Another reason to understand who they are is that they have an opportunity for influence far beyond the legislature. The legislature often contains future top leaders. Sam Rayburn was elected speaker of the Texas House of Representatives in 1911 and went on to become the longest-serving speaker of the U.S. House of Representatives. Texas leaders who served in the legislature include U.S. Senator Kay Bailey Hutchison, 12 of 30 U.S. representatives, Lieutenant Governor Rick Perry, and Agriculture Commissioner Susan Combs.

Constitutional Provisions Affecting Legislators

The Texas Constitution sets out the length of legislative terms of office, the requirements that a person must meet to serve as a legislator, the provisions for legislators' pay, and the provisions limiting what a legislator may do in office. These requirements are shown in Table 8.4.

Length of Terms   Representatives are elected for two-year terms and senators for four-year terms, with no limit on the number of terms they may serve. Senate elections are staggered—15 seats are up for election, then two years later, the other 16 are up for election. After redistricting sessions, such as 2001, all senators must run because new district boundaries are drawn. Senators draw lots to see who serves a two-year term and who gets a four-year term, so that membership terms return to a staggered system.

Compensation   Texas legislators are among the lowest paid in the nation. Legislative salaries are established in the constitution at $600 per month, for each month of the term of office, or $7,200 per year. Nationwide, state legislative salaries range from $78,624 in California and $57,500 a year in New York to $200 in New Hampshire (and no per diem).[11] Some states also pay salary supplements to leaders.

Table 8.4   CONSTITUTIONAL REQUIREMENTS AFFECTING LEGISLATORS

	Senate	House
Residency	5 years in Texas; 1 year in district	2 years in Texas; 1 year in district
Minimum age	26 years	21 years
Term of office	4 years	2 years
Both the Senate and the House		
Citizenship	United States	
Voting status	Qualified (registered) voter	
Salary	$600 per month	
Conflict of interest	Must disclose any personal interest in a bill; may not hold any other state office or contract	

Source: Texas Constitution, Article 3.

Texas legislators' pay was last raised, by constitutional amendment, in 1974. In 1991, voters amended the constitution to allow the new Ethics Commission to propose a higher salary, subject to approval by the voters. The commission may also propose higher salaries for the speaker and the lieutenant governor. The commission has taken no action under this new authority.

Legislators also get a **per diem** (per day) allowance to cover room and board expenses when they are engaged in state business. During regular sessions, legislators typically rent apartments; during other trips to Austin, they usually rent hotel rooms. The 1991 constitutional amendment allows the Ethics Commission to set the rate at an amount no higher than the maximum federal tax deduction for business expenses. The commission adopted the rate of $118 per day for 1999.

Variables Affecting Members' Elections

Two variables involving legislative elections are significant in determining who the members of the legislature are. First, members run from districts, so we examine how the lines for those districts are drawn. Second, members may run for re-election to an unlimited number of terms, so we examine the stability or turnover in legislative membership.

Redistricting   Legislators are chosen in **single-member districts** (each legislator represents a separate, distinct election district). Because districts become unequal in population size over time, the U.S. and the Texas Constitutions require that the district lines be redrawn every decade to assure citizens equal representation, regardless of where they live.[12] The legislature redistricts in the year after the federal census, such as 2001.

The ultimate goal of redistricting is to create districts with equal-sized populations. Based on an estimated 2000 census of 20 million Texans, the ideal Texas Senate district size is about 645,000 constituents, and the ideal Texas House district size is about 133,000 constituents. Reaching that goal of equality is a process laden with political intrigue and hidden traps. Political parties, incumbents running for reelection, courts, the U.S. Justice Department, and racial and ethnic groups are the primary players in redistricting politics, and their goals are often at odds. Legislators often gerrymander districts, drawing the lines to enhance or diminish the power of one party or of one racial or ethnic group.

The U.S. Voting Rights Act declares that states with a history of electoral discrimination against minority groups—including Texas—must preclear redistricting plans with the U.S. Justice Department or the U.S. District Court of the District of Columbia. Also, the U.S. Supreme Court has ruled that redistricting raises constitutional questions of equal representation, so courts (federal and state) have jurisdiction to review redistricting plans. The court is divided over the issue of racial gerrymandering and has given mixed signals about it in cases such as *Shaw v. Reno* (1993) and *Hunt v. Cromartie* (1999).[13]

Before 1970, when there were few Republican legislators in Texas, redistricting rarely raised questions about party representation. Incumbent legislators simply bargained for the best district from which to win reelection. As Republicans, Mexican Americans, and African Americans increased their representation, it came at the expense of Anglo Democrats, making redistricting battles more partisan and race conscious.

In 1981, Democrats had their usual majority in the legislature, giving them an advantage in redistricting. However, the Republican governor could veto a redistricting plan, so Republicans had a strong bargaining chip. In 1991, Democrats still had a majority, and Democrat Ann Richards had just been elected governor. Republicans, Mexican Americans, and African Americans all proposed redistricting maps that would be to their greatest advantage. Anglo Democratic incumbents wanted to protect their seats, but they knew that if they protected themselves too strongly, the courts could reject their plan and write their own plan. That is exactly what happened.

The new districts drawn by the courts for 1993 resulted in an increase for Republicans in the Senate and for minorities in both chambers. The court decision for the Senate was highly controversial. The federal judges had been appointed by Republican presidents. One judge, a former Republican Texas state representative, had contact with a Republican legislator in drafting the court plan and was later censured for his actions. In 1993, the new Senate redrew lines in a way that would benefit minorities but would not benefit Republicans so much. A federal district court upheld this new plan. In 1994, Republicans still gained an additional seat. In 1995, a group of Republican voters sued the state to overturn the House plan. The House negotiated with the plaintiffs and redrew some districts in metropolitan areas, and the U.S. Justice Department and a federal court panel approved the new plan. The 1990s redistricting skirmishes led to increased Republican representation, including Republican majority Senates in 1997 and 1999.

Reelection Rates and Turnover of Membership In the early years, more than four-fifths of Texas legislators served a single term and did not seek reelection.[14] In modern times, most incumbents seek reelection, and most are successful. Many legislators make a career of politics. Across the United States, out of a sense of frustration that the system of representation and election is biased in favor of incumbents staying in office, a new term-limitation political movement is astir. As of 1999, 18 states had adopted state legislature term limitations.[15] However, Texas does not have initiative and referendum[16]—the method used to force **term limits** in most states—and it is unlikely that the Texas legislature will approve limits for themselves.

In the year 2000, the dean (the longest-tenured member) of the Senate was Carlos Truan, who had served 23 years in the Senate and 8 years in the House. Representative Tom Uher, the dean of the House, had served 32 years. The average tenure, though, was seven years in the Senate and seven years in the House.

Incumbency reelection rates are more than 90 percent in 10 of the largest states. The average turnover in state legislative races in 1994–1996 was 20 percent.[17] The turnover rates for the Texas House were 18 percent in 1996 and 16 percent in 1998; the turnover rates for the Texas Senate were 19 percent in 1996 and 6 percent in 1998.

Personal and Political Characteristics of Members

An examination of member characteristics, such as party affiliation, ideology, occupation, race, gender, and age, can describe who represents us in the legislature and can show whether there are distinctive patterns to that representation. Table 8.5 presents figures for the past 30 years on party, gender, and race characteristics of the legislative membership.

Occupation, Education, and Religion In the nineteenth and early twentieth centuries, nearly half of state legislators were farmers and about half were lawyers, business people, and other professionals. The majority of legislators were probably middle class. In state legislatures today, the number of business owners, farmers, and attorneys is declining, and the number of teachers, preachers, public organizers, and former legislative aides being elected to legislatures is increasing. Nationally, the percentage of legislators who are attorneys declined from 30 percent in 1960 to 16 percent in 1986.[18] In Texas, however, in 1999, 42 percent of senators and 35 percent of representatives were attorneys, and 58 percent of senators and 50 percent of representatives were business people. One possible explanation is the low level of pay, which ensures that most legislators must have flexible schedules and must be able to take off work without losing their jobs.

In 1999, every senator and all but five House members had attended some college, and a majority of legislators had graduate degrees. Understandably, more Texas legislators have law degrees than any other type of graduate degree, with Master's degrees second.

Table 8.5 **LEGISLATIVE MEMBERSHIP**

The party, gender, and racial and ethnic composition of the legislature has changed considerably over the past 30 years (though it still does not mirror the population of Texas).

Texas House of Representatives

	Democrats	Republicans	Men	Women	Anglo	African American	Hispanic
1971	140	10	149	1	139	2	10
1973	133	17	145	5	131	8	11
1975	134	16	143	7	128	9	13
1977	132	18	140	10	120	13	17
1979	128	22	139	11	119	14	17
1981	114	36	139	11	120	13	17
1983	113	37	137	13	118	12	20
1985	98	52	135	15	118	13	19
1987	94	56	136	14	117	13	20
1989	93	57	134	16	117	13	20
1991	93	57	132	18	117	13	20
1993	93	57	125	25	112	14	24
1995	88	62	121	29	110	14	26
1997	82	68	120	30	108	14	28
1999	78	72	117	33	108	14	28

Texas Senate

	Democrats	Republicans	Men	Women	Anglo	African American	Hispanic
1971	29	2	30	1	29	1	1
1973	30	1	30	1	29	0	2
1975	28	3	30	1	28	0	3
1977	28	3	30	1	27	0	4
1979	27	4	30	1	27	0	4
1981	24	7	30	1	27	0	4
1983	26	5	31	0	26	1	4
1985	25	6	30	1	26	1	4
1987	25	6	28	3	23	2	6
1989	23	8	28	3	23	2	6
1991	23	8	27	4	24	2	5
1993	18	13	27	4	23	2	6
1995	17	14	27	4	24	2	5
1997	14	17	28	3	22	2	7
1999	15	16	28	3	22	2	7

Sources: Membership Profiles compiled by the Texas Legislative Reference Library; Texas Legislative Service Legislative Membership Directories; authors.

With the diversification of the legislature since the 1970s has come a broadening of the representation of religious denominations. While Baptists traditionally had the highest number of members in the legislature, by the 1990s, Catholics were the largest group, followed by Baptists, Methodists, and Episcopalians.

Gender, Race, and Age   Historically, the membership of most state legislatures has been Anglo male Democrats. The recent trend in legislatures is an increase in minorities and women. Nationwide, women constituted only 4 percent of state legislators in 1969. By 1997, 21 percent of state legislators were women. African Americans constituted only 2.2 percent of state legislators in 1970; by 1991, 5.8 percent of state legislators were African American. Hispanics are still less than 2 percent of state legislators, though they exceed 10 percent in Arizona, Colorado, New Mexico, and Texas.[19]

African Americans were a vital part of the political process in Texas in the 1860s and 1870s. During Reconstruction, African Americans were elected to the Constitutional Convention of 1868 and to the Texas legislature from 1869 to 1874. The end of Reconstruction, however, brought about the end of representation for African Americans when white supremacists regained power. The nine African-American representatives and two African-American senators in the 1871–1872 legislature were not surpassed in number until 1977. The Constitutional Convention of 1875 included a small number of African-American delegates. A few African Americans won election to the legislature and served until 1895—the last year that an African American served in the legislature until Barbara Jordan, Curtis Graves, and Joseph Lockridge won elections to the Texas legislature in 1966.[20]

In the 1999 House membership of 72 Republicans, 71 were Anglo and 1 was Hispanic; of 78 Democrats, 38 were Anglo (49 percent of Democrats), 26 Hispanic (33 percent), and 14 African American (18 percent). In the Senate, all 16 Republicans were Anglo. Of Senate Democrats, 7 were Anglo, 6 Hispanic, and 2 African American.

Most Texas legislators are in their 40s or 50s in age. House members tend to be young to middle-aged, while senators tend to be middle-aged to older—though there certainly are exceptions. In 1999, one House member was in his 20s, and four were in their 70s. The youngest two senators were 43 years old, while the oldest was 66 years old.

Political Party   Historically, Democrats have won far more seats in the Texas legislature than have Republicans. Republicans only had a majority in 1870 (until winning a majority of the Senate in 1996 and 1998). This Democratic dominance in Texas is overwhelming but also reflects that in the twentieth century Democrats have typically controlled about two-thirds of *all* state legislative chambers. Thus, the strength of Republicans in state legislatures in the 1990s was either an exception or evidence of a new trend. Democrats have won back some that they lost. In 1999, Democrats controlled 26 state senates, compared to 23 for Republicans; Democrats controlled 25 state houses of representatives, compared to 23 for Republicans, with one split. Table 8.5 demonstrates the growth of the Republican Party in the Texas legislature.

Critical Thinking Exercise: Review the information in Chapter 2 on the changing demographics of Texas population. What is the membership of the legislature likely to look like in 10 years? 20 years? What would cause the legislative membership balance to reflect or not reflect changes in the population?

Ideology   The four kinds of ideology described in Chapter 2 can be useful in analyzing legislative voting patterns. Several groups rank legislators' votes on ideological dimensions—though they are usually two-dimensional, rather than four-dimensional. The groups or publications simply choose record votes on issues that are most important to them, given their policy perspectives, and see whether legislators agreed with them. Of course, these results tend to be skewed, because groups choose issues that clearly divide legislators.

A source frequently used to measure liberalism and conservatism is the voting analysis by the *Texas Observer,* a liberal publication. For the 1995 session, the *Texas Observer* scores reflect that of House Democrats, 38 percent were liberal, 36 percent moderate, and 26 percent conservative. Of House Republicans, 100 percent were conservative. Of Senate Democrats, 41 percent were liberal, 47 percent moderate, and 12 percent conservative. Of Senate Republicans, 100 percent were conservative.[21] For the 1999 session, the Young Conservatives of Texas ranked House Democrats as 84 percent liberal and 16 percent moderate. Of House Republicans, 99 percent were ranked conservative and 1 percent moderate.[22]

It is difficult to find analyses of voting patterns that take into account populism and libertarianism. Recall from Chapter 2 that we focused on differences in equality and liberty in our definitions of ideology. For the 1995 and 1999 sessions, we identified for each session five votes in the House on equality and five on liberty measures, based on the description of those ideologies we presented in Chapter 2, to measure the four-part ideological framework.[23] This analysis reveals an ideologically divided House. In 1995, of the 149 voting members (the speaker did not vote), 50 were conservative, 44 were libertarian, 42 were liberal, and 13 were populist.[24] In 1999, the House was even more polarized, with a trend toward libertarianism over traditional conservatism. There were 72 libertarians, 45 liberals, 28 populists, and 4 conservatives (Figure 8.1). The voting pattern shows that legislators were far more divided on issues of equality than they were on issues of liberty and order. Thus, whereas issues about personal freedom may be intensely debated, legislators are more likely to compromise on those issues. They are more likely to be staunchly for or against proposals for greater equality.

Moreover, there is a distinct difference between legislative Democrats and legislative Republicans. All 28 populists were Democrats, and 43 of 45 liberals were Democrats; all 4 conservatives were Republicans, and 69 of 75 libertarians were Republicans. Thus, the center of the House Democratic party is liberal-populist, while the center of the House Republican party is libertarian.

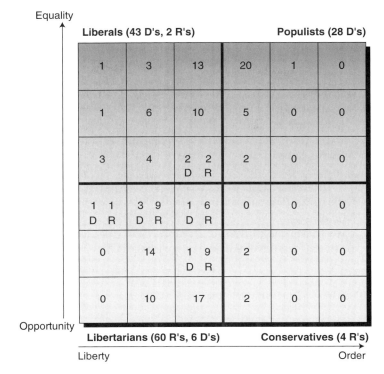

Figure 8.1 Ideological Voting Pattern in the Texas House of Representatives (1999)
Based on 5 roll-call votes selected on equality/opportunity and 5 roll-call votes selected on liberty/order. Record votes 34, 121, 225, 262, and 398 were used to measure legislators' placement on the equality/opportunity axis. Record votes 69, 150, 368, 407, and 468 were used to measure legislators' placement on the liberty/order axis. For instance, on Record Vote 121, an aye vote was a vote to table (kill) an amendment to phase out financial aid to undergraduate teaching candidates; it was categorized as a vote for "equality" and against "opportunity." On Record Vote 150, an aye vote was a vote for a bill containing bicycle safety measures, including requiring children to wear bicycle helmets; it was categorized as a vote for "order" and against "liberty." Each legislator was then placed on the 36-point grid based on the 36 possible combinations of scores, from 0–0 to 5–5.

ORGANIZING FOR POWER AND INFLUENCE IN THE LEGISLATURE

All legislators are equal: each has one vote. In terms of influence, however, those who gain positions of authority within the institution wield significantly more power. The relationships among leaders, legislators who support them, legislators who oppose them, and outsiders affect policy outcomes, political careers, and public perceptions of the legislature. The process of leadership selection and the methods that leaders use to push their policy priorities and to keep themselves in power are crucial in understanding how the legislature works.

In order to pass bills, legislatures must have vehicles for organizing the leadership and its supporting coalition; if the legislature is open and democratic, there will also be vehicles for organizing opposition. In most legislatures, political parties serve as those vehicles, but not in Texas (see Chapter 4). An organization of legislators who are all affiliated with the same political party is called a **legislative party caucus** (e.g., the House Republican Caucus). In the absence of parties, strong factions and strong leaders rule. There were no party caucuses in Texas until the 1980s. The result is that a strong party system is now antithetical to the system of strong speakers and lieutenant governors that has evolved in its absence.[25] It remains to be seen whether party caucuses will merely coexist in a subservient position with the leadership or will manage to become a new power center.

In this section, we examine how Texas legislators organize to pass or to block legislation. We must examine the House and the Senate separately, though, because they have some important differences in their leadership and opposition patterns. Some of these differences are rooted in the constitution and some in the rules and traditions of each chamber.

Leadership and Opposition in the House

The constitution requires that the representatives elect one of their members to be the head of the House, and that person is called the speaker. In the 1800s, by custom, a speaker would serve one two-year term. A few served two terms, and one served three nonconsecutive terms. By the middle of the twentieth century, two terms was the norm.

In reaction to Gus Mutscher's campaign (before his conviction on bribery charges) for a then-unprecedented three consecutive terms as speaker, and believing that much of the source of the legislature's problems was concentration of power in the hands of the speaker, the 1973 reformers proposed limiting speakers to one term of office. They lost that battle, but in a move that they have since regretted, they won a vote to make the balloting for speaker open and public. Now legislators vote publicly on a speaker who is seeking reelection—with the fear of retaliation from a newly reelected speaker and his or her allies against any who opposed them. So, few do. Since the change to open balloting, we have witnessed the longest speakerships in Texas history. Bill Clayton served four terms (1975–1982). Gib Lewis followed with five terms (1983–1992), and Pete Laney (1993–present) announced in 1999 that he would seek a fifth term for 2001.

The Speaker's Race   The campaign to determine who shall be speaker for the biennium, called the **speaker's race,** is the cornerstone of the legislative process in the House. A representative who wishes to be speaker announces his or her intentions and asks legislators to sign pledge cards of support. While it may seem that this would be a simple, in-house process, in reality, it is a statewide campaign, with victorious candidates now raising (typically from lobbyists) and spending huge amounts of money to get the required 76 votes. When Speaker Gib Lewis retired in 1992, he had a balance of more than $400,000 in his speaker's campaign fund!

Some of the campaign money is spent in travel and phone expenses. The candidates travel the state to attend the proverbial barbecue fund-raisers for fellow legislators, in a mutually beneficial effort to show support for and to court the local legislator. In addition, much of the campaign money is spent to help elect legislators who will be pledged to the speaker candidate; thus, the speaker's campaign becomes a quasi-party organization. The speaker becomes a leader in recruiting and supporting other political leaders, in a fashion similar to other states, though not in the partisan format of other states. Speakers and legislative party caucuses in a majority of states provide such assistance to legislative candidates.[26]

The Texas House speaker's race really never ends; instead, it becomes the center for organizing the leadership team (the **speaker's lieutenants** or the **speaker's team**) and wielding influence within the House. A speaker who is running for reelection relies on help from lieutenants in circulating pledge cards and persuading legislators to support him or her. When a speaker retires, the lieutenants vie among themselves for the office. Savvy lieutenants will seek pledge cards for the speaker who is running for reelection and simultaneously for themselves for the future.

House Leadership and the Political Parties Republicans have controlled the House during only one session, in 1870. Today, there are no party nominees for speakership, and parties are not the basis of the competition. Personal and factional groupings dominate the selection process, with the conservative Democratic faction almost always winning. In 1971, the *Dallas News* wrote, "the Texas House of Representatives, with minor exceptions, has been under conservative Democratic control since we first reported its happenings during the 1930's."[27]

House Democratic leaders have often supported bipartisanship and eschewed efforts to create party caucuses. Speaker Clayton told reporters, "It's bad business if we let party politics interfere with the issues." In opposing the formation of the House Democratic Caucus in 1981, Representative Gib Lewis said, "We have always voted for or against legislation on its merits and not on whether it was supported or introduced by a Democrat or a Republican. That is why we always have had stability in state government." Later as speaker, when he was confronted with Republican unity against the governor's tax proposal, he decried the end of the nonpartisan legislative system, saying, "I hate to see us degenerate to this level."[28] More recently, Speaker Laney appears to be more open to party organization, especially after some Republicans organized an effort to defeat him in 1998. He has met with the Democratic Caucus, though it has never organized to influence the passage of legislation.

The Speaker's Influence over Committees Speakers have the ability to "stack" important committees with legislators from the faction that controls the House. Historically, there were no restraints on the speaker's powers to assign representatives to their committees. Because of the perception that speakers used these assignments to reward their friends with appointment to the most important committees and to punish their enemies with appointment to the least desired committees, the reformers in the mid-1970s won a limited seniority system that the speaker must consider in some of his or her appointments. Before the reforms, conservatives, reflecting the ideology of the speakers, were substantially overrepresented on key committees. Since the reforms, conservatives have still been overrepresented on those committees, but to a lesser degree.[29]

Pledge cards become a tool of power in an environment where a speaker may seek reelection. A key part of a speaker's coalition involves the implicit presumption that those who support the winning candidate will be rewarded with choice committee assignments and chair appointments. However, explicit commitments violate both the constitutional oath of office and state law. Legislators say off the record that speakers have extorted reelection pledge card signatures before making their committee assignments, one of the strongest powers that the speaker has over House members. Such a practice certainly appears to violate the democratic principle of nontyranny but is usually hidden from public view and does not give rise to a public reaction. This "extortion" system became so explicit in the Mutscher era that one of the reforms of 1973 was the adoption of a state law to legally define the promise of an appointment to a committee chair or vice chair position in exchange for a pledge in the speaker's race as a bribe.

House Opposition and the Political Parties   Opposition to the speaker and the speaker's team is not organized along party lines. Indeed, since the mid-1970s, the Democratic speakers have relied on Republicans as a part of their coalition to win office and have rewarded them with committee chair positions. In 1999, Speaker Laney appointed 23 Democrats and 14 Republicans as chairpersons.

Even Republicans long resisted organizing, gaining greater leverage by being part of the conservative leadership coalition. Republican Representative Tom Craddick said during Clayton's tenure that "we're not going to do anything in the way of organizing. Under Clayton, Republicans have been treated real fairly. It hasn't been Republicans versus Democrats." Later, he stated, "it's more to [our] benefit for us not to have" a caucus. Even when Republicans gained in numbers, they resisted organizing. One Republican said that a caucus would "polarize the members on party rather than on philosophy and issues."[30] A Republican Party Caucus was not formally organized until 1989, with Craddick as its chair. He served as its chair until 1999.

Organizing in the House Through Nonparty Caucuses   A **nonparty legislative caucus** is a group of legislators organized around some attribute other than party affiliation. In the absence of strong parties, opposition is usually ad hoc, with legislators who oppose the speaker on one issue supporting him or her on others. In some sessions, nonparty caucuses, including county and regional delegations, ad hoc issue groups, and ideological groups, have served as opposition vehicles. In the sessions immediately after Sharpstown, the legislature was closely divided, with reformers coalescing into a bloc to support Speaker Daniel, then to oppose Speaker Clayton and his conservative bloc. The 1973 session is the only one in the past 30 years in which conservatives have been in opposition to the speaker—and about 35 of them, including Clayton, formed a loose opposition caucus that year.[31]

A caucus called the House Study Group (HSG) formed in 1975 and was generally in opposition to Clayton's team. The result was warfare between the two camps.

For 20 years, the speakers' teams tried to eliminate the HSG. Clayton said that he did not believe it was proper to create groups outside the formal committee structure. Despite the long history of factions in the legislature, Clayton's aide said that Clayton opposed the HSG because "he's afraid it will factionalize the House." Pete Laney, then Clayton's House Administration Chair, told reporters "I don't think we need to use state money to have all these groups working for and against legislation." In a clear statement of support for a majoritarian democracy, rather than a pluralist one, one of his committee members said, "A committee hears testimony, studies, then this study group takes the same bill and studies it also, so they're not taking the word of the committee that was set up by the majority of the members of the House."[32] While the repeated attempts to kill the HSG failed, they did succeed in changing it from an opposition caucus to a staff-research office named the House Research Organization (HRO), which now serves all House members.

During the long speakership of Gib Lewis, opposition virtually disappeared except when Republicans left the leadership coalition on selected issues. When the legislature was fighting Republican Governor Bill Clements on tax or school-finance issues, Republican legislators would oppose the speaker's bills. It put a strain on Lewis's leadership coalition because seven committee chairs were Republicans.

In 1985, Republicans and a few conservative Democrats, including Speaker Lewis and Representative Laney, formed the Texas Conservative Coalition. It helped defeat a health-care proposal in 1985, triggering a special session to pass it. By 1993, the Conservative Coalition was using parliamentary points of order and staff research to effectively oppose legislation. In 1994, moderate and liberal Democrats formed a new caucus, called the Legislative Study Group, to counter the influence of the Conservative Coalition.

In 1993, the House Administration Committee eliminated the partial public funding for caucuses. By 1999, Speaker Laney stripped them of Capitol office space.

Leadership and Opposition in the Senate

The constitution designates a leader for the Texas Senate, though in a manner very different from the designation of the House speaker. The constitution says that the lieutenant governor shall serve as the president of the Senate, though he or she is not a member of the Senate and may not vote except in the case of a tie vote. In the case of a vacancy in the lieutenant governorship, the Senate would elect a new lieutenant governor.

Thus, there is typically no battle over who the top leader will be. In the small Senate, especially with weak political parties, leadership and opposition is typically organized on an ad hoc basis and is heavily influenced by the personal relationships the senators and the lieutenant governor establish with each other.

The Role of the Lieutenant Governor   Lieutenant governors were elected to two-year terms of office until 1974, when the term was lengthened to four years. Many lieutenant governors use the post as a political steppingstone. As a statewide elected official, the lieutenant governor gains more attention than the House speaker does and is more often mentioned as a possible candidate for higher office. Most of the early lieutenant governors served one term and went on to serve as governor. Three people have served as speaker, lieutenant governor, and governor.[33]

Beginning in the 1890s, multiple two-year terms for lieutenant governors became the norm. The first three-consecutive-term lieutenant governorship occurred from 1907 to 1912. Now, the pattern is one of long tenureships. Ben Ramsey served from 1951 through 1961; Bill Hobby served from 1973 through 1990; and Bob Bullock served from 1991 through 1998.

The lieutenant governor of Texas is one of the most powerful lieutenant governors in the states. Across the nation, 26 lieutenant governors preside over their senates, 25 can vote only in the case of a tie, and 6 appoint committees.[34] The Texas lieutenant governor has all those powers and appoints the committee chairs. However, it is not the constitution that gives the lieutenant governor significant powers over the Senate. The senators themselves decide how to write the Senate rules, and historically, they have written the rules to give the lieutenant governor real power over them: the power to appoint committee chairs, assign members to committees, and refer bills. In most other states, these powers are wielded by party leaders or through a seniority system. In the absence of a majority party leader in the Texas Senate, the Senate president is the most powerful force in the Senate.

Coalition Building in the Senate   Lieutenant governors are thus responsible for guiding legislation through the Senate, and they must appoint allies as key committee chairpersons, place allies on the important committees, and build a leader-

Lieutenant Governor Rick Perry uses his persuasive skills in the chambers of the Texas Senate in 1999, in his role as Senate president.

ship coalition—recognizing that senators will also become leaders in the policy areas that are most important to them.

Partisanship was never a factor in this coalition building because there were no Republicans, and there was not a Republican lieutenant governor in the twentieth century until Rick Perry in 1999. As Republicans gained in numbers under the long tenureship of Lieutenant Governor Hobby, he included them in his coalition. In 1991, new Lieutenant Governor Bob Bullock adopted a more partisan approach, stripping Republicans of their committee chair positions. In 1993, when Republicans for the first time gained more than one-third of the Senate, Bullock reversed himself and appointed Republicans as committee chairs. In 1999, Perry appointed Republicans to 11 leadership positions and Democrats to 8. Lieutenant governors know that their legislative powers depend on senators voting them those powers and that they cannot afford to have a large bloc of senators opposed to them.

As in the House, a conservative faction has typically dominated the Senate. The current manifestation of this leadership faction is a Republican-conservative Democratic combination. Liberal Democrats have typically been the opposition. Unlike in the House, the opposition in the Senate has a strong protector—the **Senate two-thirds rule.** As a means of controlling the flow of legislation, the Senate requires every bill to win a vote of two-thirds of the senators before it can be considered. So if an opposition bloc has at least one-third of the senators, the leadership bloc must bargain with it to get the bill passed. This rule makes the leadership-opposition blocs more fluid in the Senate. This protection of minority rights enhances pluralist democracy in the Senate, in stark contrast to the House. In the final section of this chapter, on the legislature and democracy, we provide an example of how this rule influences the Senate.

THE LEGISLATIVE PROCESS

In the scenario with Chapter 1, you learned that it was a series of bills that the legislature passed in several sessions that created the requirement that students take this college course, and those bills changed as they went through the legislature. Now it is time to study the **legislative process**—the method the legislature follows in passing legislation. We look at the different kinds of legislative documents known as bills and resolutions, the significance of legislative rules, and the step-by-step process in how a bill becomes a law.

What Is a Bill? What Is a Resolution?

When the legislature adopts or amends a state law, it is through a document called a bill. Other adoptions by the legislature are called resolutions. There are different kinds of resolutions. Thus, anything that the legislature considers will be labeled a bill, a joint resolution, a simple resolution, or a concurrent resolution.

When the legislature wants to create a new law, called a statute, or amend an existing one, it must do so by passing a bill—either a House Bill (SB) or a Senate

Bill (SB). The constitution specifies the form that every bill must take. It must have each component (e.g., an enacting clause), or it is subject to being ruled in violation of the requirements and thrown out by the legislature itself or by a court.

A **joint resolution** either proposes an amendment to the Texas Constitution or ratifies an amendment to the U.S. Constitution. It is called either a House Joint Resolution (HJR) or a Senate Joint Resolution (SJR). A **simple resolution** goes through only one chamber (such as the resolution to adopt House rules or a resolution commending a citizen). It is called either a House Resolution (HR) or a Senate Resolution (SR). A **concurrent resolution** expresses the will of both chambers, though there is no authority of the force of law behind it (for instance, telling the U.S. Congress what the Texas legislature thinks it should do). It is called either a House Concurrent Resolution (HCR) or a Senate Concurrent Resolution (SCR).

Rules, Procedures, and Internal Government

Article 3 of the Texas Constitution includes numerous rules governing the legislative process, including setting out a designated regular order of business for a legislative calendar. It provides broad rules, but it also contains more specific rules—restrictions so specific that the legislature often overrides them. For instance, the part of the regular order of business limiting the legislature to some types of action early in the session and others later in the session is routinely suspended at the beginning of each session, as the House did in 1999 through HR 3. The rules adopted by the House and the Senate embody the constitutional limitations, plus more specific rules needed for smooth working, or for power wielding, in the legislature.[35]

The House and Senate adopt separate resolutions setting members' office budgets, policies for employees, the administrative authority of the leadership, and the governing of caucuses. For the 1999–2000 biennium, the House set the monthly allocation to each member at $9,750. This money is spent for staff salaries, office equipment, mailing expenses, and member per diem expenses. The Senate gave each of its members $25,000 for staff salaries alone.

In most sessions, the adoption of the rules and the housekeeping resolutions in the House is routine and noncontroversial, partly because they are considered the prerogative of the speaker, and the speakers have been so powerful that few representatives have dared to challenge them. However, 1993 was different. As Speaker Gib Lewis's tenure went on, and with his second misdemeanor conviction (both for failure to report financial information), a revolt brewed against his rules and his power. With his announced retirement and the resulting speaker's race, rules reform became a key part of the contest.

In 1992, Speaker Lewis appointed a House Select Committee on Rules. The winning speaker's race candidate, Pete Laney, adopted most of the recommendations of that committee in his proposed rules package, and they were approved by the House in 1993. Most of these changes reflected a desire by reform advocates for a more open process of setting bills for House consideration, more time to study bills and amendments, and more restrictions on committee chairs' ability to make unilateral decisions.

How a Bill Becomes Law

In order to promote deliberation, the constitution requires that a bill be read on three separate days in each chamber of the legislature. It must also pass both chambers in identical form. A legislator files a bill or resolution, and a clerk assigns it a number. The same bill might be introduced in the House and Senate, with different numbers (e.g., HB 425 and SB 227 could be the same bill). Though there is no requirement that a bill be introduced in both chambers, it helps speed the process, allowing simultaneous House and Senate hearings. Figure 8.3 summarizes the basic steps by which a bill is enacted into law in the Texas legislature.

Each day, the speaker in the House and the lieutenant governor in the Senate announce the **first readings,** in which the clerk of each body reads aloud the caption for each bill or resolution. The caption is a brief statement at the beginning of a document, describing what the bill or resolution does. The speaker or lieutenant governor then refers the bill or resolution to a committee, under the rules setting out the jurisdictional areas of each committee.

Most committees get more bills referred to them than they can reasonably consider. Even when a legislator requests a hearing, there is no requirement that the chairperson schedule the bill for one. While this practice in other states has led to revolts against the leadership, it has not been seriously challenged in Texas. So why does a committee chair decide to let the committee consider a bill or decide to kill the bill by not setting it on the agenda? Such decisions are usually made privately, with no public discussion, and are influenced by the position of the House speaker or the Senate president, by the lobbying of interest groups, and by the political needs of the chair and the bill's author.

Most bills are considered in public hearings, in which citizens may testify for or against the bill, but House committees may consider bills in formal meetings, in which testimony is usually not accepted. Because of the post–Sharpstown reforms and the demand for a more open process, a committee must post notice of a public hearing at least five days in advance of the hearing.

Public hearings must be open to all, and votes must be taken in open meetings. The chair will lay out the bill and call on the author to explain it. The committee hears testimony from witnesses for the bill, witnesses against the bill, and neutral witnesses. The committee may also call on resource witnesses, who are usually state agency representatives who do not officially take a position for or against the bill, but who provide technical information on the subject. In reality, many bills are drafted by agency officials. Agencies run programs and constantly see the need for updating or changing the laws, so they often come to the legislature with a package of proposals. Interest groups also prepare bills that would instruct a state agency, so agency officials push hard for the passage or defeat of such bills. After hearing testimony, the chair closes the testimony, and the members then discuss the bill. They may at that point amend the bill, approve it, defeat it, send it to a subcommittee, or take no action on it.

A subcommittee chair decides whether to have a public hearing or a formal meeting. Often, subcommittee meetings are brief huddles at the floor desk of the

This diagram displays the sequential flow of a bill from the time it is introduced in the House of Representatives to to final passage and transmittal to the Governor. A bill introduced in the Senate would follow the same procedure in reverse.

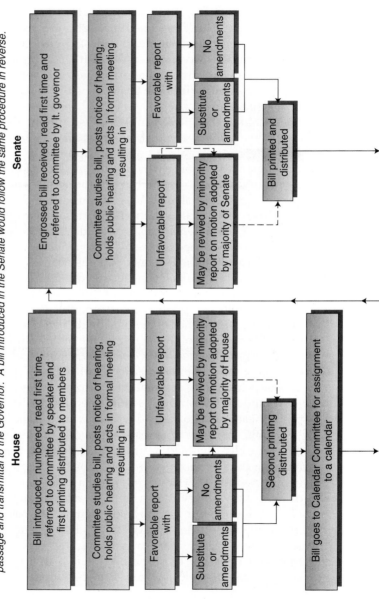

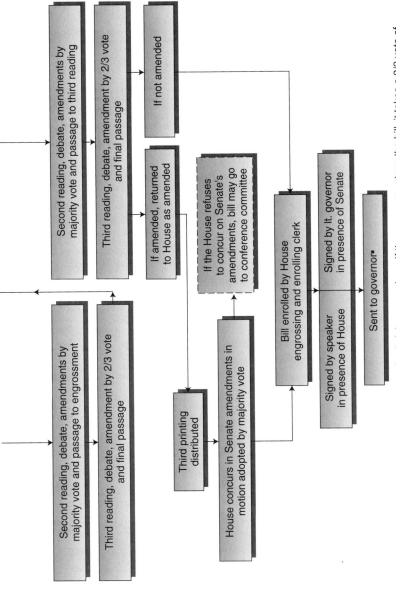

Figure 8.2 Basic Steps in the Texas Legislative Process

Source: Texas Fact Book 1996. Legislative Budget Board, Texas Legislative Council.

* If the governor signs the bill or refuses to sign it, it becomes law. If the governor vetoes the bill, it takes a 2/3 vote of both the House and the Senate to override the veto and make the bill law.

chairperson. Such meetings, though public, are rarely tape-recorded and frequently occur with no one present other than the subcommittee members and staff members. These meetings are good examples of the thwarting of deliberative democracy because there is little discussion, and the members simply ratify decisions made in private meetings of legislators and lobbyists. Action by the subcommittee is in the form of recommendations by majority vote to the full committee, which considers subcommittee reports in its regular meetings and usually adopts them as drafted.

At this point in the legislative process, the House and the Senate diverge considerably. In both chambers, all bills reported from committee are referred to a procedural committee. Bills in the House go to the Calendars Committee or, if the substantive committee requests it, to the Local and Consent Calendars Committee.[36] In the Senate, bills reported from committee are referred to a procedural committee, but it is an informal process that determines the fate of legislation in the Senate.

The House Calendars Committee   The Calendars Committee sets the daily calendar for the House.[37] How a bill makes it onto—or is kept off—the daily calendar is one of the more controversial topics in the Texas House. Until 1993, the Calendars Committee could simply refuse to consider a bill that a committee had reported to it. While Calendars Committee meetings were open to the public, the unwritten rule was that no legislators, staff members, or lobbyists were to attend the meetings on penalty of automatically having the bill killed. The typical process was that *any one member* of the committee could kill a bill, with no public vote and with no one knowing who killed it or why it was killed. While this practice may protect minority rights and thus advance pluralist democracy and deliberation, the manner in which it is exercised may thwart deliberation and thus support a process of tyranny rather than nontyranny.

The 1993 reforms changed several aspects of Calendars Committee operations. While the committee had been required to lay out the calendar at least 24 hours in advance, this requirement was sometimes violated. One reform requires the committee to distribute the daily calendar to each representative at least 36 hours in advance, and the committee has complied with the rule. Another reform requires the committee to take a public vote on each bill, within 30 days of receiving it, on whether to place it on a calendar. The committee circumvents this requirement by setting the bills that it wishes to set, then adopting a universal motion to not set all other bills on a calendar. Other reforms include requirements of advance public posting of the meetings and opening the meetings to the public and other members.

The committee, however, cannot escape controversy. On a crucial day late in the session in 1997, Republican Representative Arlene Wohlgemuth, in retaliation for a bill not getting set on a calendar, called a point of order that a Calendars Committee meeting had not been properly announced. The speaker sustained the point of order, killing all bills on the calendar (effectively killing them for the rest of the session). Wohlgemuth's action came to be known as the 1997 Memorial Day Massacre. On the last day of the session, another Republican legislator and the

Democratic Calendars Committee chair exchanged personal privilege speeches attacking and defending the committee.

The Senate Calendaring Function   The Senate Administration Committee sets a Local and Uncontested Calendar to consider noncontroversial bills, but for significant bills, there is no committee to advance or kill bills approved by the standing committees. Instead, the process used to winnow the number of bills is a rule that requires a two-thirds vote to consider any bill out of its regular order. A senator whose bill has been approved by committee must give written notice of intent to move to suspend the regular order of business. This daily listing of notices is called the Intent Calendar.

By tradition, at the beginning of each legislative session, a senator will introduce a frivolous bill with no intention of ever asking for a vote on it in the full Senate. As an example, in 1999, Senator Chris Harris introduced SB 69, establishing a "County Park Beautification and Improvement Program," which served as this bottleneck bill. The bottleneck bill is the first bill to be approved by any committee, so it is then placed at the top of the order of business. Thus, *every* bill except that one is always out of order, so long as the author of that bill does not request a vote on it. So, before any other bill can be considered, the Senate must first vote to suspend the rule governing the regular order of business. That motion requires a two-thirds vote and must be made for every bill. This two-thirds rule is a method by which the Senate assures deliberation and compromise. It protects any minority that has at least one-third of the senators because they can block passage of a bill.

The Bill Reaches the Floor   The chamber of the House, and likewise the chamber of the Senate, is often referred to as the "floor" where legislative action occurs. At the beginning of each legislative day, the speaker or president calls the members to order and the roll is called to ascertain whether a **quorum** (a required minimum of two-thirds of the members) is on the floor. After such housekeeping measures (as a prayer, announcements, introductions) and first readings of bills, the members consider the bills on final or **third reading.** These are bills that have already been approved on second reading and require only the usually perfunctory final vote. Then bills on **second reading** are presented, and this is when the real debate occurs.

In the House, the speaker calls a bill from the calendar for second reading and recognizes the bill's author or, in the case of a Senate bill, the House sponsor, who explains the bill. Any member may ask the author questions. After the author's opening statement, any member may speak for or against the bill or may offer **amendments,** and any other member may question the speaker. The author is limited to 20 minutes to open debate on the bill and 20 minutes to close it. All other speakers are limited to 10 minutes, including any interruptions from questioners. Members take the full allotment of time only on major or controversial bills. Conceivably, debate on a bill could take days. In reality, this rarely happens.

Senator Gonzalo Barrientos (Democrat-Austin), on the Senate floor, filibustering against a bill that he opposes. On his desk are flowers sent into the chamber by his supporters to give him encouragement.

In the Senate, the president recognizes a senator to suspend the regular order of business so that the Senate may consider a bill on second reading, and the senator explains the bill. There could be discussion at this point if the bill is controversial. Otherwise, the rules-suspension vote is quickly taken, followed by further explanation, any amendments, and the second reading vote. Unlike the House, the Senate has no time limits on debate, creating the **filibuster** as a tactical tool. A senator may hold the floor for an unlimited amount of time and thus can try to kill a bill by refusing to allow a vote on it.

An amendment must be **germane** to the bill—that is, related to the topic; but germaneness is a matter of interpretation by the House speaker or Senate president. Amendments can drastically alter a bill and thus become powerful tools in the hands of opponents to the bill. The consideration of amendments is a critical part of the legislative process for both sides, and a controversial bill has the potential for lengthy debate and twists and turns in tactical victories and defeats.

When a vote is called in the House, the speaker may call for a voice vote or for a vote on the House's voting machine. A voice vote is simply audible "aye" or "nay" votes by the whole group of members, with the speaker judging which group is the largest. It is typically used on noncontroversial matters. In a division vote, each member votes on the voting machine, but this voting is only for the purpose of enabling the speaker to judge more accurately which side has won; it is then erased. Record votes are those votes, usually made by machine but occasionally by roll-call votes, printed in the *House Journal*, the official record of House proceedings. The speaker usually does not vote. He or she could vote, either to create or break a tie, or to show the leadership position on a crucial bill.

The Senate does not use a voting machine. Some votes are simple voice votes *en masse*, if the presiding officer expects a unanimous or nearly unanimous aye vote. However, many votes require each senator to state his or her vote orally, as the names are called alphabetically from the roll of senators. Such roll-call votes are recorded in the official *Senate Journal*. The Senate president may not vote unless there is a tie.

In the chamber in which the bill originates, when the final vote on a bill on third reading is favorable, the bill is considered an **engrossed bill** and is then sent to the other chamber by a staff messenger. It then goes through the referral and committee process and may or may not ever make it to the floor of the second chamber.

Two Bills into One: The Final Stages   The Texas Constitution requires that, in order to become law, a bill must be adopted by both houses in exactly the same form. Many bills are amended in the second chamber, so an additional step is required to meet this requirement. The original chamber could simply vote to concur with the amendments placed on the bill by the other chamber, or it may vote to not concur and request a conference committee to adjust the differences between the two versions of the bill.

Conference committees have five House members appointed by the speaker and five senators appointed by the lieutenant governor. If the conferees cannot reach a compromise, the bill is dead. If they do reach a compromise, this new version of the bill is presented to each chamber, which must approve it with no further amendments by majority vote.[38] For instance, in 1999, the House passed HB 1, the state appropriations bill. The Senate then passed HB 1 but with different amounts of money for many programs. The conference committee worked for weeks to adjust the differences. It finally produced a compromise bill, which the House and Senate then approved in floor votes.

Approval of the Final Document   If a bill achieves final approval, it is then an **enrolled bill** and is sent to the governor. The governor may sign the bill into law, **veto** the bill (nullify its passage), or ignore it, in which case it becomes law without his or her signature. In Chapter 9, we examine governors' vetoes more closely.

If the governor vetoes a bill, the legislature may consider a motion to override the veto, which requires a two-thirds vote. However, most vetoes happen late in the session or after the legislature has adjourned, so there is no chance to attempt an override. Vetoes of regular-session bills may not be overridden by a subsequent special session.

LEGISLATIVE STAFF

Staffing and information development has been a focal point in institutional development of state legislatures. Legislators, especially part-time legislators such as Texas has, do not have the time or resources to do all of the work required to conceive, develop, and pass legislation. Staff members do much of the work in developing information. Deliberative democracy can be enhanced with increased availability of information, though a burdensome staff structure could also thwart access to lawmakers.

Early efforts at increasing legislative information were aimed at establishing state libraries, interim committees to gather information between sessions, and **Legislative Councils**—centralized staffing operations to provide bill drafting, policy research, and program evaluation services. By the 1960s, most state legislatures found centralized staffing inadequate. One staff office could not be specialized enough or attentive enough to the needs of individual legislators or committees, so legislatures began providing staff members for standing committees, individual legislators, and caucuses.

Some large states, such as Michigan and California, have significant party staff capabilities. In Michigan, most of the legislative staff is organized along partisan lines. In California, partisan professionals staff most of the committees.[39] In 1999, the Texas House Democratic Caucus had no staff members, and the Texas House Republican Caucus had only one. In the Senate, the Democratic caucus had two staff members.

The result of increased use of individual staffing, institutional staffing, and group staffing is a much larger legislative staff than in the recent past, though Texas still has substantially fewer staff members than New York or California. However, there has been a political backlash against the larger staffing levels. As term limits took hold in California in the 1990s, new legislators cut staffing substantially.[40] In 1998, there were 2138 full-time-equivalent legislative staff members in Texas, including 1327 in the legislators' offices, committees, and groups; 393 in the Legislative Council; 254 in the State Auditor's Office; 118 in the **Legislative Budget Board (LBB);** 34 in the Sunset Commission; and 12 in the library.[41]

Staffing for Technical Assistance, Specialized Information, and Political Assistance

The Texas legislature created its Legislative Council and LBB in 1949. Both entities are joint committees chaired by the lieutenant governor. They operate only during the interims, though the staffs operate year-round.

The Legislative Council has ten representatives, five senators, and the lieutenant governor and speaker as members. The council's attorneys and other staff members draft bills, conduct policy studies during the interim between sessions, and produce such documents as committee schedules, legislative calendars, and bill-status information.

The LBB has four representatives, four senators, and the lieutenant governor and speaker as members. The LBB's staff analysts prepare the state budget and conduct evaluations of agencies' programs. We take a closer look at the role of the LBB in Chapter 14.

By the 1970s, committees were typically served by two or three staff members hired by the committee chairperson. The expertise and duties of committee staff members varies considerably, with each chair having different priorities. In 1999, the House created a House Bill Analysis Office as a vehicle to centralize the analyses that had previously been prepared by each committee's staff.

Individual representatives did not have staff members—or offices—until the 1960s. Before then, they used a common pool of secretaries. Now legislators receive a monthly account to pay for office expenses, including staff. A typical representative hires three to five staff members in Austin, plus one or two district staff members. Senators hire about five to ten capitol staff members plus district staff. The staff provides constituent services, administrative support, and assistance in drafting legislation, negotiating with staff and lobbyists, and preparing support materials

Battles over Control of House Staffing

When the legislature decided to allow individual legislators to hire staff members, legislators gained the opportunity to wield a resource independent from the House speaker, Senate president, committee leaders, and lobbyists. Over the years, as groups of representatives pooled their staff resources to maximize their effectiveness, the speaker's team repeatedly tried to block such efforts, an action seemingly at odds with the principles of political equality and deliberative democracy.

The Dirty Thirty and its successors used staff resources as a tool of opposition to the speaker's team in the 1970s. Speaker Clayton's House Administration Committee barred joint staffing in 1976, but the House showed its displeasure by reversing that decision. Although Speaker Lewis's House Administration Committee voted in 1986 to abolish the House Study Group (HSG) and set up another research group, the decision was reversed a few months later. The HSG was reconstituted as the House Research Organization (HRO), and all 150 members automatically got access to its staff work. In 1993, the House Administration Committee announced that it was cutting off the HRO's funding, but a coalition of House members turned back the attempt, and the funding was restored. In 1999, the HRO operated with a staff of ten researchers and three administrators and support staff, providing bill analyses and analytical reports.

In 1985, the House Administration Committee voted to allow public funds to be used for staffing the new Conservative Coalition and other caucuses. This suggests that perhaps, in seeking to control groups and staffing arrangements, the leadership may not be driven by a majoritarian democracy mind-set as much as it is driven by ideological commitment. Once joint staffing had shown its worth for the opposition bloc, conservatives in the leadership decided to use it for their agenda, too. In 1994, the House Administration Committee voted to stop funding all caucuses, and after the 1997 session, caucuses were forced to move their offices outside the Capitol.

Senate Staffing

Staffing in the Senate is more extensive and more readily accepted. One result is that individual senators' staffs and committee staffs are larger and better paid. In 1979, several moderate to liberal senators decided to emulate the HSG by forming the Senate Independent Research Group. The effort lasted only one session. Later, Lieutenant Governor Hobby established a Senate Bill Analysis Office, and it was expanded under Lieutenant Governor Bullock as the Senate Research Center. It is still in use under Lieutenant Governor Perry, producing bill analyses and doing issue research.

INFLUENCES ON LEGISLATIVE BEHAVIOR

Legislators must interact with the governor, other executive-branch officials, judges, voters, lobbyists, reporters, staff members, party officials, and officials from the federal government and from other states. The legislature is also a social system and must be understood in the context of the norms of behavior and roles that legislators take with each other, from "backscratching" to "logrolling" (see Table 8.3 on legislative lingo).

The influences on how a legislator votes and provides leadership on policy issues are many and often conflicting. In deciding either how to vote on a particular bill or which bills to sponsor, a legislator asks such questions as these: Which of my constituents will benefit from or be harmed by this bill? How much support will I get from them for the bill and in my reelection campaign? Will it generate opposition in my district? Who can I gather into a coalition of support for the bill? Which lobbyists will support me, and which will oppose me? Will they be more or less likely to finance my campaign or an opponent's because of this bill? How will the media play the issue? Does the leadership support the bill? Can I win support from my fellow legislators? Will the bill help or hurt my reputation with them? What do I need to do to get the governor's support? Often, such legislative decision making must be made quickly and can come back to haunt a legislator, as happened in Sharpstown.

Relations with the Governor

Governors may be weak in their control of the executive branch, but they are stronger players in the legislative process. Governors have leverage to push their agenda through the give-and-take of legislative politics because they have some things that legislators want, such as an emergency declaration for their bills

The 1999 legislative passed utility deregulation legislation, and Governor Bush signed the bill into law. Here, at the ceremonial bill signing, Governor Bush holds an electric utility meter, with Senator David Sibley, and Representatives Steve Wolens and Debra Danburg.

(which allows the bills to be heard early in a legislative session), adding their bills to a call for a special session, or signing their bills into law. During special sessions, for instance, governors may refuse to add a bill to the agenda until or unless the legislator pledges support of the item that the governor is pushing the legislature to adopt.

Relations with Lobbyists

A recurring issue in public policy is the proper role of lobbyists and their relationship with legislators. In Chapter 5, we defined a lobbyist as one who tries to influence the actions of government officials. In the 1960s and 1970s, state legislatures passed many "open-government" measures, including stricter requirements for lobbyists to register, so that the public would know who was seeking to influence state government. During the 1999 legislative session 1579 lobbyists registered with the Texas Ethics Commission—about seven for every legislator.

Lobbyists legitimately approach the legislature to protect the interests of the members of their group through public-policy changes. In trying to persuade legislators, they provide information that legislators need to evaluate the issue; thus, lobbyists can be an invaluable resource to legislators in their quest for deliberative democracy. For instance, in the 1999 battle over deregulating electric utilities, the legislature got information from private utilities, municipal utilities, electric co-ops, environmental groups, and consumer groups. Everyone knew that the information came from groups with different goals, providing the technical information the legislature needed, as well as supporting particular policy proposals that different legislators favored.

That role as an information source also makes lobbyists power players, and they can become protective of their influence with legislators by monopolizing access to legislators and potentially thwarting deliberative democracy. One lobbyist justified his opposition to a stronger legislative staff by saying to one of the authors that "as long as the representative has analysis, he abdicates [decision-making responsibility] and doesn't need to talk to me." Party caucuses and leaders can also present competition for lobbyists. Upon the formation of the Senate Democratic Caucus in 1983, a senator said, "when the party starts taking positions on issues, lobby influence will be diminished."[42]

The Ethics of Lobbying

While most lobbyist-legislator contact happens with complete legitimacy, there are so many questionable contacts and practices that questions about ethics recur in legislative politics. Exposure of Frank Sharp's bribery of legislators led to the largest wave of Texas government reforms in modern times. Since the Sharpstown scandal, we have experienced the federal government's attempt to ensnare corrupt legislators through its "Brilab" sting operation (Speaker Clayton was accused of accepting a bribe but was acquitted in 1980); stories of outlandish spending by lobbyists on the "wining and dining" of legislators; and a chicken magnate, Lonnie "Bo" Pilgrim, walking around the Senate floor in 1989 handing out checks to senators as he was talking with them about his support of Governor Clements's workers' compensation proposals.

Often, the questionable activities concern the blurring of the line between lobbying activities and election and campaign activities. The same individuals who are the most successful lobbyists, primarily business representatives, are also deeply involved in contributing money for legislative campaigns. Legislators need money for the next campaign, and interest-group leaders want access to and influence with legislators, so the campaign finance game is a symbiotic relationship. Legislators and lobbyists both get what they need.

Questions recur about whether campaign finances, wining and dining, and officeholder accounts taint public policy and political equality, including repeated news stories about lobby-paid junkets to Mexico, Las Vegas, and various resorts; stories about legislators paying their mortgages or buying their cars with political funds; and demands from public-interest groups for limits on lobbyists' expenditures. Ann Richards's successful 1990 campaign capitalized on perceived unethical conduct. The result was that the 1991 legislature passed an ethics-reform bill. The new law restricted the amount of money that lobbyists can spend, increased their reporting requirements, and established the Texas Ethics Commission.

THE LEGISLATURE AND POLITICAL CHANGE

The legislature is the arena where citizens are represented in state government. Perhaps more than other political institutions, the legislature is a lightning rod for public anger, energy, and passion. "There ought to be a law!" is usually idle coffee shop talk. However, in periods of intense creedal passion and with organizations to steer and lead it, that passion becomes more targeted: "Why doesn't our legislature clean up this mess!" Sometimes the swelling of public participation causes the legislature to react against the perceived wrongdoer, as it did in the 1890s by creating the Railroad Commission to regulate railroads or in the 1970s by creating the Public Utility Commission to restrain utility rate hikes. At other times, the legislature itself is the subject of public wrath, as it was in the Sharpstown scandal and its aftermath. When creedal passions are inflamed, the legislature can become the target of the public's demand to realign institutional and policy realities with their ideals of democracy and fairness. Yet such passions run into powerful resistance in the legislative setting.

Political scientist E. E. Schattschneider argued that if public policy conflicts were confined to a small group of actors in traditional institutions, those with more power would usually win. If, however, **socialization of conflict** happened and the conflict broadened to include a wide array of actors, the weaker group's chance of winning would increase.[43] Periods of creedal passion broaden conflict. The Sharpstown scandal provides a powerful example of the difference between "privatized" conflict as the norm in legislative politics and socialized conflict when the public becomes more involved.

Power is wielded through tight control of the committees and the flow of bills, especially through the House Calendars Committee. When policy conflicts become socialized, media scrutiny and concerns about electoral consequences can create pressures on these centers of power and can empower the legislative opposition. An opposition must have some tools of power to be effective, however. Staffing and information can serve as socializing agents and as tools of power by providing an internal mechanism for access to legislators previously unavailable to groups outside the traditional power channels. Nonlegislative actors can also serve as socializing agents, attempting to capitalize on creedal passions and to draw the public into the fray through media coverage, mass meetings, and grassroots mobilization.

At a 1991 reunion of the Dirty Thirty, a member said that they would not have been successful in pushing for open-government reforms except for the Sharpstown scandal, which provided "a ready vehicle for media attention and getting our message across to the people."[44] The Sharpstown scandal occurred in the midst of the broader 1960s–1970s reexamination of institutions. The bribery of public officials violated the sense of political equality; the leadership reaction violated the sense of nontyranny; and manipulation of the existing legislative process violated the sense of deliberation.

The 1973 institutional reforms were a reaction to this creedal passion. They continue to stand out as a prime example of the impact of creedal passion in twentieth-century Texas politics. There have been other instances of public outrage since then but all with far more limited consequences. When "Bo" Pilgrim walked around the Senate floor handing out checks, the perceived bribery violated the public's sense of political equality. However, the prevalent reaction was cynicism. Some attempted to bring practice and institutions into accord with principles and beliefs, but both public participation in the 1991 ethics legislation and the legislation itself were more limited in their impact on political and institutional realities than were the 1973 changes.

THE LEGISLATURE AND DEMOCRACY

Legislatures present an excellent forum for deliberative democracy, but there are also powerful disincentives to deliberation. Thus, we must examine the conditions that encourage or discourage deliberation. It is ironic and instructive that the best examples compelling the legislature toward deliberation are norms and rules that protect minorities. As Chapter 1 suggested, deliberation seems more likely when the decision rules allow a minority veto. The two-thirds rule and the threats of filibusters are the twin enforcers of deliberation in the Senate, and the 1979 **"Killer Bee"** incident provides a colorful example of what can happen when the norms are violated.[45]

In 1979, former Democratic Governor John Connally was running for the Republican nomination for President and needed a home-state presidential primary election to bolster his campaign. Legislators were willing to create the primary, but conservative Democrats would have been damaged if it were held simultaneously with the state primaries. Because of the state's primary system, conservative voters could have abandoned the Democratic primary if faced with the juicy choices that the Republican primary would have held in the expected slugfest involving Ronald Reagan, John Connally, and George Bush.[46] So conservative Democrats, with the support of Lieutenant Governor Hobby, wrote a bill to create a presidential primary in March, separate from the May state primaries.

Liberal Democrats protested the separate primary and had the necessary one-third votes in the Senate to block it from coming up, under the Senate two-thirds rule. As the session dragged on, Hobby grew frustrated with the minority and their ability to block bills; he derided them as "killer bees." He decided to circumvent them and to bring the presidential primary bill up through a creative parliamentary ruling that would have had the effect of suspending the two-thirds rule for this one bill, that is, he moved to use majoritarian democracy rather than the pluralist democracy that the Senate rules and tradition required.

In retaliation, the Killer Bees disappeared, preventing the Senate from meeting at all because the quorum requirement is two-thirds. Hobby sent the police to arrest them, and after five days of botched maneuvers across the state and into Oklahoma and Mexico, which resulted in national media coverage of the search, Hobby relented. The Killer Bees returned, and the two-thirds rule was preserved. Deliberation and negotiation with minority factions in the Senate—the principle of pluralist democracy, rather than majoritarian democracy—was preserved.

The committee system presents the best opportunity for deliberative democracy, and indeed, long hearings can convince an observer that legislators seriously consider the options to and consequences of policy changes before them. Experts, citizens, and government officials provide a great deal of complex information for committees to consider.

At other times, legislators' derogatory references to committee hearings as "dog-and-pony shows" cast doubt on the actual deliberation that goes on. Certainly, many hearings actually are deliberative; others are window dressing for the deal that has already been cut in behind-the-scenes negotiations and deliberations with lobbyists. These private deliberations are critical to the policy outcomes in the legislative process; they are also the chief forum for privatized conflict, with little chance for socializing the deliberations to include a broader public.

Finally, the House Calendars Committee provides the best example of nondeliberative democracy in the legislature. For years, the committee met in secret. Because this committee is virtually absolute in its power to determine what the House will consider, the nondeliberative nature of its decisions is one of the most powerful aspects of Texas legislative politics. The 1993 reforms provide the possibility of the introduction of deliberative democracy in the committee's decision-making process. Yet a review of the committee's minutes since 1993 revealed that the committee went through the formal procedures required to meet the new rules without changing the real decision-making process. The meetings typically lasted one to five minutes, as the members quickly ratified the list of bills brought in by the committee chair. Clearly, the real decision making was made in the behind-the-scenes nondeliberative process.

The legislature has the mechanisms required for deliberative democracy—committees, public hearings and debates, and open votes. However, the legislature operates in the broader environment of the political system and the political economy, in which deliberative democracy may not be as important as having particular actors, such as interest groups, businesses, public officials, etc., win their policy battles. If deliberative democracy hurts an actor's chances for winning, as it might, if the conflict is socialized, and if that actor is powerful or skillful enough to win by another means, then he or she will pursue other means. The legislature is not only a battleground over public policy, then, but also a constant battleground over the nature of democratic decision making itself. The concentration of power in the hands of the Senate president and the House speaker provides compelling evidence of a majoritarian rather than a pluralist form of democracy in the Texas legislature. Moreover, the weakness of legislative party caucuses strengthens the leadership and, thus, the majoritarian tendency. However, interest group activity, redistricting challenges, and ideological differences among the membership can act as a brake on majoritarianism and assert pluralist democracy that would seem to be a natural part of a legislative process.

SUMMARY

The Texas legislature is the key political institution providing representation for citizens in the governmental process. In analyzing how it represents us, we examined its structure, its rules and procedures, and its membership characteristics.

We then focused on the issue of how leaders run the legislature and on the role of opposition to the leadership. Finally, we examined outside influences on legislative behavior, including the governor, interest groups, media, and even public opinion, which is sometimes inflamed by creedal passion.

Comparison of the effects of the 1973 legislative reforms with the 1993 reforms demonstrates the power of periods of creedal passion. The public's demand—through their decisions in the 1972 elections—for realigning institutional processes with the ideal of open, fair, and deliberative democracy, led to the passage of new laws that still affect state politics today. The more modest public outrage and involvement in the lobby scandals of the late 1980s and early 1990s resulted in a new ethics bill and new House rules, which did little to expand deliberative democracy in the legislature.

KEY TERMS

Sharpstown scandal
bill
Dirty Thirty
incumbents
turnover rate
redistrict
impeach
legislative leadership
legislative opposition
bicameral
impeachment
biennial legislature
regular session
special (or called) session
Senate president
pro-tempore (pro-tem)
House speaker
committee
representation
per diem
single-member districts
term limits
legislative party caucus

speaker's race
speaker's lieutenants
speaker's team
nonparty legislative caucus
Senate two-thirds rule
legislative process
joint resolution
simple resolution
concurrent resolution
first reading
quorum
third reading
second reading
amendments
filibuster
germane
engrossed bill
enrolled bill
veto
Legislative Council
Legislative Budget Board (LBB)
socialization of conflict
Killer Bees

SUGGESTED READINGS

Bositis, David A. *Redistricting and Minority Representation: Learning from the Past.* Washington, D.C.: University Press of America, 1998.

Brewer, J. Mason. *Negro Legislators of Texas,* 2d ed. Austin, Tex.: Jenkins, 1970. (1st ed., 1935.)

Gray, Virginia, Hansen, Russell, and Jacob, Herbert, eds. *Politics in the American States: A Comparative Analysis*, 7th ed. Washington, D.C.: Congressional Quarterly Press, 1999.

National Conference of State Legislatures. *Redistricting Law 2000*. Denver, Colo.: NCSL, 1999.

Pittman, H. C. *Inside the Third House: A Veteran Lobbyist Takes a 50-Year Frolic Through Texas Politics*. Austin, Tex.: Eakin Press, 1992.

Rosenthal, Alan. *Legislative Life: People, Process, and Performance in the States*. New York: Harper and Row, 1981.

———. *Governors and Legislatures: Contending Powers*. Washington, D.C.: Congressional Quarterly Press, 1990.

Vega, Arturo. "Gender and Ethnicity Effects on the Legislative Behavior and Substantive Representation of the Texas Legislature," *Texas Journal of Political Studies* 19, no. 2 (1997): 1–21.

NOTES

1. The sources for this material include Charles Deaton, *The Year They Threw the Rascals Out* (Austin, Tex.: Shoal Creek Press, 1973); Harvey Katz, *The Shadow on the Alamo: New Heroes Fight Old Corruption in Texas* (Garden City, N.J.: Doubleday, 1972); Sam Kinch and Ben Proctor, *Texas Under a Cloud* (Austin, Tex.: Jenkins 1972); Mickey Herskowitz, *Sharpstown Revisited: Frank Sharp and a Tale of Dirty Politics in Texas* (Austin, Tex.: Eakin Press, 1994); the official *House Journal.*

2. Sam Kinch, *Dallas News,* 10 July 1971; *Austin American-Statesman,* 13 May 1971.

3. Sam Kinch, *Dallas News,* 10 July 1971; *Dallas News,* 14 July 1971; *Ft. Worth Star-Telegram,* 27 April 1972.

4. *Houston Post,* 27 September 1971.

5. *Austin American-Statesman,* 1 December 1971; *Houston Post,* 7 December 1971.

6. The numbering of the legislative sessions was not changed when the current constitution was adopted. Thus, the 1st Legislature convened in 1846, when Texas joined the United States; the first legislature to meet under our current constitution (in 1876) was the 15th Legislature.

7. Kendra Hovey and Harold Hovey, *Congressional Quarterly's State Fact Finder 1999: Rankings Across America* (Washington, D.C.: Congressional Quarterly Press, 1999), 95.

8. There are several ways that state officials may be removed from office. Article 15 of the Texas Constitution lists elected officials subject to impeachment by the House and trial by the Senate. A following provision then adds that "the legislature shall provide by law for the trial and removal from office of all officers of this State, the modes for which have not been provided in this Constitution." Still another provision says that judges may be removed on "address" of the legislature, by two-thirds vote of each house.

9. Larry Sabato, *Goodbye to Good-Time Charlie: The American Governorship Transformed*, 2d ed. (Washington, D.C.: Congressional Quarterly Press, 1983), 79; Alan Rosenthal, *Governors and Legislatures: Contending Powers* (Washington, D.C.: Congressional Quarterly Press, 1990).

10. In 1999, voters approved a constitutional amendment requiring the Senate, in the case of a vacancy in the office of lieutenant governor, to elect a lieutenant governor from among its members.

11. Council of State Governments, *Book of the States 1998–99,* vol. 32 (Lexington, Ky.: Council of State Governments, 1998).

12. The Texas Constitution actually allowed for unequal-sized Senate seats, but in 1962, the U.S. Supreme Court declared in *Baker v. Carr* that state legislatures must reapportion to a one-person–one-vote standard.

13. See National Commission of State Legislatures, *Redistricting Law 2000* (Denver, Colo.: National Commission of State Legislatures, 1999).

14. Ralph A. Wooster, "Membership in Early Texas Legislatures, 1850–1860," *Southwestern Historical Quarterly* 69 (October 1965): 163–173.

15. Virginia Gray, Russell Hanson, and Herbert Jacob, *Politics in the American States*, 7th ed. (Washington, D.C.: Congressional Quarterly Press, 1999), 168.

16. For more information on initiative and referendum, see Shaun Bowler, Todd Donovan, and Caroline Tolbert, eds., *Citizens as Legislators: Direct Democracy in the United States* (Columbus, Ohio: Ohio State University Press, 1998).

17. Hovey and Hovey, *State Fact Finder*, 100.

18. Wooster, "Membership in the Early Texas Legislatures," 163–173; Alan Rosenthal, "The Legislative Institution In Transition and at Risk," in *The State of the States*, ed. Carl E. Van Horn (Washington, D.C.: Congressional Quarterly Press, 1993), 122.

19. Rosenthal, "The Legislative Institution," 122.

20. See J. Mason Brewer, *Negro Legislators of Texas*, 2d ed. (Austin, Tex.: Jenkins, 1970); 1st ed., 1935.

21. See the *Texas Observer*, 16 June 1995. The *Observer* did not publish a vote analysis for 1999.

22. "Legislators Rankings," [sic] Young Conservatives of Texas Baylor Chapter, no date. Accessed 1 March 2000. http://www.baylor.edu/~YngConsrvOfTX.html.

23. Any such ranking is partly an artifact of the votes chosen. Different record votes could have produced different results, and absences can influence one's ranking.

24. For a description of the 1995 votes, see the 1st edition of this textbook.

25. For a description of this nonparty speaker system and the current birthing of parties that threatens to undo that system, see Keith Hamm and Robert Harmel, "Legislative Party Development and the Speaker System: The Case of the Texas House," *The Journal of Politics* 55 (November 1993): 1140–1151.

26. Rosenthal, "The Legislative Institution," 131–132; and Stephen A. Salmore and Barbara G. Salmore, "The Transformation of State Electoral Politics," in *The State of the States*, ed. Carl E. Van Horn (Washington, D. C.: Congressional Quarterly Press, 1993), 67.

27. *Dallas News*, 30 December 1971.

28. *Dallas Times-Herald*, 16 January 1981; *Houston Post*, 16 January 1981; *Dallas Morning News*, 22 July 1987.

29. Gary Moncrief, "Committee Stacking and Reform in the Texas House of Representatives," *Texas Journal of Political Studies* 2 (Fall 1979): 47.

30. *Dallas Times-Herald*, 1 December 1980; *San Angelo Standard Times*, 13 February 1983; *Austin American-Statesman*, 11 January 1981.

31. *Houston Post*, 1 September 1973.

32. *Houston Post*, 20 April 1976; *Houston Post*, 16 January 1977; *Dallas Times-Herald*, 10 June 1975; tape recording, House Administration Committee, 14 May 1975.

33. The three were James Wilson Henderson, Hardin Richard Runnels, and Coke Stevenson. Texas Legislative Council, *Presiding Officers of the Texas Legislature, 1846–1995*, rev. ed. (Austin, Tex: 1995), 21, 25, 77.

34. Council of State Governments, *Book of the States 1998–99*, vol. 32 (Lexington, Ky.: Council of State Governments, 1998), 48.

35. For more detailed information, see House Research Organization, *Session Focus*, "How a Bill Becomes Law: 76th Legislature," 29 January 1999 and *Daily Floor Report*, 13 and 14 January 1999, for discussion of proposed Rules and Housekeeping Resolutions.

36. The Local and Consent Calendar is supposed to be reserved for noncontroversial bills (though sometimes, a controversial matter will be sneaked through on it). Bills on this calendar are not usually debated. If they are contested, they will be pulled from this calendar.
37. This daily calendar actually includes several calendars. Bills are considered on Major State, General State, Emergency, Resolutions, Constitutional Amendments, or Senate Calendars.
38. Technically, the rules only require that a majority of members of the conference committee from each chamber sign the report. This loophole allows "phantom" meetings—some conference committees never meet. The chairs simply negotiate the language behind closed doors, then present it to the others for their signatures—another example of legislative processes that thwart deliberative democracy.
39. Rosenthal, "The Legislative Institution," 127.
40. Thad Beyle, *State Government: Congressional Quarterly's Guide to Current Issues and Activities, 1998–1999* (Washington, D.C.: Congressional Quarterly Press, 1998), 71.
41. Alan Rosenthal, *Governors and Legislatures: Contending Powers* (Washington, D.C.: Congressional Quarterly Press, 1990), 46; Rosenthal, "The Legislative Institution," 120; Marilyn Duncan, ed., *Guide to Texas State Agencies,* 10th ed. (Austin, Tex.: LBJ School of Public Affairs, 1999), 3, 7, 9, 11, 13, 14.
42. *Ft. Worth Star-Telegram,* 13 January 1983.
43. E. E. Schattschneider, *The Semi-Sovereign People* (New York: Holt, Rinehart & Winston, 1960).
44. *Dallas Morning News,* 24 April 1991.
45. See Robert Heard, *The Miracle of the Killer Bees* (Austin, Tex.: Honey Hill, 1981), for an account of the incident.
46. Ironically, in the 2000 presidential primaries, George W. Bush complained that crossover Democratic votes for John McCain hurt his bid for the Republican nomination.

9 The Governor of Texas

★ Scenario: George W. Bush—Policy Change, Political Change, and Governors

Governors often emerge as high-profile issue leaders and, as a result, gain popularity and win policy battles within the executive branch or with the legislature. Governors have the opportunity to forge a direct electoral bond with voters. As campaigners, they have the potential to embrace and to try to lead political movements. An excellent example of an executive official emerging as a high-profile policy leader is Governor George W. Bush, who targeted education and taxes as his legislative issues. The political environment was different in each of his legislative sessions. In 1995, he faced a solidly Democratic legislature; in 1997, a majority of the Senate was Republican; and by 1999, both a majority of the Senate and the lieutenant governor were Republican. He won some and lost some of his legislative initiatives, yet he emerged from the sessions politically strong. In an era lacking in creedal passion, what is the ultimate outcome of such gubernatorial leadership?

Nineteen hundred ninety-four was a watershed Republican year across the nation. In Texas, Republican George W. Bush beat popular Democratic Governor Ann Richards in her bid for reelection. In the 1995 legislative session, Governor Bush advocated changes in education, welfare, civil justice, and juvenile justice policies, and the legislature enacted significant changes in each of those areas. The legislature approved a new education code, a complete overhaul of the welfare system, a victory for "tort reform" forces, and tougher juvenile justice laws. Bush emerged from the session with a reputation for pragmatism, effectiveness, and success.

For the 1997 session, Governor Bush announced his education and tax goals. With a strong economy and a looming budget surplus, he proposed an ambitious plan to dramatically reduce local school property taxes and to increase some state taxes in exchange. Democratic Lieutenant Governor Bob Bullock and Speaker Pete Laney were skeptical.[1] With Bush's proposal coming just after the election in which Republicans had gained legislative seats, they were also wary of the political consequences of a big tax policy victory for Bush. Thus, the partisan element in the legislative dialogue with the governor was much stronger in the 1997 legislative session than in 1995.

Governor Bush played on the fact that Texas's property taxes are among the highest in the nation. Since these are primarily school taxes, his initiative effectively reopened the politically volatile question of school financing, which had only recently been settled (see Chapter 14). Moreover, any tax cut ultimately shifts the tax burden among taxpayers. *Texas Monthly,* though usually laudatory of Governor Bush, wrote that the beneficiaries of his proposal would be refineries, chemical plants, and heavy manufacturing, while the losers would be groceries, restaurants, retailers, high-tech manufacturing companies, and partnerships.[2] In the end, Bush's tax proposal was amended away, until all that was left was an increase in the tax exemption for homeowners. However, the public did not view the failure of his major tax overhaul proposal as a failure of his governorship or his leadership.

By 1999, with his presidential campaign revving up, Bush did not spend as much time with legislators as he had previously,[3] and he again had a mixed session. Bush continued his quest for lower school taxes and for education policy changes. He began the session by advocating a pilot school vouchers program that would allow some students to use public funds to attend private schools. Near the end of the session, he lobbied fence-sitting Republican senators for vouchers, but he was not able to persuade them, and the voucher effort died. In the education arena, he advocated ending the social promotion of students (i.e., promoting students to the next grade, even if they are failing). The legislature passed a modified version of his proposal, adding Democratic amendments providing funding for intensive instruction of those students.

Also, once again, he proposed tax cuts without first lining up legislative support. The session began with a sizable projected revenue surplus. Bush called for $2.6 billion in tax cuts and said that if any surplus money remained, he would support a pay raise for teachers. The legislative session became a battle between tax cuts—supported by Republicans—and increased spending for education, supported by both parties, but with Democrats advancing the more aggressive pro-

Texas Federation of Teachers President John Cole, leading a teacher rally during the 1999 legislative session. Teachers and Democrats repeatedly emphasized the need for additional money in education, making it more difficult for Governor Bush and Republicans to win a large tax cut.

posals. Soon, the projected surplus was all spoken for. Republican senators proposed further tax cuts and suggested cutting spending for kindergarten $250 million to pay for them, giving Democrats a softball to swing away at. Republicans insisted on large tax cuts first; Democrats insisted on increased education spending first.

House Republicans won sizable tax cuts in House floor battles. Meanwhile, Democratic House committee chairman Paul Sadler held the school finance bill hostage, waiting for the final revenue estimate so that he could propose teacher pay raises. Four Democratic legislative caucuses held a joint press conference to demand that the comptroller release the final revenue estimate and to focus attention on education issues. With only two weeks remaining in the session, new Republican Comptroller Carole Rylander (see Chapter 10) increased the estimate of the budget surplus—enough, she said, for "really significant" tax cuts.[4] In the end, in time-honored legislative tradition, the compromise spent more money for education than Bush and Republican legislators wanted, and tax cuts were larger than Democrats wanted.

Thus, over three legislative sessions, Governor Bush persistently led efforts for education policy changes and for tax cuts. He claimed that his efforts won billions in tax cuts for Texans, and he campaigned for the presidency on that record. After the 1997 session, however, the *Texas Observer* argued that some homeowners received no tax cut at all. And after the 1999 session, the Texas Education Agency surveyed school districts. The agency's figures showed no overall change in the tax rates: decreases in some categories were balanced by increase in others, leaving no net change in taxes.[5]

No policy leadership happens in a vacuum. Governor Bush's education policy proposals built upon earlier efforts at reform. He came into office with an accountability system already adopted by the legislature in 1993, requiring annual exams (Texas Assessment of Academic Skills, or TAAS). He implemented and expanded the new system. As *Time* magazine reported, "In part, he's been lucky. When he took office, Bush was the beneficiary of a decade's worth of reform efforts beginning with Ross Perot's mid-'80s movement to reduce class sizes and install statewide testing and accountability. By [1993 the legislature had repealed the state education code and the 1995] legislature was at work on a new one that would push authority down to the local school districts. Like any gifted politician, Bush commandeered the train, adding some cars of his own and taking credit for laying its track. But then he drove it further."[6]

Governor Bush was able to work with the legislature by using his informal powers, including personality, persuasion, and the aura of presidential politics. Bush has stated that "People say the Texas governor is a weak position. Only a weak person makes it a weak position." His legislative liaison has commented that "for Bush, everything is personal. He needs to have the personal relationship. . . ."[7] His experience demonstrates that formal powers may be less important to a governor's pursuit of policy goals than informal powers. A governor's success is also tied to prior policy groundwork and to political dynamics, such as election trends and partisan trends. ★

INTRODUCTION

The top political leader and the top official of the executive branch of Texas state government is known as the "governor."[8] The governor is sometimes referred to as the "chief executive officer" of Texas. George W. Bush was elected governor in 1994 and reelected in 1998. However, power and policy implementation is not centralized in Governor Bush's office; rather, we have a **plural executive,** with power divided among several independently elected officials and more than 100 executive boards and commissions.

The governor has little direct power over state agencies. This fragmented government is a two-edged sword. It increases the chance for conflicts over policy making, but it enhances the opportunity for policy innovation and experimentation, due to the diversity and number of independent and powerful officeholders. In some senses, the Texas governor is simply one of many equals inside Texas government.

The governor is not even assured of the support and cooperation of the lieutenant governor. Texas does not have a party ticket or a team system. Twenty-four states try to ensure some executive cooperation by electing the governor and lieutenant governor on a single ticket so that it is impossible for them to be from different political parties. Only eight states have a governor–lieutenant governor

Te★as*Index*

State Governors

Governor's salary, 1998:

Texas—$115,345 (7th)

California—$114,286 (8th)

New York—$130,000 (1st)

Florida—$97,850 (19th)

Frequency of meetings of governor's cabinet:

Texas—(no cabinet)

California—(2 weeks)

New York—(governor's discretion)

Florida—(2 weeks)

Governors who became President of the United States:

Texas—none

California—Ronald Reagan

New York—Martin Van Buren, Grover Cleveland,

Theodore Roosevelt, Franklin D. Roosevelt

Florida—none

Maximum number of terms allowed:

Texas—unlimited

California—2

New York—unlimited

Florida—2

Joint election of governor/lieutenant governor:

Texas—no

California—no

New York—yes

Florida—yes

team as we have with the president and vice president, where the candidate running for governor gets to choose the candidate running for lieutenant governor.[9] Three times, Texas has had a Republican governor and a Democratic lieutenant governor.

Because Texas governors are not assured of control of state government, they must build strong outside support. That could consist of support from the economic powers, popular support among the voters, or both. In this chapter, we examine how the Texas governorship developed and what the current office is like. Then we look at the powers of the governor within the executive branch and compare those with the powers of governors in other states. We then assess the governor as a political leader. With that material, and drawing on the example of George W. Bush's governorship, we then evaluate the Texas governorship, political change, and forms of democracy.

INFLUENCES ON THE DEVELOPMENT OF THE TEXAS GOVERNORSHIP

The issue of how the governor will be chosen is one that has its roots in decisions made long ago in the emerging political systems of the United States and Mexico. Spanish kings sent representatives of the crown to what is now Texas in the 1500s. In 1691, the king designated the first *Governador de Tejas*—Don Domingo Teran de los Rios—who, in addition to governing, drove cattle from Mexico and established the first herds in Texas.[10] The Mexican Constitution of 1824 and the 1827 Constitution of the State of Coahuila y Tejas established a governor and an executive council and gave the governor the power to rule by decree.

Far to the east, in the British colonies, governors also represented and served at the pleasure of a monarch—in this case, the British Crown. Only two of the governors were elected. These early American governors were weak. They shared power with executive councils and with other statewide officials and were subordinate to the colonial legislatures.[11]

Under the Republic of Texas, the chief executive was the president, who ruled with a **cabinet** of top officials appointed by and responsible to the chief executive. When Texas joined the United States in 1845, it was with a relatively powerful governor. The governor, who was elected to a two-year term of office, appointed almost all state officials, including judges, though the comptroller and the treasurer were elected by the legislature. By 1850, the constitution was amended to provide for the direct election of judges, the attorney general, comptroller, treasurer, and land commissioner. The Confederate Constitution of 1861 was similar to the 1845 one in the governor's powers.[12]

The 1866 constitution included a four-year term of office for the governor, with a limit of two consecutive terms, and **gubernatorial** (meaning of or by the governor) appointment of all officials but the comptroller and the treasurer. A new power for the governor was the line-item veto, which had been used in the Confederacy. The 1869 constitution retained a four-year term. The governor could appoint local officials and state police and could impose martial law. However, as a scholar of the Texas governorship wrote, "more disintegration of the executive power than ever was effected." The lieutenant governor, comptroller, treasurer, land commissioner, and public-instruction superintendent were all elected to four-year terms.[13]

The 1876 constitution further decentralized and limited state government. The governor's term was reduced to two years, and the governor's salary was reduced from $5,000 to $4,000. While we have amended this constitution many times since its adoption, the basic structure of executive power remains the same today—a weak governor, who must share power, both with others in the executive branch and with a strong legislature. Texas has had 30 governors under this constitution (Table 9.1).

THE OFFICE OF THE GOVERNOR

The terms of office for the governorship are set by the constitution. The roles that the governor plays are set by constitutional mandate, legislative mandate, and

Table 9.1   TEXAS GOVERNORS, 1876–2000

Number	Governor	Party	Term	Years served	Birthdate	Age	Left by	Occupation
1	Richard Coke	D	1	2+ (1874–1876)	3-13-1829	43	Resigned	Lawyer/farmer
2	Richard B. Hubbard	D	1+	3+ (1876–1879)	11-1-1832	44	Defeated	Lawyer
3	Oran M. Roberts	D	2	4 (1879–1883)	7-9-1815	63	Retired	Lawyer/educator
4	John Ireland	D	2	4 (1883–1887)	1-1-1827	56	Retired	Lawyer
5	Lawrence Sul Ross	D	2	4 (1887–1891)	9-27-1838	48	Retired	Farmer/soldier
6	James S. Hogg	D	2	4 (1891–1895)	3-24-1851	39	Retired	Lawyer/editor
7	Charles A. Culberson	D	2	4 (1895–1899)	6-10-1855	39	Retired	Lawyer
8	Joseph D. Sayers	D	2	4 (1899–1903)	9-23-1846	57	Retired	Lawyer
9	Samuel Lanham	D	2	4 (1903–1907)	7-4-1846	56	Retired	Lawyer
10	Thomas M. Campbell	D	2	4 (1907–1911)	4-22-1856	50	Retired	Lawyer; railroad exec.
11	Oscar B. Colquitt	D	2	4 (1911–1915)	12-16-1861	49	Retired	Lawyer/editor
12	James E. Ferguson	D	1+	2+ (1915–1917)	8-31-1871	43	Impeached	Banker/lawyer/farmer
13	William P. Hobby	D	1+	2 (1917–1921)	3-26-1878	39	Retired	Editor
14	Pat M. Neff	D	2	4 (1921–1925)	11-26-1871	49	Retired	Lawyer/educator
15	Miriam A. Ferguson	D	1	2 (1925–1927)	6-13-1875	49	Defeated	Housewife
16	Dan Moody	D	2	4 (1927–1931)	6-1-1893	33	Retired	Lawyer
17	Ross Sterling	D	1	2 (1931–1933)	2-11-1875	55	Defeated	President of Mobil Oil
	Miriam A. Ferguson[a]	D	1	2 (1933–1935)	6-13-1875	57	Retired	Housewife
18	James V. Allred	D	2	4 (1935–1939)	3-2-1899	35	Retired	Lawyer
19	W. Lee O'Daniel	D	1+	2+ (1939–1941)	3-11-1890	48	Resigned	Businessperson/salesperson
20	Coke Stevenson	D	2+	5+ (1941–1947)	3-20-1888	53	Retired	Lawyer/banker/rancher
21	Beauford Jester	D	1+	2+ (1947–1949)	1-12-1893	54	Died	Lawyer
22	Allan Shivers	D	3+	7+ (1949–1957)	10-5-1907	41	Retired	Lawyer
23	Price Daniel	D	3	6+ (1957–1963)	10-10-1910	46	Defeated	Lawyer/educator/rancher
24	John Connally	D	3	6 (1963–1969)	2-27-1917	45	Retired	Lawyer/rancher
25	Preston Smith	D	2	4 (1969–1973)	3-8-1912	56	Defeated	Businessperson
26	Dolph Briscoe	D	2[b]	6 (1973–1979)	4-23-1923	49	Defeated	Rancher/banker
27	Bill Clements	R	2[c]	4 (1979–1983)	4-13-1917	61	Defeated	Oilman
28	Mark White	D	1[c]	4 (1983–1987)	3-17-1940	42	Defeated	Lawyer
	Bill Clements[a]	R	1[c]	4 (1987–1991)	4-13-1917	69	Retired	Oilman
29	Ann Richards	D	1[c]	4 (1991–1995)	9-1-1933	57	Defeated	Teacher/campaigner
30	George W. Bush	R	2[c]	8? (1995–present)	7-6-1946	48	—	Oilman/businessperson

[a]Miriam Ferguson and Bill Clements served nonconsecutive terms as governor.
[b]Briscoe served one two-year term and one four-year term.
[c]Served four-year terms.

Sources: Garland Adair, *Texas Pictorial Handbook* (Austin, Tex.: Texas Memorial Museum, 1957). William Atkinson, *James V. Allred: A Political Biography,* (Ph.D. diss. TCU, 1978). Biographical Files—Governors of Texas, in the Center for American History, University of Texas. Robert A. Calvert and Arnoldo DeLeon, *The History of Texas* (Arlington Heights, Ill.: Harlan Davidson, 1990). Council of State Governments, *The Governors of the States, Commonwealths, and Territories 1900–1980* (Lexington, Ky.: Council of State Governments 1981). *Dallas Morning News,* 7 March 1991, Fred Gantt, *The Chief Executive in Texas: A Study in Gubernatorial Leadership* (Austin, Tex.: University of Texas Press, 1964), App. III. Ross Phares, *Governors of Texas* (Gretna, La.: Pelican, 1976). *Texas Almanac* (Dallas, Tex.: A. H. Belo Corp., 1992). *Who's Who in the South and Southwest,* 16th ed. (1978–79); 18th ed. (1982–83), Chicago: Marquis Who's Who).

custom. Some of these roles encompass real powers and functions of the governorship, while others appear to be little more than ceremonial.

Requirements and Roles

The constitutional requirements for being governor of Texas are minimal. One must be at least 30 years of age, a U.S. citizen, and a Texas resident for the five years immediately preceding the election. The youngest governor has been Dan Moody, inaugurated at the age of 33.

Chief of State   The governor serves as the **chief of state**—the official head of and representative of the State of Texas in its relationships with the national government, other states, and foreign dignitaries. Relations with foreign countries are generally informal because the U.S. president is in charge of foreign affairs, but increasingly, the states (including Texas) are pursuing international initiatives of their own.

Because of the Texas–Mexico border, Texas governors have frequently been involved in U.S.–Mexico relations. Governor Colquitt proclaimed Texas neutrality in the Mexican Revolution, then later urged U.S. intervention. Governor Jim Ferguson called for a U.S. invasion of Mexico during the era of Pancho Villa's raids across the border. Governor Hobby and Mexican President Alvaro Obregon became friends and traded visits. Governor Allred visited Mexico to promote President Franklin Roosevelt's Good Neighbor Policy. Governor Stevenson created the Texas Good Neighbor Commission and accompanied President Roosevelt to Mexico. Since then, Texas governors have visited Mexico on numerous occasions, including Governor Bush, who is fluent in Spanish.

Governors have little in the way of formal relations with the national government. They may not hold state and national offices simultaneously. Nonetheless, governors receive or approve some federal grants to their states, often serve as informal advisers to the president, and often are the president's key political figures in the states. Governors also communicate with each other to coordinate the states' positions on national issues. The National Governors' Association and the Office for Federal–State Relations serve as vehicles for governors in the nation's capital. A Texas state agency, the Texas **Office of State–Federal Relations** (the director of which is appointed by the governor), has offices in Austin and Washington, D.C.

Commander in Chief of the State Militia   Article 4, Section 7 of the Texas Constitution states that the governor is the "**Commander-in-Chief** of the military forces of the State," and has the power "to call forth the militia to execute the laws of the State, to suppress insurrections, repel invasions, and protect the frontier from hostile incursions by Indians or other predatory bands." Using the militia this way to "execute the laws" is martial law.

The "Texas Volunteers" became the "State Militia" when Texas entered the Union. When Congress passed the National Guard Act in World War I and gave federal money to support state militias, it was renamed the Texas National Guard and includes the Army Guard and the Air Guard; it has about 22,000 troops. A Texas State Guard Reserve Corps supplements the National Guard. If the National Guard is called to duty outside the state, then the 1400-member State Guard can be called to duty within the state.[14]

The uses of the guard have been varied. Governors have called out the troops to police violent cross-border raids on the Rio Grande, suppress race riots, stop East Texas oilfield clashes, break labor strikes, and respond to natural disasters.[15] Martial-law powers aimed at social problems were used frequently in the days of the Texas Republic and of early statehood, then again repeatedly from 1915 to the 1930s. Modern governors use the National Guard primarily for responses to natural disasters.

Chief Executive Officer   Article 4, Section 1 of the constitution designates the governor as the **chief executive officer** of Texas. Primarily through the power of making appointments to boards and commissions that set policies for agencies, the governor is considered the head of the executive branch of state government, though the fragmented organization of executive power makes this title one that depends largely on the political and personal skills of the governor.

While most agency directors cooperate with the governor in policy implementation, there have been hostilities. Governor Jim Ferguson met with boards, ordered them to act according to his wishes, and threatened the removal of board members if they did not comply. Governor W. Lee O'Daniel blasted the lack of gubernatorial control over boards, particularly the staggered terms of members (see Chapter 10).[16]

Other executive officials are frequently interested in becoming governor themselves. Thus, there are frequent clashes between governors and other officials. Governors Jim and Miriam Ferguson feuded with Attorney General Dan Moody. Moody, in turn, ran against and beat Governor Miriam Ferguson. Governor Price Daniel and Attorney General Will Wilson feuded over tax policies.[17] Governor Dolph Briscoe and Attorney General John Hill had policy differences, and Hill then ran against and beat Briscoe for the governor's nomination. Democratic Attorney General Mark White clashed with Republican Governor Bill Clements, then beat Clements for the governorship. Democratic Land Commissioner Garry Mauro and Governor Bush squared off over coastal and other issues, then Mauro ran as the Democratic nominee against Bush in 1998, but lost.

Chief Budget Officer   In 1931, the legislature designated the governor as the state's **chief budget officer**—presumably the official responsible for preparing the budget proposal and for overseeing its implementation. However, the same law gave the State Board of Control the responsibility of preparing the budget. The governor had no budget staff. Through the 1940s, the governor typically just gave the legislature the Board of Control's budget, with a few comments.[18]

In 1951, the legislature and Governor Shivers moved the budget function directly into the governor's office, where it has remained.[19] However, that was also the first session for the new Legislative Budget Board (LBB), and the legislature has consistently ignored the budget developed by the governor's office, in favor of the budget developed by legislative leaders in charge of the LBB.[20] Thus, the title and function of the governor as chief budget officer are largely ceremonial. (See Chapter 14 for more on the budgetary process.)

Chief Law Enforcement and Judicial Officer   Because of the governor's powers over the Department of Public Safety, judicial vacancies, pardons, parole, and clemency, he or she has a limited role in law enforcement. The original 1876 constitution gave the governor almost absolute power in **clemency**, reducing prison terms. Governors received and granted thousands of requests for clemency and pardons, and there were recurrent rumors of bribery. Governor Moody and the legislature created a Board of Pardons and Paroles in 1929, and Governor Allred had it put into the constitution in 1936, thus reducing the governor's powers, as well as the pressure on governors.[21]

Chief Legislator   The governor has become a powerful figure in legislative politics, as we saw in the chapter scenario. A governor accomplishes this by delivering **governor's messages** that pronounce policy goals and budget priorities, issuing "emergency" messages designed to speed favored bills through the legislative process, threatening to veto bills and thus gaining a seat in negotiations over bills,

Each legislative session, the governor addresses the legislature and occasionally drops by to visit and lobby for legislation. Here, Governor George W. Bush and Speaker Pete Laney are at the podium in the House chamber during the 1999 session.

calling special legislative sessions, setting the agenda for special sessions, signing bills into law, and vetoing bills.

Party Leader   Party leadership is a nominal role in Texas. Historically, the governor got to choose the chairperson of his or her political party, though that is less direct or certain today (see Chapter 4). The party usually works to advance the success of the governor. Legislative members of the governor's party also rally around the governor as their leader when there are partisan battles, which occur more frequently now, with Texas's emergence as a two-party state.

Terms of Office

The constitution sets the length of the term of office for the governorship, methods for removing a governor from office, and the line of succession in the event of a vacancy in the office. The constitution originally set the governor's salary, though the legislature now does so.

Length and Number of Terms   The length of the term of office for the governor is four years. It was established as a two-year term in the original 1876 constitution and remained two years until it was amended in 1974.[22] Texas was later than most states in lengthening the governor's term of office. All states now have four-year governorships, except for New Hampshire and Vermont.[23]

Governors across the United States are now serving longer tenures, too, due to multiple reelections.[24] Ten states, including Texas, have no limit on the number of terms of office their governors may serve. One state limits its governor to three terms; 23 states limit their governors to two terms; and 16 states allow more than two terms if they are not consecutive, with various ways of defining a consecutive term.[25] In recent times, less than half of the gubernatorial elections have resulted in an incumbent being reelected.[26]

Until the 1940s, no Texas governor had served more than two terms. Table 9.1 lists Texas governors and the number of terms that they served. Virtually all governors won two terms when the terms were two years long. From the 1940s to the 1970s, a three-term tradition was maintained.[27] Dolph Briscoe was elected governor in 1972. When he won reelection in 1974, it was for the new four-year term. In 1978, he ran for another four-year term but was defeated in the Democratic primary—partly on an appeal by his opponent against having an unprecedented ten-year governor. Bill Clements served one four-year term and was defeated by Mark White, who served a single four-year term before being defeated himself by Clements. Clements then served another four-year term. Ann Richards served a single four-year term, then lost her race for reelection in 1994. George W. Bush beat her, and then won reelection in 1998. He is the first governor to win back-to-back four-year terms and, if he serves out his second term, will become the governor with the longest consecutive governorship.

Critical Thinking Exercise: Given Texas's history of limited government and given the recent national movement for term limitations, why does Texas not have a term limit for its governor? Would you support such a limitation? What effect might a term limit have on the governor's exercise of power?

Salary   In the state budget for fiscal year 2001, the Texas governor is paid $115,345. In all of Texas's constitutions up until 1954, the governor's salary was set in the constitution. It was originally $4,000 in the 1876 constitution.[28] Voters repeatedly defeated salary increases before a $12,000 salary was approved in 1935. In 1953, the constitution was amended to allow the legislature to set the governor's salary. It quickly became one of the highest governor's salaries in the nation. The salary level stagnated in the 1990s, and the comparative ranking slipped. In 1998, the governor was paid $115,345, which ranked seventh in the nation, while the highest governor's salary was New York's, at $130,000.[29]

Impeachment

One Texas governor has been impeached, convicted, and removed from office. In 1917, Jim Ferguson angered legislators and University of Texas (UT) alumni by vetoing UT appropriations in order to force changes that he wanted. Legislators resurrected old allegations that he had misused public money, impeached him, and convicted him. He was removed from office and barred from holding office again. He later successfully ran his wife Miriam for governor, under the slogan, "Two Governors for the Price of One."

Succession   Article 4, Section 17 of the constitution provides for **succession.** The lieutenant governor succeeds to the governorship if there is a vacancy. Since 1876, four lieutenant governors have done so. Richard Hubbard became governor when the first governor under the new constitution, Richard Coke, resigned in 1876 to become U.S. Senator. William Hobby did so when Governor Jim Ferguson was removed from office in 1917. Coke Stevenson did so when Governor O'Daniel won a special election to the U.S. Senate in 1941, and Allan Shivers did so when Governor Jester died in 1949. In 2000, George W. Bush was running for the presidency. Should Governor Bush win and then resign his governorship in midterm, Rick Perry would become governor. Voters amended the constitution in 1999 to assure that in such event, the lieutenant governor would have to resign that office upon succeeding to the governorship, and the Senate would select a new lieutenant governor.

POWERS OF THE GOVERNOR

How much power and what kinds of power a governor has depends on constitutional provisions, the era and political times in which a governor serves, and the relative power of other governmental officials. Regardless of how these factors have changed, Texas governors have always been weaker than governors in most other states.

Characteristics of Strong Governorships

Political scientist Joseph Schlesinger devised a scale to measure the power of governors, using data from 1960–1961. These data have been updated periodically since then. Schlesinger used four variables: (1) tenure—length of term of office, limits on number of terms; (2) appointments—power to appoint heads of executive agencies; (3) budget—budget-preparation power; and (4) signing and vetoing of bills-veto and line-item veto authority, time to consider legislation before signing or vetoing it, difficulty of legislative ability to override. Schlesinger found that strong governorships were typically in large, urbanized, wealthy, nonsouthern states, with a strong level of party competition.[30] Table 9.2 lists the generally accepted characteristics of a strong governor.

Table 9.2 CHARACTERISTICS OF A STRONG GOVERNOR

Scholars of the American governors have suggested more than a dozen characteristics that indicate a strong governorship.

- Four-year term of office
- No limit on reelection
- Leader of political party
- State has strong party system
- Call special elections/appoint replacements
- Appoint judges
- Appoint commissions, boards
- Appoint and remove heads of agencies
- Govern with cabinet-type leadership
- Develop budget for all executive agencies
- Call special legislative sessions
- Set agenda of special legislative sessions
- Veto bills
- Return bills to legislature for changes
- Legislature can recall bills to add governor's demands
- Veto line items in appropriations bills
- Reduce appropriations

Sources: Joseph Schlesinger, "Politics, the Executive," in *Politics in the American States: A Comparative Analysis,* 1st and 2d eds., eds. Herbert Jacob and Kenneth Vines (Boston: Little, Brown, 1965 and 1971); Thad Beyle, "Governors," in *Politics in the American States: A Comparative Analysis,* 5th ed., eds. Virginia Gray, Herbert Jacob, and Robert Albritton (New York: HarperCollins, 1990); Thad Beyle, "Governors: The Middlemen and Women in Our Political System," in *Politics in the American States: A Comparative Analysis,* 6th ed., eds. Virginia Gray and Herbert Jacob (Washington, D.C.: Congressional Quarterly Press, 1996); Thad Beyle, "The Governors," in *Politics in the American States,* 7th ed., eds. Virginia Gray, Russell Hanson, and Herbert Jacob (Washington, D.C.: Congressional Quarterly, 1999); Larry Sabato, *Goodbye to Good-time Charlie: The American Governorship Transformed,* 2nd ed. (Washington, D.C.: Congressional Quarterly Press, 1983), 77.

Moralism and Restriction of Governors' Powers

Nationwide distrust of government and governors in the eighteenth and nineteenth centuries led to restrictions on the power that governors could wield and on their terms of office. All but three of the original states had one-year terms of office for governors, some had term limits, and the Virginia and South Carolina governors were even appointed by the legislature! Only the Massachusetts and New York governors had veto power in the early years of the federation. In the Jacksonian era, the powers of governors were increased somewhat. Terms were extended to four years, and appointment, veto, and clemency powers were increased. Their powers were checked, though, by the increasing election of other executive officials.[31] Gradually, throughout the twentieth century, states lifted many of the gubernatorial restrictions and empowered their governors. At the start of the twenty-first century, most governors have significant powers.

Restriction of the power of governors is an example of moralism at work, and Texas was a practitioner of such moralism, especially in reaction to the strong government set up during Reconstruction. Under the 1869 constitution, the governor had complete control over voter registration, could appoint the governing bodies of towns and cities, and had control of the militia and the state police. Under Republican Governor E. J. Davis, the militia and the state police were despised by some. (Of course, racial politics also influenced people's attitudes.) A much later historical analysis argued that "the police force was used so often to enforce the arbitrary will of the governor that it became an emblem of despotic authority."[32]

In 1872, the voters rebelled and elected an antiadministration legislature, which triggered adoption of a new constitution. The desire to punish Davis and to prohibit future governors from becoming powerful led constitutional convention delegates in 1875 to adopt provisions that reduced the governor's salary, elected a plethora of other officers independent from the governor, and restricted the governor's appointment and removal powers.[33]

Comparing the Texas Governor with Other Governors

A comparison of the 50 governors around the United States reveals substantial differences among them, particularly some interesting contrasts with the Texas governorship. Whereas 41 states have some kind of cabinet system in which the major agency directors are selected by and responsible to the governor, Texas does not.[34] Texas has a plural executive. Most agency directors are appointed by boards, rather than directly by the governor; some agency directors are elected; there is no systematic, ongoing process for the governor to coordinate executive agency policies; and it is virtually impossible for the governor to fire a board member or an agency head. (See Chapter 10 for a discussion of reorganization efforts.)

On Schlesinger's 1960–1961 scale, the Texas governor tied for the weakest of the 48 governors when all variables were combined. When he updated his scale using 1968–1969 data, Texas ranked fiftieth, and Schlesinger commented that "Texas is the only populous state where the governor's formal strength is low."[35] Political scientist Thad Beyle has updated the rankings numerous times since then; in his rankings, Texas always ranked forty-eighth or forty-ninth, until he changed the variables in 1999, with Texas ranking twenty-eighth. Table 9.3 shows Texas rankings. Texas is also a weak-governor state on the four individual variables. For instance, Texas is the only governor with weak budget-making power, and only Texas, Georgia, Mississippi, South Carolina, and Oklahoma governors are very weak in appointment powers.[36]

Constitutionally, it is apparent that the Texas governor is weak, as we concluded in Chapter 3. Governors may be able to amass and exercise more strength, though, in the political arena, where appearance, charisma, and bluff may count more than constitutional reality. In 1994 and 1999, Beyle compared the "personal power" of the governors. As we might guess from the chapter scenario on Governor Bush's influence, Texas's governor ranked significantly higher on personal power than on the institutional powers rankings. Further, the legislature and the voters have strengthened the Texas governorship in recent years. Today,

Table 9.3   POWERS OF THE TEXAS GOVERNOR COMPARED TO OTHER GOVERNORS

Four snapshots of governors in the United States show that Texas governors have long been weaker than governors in other states.

	Number of points (and comparative rank)			
Characteristics	**1960–1961**	**1968–1969**	**1990**	**1999**
Tenure	2 (33rd)	2 (41st)	5 (1st)	5 (1st)
Appointments	1 (38th)	1 (41st)	2 (46th)	3.5 (10th)
Budget	1 (41st)	1 (45th)	1 (50th)	2 (49th)
Veto	3 (14th)	3 (41st)	5 (1st)	5 (1st)
Budget changing			1 (^{a})	
Legislative strength			2 (33rd)	
Separately elected officials				1 (41st)
Gubernatorial party control				3 (20th)
Combined	7 (48th)	7 (50th)	16 (49th)	(28th)

^{a}For 1990, Beyle added a new category comparing the governor's power vis-à-vis legislative budget-changing power. He found only 4 states where the governor had any significant power over the legislature, and 43 states, including Texas, where the governor was "very weak."

Sources: Joseph Schlesinger, "Politics, the Executive," in *Politics in the American States: A Comparative Analysis*, 1st ed., eds. Herbert Jacob and Kenneth Vines, (Boston: Little, Brown, 1965), 220–229 and 2d ed., 1971, 225–234. Thad L. Beyle, "Governors," in *Politics in the American States*, 5th ed., eds. Virginia Gray, Herbert Jacob, and Robert Albritton (New York: HarperCollins, 1990), 574. Thad L. Beyle, "The Governors," in *Politics in the American States*, 7th ed., eds. Virginia Gray, Russell Hanson, and Herbert Jacob (Washington, D.C.: Congressional Quarterly, 1999), 210–211.

the governor can appoint more high-level positions than ever before, and he or she has (limited) budget execution authority (see Chapter 14). Also, a 1980 amendment (Article 15, Section 9) allows the governor, for the first time under our current constitution, to remove from office gubernatorial appointees—but only with a two-thirds vote of the Senate and only his or her own appointees, not previous governors' appointees. No governor has yet used this power.

Staff and Budget

The responsibilities of the governor's staff are broad: developing the governor's budget proposal and policy recommendations; performing public relations; serving as liaison with local, state, and federal agencies and with the legislature and party officials; answering correspondence and visiting with citizens who call on the governor; and contacting and negotiating with lobbyists. These duties change with the priorities and organizational preferences of each governor.

Nineteenth-century governors typically had two or three staff members. The growth in the number of state boards and commissions, with the governor as ex officio member of many of them, brought an increase in the governor's staff to about eight in the 1920s and 1930s. Since the mid-1900s, the governor's staff size has grown tremendously. Governors Clements, Richards, and Bush each had about 200 staff members. Measuring staff size, though, is difficult, because governors can persuade agency heads to pay for staff members that are then loaned to the governor and do not appear on the governor's payroll.

The amount of money that the legislature appropriates for the operations of the Office of the Governor depends on what functions the legislature and the governor choose to place under the Office of the Governor. The organization of Governor Bush's office is shown in Figure 9.1. While the governor's appropriations may exceed $100 million a year, only about $7 million of that is for the narrower Governor's Office, and the remainder is for discretionary funds and the suboffices included in the governor's budget. In fiscal year 2000, the budget of the Office of the Governor was $107 million, and in 2001, $95 million. These figures include monies for such categories as the governor's mansion, the governor's ombudsman, grants, music and film industry marketing, information on disability policies, transportation coordination, women's groups, and immigration/refugee assistance.

Appointments to the Executive Branch

Article IV, Section 12 of the constitution details the method for filling vacancies in the executive branch: "All vacancies in State or district offices, except members of the Legislature, shall be filled unless otherwise provided by law by appointment of the Governor." The governor appoints more agency heads today than ever before (Table 9.4). Recent additions to the governor's appointment powers include

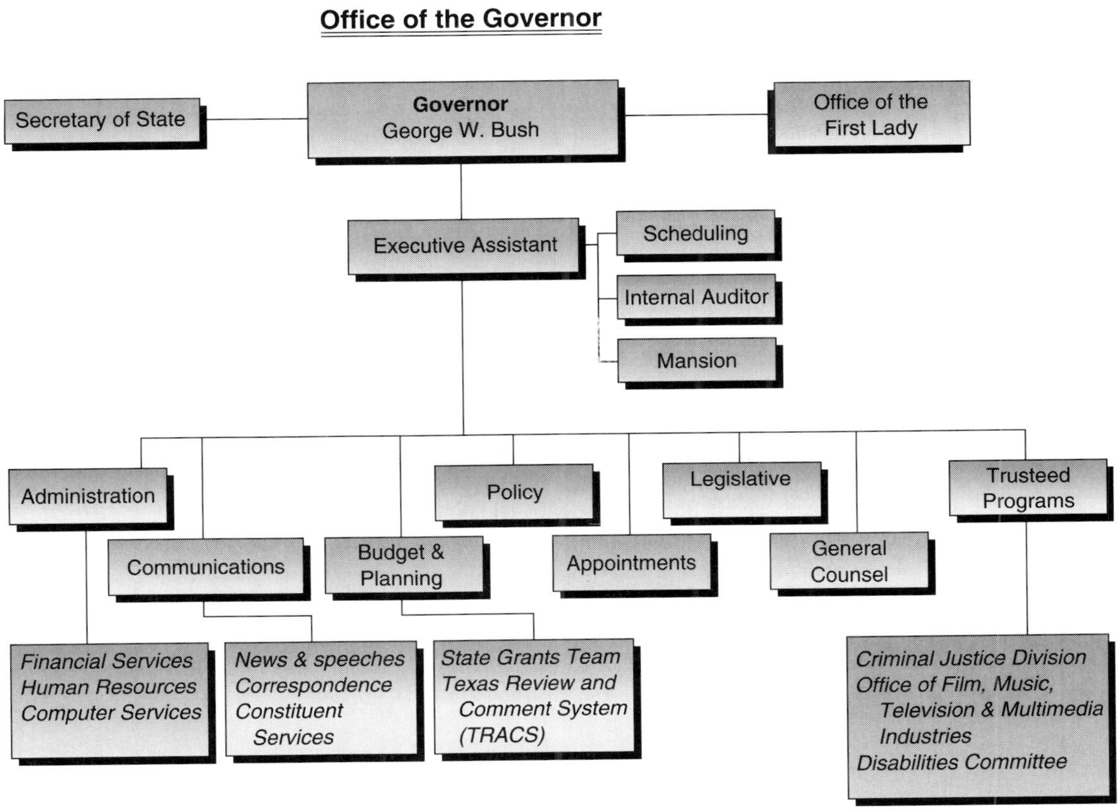

Office of the Governor

```
Secretary of State        Governor                Office of the
                         George W. Bush            First Lady

                      Executive Assistant  —  Scheduling

                                             Internal Auditor

                                             Mansion

Administration       Policy        Legislative      Trusteed
                                                    Programs

   Communications   Budget &      Appointments   General
                    Planning                     Counsel

Financial Services  News & speeches   State Grants Team    Criminal Justice Division
Human Resources     Correspondence    Texas Review and     Office of Film, Music,
Computer Services   Constituent        Comment System        Television & Multimedia
                    Services           (TRACS)               Industries
                                                            Disabilities Committee
```

Figure 9.1 Organization of Governor George W. Bush's Office

Governors have some leeway in how they organize the programs in their offices. Governor George W. Bush has organized his programs and staff as indicated above.

Source: Office of the Governor; Legislative Budget Board, *Legislative Budget Estimates for the 2000–01 Biennium,* January 1999.

education commissioner, health and human services commissioner, and transportation director. However most appointments are to boards, commissions, and advisory panels. (See Chapter 10 for more details on these state agencies.) The governor makes several hundred appointments a year, though the number varies from year to year.[37]

A 1933 court case determined that the legislature may designate someone other than the governor to make an appointment, and no Senate confirmation would be required. However, if the legislature does not provide an alternative means, the governor appoints.[38] Some analysts argue that the legislature can specify a gubernatorial appointment without requiring Senate confirmation.

Table 9.4   STATE AGENCY HEADS APPOINTED BY THE GOVERNOR

As recently as the 1970s, Texas governors appointed only a handful of the heads of executive agencies. While most such heads are still not appointed by the governor, the list of those who are appointed by the governor is growing longer.

Adjutant General
Chief Administrative Law Judge
Architect of the Capitol (appointed by State Preservation Board, which is chaired by the governor)
Executive Director, Criminal Justice Policy Council
Commissioner of Education (nomination made by the Board of Education)
Fire Fighters Pension Commissioner (nomination by State Firemen's and Fire Marshals' Association)
Commissioner of Health and Human Services
Executive Director, Department of Housing and Community Affairs
Commissioner of Human Services (nomination made by Board of Human Services)
Insurance Commissioner
Presiding Officer, Private Sector Prison Industries Oversight Authority
Public Insurance Counsel
Public Utility Counsel
Secretary of State
Executive Director, Office of State–Federal Relations

Source: Marilyn Duncan and Mary J. Powell, *Guide to Texas State Agencies,* 10th ed. (Austin, Tex.: LBJ School of Public Affairs, 1999).

Indeed, there are several positions that the governor fills without confirmation, though there are others that the Senate does confirm without express provisions for confirmation.[39] Custom and the balance of political power seem to dictate on a case-by-case basis whether confirmation will be required.

While presidential appointment requires only a simple majority confirmation in the U.S. Senate, Texas gubernatorial appointments require consent of the Texas Senate in a vote of at least two-thirds of those present [Article 4, Section 12(c)]. Because most appointments are made while the legislature is not in session, when the Senate convenes in regular or special session, it may take up appointments made during the interim. Appointees serve, sometimes for a year or more, until the Senate meets and confirms or rejects the nomination. **Senatorial courtesy** is a norm that requires the governor to preclear a nominee with the senator in whose district the nominee resides. Senatorial courtesy and the recent growth of a two-party legislature mean that a governor must be sensitive to senatorial concerns or risk either embarrassment or a political battle.

A 1999 appointment attempt by Governor Bush demonstrates how senatorial courtesy actually works. Bush wanted to reappoint Public Utility Commissioner Judy Walsh, who is from Austin, when her term expired August 31. However, opponents of Walsh convinced Austin's Senator Gonzalo Barrientos to oppose the nomination. Governor Bush recognized the norm of senatorial courtesy and assumed that the Senate would then reject the nomination if he submitted it. However, since the legislature was not in session, the governor simply did not appoint anyone, which left Walsh in the position until he would make a new nomination when the Senate next convened.[40]

The election of Republican Bill Clements provided the first test of how party clashes would affect appointments. Governor Clements made 105 "lame-duck" appointments after he was defeated in 1982, and early in 1983, new Democratic Governor Mark White and the Democratic Texas Senate found a way to negate most of the appointments. The Senate returned 59 to White unconfirmed, with 2 more later rejected. White then reappointed 11 of Clements's picks but ignored the others and made his own nominations.[41] The legislature then approved, and voters ratified, a constitutional amendment shifting the dates of some appointments to take away the chance of so many lame-duck appointments. When George W. Bush became governor, the Senate Nominations Committee—chaired for the first time by a Republican—stalled several of Ann Richards's unconfirmed interim appointees, refusing them hearings, so Bush could fill those positions.

For some appointments, the governor is free to nominate anyone; for others, the law requires people from certain categories to be nominated (e.g., the "general public," engineers, health professionals), or it requires the governor to nominate from a list submitted by the board or even by a private group.

Analysis of appointees reveals that governors tend to appoint people like themselves and their allies. Because all but two governors have been male, all but two have been Democrats, and all have been Anglo, it should not be surprising that Anglo, male Democrats have historically dominated state boards and commissions. A 1989 Senate study covering the appointees of Governors White and Clements found a large percentage of Anglos and males among the appointees (Table 9.5.) **Over-** and **underrepresentation** is higher or lower numbers than would be expected based on the group's numbers in the general population. For governors' appointees, those who were overrepresented in appointments were Anglos and males, while women, African Americans, and Mexican Americans were all underrepresented.

The pattern of appointments has changed only marginally in the past two decades, with the significant exception of Ann Richards. Governor Clements brought in more Republicans but reduced the number of minorities appointed. Governor White appointed more women and minorities than did his predecessors, though still in numbers far below their presence in the population.[42] Ann Richards made a public issue of the gender and race of appointees. She is the only governor to appoint numbers of women and racial and ethnic minorities in approximate proportion to their presence in the population. Her pledge to do so gave a boost to her 1990 campaign. By the end of her term, 45 percent of her appointees were women; 19 percent were Mexican American; and 14 percent were African American (Table 9.5). Governor Bush has not appointed as many women and minorities; at the end of his first term, one-third of his appointees were women, 11 percent were Mexican American, and 7 percent were African American.[43]

Table 9.5   ANALYSIS OF GUBERNATORIAL APPOINTMENTS

Historically, governors' appointees to state offices have been Anglo males. Recent data demonstrate some diversification of appointees, but Anglo males are still dramatically overrepresented, and others are underrepresented, compared to the population as a whole. Governor Richards's appointees were very close to the proportion of groups in the Texas population. Analysis of Governor Bush's appointees indicate that he made fewer minority and women appointments than Governor Richards but more than earlier governors.

	Texas population 2000 (est.)	Appointees of Governors White and Clements[a]	Governor Richards's appointees	Governor Bush's appointees
Gender				
Male	49.5%	79.6%	55%	67%
Female	50.5	21.4	45	33
Race/ethnic group				
White	54.5	87.3	65	82
Mexican American	31.0	6.1	19	11
African American	11.4	5.6	14	7
Other	3.1	1.0	2	N/A

[a]Of the 1389 gubernatorial appointees identified, 947 responded to a survey taken in 1989.
Source: Texas State Data Center, *Population Projections for Texas,* February 1998; Clements and White appointees adapted from Senate Nominations Committee, "Analysis of Gubernatorial Appointees to Agencies, Boards and Commissions," 8 December 1989; list from Office of Governor Ann Richards, 13 October 1994; Governor Bush's nominations 1995–1998 from Wayne Slater, "Bush Steps Up Number of Hispanic Appointees," *Dallas Morning News,* 12 October 1999, p. A1.

Critical Thinking Exercise: Does the gender and racial/ethnic makeup of gubernatorial appointees matter? Would public policy in Texas be any different if nearly all appointees were women? If most were Mexican American and African American?

In addition to the significance of homogeneity or diversity of appointees, another issue has also dominated analysis of gubernatorial appointees—that of the role of campaign donations. In his gubernatorial campaigns, Bush collected about $2.4 million in contributions from people he appointed to state positions.[44] Often, key appointments go to the governor's largest campaign contributors. Of Governor White's early appointments, 27 percent were campaign contributors.[45] Governor Richards appointed her largest contributor to the Parks and Wildlife Board. Another large contributor was appointed chair of the UT Board of Regents. George W. Bush has kept this tradition alive by appointing big contributors to key posts, including Allan Polunsky, Chair of the Board of Criminal Justice; David Laney, Chair of the Transportation Commission; Donald Evans, Chair of the UT Board of Regents; and Tony Sanchez, UT Board of Regents.

Such appointments—which appear to happen regardless of the party, ideology, or gender of the governor—generate news stories and public-interest group complaints, and they probably reinforce or raise the level of cynicism about government being for sale. No governor (or candidate for governor) has made an issue of the economic or campaign finance clout of appointees. While this has been an issue among some public-opinion leaders, it has not stirred the public, who seem to accept it as a part of their cynicism regarding the use of public power.

SOCIAL AND POLITICAL CHARACTERISTICS OF GOVERNORS

People who win the governorship bring to office with them their social characteristics and their political experience. Examining such factors as race, gender, age, education, religion, party, ideology, and previous experience of those who have served as Texas governor reveals patterns showing who is likely to win the governorship. Such an examination may also spotlight some key variables in governors' behavior.

Race, Gender, and Age

American governors have been almost exclusively white males. Hispanic governors have been elected only in New Mexico in 1916, 1918, 1974, and 1982 and Arizona in 1974; only 1 African-American governor has been elected, in Virginia in 1990. Women have had better success in recent years across the nation. Still, only a total of 16 women have ever served as governors, and only 11 of those were elected in their own right. Three women served as governors in 1999.[46]

In Texas, only Anglos have won the governorship. Two women have won. Miriam Ferguson won the governorship twice in the early twentieth century, although she was seen as a stand-in for her impeached and convicted husband. Ann Richards's election in 1990 was the first time a woman was elected in her own right in Texas. Given that women are winning more statewide offices (Kay Bailey Hutchison as Texas treasurer and U.S. senator; Martha Whitehead as Texas treasurer; Carole Rylander as Texas railroad commissioner and comptroller; Susan Combs as agriculture commissioner), it is likely that more women will run for the governorship in the future. Dan Morales's election as attorney general in 1990 and 1994 placed a Mexican American, for the first time, in an office seen as a stepping-stone to the governorship. No African American has won a statewide executive position,[47] although some have won U.S. congressional and state judicial seats and could be seen as viable gubernatorial candidates in the future.

The average age of the nation's governors at their first election has been declining. In the 1940s, the average age was 51 years. From 1951 to 1981, the average age was 47. Bill Clinton helped bring down the average; he was 32 years old when he was first elected Arkansas governor in 1979.[48] In Texas, the average age at the time of inauguration is 49 years old (see Table 9.1). Most have been in their 40s. Bill Clements was 61 and then 69 years of age at his two inaugurations; Mark White was 42; Ann Richards was 57; and George W. Bush was 48 years old.

Education and Religion

Almost all state governors now have college degrees, and it has been 50 years since Texas had a governor without a college degree. Twenty-one of the 30 governors Texas has had since adoption of our 1876 constitution had some college education, with the University of Texas and Baylor being most heavily represented. Most also have graduate degrees in law.

Protestants have been significantly overrepresented among American governors, and Catholics and Jews have been underrepresented. Almost all Republican governors have been Protestant (92 percent).[49] All Texas governors have been Protestant. In 1958, a Catholic, then-State Senator Henry B. Gonzalez (later longtime U.S. Congressman from San Antonio), ran for governor. Some opposed him because he was Catholic; he lost the race.

Party and Ideology

Across the United States, governors' elections typically stay within the two-party system; Maine's Independent Angus King and Minnesota's Reform Party Governor Jesse Ventura are exceptions. In the twentieth century, there have been six Independent (nonpartisan) governors, and half of those have come in the 1990s. Democrats were dominant in winning governorships for most of the twentieth century. Republicans held a majority of the governorships only in 1951–1953, 1967–1970, and 1995–2000. In 1999, the breakdown was 31 Republicans, 17 Democrats, 1 Reform, and 1 Independent.

Texas has had a history of Democratic dominance of the governorship. Bill Clements and George W. Bush were the only Republican governors since the adoption of the 1876 constitution. In Chapter 4, we examined this one-party history. Because the legislature was Democratic until 1997, the Clements and Bush administrations are the only time periods of **divided government** with one party in control of the governorship and the other party in control of the legislature.

A governor's ideological posture may play an important role in his or her power base, depending on the factional strengths of the era, his or her appeal to voters, and his or her relationship with legislators. Using the four ideological categories developed in Chapter 2 and historical data and evaluations, we have classified Texas governors on the two axes: liberal/conservative and populist/libertarian. Figure 9.2 shows that, at least for the past 60 years, Texas has had governors concentrated in the conservative quadrant, with one liberal, one populist, and no libertarians. After Jimmie Allred's governorship in the 1930s, conservatives dominated the governorship. Ann Richards was moderately liberal. George W. Bush appears to be conservative with some indications of libertarianism.

Prior Experience

Lawyers have constituted more than half of all twentieth-century governors of the American states. From 1951 to 1981, 49 percent of governors were lawyers, 8 per-

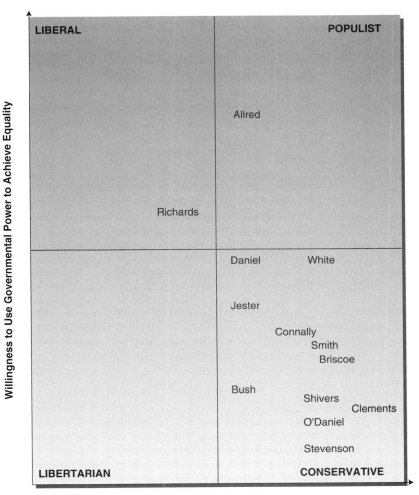

Figure 9.2 Ideology and Governors, 1935–2000

Since governors do not cast votes, as legislators do, it can be difficult to categorize them according to the four ideologies. We can, however, use their speeches, messages to the legislature, vetoes, and general philosophy to suggest where they might best fit in the grid of the four ideologies.

cent were lawyer/businesspeople, and 20 percent were businesspeople. Lawyers and businesspeople constituted the majority of governors in every state. Republican governors are more likely to be businesspeople, and Democrats are slightly more likely to be lawyers.[50] Before their electoral careers, most Texas governors were lawyers or businesspeople. Of the 30 Texas governors since 1876, 20 have been lawyers (see Table 9.1). The most recent governors have included a small business owner (Smith), a rancher/banker (Briscoe), an oil company owner (Clements), a lawyer (White), a teacher/campaign manager (Richards), and a businessman (Bush).

Legal or business careers are not usually enough alone to gain one the governorship. Prior elective service is almost always a part of the experience of winning gubernatorial candidates, though the percent of no-prior-office governors in the nation rose in the recent decades.[51] In Texas, John Connally, Bill Clements, and George W. Bush were successful in making the governorship their first elective office. Often, governors have held more than one prior elective office, and sometimes they have even lost previous elections. (Bush lost a 1978 race for the U.S. Congress.)

A **penultimate office** is the last office held. Across the nation, from 1950 to 1980, the penultimate office prior to the governorship was the legislature (24 percent), state elective office (22 percent), law enforcement (19 percent), administrative office (10 percent), U.S. Congress (9 percent), and local elected office. The prominent officeholders, however, do not always win the governorship. In all the governors' races in the nation from 1977 to 1993, only 17 of 61 lieutenant governors running for governor won; only 14 of 53 attorneys general won; and only 9 of 26 house speakers won.[52]

In Texas, the penultimate elective offices have been lieutenant governor (5), attorney general (5), member of the U.S. House of Representatives (2), railroad commissioner (2), and U.S. senator, Texas Supreme Court justice, Texas legislator, and Texas treasurer (1 each). Since the 1960s, Lieutenant Governor Ben Barnes, Attorneys General John Hill and Jim Mattox, and Land Commissioner Garry Mauro lost races for the governorship, while Lieutenant Governor Preston Smith, Attorney General Mark White, and Treasurer Ann Richards won. Few incumbent or former U.S. senators run for a governorship. Only 10 did so across the nation from 1950 to 1980, and only 4 of those won: in Arizona, North Carolina, South Carolina, and Texas (Price Daniel).[53]

Postgubernatorial Careers

In modern times, close to half of American governors have gone on to serve in some other public capacity. Most Texas governors have gone back into law or business.[54] Some have sought other elective office or comeback bids for the governorship, usually unsuccessfully. Miriam Ferguson won one and lost three comeback attempts. More recently, Preston Smith and Mark White tried unsuccessful comeback bids. Bill Clements was successful in a comeback bid in 1986.

Because of Texas's size in the Electoral College, the formal voting mechanism for the U.S. presidency, Texas governors are often mentioned as candidates for the presidency or vice presidency. While no Texas governor has won the presidency,[55] Jim Ferguson ran for U.S. president in 1920 on the American Party ticket,[56] and John Connally ran unsuccessfully for the Republican presidential nomination in 1980.

The governorship is sometimes a springboard to the U.S. Senate in many states, though rarely in Texas. Only three former Texas governors have served in the U.S. Senate: Richard Coke, Charles Culberson, and W. Lee O'Daniel. Former governors running for the U.S. Senate and losing include John Ireland, Thomas Campbell, Jim Ferguson, Dan Moody, James Allred, and Coke Stevenson.

Former Texas governors have served in several state administrative posts and as trustees for the state colleges and universities, and some have received federal appointments. For the past few governors, Price Daniel won election to the Texas Supreme Court, John Connally served in President Nixon's cabinet, Preston Smith chaired the Texas College and University System Board of Trustees, and Bill Clements served as Chair of the Board of Trustees of Southern Methodist University (SMU) before regaining the governorship.

THE GOVERNOR AS A POLITICAL LEADER

If the Texas governor is constitutionally weak, then the governor's skill in wielding political power becomes even more important in his or her success at governing. The last sentence in Fred Gantt's study of the Texas governorship through the middle of the twentieth century is, "Instead of the 'Chief Executive of Texas,' under existing laws he might more accurately be labeled the 'Chief Persuader of Texas.' "[57] In more recent years, an analysis of Ann Richards's governorship concluded that she "pushed the powers of a weak office to their limits."[58] The political leadership that a governor is able to provide flows from the governor's skills and previous experience, as well as similarity in party, philosophy, ideology, and life experiences with other decision makers.

Of course, these skills must be honed in the electoral arena in order to win the governorship. All Texas governors have sought reelection; governors must, then, maintain those electoral connections while in office. Because Texas political parties have been weak, governors have had to build and sustain personal followings and organizations. Of course, campaign money is essential, and governors must raise money while they are in office, both to pay off any previous campaign debt and to prepare for the next campaign. These electoral linkages help build the visibility of the governor, as well as an image of strength—which in turn helps him or her in wielding governmental power in battles with other officials and private interests (see Chapters 4 and 7).

Public Opinion Leadership

Especially because of their weak constitutional powers, Texas's governors resort to public opinion leadership to increase their power with other officeholders. Invariably, their opponents see such initiatives as public-relations efforts to boost the governor's political fortunes. Governors hold news conferences either on a regular basis or whenever they believe that such conferences would be beneficial to them. Sometimes they go outside of Austin to try to stir up public support for their policies. Governor Clements tried an antitax tour during a legislative session. Governor Richards tried a "tour of state government" to promote dialogue

George W. Bush is inaugurated as Governor in January 1995. His father, former President George Bush, is sitting in the front row at the far left. House Speaker Pete Laney and Lieutenant Governor Bob Bullock are sitting to either side of the Governor.

between state officials and citizens in several locations across the state. Governor Bush spoke around the state about his tax and education proposals.

In Chapter 6, we explored the use of the media in Texas politics. Modern governors have sometimes had their own television shows. When Bill Clements went through a period of strained relationship with the media, he stopped showing up for the taping of the show, and its name had to be changed from "The Governor's Report" to "Capitol Report." Governor White ran television commercials to build support for higher teacher salaries and made trips during legislative sessions to key legislators' districts.

Relationship with the Legislature

To be a successful governor, one must succeed in pushing a program through the legislature and in killing unwanted legislative measures. To do so, a governor must develop good personal or working relationships with key legislators and must use the powers of the governorship to assist the legislative process and, sometimes, to thwart it. Speaker Laney has said of Governor Bush, "The governor has no power except what the legislature gives him or he takes with the force of his own personality. Bush recognized that, so he wanted to work with us from the get-go."[59]

The constitution requires the governor to give an opening, a budget, and a closing message to the legislature. The opening message has come to be known as the "State of State" message. Together with the budget message, these are the formal vehicles governors use to convey their wishes to the legislature. Governors also make "emergency proclamations," which put governors' favored bills ahead of others on the legislative schedule.

A governor uses a grab bag of tools to win his or her legislative agenda, including direct appeals to voters, pleas from citizen study groups, pressure from lobbyists, breakfasts for legislators, entertainment (including evenings at the governor's mansion), individual legislative conferences, floor leaders, and staff representatives working the floor.[60]

The presence of a hostile lieutenant governor or House speaker could, of course, seriously damage the governor's chances of success. Such a possibility was an underlying theme in the 1998 lieutenant governor's race. The governor has no role in the selection of the lieutenant governor because the office is elective. Governors can try to influence the 150 House members who select the speaker, but to do so is politically risky. In the early twentieth century, governors sometimes became involved in House speaker races. Governors Colquitt, Sterling, and Allred supported unsuccessful candidates for speaker. As Miriam Ferguson began her term as governor in 1933, Jim Ferguson successfully supported Coke Stevenson for speaker.[61]

Since the 1930s, no governor has openly endorsed or campaigned for a speaker candidate, although they sometimes play a quiet and behind-the-scenes role in the speaker's race. John Connally used the ultimate gubernatorial power to influence the selection of a speaker. When he had differences with Speaker Byron Tunnell, he appointed Tunnell to the Railroad Commission, thus opening up the speakership. To ensure that he would get a new speaker whom he liked, he and his lobbyist friend Bob Bullock tipped off young Representative Ben Barnes about the appointment. Barnes used the tip to gear up his ultimately successful campaign for the speakership before anyone else could get organized.[62]

Patronage, rewarding certain behavior with employment, is a tool that governors of many states use to win legislative favor, by giving jobs to those recommended by legislators. The patronage power of Texas governors is exceedingly weak, though governors can use appointments of legislators themselves to executive positions as rewards or enticements.

A key power of governors is the ability to call special sessions of the legislature (all governors have this power) and to set the agenda for the special session (governors of 37 states, including Texas, can set the agenda).[63] The Texas governor's ability to control the agenda of special sessions extends only to regular legislative acts and not to appointments or impeachments. In 1917, Governor Jim Ferguson vetoed the appropriations for UT, then called a special session to consider new appropriations. During that special session, the legislature impeached him. Ferguson claimed that the legislature could not act on impeachment because he had not added it to the agenda of the special session, but the Texas Supreme Court upheld the legislature.[64]

The **veto**—the power to nullify bills passed by the legislature—is one of the governor's most potent legislative weapons. Only the North Carolina governor has no veto power. All of Texas's constitutions have given the governor the veto power, with the condition that the legislature may **override,** or cancel, the veto by a vote of two-thirds in each chamber.[65] Article 4, Sections 14 and 15 of the Texas Constitution give the governor the power to veto bills, concurrent resolutions, and items of appropriations.[66] When the governor receives a bill passed by the legislature, he or she has 10 days to sign or veto the bill. However, if the end of the legislative session occurs in that 10-day period, the governor has 20 days from adjournment to consider the bills.

At the national level, if the U.S. Congress passes a bill and adjourns and the president does not sign the bill, it dies. This is called a "pocket veto"—the president just pockets the bill and ignores it. In Texas, if the governor does not sign a bill, it becomes law anyway—Texas does not have the pocket veto.[67]

The mere existence of the veto power allows a governor to *threaten* to veto bills, which places the governor squarely in the middle of the negotiating, bargaining, and wheeling and dealing of the legislative process, as legislators seek to compromise in order to avoid a veto. Such threats can be made privately to legislators or in public.

Republican Governor Clements often resorted to vetoes and threats to veto in his dealings with the Democratic legislature. Clements vetoed more bills and resolutions than any other governor—184. Ann Richards wanted to maintain good relations with her fellow Democratic leaders in the legislature. She told the legislators in her first session that she would not resort to such threats and constant use of the veto. By her second legislative session, she was publicly and frequently threatening to veto a concealed handgun bill. The legislature amended it in response to her threats and passed it, but she vetoed it as unacceptable. The legislature passed the bill again in 1995, and Governor Bush signed it. Governor Bush vetoed 24 bills in 1995, 36 in 1997, and 31 in 1999—numbers typical of his predecessors.[68]

In Texas, most bills are passed in the last 10 days of the session. Consequently, most vetoes occur after adjournment, and the legislature has no chance to vote to override. There is not even a veto message because the legislature is not there to receive it. Thus, most vetoes are not challenged by the legislature. There have been only 76 veto override attempts under the current constitution, and only 26 of these have been successful. Governor Clements had 1 veto overridden in 1979, and there have been no override attempts since then.[69]

A variation of the veto authority is the **line-item veto.**[70] For bills that appropriate state money, this power allows the governor to select one or more lines of appropriations and veto them, while signing the rest of the bill into law. Line-item veto authority was used in the Confederacy and has been brought forward into Texas constitutions since 1866. Forty-four governors now have this power.[71] While the power is usually used to void a program that the governor opposes, in

1989, Governor Clements used it to abolish an entire state agency—the Advisory Commission on Intergovernmental Relations. In some legislative sessions, the governor vetoes only a handful of line items; in other sessions, governors have vetoed up to 26 items.

Because the major appropriations bill is always passed at the end of a session, the legislature adjourns and then has no chance to override any line-item vetoes. Thus, the line-item veto can be a powerful weapon, and every recent governor has used it. However, the legislature has learned to mitigate against it by organizing material in the appropriations bills in such a manner as to limit the usefulness of such a veto by lumping programs together and by using "riders" to describe programs and funding levels, rather than line items for those programs.

GOVERNORS AND POLITICAL CHANGE

Governors are in a unique position to influence political change. They can use the media and personal appearances to garner public attention on an issue. They can use personal skills to influence legislators and executive officials to adopt changes, and they can use constitutional and statutory powers to win changes in the government and in policies—though as we have seen, these powers are not that strong. A governor with strong personal and political skills can become a driving force for change. A governor with weaker skills, or who is not liked by other leaders, has little chance for effecting real change.

Fred Gantt devised a typology of governors, comprising these categories: Strong Leader, Showman, Figurehead, Man of the People, Grafter, and Reformer. A *strong leader,* Gantt suggested, is one who has a reasonable understanding of human nature, attractive personal characteristics, persistence, courage, and independence. A *showman* is one who uses gimmicks and theatrics to entertain and attract attention. A *figurehead* is weak, colorless, with little courage, no fresh ideas, and no leadership qualities. A *man of the people* is not an originator, has no definite ideas, and has no outstanding qualities but is liked by the people and governs with few major changes in policies. A *grafter* is one who fills offices with friends, influences purchases from particular sources, and does favors for a retainer. Finally, a reformer carries out specific policy reforms in office, as promised in campaigns.

Gantt suggested only a few governors that he would place in these categories. Table 9.6 shows Gantt's classification, plus the authors' update for recent governors, with the exception that the category "Man of the People" is changed to "Status Quo Manager." Because it is difficult to judge contemporary officials without the passage of time and analysis, any placement of Ann Richards and George W. Bush is tentative. These categories can be useful in assessing a governor's success in leading political change, but they rely more on personality than on the broader environment. Most governors are status-quo managers, unable or unwilling to effect significant political change. Reformers, able and willing to effect change, seem to coincide with periods of creedal passion.

A significant variable in a governor's ability to influence political change is the reaction of the public to political events of the era. If creedal passion leads to

Table 9.6 GOVERNORS AND POLITICAL CHANGE

Political scientist Fred Gantt first suggested a typology of Texas governors and their role in political change. The most recent governors seem to fit best into the "Status Quo Manager" category.

Strong leader
Allan Shivers
John Connally

Figurehead
Miriam Ferguson

Grafter
(None suggested)

Showman
W. Lee O'Daniel

Status quo manager[a]
Sul Ross
Charles Culberson
Coke Stevenson
Beauford Jester
Price Daniel
Preston Smith
Dolph Briscoe
Bill Clements
Mark White
Ann Richards?
George W. Bush?

Reformers
James Hogg (railroads)
Dan Moody (prisons; highways)
James Allred (social welfare)
Ann Richards? (insurance; ethics; appointments)

[a]Gantt's label for this category was "Man of the People."
Sources: Fred Gantt, *The Chief Executive in Texas: A Study in Gubernatorial Leadership* (Austin, Tex.: University of Texas, 1964), 44–49, and authors.

intense public involvement in politics because of a perceived dissonance between an ideal and reality, it would appear that governors have not often been the targets of such passion, though elections have occasionally been outlets for creedal passion. Perhaps single executives are better able to respond to popular movements than are institutions, such as the legislature. Also, perhaps in an era of creedal passion, the governor is able to provide passionate leadership on the cleavage issue, so he or she does not become the target of the public.

Governor Jim Hogg was successful in riding the wave of populism during his terms as governor from 1891 to 1895. He responded to the creedal passion for regulation of powerful railroads by successfully championing the creation of the Railroad Commission. Governors Jim and Miriam Ferguson were certainly popular governors. After the legislature impeached and convicted Jim Ferguson, the voters then thwarted the will of the legislature, surreptitiously electing Ferguson two more times by putting his wife in the governor's seat with Jim exercising the real power. However, there was not really much creedal passion in the voters' action. It seemed to stem from personalities and factional politics. During the Great Depression, Governor Jimmy Allred successfully led the wave of creedal passion to realign the system to provide more services for the poor. Governor Allan Shivers initiated popular votes on integration in the 1950s to demonstrate convincingly that Texans (i.e., the Anglo Texans who could vote) were against it. Nonetheless, such issue leadership does not seem to have emerged from creedal passion in the populace, except in the populist and the Great Depression eras.

In modern times, the only thing approaching creedal passion aimed at the governorship has come in the midst of scandals. Governor Preston Smith was trounced when he ran for reelection in 1972 after his involvement in the Sharpstown affair (see Chapter 8). The legislature's ethics scandals of the late 1980s and early 1990s triggered initiatives by public-interest groups to tighten state ethics laws. Ann Richards capitalized on the issue by making ethics reform a central part of her 1990 race for governor, and she coupled that with attacks against the insurance industry and the cozy relationship between state regulators and the industry.

Many citizens believe that private interests control public officials. Some also believe that officials make decisions that both benefit private entities and harm the public. At first glance, it might seem that citizens' beliefs would lead to movements to square reality with their ideals. More often than not, it seems that complacency and cynicism rule the day. People do not seem to believe that they have much power to affect executive officials. Perhaps they even rightly perceive that the governor has little real power to lead the executive branch and to effect political change.

An example of the difficulty of assessing the role of governors in political change—and in categorizing governors—involves the 1989 changes in workers' compensation policies that were pushed by Governor Clements. Long a goal of the business community, restriction of access to workers' compensation was recommended in 1988 by a special legislative committee. Labor unions and trial lawyers opposed the changes, which the business community called "reforms." Labor and trial lawyers were able to defeat the bill in the regular session. Governor Clements vowed that he would call the legislature back into special session, and he would continue calling them back until he got the bill he wanted. He made good on his promise. The first special session ended with no bill. He called a second session, which ended with no bill. He called a third session. In the third session, just enough senators formerly allied with labor and trial lawyers were convinced to abandon the coalition, and the changes were adopted. Thus, persistence and the power of keeping legislators in Austin, away from their income-earning occupations, proved powerful for Governor Clements.

In Table 9.6, we list Clements as a status quo manager. Whether the victory of business lobbyists over labor and trial-lawyer lobbyists could be called "reform" may depend on one's perspective. Because Clements proposed *change,* we could argue that he was a reformer. In the broader context of the Texas political economy, however, an environment that strongly favors business over labor and consumers, Clements was pushing a "change" that gave more power to the already powerful. Politics is not static; hence, a status-quo manager may sometimes have to champion change in order to maintain the existing balance of power.

> **Critical Thinking Exercise:** Governor Bush championed what he called *reforms* of welfare, juvenile justice, education policy, and tax policy. Would you argue that he was a reformer, a status quo manager, or something else? Why?

GOVERNORS AND DEMOCRACY

The forms-of-democracy concept that we introduced in Chapter 1 is more difficult to apply to the governor than to the legislature because *majoritarian* and *pluralist* apply more to multimember bodies or to voting. Perhaps the existence, and persistence, of a plural executive, with multiple elected officials, confirms both an ongoing mistrust of concentrated power and the desire to have pluralist democracy by having a plural executive.

The existence of a plural executive does not necessarily equate with pluralist democracy or even with deliberative democracy. In Chapter 1, we listed the conditions for deliberative democracy. Deliberation requires genuine and open discussion with negotiation and compromise. Texas's plural executive is more exactly several separate, competing government structures. Deliberation is not built into the system—if it happens, it is by circumstance or the necessities of political power.

> **Critical Thinking Exercise:** Do we really even expect democracy in the executive branch? What would that mean? If democracy includes open discussion and dialogue, is that possible with a single officeholder, as compared to a legislature or even a multimember executive?

The singular victory of a candidate for the governorship would seem to enhance the chances for majoritarian democracy. Perhaps the *weakness* of the Texas governorship would push the executive to deliberation with the legislature in a way that could produce pluralist democracy. However, if the executive is by design not a pluralist democracy and the legislature itself is not a pluralist democracy (see Chapter 8), it is unlikely that a pluralist democracy could emerge from the interactions of the two.

SUMMARY

Texas governors are weak, compared with other governors, and they must share political power with legislative and other executive leaders. The Texas governorship, however, is still a keenly sought-after office. The governor is the focus of media and public attention, and if he or she has strong personal skills, the governor can influence the legislature and executive agencies. Institutional powers, while they may be weak in comparison with other governors, still give the governor enough power to gain the attention of other policy makers and to make him or her a central player in policy making. Texas voters apparently feel some degree of ambivalence about their governors, since George W. Bush is the only governor since 1974 to win reelection.

KEY TERMS

plural executive	succession
gubernatorial cabinet	senatorial courtesy
chief of state	over- and underrepresentation
Office of State-Federal Relations	divided government
Commander-in-Chief	penultimate office
chief executive officer	patronage
chief budget officer	veto
clemency	override
governor's message	line-item veto

SUGGESTED READINGS

Beyle, Thad, ed. *Governors and Hard Times.* Washington, D.C.: Congressional Quarterly Press, 1992.

Gantt, Fred, Jr. *The Chief Executive in Texas: A Study in Gubernatorial Leadership.* Austin, Tex.: University of Texas Press, 1964.

Hendrickson, Kenneth, Jr. *The Chief Executives of Texas: From Stephen F. Austin to John B. Connally, Jr.* College Station, Tex.: Texas A&M Press, 1995.

Ivins, Molly, and Lou Dubose. *Shrub: The Short but Happy Political Life of George W. Bush.* New York: Random House, 2000.

Morris, Celia. *Storming the Statehouse: Running for Governor with Ann Richards and Diane Feinstein.* New York: Scribner's Sons, 1992.

Munutaglio, Bill. *First Son: George W. Bush and the Bush Family Dynasty.* New York: Times Books, 1999.

Sabato, Larry. *Goodbye to Good-Time Charlie: The American Governorship Transformed,* 2d ed. Washington, D.C.: Congressional Quarterly Press, 1983.

Tolleson-Rinehart, Sue. *Claytie and the Lady: Ann Richards, Gender and Politics in Texas.* Austin, Tex.: University of Texas Press, 1994.

NOTES

1. See Paul Burka, "The Honeymoon Is Over," *Texas Monthly*, January 1997.
2. Gregory Curtis, "Scattered Applause," *Texas Monthly*, March 1997.
3. Paul Burka, "Not So Rosy," *Texas Monthly*, May 1999.
4. Nate Blakeslee, "Guv'nor Crunch," *Texas Observer*, 28 May 1999.
5. Louis Dubose, "On the Record: Twelve Questions the National Media Should Ask Governor Bush," *Texas Observer*, 25 June 1999; Texas Education Agency, "October Tax Rate Survey Results," updated 10 February 2000. Accessed 5 March 2000, *http://www.tea.state.tx.us/school.finance/rates.html*; Dick Lavine correspondence, Center for Public Policy Priorities, 2 February 2000.
6. Anne Lewis, "Why the Big Gains?" *Education Digest*, October 1999, 71–73; Siobhan Gorman, "Bush's Lesson Plan," *National Journal*, 7 August 1999, 2300–2303; Eric Pooley, "The Bush Formula," *Time*, 16 November 1998, 60–62.
7. Eric Pooley, "Who is the Real Reformer," *Time*, 21 February 2000, 26.
8. In the first years of the United States, New Hampshire and Georgia designated their top official as the "president," but both states switched the title to "governor" by 1792. All states since then have had "governors." Larry Sabato, *Goodbye to Good-Time Charlie: The American Governorship Transformed*, 2d ed. (Washington, D.C.: Congressional Quarterly Press, 1983), 11.
9. Council of State Governments, *Book of the States 1998–99*, vol. 32 (Lexington, Ky: Council of State Governments, 1998), 17–18.
10. Fred Gantt, Jr., *The Chief Executive in Texas: A Study in Gubernatorial Leadership* (Austin, Tex.: University of Texas Press, 1964), 15–16. Charles Polzer lists 31 Spanish governors of Texas from 1717 to 1823. "Documentary Relations of the Southwest," in *Biographical Files—Governors of Texas* (Austin, Tex.: Center for American History, University of Texas, 1977).
11. Sabato, *Goodbye to Good-Time Charlie*, 2–4.
12. See constitution of 1845 and amendment of 1850. *See also* Gantt, *The Chief Executive in Texas*, 20–27.
13. Gantt, *The Chief Executive in Texas*, 30–31.
14. Ibid., 155; Adjutant General's Department, *Agency Strategic Plan for the 1995–1999 Period*, 15 June 1994.
15. Gantt, *The Chief Executive in Texas*, 42–43, 158–163; Harry Krenek, *The Power Vested: The Use of Martial Law and the National Guard in Texas Domestic Crisis . . . 1919–1932* (Austin, Tex.: Presidial Press, 1980); Curren McLane, *A History of the Texas State Guard* (Austin, Tex.: Texas State Guard, 1983); Adjutant General, *Agency Strategic Plan, 1994*.
16. Gantt, *The Chief Executive in Texas*, 112, 135.
17. Ibid., 112, 115.
18. See the General Laws of Texas, 42nd Legislature, Regular Session, Chapter 206; Stuart A. MacCorkle and Dick Smith, *Texas Government*, 2d ed. (New York: McGraw-Hill, 1952), 99, 160.
19. Gantt, *The Chief Executive in Texas*, 99.
20. MacCorkle and Smith first commented on this occurrence in the 1951 session. *See* MacCorkle and Smith, *Texas Government*, 99.
21. Gantt, *The Chief Executive in Texas*, 151–152.
22. The 1827 constitution included a 4-year term with a one-term limit. The constitution of the Texas Republic limited the president to a single 2-year term. Sam Houston served two nonconsecutive terms. The 1845 and 1861 constitutions included a 2-year term with a limit of no more than 4 years in a 6-year period. The 1866 constitution included

a 4-year term with a limit of no more than 8 years in a 12-year period. The 1869 constitution had the most liberal provisions—a 4-year term of office, with no term limits. Gantt, *The Chief Executive in Texas,* 335.

23. Council of State Governments, *Book of the States 1998–99,* vol. 32, 17–18.

24. Sabato, *Goodbye to Good-Time Charlie,* 99.

25. Council of State Governments, *Book of the States 1998–99,* vol. 32, 17–18.

26. About three-fourths of incumbents have been eligible to seek reelection, about three-fourths of those eligible did seek election, and about three-fourths of those who sought reelection were successful. Thad Beyle, "The Governors, 1992–93," in *Book of the States 1994–95,* vol. 30 (Lexington, Ky.: Council of State Governments), 36.

27. Allan Shivers served part of Jester's term and three of his own terms, for a total of 7½ years—still the longest consecutive governorship in Texas history; Clements's total of 8 years is the longest, but they were not consecutive terms.

28. The President of the Texas Republic was paid $10,000 a year, as specified in the constitution. The salaries for the governors under the constitutions from 1827 until 1876 varied from $2,000 to $5,000. The 1876 constitution reduced the salary from $5,000 to $4,000. Gantt, *The Chief Executive in Texas,* 335.

29. Ibid., 38; Council of State Governments, *The Governor: The Office and Its Powers* (Lexington, Ky.: Council of State Governments, 1972); *Book of the States 1998–1999,* vol. 32, 20.

30. Joseph Schlesinger, "Politics, the Executive," in *Politics in the American States: A Comparative Analysis,* eds. Herbert Jacob and Kenneth Vines (Boston: Little, Brown, 1965), 220–229.

31. Sabato, *Goodbye to Good-Time Charlie,* 4–6.

32. Citizens Advisory Committee on Revision of the Constitution of Texas, "Interim Report to the 56th Legislature and the People of Texas," 1 March 1959, 20–21.

33. See Gantt, *The Chief Executive in Texas,* 29–33; Seth McKay, "Making the Texas Constitution of 1876," (Ph.D. diss., University of Pennsylvania, 1924).

34. In Maine, New Hampshire, New Jersey, and Tennessee, the governor is the *only* statewide elected official and names all other officials. Council of State Governments, *Books of the States, 1998–99,* vol. 32, 17–18, 27.

35. Ibid., 225–234; Schlesinger, "Politics, the Executive."

36. Virginia Gray, Herbert Jacob, and Robert Albritton, *Politics in the American States,* 5th ed., (New York: HarperCollins, 1990), app. 6.1–6.7; Thad Beyle, "Governors: The Middlemen and Women in Our Political System," in *Politics in the American States: A Comparative Analysis,* 6th ed., eds. Virginia Gray and Herbert Jacob (Washington, D.C.: Congressional Quarterly Press, 1996); Thad Beyle, "The Governors," in *Politics in the American States: A Comparative Analysis,* 7th ed., eds. Virginia Gray, Russell Hanson, and Herbert Jacob (Washington, D.C.: Congressional Quarterly Press, 1999).

37. It is not clear exactly how many appointments a governor makes. A 1982 analysis states that there are about 4000 appointments, with about 2000 subject to confirmation. A 1989 Senate study, however, counted only 1389 appointees. Governor Bush made about 3400 appointments in just over four years in office. See Senate Nominations Committee, "Analysis of Gubernatorial Appointees to Agencies, Boards and Commissions," 8 December 1989, p. 1. Charles Wiggins, Keith Hamm, and Howard Balanoff, "The 1982 Gubernatorial Transition in Texas," in *Gubernatorial Transitions: The 1982 Elections,* ed. Thad Beyle, (Durham, N.C.: Duke University, 1985), 396; Wayne Slater, "Bush Steps Up Number of Hispanic Appointees," *Dallas Morning News,* 12 October 1999, p. A1.

38. The case is *Denison v. State.* Texas Legislative Council, "Staff Memo to Senate Committee on State Affairs, Subcommittee on Nominations," 26 January 1981.

39. George Braden, *The Constitution of the State of Texas: An Annotated and Comparative Analysis,* vol. I (Austin, Tex.: Texas Legislative Council, 1977), 327–331. *See also* Legislative Council, "Staff Memo," pp. 4, 13.

40. Bruce Hight, "Senator Blocks Utility Official," *Austin American-Statesman,* 28 September 1999, pp. C1, C2; Bruce Hight, "Senator: PUC Decision Was 'Difficult'," *Austin American-Statesman,* 29 September 1999, p. D2.

41. Wiggins, Hamm, and Balanoff, "The 1982 Gubernatorial Transition," 396.

42. See Chandler Davidson, *Race and Class in Texas Politics* (Princeton: Princeton University Press, 1990), 237.

43. Wayne Slater, "Bush Steps Up Number of Hispanic Appointees," *Dallas Morning News,* 12 October 1999, p. A1.

44. Ibid.

45. Wiggins, Hamm, and Balanoff, "The 1982 Gubernatorial Transition," 398.

46. See "Women in Statewide Elective Office," Center for the American Woman and Politics, 20 January 2000. Accessed 2 March 2000, http://www.cawp.rutgers.edu and "The Governors, Political Affiliations, and Terms of Office," National Governors Association, no date. Accessed 2 March 2000, http://www.nga.org/Governor.GF19980508.html.

47. Governor Bush's appointee to the Railroad Commission, Michael Williams, ran for election to the seat in 2000. Should he win, he would be the first African American to win a statewide executive office.

48. Sabato, *Goodbye to Good-Time Charlie,* 31.

49. Ibid., 26–27.

50. Ibid., 41.

51. Ibid., 43–44.

52. Ibid., 38–39; Beyle, "The Governors, 1992–1993," 38.

53. Sabato, *Goodbye to Good-Time Charlie,* 41.

54. Ibid., 45; Gantt, *The Chief Executive in Texas,* 66.

55. George W. Bush was running for the presidency as this textbook was being written.

56. Gantt, *The Chief Executive in Texas,* 65.

57. Ibid., 327.

58. Richard Murray and Gregory Weiher, "Texas: Ann Richards, Taking on the Challenge," in *Governor and Hard Times,* ed. Thad L. Beyle (Washington, D.C.: Congressional Quarterly Press, 1992), 186.

59. Eric Pooley, "Who is the Real Reformer," 26.

60. For descriptions and examples of governors' legislative prowess, see Gantt, *The Chief Executive in Texas,* 42, 237–238, 244–254.

61. William Atkinson, "James Allred: A Political Biography, 1899–1935." (Ph. D. Diss., Texas Christian University, 1978), 275.

62. See John Connally, *In History's Shadow—An American Odyssey* (New York: Hyperion, 1993), 226; Ann Fears Crawford and Jack Keever, *John Connally: Portrait in Power* (Austin Tex.: Jenkins, 1973), 183–186.

63. Council of State Governments, *Book of the States 1998–99,* vol. 32 (Lexington, Ky.: Council of State Governments, 1998), 65–66.

64. *Ferguson v. Maddox,* 1924; Gantt, *The Chief Executive in Texas,* 221.

65. Gantt, *The Chief Executive in Texas,* 39. Most states require a two-thirds vote to override, but six require three-fifths and five others require a simple majority. Council of State Governments, *Book of the States 1998–99,* vol. 32 (Lexington, Ky: Council of State Governments, 1998), 22. The Texas Constitution is confusing in its language about overrides of vetoes. It says that an override requires a vote of two-thirds of the members present in the chamber that passed the bill first, and two-thirds of the elected

members of the chamber that passed the bill last—or, if it is a line-item veto, two-thirds of the members present in each chamber.

66. An Attorney General Opinion (M-1167) declared that joint resolutions cannot be vetoed. Texas Legislative Council, "Gubernatorial Veto: Powers, Procedures, and Override History," staff memorandum, 22 May 1990.

67. The President of the Republic of Texas had pocket-veto authority. If he refused to sign a bill passed in the last five days of a session, the bill died. No constitution since statehood has included pocket-veto authority. Braden, *The Constitution of the State of Texas*, 333.

68. House Research Organization, *Special Legislative Report*, "Vetoes of Legislation" #193 (1995); *Special Legislative Report*, "Vetoes of Legislation—75th Legislature," #75-16 (1997); *Focus Report*, "Vetoes of Legislation—76th Legislature," (June 25, 1999).

69. Texas Legislative Council, "Gubernatorial Veto: Powers, Procedures, and Override History," staff memorandum, 22 May 1990. *See also* Fred Gantt, "The Governor's Veto in Texas: An Absolute Negative?" *Public Affairs Comment*, 15, no. 2 (March 1969), University of Texas Institute of Public Affairs.

70. Presidents of the United States do not have line-item veto authority. In 1996, Congress created, by law, line-item veto authority for the president. Since the U.S. Constitution's language on presidential vetoes does not include any line-item veto authority, the Supreme Court later declared it unconstitutional.

71. Gantt, *The Chief Executive in Texas*, 39; National Governors Association, "NGA Issue Brief: Gubernatorial Line-Item Veto Authority," 20 September 1996. Accessed 2 March 2000, http://www.nga.org/Pubs/IssueBriefs/1996/960920Line-Item Veto.asp.

10

The Executive Branch

★ Scenario: Governing Public Education

In the 1970s and 1980s, Mel and Norma Gabler were the sometimes lonely citizen watchdogs in an effort by religious conservatives to influence school textbook selection and content before the State Board of Education. By the 1990s, religious conservatives sat on the board, directly influencing those decisions. There are, however, many centers of power in public education policy, making it an excellent example of the fragmentation of institutions and authority in Texas state government. Public education is governed by an elected State Board of Education, a commissioner of education appointed by the governor, a large bureaucracy (the Texas Education Agency, or TEA), and local and regional entities. In the 1990s, those entities sometimes warred with each other, with the legislature, and with interest groups. Elections to the board became a battleground between religious right forces and traditional public education forces, and those differences carried over into policy battles.

The constitution (Article 7, Section 8) establishes the State Board of Education, but allows the legislature to decide how the members will be selected and what duties they will have. The legislature created a 23-member board, elected statewide. In the mid-1980s, Ross Perot led an education reform effort in Texas. Perot concluded that the board was hostile to reforms, and he persuaded the legislature to change it to an appointed board until the reforms were in place. In the late 1980s, the legislature then established a 15-member board elected from districts.

By the 1990s, the legislature had given the governor the authority to appoint both the chair of the State Board of Education and the commissioner of education; thus, Governors Ann Richards and George W. Bush were more directly responsible for education policy than earlier governors. In 1995, Governor Bush appointed Mike Moses as commissioner and Republican board member Jack Christie as chairman of the board.

As religious conservatism grew in the 1970s and 1980s, its proponents became interested in how and what children are taught in public schools. In 1988, televangelist and Christian Coalition founder Pat Robertson ran for the Republican nomination for president. Although he lost, from that time on, religious conservatives learned how to organize in politics. In Texas, they recruited, funded, and campaigned for candidates for the State Board of Education. The Gablers were no longer alone. The Texas Christian Coalition, Texas Eagle Forum, and American Family Association all joined the battle. They focused on issues such as sex education, phonics, public vouchers for private school education, creationism, and textbook content. For instance, the president of Texas Eagle Forum declared that biology textbooks adopted by the board "are anti-creation and anti-Christian."[1] Religious conservatives found a powerful ally in San Antonio millionaire James Leininger, who funded a political action committee (PAC) called Texans for Governmental Integrity.[2] In 1992, he helped San Antonio dentist Robert Offutt and other religious right candidates for the board. Offutt was elected, became an outspoken leader on the board, and recruited others to run. With more victories in the 1994 elections, religious conservatives, all Republicans, had a strong minority bloc of six. Christian Coalition executive director Ralph Reed, in a visit to Texas, declared that "we can praise God for this happening, not only in Texas, but all over the country."[3]

Their victories galvanized public education politics. The Texas Federation of Teachers and Texas State Teachers Association both organized to oppose the religious conservatives. A new interest group also formed to oppose them. When Governor Richards lost her reelection bid in 1994, her daughter Cecile became convinced that organizing by religious conservatives was a key factor in the loss. "The whole tone and feeling about politics had changed, just in four years. I was really alarmed by the whole dynamics of politics. I was really concerned that people were feeling very hateful. They were on a mission to eradicate these 'godless, anti-family' officials they thought were ruining the country," she said. In early 1995, she attended a meeting of the State Board of Education. "The religious right testified on every issue," she said. She turned to a friend and asked " 'When does our side come on?' And she said there wasn't anybody."[4] So, Cecile Richards founded the Texas Freedom Network to counter the influence of religious conservatives on education policy and politics.

State Board of Education meeting, March, 2000. Chairman Chase Untermeyer leads the meeting. A vote board on the wall shows the names of all members of the board.

In 1995, the legislature rewrote the Education Code to increase local school board control. The new law stripped the State Board of Education of its role in textbook selection, teacher certification, nomination of the commissioner, and other areas. The board could no longer reject textbooks, but it could classify them as "conforming" or "nonconforming" with curriculum standards. Religious conservatives on the board insisted they still had the right to screen the content of textbooks. That reaction angered legislative leaders. Bill Ratliff, Republican chair of the Senate Education Committee, ordered his staff to attend all meetings of the board and report to him on their activities.[5] The attorney general later ruled that the legislature had, indeed, stripped the power from the board. "In great contrast to its former authority, the board's powers are now expressly limited, and powers not assigned to the board are reserved to local school districts," he wrote. Governor Bush and legislative leaders publicly endorsed the decision.[6]

In 1996, James Leininger, along with Wal-Mart heir John Walton, funded the new A + PAC for Parental School Choice. The PAC spent more than $300,000 in the primary and general elections, most of which went to candidates for the State Board of Education.[7] In the Republican primaries, religious conservative board members recruited a candidate to run against Chairman Christie, and Leininger helped fund the campaign. With assistance from supporters of Governor Bush, Christie beat back the challenge,[8] and Bush reappointed him board chairman.

In the 1997 legislative session, Democratic legislators proposed bills to limit the board's authority to constitutional duties only. "It basically abolishes the board," said one legislator. Christie responded, "I have warned some of the members of the board that extremist viewpoints disturb a great majority of the state legislators. When you have an agenda that criticizes everything the public schools do except the lunch menu, you get tired of hearing it." The board members he was criticizing did not back down. "There have been more and more board members elected to the board that are not willing to be a rubber stamp for TEA," said board member Robert Offutt.[9]

Also in 1997, Governor Bush, Commissioner Moses, and Chairman Christie supported adoption of new curriculum standards, including adoption of a modified version of Goals 2000, a nationwide curriculum reform effort. Governor Bush especially wanted Goals 2000 federal money for his reading skills initiative. Religious conservatives said that Goals 2000 would lead to a federal takeover of Texas public schools and opposed the effort. Board member Donna Ballard led the opposition for the religious conservatives, but the board approved the new standards on a 9-to-6 vote. "Hell hath no fury like a woman scorned," Ballard responded, and she and other religious conservative board members threatened to sue their own board to stop the standards.[10]

From his appointment in 1995 up through the curriculum standards battle, Commissioner Moses had increasingly strained relations with the minority bloc. Finally, he wrote a blunt and undiplomatic letter to religious conservative board members, saying that they were not working in good faith with him. He wrote that he was "tired of the suspicions and ongoing insinuations of mistrust." He urged them to move away from "pettiness and politics." Then, he told them not to speak to him outside of board meetings unless the board chair or vice chair was present. They objected to the letter. Other board members supported him in criticizing the minority bloc. Said one Democratic board member, "You never know what cloud these people are coming off of."[11] The battles continued. Later that year, Offutt called on Governor Bush to oust Christie as chair.[12] (He didn't.) Shortly thereafter, Ballard resigned from the board when she moved to El Paso, outside of the district she represented.

In the 1998 elections, no Democrat won any statewide race. In the State Board of Education races by districts, however, Democrats still won. Donna Ballard ran again, but lost 40 percent to 60 percent. The party balance on the board remained nine Republicans and six Democrats. The number of religious conservatives remained at six, but with occasional support from others, they sometimes fashion a majority. In 1999, the board ordered textbook publishers to change their books to reflect more phonics. A Democratic board member warned that the action violated state law, and publishers threatened to sue. Lawmakers again floated proposals to restrict the board's authority.[13] In 2000, Offutt campaigned against George W. Bush in Iowa, then was defeated in the Republican primary election by a Bush-backed candidate. ★

INTRODUCTION

In this chapter, we examine the executive branch of state government. Although the executive, legislative, and judicial branches are coequal parts of government, the executive agencies account for 99 percent of the state's budget. An agency in the executive branch of government consists of the person or body in charge of the agency, its staff, and its rules and procedures.

You probably use the term **bureaucracy** to refer to government agencies. Citizens usually dislike bureaucracy, but it has become the standard method of social organization for both governmental and private organizations. German sociologist Max Weber, the leading theorist on the nature of bureaucracies, defined bureaucracies as organizations that operate under hierarchical authority, specialization of function, and management by fixed rules.[14]

Why is there government bureaucracy? Its purpose is to **implement,** to put into effect, to *execute* legislative policy, hence the term *executive* branch. Legislatures are chiefly responsible for creating public policies (**policy making**). Bureaucracies are supposed to translate legislative intent into working public policy, that is, to implement the wishes of the legislature. Agencies do so by **rule making** (adopting standards and processes by which they operate and make decisions); regulation of private activities; and provision of services and products. However, as they attempt to understand and to implement legislative intent, agency officials often must fill out the details that are missing in legislation and thus sometimes also *make* policy.

As the Texas legislature creates executive agencies or gives them new programs to administer, it is involved in the never-ending necessity of deciding how much power and freedom to give agencies and how best to organize them.

Te★as*Index*

State Government Bureaucracy

Number of full-time equivalent (FTE) state employees (1998):
Texas—268,005
California—335,353
New York—251,587
Florida—176,953

Number of state employees per 10,000 population (1998):
Texas—143 (43rd)
California—103 (50th)
New York—139 (39th)
Florida—119 (48th)

Average annual salary of full-time state employees (1995):
50-state average—$32,700
Texas—$33,377
California—$45,245
New York—$42,605

Agencies are organized in a host of ways (Figure 10.1), but there are three basic patterns.

First, there are those agencies headed by one person (though the head position is called different things in different agencies). Some are appointed by the governor, such as the Texas secretary of state. A few of those agency heads are elected by the people, such as the Texas comptroller of public accounts. Those statewide elected officials are significant because of their prominent role in policy making and in public-opinion leadership.

Second, there are those agencies run by a part-time, unpaid board or commission. Those two terms are used interchangeably. The members of most governing boards are appointed by the governor. In most cases, the board hires a person to run the agency. The Texas Department of Health is an example of such an agency. It is run by the Texas Board of Health, appointed by the governor, and the board hires the commissioner of health.

Third, there are a few agencies run by a full-time, paid commission. These include the governor-appointed Public Utility Commission (PUC), Texas Natural Resource Conservation Commission (TNRCC), Texas Workforce Commission, and Board of Pardons and Paroles, and the elected Texas Railroad Commission. Commission members may or may not hire an executive director to assist them in running the agency.

Citizens have little direct control over agencies, except over the six with heads or boards that are elected. Thus, if citizens believe that agencies are not being responsive or are acting in a way to favor special interests, they must voice their

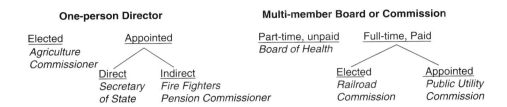

Figure 10.1 Texas State Agency Organizational Leadership Schemes
State agencies have different leadership structures and different ways of being authorized.
Examples showing six patterns are shown.

criticism to the legislature and the governor. The creation of the PUC in 1975 is an example in which the legislature responded to public pressure by creating an agency. Citizens often complain to legislators about how agencies are doing their job. This is a very indirect way of effecting change. Indeed, the legislative process can insulate agencies from public pressure if legislators are sympathetic to special interests.

In this chapter, we examine the different types of state agencies, highlighting some of the most significant agencies. Table 10.1 highlights the 20 largest agencies by spending level and the 20 largest agencies by employment level. Any such ranking is difficult to establish. For instance, the University of Texas (UT) at Austin ranks twelfth in spending and fifth in employment, and Texas A&M University at College Station ranks sixteenth in spending and seventh in employment. If the UT System, which is governed by a single board or trustees, were considered one agency, it would account for $2.5 billion in spending, ranking fifth, and it would have more than 65,000 employees, ranking first. The Texas A&M University System would account for $954 million in spending, ranking ninth, and it would have nearly 24,000 employees, ranking third.

We also look at how the governor and legislature attempt to influence and change agencies by periodically reorganizing agencies, by reviewing and abolishing agencies, and by reviewing agency expenditures, rules, regulations, and performance. In examining how these bureaucracies are involved in political change, we introduce and examine the concepts of the iron triangle and the revolving door. Finally, in looking at bureaucracies and forms of democracy, we revisit the State Board of Education and the Texas Education Agency.

ELECTED STATE OFFICIALS

In the American Creed, we place a high value on elections. We assume that elected officials are more responsive to citizens, and thus more democratic, than nonelected officials. Elected officials may not have any more authority than appointed officials, but election seems to give them more legitimacy in the eyes of citizens. Certainly being a part of the electoral process gives them more political power than appointed officials.

Table 10.1   TOP 20 STATE AGENCIES: RANK BY BUDGET AND BY EMPLOYMENT

While Texas has more than 200 state agencies and institutions of higher education, most of them are small. Generally, the largest agencies in spending are also large in numbers of employees.

Agency	FY 2000 budget		FY 1999 FTEs[a]	
	In millions	Rank	Number	Rank
Texas Education Agency	$11,398.9	1	820	—[b]
Department of Health	6,438.9	2	5,546	11
Department of Human Services	3,536.1	3	14,888	3
Department of Transportation	3,507.8	4	14,306	4
Department of Criminal Justice	2,084.3	5	41,788	1
Department of Mental Health/ Mental Retardation	1,627.5	6	22,251	2
Teachers Retirement System	1,247.9	7	380	—
Texas Workforce Commission	841.8	8	3,820	19
Employees Retirement System	834.9	9	290	—
UT M.D. Anderson Cancer Center	602.3	10	8,510	8
Protective and Regulatory Services	572.3	11	6,184	10
UT at Austin	499.1	12	13,506	5
UT Medical Branch at Galveston	464.9	13	13,495	6
Texas Lottery Commission	392.7	14	312	—
TNRCC	369.4	15	2,802	—
Texas A&M University at College Station	343.6	16	9,730	7
Department of Public Safety	312.1	17	6,818	9
Texas Rehabilitation Commission	263.5	18	2,421	—
Attorney general	251.6	19	3,613	—
Higher Education Coordinating Board	194.3	20	255	—
Texas Tech University	140.7	—[b]	5,027	12
UT Southwestern Medical Center	123.5	—	5,013	13
University of Houston	169.5	—	4,854	14
UT Health Science Center Houston	139.2	—	4,512	15
Texas Youth Commission	188.2	—	4,420	16
UT Health Science Center San Antonio	130.2	—	4,278	17
Texas Tech Health Science Center	81.4	—	4,218	18
University of North Texas	120.1	—	3,587	20

[a]FTE - Full-time equivalent employee, 2nd quarter FY 1999.
[b]Blanks indicate agencies not ranked in top 20.
Source: Legislative Budget Board, *Legislative Budget Estimates for the 2000–01 Biennium,* January 1999; Senate Bill 4 as enrolled, with vetoes, 76th Legislature, Regular Session; Marilyn Duncan and Mary Jo Powell, *Guide to State Agencies,* 10th ed. (Austin, Tex.: LBJ School of Public Affairs, 1999), App. M and N; State Auditor, *A Quarterly Report of Full-time Equivalent State Employees for the Quarter ending February 28, 1999.* May 1999, Report #99-705.

Table 10.2 ELECTED STATE OFFICIALS

Texas elects three of the five major officials that most states elect. Texas also elects other officials that are appointed officials in most other states.

State officials	Number of States that elect	Texas elects
Governor	50	✓
Lieutenant governor	41	✓
Attorney general	38	✓
Secretary of state	36	
Treasurer	35	*a*
Auditor	25	
Commissioner of education	14	
Superintendent of education	1	
Agriculture commissioner	9	✓
Comptroller	9	✓
Education board	7	✓*b*
Insurance commissioner	6	
Labor commissioner	5	
Land commissioner	4	✓
Railroad commissioners	2	✓
Corporation commissioner	2	
Revenue commissioner	2	
University board of regents	2	
Public service commissioner	2	
Adjutant general	1	
Election administrator	1	
Commissioner of mines	1	
Executive council	1	

*a*The treasurer was elected until voters abolished the office by constitutional amendment in 1995.
*b*The Board of Education has 15 members, elected by districts.
Source: Council of State Governments, *Book of the States, 1998–99.* vol. 32 (Lexington, Ky.: Council of State Governments, 1998).

In the Texan Creed, we elevate this principle to an even higher level. Texas elects a lot of executive agency heads in statewide elections. The median number of statewide elected officials for the 50 states is 6. In Maine, New Hampshire, and New Jersey, only the governor is elected. Texas ranks seventh among the states, electing 9 statewide officials plus the State Board of Education, whose 15 members are elected from districts.[15] Nearly half the states have reduced the number of elected state officials in recent decades. Texas joined this trend in 1995, when voters amended the constitution to abolish the position of state treasurer. Table 10.2 shows how many states elect which state officials.

> **Critical Thinking Exercise:** What might happen if our national government were organized like our state government is—that is, if we elected not only the president, but also the attorney general, secretary of the treasury, secretary of agriculture, secretary of the interior, and interstate commerce commission? What if some of them were Democrats and some Republicans? Do these factors affect public policy?

Attorney General

Next to the governor and the lieutenant governor, the **attorney general** is the most significant elected state official. The attorney general serves as the chief counsel for the State of Texas. Because the attorney general is elected, he or she is independent from the governor, and indeed, the governor has his or her own legal adviser. Conflicts are inevitable, as the governor attempts to direct state policies and agencies, while the attorney general may have priorities or legal opinions different from those of the governor and the governor's legal staff. In most years since 1978, governors and attorneys general have even been from different parties. Often, attorneys general have ambitions to run for governor, which can impede cooperation. In Chapter 9, we reviewed cases where governors and attorneys general clashed and where attorneys general challenged incumbent governors, sometimes defeating them in the next election.

As the state's chief lawyer, the attorney general may issue advisory opinions to state and local officials on the legality of their actions, as Attorney General Dan Morales did over the issue of the State Board of Education's authority to review textbook content. Public officials request an Attorney General's Opinion when they are uncertain about a law or when they think that the attorney general will rule in their favor in a dispute with private groups or other public officials. These Attorney General Opinions have the force of law for agency officials, until or unless a court rules otherwise.

As chief counsel to state agencies, the attorney general and the hundreds of assistant attorneys general represent most agencies in litigation. When an agency sues a private individual or organization to force compliance with a state law or agency regulation, the attorney general's office usually provides the attorney for the agency. When someone sues a state agency, charging violation of a law or of the state or federal constitution, the attorney general must defend the agency. For example, in Chapter 14, we examine the lawsuits brought by San Antonio resident Demetrio Rodriguez and the Edgewood Independent School District against the Texas Education Agency. Throughout the years that those school-finance cases were being heard in state and federal courts, the attorney general defended the agency, arguing that its actions were legal and that state laws were constitutional.

In Chapter 11, we review the state court system. If the attorney general loses a lawsuit in the lower courts, he or she must decide whether to appeal the case. Such a decision may rest on how extensive the effects of the loss would be. For instance, if a company sues a state agency, claiming that the agency's contract for work was violated, the attorney general may choose not to appeal a loss. However, in a situation such as the school-finance cases, a loss had ramifications for the whole of Texas society, so the attorney general appealed to the highest court. Indeed, if the attorney general does not appeal a case with broad policy implications, he or she is sometimes subject to public and political criticism, or even to electoral opposition.

While election campaigns for attorney general often focus on criminal issues, the attorney general has little authority in the field of criminal law and focuses instead on civil law. The attorney general may commence civil proceedings in areas where the legislature has given him or her jurisdiction. For instance, the attorney general is authorized to sue under the state's Deceptive Trade Practices Act. The attorney general has limited subpoena powers. In criminal matters, he or she may assist local prosecutors on request, but only if a state interest is involved.

The attorney general has continuous opportunities to provide public-policy leadership by deciding what kinds of cases to emphasize and draw public attention to. Attorney General Jimmie Allred (1931–1935) sued major oil companies under the state's antitrust laws. Attorneys General John Hill (1973–1979) and Mark White (1979–1983) emphasized consumer-protection cases. Attorney General Jim Mattox (1983–1991) sued numerous companies to force compliance with consumer safety, antifraud, and environmental statutes. Attorney General Dan Morales (1991–1999) sued tobacco companies on health-related issues.

Often attorneys general are pulled into public-policy leadership in areas that are not of their own making. Mattox and Morales devoted a massive amount of staff time to resolving the *Ruiz* case concerning state prison management (see Chapter 11). Morales signed an agreement that returned much of prison policy to the control of the state—though Republicans criticized his settlement. Mattox and Morales also had to devote considerable resources to a new policy area, child-support collection. Also, Morales staff members spent much time on redistricting issues as a result of numerous lawsuits in state and federal courts over the legislature's redistricting plans for the U.S. Congress and the Texas legislature (see Chapter 8).

In 1998, Jim Mattox won the Democratic nomination in a comeback attempt, but lost the general election to John Cornyn, the first Republican so elected. Cornyn served on the Texas Supreme Court from 1990 to 1998. In 1999, Attorney General Cornyn attacked the tobacco settlement that Morales had agreed to, trying to undo attorney fee provisions and trying to get courts to investigate the state's attorneys, including Morales. He also issued an opinion rescinding Morales's *Hopwood* opinion (see Chapter 1).

Comptroller of Public Accounts

The **comptroller** is the state's tax collector. The comptroller has offices across the state, and even in other states, to ensure that Texas collects what is due it. Chapter 14 details the types and amounts of taxes that the comptroller collects. As of 1996, with the constitutional amendment abolishing the office of state treasurer, the comptroller is now also the state's money manager. What makes the comptroller a powerful statewide official, though, is that he or she is responsible for estimating the amount of revenue the state will have coming in, and the legislature may not appropriate more than that amount (except by a four-fifths vote). Thus, the comptroller becomes a significant legislative player.

The revenue-forecasting function requires the comptroller to have a sophisticated economic analysis capability. The agency includes a large economic and policy research staff, which has become one of the state's most respected economic-forecasting centers. Still, part of the comptroller's power in the legislative process is that the forecasts are built on assumptions, and those assumptions can be changed. For instance, the comptroller can increase or decrease the projected state revenues by increasing or decreasing the assumed sales price of a barrel of oil. Thus, if the comptroller wants to influence the amount of money available to the legislature (as we saw in the scenario for Chapter 9), the revenue estimating process can accommodate those tactics. Chapter 14 examines the budget process in more detail.

Longtime Comptroller Bob Bullock (1975–1991) used the high-profile nature of the office to boost his standing with voters and then served as lieutenant governor (1991–1999). As comptroller, his staff, known as "Bullock's Raiders," was aggressive in collecting overdue taxes from delinquent business taxpayers. Bullock was also an important voice in modernizing the tax laws in the 1980s.

John Sharp served as comptroller from 1991 to 1999, after service as state representative, state senator, and railroad commissioner. Governor Richards and the legislature turned to him for assistance with a wide range of activities, demonstrating the scope, flexibility, and influence of this statewide elected office. Much of Sharp's energy was focused on performance evaluations of state agencies. His office was also given the task of starting up the new state lottery, which was later reorganized into the new Lottery Commission. In 1998, Republican Carole Keeton Rylander defeated Democrat Paul Hobby (son of former Lieutenant Governor Bill Hobby), to become the first Republican comptroller. She rose from local politics, having served on the Austin school board and as mayor of Austin. She lost a race for Congress, was appointed to the Insurance Board, then won a seat on the Railroad Commission.

Treasurer

Until the voters abolished the office in 1995, the **treasurer** managed the state's funds. Ann Richards served as treasurer from 1983 to 1991, before being elected governor in 1990. In 1990, for the first time in history, a Republican—Kay Bailey Hutchison—won the job as treasurer. She did not serve long enough, though, to put much of her own stamp on the office. She won a special election for the U.S. Senate seat vacated by Lloyd Bentsen when he became President Clinton's secretary of the treasury. Governor Richards then appointed Martha Whitehead as state treasurer. Whitehead championed a long-voiced suggestion that her position and its staff and duties be combined with the comptroller's office. She ran for election to the position in 1994 on that pledge and won. Because abolition of the office required a constitutional amendment, she then convinced the legislature to propose a constitutional amendment, and the voters responded in November 1995 by voting to abolish the office.

Land Commissioner

The **land commissioner** is more significant in Texas than in most other states that have such an office because the state owns and manages so much land. The Republic of Texas constitution of 1836 validated all Spanish and Mexican land grants and recognized existing property rights, and the first Congress of the Republic of Texas established the General Land Office and commissioned surveys of the state.[16] The 1845 terms of annexation to the United States gave to the state "all the vacant and unappropriated lands lying within its limits."[17] The land commissioner is responsible for managing and leasing the property.

As oil was discovered in the early twentieth century, the land commissioner enjoyed newfound importance. Oil revenues from state-owned land pumped up funds for schools and universities, to which the land-generated revenues are constitutionally committed (see Chapter 14). Also, the land commissioner was given responsibility for the new Veterans Land Program in 1946, a program that loans money to veterans for the purpose of buying a homestead. Now the program includes loans for houses as well as land.

With the increased responsibilities also came pressure to distribute resources in ways that the legislature may not have intended. Land Commissioner Bascom Giles (1938–1955) was convicted of bribery and theft for his role in misusing veterans' land bond money. Land Commissioner Jerry Sadler (1961–1971) became known for his aggressive way of interacting with other officials in performing his duties, sometimes to the point of fistfights. Largely because of the notoriety brought on by his fights, Sadler was defeated by a state legislator from Austin, Bob Armstrong. Armstrong served from 1971 to 1983. He later served on the Parks and Wildlife Commission, Governor Richards appointed him as her energy adviser, and President Clinton appointed him as assistant U.S. secretary of the interior in 1993.

Garry Mauro, former executive director of the Texas Democratic Party, served as land commissioner from 1983 to 1999. Mauro expanded the scope of the land-management functions of the office by focusing on the natural gas resources on those lands and through market promotion of those resources. He promoted the use of natural gas, especially in vehicles, and won passage of a new state law requiring state and local vehicle fleets to purchase vehicles that can use multiple fuels, including natural gas. Mauro also aggressively turned the land-management responsibilities of his office into environmental protection programs, such as beach cleanups, corporate recycling programs, and coastal-zone management. In 1998, Mauro won the Democratic nomination for governor but lost the general election to Governor Bush.

Mauro was succeeded by David Dewhurst, the first Republican to win the office. Dewhurst had served in the Air Force, Central Intelligence Agency, and State Department, then founded a Houston energy and investments company. He had not previously held an elective office.

Agriculture Commissioner

The **agriculture commissioner** is the only one of the statewide elected officials whose job was created by the legislature instead of by the constitution. The job of the commissioner is both to promote agricultural interests in the state and to regulate them. The Texas Department of Agriculture administers promotion campaigns for Texas commodities and encourages use of Texas products through labeling them as Texas-made. Traditional regulatory programs include monitoring the accuracy of weights and measures, regulating the safety of grain warehouses, and ensuring compliance with pest-control regulations and with egg- and seed-labeling requirements.

John White served as agriculture commissioner for 27 years, from 1950 until he was appointed assistant U.S. secretary of agriculture by President Carter in 1977. Governor Briscoe appointed Reagan Brown to succeed him, and Brown won the 1978 election to fill out the rest of the term. He then lost his bid for reelection to Jim Hightower in 1982 in the Democratic primary. Hightower had been head of an agricultural-policy think tank in Washington, then had been editor of the liberal *Texas Observer,* putting a definite populist voice to its coverage.

As agriculture commissioner from 1983 to 1991, Hightower initiated and won legislative approval for new programs, such as tighter regulation of pesticide use, education programs for farmworkers who use pesticides (the right-to-know statute), organic food certification, revitalization of farmers' markets, and national promotion of Texas foods. Hightower won reelection by a large margin in 1986. He was defeated by Rick Perry in the general election in 1990—the first time that a Democrat other than governor had lost an executive office to a Republican.

Perry, a Democratic state representative who had led the effort to limit Hightower's powers and his pesticide regulatory authority, switched to the Republican Party to run against Hightower. Perry, who also won reelection easily in 1994, de-emphasized Hightower's new programs and reemphasized the traditional role of the department. In 1995, the Farm Bureau and Commissioner Perry urged the legislature to repeal the farmworker right-to-know law, but they failed. In 1998, Perry was elected lieutenant governor (see Chapter 7 scenario).

Perry was succeeded by Susan Combs, a lawyer-rancher who served in the Texas House from 1993 through 1996 from Austin and then as U.S. Senator Kay Bailey Hutchison's state director. She is the first woman to hold the post.

Railroad Commissioners

The three railroad commissioners are elected in statewide elections. Whereas other state officials are elected to four-year terms, railroad commissioners are elected to six-year terms, on a **staggered term** basis (one seat is up for election every two years). The **Railroad Commission** was the highest achievement of populists in the 1890s. Populists demanded regulation of railroads, and they insisted that the people have direct control over those regulators by electing them. Over the years, other regulatory duties have been added to the agency's responsibilities.

In the early twentieth century, big oil companies wanted to produce, transport, refine, and sell oil and gas but were stymied by another populist victory, a state law forbidding monopoly market concentration.[18] The compromise that was finally reached allowed them an integrated business operation, with the trade-off of having regulation of oil and gas pipeline transportation. Because the Railroad Commission already regulated a form of transportation, it was given this authority over the oil and gas industry. Regulation of trucking and mining came later. Today, the federal government has usurped much of the agency's regulatory responsibilities for railroads and trucking, leaving oil and gas regulation as its primary function. It is the oil and gas industry that has the most influence at the agency. Longtime Commissioner Ben Ramsey stated flatly that the Railroad Commission was "industry's representative in state government," and Commissioner Jon Newton stated once that the Commission was a captive of the oil and gas industry.[19]

From the 1994 elections, for the first time in Texas history, all three railroad commissioners were Republicans, and that has remained the case since then. In 1999, the commission included Charles Matthews, Michael Williams, and Tony Garza. Matthews was mayor of Garland and had served on a power authority board before beating longtime commissioner Jim Nugent in 1994. Williams is the first African American to serve as railroad commissioner. Governor Bush appointed him

The Texas Railroad Commission holds a public hearing in 1999. Members are, from left to right, Tony Garza, Michael Williams, and Charles Matthews.

in 1998 and, should he be elected in 2000, he would be the first African American elected to statewide executive office in Texas. Williams had served President Bush as assistant secretary of education for civil rights and had served as general counsel to the Texas Republican Party. Garza served as the first Republican county judge in Cameron County, then Governor Bush appointed him secretary of state. In 1998, he became the first Republican Mexican American to win statewide office.

State Board of Education

As we learned in this chapter's scenario, the 15-member elected State Board of Education sets policy for the Texas Education Agency. While the state has always had a presence in education, the nature of state leadership has evolved. Beginning in 1866, Texas had a superintendent of public instruction, who was usually elected statewide. There was also an advisory Board of Education. Superintendent Annie Webb Blanton (1919–1923) was the first woman elected to statewide office in Texas. In 1949, the Board of Education was enlarged and made an elected board, with the new commissioner of education to be appointed by the board, with Senate confirmation.

As a part of Governor White's education reforms developed by the Perot Commission in the early 1980s, the board was reduced in size to 15 members. It was also changed to an appointed board, because the elected board members were viewed as hostile to the reforms. The legislature (and later the voters) required, though, that the board revert to an elected board once the reforms were in place. The elected board recommended to the governor a person for appointment as commissioner of education. In 1995, the governor was given sole authority to appoint the commissioner, with Senate confirmation.

The elected board became quite controversial in the 1990s, as indicated in the chapter scenario. In 1995, the legislature rewrote the education code, including provisions limiting the powers of the board and taking away its role in selecting the commissioner. In 1999, Governor George W. Bush appointed Chase Untermeyer to fill a vacancy on the board and to serve as chair. Untermeyer was a former state representative and a longtime aide to George H. W. Bush when he was congressman, vice president, and president.

APPOINTED STATE OFFICIALS

As discussed in Chapter 9, the governor appoints few directors of state agencies, though the number has grown in recent years. Historically, the most significant appointment that the governor makes is the Texas secretary of state. In modern times, the governor has been given authority to appoint regulatory commissioners in the fields of utilities, environmental protection, insurance, and health and human services. These positions, plus the public advocates before those commissioners, are the most important people that the governor gets to appoint to run agencies. A person appointed directly by the governor is generally seen to be more powerful than those appointed by boards or commissions by virtue of access to the governor and of being part of the governor's political team. However, the distribution of elected officials, appointed officials, and boards and commissions is not based on rational assumptions as much as it is on political power and personalities in power at the time the decisions were made. Table 9.4 listed 15 heads of agencies and 11 regulatory commissioners appointed directly by the governor. Five of those commissioner appointments, though, are for river authorities, which are not statewide positions. Table 10.3 demonstrates the array of agencies, heads of agencies, and boards and commissions in relation to the governor. Those in the chart next to the governor are generally seen as being more responsive to the governor than those that are farther away.

Secretary of State

The first appointment made by an incoming governor, and a key one, is the Texas **secretary of state.** This officer is literally the secretary for the State of Texas—the keeper of the records. Election data and filings, state laws and regulations, public notifications through the *Texas Register,* and corporate charters are examples of records managed by the secretary of state.

The secretary of state serves as the state's chief elections officer—registering voters, making sure that counties conduct the elections properly, and collecting and certifying election results. In this capacity, the secretary is one of the most important political officials inside state government. The secretary is a key liaison between the governor and both the political party and elected officials across the state.

Secretaries of state have a golden opportunity to create a statewide political base. In fact, many secretaries run for statewide elective office after serving the governor. After stints as secretary of state, Crawford Martin, John Hill, and Mark White ran successfully for attorney general; Bob Bullock ran successfully for comptroller and lieutenant governor; and Tony Garza ran successfully for railroad commissioner.

Governor White appointed the first African-American woman to the post, Myra McDaniel. As a part of her pledge to ensure ethical government, Governor Richards appointed as her secretary of state John Hannah, a former member of the legislature's Dirty Thirty (discussed in Chapter 8) and a federal prosecutor known for prosecuting corrupt officials. After President Clinton named Hannah as a federal district judge, Richards appointed Ron Kirk, an African-American attorney. Kirk mounted an aggressive voter-registration and get-out-the-vote drive for the 1994 elections, but the Democrats lost the governorship, and he returned to Dallas and won election as mayor.

Governor Bush appointed Tony Garza as his secretary of state, the second Mexican American appointed to the post. Garza was the only Republican county judge in South Texas, and in 1994, he had run unsuccessfully for the Republican nomination for attorney general. Garza resigned in 1997, then won election as railroad commissioner in 1998. Bush appointed Alberto Gonzales as his new secretary of state. Gonzales served until 1999, when Bush appointed him to the Texas

Table 10.3 PROXIMITY OF AGENCY HEADS, BOARDS, AND STAFF TO THE GOVERNOR

Governors have the most control over officials they appoint and the least control over officials elected by the voters. Analysis of the largest and/or most significant agencies shows that the heads of most of these agencies are not controlled directly by the governor; but rather are buffered by a board or are elected by the people.

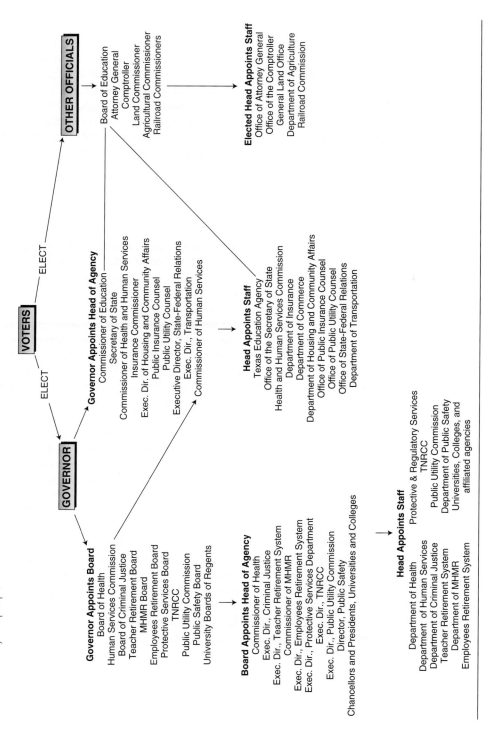

VOTERS

ELECT

ELECT

GOVERNOR

OTHER OFFICIALS

Governor Appoints Head of Agency
Commissioner of Education
Secretary of State
Commissioner of Health and Human Services
Insurance Commissioner
Exec. Dir. of Housing and Community Affairs
Public Insurance Counsel
Public Utility Counsel
Executive Director, State-Federal Relations
Exec. Dir., Transportation
Commissioner of Human Services

Board of Education
Attorney General
Comptroller
Land Commissioner
Agricultural Commissioner
Railroad Commissioners

Head Appoints Staff
Texas Education Agency
Office of the Secretary of State
Health and Human Services Commission
Department of Insurance
Department of Commerce
Department of Housing and Community Affairs
Office of Public Insurance Counsel
Office of Public Utility Counsel
Office of State-Federal Relations
Department of Transportation

Elected Head Appoints Staff
Office of Attorney General
Office of the Comptroller
General Land Office
Department of Agriculture
Railroad Commission

Governor Appoints Board
Board of Health
Human Services Commission
Board of Criminal Justice
Teacher Retirement Board
MHMR Board
Employees Retirement Board
Protective Services Board
TNRCC
Public Utility Commission
Public Safety Board
University Boards of Regents

Board Appoints Head of Agency
Commissioner of Health
Exec. Dir., Criminal Justice
Exec. Dir., Teacher Retirement System
Commissioner of MHMR
Exec. Dir., Employees Retirement System
Exec. Dir., Protective Services Department
Exec. Dir., TNRCC
Exec. Dir., Public Utility Commission
Director, Public Safety
Chancellors and Presidents, Universities and Colleges

Head Appoints Staff
Department of Health
Department of Human Services
Department of Criminal Justice
Teacher Retirement System
Department of MHMR
Employees Retirement System
Protective & Regulatory Services
TNRCC
Public Utility Commission
Department of Public Safety
Universities, Colleges, and affiliated agencies

Supreme Court to fill a vacancy there. In February 1999, Bush appointed as secretary of state Elton Bomer, who was his insurance commissioner and who had previously been a Democratic state representative.

Public Utility Commissioners

The **Public Utility Commission (PUC)** has jurisdiction over telephone and electric power companies, while the Railroad Commission retains authority over gas companies. The three members of the PUC are appointed to staggered six-year terms by the governor. The public utility commissioners have a role that is largely **quasi-judicial.** The agency was created in 1975 in a storm of public sentiment to limit rapidly rising utility rates. The governor, however, did not support the movement, and the early commissioners were generally perceived as sympathetic to utility companies. In the 1982 gubernatorial election, Mark White ran against Clements partly on the issue of high utility rates and the record of Clements's appointees approving those rates. White won the election and appointed a commissioner seen as a strong consumer advocate. He then mounted a campaign to pressure the other commissioners to resign. While they were not legally obligated to do so, they did resign as White demanded, and he appointed new commissioners who were generally perceived as neither strong consumer advocates nor strong industry allies. Clements won the governorship back in 1986 and appointed two strong industry allies. Governor Richards appointed the first Asian American and a woman as commissioners. They were generally seen as moderates. Governor Bush appointed Pat Wood III and Brett Perlman, both lawyers, and Judy Walsh, an accountant. (See Chapter 9 for the 1999 senatorial effort to block Walsh's reappointment.)

In 1995, the legislature redrafted the PUC's statute. Deliberations focused on telecommunications and utility industry deregulation, as both technological developments and anticipated federal changes away from regulation and toward competition framed the debate. While the telecommunications bill passed, the utility deregulation bill failed. In 1997, the legislature approved a utility deregulation bill. Most monopoly electric utilities must split into transmission and distribution companies, power generating companies, retail providers, and independent system operators. One goal is to guarantee residential customers choice of providers, though the PUC must maintain a no-call list for customers who don't want telephone solicitation about electric service. The PUC will still regulate transmission and distribution, but rates for power generating and retail will be deregulated as of January 1, 2002. In 2004, the PUC will rule on the cost base utilities are using and may modify rates at that one time. The PUC's role will then be to monitor abuses of market power, provide remedies, and oversee and review power grid procedures.

Texas Natural Resource Conservation Commissioners

In 1991, responding to pressure from environmental groups energized by the highly visible twentieth anniversary of Earth Day in 1990, the legislature combined many of the state's environmental programs into a new agency, the **Texas Natural Resource Conservation Commission (TNRCC),** and abolished the Air Control Board and the Water Commission. The three TNRCC commissioners are appointed by the governor to staggered six-year terms. Commissioners have a quasi-judicial role in contested cases, but they have significant policy roles that make them the real powers in running the agency.

Businesses that will be emitting pollutants into the air or water must seek permits from the commission and must comply with regulations to limit the amount of those emissions. Thus, the commission becomes a lightning rod for conflicts between, on the one hand, environmental and neighborhood groups seeking to restrict activities that could pollute, and on the other hand, businesses seeking to keep costs down while using modern industrial techniques and expanding or beginning new operations supplying products to the marketplace.

Since its creation, the legislature has considered scores of bills to scale back the environmental authority of the agency, and some of them were adopted. SB 14 is a "property rights" bill that passed in 1995; while it has many exemptions, it requires TNRCC and other agencies to evaluate the costs of environmental regulation to property owners, and it could force the state to abandon regulations that might lower private-property values. The legislature has also scaled back the public participation provisions that the agency must follow. A 1999 bill would have abolished contested case hearings. The legislature passed a modified version that keeps most contested case hearings but changes public comment provisions.

Insurance Commissioner

Because of the need to know whether insurance companies have assets sufficient to pay their claims, and because out-of-state companies proved difficult to pursue if customers had complaints of fraud, Texas has long had a public official or public body to oversee or regulate the insurance industry. In 1876, the legislature created the Department of Insurance, Statistics, and History, with a commissioner. The legislature has periodically reorganized the state agency, sometimes having a multimember body of commissioners and sometimes a single commissioner. In 1993, the three-member State Board of Insurance was replaced by a single commissioner appointed by the governor. The commissioner runs the Department of Insurance and is one of the few single executive heads appointed directly by the governor. Again, the commissioner has a high level of independence because the governor can remove the commissioner only under extraordinary circumstances. The commissioner's job is to monitor the health of the insurance industry and, within new confines voted in by the legislature, to regulate insurance rates.

Just as Mark White had run against the pro-business slant of Bill Clements's public utility commissioners, in 1990 Ann Richards ran against what she and consumer advocates saw as the pro-insurance-company slant of Clements's Insurance Board members. Again taking a page from White, Richards demanded and eventually got the resignations of the board members and appointed her own. The legislature then abolished the board in 1993 and created the single insurance commissioner. Governor Richards went out of state to select as the first commissioner Robert Hunter, known as the premier consumer advocate in the field of insurance regulation. Governor Bush appointed Democratic State Representative Elton Bomer as his first insurance commissioner. When Bomer became his secretary of state in 1999, he appointed Jose Montemayor as insurance commissioner. Montemayor is an accountant who had been associate commissioner.

In 1995, the legislature passed a bill regulating health maintenance organizations (HMOs). Insurance companies (the primary owners of HMOs) fought against the bill. When it passed, they persuaded Governor Bush to veto it. Bush then requested Commissioner Bomer to write new rules governing HMOs. In 1997, the legislature passed a bill allowing patients to sue their HMOs for malpractice—one of the first such laws in the nation.

Public Counsels

In recent years, as conflicts grew over regulatory policies, public-interest groups charged that regulatory agencies were captured by business interests and were not adequately protecting consumers. A concept that gained some acceptance is that of **public counsels** to serve as advocates for the public before governmental agencies. The legislature gave the governor power to appoint a public insurance counsel and a public utility counsel. These attorneys are heads of small agencies separate from the Department of Insurance and the Public Utility Commission. The counsels and their staffs examine rate hike requests and other regulatory matters before the regulatory agencies, then they go before the regulators to argue for their position, which is usually for rate reductions or for lower rate increases than the private companies have requested or the regulatory agency staff has recommended.

Commissioner of Health and Human Services

Health and human service programs are administered in Texas by numerous state agencies. Governor Richards proposed consolidating and merging these services into one agency, using the slogan "one person, one trip." Comptroller Sharp, in urging consolidation, wrote that "This fragmentation produces well-documented agency-wide problems such as a failure to maximize federal funds, inconsistency in rate-setting and contracting and a failure to coordinate client transportation services."[20]

In 1991, the legislature partially agreed by creating a new position, the commissioner of health and human services. Nicknamed the "health and human services czar," the commissioner does not run the 13 agencies under his or her umbrella but is supposed to *oversee* the massive health and human services programs scattered across the agencies. The primary ones are the Departments of Health, Human Services, Mental Health and Mental Retardation, and Protective and Regulatory Services. The commissioner is appointed directly by the governor, unlike the heads of the agencies that the commissioner oversees, who are appointed by boards and commissions. In 1998, Governor Bush appointed Don Gilbert as commissioner of health and human services. He had previously served as commissioner of mental health and mental retardation. In 1999, voters rejected a constitutional amendment that would have increased the tenure and powers of the commissioner and allowed the governor to fire him or her.

Boards and Commissions

Most state agencies are organized with a multimember policy-making body and a staff under the direction of the policy-making body. Some of these bodies are called **boards,** some are called **commissions,** and a very few are called councils or authorities. Collectively, these bodies are often referred to as the "board and commission" system of government.

Of all executive-branch agencies receiving state appropriations, 6 have single elected heads, 8 have single heads appointed by the governor, and there are 101 boards or commissions (plus 50 locally elected community college boards of trustees). Some boards or commissions govern more than one agency. For instance, the 10 boards of trustees of the state's colleges and universities run 37 general academic institutions, 9 medical schools, and 9 major services.

Boards and commissions are used for large and small agencies. The most common sizes of the boards or commissions are 3 or 9 members, though a few have more members. A 1999 constitutional amendment standardized most boards at 3, 5, 7, or 9 members. A board or commission may have no staff, a handful of staff members, or a large bureaucracy. The Board of Criminal Justice, for instance, hires a full-time, well-paid, and powerful executive director, who oversees a staff of 42,000.

In almost all cases, members of these policy-making bodies are appointed by the governor, with Senate confirmation. A few have statutorily designated membership from agency heads or elected officials. It is these appointments to boards and commissions that constitute the bulk of the governor's appointments. However, for most boards, the terms of members are six years, and the terms are staggered, so a governor is not usually able to gain control of a majority of a board until late in his or her term of office. Even then, there is no assurance that members will do as the governor wishes because the governor may not fire the members. The governor may request the removal of an official that he or she appointed, but it requires approval of two-thirds of the Senate, and no such removal has ever occurred.

Other than the full-time, paid members of the PUC, the TNRCC, the Workforce Commission, the Board of Pardons and Paroles, and the Railroad Commission, the members of these boards and commissions are not paid. They are volunteer, part-time positions. Members' expenses are reimbursed when they travel to meetings, but they do not get pay for their work. Most boards or commissions meet monthly or quarterly. They may work through smaller committees of members, with additional meetings of those committees.

ORGANIZATION AND REORGANIZATION OF STATE AGENCIES

Legislatures create executive agencies to respond to particular problems. How they organize the agencies is determined by the nature of the problem, the personalities and political dynamics at work, and the organizational structure that is in vogue at the time. All of those variables can change over time, so there are recurring **government reorganization** efforts. Federal reorganization efforts have sometimes spurred state action. The reorganization initiatives from the federal Taft Commission in 1911 and Hoover Commission in 1949 and 1953 triggered state-level reorganization efforts. The 1980s and 1990s also witnessed state-level reorganization efforts. Since 1985, every state has implemented an executive-branch reorganization program.[21]

In 15 states (not including Texas), state constitutions allow their governor—as chief of the executive branch—to reorganize the executive branch, subject only to legislative veto.[22] In Texas, the ongoing question of how much power the governor should have over executive agencies is often entwined with questions of reorganizing the executive branch. Though the Texas governor is chief executive, as we learned in Chapter 9, he or she has little direct authority over executive agencies. For example, though the constitution says that the governor may require reports from agencies, there is no means of discipline or sanctions.[23]

There have been numerous attempts to fundamentally reorganize the executive branch, some by legislative initiative, some by gubernatorial initiative, and some by calls for a new constitution (see Chapter 3). In 1931, the Texas legislature created a committee to reorganize state government.[24] Its reorganization plan suggested a cabinet-style government to strengthen executive coordination, but only parts of it were enacted.

Governors' initiatives to reduce the fragmentation of executive authority and to increase the authority of governors usually fail. Because major reorganization has been difficult to pass, governors have frequently used piecemeal reorganization of the executive branch, either on an informal basis or with legislative authorization, to effect minor policy changes or shifts in priorities.

The failure of the 1974 Constitutional Convention (see Chapter 3) triggered the creation of the Hobby-Clayton Committee in 1975 to reorganize state government. It was mandated to conduct "a comprehensive review of governmental structure and administration." The committee's report cited the history of federal and state reorganization efforts, noting that "Texas has not actively participated in the evaluation/reorganization movement in the past." It said that the only previous major reorganization plan was the 1931 one. The Hobby-Clayton Committee made scores of recommendations, many of them changes that would increase the governor's powers and that would change state policies, rather than simply reorganize agencies.[25] Again, the legislature enacted some of the recommendations and ignored others.

In the 1990s, the Texas legislature and the governor were involved in an ongoing effort to systematically reorganize state agencies. Governor Richards and

Comptroller Sharp developed proposals for executive reorganization, with the stated objective of saving taxpayer dollars. Sharp and his staff, working with interagency task forces, produced a comprehensive analysis of state agencies and programs. He recommended a cabinet form of government, excluding the elected state officials, or that each incoming governor be allowed to remove all board and commission members and make new appointments. He identified 14 health and human services agencies, 15 environmental agencies, and 43 licensing and regulating agencies, and called for consolidation of programs into fewer agencies.[26]

Trumpeting Sharp's recommendations, Governor Richards stated that "under our proposals, Texas will eliminate 58 agencies through consolidation and streamlining."[27] The legislature adopted some, but not all, of Richards's and Sharp's recommendations. Proposals such as a governor's cabinet that would concentrate power in the governorship were not approved. In 1991, the legislature abolished some agencies, consolidated others, renamed some, shifted functions across some of them, and even created some new agencies. In the restructuring, the governor got to appoint the commissioner of education and a new commissioner of health and human services and gained control of the Department of Commerce, Department of Housing and Community Affairs, and the Film and Arts Commission.

In 1992, Governor Richards initiated a new phase of reorganization by having Comptroller Sharp begin a long-range study of the future in Texas, a project called "Forces of Change." The comptroller now has an ongoing agency review process, and Comptroller Rylander is performing that function.

CONTROLLING BUREAUCRACY

Legislatures may delegate decision-making authority to executive agencies—a practice long recognized by courts. In creating executive agencies, creating policy programs, and delegating authority to agencies, legislature do not then wash their hands of responsibility for those programs. They have a duty to oversee what they have created and delegated. **Legislative oversight** of the bureaucracy includes review of expenditures, review of rules and regulations, performance reviews, audits, sunset review (in which the continuing need for an agency is evaluated), review of staff sizes and functions, and response to constituent complaints about agencies. Numerous states have upgraded their audit staff and their program-evaluation capabilities. Sixteen states have even adopted legislative vetoes of administrative rules and regulations, though eight state courts have thrown them out as unconstitutional violations of separation of powers.[28]

The Sunset Process

Sunset is a concept of establishing a date at which agencies will cease to exist (the *sun* will *set* on them) unless the legislature renews them. Sunset forces a review of executive agencies and programs. It was first adopted in Colorado in 1976 and is now in use in about three-fourths of the states.[29] The Texas Sunset Act was adopted in 1977. While the motivation for the movement was to review and abolish some agencies, ironically, the first step was to create a new agency—the Sunset Advisory Commission. It consists of four state senators, four state representatives, one public member appointed by the lieutenant governor and one public member appointed by the speaker. Under the Texas system, each state agency is given a 12-year life span.

Each biennium, agencies that are then nearing the end of their 12-year life span submit a self-evaluation report to the Sunset Advisory Commission. The commission staff reviews the reports and conducts its own investigations. The commission then makes recommendations to the next legislature. If the commission recommends continuation of an agency, it drafts legislation, always with changes in the structure or procedures of the agency.

In addition to agency-specific recommendations, the first commission adopted a set of across-the-board "**good government**" recommendations for all agencies to open themselves up to public participation and scrutiny and to minimize conflicts of interest (Table 10.4). Early Sunset Commission analyses clearly reflect that the staff, and perhaps commission members, believed that agencies had been captured by private interests:

> The first two commissions, appointed in 1977 and 1979, focused on breaking the hold that trade associations had over professional licensing agencies and re-establishing an arms-length relationship between the regulated and the regulators. The commission recommended imposing controls on agencies that for years had escaped serious legislative oversight. Commission actions to impose these controls were fiercely opposed by lobby groups and trade associations surrounding the agencies.[30]

Table 10.5 shows the results of sunset review since 1979. Clearly, it has been a significant tool in the legislature's attempt to control bureaucracy. Just as clearly, it has become a target for those wary of the repeated battles that ensue, as interest groups, agencies, and their defenders and detractors clash over how policy programs will be organized and implemented. Because of those intense battles, in 1993, Governor Richards, Lieutenant Governor Bullock, and Speaker Laney supported repeal of sunset review, but the effort died. The 1999 legislature reviewed 25 agencies, continuing 23 of them, abolishing 1, and merging 1.

Table 10.4   SUNSET "GOOD GOVERNMENT" PRINCIPLES

- Public membership on governing boards
- Conflict-of-interest regulation
- Career ladders for employees
- Merit-pay systems
- Public notification of hearings and opportunity for public testimony
- Placement of state funds in state treasury
- Establishment of a complaint process
- Adoption and implementation of an equal-opportunity policy

Table 10.5   SUNSET AND TEXAS STATE AGENCIES

The Texas legislature began using sunset in 1979 as a tool to oversee and control state agencies. It has resulted in the abolition of several agencies and merger of others.

Number of State Agencies

Year	Reviewed	Continued	Abolished	Abolished and transferred	Merged/separated
1979	26	12	8	1	5
1981	28	22	2	3	1
1983	32	29	3	0	0
1985	31	24	6	0	1
1987	20	18	2	0	0
1989	30	25	3	2	0
1991	30	22	3	3	2
1993	30	19	0	1	10
1995	18	17	0	1	0
1997	21	19	0	0	2
1999	25	23	1	0	1
1979–1999	291	230	28	11	22

Source: Texas Sunset Advisory Commission, "Sunset Report to the 76th Legislature," 1999.

Critical Thinking Exercise: What effect has Sunset had on interest group involvement in executive and legislative politics? What effect does it have on the iron triangle? What role has the sunset process played in political change?

Staff Size and Pay

Since World War II, state and local governments—not the national government—have grown considerably in size. Across the nation, state government employment grew from 1.5 million in 1960 to 4.0 million by 1998.[31] A favorite method of legislative review and control of agencies is to monitor and then to increase or reduce staff size. Legislators and governors often vow to cut the number of state employees as a way of reducing the budget and as a way of controlling bureaucracy. Governor Clements vowed to cut 25 percent of the state workforce; when he left office, it was larger than when he took office. More recently, the legislature has adopted caps on numbers of employees that the agency may employ. One result of this policy is increased contracting for services.

Numbers of employees are usually measured in units known as **full-time equivalent (FTE)** workers. That is, if you have five full-time employees and two half-time employees, then you have six FTEs. In 1999, the number of FTE state workers in Texas was approximately 267,000.[32] Another measure used to compare government employees across states is to modify the figures for the population in the state. In 1998, the number of FTE state workers per 10,000 population in Texas was 136. Smaller states generally have larger numbers. Of course, these numbers can be skewed by more heavy reliance on private contractors. The State of Texas is currently contracting with nearly 30,000 contractors.

The legislature adopts pay scales, titled the Classification Salary Schedule and the Exempt Salary Schedule, as a part of the appropriations bill. The bottom of the salary schedule for fiscal year 2001 is $14,376, while the top is $164,376. The top earners are physicians, highest-level investment managers and actuaries, and the deputy comptroller. However, some officials are allowed to accept private pay supplements. While such a policy raises questions of conflicts of interest, state leaders have decided that they will not get qualified people for some positions without extremely high pay levels, and they do not want to be on record as approving those pay levels, so they authorize them to raise private money as a pay supplement. Typically, college football coaches, physicians at state hospitals and medical facilities, university chancellors, university presidents, some professors in endowed chairs, and the heads and investment officers of pension funds get supplements from private funds, making them the highest paid state employees.

BUREAUCRACIES AND POLITICAL CHANGE

Executive agencies have the primary role of implementing decisions made by the legislature. However, they also play key policy-making roles, and their freedom to interpret legislative intent makes them policy powerhouses. Throughout the history of government regulation, the relationship between regulating agencies and private interests has been at the center of public discourse, as we have seen with the PUC, the Railroad Commission, and the Department of Insurance. Those relationships are at the center of examining the role of bureaucracies in political change.

Political scientist Marver Bernstein described the evolution of agencies, from their creation in an atmosphere of public outrage at perceived abuses at the hands of private industry (what we would call an era of creedal passion), to their original role as independent watchdogs over the industry, to an unintended role as an agency captured by the private interests, consistently making decisions favorable to those interests. This final stage of **captured agency** "is marked by the commission's surrender to the regulated. Politically isolated, lacking a firm basis of public support, lethargic in attitude and approach, bowed down by precedent and backlogs, unsupported in its demands for more staff and money, the commission finally becomes a captive of the regulated groups."[33]

The Texas Railroad Commission fits Bernstein's model. Born as the fruit of populists' anger at railroad company rates and practices, the commission at first responded to the public's demand for lower rates. By the time the agency's largest role was to regulate the oil and gas industry, it was so fully captured by that industry that it ran an ad (sponsored by two industry associations) claiming that "Since 1891 the Texas Railroad Commission has served the oil industry."[34]

The PUC has had a similar history to that of the Railroad Commission. Attempts at creating a new state agency had stalled for years. In the 1970s, the populace was stirred up over high utility rates and the appearance of favoritism to utility companies by government institutions. This popular participation, triggered by economic crisis, brought about political change and the creation of the PUC. However, key state leaders still opposed an adversarial regulatory relationship with the industry, governors appointed commissioners sympathetic to the industry, and the agency quickly became captured by the industry. In the 1980s, political change was triggered again by the electoral needs of new gubernatorial candidates in a political environment that was experiencing voter realignment (see Chapter 4).

Such closeness of regulators and industry often fuels public cynicism about the fairness of government actions. It also fuels debates among analysts and regulators about the proper course of regulatory action—whether agencies serve the public better by being adversarial or even confrontational with industry, or by considering industry a client to be saved, which is known as a **clientele relationship.** Legislators can be allies of this relationship. Often legislators become staunch defenders of a private industry, an agency that is close to an industry, or both. Longtime chair of the House Appropriations Committee Bill Heatly was a defender of programs and agencies that he favored and an advocate of a clientele relationship between agencies and interest groups. If a legislative evaluation was critical of a program he supported, he criticized the evaluation as suspect. At a 1982 hearing over the budget for the Department of Mental Health and Mental Retardation, Heatly challenged the legislative staff evaluation and suggested that if the agency did not request an evaluation, the evaluation had no validity. In a committee hearing on the Department of Health, when questions arose about its regulation of nursing homes, he stated that "an agency is supposed to help an industry that they regulate. The Insurance Board does. All other regulatory agencies do, but this one doesn't. They're supposed to help the people that they regulate."[35] His comments reflect the traditional conservative ideology of pro-business public policy.

One practice that tends to reinforce close relations between private interests and public regulators is the **revolving door,** in which there is an ongoing exchange of personnel between the two. Most often, employees of the agency quit and go to work for the industry that they had regulated, then they often turn around and lobby the agency for their new private employer. Sometimes it happens in reverse, or even in a revolving fashion, as in the 1970s, when a Texas Air Control Board official quit, worked for a company regulated by the agency, then returned to the agency as its executive director. Industry and many agency officials argue that such exchanges help to ensure that regulators know the industry that they are regulating. Critics charge that it is a key method that private groups use to capture agencies. Employees hoping to get better-paying jobs with the industry will be tempted to make decisions for personal or industry benefit, not for public benefit. Also, businesses have ready access to decision makers if their lobbyists are former agency officials.

The revolving door periodically becomes a public issue, particularly when an explicit decision benefiting a private interest can be tied to the role of one individual, first as a regulator, then as a representative of private industry. Governor

Richards and numerous state officials proposed to "lock" the revolving door of most agencies, as it was already locked at the PUC, by prohibiting officials from working for a regulated industry for a period after leaving the agency. The legislature extended the revolving door lock to the TNRCC and the Department of Insurance. Then the legislature applied a limited revolving door restriction to all regulatory agencies. The general revolving door statute applies only to officers and employees with exempt or high-end pay classifications.

> **Critical Thinking Exercise:** If the revolving door is allowed, what implications might that have for its policy decisions? If it is locked, what implications might that have for its ability to recruit and attract skilled employees?

Another role that agencies play in the **policy process** (policy making, policy implementation, and policy evaluation) is described by a model known as the **iron triangle** (see Figure 10.2). This model postulates that public policy making is controlled by three entities: private interest groups, regulatory agencies, and legislative committees specializing in that policy area. The three share common interests and goals and control key decision-making forums so much that their control is iron-tight—they form an iron triangle of policy control. Sometimes, legislators

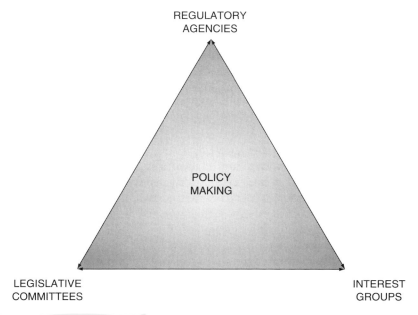

Figure 10.2 The Iron Triangle

The iron triangle model suggests that public policy making is largely controlled by private interest groups, regulatory agencies, and legislative committees. The iron triangle demonstrates the close relationship that develops between and among those three.

and legislative aides become executive officials, further strengthening the policy and political ties between the two branches. Examples include former state representatives Rick Perry, agriculture commissioner; Susan Combs, agriculture commissioner; and Elton Bomer, insurance commissioner, then secretary of state.

The closeness of private interests in Texas to legislators, through lobbying and campaign contributions, as was noted in Chapter 7, and to executive agencies, through influence on gubernatorial appointments and through the revolving door, lends strength to the iron-triangle model. In creating the PUC in a period of creedal passion in the 1970s, legislators were concerned enough that they locked the revolving door.

The captured agency theory, the iron-triangle model, and the existence of the revolving door suggest that the role of executive agencies in political change is closely tied to the power of the private sector and the power of the legislature, which limits their role in political change to that of a dependent or follower role, rather than that of an independent or leader role. However, other models may also explain bureaucracies and political change. As we saw with the State Board of Education, ideological battles can set officials against each other and interest groups against each other in a way that triggers a change of the process to circumvent the clashes.

BUREAUCRACIES AND DEMOCRACY

Bureaucracies are, in one sense, inherently undemocratic. Their officials are not elected (except, of course, for the governor and six Texas executive agencies run by elected heads or boards). However, if democracy involves, at its core, the idea of deliberation, then bureaucracies may be a key part of the democratic process. The state's rule-making process, spelled out in the **Administrative Procedures Act,** requires agency officials to seek written public comments, and agencies sometimes have public hearings before adopting rules and regulations. Such deliberation would seem to bolster the idea of a participatory, pluralistic democracy.

The iron-triangle model would suggest otherwise. Indeed, if one follows the proposed rules and regulations as first published by agencies in the *Texas Register,* the written comments received, and the revisions and final rules, it appears that in many cases, the agencies are merely going through the motions of including the public, while the decisions have already been made, or are made in consultation with the key private interests involved, out of the public eye—hardly a picture of the reality of policy making meshing with the public's ideal of government. Indeed, that is what a Texas court ruled in 1999 in a case invalidating some rules of the TNRCC.[36] Politics at the State Board of Education would tend to suggest a pluralistic democracy, full of participation, yet such an environment may be difficult to sustain in an executive agency setting. The legislature has changed the board to an appointed board before, and may well do so again as a result of controversy that the board's public discussions and differences continue to generate.

SUMMARY

Executive agencies are created to respond to public problems, and they are supposed to implement policies as instructed by the legislature. State agencies in Texas are organized with a policy-making board or commission, or with a single head appointed by the governor or elected by the people. Periodically, the state reorganizes the agencies in an attempt to improve problem-solving capabilities. Each agency must undergo sunset review every 12 years to determine whether to continue the agency or to change its structure and procedures.

The relationship between agencies and private interests is a key variable in understanding the role that agencies play in policy making and policy implementation. While such agencies as the Railroad Commission and the PUC were created from a wave of creedal passion with people demanding strong government regulation of business, those agencies are now often seen as being captured by the private interests they regulate. The iron triangle creates a strong bond that often mitigates against political change, and the revolving door of people from the agencies to the private sector and back further forges the bond.

KEY TERMS

bureaucracy
implement
policy making
rule making
attorney general
comptroller
treasurer
land commissioner
agriculture commissioner
staggered terms
Railroad Commission
secretary of state
Public Utility Commission (PUC)
quasi-judicial
Texas Natural Resource Conservation
   Commission (TNRCC)

public counsels
boards and commissions
government reorganization
legislative oversight
sunset review
"good government"
full-time equivalent (FTE)
captured agency
clientele relationship
revolving door
policy process
iron triangle
Administrative Procedures Act

SUGGESTED READINGS

Comptroller of Public Accounts. *Challenging the Status Quo: Toward Smaller, Smarter Government*. 1999.

Duncan, Marilyn, and Mary Jo Powell. *Guide to Texas State Agencies*, 10th ed. Austin, Tex.: LBJ School of Public Affairs, 1999.

Lauderdale, Michael, *Reinventing Texas Government.* Austin, Tex.: University of Texas Press, 1999.

Prindle, David. *Petroleum Politics and the Texas Railroad Commission.* Austin Tex.: University of Texas Press, 1981.

Sunset Advisory Commission. *Guide to the Texas Sunset Process.* 1999.

NOTES

1. Terrence Stutz, "Education Board Battle Taking Shape," *Dallas Morning News,* 7 March 1998, p. A1.
2. Terrence Stutz, "$200,000 Raised for Religious Conservatives," *Dallas Morning News,* 16 October 1996, p. A17.
3. Terrence Stutz, "Education Board," p. A1.
4. Nancy Kruh, "The Daughter Also Rises," *Dallas Morning News,* 5 July 1996, p. C1.
5. Terrence Stutz, "State School Board Monitored," *Dallas Morning News,* 22 September 1995, p. D11.
6. Terrence Stutz, "AG Issues Opinion on Textbooks," *Dallas Morning News,* 22 November 1996, p. A27.
7. Terrence Stutz, "$200,000 Raised," p. A17.
8. Terrence Stutz, "Education Board," p. A1.
9. Cindy Ramos, "Proposals Aim to Cut Power Given to State School Board," *San Antonio Express-News,* 18 March 1997, p. A7.
10. Terrence Stutz, "State Education Board Approves Overhaul of Curriculum Standards," *Dallas Morning News,* 12 July 1997, p. A27.
11. Carlos Sanchez, "Texas School Chief 'Tired of Mistrust' from Board Critics," *Fort Worth Star-Telegram,* 3 October 1997, p. 1.
12. Terrence Stutz, "Education Board," p. A1.
13. "Around the Capitol," *Capitol Update,* Texas State Directory Press, 26 November 1999, p. 2.
14. Max Weber, *Essays in Sociology,* eds. and trans. H. H. Gerth and C. Wright Mills (London: Oxford University Press, 1946).
15. Council of State Governments, *Book of the States 1998–99,* vol. 32 (Lexington, Ky.: Council of State Governments, 1998), 33.
16. Virginia H. Taylor Houston, "Surveying in Texas," *Southwestern Historical Quarterly* 65 (October 1961): 216.
17. How much land this represented is uncertain, since even the boundaries of the state were in dispute.
18. For a history and analysis of the Railroad Commission, see David Prindle, *Petroleum Politics and the Texas Railroad Commission* (Austin, Tex.: University of Texas Press, 1981).
19. Prindle, *Petroleum Politics,* 20, 112, 117.
20. Comptroller of Public Accounts, *Breaking the Mold: New Ways to Govern Texas* (1991), 43.
21. Council of State Governments, *Book of the States 1992–93,* vol. 29, (Lexington, Ky.: Council of State Governments, 1992), 59.
22. Larry Sabato, *Goodbye to Good-Time Charlie: The American Governorship Transformed,* 2d ed. (Washington, D.C.: Congressional Quarterly Press, 1983), 62.
23. Article 4, Section 24. See also Fred Gantt, Jr., *The Chief Executive in Texas: A Study in Gubernatorial Leadership* (Austin, Tex.: University of Texas Press, 1964), 111.
24. Joint Advisory Committee on Government Operations, "Final Report to the Governor of Texas and Members of the 65th Texas Legislature," January 1977.

25. Ibid.
26. Comptroller of Public Accounts, *Forces of Change: Shaping the Future of Texas,* 1993, 227; Comptroller of Public Accounts, *Breaking the Mold,* 38.
27. Office of the Governor, *Building from the Blueprint: A Plan for Texas State Government* (1991), 8.
28. William Gormley, Jr., "Accountability Battles in State Administration," in *The State of the States,* ed. Carl E. Van Horn (Washington, D.C.: Congressional Quarterly Press, 1993), 172.
29. Alan Rosenthal, *Governors and Legislatures: Contending Powers* (Washington, D.C.: Congressional Quarterly Press, 1990), 190.
30. Texas Sunset Advisory Commission, "Sunset Review in Texas: Summary of Process and Procedure" (October 1993), 23.
31. Sabato, *Goodbye to Good-Time Charlie,* 169; U.S. Census, "State Government Employment," March 1998. Accessed 5 March 2000, http://www.census.gov/ftp/pub/govs/apes/98stus.txt.
32. State Auditor, *A Quarterly Report of Full-time Equivalent State Employees for the Quarter ending February 28, 1999.* May 1999, Report #99-705.
33. Marver Bernstein, *Regulating Business by Independent Commission* (Princeton, N.J.: Princeton University Press, 1955), 90.
34. *Texas Almanac 1972–1973.* (Dallas, Tex.: A. H. Belo Corp., 1971), 397.
35. Molly Ivins, *Dallas Times Herald,* 13 February 1983.
36. *ACCORD Agriculture v. TNRCC,* 1999. Tex. App. no. 03-48-00340-cv.

The Texas Justice System: The Law, the Courts, and Criminal Justice

★ Scenario: Winning the Gavel—Steve Mansfield and the Judicial Selection Process

In November 1994, Texas held a general election. On the ballot were several statewide offices, including two positions on the Texas Court of Criminal Appeals. Steve Mansfield won one of them. Shortly before the election, a number of inconsistencies and misstatements were discovered about Mansfield's description of himself. For instance, it was revealed that he may have lied about his birthplace being Houston, Texas, when it was actually Brookline, Massachusetts. Mansfield did not move to Texas until 1984. He then spent nine years doing pension and tax work for two insurance companies, in spite of having claimed to have been a practicing attorney in Texas since 1980. He did not receive a license to practice law in Texas until 1992. The pension and tax work for the insurance companies did not require a license, but when he did apply for a license, the Board of Law Examiners, the agency responsible for licensing attorneys to practice in Texas, investigated an allegation that Mansfield was in arrears on child-support payments. Mansfield had also said that he had never run for public office before, when he had actually run for the United States Congress twice in New Hampshire.

In addition to these discrepancies, there were more serious allegations. Mansfield was accused of creating a fictional legal career to exaggerate his legal experience. Mansfield had claimed that he had extensive criminal law experience in Florida and Illinois. None of that appears to be true; indeed, it seems that the only experience Mansfield had with the legal system in Florida was a $100 fine for practicing law without a license in 1986. Outside of Florida, it has been alleged that he was once arrested for possession of marijuana.

The only criminal law experience that Mansfield had as an attorney was a few misdemeanor cases in the 1970s, shortly after he got out of law school. There is no evidence that he ever handled a felony case. Because the Texas Court of Criminal Appeals is the court of last resort for criminal cases, it seems somewhat odd that one of its justices would have no experience in serious criminal cases. Mansfield had also claimed that he had written extensively on criminal law, but no evidence was offered to support the assertion. The State Bar of Texas—the professional association of Texas lawyers—gave Mansfield a public reprimand for professional misconduct because he lied during the election, but it did not suspend or revoke (disbar) his license to practice law.

Following these revelations, the Board of Law Examiners reviewed the evidence concerning the allegations that Mansfield had been in arrears on child-support payments when he applied for his law license, but it announced in July 1995 that no action would be taken against Mansfield. Texas Attorney General Dan Morales reviewed the constitutional requirement that a candidate for any of the appellate courts in Texas have 10 years experience as a practicing attorney and/or a judge. Morales ruled that the constitution did not specify that the experience had to be in Texas, but that it could be anywhere. The experience that Mansfield accumulated in Texas, Illinois, and Florida in civil cases met the requirement.[1]

His troubles did not end with his election. Shortly after taking the oath of office, Mansfield made the news again. A complaint was filed against him for mistreating his three Pomeranians. During work, Mansfield left his dogs inside his car, which was parked inside the Capitol garage. The dogs had food, water, and pet toys, and Mansfield would walk them around the Capitol grounds during his lunch break. A Humane Society investigator did not file charges but did suggest that Mansfield should leave the dogs at home. In 1998, he was arrested for scalping University of Texas football tickets outside the stadium before the Texas-Texas A&M game. The Texas Commission on Judicial Conduct reprimanded him, and after pleading no contest to trespassing, he was sentenced to six month's probation, a $300 fine, and 30 hours of community service. Mansfield protested that he did not know he was doing anything wrong, but he was issued a criminal trespass warning by one officer, who explained that selling the tickets on university property was prohibited. A second officer arrested Mansfield when he attempted to sell the tickets only a few minutes after receiving the warning. To make appearances even worse, he sold the tickets given to him by the university for three

Judge Steve Mansfield (right) takes the oath of office as a judge on the Texas State Court of Criminal Appeals, one of Texas's two supreme courts, in January 1995.

times their face value of $38.[2] Because of this seemingly endless string of incidents, Mansfield has often been referred to as the "poster boy" for judicial reform.

Texas elects its judges in partisan elections. It also has two supreme courts: the Texas Court of Criminal Appeals and the Texas Supreme Court. Supreme courts are held in high regard by most citizens. Probably because of the identification with the United States Supreme Court, the Texas Supreme Court is better known than the Texas Court of Criminal Appeals, which operates in relative obscurity. Many Texans do not know who serves on this court, even though its judges are elected in statewide elections. Mansfield apparently decided to run for the court because he was upset when the court overturned the conviction of a person who committed murder during a carjacking. Mansfield paid the $3,000 filing fee to run in the Republican primary election. He had no party ties, no base of support, and no name recognition, but he toured the state visiting courthouses, party activists, and victim's rights groups. He won the primary election against another unknown candidate and rode a Republican tide to victory in November.

After vacillating between running and not running for reelection in 2000, Mansfield decided not to file for the Republican primary election. Three Republicans had filed for his place on the court, and perhaps he decided that he had become too well known. The problems associated with the election of Mansfield to one of the Texas supreme courts and the other problems associated with the Texas judicial system are discussed in this chapter.★

INTRODUCTION

Of the three branches of government—executive, legislative, and judicial—the judicial branch is the least visible and the least understood. The judicial branch is designed to serve three purposes:

1. To administer a system in which those accused of a crime may be tried and punished
2. To administer a system in which disputes among individuals can be settled within a set of rules
3. To interpret the law

Because the law is the main tool of the judicial branch, the types of law and the basis for laws are briefly considered first. The court system of Texas—where the law is interpreted and administered—is discussed next, including an accounting of its problems and structural shortcomings. The method of selecting judges is also considered. The final part of the chapter briefly examines the criminal justice system, which becomes operative when the law is broken and someone is convicted and sentenced for the crime.

THE BODY OF LAWS: THE BASIS OF THE JUDICIAL BRANCH

Judicial branches in the United States and, hence, in Texas operate under the rule of law. The judiciary does not operate in a vacuum and rule by whim. Judges may not arbitrarily make decisions but do so within the context of a set of rules or laws. This section has two parts. The first discusses the sources of law and describes how laws are created from such sources as constitutions and government agencies, as well as legislatures and precedent. The second describes the two basic types of law: criminal and civil.

Sources of the Law

The "law" is generally conceived as something that is created by the United States Congress, state legislatures, and city councils. While all of the preceding sources are legitimate, the law in Texas may also come from government agencies, boards and commissions, and other forms of local government. The law has four general sources: (1) the common-law tradition, (2) constitutions, (3) statutes and ordinances, and (4) administrative rules and regulations.

Common Law   The **common law** tradition is a legacy of the English influence on the United States and Texas. England has no written constitution. However,

Te★as*Index*

Crime, Courts, and Judges

Crime rate per 100,000 population—1998
Texas: total–5112, violent—565, murder—6.8
California: total–4343, violent—704, murder—6.6
New York: total–3589, violent—638, murder—5.1
Florida: total–6886, violent—939, murder—6.5

Capital punishment: Number of prisoners on death row—1998
Texas—451
California—512
New York—1
Florida—372

Courts of last resort—1998
Texas: 2, supreme court and court of criminal appeals, 9 justices each, election
California: 1, supreme court, 7 justices, appointed by governor
New York: 1, court of appeals, 7 justices, appointed by governor from Judicial Nomination
Commission, Senate confirmation
Florida: 1, supreme court, 9 justices, selected by the court

Compensation of judges—1998
Texas: supreme court, $113,000; district courts, $101,700 to $111,000
California: supreme court, $131,085; superior courts, $107,390
New York: court of appeals, $125,000; supreme courts, $113,000
Florida: supreme court, $137,314; circuit courts, $110,754

Prison Population—1998
Texas—144,510
California—161,904
New York—72,638
Florida—67,224

Adults on Probation—1998
Texas—443,758
California—324,427
New York—190,518
Florida—239,021

Adults on Parole—1998
Texas—112,022
California—110,617
New York—59,548
Florida—7,421

judges in England have been making rulings on cases for several hundred years. The compendium of those rulings constitutes the "common law" of England. Much of that system crossed the Atlantic with the first immigrants from England and became a part of U.S. law. The early immigrants into Texas from elsewhere in the United States brought that tradition with them, and Texas adopted much of it. Some of it has been codified into formal statutes, but much of it has, of course, been modified under the influence of Spanish and Mexican law and by the rulings of courts in the United States as a whole and in Texas in particular. However, the common law tradition remains the basis for much of current Texas law.

Judicial interpretation occurs when judges apply the rule of law to cases. The law tries to be as precise and as all encompassing as it can be, but it cannot specifically address all possible circumstances. While many cases may be similar in nature, no two cases are exactly alike. Judges must decide how the law will be applied in each case. The decision rendered in a particular case is an interpretation of the law. The particular way that a judge interprets the law is dependent on many variables. Judges may be influenced by political ideology, by their perception of the role of a judge, and by precedent.

A precedent is a ruling made by a previous court that governs the way cases are interpreted by subsequent courts. One of the fundamental principles of judicial interpretation is "treat like cases alike." When a case comes before a judge, the judge searches previous cases to determine if there are any "like" it. If cases are found to be like the one currently before the court, then the rulings in those previous cases will be looked at. Unless the judge can find a compelling reason not to, the rulings in those prior cases will be applied to the current case. The ruling, or precedent, established in the prior case or cases will be used to decide the current case. Of course, the determination is sometimes made that the precedent was wrong and is overturned. Sometimes the determination is made that no precedent exists and the judge can then interpret the law and set a new precedent.

Constitutions   Constitutions are also a source of law, indeed, the most fundamental source of law for the citizens of Texas and the rest of the United States (see Chapter 3). They provide the foundation and framework for the laws that follow from it. Any statutes, ordinances, and administrative laws in Texas that appear to contradict any provisions of the Texas and U.S. Constitutions are open to being challenged as unconstitutional. Even the elements of the common law that came from the English tradition must eventually conform to the appropriate constitutions.

Statutory Law   **Statutes** are passed by the United States Congress and the state legislatures. Under the federal system of government used in the United States, Texas is subordinate to and constrained by the national government, meaning that Texas may do what it wishes *unless* it is prohibited from doing so by the national government. That leaves Texas with considerable discretion and autonomy. As Chapter 8 points out, the Texas legislature passes more than 1000 bills each regular session every two years. Statutes (statutory law) are what most people are referring to when they talk about the "law." If asked to describe the law, many people would probably discuss it in terms of the criminal law, also called "the penal code," but the law covers a host of other areas as well, such as contracts, workplace safety, and environmental protection. Statutes have replaced much of the common law and are used to fill out constitutional provisions, but they are also used to authorize other agents to make laws.

Ordinances are statutes passed by city councils (see Chapter 12). Traffic laws, building codes, and the regulation of nonsmoking areas in restaurants are all common examples of ordinances. The ability of cities in Texas to pass ordinances is a further extension of the federalist system of government: Cities, or at least home-rule cities, may do almost anything they wish *unless* prohibited by the state and/or national governments.

Administrative Law   **Administrative law** consists of rules and regulations, primarily issued by executive agencies (see Chapter 10). Quasi-judicial bodies, such as municipal boards of adjustment, make rulings on local administrative matters, which can only be overturned by a court of law, and those rulings are also considered administrative law. Why are these entities allowed to produce law? Legislators often pass laws on matters about which they have very little expertise or personal experience. That lack of expertise dictates that the legislature must pass laws with rather broad mandates that define desired outcomes—such as soil and water conservation or the regulation of public utilities—but these laws often have very little in the way of actually dictating how those outcomes should be obtained. As a result, such executive agencies as the Public Utility Commission are often granted extraordinary authority and discretion in the implementation of the law, which requires creating rules and regulations. In effect, the legislature has granted these agencies the authority to create law in its place.

The Types of Law

All laws are organized into two codes: criminal and civil law. Essentially, the two codes are distinguished by how society views violations of its rules.

The Criminal Code   **Criminal law**—also called the criminal code or the penal code—deals with acts that are considered an offense against society. If something is deemed a criminal offense, then society has made the determination that the offense is considered of sufficient gravity that society at large should punish the perpetrator. Such crimes as murder, robbery, shoplifting, loitering, and embezzlement are criminal offenses, even though the number of people affected by a particular crime may be quite small. Crimes are classified into misdemeanors, which are considered to be less serious, and felonies, which are more serious crimes. The enforcement and prosecution of criminal law and the punishment of those who break it takes place within the criminal justice system, discussed in more detail later in the chapter.

The Civil Code   **Civil law** arises from disputes between individuals. In the legal system, an individual may be a person, a corporation, an institution (such as a university), or even a government agency. Civil law is usually associated with the filing of a lawsuit. When one party sues another, the implication is that one party has been harmed by the other. Civil law serves the purpose of rectifying the harm suffered. The actions of one person have caused another person to suffer a decrease in the level of welfare. A lawsuit restores the level of welfare. Civil suits may result from the harm caused by such things as discrimination in employment, slander, a breach of contract, or personal injury.

People are probably most familiar with civil-law news stories chronicling the spectacular monetary awards given to people injured in some way through someone's negligence. Because the law treats a corporation as an individual, that "someone" could be a company. **Torts,** which are claims of injury, have created much controversy over the years. Plaintiffs' lawyers and defendants' lawyers have often been engaged in political battles over the need for tort reform.

Much of the attention to torts comes from the news media, which tend to focus on spectacular lawsuits that result in substantial damage awards, such as the infamous case of the woman who was burned after trying to hold a cup of McDonald's coffee between her legs and to drive at the same time. McDonald's was found negligent. However, the vast majority of cases are civil suits that do not involve large sums of money. Indeed, most civil suits are settled out of court. Similarly, most criminal cases are plea bargained, meaning that the accused pleads guilty to a lesser charge to avoid prosecution on a more serious crime. One might wonder then why the court system and judges should be studied if most cases never get to them. Out-of-court settlements and plea bargains are indirectly affected by the judicial system, as the courts and judges set the tone for what will happen in plea bargains and out-of-court settlements.

Critical Thinking Exercise: Administrative law is troubling because it is created by bureaucracies that are not democratically elected. Much of it is written by bureaucrats that are not even directly appointed by an elected official. How does the creation of administrative law affect the democratic process?

THE JUDICIAL BRANCH

This part of the chapter focuses on the judicial branch, beginning with the jurisdictions of the courts in Texas and various proposals for reform. As the Mansfield scenario illustrates, the selection of judges has been the subject of discussion and controversy in Texas for a number of years. The various rationales for and methods of selection are examined next.

Organizing Principles of the Judicial Branch

The judicial branch in the State of Texas is somewhat complicated. Indeed, some observers have argued that there is no clearly discernible—or at least logical—system as such. Understanding the types of courts requires some understanding of jurisdiction, which refers to the categories of cases the courts are empowered to hear. There are several types of jurisdiction, but the two most basic kinds are original and appellate jurisdiction.

Original Jurisdiction   **Original jurisdiction** means that a court may conduct hearings that deal with the matters of fact in a case—trials. A court of original jurisdiction determines a person's guilt or innocence. There are courts of original jurisdiction at the local, county, and state levels, distinguished from each other by the types of cases being heard (for example, civil vs. criminal, misdemeanors vs. felonies, state laws vs. municipal laws).

Courts of original jurisdiction at the local and county levels are called courts of limited jurisdiction because they are far more limited in the types of cases they can hear than are the state courts of general jurisdiction, also called district courts. In some areas, some district courts—also called state trial courts of special jurisdiction—have divided their responsibilities for efficiency. For instance, such a court might only hear divorce cases.

Appellate Jurisdiction   **Appellate jurisdiction** refers to the ability to conduct hearings that deal with matters of proper trial procedure or constitutional rights; appellate courts review trials, as when the defense feels that proper procedure was not pursued in a hearing that led to a conviction. These procedures govern many aspects of court behavior and are intended to help ensure that a hearing is fair and will result in a just verdict. For example, juries are usually told that in reaching a verdict, they may only consider evidence presented in court.

An appellate court's determination that proper procedure has not been followed and/or that constitutional rights have been violated does not mean that a person is innocent, only that the case will be returned to the trial court. That court may then dismiss the charge in a criminal case or dismiss the case in a civil suit—or retry the case without making the same mistakes again. Courts of original jurisdiction can also be appellate courts for lower courts.

The Structure of the Judicial Branch

The state constitution applies the organizing principles just described to create the different types and levels of courts. Texas's judicial branch is quite decentralized, like much of the rest of state and local government in the state, with the various

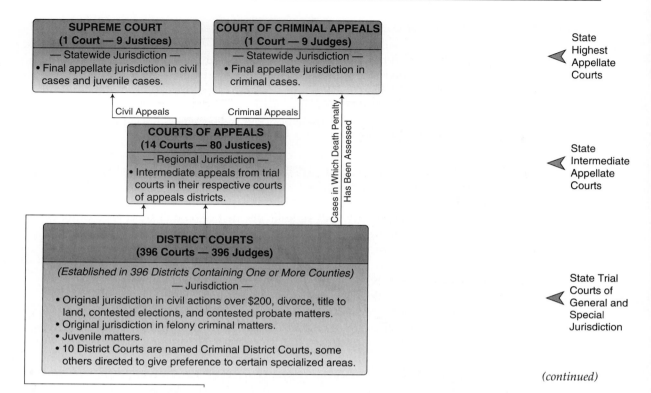

Figure 11.1   The Court Structure of Texas

This figure shows the bewildering array of jurisdictions, levels, and kinds of courts in the state judicial branch.

Source: Office of Court Administration.

lower courts particularly overlapping in their responsibilities. The Office of Court Administration, an official state organization, categorizes the various courts into five basic types:

1. Local trial courts of limited jurisdiction
2. County trial courts of limited jurisdiction
3. District courts, also called state trial courts of general and special jurisdiction
4. State intermediate appellate courts
5. State highest appellate courts[3]

Each type of court is discussed in turn next. (Figure 11.1 illustrates the current system of courts in Texas.)

Local Trial Courts   Local trial courts of limited jurisdiction include municipal courts and justice of the peace courts. The first type, **municipal courts,** have been established in approximately 850 cities in Texas with approximately 1122 judges.

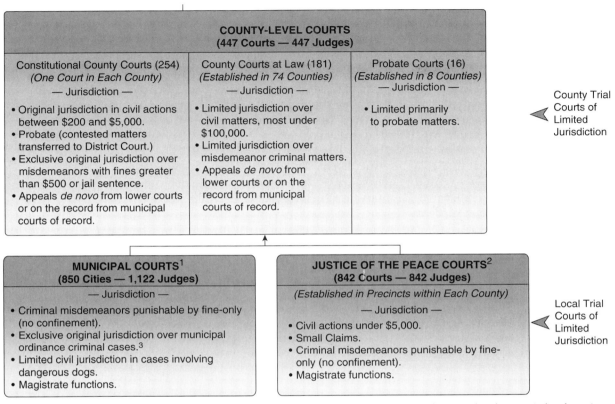

COUNTY-LEVEL COURTS
(447 Courts — 447 Judges)

Constitutional County Courts (254) *(One Court in Each County)* — Jurisdiction —	County Courts at Law (181) *(Established in 74 Counties)* — Jurisdiction —	Probate Courts (16) *(Established in 8 Counties)* — Jurisdiction —
• Original jurisdiction in civil actions between $200 and $5,000. • Probate (contested matters transferred to District Court.) • Exclusive original jurisdiction over misdemeanors with fines greater than $500 or jail sentence. • Appeals *de novo* from lower courts or on the record from municipal courts of record.	• Limited jurisdiction over civil matters, most under $100,000. • Limited jurisdiction over misdemeanor criminal matters. • Appeals *de novo* from lower courts or on the record from municipal courts of record.	• Limited primarily to probate matters.

County Trial Courts of Limited Jurisdiction

MUNICIPAL COURTS[1]
(850 Cities — 1,122 Judges)
— Jurisdiction —
• Criminal misdemeanors punishable by fine-only (no confinement).
• Exclusive original jurisdiction over municipal ordinance criminal cases.[3]
• Limited civil jurisdiction in cases involving dangerous dogs.
• Magistrate functions.

JUSTICE OF THE PEACE COURTS[2]
(842 Courts — 842 Judges)
(Established in Precincts within Each County)
— Jurisdiction —
• Civil actions under $5,000.
• Small Claims.
• Criminal misdemeanors punishable by fine-only (no confinement).
• Magistrate functions.

Local Trial Courts of Limited Jurisdiction

[1] Some Municipal Courts are courts of record — appeals from those courts are taken on the record to the county-level courts.
[2] All Justice of the Peace Courts and most Municipal Courts are not courts of record. Appeals from these courts are by trial *de novo* in the county-level courts; and in some instances to the district courts.
[3] An offense that arises under a municipal ordinance is punishable by a fine not to exceed: 1) $2000 for ordinances that govern fire safety, zoning, and public health; or, 2) $500 for all others.

Figure 11.1   The Court Structure of Texas—*Continued*

Municipal courts have original jurisdiction over (a) criminal misdemeanors with fines less than $500 and (b) municipal ordinance violations. Municipal courts may also levy limited civil penalties in cases involving dangerous dogs and may act as magistrates.[4] Magistrates perform such duties as conducting examining trials (preliminary hearings for county and district courts to determine whether enough evidence exists to hold someone for trial), issue search and arrest warrants, and give statutory warnings.

In fiscal year 1998, municipal courts in Texas had 6,725,706 cases filed in them. Of that, 77.9 percent were for traffic violations[5]—hence, the popular title of traffic courts given to many municipal courts. The rest of the cases involved violations of municipal ordinances, such as health and building codes. Municipal courts in Texas also conducted emergency mental-commitment hearings, driver's license suspension hearings, and inquests (hearings to determine the cause of death), among other duties.

The second type of local trial courts comprises the **justice of the peace courts.** There are 842 justice of the peace courts in Texas, each with one judge, established in precincts within each county. Justice of the peace courts have original jurisdiction over civil cases involving less than $5,000 and act as small-claims courts. In small-claims court, the parties to a dispute each present their sides of the case without the benefit of having attorneys present. The judge then renders a decision in the case, based on the evidence and testimony given in court. The amounts of money involved in such cases are usually too small to justify retaining an attorney, but the grievances are nevertheless significant to the claimants. For example, a person may feel that a mechanic did $200 of unnecessary work on his car and may take the mechanic to court to get the money back, but a lawyer would cost more than that just to try the case. Justice of the peace courts provide an inexpensive alternative for such cases. Justice of the peace courts act as the real "people's courts."

Justice of the peace courts have original jurisdiction over criminal misdemeanors involving a fine of less than $500 dollars. Justices of the peace also act as magistrates.[6] During fiscal year 1998, 2,587,908 cases were added to justice of

This hearing in a small courtroom is about civil liability for alleged injury to the plaintiff. Most courtrooms in Texas are for municipal, justice of the peace, and county courts; and most of the cases heard in them are unassuming and undramatic.

the peace dockets. Of those cases, 90.5 percent (2,341,191) were criminal cases. The remaining 9.5 percent (246,717) were civil cases, of which 25 percent (61,679) were small-claims cases. In addition, justice of the peace courts also held peace-bond hearings, examining trials, driver's license suspension hearings, and inquests, and they issued search warrants and more than 650,000 arrest warrants.[7]

County Courts There are three basic kinds of **county courts:** (1) constitutional county courts, (2) county courts at law, and (3) probate courts. There are 254 constitutional county courts in Texas, one for every county in the state. They have original jurisdiction in civil matters involving $200 to $5,000 and in probate cases. However, if the probate is contested, the case is then transferred to a district court (see subsequent discussion). Constitutional county courts have exclusive criminal jurisdiction over misdemeanors that have a fine greater than $500 or that have a jail sentence.

Constitutional county courts also have appellate jurisdiction over cases from municipal and justice of the peace courts.[8] Very few municipal courts and no justice of the peace courts are **courts of records,** meaning that there is no transcript of the trial. Without a transcript, there is no record of the proceedings for the appellate court to review for procedural and/or constitutional violations. As a result, appeals from most municipal courts and all justice of the peace courts are heard *de novo*—which essentially means that the trial is conducted again.

The second type of county court—county courts at law—was essentially formed to take over the judicial functions of the county judge, who oversees the constitutional county court. In fact, not every county has a county court at law. There are 181 county courts at law in Texas, established in 74 counties. In addition to having judicial duties, the county judge also serves on the county commissioners court (the county's legislative body) and acts more or less as the chief executive officer for the county (see Chapter 12). In highly populated urban counties, such as Dallas or Harris, the county judge's time is usually taken up with the legislative and executive duties of the office.[9] County courts at law then assume the judicial duties of the county judge. Some counties have several county courts at law, with each having a different jurisdiction, which is also why county courts as a whole are considered courts of limited jurisdiction.

The state legislature has created county courts at law—with original criminal and/or appellate jurisdictions—according to the needs of each county's court system. As a result, during nearly every session, the legislature creates new county courts at law with varying jurisdictions, and it changes the jurisdictions of existing courts. This creates a bewildering array of county courts at law, which makes categorization almost impossible. Although this is in keeping with the state's commitment to decentralized government, it has also engendered problems, discussed later in this chapter.

County courts at law have limited original jurisdiction in civil cases, usually in those involving less than $100,000. They also have limited original jurisdiction in criminal cases involving misdemeanors. The appellate jurisdiction of county courts at law is the same as that of the constitutional county courts.

The third type of county court—probate courts—specializes in the disposition of a person's estate after death. A total of 16 probate courts have been established in eight counties in Texas.[10] In 1999, the legislature authorized money for associate judges to deal with the needs of children in the foster care system. The presiding judge of the administrative judicial region may appoint associate judges to hear substitute care and child protective services cases. The judges may be appointed where needed to relieve a backlog of cases. In the jurisdictions where the associate judges are appointed, the cases must be referred to them.

County courts of all types added 682,693 cases to their dockets in fiscal year 1998. Of that number, 82 percent (559,867) were criminal cases. The largest categories of criminal cases were theft, with 38.3 percent of cases, and driving while intoxicated (DWI) and driving under the influence of drugs (DUID), totaling 18.5 percent of cases. Civil cases accounted for 15.6 percent (106,577) of the total number. The rest of the cases involved juvenile, probate, and mental-health commitment hearings (to determine the mental competency of a person).[11]

District Courts The state courts of general and special jurisdiction are usually referred to as **district courts,** of which Texas has established 396. They have original civil jurisdiction in cases involving more than $200, all land title disputes, divorces, contested elections, and contested probate matters. The district courts also have original criminal jurisdiction in all felony cases and all cases involving juveniles.

District courts can be designated courts of special jurisdiction for the sake of efficiency and expertise. At least 10 district courts have been designated as criminal district courts and try only criminal cases. In some counties, there are district courts that deal exclusively or almost exclusively with divorce or juvenile cases.[12]

District courts added 544,590 cases to their dockets during fiscal year 1998. Of that total, 64 percent (443,095) were civil cases, 31 percent (215,958) were criminal cases, and 5 percent (37,261) were juvenile cases. By far the largest category of criminal cases was for drug-related offenses, with 32 percent (69,107) of the total. Homicides were the smallest category, with 1 percent (2,160) of the total of criminal cases. The largest category of civil cases was family law matters other than divorce, with 36 percent (159,514) of the total of civil cases.[13]

Intermediate Courts of Appeal Texas is divided into 13 regions, with one **court of appeal** each in 12 of those 13 regions. Because of the size of the caseload, two courts of appeal serve the Houston area, the First and Fourteenth Courts of Appeal, so that there are a total of 14 intermediate appellate courts with 80 justices. All of these courts have appellate jurisdiction over appeals from courts of original jurisdiction in their respective regions. The jurisdiction of the courts of appeal extends to all cases except those involving the death penalty, which are appealed directly from the trial court to the Court of Criminal Appeals.[14]

A total of 11,566 cases were filed in the courts of appeal during the 1998 fiscal year. There were 6,375 criminal and 5,191 civil cases filed. The average amount of time it took to dispose of cases was 1.8 months for criminal and 8.5 for civil.[15] Justices on the courts of appeal usually sit in panels of three, deciding cases by majority rule.

The Supreme Courts The state's highest appellate courts are the **Texas Supreme Court** and the **Texas Court of Criminal Appeals.** The Texas Supreme Court has only civil jurisdiction, and the Texas Court of Criminal Appeals has only criminal jurisdiction. Both are **courts of last resort,** meaning that they are the last state courts to which a person can appeal a case, although a person who claims that the United States Constitution, a United States treaty, or a federal law has been violated may next appeal to the United States Supreme Court.

Texas's bifurcated (dual) supreme court system (shared only with Oklahoma among the 50 states) dates from 1876, when the current Texas Constitution created the court structure. At that time, the two supreme courts were the only appellate courts, and two separate supreme courts, one for civil cases and one for criminal cases, made sense. Over time, however, the caseloads of the supreme courts grew to unmanageable proportions. As the state's population increased, so did the number of cases handled by the lower courts. The number of cases appealed to the supreme courts also grew proportionately. Hence, the courts of appeal were created in 1891 to relieve the burden. The courts of appeal were initially given jurisdiction only over civil cases. The courts of appeal were given jurisdiction over criminal cases in 1981 after the caseload of the Court of Criminal Appeals became too great.

Each of the supreme courts in Texas has nine members. The Texas Supreme Court always hears cases *en banc,* with all nine justices. The Texas Court of Criminal Appeals, however, may sit in panels of three judges, except for capital murder cases, but it almost never does. For each court, decisions are the result of a majority vote.

Each of the supreme courts in Texas considers several kinds of applications for review in performing its functions. When a person applies to the Texas Supreme Court for a **petition for review,** formerly called **writs of error,** it means that the court is being asked to determine whether the person's procedural and/or constitutional rights were violated. When the Texas Supreme Court issues a petition for review, it has decided to review the case. In fiscal year 1998, the Texas Supreme Court received 1054 petitions for review and granted 89 of them. A refusal to grant a petition for review upholds the ruling of the lower court. The Texas Supreme Court also issues **writs of mandamus,** which are orders to corporations, persons, or state officials to perform certain acts. For example, a state official may be ordered to enforce a law that had previously not been enforced. Both the Texas Supreme Court and the Texas Court of Criminal Appeals issue writs of habeas corpus. A **writ of habeas corpus** is an order to an official holding a person in custody to bring that person before a court to inquire into whether that person is being held legally. In addition, the Texas Court of Criminal Appeals reviews applications for discretionary review, which serve the same purpose as the Texas Supreme Court's petitions for review. In fiscal year 1998, the Texas Court of Criminal Appeals received 1983 petitions for discretionary review and granted 173.

The Texas Supreme Court issued 222 opinions during the 1998 fiscal year. An opinion outlines the reasons for the court decision and in essence establishes what the law means on the point or points raised in the appeal. During that same period, the Texas Court of Criminal Appeals issued 652 written opinions, of which 417 were opinions of the court that actually disposed of a case, meaning that the court actually rendered a judgment as to whether procedural and/or constitutional rights were violated. The rest of the written opinions were dissents, concurrences, and opinions on rehearings. Dissents are written by justices who disagree with the opinion of the court majority and wish to have a written record of why they disagree. Concurrences are written by those justices who agree with the opinion of the court majority but for reasons different from those of the justices in the majority.

The Texas Supreme Court performs several administrative duties in addition to its judicial responsibilities. It is responsible for establishing the administrative rules that govern civil courts in Texas. It also conducts proceedings for the removal of judges. Furthermore, the Texas Supreme Court approves the establishment of law schools in Texas and appoints the members of the Board of Law Examiners, which prepares the bar exam. The Texas Supreme Court determines who passes the exam and then certifies successful applicants to practice law in Texas.

Criticisms of the Judicial Branch

The Texas court system can be criticized on two grounds. First, as can be seen from the preceding discussion, many courts have overlapping jurisdictions. Many civil cases and some criminal cases could be heard in a justice of the peace court, a constitutional county court, a county court at law, or a district court.

A good lawyer can "judge shop," manipulating the system to place a case in the court perceived to have the most sympathetic judge for that type of case. Worse, a particular judge may be sympathetic to a particular lawyer because the lawyer bought a favorable hearing through donations to the judge's election campaign.

Second, the decentralization of the court system in Texas has drawn criticism as well. The system may have made sense in the nineteenth century, when the state lacked rapid or reliable communications. However, in the current era, many have argued that a simplified system would serve the needs of the citizens of Texas much better.

Since the enactment of the 1876 constitution that defined the current system, there have been periodic attempts to reform the structure of the court system and the election of judges. In the 1940s, much of the country, including Texas, began to examine a method of nominating and electing judges that has become known as the Missouri Plan. A conference held in 1964 identified problems with the court system in Texas without making specific proposals.[16] The attempt at constitutional revision in 1974 and 1975 (see Chapter 3) prompted renewed efforts to reform the structure of the court system, largely based on the work of the Texas Chief Justice's Task Force on Judicial Reform.[17] In 1990, the Texas Research League published an extensive report on the Texas judicial system.[18] All of the reports tend to have the same conclusion: the Texas court system needs to be reformed. All agree that overlapping jurisdictions produce confusion and the possibility of corruption. Many courts are overloaded, producing pressure for out-of-court settlements in civil suits and for plea bargains in criminal cases, which may be inappropriate and may result in justice not being served.

Reforming the Court Structure

Proposals for structural reform focus primarily on unifying the court system and simplifying the structure. The proposals generally follow the steps outlined here. (Figure 11.2 illustrates one such proposal.) First, municipal courts would have to be retained. Particularly for home-rule cities in Texas (see Chapter 12), a municipal court system would be imperative for the adjudication of charges that arise from the violation of city ordinances.

It is not clear, however, that all of the county courts need to be retained. The distinction between the constitutional county courts and the county courts at law does not need to be maintained; separate justice of the peace courts probably do not need to be maintained, either. The existing justice of the peace courts, constitutional county courts, county courts at law, and probate courts could be combined into one level of local trial courts of limited jurisdiction.

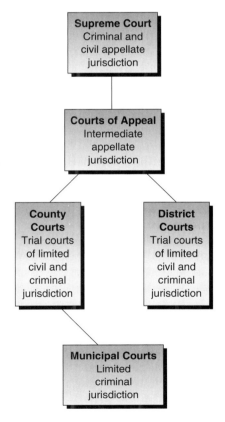

Figure 11.2   A Proposal for a Revised and Simplified Texas Judiciary
Note that the number and kinds of courts have been decreased and that there are fewer ways for a case to climb through the appeals process.

This new type of county court would have original criminal jurisdiction over all misdemeanors. The limits on original civil jurisdiction would have to be determined by the caseload. County courts might handle civil cases involving less than $5,000, for instance, while the higher district courts might handle civil cases in excess of that amount. The new county courts could be given magistrate duties, or a separate system of magistrates could be devised.

The district courts would be retained more or less as they now stand. They would have original criminal jurisdiction over all felonies and original civil jurisdiction over cases that involved amounts over the limit set as the maximum for the county courts. Both the county and district courts would retain their respective special jurisdictions, such as probate for the county courts and divorce for district courts. Also, as they do now, both county and district courts could specialize in those counties with multiple districts. For example, some district or county courts could be designated as criminal courts, with exclusive jurisdiction in criminal matters.

The courts of appeal would be left pretty much intact, although the geographic zones could be redrawn to equalize caseloads. The Houston area would be much better served by dividing the present single district into two districts. For those districts that are staffed by more than three justices, new districts could be created so that all districts have three justices.

The courts of appeal would have appellate jurisdiction over all criminal and civil cases. Whether to add appellate jurisdiction over capital cases—criminal cases involving the death penalty—to the courts of appeal is a debatable issue. Perhaps the Texas Court of Criminal Appeals was given exclusive appellate jurisdiction in capital cases as an indication of the importance of the issue. One could argue, however, that the gravity of the execution of a convicted person would be better served by the possibility of two reviews, first by a court of appeals and then by a supreme court. Automatic appeal to the next level could also be built into the system for capital cases.

Most proposals for reform of the court system in Texas call for the merger of the two supreme courts, the Texas Supreme Court and the Texas Court of Criminal Appeals, into one supreme court. Many point out that the United States court system works very well with one supreme court. However, the Texas Research League study argues that the two courts have never handled their caseloads very well.[19] As a result, there is no reason to believe that one court could do any better. On the other hand, a restructuring of the courts of appeals might make a one-supreme-court system work.

Many proposals for reform have been put forward over the years; none has been carried out. In most respects, the current court system is the same as that created in 1876. Many adjustments have been made to the system over the years, but the basic structure of a highly decentralized, locally controlled system remains. Every study of the court system in Texas has resulted in a call for reform, but the current structure is the product of a statutory constitution. Therefore, any fundamental change in the court structure is going to require constitutional amendment or constitutional revision.

Constitutional amendments must be voted on by the people of the state of Texas. The issues involved in the court system in Texas are rather abstract and obscure to most voters. Although plagued by many problems, the court system has not undergone a serious enough scandal in its operations to arouse people from their complacency. Not even the growing concern with crime in the past several years has produced a call for reform of the court system. For a period of creedal passion to occur, the gap between the ideals and the existing institutions must produce a period of moralism. Perhaps only if the crime rate and the court system can be sufficiently linked will a period of creedal passion be engendered.

Judges and Judicial Selection

The people responsible for dispensing justice within the court system are lawyers and judges. Judges in Texas have been the subject of much discussion as to their qualifications because of such episodes as the controversy surrounding the election of Steve Mansfield, described at the beginning of this chapter. Many of those discussions have paralleled movements to reform the court structure. Indeed, the selection of judges in Texas has generally created more interest among the general public than has the court structure but without yet producing a wave of creedal passion. This section focuses on the qualifications required of the various judges in Texas (Table 11.1) and the various methods by which judges are selected in Texas. Attention is directed to the rationale for the three basic methods of judicial selection and the efficacy of those methods.

Judicial Qualities and Qualifications   The qualifications for judges in Texas are not strict in most cases. For some positions, no more legal experience than being a qualified voter or "well informed in the law" is necessary. Evidently, anyone who can get elected to the office is "well informed in the law." For other positions, as with county courts at law, judges must be practicing attorneys. It is not clear whether a person can rise to the top courts in Texas without being a licensed attorney or having practiced law. However, if a person could serve as a municipal court of record judge for four years (such as for an El Paso municipal court), then serve as a district judge for at least six years and otherwise be qualified, then it appears that the person could serve on an appellate court.

Concern over the qualifications of judges has engendered many discussions of the method of selection of judges in Texas. Does the current method of selection produce a gap between the institutions and the ideals? Answering this question requires an understanding of the characteristics that a judge is expected to display:

1. **Independence** of outside pressures on the courtroom—judges are supposed to adjudicate cases on the basis of the law, not on the basis of outside concerns, such as public opinion, the media, or the preferences of public officials
2. **Accountability** for their actions on the bench

Table 11.1   JUDICIAL QUALIFICATIONS

Court	Term of office	Salary, 1998	Qualifications
Municipal courts	2 or 4 years, varies by city	Set by city, highly variable	Determined by the city
Justice of the Peace courts	4 years	Set by county, highly variable	None
Constitutional county court	4 years	Set by county, highly variable	Must be "well informed in the law"
County courts at law	4 years	Set by county, highly variable	25 years of age, county resident for 2 years, licensed attorney in Texas, served as judge or practiced law 4 years
District courts	4 years	$101,700, may be supplemented by the county	Citizen, district resident for 2 years, licensed attorney in Texas, practicing lawyer or judge for 4 years
Courts of appeal	6 years	Chief Justice: $107,850 Justices: $107,350, may be supplemented by counties in the district	Citizen, 35 years of age, practicing attorney or judge of a court of record for ten years
Texas Court of Criminal Appeals	6 years	Presiding judge: $115,000 Judges: $113,000	Same as courts of appeal
Texas Supreme Court	6 years	Chief Justice: $115,000 Associate Justices: $113,000	Same as courts of appeal

3. Sufficient **intellectual qualifications** for the job—in other words, judges should be knowledgeable of the law and the function they serve in the courtroom; judges are also expected to exercise judgment, in the sense that they should have both common sense and wisdom

The ideals of independence and accountability are contradictory. If the independence of a judge is increased, then the accountability is decreased, and vice versa. United States Supreme Court justices are given life tenure on the bench to enhance their independence, but life tenure establishes little accountability. A small-town judge, elected by people who know her or him personally, probably has high accountability but little independence. The selection method should ideally try to focus on at least one of these qualities.

Emphasizing Accountability: Judicial Elections   All judges, with the exception of some municipal court judges appointed by city councils and those appointed to fill vacancies, are elected by partisan ballot in Texas. **Partisan elections** are those in which people are identified on the ballot by partisan affiliation. An individual runs as a Democrat, a Republican, a Libertarian, or a member of another political party. Elections are designed to emphasize accountability. In a democratic society, the ultimate accountability comes through elections. Public servants can be held directly responsible for their actions by the voters.

Some observers of and participants in the Texas judicial system criticize partisan elections for a number of reasons. For an electoral system to function effectively, voters need to deliberate on the issues and the candidates (see Chapter 1). Effective deliberation requires that voters have complete information concerning the candidates and issues. The level of information that exists on candidates in judicial elections is usually sparse, to say the least. Many voters are only vaguely aware of the candidates, if at all. In 1999, the legislature passed legislation that would authorize the Secretary of State to publish information via the Internet on judicial candidates, but Governor George W. Bush vetoed the bill.

Consequently, the election of the majority of judges in Texas depends either on party identification or name recognition. In other words, individuals are elected because they are a member of a particular party or because they have a name that is recognizable to the voters. Name recognition can be built through advertising, such as the 10- to 30-second television spots that do little more than put the person's name on the screen. It is a truism of politics, however, that a recognizable name will be voted on more often than a name that is not, other information being equal. Name recognition can also come through simply having a name that is easy to recognize or is familiar.

The election of judges because they are members of a particular party has engendered at least two proposals for reform of the current partisan system. One would be to elect judges on a nonpartisan basis. Candidates for judicial office would not be identified by party affiliation. There is precedent for such a method. Local elections for city councils and special district boards in Texas are conducted on a nonpartisan basis. **Nonpartisan elections** are a legacy of the progressive movement of the early 1900s. They are, of course, designed to remove the influence of party politics from the electoral process. However, as Chapter 4 discusses, the importance of parties has declined significantly since the populist era, and they no longer play the role they once did.

Making elections nonpartisan will not necessarily result in a greater level of information on the qualifications of the candidates. There is no reason to believe that press coverage will increase or that citizens will have a greater desire for information. Indeed, the logical result would be an even greater reliance on name recognition.

The second variation on elections would be to discount straight-ticket voting. Texas allows voters to cast a straight ticket. With one mark on the ballot, a person can vote for all the Republicans, all the Democrats, or even all the Libertarians. This would indicate that judicial contests are being decided by party identification. By not allowing straight-ticket voting in judicial contests people would be forced to vote for judges on a position-by-position basis. It is highly questionable whether this would somehow generate more information on the qualifications of those running for office. One could still vote for all of the candidates of a particular party. The logical result would be that turnout in those races would decline and that name recognition rather than party identification might be relied on more.

While the candidates in a judicial race are often obscure to most voters, the issues involved are often even more obscure. At the trial-court level, judges may run on a platform of law and order, but it is usually put in vague terms. Issues on a substantive level that often influence races for the city council or the state legislature rarely exist at the trial court level. Campaigns run on a platform to "reduce the court's docket," for instance, do not appeal to the public. The only real issue is the candidate's qualifications.

The appellate level, however, can have an issues debate of a sort. The Texas Supreme Court in recent years has been the subject of a battle between plaintiffs and defendants in civil suits. The Texas Trial Lawyers Association is a special interest group generally made up of lawyers who represent plaintiffs in lawsuits. Groups representing defendants have also tried to influence the outcome of judicial races. Through their individual members and PACs, both groups have contributed vast sums of money to judicial contests in recent years (see Chapter 5). This raises the specter of lawyers trying to influence judicial decision making through campaign contributions. This further raises the possibility of a lawyer shopping for a judge and perhaps "buying" one through campaign contributions.[20]

In 1987, a *60 Minutes* segment entitled "Is Justice for Sale?" reported on the $11 billion settlement in the Pennzoil lawsuit against Texaco, noting the cam-

In two segments, in 1987 and 1998, *60 Minutes* correspondent Mike Wallace asked, "Is Justice for Sale in Texas?" Many Texans feel that large campaign contributions from lawyers and parties who have cases pending before the Supreme Court create the perception of impropriety.

Source: Ben Sargent, *Austin American-Statesman.* By permission.

paign contributions of Joe Jamail, the principal lawyer for Pennzoil. The report documented unethical activities by several justices on the Texas Supreme Court, precipitating a movement to reform the court. Nevertheless, a 1998 report by Texans for Public Justice argued that candidates for the Texas Supreme Court still get a significant percentage of their campaign contributions from lawyers, law firms, and PACs representing litigants before the court. Seven Supreme Court justices elected since 1994 raised more than $9 million in contributions over $100 for their most recent reelection contests, and 40 percent of those contributions were from lawyers and parties that had official business on the court's docket between 1994 and 1997. The report concluded that Supreme Court justices " . . . continue to sully the court's reputation by raising millions of dollars from parties and lawyers who have business before the court."[21] On November 1, 1998, *60 Minutes* provided an update on justice in Texas, citing evidence from the Texans for Public Justice report and calling for judicial reform in Texas.[22]

The relationship between money and politics, especially the direction of the relationship, is difficult to discern. In the realm of judicial politics the possible relationships can be characterized as follows: Do lawyers contribute to the campaign of a particular judge because:

1. They wish to use the influence that money can buy to get a judge to vote a certain way?
2. The judge has demonstrated a record for voting or ruling for one side or the other?
3. Based on what they know about the judge, they believe the judge will display a favorable record if elected?

In other words, do votes follow the money, or does the money follow the votes? Does a judge on a supreme court vote in a certain way because of campaign contributions, or are the contributions made because the judge voted in a certain way? Of course, except in cases of flagrant bribery, it is impossible to determine the answer.

Still, it is a troubling issue. Elections are supposed to ensure accountability, but accountability to whom and for what? At least to some extent, it is expected that executives and legislators would cater to special interest groups. At the very least, it is not surprising to discover that they have done so. Nonetheless, when the judiciary does so, it is taken as unseemly. This is the nightmare of judicial accountability. While the judiciary is supposed to be accountable for its actions, it is also supposed to adjudicate cases based on the law, not on political or personal whim.

Emphasizing Independence: Judicial Appointment Selecting judges through some **appointment** process generally stresses the independence of judges. As noted previously, some municipal court judges are appointed by city councils. Appointment systems usually follow the pattern in which an executive nominates individuals, who are then confirmed by a legislative body. The United States judiciary provides a classic example. The U.S. president nominates individuals for the national judiciary. The U.S. Senate must then confirm the appointment. If Texas were to adopt such a system, state judges (appellate and district) could be nominated by the governor and then confirmed by the Senate. County judges could be appointed by the commissioners' court.

One could question how much independence is gained from the appointment process. On the one hand, appointment frees the prospective judge from campaigning for office and particularly from the onus of seeking campaign funds. On the other hand, the prospective judge must be politically shrewd enough to receive a nomination and a confirmation. Surely, they must face some political pressure to conform to the wishes of the executive who nominated them and to those of the confirmation body.

The president of the United States no doubt nominates people who meet the president's standards of ideology and perhaps judicial philosophy. The Senate of the United States, particularly with Supreme Court nominees, often displays a concern with a candidate's ideology or judicial philosophy. We could expect the same of the governor and Senate of Texas.

The degree of independence of a judge is a function of what happens after the nomination and confirmation. At the national level, for example, federal judges are given life tenure, under conditions of "good behavior." Only resignation, death, or impeachment and removal can separate a person from a federal judgeship. However, if a judge has a fixed term in office after nomination and confirmation, as is common in many states, then independence is somewhat reduced by the prospect of facing renomination and reconfirmation. This can be mitigated by the prospect of going through the process with a different set of individuals at the end of the term. This would, of course, depend on the length of the term in office and the reelection success of those who previously nominated and confirmed the judge.

Introducing Quality: The Missouri Plan   Election and appointment emphasize accountability and independence, respectively. Neither of the two methods of selection addresses the issue of quality. Election may result in the best politician, not necessarily the best judge, being put on the bench. Appointment may result in having the friends of the governor become judges—again, not necessarily the best qualified persons for the job. The concern over quality led to the creation of the **Missouri Plan,** a type of merit plan. In 1940, Missouri became the first state to adopt such a plan. As a result, the term *Missouri Plan* has become almost synonymous with a merit-selection plan. As of 1995, 12 states had adopted some type of Missouri Plan. There are almost as many variations on the plan as there are states that have adopted it. However, all such plans have three basic features in common:

1. A judicial selection commission
2. Appointment
3. Retention elections

Judicial-selection commissions are designed to introduce the ideal of quality into the selection process. Commissions are typically made up of one-third lawyers, one-third judges, and one-third laypersons, anyone who is neither a lawyer nor a judge. Some states also include a dean of a law school in the state and the chief justice of the supreme court. The purpose of the judicial-selection commission is to identify the best qualified individuals for the job. Ideally, the commission would do this without regard to factors other than the person's legal credentials, experience, and record. Typically, judicial-selection commissions are required to submit a list of three candidates at the end of the search.

Judicial-selection commissions have often been accused of replacing more straightforward party and electoral politics with the politics of the state's bar association.[23] After all, two-thirds of the commission is made up of lawyers. It is true that most judges are lawyers. One could argue, however, that judges have a perspective different from lawyers. Judges perform a different function than lawyers do in the American legal system. Judicial-selection commissions have drawn criticism for being extensions of the governor. The members of the commission must be chosen by some method. Typically, the governor selects the members of the commission. To the extent that the governor chooses individuals with the same ideology or judicial philosophy that the governor has, the commission may submit candidates that are no different from what the governor would have chosen. That can be mitigated by allowing persons other than the governor to pick commission members. In Texas, the lieutenant governor and the speaker of the House could be allowed to place individuals on the commission. The commissioners could also be given staggered terms that are longer than the term of the governor.

The judicial-selection commission submits a list of names to the official, who will then make an appointment. Typically, this official would be the governor. The governor would then nominate one person from that list for the vacancy. At that point, the nomination could go to the legislature for confirmation. After serving for a year or two, the judge would then face a retention election—basically a referendum on the judge with no other name on the ballot. Voters simply vote to retain the judge in office or to remove her or him. If retained, the judge would then serve a term of longer duration or even be given life tenure. If rejected, the process would start over again with the judicial-selection commission.

The Missouri Plan was designed to meet the characteristics of accountability, independence, and—most important—quality. The Missouri Plan was designed to produce better judges than either election or appointment. An examination of the Missouri Plan convinces most people that it will produce better judges. It is supposed to, and it should, but does it? There is no evidence that the method by which judges are selected correlates with the quality of judges. In other words, no definitive relationship can be found between whether a judge is doing a good job or a bad job and the method by which he or she was chosen. All methods seemingly produce a few outstanding judges, many very good judges, and a few bad ones.[24] Why does it not matter? The answer is unclear. One possible explanation is that regardless of the method of selection, the applicant pool is roughly the same. Certainly, people who would run for an office would allow themselves to be appointed to that position or to be selected by a commission. In other words, regardless of the method of selection, the process involves choosing from essentially the same pool of people.

Which Method Should It Be?   If it makes no difference how judges are selected, then what should be the preferred method? Perhaps a simple appointment system should be because it is the cheapest and easiest. However, the traditional characteristics of accountability, independence, and quality are not the only possible aims of a method of selection.

The election system in Texas has drawn criticism because of the lack of minority judges. African Americans and Hispanics are not represented on the bench in proportion to their numbers in society. Judges for courts of appeal, district courts, and county courts at law are elected in district-wide, at-large elections. For courts of appeal, the state is divided into 13 different geographic regions. All of the judges for each of the districts are elected by the voters in that district. District and county court-at-law judges are elected on a countywide basis. In large, urban counties the ballot may have more than 50 judicial contests on it.

At-large elections can produce results that may be discriminatory in nature. In *Rangel v. Mattox* and *LULAC v. Clements,* both 1988 cases, the plaintiffs argued that the at-large system results in minorities being underrepresented in the courts as judges and the system was thus a violation of the 1965 Voting Rights Act. One of the court-of-appeals districts in South Texas covers 20 counties and was 56 percent Hispanic in 1988. However, only one of the six elected judges was Hispanic. The solution that has been proposed is to go to a single-member district system. See Chapter 12 for a discussion of at-large vs. single-district systems for city council elections.

The question of minority representation raises a number of issues. In a district that is 56 percent minority, the problem is not discrimination in the sense that individuals are legally prohibited from voting or running for office because of racial or ethnic affiliation. Under those circumstances, low voter turnout among minorities is the problem, although low voter turnout may be the legacy of past discrimination. However, there are districts and counties that have substantial numbers of ethnic minorities—even close to 50 percent—that do not constitute a majority. If votes are cast along racial or ethnic lines, then minorities may have no representation on the bench. The problem, however, may be the lack of candidates rather than the lack of voters. Delbert Taebel has found that in urban counties in Texas, voters in general elections "vote consistently and overwhelmingly along party lines" without regard to race.[25] However, party affiliation does seem to be more polarized along racial and ethnic lines. That is, Anglos seem to be moving toward overwhelming support of the Republican Party, while African Americans and Hispanics still tend toward overwhelming support of the Democratic Party (see Chapter 4).

Critical Thinking Exercises: Given the previous discussion of the court system, how would you restructure the system to make it more efficient and why? Speculate further about the possible reasons for the method of selection of judges not being correlated to performance on the bench.

THE CRIMINAL JUSTICE SYSTEM

The approach to criminal justice systems in the United States consists of three basic parts:

1. Law enforcement and prosecution
2. The court system
3. The correctional system

Law-enforcement officials are responsible for the apprehension of suspects in a crime. Public prosecutors are responsible for securing a conviction of those accused of a crime through either a trial or a plea bargain. After the court system determines guilt or innocence, the correctional system enforces any required acts, such as punishment or psychiatric treatment, on convicted offenders.

Enforcing the Law: The Police, Sheriffs, Highway Patrol, and Texas Rangers

Law enforcement, like the judicial system in Texas, is highly decentralized. For most Texans, the primary provider of law enforcement or police protection is a city police department. City police departments are responsible for enforcing city ordinances, state laws, and national laws within the city's limits. For those Texans who live outside a city's limits the primary provider of law enforcement is the county sheriff's department. (See Chapter 12 for more discussion of city and county law enforcement.) The Texas Department of Public Safety (DPS) provides law enforcement and police protection on the state's highways. The Texas Rangers, a unit of the DPS, acts as the state's investigations department.

Representing the People: Prosecuting Crimes

The prosecution of crimes is also highly decentralized. County attorneys and district attorneys are responsible for the prosecution of criminal defendants. These attorneys are elected and serve either a county or a multicounty district. County attorneys are attached to the county court system and usually prosecute misdemeanors. District attorneys are attached to district courts and usually prosecute felonies. There is no centralized prosecutor's office in Texas. At the national level, the United States attorney general is the chief prosecutor for the nation. Texas has no such counterpart. The attorney general of Texas is not responsible for criminal prosecutions (see Chapter 10).

Prosecution begins with either a bill of information or an indictment. A bill of information is issued for misdemeanor charges. A complaint may be filed by any competent person. A complaint is a statement swearing that a person has committed a particular offense. On the basis of the complaint the county or district attorney may then issue a bill of information formally charging the person with a misdemeanor offense.

Grand jury indictments may be used for misdemeanor offenses, but they rarely are. To charge a person with a felony, however, requires indictment by a grand jury. Grand juries are composed of 12 individuals either selected at random or by a judge from a list of names recommended by a grand jury commission. The grand jury's function is to determine whether enough evidence exists to charge a person with a crime, not to determine his or her guilt or innocence. Grand juries operate in secret. Although empowered to investigate all criminal matters, they usually deal only with felonies. Grand juries rely heavily on the evidence presented to them by the county or district attorney. After presentation of evidence and deliberation, the grand jury may return either a true bill (an indictment) or a no bill (failure to indict).

If charged with a misdemeanor or felony offense, a person has a right to trial by a jury. The right to a jury trial is often waived either by pleading guilty to the offense, by pleading guilty to a lesser offense (plea bargaining), or by submitting to trial by the judge, who then acts as both judge and jury. Misdemeanor offenses require a 6-person jury, while felony trials require a 12-person jury. In either case, a guilty verdict requires a unanimous decision by the jury.

All jurors serving on either grand juries or trial juries must meet the same qualifications. A juror in Texas must be (a) a citizen of the United States and the state of Texas; (b) at least 18 years of age; (c) of sound mind; (d) able to read and write, unless literate jurors are unavailable; and (e) neither convicted of a felony, nor under indictment or accusation of theft or a felony.

A venire (jury panel) is chosen at random from a county's list of registered voters, licensed drivers, and Department of Public Safety identification card holders. From the venire, a **petit (trial) jury** is chosen by the prosecution and the defense. Either side may dismiss a potential juror by a peremptory challenge or a challenge for cause. A peremptory challenge is one in which no reason has to be given for dismissing a potential juror. In a capital felony case each side has up to 15 peremptory challenges, in other felony cases up to 10, and in misdemeanor cases up to 5. Challenges for cause have no limits set on the number, but reasons must be given for the challenge. The presiding judge in the case then decides whether to dismiss the juror.

The Fulfillment of Justice: The Correctional System

The correctional system in Texas—and across the United States—has long been the subject of much controversy. Indeed, it has evolved a great deal since Texas became a state, most of all during this century. Many of the controversies surrounding correctional systems have remained fairly consistent. Historically, correctional systems have placed emphasis on two objectives:

1. *Retribution.* Underlying **retribution** is the basic idea that a person who harms another in some way should be punished for the act of inflicting harm. Retribution can be summed up with the Biblical quote, "an eye for

an eye, a tooth for a tooth." Retribution also implies that only the guilty should be punished. The notion of "innocent until proven guilty" has part of its justification in the objective of retribution.

2. *Rehabilitation.* **Rehabilitation** implies that a crime has been committed for a reason that is correctable in some sense. Therefore, criminals can be made into productive citizens with the proper rehabilitative measures, such as job training or drug counseling.

The emphasis that a correctional system places on retribution or rehabilitation affects the way crime and criminals are treated. That emphasis is a reflection of the ideologies affecting public policy. Both liberals and libertarians place an emphasis on liberty and personal freedom over order and the formal and legal restraint of society over human behavior. Therefore, they are more likely to favor lighter sentences and alternative sentencing programs, which are programs other than incarceration in a state prison. Examples include drug-rehabilitation programs, supervised probation, house arrest, and electronic monitoring of persons subject to house arrest. Because liberals and libertarians tend to regard human nature as basically good, they also tend to place more emphasis on rehabilitation. Conservatives and populists, on the other hand, emphasize order over liberty. Therefore, they tend to stress retribution rather than rehabilitation.

The Adult Corrections System   The Board of Criminal Justice oversees the criminal justice system. The correctional part of the criminal justice system in Texas is administered by the Division of Corrections, a part of the Department of Criminal Justice. It is responsible for the prison system and for probation and parole. Texas uses a graded system of penalties to define the seriousness of a crime. There are two basic groups: misdemeanors and felonies. Misdemeanors are considered minor crimes, while felonies are considered the more serious crimes. Examples of the types of offenses and the penalties attached to them can be found in Table 11.2.

Notice that there is rather wide discretion in the amounts of fines and the lengths of jail sentences that may be imposed. Why give judges and juries discretion in the matter of fines and sentences? The administration of justice tries to take account of individual circumstances, both good and bad. One of the ideals of the American Creed is that of individualism. As such, the political process should take into account individual preferences. That belief is extended to the criminal justice system through the notion of taking individual circumstances, or what is usually referred to as mitigating circumstances, into account when assessing penalties.

Once convicted, a criminal may receive probation, be incarcerated, and/or be fined. Probation means that the offender will not be sent to prison but will be put under some type of supervision. The supervision may range from (a) nothing more than being required not to commit another crime as a condition of staying out of jail to (b) house arrest. Incarceration may take place in a county jail, a state jail, or a state prison. If the sentence is less than one year, it will usually be served in a county jail. If the sentence is one year or longer, then it is usually served in a state prison. State jails were created in 1993 to house nonviolent offenders convicted of state jail felonies. Although conviction of a state jail felony technically

Table 11.2   THE TEXAS SYSTEM OF GRADED PENALTIES

Offense	Maximum punishment	Examples
Capital felony	Execution	Capital murder
First-degree felony	5–99 years or life; $10,000 fine	Aggravated sexual assault; theft of property valued at $200,000 or more
Second-degree felony	2–20 years; $10,000 fine	Tampering with a consumer product; theft of property valued at $100,000 or more but less than $200,000
Third-degree felony	2–10 years; $10,000 fine	Drive-by shooting without injury; theft of property valued at $20,000 or more but less than $100,000
State jail felony	180 days to 2 years; $10,000 fine	Credit card or debit card abuse; theft of property valued at $1,500 or more but less than $20,000
Class A misdemeanor	1 year; $4,000 fine	Burglary of a vehicle; abuse of a corpse; theft of property valued at $500 or more but less than $1,500
Class B misdemeanor	180 days; $2,000 fine	Silent or abusive calls to a 911 service; prostitution; theft of property valued at more than $20 but less than $500
Class C misdemeanor	$500 fine	Assault without bodily injury; attending a dog fight; theft of property valued at less than $20

does not carry with it a prison sentence, judges may order up to one year of incarceration as a condition of probation.

The prison system in Texas had been under scrutiny for some time. In 1971, David Ruiz, a prisoner, filed the court case of *Ruiz v. Estelle* in U.S. District Court in Tyler. Ruiz alleged that the Texas prison system violated the Eighth Amendment to the United States Constitution's prohibitions against cruel and unusual punishment. The major complaints in the *Ruiz* case were overcrowded conditions and the lack of medical care. In particular, Ruiz was concerned with the practice of putting two or more inmates in a cell designed for one person. The Supreme Court of the United States agreed with Ruiz. *Ruiz v. Estelle* started a 20-year controversy over the prison system in Texas.

The U.S. court system eventually took over the prison system in Texas. Court control was not relinquished until 1994. The federal court mandated that Texas could not allow the number of inmates to exceed 95 percent of maximum capacity. As a result, over the course of several years, either new prisoners could not be admitted to the prison system, or existing prisoners had to be released early to allow new prisoners in. Not allowing new prisoners in meant that many county jails were overcrowded. As a result, many of those jails became the subjects of lawsuits. The problem became so acute at one point that counties successfully sued the state for reimbursement to those counties that held prisoners who would normally have been transferred to the state prisons. Releasing prisoners early led to individuals serving a fraction of the time they had been sentenced. At the same time, the number of crimes committed by persons who had been previously convicted of other crimes—called the recidivism rate—rose.

By the late 1980s and early 1990s, the state had launched a major prison construction program. While it has been popular to blame the U.S. courts for the overcrowding in Texas prisons, that is not quite fair. After all, the major complaint of the Ruiz case was overcrowding. Overcrowding existed long before the U.S. district court's intervention. There are at least five factors that have contributed to the problem over the years.

1. The population of Texas has continued to grow decade after decade, especially during the 1970s and 1980s. As population grows, so does the number of criminals. Even if the percentage of criminals remains the same, as the population grows, so does the number of criminals.

2. Texas is also a relatively young state. The average age of Texans is below that of the national average. This means that Texas has a fairly substantial number of young males, the group most responsible for crime. Crime statistics are clearly correlated with the number of 18- to 30-year-old males in a given area. If that group goes up in number, then crime goes up. If that group goes down in number, then crime goes down.

3. Texas has engaged in renewed emphasis on retribution rather than rehabilitation. Although overall crime rates have actually declined in the United States in the past decade or so, the incidence of violent crime went up for a number of years. This produced a "lock 'em up and throw away the key" mentality on the part of many in the general public.

4. During the 1980s, the Reagan administration declared a war on drugs. Penalties for buying, selling, and using drugs were increased at the national level. Many states, including Texas, followed the pattern, resulting in more people being sentenced to prison for longer terms for drug offenses.

5. Perhaps the most important reason for overcrowding in Texas prisons was the response of the state to the looming crisis. Basically, the response was to ignore the problem. During Bill Clements's first term in office (1977–1981) and Mark White's term (1981–1987), the State of Texas refused to build any new prisons. By ignoring the problem when it was still manageable, the problem only grew worse.

The U.S. courts may have made a bad problem worse, but they certainly did not invent it.

In response to the problem of overcrowding, Texas launched a major prison-building program. The $2.3 billion building program almost tripled prison capacity over a four-year period. By 1995, the state had approximately a 145,000-bed capacity, compared to only 50,000 in 1990. Approximately 97,000 of the beds are in prisons that will increasingly be reserved for violent and repeat offenders. About 13,000 beds are in transfer and detention facilities used primarily as holding facilities for prisoners awaiting transfer to a state prison.

The $2.3 building program resulted in many new prisons for Texas, such as the one pictured above.

Approximately 10,000 beds are devoted to substance-abuse felony treatment centers, used primarily by first-time offenders with severe drug and/or alcohol problems. About 25,000 beds are devoted to the state jails. The building program has been expensive. The state issued bonds to fund the new facilities, so both principal and interest will have to be paid.[26] Operating the correctional system costs approximately $40 per prisoner per day.

The Juvenile Corrections System   Juvenile justice has undergone tremendous changes in the past couple of decades. A system that was originally designed to handle juvenile delinquency is increasingly asked to deal with what are at least perceived to be hard-core criminals. While overall crime rates, including violent crime rates, have declined recently, violent crime rates committed by youths have escalated in the past few years. The state has tried to respond to this trend in a variety of ways.

One of the responses has been to lower the age at which a juvenile can be tried as an adult. Under the original juvenile justice system, anyone under age 18 years was considered a juvenile and was treated as such, regardless of the crime committed. Rather than a system for the punishment of juvenile offenders, the system served as a mechanism for giving juvenile offenders a second chance. However, as the incidence of violent and repeat offenders has risen, and as the nature of the crimes committed by juveniles has changed to more closely resemble those committed by adults, calls for reform have been made. One of the changes has been to certify many juveniles as adults. This means that a juvenile will be treated as an adult for the purpose of trial and sentencing. The age at which a juvenile may be certified as an adult by a judge was lowered to 14 years in 1995.

Another of the responses to juvenile crime has been passage of the Determinate Sentencing Act. Under the original juvenile justice system, juvenile records were sealed or destroyed upon the eighteenth birthday of the offender. Upon reaching the age of 18, the juvenile received a chance to start over. The assumption was made that youths could not be held accountable for their crimes.

The juvenile justice system clearly reflected a belief in rehabilitation as its primary objective. The incidence of repeat and violent offenders has convinced many in both the adult and the juvenile systems that rehabilitation is a failure. There is also a perception among juveniles that they can do anything they want until they reach age 18. At that time, they can start over with a clean record.

The Determinate Sentencing Act allows the criminal justice system to retain custody of a person for up to 40 years after being convicted of a crime. Upon reaching the age of 18, a juvenile can be transferred to the adult system. The cumulative length of time spent in both systems cannot exceed 40 years. The act has drawn some criticism because it is quite possible for a juvenile ultimately to spend a considerably longer amount of time in the system than an adult who committed the same crime.

In 1999, the legislature responded to gang activity in Texas by passage of a number of laws. The Texas Department of Public safety is now required to maintain a statewide criminal street gang database in accordance with federal law. The Office of the Attorney General is now required to maintain an electronic database that compiles information on street gangs, such as colors and recruiting efforts. Only law enforcement officials have access to the database. It is a criminal offense to coerce or solicit a child to participate in gang activity. It is also a criminal offense to recruit members for a gang if commission of a felony is required for membership.

Critical Thinking Exercise: Given your political ideology, should retribution or rehabilitation be the basis of the correctional system in Texas? Explain why you would emphasize one rather than the other.

THE COURTS, CRIMINAL JUSTICE, AND POLITICAL CHANGE

The judicial system in Texas is in most ways the same now as when it was constructed in 1876. The state legislature has changed the judicial system in a piecemeal fashion, with the legislature creating more trial courts and courts of appeal in an effort to meet the rising caseload. The incidence of overlapping jurisdictions, combined with problems in the election of judges, has raised questions in the media and the academic community about the integrity of the system. The greatest chance for reform probably came during the 1970s when the constitutional reform effort was underway. Like the numerous previous attempts, however, the effort failed. The ideals of the judicial system are difficult to articulate to the general public. It is, therefore, difficult for the public to perceive the gap between the ideals and the institutions. In spite of the problems of the court system in Texas, no period of creedal passion has developed that would change it.

Just as there have been repeated calls for reform of the court system in Texas, there have been calls for a change in the method of selecting judges. Again, the press and the academic community have been the primary instigators of such calls. They have also been joined by prominent politicians from time to time. John Hill, former attorney general, resigned from his seat on the Texas Supreme Court to campaign for the adoption of a Missouri Plan for Texas. In spite of these strong efforts, attempts at changing the method of selecting judges in Texas have also failed.

A democratic political system responds to demands from the public, especially when those demands are overwhelming. There has been a fairly remarkable shift in the criminal justice system in the past few years. The adult system, never really having embraced rehabilitation as its primary objective, reflects an even greater emphasis on retribution. The rise in violent crimes has created a public call for protection. The American and Texan Creeds can only be pursued in a society that is relatively peaceful. The creeds also demand that individuals respect the rights of others, at least in the minimal sense of not interfering with or harming others. A breakdown in law and order threatens the level of respect that is needed for the ideals to flourish.

The juvenile justice system has undergone an even greater change than the adult system. The reasons for the changes in both systems are essentially the same. The primary objective of the juvenile justice system was originally the rehabilitation of youths. The response to the rising rate of violent crime among youths has produced calls for more adult treatment of juvenile offenders. This is also a response to the threat posed by the perceived breakdown of law and order. The changes in the adult and juvenile justice systems have not occurred during a period of creedal passion in the sense that the changes have closed the gap between the ideals and the institutions, as much as they have been a response to a perceived threat to those ideals.

> **Critical Thinking Exercise:**   The juvenile system used to emphasize the objective of rehabilitation. There is a noticeable shift to retribution in the treatment of juveniles. Is that shift justified and on what basis?

THE COURTS, CRIMINAL JUSTICE, AND DEMOCRACY

Though people in Texas in particular and in the United States as a whole do not often associate the courts with democracy, people often pride themselves on the attention that is paid to individual rights and liberties. In many respects, the courts are the final arbiters and defenders of those rights. (See Chapter 13 for a discussion of civil rights and civil liberties in Texas.) The ideal of democracy has been served in Texas by the popular election of judges. However, it is unclear whether the election of judges meets the conditions of democracy or serves justice, or whether it should attempt to do both at the same time.

Deliberation over the qualifications of those running for judicial office is virtually nonexistent. Deliberation is hampered by the lack of information available on the candidates. The issues involved in judicial elections are little understood by the citizens and are usually given little attention by the press. Thus, judicial elections tend to be won on party affiliation and name recognition rather than on qualifications. This was the case with the election of Steve Mansfield to the Texas Court of Criminal Appeals in 1994 and in the election of other judges in 1996 and 1998.[27]

The condition of nontyranny is satisfied in a formal sense, but judicial elections tend to suffer from low voter turnout. Even in statewide races, the number of people who vote for supreme court justices is usually considerably less than the number who vote for the governor. Turnout is even lower at the local level. Judicial elections may be controlled by a relatively small number of voters. That small number may, of course, constitute a special interest.

A criminal justice system has as its ultimate objective the preservation of society. The conditions for democracy are obtainable only in a society where respect exists for the rights of others. The punishment of those that do not respect the rights of others is a mechanism for trying to ensure those rights.

The condition of deliberation requires that people have access to complete information. It also requires that people be able to discuss and exchange ideas freely and without coercion. One of the aims of a criminal justice system is to help ensure a climate in which free discussion can take place. The condition of nontyranny requires that a majority not ignore the rights of the minority. In establishing criminal laws, the majority defines the behaviors that are abhorrent to society. In enforcing those laws, the criminal justice system must protect the rights of the minority—accused criminals—by ensuring that the criminal justice process is fair and equitable. The criminal justice system must balance the interests of the majority and the interests of the minority.

Critical Thinking Exercise: Ideally, judges are supposed to be free of the kind of political pressure that exists in a democracy. On the other hand, judges are supposed to serve the interests of democracy. How do you explain the contradiction?

SUMMARY

This chapter has examined the judicial system in Texas. The structure of the courts is fragmented and highly decentralized. While the system may have been adequately designed for rural, 1870s Texas, its current applicability to Texas has been questioned. In spite of repeated attempts at reform, the system is very similar to the way it looked when initially established. It is characterized by too many courts with too many overlapping jurisdictions.

The overlapping jurisdictions of courts and the election method of judge selection in Texas have created a number of perceived problems. Judges may be bought or at least heavily influenced by patrons and interest groups. The quality of judges has been questioned. As a result, there has been an ongoing debate in Texas concerning the method of selection of judges for some time. However, the evidence suggests that there is no correlation between the method of selection and the quality of a judge's performance.

The criminal justice system may be guided by one of two objectives: retribution or rehabilitation. The objective that is going to be paramount in the criminal justice system is a function of ideology. As a result of the emphasis placed on retribution and of the mistakes in the past, the prison system in Texas has experienced severe overcrowding problems. The overcrowding in the prisons has forced major changes in the way convicted individuals are handled by the system. Perhaps the biggest pressure for change has come from the rising incidence of violent crime among youths. Juvenile corrections have changed remarkably over the past 30 years.

KEY TERMS

common law	Texas Supreme Court
statutes	Texas Court of Criminal Appeals
ordinances	courts of last resort
administrative law	petition for review
criminal law	writs of error
civil law	writs of mandamus
torts	writ of *habeas corpus*
original jurisdiction	independence
appellate jurisdiction	accountability
municipal court	intellectual qualifications
justice of the peace courts	partisan election
county court	nonpartisan election
courts of record	appointment
de novo	Missouri Plan
district court	retribution
court of appeal	rehabilitation

SUGGESTED READINGS

Champagne, Anthony, and Judith Haydel, eds. *Judicial Reform in the States.* New York: University Press of America, 1993.

Davidow, Robert. "Judicial Selection: The Search for Quality and Representativeness," *Case Western Reserve Law Review* 31 (1981): 409–464.

Johnson, Orrin, and Laura J. Urbis. "Judicial Selection in Texas: A Gathering Storm?" *Texas Tech Law Review* 23 (1992): 525–569.

Taebel, Delbert A. "On the Way to Midland: Race or Partisanship? A Research Note on Comparative Voting in Urban Counties in Judicial Elections," *Texas Journal of Political Studies* 12 (Fall/Winter 1989–1990): 20–21.

Texas Research League. *Texas Courts: A Study by the Texas Research League,* 3 reports Austin, Tex.: Texas Research League, 1990–1992.

NOTES

1. Ben Wear, "State Judge Reprimanded for Lies from His Campaign," *Austin American-Statesman,* 15 July 1995, pp. B1–B2; Thomas Whatley, ed. *Texas Government Newsletter,* 3 July 1995, 1.

2. Stuart Eskenazi, "Dissed Robes," *Dallas Observer Online,* 18–24 November 1999. Accessed 18 November 1999, http://www.dallasobserver.com/issues/current/feature2.html.

3. The data on the courts in Texas were obtained from the Office of Court Administration, *Texas Judicial System, Annual Report* for the 1998 fiscal year, the latest information available at time of publication. The data obtained by the Office of Court Administration are dependent on the separate courts reporting to the office. Evidently, not all courts actually send a report in, so all numbers are approximate.

4. Ibid.

5. Ibid.

6. Ibid.

7. Ibid.

8. Ibid.

9. The qualifications for the two offices are not the same. Constitutional county judges only need to be "well informed in the law," while county court at law judges must be licensed attorneys. There is some question, then, as to the ability of a constitutional county judge to be a good judge. This issue is discussed later in this chapter.

10. Office of Court Administration data.

11. Ibid.

12. Ibid.

13. Ibid.

14. Ibid.

15. Ibid.

16. *Consensus Statements and Principal Addresses from the Texas Conference on Judicial Selection, Tenure and Administration,* Austin, Texas, 16–18 April 1964. Sponsored by the State Bar of Texas.

17. Texas Chief Justice's Task Force on Judicial Reform, *Justice at the Crossroads: Court Improvement in Texas,* Austin, Texas, 1972.

18. Texas Research League, *Texas Courts: A Study by the Texas Research League,* 3 Reports (Austin, Tex.: Texas Research League, 1990–1992).

19. Texas Research League, *Texas Courts: A Study by the Texas Research League,* Report 2 (Austin, Tex.: Texas Research League, 1991), 25–27.

20. See Sheila Kaplan, "The Very Best Judges That Money Can Buy," *U.S. News and World Report,* 29 November 1999, 35–36, reporting U.S. Supreme Court Justices Kennedy and Breyer discussing the dangers of the role that campaign money plays in judicial races.

21. Texans for Public Justice, "Payola Justice: How Supreme Court Justices Raise Money from Court Litigants." Conclusion, February 1998. Accessed 8 November 1998, http://www.tpj.org/reports/payola/conclusions.html.

22. See Osler McCarthy, "A Better Way to Choose Judges?" *Austin American-Statesman,* 8 November 1998, pp. J1, J6.

23. In order for a person to be allowed to practice law in a given state, a license must be obtained from the state bar. The bar is essentially an association of lawyers. The state bar exam must be passed, and dues must be maintained. The bar is then, essentially, a professional organization with certification powers.

24. Rex C. Peebles, "Good Judges and the Method of Selection," unpublished paper, 1987. See also Victor E. Flungo and Craig R. Ducat, "What Difference Does Method of Judicial Selection Make? Selection Procedures in State Courts of Last Resort," *Justice System Journal* 5 (1979): 20–46; and Jona Goldschmidt, "Merit Selection: Current Status, Procedures, and Issues," *University of Miami Law Review* 49 (Fall 1994): 1–126.

25. Delbert A. Taebel, "On the Way to Midland: Race or Partisanship: A Research Note on Comparative Voting in Urban Texas Counties in Judicial Elections," *Texas Journal of Political Studies* 12 (Fall/Winter 1989–1990): 20–21.

26. Thomas L. Whatley, ed., *Texas Government Newsletter,* 27 March 1995, 2.

27. See Stuart Eskenazi, "Dissed Robes," *The Dallas Observer Online*, 18–24 November 1999. Accessed 18 November 1999, http://www.dallasobserver.com/issues/current/feature2.html.

12

The Local Governments: Cities, Counties, and Special Districts

★ **Scenario: Local Government and Sports Arenas— Strange Bedfellows?**

People often consider that government is separate from their private lives. However, government at all levels is involved in your life. The connections be-tween the public and private sectors often take rather odd forms. One such form is the partnership that exists between cities and sports teams. Sports teams can bring prestige and tax dollars to a city, especially if the team is doing well. A winning team will generate greater attendance at games and, therefore, generate greater tax revenue from expenditures at the arena and at surrounding businesses.

The State of Texas and its cities have been involved in the construction of sports arenas for many years.[1] The legislature in 1989 approved a bill that would allow certain counties to form sports districts for the purpose of building new sports facilities. In the 1995 session, legislation was passed that would allow cities and counties or a combination of the two to designate sports venue districts. These districts can issue bonds to build sports venue projects, such as arenas or stadiums, once they have been approved by a local referendum. The project can then be funded through a variety of mechanisms, such as a half-cent sales tax and car rental, admissions, parking, and hotel occupancy taxes.

On November 2, 1999, the cities of San Antonio and Houston held referendums on the issue of building new sports arenas for the Spurs and the Rockets, respectively. The vote was expected to be close in both cities, but it actually turned out to be rather lopsided with voters approving the new arena in San Antonio and rejecting it in Houston by convincing margins. Approximately 60 percent of voters approved the referendum in San Antonio, while approximately 55 percent rejected the referendum in Houston.

The San Antonio Spurs play in the six-year-old Alamodome, an arena originally designed for football. In spite of winning the NBA Championship in 1999, the Spurs organization argued that they needed a new arena to be profitable. A new arena would give them a smaller venue with skyboxes closer to the court. The Spurs had said that they would have to consider moving to another city without a new arena. Tim Duncan, the Spurs superstar, had also let it be known that the vote would be a consideration in his decision to re-sign with the Spurs.

The Alamodome was designed for football rather than basketball. The San Antonio Spurs will soon play in a new arena, which will be funded primarily through taxes on rental vehicles and hotel and motel rooms.

The Spurs new arena will be built east of downtown and seat 18,500 people. Construction will cost approximately $175 million, only $28 million of which will be paid by the team. The rest will be financed from higher car rental and hotel and motel taxes. Houston also planned to build an 18,500 seat arena that Rockets owner Les Alexander intended to lease for 30 years. He also planned on moving his WNBA Comets and arena football Thunderbears teams into the new venue. The cost would have been approximately $160 million, half to come from Alexander and half from the Harris County-Houston Sports Authority. The Authority is a special district that controls the money from car rental and hotel-motel tax increases approved by voters in Houston in 1996. The Authority also would have controlled ticket and parking taxes at the new arena.

The propositions before the voters in San Antonio and Houston were similar in size and cost. The private share of the cost of the arena was much higher in Houston than in San Antonio. Both cities argued that the public share of the costs would be primarily borne by tourists and other visitors to the city. Other public financing would have come from those that used the arena. Taebel, Hissong, and Daniel have demonstrated that public financing of sports venues can be successfully "sold" to the voters when they feel that someone else is going to pay for it.[2]

What accounts for the success of San Antonio and the failure of Houston? Many consider subsidizing sports venues with public money welfare for the rich, or corporate welfare. Ironically, the public share in Houston would have been much smaller than the share will be in San Antonio. Both were able to demonstrate that most, if not all, of the public funding would come from visitors and those that actually used the arena. No general revenue funds would be spent to build the arenas. Houston had even created a special purpose government whose sole purpose was to handle the public financing of the project. In the final analysis, perhaps a nonpolitical issue made the difference: San Antonio had produced an NBA Champion that year and Houston had not. ★

INTRODUCTION

On a day-to-day basis, people are more likely to come into contact with local government than any other type or level. If a person's home is on fire, there is no one in the national or state government to contact. Fire protection is a local function, either through a local government, a volunteer fire company, or—as is sometimes the case in Texas—a joint public-private effort. Police protection, garbage collection, and water and sewer services are local government functions. Education, too, is largely locally governed. The independent school districts (ISDs) most people are familiar with are local governments. Even community colleges, one of the fastest-growing segments of higher education, are local governments. Local government is the level of government that is the closest to most people, and strong local government can provide opportunities for democracy that exceed those possible at the state or national level.

In spite of these facts, local government remains somewhat of a mystery to many people. Participation rates are lower for local elections than for state or

Te★as*Index*

Local Governments in the States

States ranked by degree of authority granted to local governments:
Texas: Composite, 11; city, 1; county, 43
California: Composite, 18; city, 17; county, 17
New York: Composite, 35; city, 44; county, 25
Florida: composite, 26; city, 30; county 14

Number of local governments, 1997:

Total:
Texas—4700
California—4607
New York—3413
Florida—1081

Counties:
Texas—254
California—57
New York—57
Florida—66

Municipalities:
Texas—1177
California—471
New York—1544
Florida—394

School Districts:
Texas—1043
California—999
New York—706
Florida—67

Other Special Districts:
Texas—2182
California—3010
New York—1126
Florida—526

Residential property tax rates per $100 of valuation, 1996:
Houston, Texas: $2.61
Los Angeles, California: $1.05
New York City, New York: $10.73
Jacksonville, Florida: $1.11

national elections. Indeed, many people are unaware of the types of responsibilities of local governments in Texas. This chapter discusses the three basic types of local governments in Texas: cities, counties, and special districts. Novel solutions to governmental problems, including bodies that help other units of government work together (for example, councils of government and metrogovernment) are also covered.

CITIES

As of 1999, there were 1197 incorporated areas or cities in Texas, all of which received a charter of incorporation from the state to operate as a municipality known as **municipal incorporation.** A charter is the constitution of a city, defining its fundamental structures and processes. To receive a charter, a majority of the residents of a geographically designated area with at least 200 people must approve the incorporation.

The Types of Cities

There are two basic types of city in Texas: general law and home rule. An area of 5000 or less in population may only incorporate as a general-law city, but an area of more than 5000 in population may choose to incorporate as a home-rule city instead. We first consider general-law cities.

A **general-law city** operates under the general laws of the State of Texas. In other words, the city may only do what the State of Texas allows it to do. While they are fairly restricted by the state charter, they often provide basic services, such as police, fire protection, and water and sewer service. About 80 percent of all Texas cities have general-law charters, almost all of which have fewer than 5000 residents.

There are at least two reasons to incorporate. First of all, such services as police, fire protection, and water and sewer service are basic, but they are not unimportant. Second, an area may choose to incorporate to avoid annexation by another city (see "How Cities Grow" later in this chapter).

Home-rule cities, on the other hand, have much more discretion, giving them a great deal of local control. Home-rule cities may do almost whatever they wish unless prohibited by the state or national governments. Just as the national government restricts state activity to some extent, the State of Texas places some restrictions on home-rule cities. For example, cities may not levy a property tax rate higher than $2.50 per $100 of evaluation. Approximately 20 percent of the cities in Texas are home rule, and all large cities in the state have home-rule status.

A home-rule charter is not automatic, however. A city that has initially incorporated as a general-law city may adopt a home-rule charter when its population exceeds 5000 if a simple majority of the city's voters approve the change in the city's charter. Further, if the population falls below 5000, a home-rule city does not automatically become a general-law city.

The Forms of City Government

Once the decision has been made to incorporate a particular area, the voters in that area must decide on the form of government for the city.[3] The state legislature determines the various forms of government for the cities to choose from. There are three basic forms of city government in Texas:

1. Mayor-council
2. Council-manager
3. Commission

The city may also modify these three forms of city government to suit local needs and preferences, and it may create citizen advisory boards, which are one of the most common ways for municipal governments to obtain advice and guidance.

Mayor-Council Cities   The most frequently occurring form of city government in Texas is the **mayor-council.** It is also traditionally the most frequent in other states. Approximately 20 percent of the 307 home-rule cities and virtually all of the general-law cities use the mayor-council form, which is patterned after the national government and most state governments. The president or governor (or mayor) acts as the chief executive officer of the government and has powers to check the legislative branch, or **city council,** which can itself check the powers of the executive branch.

There are two types of mayor-council government in Texas: the weak mayor and the strong mayor. In the strong-mayor form of city government (Figure 12.1), the mayor is responsible for the day-to-day administration of the city, can hire and fire department heads, and may also be granted the power to veto council actions and to prepare the city budget. Weak-mayor cities (Figure 12.2), only allow the mayor to share administrative duties with the council and any elected department heads, for example, the city comptroller. There are only two large strong-mayor cities in Texas: Houston and El Paso.

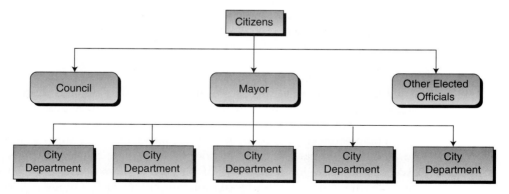

Figure 12.1   The Strong-Mayor Form of City Government

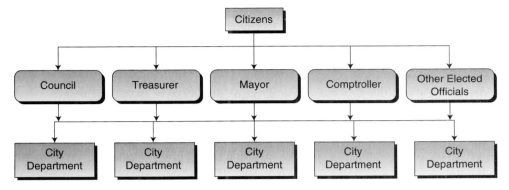

Figure 12.2 The Weak-Mayor Form of City Government

Council-Manager Cities In large, home-rule Texas cities, the council-manager form of government has become the most widespread type. Approximately 70 percent of home-rule cities use it, including Dallas, Corpus Christi, Beaumont, and Austin. Most general-law cities consider the staffing requirements of the system too expensive and tend to avoid it.

The **council-manager** form of city government (Figure 12.3) initially appeared during a national period of creedal passion at the turn of the century, directed at corrupt city officials. In the council-manager form, the mayor is reduced to little more than a figurehead and is elected either at large by the whole city or, less commonly, by the city council itself (as in San Antonio prior to 1975). The attraction of the council-manager form of city government to voters at the time is obvious. In Texas, the reaction to the regime of Governor Davis during Reconstruction resulted in a weakened governor (see Chapter 3), so the idea of weak executives was not foreign to Texans. In the council-manager form of government, the mayor is the "first among equals" on the city council. The mayor presides over the meetings of the council and may sometimes exert considerable personal influence, but in the end, the mayor has only one vote, just as the other council members do.

The essential distinguishing feature of the council-manager form of government is that the city council hires a professional **city manager** who is responsible for the day-to-day operations of the city, typically hires and fires department heads, and prepares the city budget. In most council-manager cities, the city council is a part-time body, as the city council members do not receive enough pay to make their positions full-time jobs. Consequently, a competent, politically astute city manager can become very powerful. The city manager can control the agenda of the city to a great extent—and may also become the scapegoat when things do not go well in the city. In fact, city managers are often blamed by council members for whatever has gone wrong and can sometimes be used to divert attention and blame away from the city council.

Commission Cities The **commission** form of city government (Figure 12.4) started in Texas as a result of the 1900 hurricane that wreaked havoc on the city of

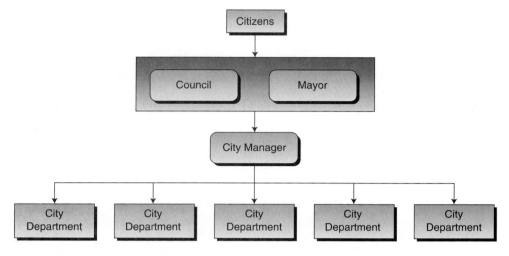

Figure 12.3   The Council-Manager Form of City Government

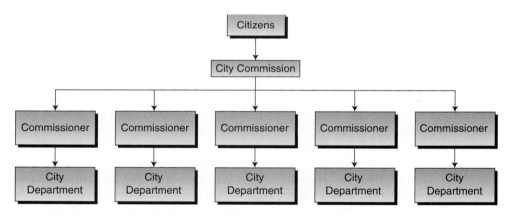

Figure 12.4   The Commission Form of City Government

Galveston. Many people were killed, and city services were crippled. The existing city government did not respond to the problems very well. The state legislature then gave Galveston permission to try the commission form of government, and Galveston pioneered and popularized the commission form in the United States.

In the commission form, commission members act not only as legislators, but also as executives. The city's administration is divided into several departments, and each member of the commission acts as an administrative head of that department, such as public safety, public works, or human services. Collectively, the commission acts as a legislative body for the city, setting the tax rate, passing the budget, passing city ordinances, and so on. The mayor is elected either by the commission or by all of the city's voters, but as with the council-manager form, the mayor has little real power, typically only presiding over meetings and acting as a spokesperson for the council.

The commission form of city government proved to be successful in Galveston, and by 1920, some 500 other cities in Texas had adopted it, including most major cities. All but a few of Texas's home-rule cities have altered their form, and most now employ the council-manager form. General-law cities may choose between the mayor-council and the commission forms, but few are now commission cities. Those that still use the commission form have generally modified their commissions so much that they hardly resemble the original.

The form was initially viewed as progressive. It eliminated the separation of powers (an executive branch—the mayor—and a legislative branch—the city council) and introduced a businesslike approach to the management of the city. The first commission in Galveston had five members, three of whom were appointed by the governor. The other two commission members were elected by the voters in Galveston. Appointment helped ensure that competent administrators would be chosen for the job. The courts later ruled that all commissioners had to be elected. That may have been the beginning of the end of commission government, because elections do not always guarantee that competent administrators will win the job. Also, coalitions among the heads of the various departments may lead to some departments getting larger budgets than others. However, the coalitions can shift every budget cycle, causing constant turmoil in reaching departmental goals and objectives. The commission form proved to be less than desirable, and consequently, very few Texas cities have retained the system or have adopted it in recent years.

Citizen Advisory Boards   Regardless of the form of city government a municipality chooses, virtually all cities use citizen advisory boards to help the city council make decisions. Some advisory boards are set up on a temporary basis to investigate particular issues and make recommendations. Many of the boards are permanent and routinely make recommendations to city councils.

Typically, the most powerful boards are planning and zoning commissions and boards of adjustment. Planning and zoning commissions make recommendations to the city council concerning requests for changes to the zoning and subdivision ordinances and exceptions to the subdivision ordinance. The city council then acts on the recommendations. Boards of adjustment grant exceptions, called "variances," to the zoning ordinance. Boards of adjustment are quasi-judicial bodies, and their decisions are final unless appealed in a court of law.

Many cities, both large and small, also have advisory boards for parks and recreation, libraries, building codes, and many other activities. There is wide variation among cities in their use of advisory boards. Cities are free to create as many as they desire. As Table 12.1 illustrates, the larger a city, the more advisory boards it tends to have. Members are appointed by the city council and usually serve two-year terms.

Keeping City Government Effective: Does the Form Matter?   It is difficult to say whether the form of city government has a significant impact on its effectiveness at fulfilling city responsibilities, but voters and politicians certainly

Table 12.1   ADVISORY BOARDS AND COMMISSIONS, 1999

Austin (pop. approx. 593,000)	Georgetown (pop. approx. 28,000)
Airport Advisory Board	Airport Advisory Board
Animal Advisory Commission	Building Standards Commission
Arts Commission	Board of Adjustment
Austin Community Education Consortium	Board of Electrical Examiners
Brackenridge Hospital Oversight Council	Convention and Visitors Board
Board of Arts Center Stage	Georgetown Enrichment Corporation
Board of Adjustment	Georgetown Housing Authority
Bond Oversight Commission	Historic Preservation Commission
Building and Fire Code Board of Appeals	Library Advisory Board
Building Standards Commission	Parks and Recreation Board
Census 2000 Complete Count Committee	Planning and Zoning Commission
Child Care Council	Williamson County and Cities Health District
Central City Entertainment Center Board	
Charter Revision Committee	
City of Austin Commission for Women	
Commission on Immigrant Affairs	
Community Development Commission	
Construction Advisory Committee	
Design Commission	
Downtown Commission	
Downtown Development Advisory Group	
Economic Development Commission	
Electric Utility Commission	
Electrical Board	
Employee's Retirement System of the City of Austin	
EMS Quality Assurance Team	
Environmental Board	
Ethics Review Commission	
Federally Qualified Health Center Board	
Historic Landmark Commission	
HIV Planning Council	
Housing Authority of the City of Austin	
Human Rights Commission	
Impact Fee Advisory Committee	
Library Commission	
Mayor's Committee for People with Disabilities	
MBE/WBE Advisory Committee	
Mechanical, Plumbing and Solar Board	
Medical Assistance Program Advisory Board	
MHMR Board of Trustees	
MHMR Public Responsibility Committee	
Mexican-American Cultural Center Task Force	

continued

Table 12.1   ADVISORY BOARDS AND COMMISSIONS, 1999—*Continued*

Austin (pop. approx. 593,000)	Georgetown (pop. approx. 28,000)
Minority and Women-Owned Business Procurement Advisory Committee	
Music Commission	
Parks and Recreation Board	
Planning Commission	
Police Civil Service Commission	
Police Retirement Board	
Police Oversight Focus Group	
Renaissance Market Commission	
Resource Management Commission	
Robert Muellar Municipal Airport Advisory Group	
Solicitation Board	
Solid Waste Advisory Commission	
State Fireman's Relief and Retirement Fund	
Telecommunications Commission	
Travis Central Appraisal District Board of Directors	
Urban Forestry Board	
Urban Renewal Board	
Urban Transportation Commission	
Water and Wastewater Commission	

seem to think so. Many Texas cities have changed form at least once over their history, and a few, such as San Antonio and Austin, have tried all three. Moreover, because different sizes and types of cities tend to favor certain forms, it is hard to compare similar cities with different forms. Moreover, almost every city tailors its adopted form somewhat, making comparisons even more problematic. The commission form is probably less effective than the council-manager and mayor-council forms, particularly because the city commission can easily become affected by political infighting and a lack of direction that might be provided more easily by a single executive officer, such as a mayor or a city manager.

Mayor-council and council-manager cities present more challenges for evaluation, particularly with the differences between weak-mayor and strong-mayor structures. In the end, the method of electing candidates for city councils may make at least as much difference in the effectiveness of city government as the actual form of that government. City council election methods are discussed next.

Electing City Councils: The Struggle for Fair Representation

The various methods of electing city councils have often produced controversy. The method of election may determine to a large extent who sits on the city council. Also, because who sits on the city council determines how the resources of the city will be allocated, the election method has a direct impact on the politics and policies of a city. Most mayors are elected at large, meaning by the entire city, but the traditional method of electing city councils in Texas is called the at-large-by-place system, which evolved from the at-large system. The usual response to calls for a change in the at-large-by-place system has been to adopt or modify the single-member district system, but there are other alternatives that may be adopted.

The At-Large and At-Large-by-Place Election Systems   The at-large election system was a part of the same progessive movement in the early 1900s that made the council-manager form of city government widespread, and most cities in Texas at the time embraced the method as a move toward good government. In an at-large election, all voters are entitled to cast votes equal to the number of members of the city council. For example, if the council had four members, then voters could cast votes, one each for their four favorite candidates. The top four vote winners would then serve as the city council. All candidates run in nonpartisan elections, meaning that the candidates do not have party-identifying labels.

Most Texas cities that first used the at-large system have changed to a variation called the **at-large-by-place system.** The city council is divided into numerically designated places. A four-member city council, for example, would have Places 1, 2, 3, and 4. Persons wishing to run for the city council would file for Place 1, 2, 3, or 4, and voters cast one vote in each of the places. The person with a simple majority of the votes cast for each place wins. If no one receives a simple majority (over 50 percent) of the vote, then a runoff election is held between the two top vote getters.

The at-large-by-place system has been praised because it only elects council members who have received the support of the majority of voters; thus, it allows the entire city to participate in the election of all city council members. It is hoped that the result is a city council that will appeal to the entire city and council members who will not be hampered by a narrow perspective from a particular part of the city. Ideally, each member will have the best interests of the city in mind when making policy decisions, assuming that the entire city participates in city council elections.

In many cities in Texas, especially rather small, homogenous communities, the at-large-by-place system probably works very well. There is much to be said for a system that encourages decisions based on the interests of the city as a whole. However, at-large-by-place election systems can also discriminate against minorities' interests, as an at-large-by-place system may result in only the majority interests being reflected on the city council. Consider a scenario with a city that is 51 percent "blue" and 49 percent "green," where these colors represent racial or ethnic groups. As long as blues only vote for blues and greens only for greens, then blues will receive 100 percent of the city council seats, and greens will receive none. If the two groups are residentially segregated, then the areas of the city that are occupied by blues may receive proportionately more in government goods and services than the areas occupied by greens.

While at-large elections may not represent intentional discrimination, their effect was to exclude minority groups from council seats in many cities, particularly African Americans and Hispanics. Indeed, under the at-large and at-large-by-place systems, no African Americans won council elections in Dallas, and only a handful did so over 30 years in Houston, even though African Americans represented a quarter or more of the population there. Hispanics were generally even less successful, and the city councils of small cities reflected the same situation. Especially in cities with significant minority populations, at-large and at-large-by-place election systems tended to produce majoritarian democracies that—unlike pluralist democracies—discouraged the expression and protection of minority-group interests. Moreover, as cities increased their territories through annexation (see "How Cities Grow" later in this chapter), they tended to absorb more affluent and Anglo citizens, changing the ethnic balance even more rapidly and eroding whatever gains had been made in representation.

Because of changes in federal law in 1975, many Texas cities subsequently were sued for violations of the federal Voting Rights Act for the diminishment of minority voting strength through the at-large election method (see the discussion of voting rights in Chapter 13). Under the Voting Rights Act, local citizens' groups and advocacy groups, such as the Mexican American Legal Defense and Education Fund (MALDEF) and the National Association for the Advancement of Colored People (NAACP), pressed cities, such as Dallas, San Antonio, Houston, and even smaller towns, such as Jefferson, to reform their election systems. These changes had to meet with the approval of the U.S. Department of Justice or the U.S. District Court in Washington, D.C., before they could be implemented. Often, cities had to adjust or to create new plans several times.

Responses to the problem of discrimination against minorities by the at-large-by-place method were to adopt one of three alternatives:

1. At-large-by-place districts with residency requirements
2. Single-member districts
3. A combination of at-large-by-place and single-member districts

In the at-large-by-place with residency requirements method, every voter can still vote for each place on the city council, but the candidates must be residents of a specified area. In a hypothetical city with four council members, the city would be divided into four geographic zones. Candidates for Place 1, for example, must live in the area designated as Place 1. Residency requirements must be narrowly drawn to stop someone who actually lives in Place 4 from claiming residency in Place 1. However, this system did not address the essential problem of minority representation or substantially assist minority candidacies because the majority group in the city can still determine who wins in each place.

Single-Member Districts and Mixed Systems   More commonly used than the at-large-by-place election system with residency requirements, the standard solution to the problems of the at-large-by-place system has been to adopt the **single-member district** system. In the single-member district system, the city is divided into geographic zones that must:

1. Be approximately equal in population
2. Be geographically as compact as possible
3. Not dilute minority voting strength by dividing neighborhoods or regions that contain significant concentrations of minorities

The last requirement virtually guarantees that a member of a minority group will be elected from such districts if they are drawn so that the minority group constitutes the overwhelming majority of voters. The single-member district method ensures at least some minority representation, assuming that the minority population is large enough to be able to constitute a majority of voters in at least one district. This is not always the case, as in Houston, where Hispanics tend to be more dispersed than African Americans and more difficult to place in a Hispanic majority district without violating geographic compactness. (See Chapter 13 for a discussion of these issues.)

Cities that adopted single-member districts typically saw rapid changes in the makeup of their city councils. Dallas, for instance, had a mixed election system that combined at-large-by-place seats with seats from single-member districts. Eight members were elected from single-member districts, and 2 members and the mayor were elected at large—usually referred to as the 8–2–1 plan. This system was challenged under the Voting Rights Act in 1988 because it still resulted in the overrepresentation of Anglos and the underrepresentation of minorities. The city decided to switch to a 10–4–1 plan, with 10 single-member districts that were smaller than the original eight; 4 at-large members; and a mayor elected at large. No election was ever held with this system, however, as the federal judge overseeing the changes found it to still be discriminatory in structure and districting. The city then proposed a 14-1 plan, with 14 small, single-member districts and a mayor elected at large.

This system, too, provoked much controversy from federal officials, advocacy groups, and local voters in the referendum on the change. However, the first election under the new system took place in 1991 and resulted in a council with two Hispanic members, four African Americans, and eight Anglos. Other cities also faced similarly tortured paths and generally greeted more pluralist councils.

Comparing Results: At-Large, Single-Member, and Mixed Systems Which system should a city adopt? Courts and advocacy groups have generally not supported mixed systems, such as the one Dallas had in 1988 or initially tried to convert to. Instead, pure single-member districts, such as Dallas's current system, have been more widely accepted by reformers. However, adoption of single-member districts does not ensure equity, and for some critics, there is no need to change or reform the at-large systems. In effect, the choice is between discrimination against minority interests with at-large elections and discrimination against majority interests with single-member districts. An observer's preference may, in the end, depend on what that observer values most: majoritarian or pluralist democracy. It is true that if the only two choices available are single-member districts and at-large elections, then single-member districts are more effective at including minorities in the political system. However, these are not the only two choices available, only the most commonly considered. Proportional representation is useful to examine briefly, if only to show that another alternative exists.

An Alternative Election System: Proportional Representation   The basic idea behind **proportional representation** is to try to ensure that those issues most supported by the greatest numbers of people are represented on the city council or any other legislative body.[4] Essentially, issues would be represented on the city council in proportion to the number of votes they received. For example, if 40 percent of the city's voters thought that the primary focus of the city council should be on public safety, then under proportional representation, 40 percent of the council would be made up of members who had the same position.

Proportional representation has the advantage of enabling the representation on the city council of both majority interests and significant minority interests without requiring that minorities be segregated as in single-member districts. Few governments at any level use this system in the United States, though it is widely used in Europe. It is not unheard of in the United States, however. Cambridge, Massachusetts, employs proportional representation for its city council elections.

There are many forms of proportional representation. One is **cumulative voting,** which allows greater opportunities for minority representation and is relatively simple. With cumulative voting, all voters get a number of votes equal to the number of places they are choosing candidates for. In a council with eight seats, each citizen would get a total of eight votes.

The crucial difference between this method and the at-large systems is that instead of having to assign one vote each to eight different candidates, the eight votes could be assigned to candidates in any combination the voter chooses. In other words, four votes could be assigned to one candidate and one vote each to four others, all eight could be applied to a single candidate, three votes could be spent on one candidate and five on a second, and so on. The idea is that groups that felt strongly about securing representation could devote all of their votes to one candidate, thereby increasing the odds of that candidate being placed on the city council. Like any proportional system, cumulative voting enhances the opportunities for minority representation without requiring that minorities be highly segregated into districts, as the single-member district system assumes.

The election of Veloria Nanze to the Atlanta, Texas, school board on May 6, 1995 marked two "firsts." She became the first African American to serve on the board, and she became the first African American elected by the cumulative voting method in Texas. Cumulative voting began in Texas in 1991 when the Lockhart Independent School District settled a lawsuit involving minority voting rights by adopting a system in which four members are elected at large and three are elected by cumulative voting. Since 1991, at least 15 cities, 32 school districts, and a hospital district have settled lawsuits by adopting cumulative voting.[5] A part of the educational reform package passed in the 1995 legislative session included a provision that would allow school districts to adopt cumulative voting to avoid legal challenges to their at-large election systems.[6]

How Cities Make Laws: Ordinances

All cities have the power to create ordinances, which are laws that are passed by the city council, the legislative branch of cities. As such, they usually apply only within the limits of a city's incorporated area. Ordinances may be passed in such areas as traffic, health and safety, building codes, and zoning, some of which apply outside the city's corporate limits.

Cities have responsibility for maintaining streets and bridges that have not been designated as state or national roadways and that are within the confines of the city limits. In addition, cities can regulate the traffic on those streets, designating speed limits, left-turn lanes, one-way streets, and stop lights and signs.

Perhaps the most important regulations that any city passes are zoning and subdivision ordinances, which are related to land use. Zoning and subdivision ordinances regulate commercial and residential activity through regulations defining areas, such as height districts, which regulate how high things may be built in a particular building zone. In many residential areas, for example, buildings may not exceed two stories.

Use districts are another common set of regulations; they designate the use to which an area may be put. Common classifications are industrial or commercial, retail, and residential, but further distinctions may be made. For example, residential areas may be refined to include single-family or multifamily housing.

A third widely found type of zoning regulation defines density districts, which help set the number of people allowed in a residential area. For example, a city may designate an area as having no more than two single-family residences per acre, or it may limit or prohibit apartment complexes from certain neighborhoods.

How Cities Grow

Relative to much of the northeastern United States, Texas cities are geographically very large for their populations and have grown very rapidly. Houston is an extreme but not an unusual example in the state, expanding from 160 square miles in 1950 to 540 square miles in 1990. Part of the reason for such growth lies in the flexibility of state laws, which have allowed many Texas cities to increase their boundaries quite aggressively.

Why do cities want to grow? They often try to increase their tax base by including businesses and residents that are located nearby but do not yet contribute to their tax revenue. Unfortunately, such quick growth can lead to problems, such as urban sprawl and uneven development strategies. This section discusses the three techniques cities use to expand their borders: annexation, strip annexation, and extraterritorial jurisdiction.

Annexation   **Annexation** is the inclusion of land into the city limits of an existing municipality. That land is typically unincorporated territory within the municipality's extraterritorial jurisdiction. Annexation is how cities grow physically. A major reason cities annex territory is to increase their tax base. As a central city grows, it tends to become surrounded by a ring of newer growth, which itself is usually surrounded by another ring of growth and so on. Most major cities in the United States and Texas have such rings of growth. As time passes, in the inner rings, the infrastructure—streets, water mains, sewage and storm drains, and other city structures—ages and begins to break down. Repairing or replacing the infrastructure is expensive. As the inner circles fall into disrepair, the value of the tax base in those areas declines as well, as business and upper- and middle-class neighborhoods move farther out. The result is that taxes taken from the areas that need repair the most are not always sufficient to pay for those repairs. Annexation allows cities to obtain areas that have or potentially have more substantial tax bases that can fund needed improvements in other parts of the city.

Who decides whether an unincorporated area can or should be annexed? Typically, the decision is made by the annexing city's city council. The residents of the area to be annexed have some input during the process, but their approval is not required. On the other hand, if one city wants to annex an already incorporated area—another city—then a referendum from both cities is necessary for approval.

Annexation in Texas is governed for the most part by the 1963 Municipal Annexation Act and the 1999 amendments to that act. There are four criteria or rules that cities must follow when annexing territory:

1. A city may annex up to 10 percent of its existing territory each year. For any area that contains 100 or more separate tracts of land with residential units located on each tract, the city must draw up an annexation plan at least three years prior to annexation. Amendments may be added to the plan, but any new territory added to the plan must wait three years before annexation. Annexation must occur within 31 days of the anniversary of the plan; otherwise, the city must wait five additional years before annexing the territory.

2. Annexed territory must be contiguous to the existing city limits. However, if the territory lies only along city limits that are solely the result of strip annexation, the city may not annex it. For any area that is annexed, but that is not contiguous to territory resulting from other than strip annexation, the extraterratorial jurisdiction (ETJ) for that territory is automatically reduced to 1 mile, regardless of the size of the city.

3. The city must provide full municipal services to newly annexed areas within two and one-half years after annexation. Cities may propose to extend this requirement up to four and one-half years if a schedule is included in the service plan, but anything beyond two and one-half years requires agreement with the landowners in the newly annexed territory. If city services are not provided within the allotted time, a resident or property owner in the annexed area may seek one of several remedies made

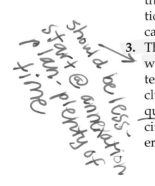
should be less- start @ annexation plan. plenty of time

available in the law. Possible remedies include the municipality's compliance with the service plan or de-annexation of the territory. If a city de-annexes property for failure to provide services, it is precluded from re-annexing the area for a period of ten years.

4. Cities may not prohibit landowners in the newly annexed territory from using their land in the manner it was used before annexation, providing that the activity was legal at the time. However, cities may impose regulations dealing with sexually oriented businesses, colonias, public nuisance, flood control, storage and use of hazardous materials, sale or use of fireworks, discharge of firearms, and prevention of imminent destruction of property or of injury to persons.

Criterion 1 favors large cities and allows them to grow at a rate faster than that of smaller cities. A city may annex 10 percent of its existing land area in the year that annexation takes place. If a city starts with 10 square miles, then in Year 1, it may annex an additional 1 square mile. In the second year, its land area is now 11 square miles, and the city may annex 1.1 square miles. One mitigating factor is the fact that a city can only bank up to 30 percent of its size. That is, if a city annexes nothing in Year 1, then in Year 2, it may annex 20 percent. If it doesn't annex anything in its second year as well, then in the third year, it may annex 30 percent. However, if it still annexes nothing that year, then it may only annex 30 percent in the fourth year.

Criterion 2—that annexed territory must be contiguous with existing city limits—simply means that the existing city and the area to be annexed must be physically connected. This prevents cities from jumping over other cities or around areas the city does not want. It also prevents cities from strip annexing through undesirable territory and then annexing more desirable territory away from the city proper.

The Criterion 3 requirement that the annexing city must provide city services to the annexed area within two and one-half years, however, is the biggest obstacle most cities face, although most cities do not have difficulty meeting this goal. In some cases, the areas to be annexed are densely populated subdivisions served by "special districts" that provide some of the services a city would normally provide. These special districts may have large amounts of debt that the annexing city must assume (see the discussion of special districts later in this chapter). The city has to determine whether the possible benefits of the additional tax base and any special districts' assets outweigh the costs of assuming the provision of services and the existing debt.

There are not many ways for an area to remove or de-annex itself from a city. The most common way is if a newly annexed area has not been provided with city services in accordance with the adopted service plan. In practice, however, it has proven to be rather difficult to demonstrate that the city has not provided services. Most annexed areas already have water and sewer service for which the city simply assumes responsibility, and the provision of most other city services is usually broadly construed so that the city can argue that they are, indeed, being provided.

Strip Annexation   Some cities also practice strip annexation, which is the practice of annexing a road and at least 500 feet on either side of the middle of the roadway. The cost to the city in terms of the provision of services is usually minimal. Even the maintenance of the roadway is sometimes funded in whole or in part by the national or state government. The 500-foot area on both sides of the roadway may encompass retail establishments that require minimal services but that may return substantial sales-tax revenue to the city. San Antonio grew especially rapidly using this technique. Cities are restricted to strip annexing no more than 3½ miles of roadway per year.

Extraterritorial Jurisdiction   The real reason for strip annexation is that it allows a city to greatly expand its **extraterritorial jurisdiction (ETJ),** which means declaring that areas outside of the city limits have been laid claim to by the city. The size of a city's ETJ is determined by the population of the city. The larger the city in population, the larger the city's ETJ can be. Because a city's ETJ extends the specified distance from any point on the city's limits, a city can strip-annex several miles of major roadways that lead out of the city proper and thus claim much more ETJ than it could without strip annexation.

There are two major reasons for claiming ETJ. First, an area that has become part of a city's ETJ cannot incorporate or be annexed by another city; it is in legal limbo. The city has added potential tax base without having to provide it with services until ready, and no other city can annex it either. The second major reason for claiming ETJ is that a city gets to exercise some degree of control over that area's growth and development. Although the city's zoning ordinances cannot be applied to an ETJ, some development regulation is possible, particularly those relating to platting and site development requirements.

As in annexation, the residents of an ETJ really have nothing to say about it. Once placed in a city's ETJ, the area may not incorporate or be annexed by another city. The only way to escape a city's ETJ is to incorporate, which requires the city's consent. If the city refuses the request for incorporation, the area's residents may petition the city to annex them. If the city fails to annex the area within six months, the area is authorized to initiate the incorporation process.

What Cities Do with Their Money: Revenues and Expenditures

Cities have several sources of revenue. One of the most substantial is the property tax, also known as the *ad valorem* tax, which is levied on the value of land and buildings. Property taxes are usually expressed as being so much per $100 of assessed value or valuation. For example, a property tax rate of 1.35 means that for every $100 a property is valued at, the owner pays $1.35 in property taxes. If the property were valued at $1,000, then the tax owed would be $10.35. The value of property is determined by tax assessors who inspect the property and recommend a valuation to the city.

Cities may also issue bonds. The issuance of bonds is a way for a city to borrow money. The city sells bonds to investors, who are in essence loaning the city money; these loans will be repaid in full at a later date, with interest. **General-obligation bonds** are used to fund projects, goods, and services that everyone in the city is generally obligated to pay for, such as streets and city buildings. The property taxes and the general-obligation bonds are directly linked, as property-tax revenue is used to pay the principal and interest on the bonds over time. **Revenue bonds** are used to fund such things as convention centers and sports arenas, which are paid for from the revenues generated by the activities created by the bonds.

Cities may also levy a 1 percent municipal sales tax on the value of goods sold within the city, subject to the same limitations as the state sales tax. In addition, cities typically levy fees for services or goods they provide.

The expenditures of a city are, of course, quite varied. However, all cities have major expenditures for such things as public safety, police and fire protection, and emergency medical services. Major expenditures also come in the area of public works, which include providing potable water and removing and treating wastewater. Most cities also maintain a storm-drainage system to help prevent flooding. Of course, the building and maintenance of streets, bridges, street signs of all kinds, and traffic signals are also considered public works. Many cities fund the collection and disposal of solid waste—trash and garbage—and some also underwrite recycling programs. Cities also commonly maintain inspection departments, parks, public swimming pools, animal shelters, libraries, museums, and airports.

Critical Thinking Exercise: The method of electing city councils has an impact on who gets represented. Which of the methods presented by the text is the best and why? Defend your answer in terms of majoritarian and pluralist democracy.

COUNTIES

Like general-law city governments, county governments in Texas may only do what the state will allow them to do. In fact, all 254 counties in Texas exist as administrative units of the state and reflect state government in structure (Figure 12.5). They do, however, have some discretionary authority, and they are staffed by locally elected officials. As a result, counties look and act like local governments and are considered by many citizens to be local governments. Indeed, for many people in rural areas, the county and one or two special districts are the only local governments with which they have contact. Counties exist primarily to enforce state law.[7]

County Government: The Plural Executive

Counties in Texas, somewhat like the state government, are run by a plural executive. The legislative functions of the county are carried out by the **commissioners**

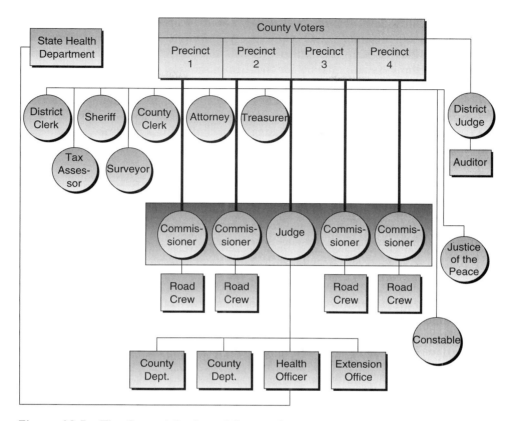

Figure 12.5   The General Outline of County Government in Texas

Source: Robert E. Norwood. *Texas County Government: Let the People Choose* (Austin, Tex.: Texas Taxpayers and Research Association, 1970).

court. The term *court* is somewhat of a misnomer because it does not conduct trials or hear appeals. The commissioners court consists of the four county commissioners and the county judge. As a collective body, it is responsible for determining the county's budget and setting the county's property-tax rate. Individually, each member of the commissioners court has executive duties, and all members are elected to four-year terms. County government is one of the few places in government in Texas or the United States that the concept of the separation of executive, legislative, and judicial powers is violated by vesting in the same group of public officials legislative, executive, and—in the case of the county judge—judicial duties (see Chapter 11).

County Judges   The **county judge** presides over the commissioners court and votes as a member of the court. However, the county judge has no veto power over the court's actions and casts only a single vote, just as the four commissioners do. As an executive, the county judge is responsible for some of the day-to-day administration of the county. This includes the administration of health and welfare programs, county parks, and libraries. Counties are responsible for operating many state programs, especially in the areas of health and welfare. The county judge is responsible for the administration of those programs. In rural counties, the county judge may still conduct trials, but in urban areas, the executive functions tend to consume all of the county judge's time, which is part of the reason for the creation of county court-at-law judges (see Chapter 11). The qualifications for running for county judge consist of being a qualified voter and being "well informed in the law."

County Commissioners   Each county in Texas is divided into four single-member districts. Each of them elects a **county commissioner,** who serves on the commissioners court with the county judge and has an equal voice in deciding the tax rate and setting the budget. Like the county judge, the commissioners also have executive duties. They share responsibility for the administration of state and county programs with the county judge in each of their respective districts. Sometimes called "road commissioners," their most traditional function is to oversee the construction and maintenance of county roads and bridges within their separate districts. This has led to many problems in the past and as a result, a few counties no longer vest their commissioners with that authority (see the section, "Keeping County Government Effective," for further explanation). The only qualification for this office is being a qualified voter.

County Sheriffs   One of the most visible members of the county's plural executive is the **county sheriff,** who is elected to a four-year term. Surprisingly enough, the position of sheriff has no special qualifications; a person need only be a qualified voter to hold the job. The county sheriff is responsible for the enforcement of state law in the county and for maintaining the county jail. In large, urban counties, the sheriff's department may employ a substantial number of deputies. In recent years, overcrowding problems and poor living conditions in the jails have caused many sheriffs to be sued for violations of rights, and both rural and urban counties have been forced to build new jails or to renovate old jails to comply with court orders. In a few small counties, the sheriff acts as the tax collector as well.

County Tax Assessor-Collectors   The county **tax assessor-collector** is elected to a four-year term, and the position has no special qualifications. The primary duty of the county tax assessor-collector is, of course, to collect taxes, including the county property taxes and fees. In some counties, the tax assessor-collector also registers voters. Most people come into contact with the tax assessor-collector when they pay their automobile registration fees. The title of tax assessor-collector is somewhat of a misnomer because the tax assessor-collector is no longer responsible for the appraisal of property for the county. Every county in Texas now has a countywide appraisal district responsible for appraising all real property in the county. All governmental entities in the county are required to use the valuation from the appraisal district.

District Clerks and County Clerks Each county may also elect two clerks, the county clerk and the district clerk. These officials are also elected to four-year terms and have no special qualifications. The **county clerk** is responsible for maintaining the records of the county courts, records of births and deaths, marriages and divorces, and transfers of property. The county clerk is also responsible for ensuring that ballots are printed and delivered to the polling places, staffing polling places, counting votes accurately, and may be responsible for registering voters. Many of the large, urban counties have hired an **elections administrator** to assume the electoral functions of the county clerk. Typically, the elections administrator is hired by the county clerk. The **district clerk** is responsible for keeping the records of the state district courts.

County Treasurers The **county treasurer** performs much the same job at the county level as the state treasurer did at the state level. The county treasurer essentially acts as the county's banker and is responsible for receiving money and paying the county's bills, keeping records of expenditures and revenues, and examining the financial records of other county officials that receive county funds. Counties with a population of more than 35,000 are required to have a **county auditor** appointed by the district judge or judges in the county. The auditor has the same responsibilities as the treasurer. In addition, the county auditor also functions as the chief budget officer and finance officer, audits all county financial records, checks monetary claims against the county, and approves the accounting system to be used by the county. Obviously, having both a county auditor and county treasurer is a bit redundant. The treasurer's position is mandated by the constitution and requires a constitutional amendment to be abolished in any county. Thus, virtually every time constitutional amendments are placed on the state ballot, one or more of them has to do with some county wishing to abolish its position of treasurer.

Minor County Officials The position of county surveyor continues to be filled in many counties. The county surveyor does any survey work needed by the county, which could be a considerable amount of work in counties experiencing rapid growth. Counties may also elect a number of other officials, including the hides inspector and the inspector of weights and measures. Most of these positions have been vacant for so long that it is not even clear what they do. Fortunately, the positions do not have to be filled; they are optional for each county, and they are filled only if someone runs for the position. Officeholders are paid only if the duties of the position are fulfilled.

What Counties Do with Their Money: Revenues and Expenditures

Counties have only two major sources of revenue: the property tax and the issuance of bonds. Like cities, counties may issue a property tax, but their property tax is subject to greater state limitations than cities face. Counties may also issue general-obligation and revenue bonds. However, because property taxes pay for the principal and interest on general-obligation bonds, state limits on the county property tax also limit the amount of general-obligation bonds that can be issued. Counties may also collect fees, the most important of which is the automobile registration fee; counties keep one-half of the revenue generated from such fees. Since 1986, the 247 counties without transit authorities have also been empowered to levy a small sales tax, the revenue of which is restricted to lowering property taxes. The tax may be one-half percent for counties with incorporated areas and one percent for counties without any cities. Almost half of the counties in Texas now have such sales taxes.

Because counties are more restricted than cities in the kinds and amounts of revenue they can raise, they also tend to have fewer expenditures. Typically, one of the largest expenditures is for law enforcement, particularly the maintenance of county jails. The building and upkeep of county roads and bridges are also quite costly. In addition, because counties are the administrative units of the state, they are responsible for much of the recordkeeping in the state. They levy fees for most recordkeeping; but they usually just pay for the activity. Finally, some counties also run parks and, in remote locales, a library system.

Keeping County Government Effective: Criticisms and Reforms

Perhaps no other unit of government in Texas has received as much negative criticism by academics and students of government as county government. Certainly, among the types of local governments, the county is considered to have the most problems. In spite of these criticisms, county government has actually changed very little since the 1876 constitution defined it. There are five aspects of county government commonly cited as needing reform:

1. **The structure of county government is very inflexible.** Urban and rural, large and small counties—spanning a wide range of climates and geography—have exactly the same structure in Texas. Many observers have stated that the solution is for the state to allow counties home-rule status, which would give the citizens of that county the ability to select the form of government that suited their needs. The state could, as it does with cities, restrict the choices of the form of government available to the counties.

2. **Having several executive officers is inefficient, compared to having only a single chief executive officer.** Because there is no single official in charge of each county, the assignment of responsibility for actions is difficult and can lead to fragmented policy and the waste of money and resources. One reform that has been suggested is to adopt a **county-manager** form of government. As with the council–manager form of city government, the commissioners court would become a purely legislative body responsible for setting the tax rate, passing the county's budget, and determining overall policy for the county. The commissioners court would hire a county manager, who would be responsible for the daily administration of the county, as well as hiring and managing the county staff—replacing

those who are now elected (for example, the county clerk). Obviously, this would be a fairly radical reorganization of county government and would put a lot of politicians out of work; the Texas Association of Counties usually rises to speak against such reforms. County government has not been the object of a period of creedal passion since the 1875 constitutional convention. The citizens of Texas seem quite content with things as they are.

3. Unlike city and state governments, county governments are handicapped by being unable to pass general laws or ordinances. Many counties have densely populated zones, such as residential subdivisions outside the limits of any incorporated area, that share the same problems as cities, without sharing the lawmaking abilities of cities to remedy those problems.

   The obvious reform would be to allow counties to change to a home-rule status, but the notion of home rule for counties is fraught with political problems. In 1933, a constitutional amendment permitting counties to apply for a home-rule charter was ratified. However, the state made the application process so difficult that no county ever received a home-rule charter, and the amendment was repealed in 1969. Life in the city and life in the country are very different, and individuals living in rural areas are probably legitimately worried that home rule for counties could lead to the passage of ordinances that may make perfect sense in a densely populated urban area but make little sense in a sparsely populated rural neighborhood.

   The best compromise might be to place a density requirement on counties before allowing them to seek home rule. In other words, a county could only receive a home-rule charter if its population per square mile exceeded a certain level. A provision could also be mandated that prevented the application of ordinances to any part of a county that had less than some specified population density.

4. Counties use a method of hiring and firing employees that does not promote professional, efficient service. The **spoils system** allows elected officials to replace any of the county's staff with their own nominees, including friends and supporters to whom they owe favors, without any formal qualifications process (see Chapter 3). Many have argued that counties should implement the **merit system,** such as the civil-service systems used elsewhere in government. Particularly in urban counties with a large county workforce, a professional system of hiring and firing may be particularly important. A civil-service system would also afford employees some protection against arbitrary firings, by instituting formal termination, grievance, and appeals procedures.

5. The system of administering county roads and bridges doesn't consistently promote good traffic management and road maintenance, especially in urban counties. Traditionally, the four county commissioners have held virtually complete authority over county roads and bridges within their respective districts. There are two basic problems with this arrangement. First, few people elected to the position of county commissioner are civil engineers or transportation experts. Decisions over where and when to

build and maintain roads and bridges are often based on politics, rather than traffic flow or safety concerns.

Second, county commissioners are under no legal obligation to coordinate their activities with each other, and they often do not, which may not improve traffic-congestion problems beyond a single district. Since 1947, the legislature has allowed counties to adopt a **unit-road system,** which brings all county roads and bridges under the jurisdiction of a professional engineer or transportation expert appointed by the commissioners court. Few counties have adopted this system.

Critical Thinking Exercise: In large metropolitan areas, county government almost seems to be unnecessary. What is your assessment of that statement? What role, if any, do county governments have to play in metropolitan areas? How would you change county government to meet that role?

SPECIAL DISTRICTS

City and county governments are general-purpose governments because they perform and serve numerous purposes, but **special districts** usually serve a single purpose and are created to supply a specific need. Although they are far more obscure than municipal and county governments, they are the most numerous type of local government. There are approximately 3200 special districts in Texas.[8] Many Texans live in one or more special districts without being aware of it. School districts, rapid transit authorities, municipal utility districts, river authorities, water control and improvement districts, and mosquito control districts are a few examples, but there are many other types as well.

How and Why Special Districts Are Formed

Depending on the type, a special district can be formally authorized through the state legislature, state boards or commissions, constitutional amendments, the county commissioners courts, and city councils. Often, local voters in the district must approve the district before it can begin operation, and the voters later approve bond sales or specific taxes.

One could legitimately ask why other governmental entities do not respond to the problems that special districts are meant to solve. The short answer is usually that other levels or departments of government either cannot or will not. The State of Texas has been reluctant to involve itself in what is perceived to be local problems. This reluctance stems from the state's libertarian and conservative legacy. The libertarian legacy demands a limited government that is not going to do too much and that will not involve itself in local problems. The conservative legacy also carries a fear that big government will ignore or override local concerns, potentially increasing state expenditures, which could necessitate tax increases. The state finds it easier to allow the creation of special districts than to address the problems itself.

County governments are also a logical alternative to special districts, but they usually do not involve themselves with problems outside their regulatory domain for a number of reasons. First, county governments may only do what the state allows them to do and are relatively restricted in their ability to respond to local concerns. Unless the state has authorized the county to address a particular problem, it is difficult for the county to act legally. Second, the state has also restricted the county's ability to raise revenue. Many times, even if the county is authorized by the state to act, the county is financially unable to respond. Last, some local problems do not respect county boundaries, as some problems may cover more than one county. In such cases, the efforts by one county may be for naught unless other counties join the effort. Such entities as the Lower Colorado River Authority were formed because the Colorado flows through many counties, but not through the whole state. Thus, pollution of the river and electrical generation along it are not statewide concerns, but neither are they in the scope of one county.

Cities are in some of the same positions as the counties when considering local problems. An issue may be something that covers parts of the city, as well as areas outside the city, but may not be countywide or statewide in nature. Consider the traffic-congestion problems faced by metropolitan areas in Texas, such as San Antonio and the Dallas-Fort Worth area. No matter what a central city does to relieve congestion, it is not going to be very effective unless the surrounding suburbs are included in the resolution of the problem. Rapid transit authorities have been created to address congestion that can cover several counties and dozens of incorporated areas. These authorities are authorized to levy a tax to raise revenues, while individual cities often feel that they are already taxing their citizens enough and are reluctant to raise taxes to fund problem solving that may not work.

Cities are also sometimes reluctant to address problems that do not face the city as a whole. The phenomenon of the creation of special districts inside the city limits occurs because the city or particular public officials will not address the needs of a particular neighborhood. Downtown development districts can be created for this reason.

The Governance and Revenues of Special Districts

The governing body of a special district is usually a multimember board of directors that makes policy for the district. The members of the board may be elected or appointed, depending on the type of district and how the district was created. For example, most water district and school board members are elected by voters. For airport authorities, board members may be either elected by voters or appointed by the county commissioners court. Depending on whether the district was created through a constitutional amendment or legislative statute, hospital district board members may be appointed by the commissioners court or by the city council, elected by voters, or partly elected and partly appointed. Mayors usually appoint members of housing authorities, and the governor appoints the members of river authorities. Regardless of how the board members are chosen, they usually select an executive director who implements the board's policies and supervises the district's employees.

Special districts in Texas derive their revenues from several sources. However, most special districts rely on a combination of some kind of tax and fees or service charges to fund their activities. For example, most water districts, such as municipal utility districts and water control and improvement districts, and hospital districts are dependent on property taxes to supplement their service charges. Transit authorities can employ a sales tax. In addition, special districts are often eligible for federal funds or state assistance. For example, airport authorities frequently receive grants from the Federal Aviation Administration for building runways and facilities. Finally, special districts can sell revenue bonds, which are repaid from fees or service charges, and if they have taxing authority, general-obligation bonds, which are repaid from taxes, to fund such capital projects as airports, water treatment plants, and water storage facilities.

The Varieties of Special Districts

Special districts are intended to focus on a huge variety of problems in Texas. Given that special districts are created for specific purposes and that the state has demonstrated a wide latitude in the creation of districts, the possible variety of special districts is limited only by the imaginations of Texas citizens. The following list will amply demonstrate their variety in Texas.

Education Districts   The most well known of all special districts are the independent school districts (ISDs). There are 1043 ISDs in Texas that bear the primary responsibility for the delivery of public education in Texas. They are governed by seven-member boards of trustees, who are usually elected to three-year terms in nonpartisan at-large-by-place elections. A few ISDs, however, such as Austin and Longview, use single-member district elections. The boards of trustees set the tax rate for the district, adopt a budget, and hire and fire the local superintendent of schools (see Chapter 14 for more information on school funding). The superintendent is responsible for the day-to-day operation of the district. The positions of superintendent and other executive directors of special districts are analogous to those of city managers in the council-manager form of city government.

There are also 50 community college districts in Texas. They are governed by nine-member boards of trustees elected by the at-large-by-place method. The boards determine the tax rate, approve the budget, and hire and fire the chancellor or president, depending on the size of the college. Large districts with a multicampus operation, as in Houston, may have several presidents, with a chancellor overseeing the presidents, while smaller colleges, such as Tyler Junior College, may only have one president. The board of trustees is also responsible for the formulation of general policy for the college, helping to provide it with goals and direction.

Water Districts   The most numerous type of special district in Texas is the water district, of which there are more than 1000. Water districts take a variety of names, but the most common are municipal utility districts, which we discuss later in this chapter, and water control and improvement districts (WCIDs). WCIDs, like municipal utility districts, can perform several functions, including flood control, hydroelectric power, navigation, water conservation, water resource data collection, and water supply. Other multipurpose water districts include water improvement districts, freshwater supply districts, river authorities, levee and flood control districts, and navigation districts. In addition, there are several single-purpose water districts, such as drainage districts, irrigation districts, and underground water conservation districts. In 1997, the legislature passed a major overhaul of the state's water policy, including provisions affecting water districts. In 1999, the legislature authorized 13 new underground water conservation districts in response to increasing concerns regarding water table levels in Texas.

Hospital Districts   In Texas, there are 98 hospital districts capable of levying a property tax and 21 hospital authorities incapable of levying a property tax. At one time, many hospital districts were owned by cities or counties but were converted for political or financial reasons to special districts so that they would stand alone as governmental entities.

Rapid Transit Authorities   There are rapid transit authorities located in Dallas, Fort Worth, Houston, San Antonio, Austin, El Paso, and Corpus Christi, including many of the communities surrounding these central areas. The authorities were created to provide mass rapid-transit systems and are allowed to levy a sales tax. Although many have been the object of criticism for doing little more than running bus services, it is also true that most Texans have demonstrated little intent to give up their cars for alternative means of transportation. Nevertheless, air pollution and traffic congestion may eventually force changes in modes of transportation. The rapid transit authorities may be in a position to provide those alternatives, as Dallas is doing now with light rail transit.

Other Types of Special Districts   The 419 housing authorities in Texas are designed to provide low-income housing, primarily through rental units. There are 3 urban-renewal agencies in Texas, focused on regenerating downtown areas and rebuilding neighborhoods. There are 8 mosquito-control districts in Texas. It is hard to believe, perhaps, that governments have been created to spray for mosquitoes, but communities on the Gulf Coast feel that mosquitoes pose enough of a nuisance and a health hazard to justify such a move. There have been 11 health districts formed in Texas.

Special districts are formed for other reasons, as well. When neither the City of Dallas nor the City of Fort Worth would commit to building a new airport, a

Parkland Memorial Hospital, located in Dallas County, is governed and funded as a special district.

special district was created to fulfill the need. Hence, the Dallas-Fort Worth (DFW) International Airport is an authority and an independent governmental agency. There are now 6 airport authorities in Texas. There are 213 soil and water conservation districts that operate in the rural areas of Texas. There are also 3 wind-erosion districts. Located primarily in the Panhandle and West Texas, they serve to mitigate the effects of dust storms. There are 5 noxious-weed-control districts in Texas. There is also one municipal power agency in Texas.

Some volunteer fire companies have been turned into quasi-governments by the creation of rural fire-prevention districts, of which there are 21 in Texas. The creation of the district allows a property tax to be assessed on all residents served by the company. The tax revenue may then be used by the volunteer fire department for the purchase of equipment, buildings, and supplies. Personnel are still volunteers.

Perhaps the most intriguing of all special districts in Texas is that of Houston's subsidence-control district. For many years, Houston obtained its drinking water from wells. However, removing the water from ground that does not have a bedrock foundation tends to decrease the soil's buoyancy, just as a sponge will collapse if the water is removed from it and a heavy object is placed on top of it. In Houston, the problem manifests itself by an overall sinking of parts of the city. The special district was formed to try to mitigate the effects of subsidence.

There is an increasing use of public-improvement districts in Texas. These districts may be created within the city limits of a municipality. Traditionally, special districts have been created outside or across city limits. However, certain areas of a city may demand or desire that a service or good be provided to that area. The city may not wish to do so because it perceives a greater demand for services or goods in another part of the city or because it simply does not feel that it can afford to provide the good or service. The competition for scarce resources may cause cities to prioritize needs and desires in such a way that a particular section's needs are not high on the list. However, the city may create a public-improvement district within that area. That area is then taxed at a rate different from that in the rest of the city, with the additional revenue used to fund the desired good or service. For example, a particular neighborhood may wish to have a park, but the city will not fund it. That neighborhood then has the city create a public-improvement district for that neighborhood. That district pays additional taxes that are dedicated to the park's building and maintenance.

Keeping Special Districts Effective: Avoiding the Problem or Focusing on Issues?

Special districts have commonly drawn criticism for two reasons: the ease of their creation and their obscurity to the public. Critics have argued that special districts are too easily created, with the result that people are then forced to carry the burden of another government, especially from those districts that levy an additional property tax. Singled out for particular attention in this regard have been municipal utility districts (MUDs).

MUDs are created to provide water and wastewater treatment for major developments, primarily residential subdivisions. When a developer makes a decision to subdivide and plat (divide the property into lots) a particular piece of property for residential use, the ultimate goal, of course, is to build houses. However, before houses can be built, the infrastructure must be put into place: roads, water mains, sewer lines, electrical lines, and gas mains, all of which cost money. Developers typically get their money after a house has been built and sold. To defray some of the expenses of developing a subdivision, developers often create a MUD to take over the maintenance and the remaining construction of the water and wastewater system. The MUD can then issue bonds that reimburse the developer for the cost of the infrastructure. Developers have been accused of taking advantage of their initial position in the subdivision to help themselves financially.

There is no doubt that developers recoup their expenses on infrastructure through the creation of a MUD faster than they would otherwise. Obviously, the creation of a special district has been beneficial to the developer. Does that mean that it is automatically detrimental to the residents of the MUD? The water and wastewater treatment systems must be put in, or the houses cannot be built if the houses are in an ETJ or a city's limits or if the builder expects to receive Federal Housing Authority (FHA) approval.[9] The homeowner will pay the cost through two means. First, a homeowner can pay through higher home prices that reflect the cost of the new systems. Second, the homeowner can pay through a property tax that will last as long as the home. In either case, the resident will pay fees for the provision of water and wastewater treatment. It is not clear that the cost of the property tax will exceed the cost of having the mortgage increased. One could argue that by creating a MUD, a mechanism has been put into place for the continued maintenance of the system after the developer has finished and moved on to another project. If no MUD has been created, it is not clear what happens to the water and wastewater systems after the developer leaves, especially in areas that lie outside a city's limits.

Special districts have also been criticized for their obscurity. Many people do not seem to be aware that they live in a special district, much less know who is running it and how. Some special districts also operate with little regulation from the state or other entities. The obscurity of special districts may emanate, however, from the fact that the district is performing the function it was established to do with relative efficiency. Often, unless something happens to produce a period of creedal passion concerning the special district complacency will be the norm.

Critical Thinking Exercise: Special districts provide a unique opportunity for local involvement that is rarely exercised by the majority of citizens. Why is that the case?

MORE THAN LOCAL, LESS THAN STATE: COORDINATION AND COOPERATION AMONG LOCAL GOVERNMENTS

The responsibilities of local and state governments increased immeasurably during the twentieth century, but governmental institutions in Texas have always evolved as the problems they were intended to face have evolved. Existing institutions change, adapt, and find novel solutions and approaches to novel problems. Local governments—cities, counties, and special districts—are no exception. This section discusses some of the problems and solutions that concern several, and often many, local governments. Some solutions, such as metrogovernments, involve creating new forms or levels of government, folding existing institutions into previously nonexistent bodies. Other solutions, such as councils of government, involve finding better ways of coordinating the activities of separate groups.

Metropolitan Solutions for Metropolitan Problems

Since 1950, more Texans have lived in urban areas than in rural areas: More than one-half of the population lives in only 10 of the 254 counties in Texas. The result is that many of the issues faced by Texans today are metropolitan problems related to urban living. The purpose of this section is to examine some of the solutions that have been proposed for such problems as managing traffic congestion; air, water, and industrial pollution; crime; development; and the decline of the tax base.

Metropolitan areas typically have a central city and surrounding suburbs, which may or may not be incorporated. A metropolitan area may also extend across two or more counties and numerous special districts and cities. The Dallas-Fort Worth metropolitan area includes the central cities of Dallas and Fort Worth, as well as the counties of Dallas, Tarrant, and arguably Collin and Denton. Hundreds of special districts are located in the same area, and within Dallas and Tarrant counties alone, there are some 40 incorporated cities.

Obviously, the problems of metropolitan areas often extend beyond the city limits of any one of the municipalities in the area. As discussed previously, the state—and most voters across the state—has an ideological and fiscal reluctance to become involved in any problems that it does not perceive as statewide in nature, so the resolution of such problems primarily falls to the entities within the metropolitan areas. Some of the solutions that Texas has used or entertained have already been discussed, such as annexation and the expansion of a city's ETJ and the creation of special districts. Sometimes, these options are not enough or not appropriate, however. Other solutions are metrogovernment, intergovernmental contracting, and various forms of privatization.

Metrogovernments   **Metrogovernment** is an idea that has been discussed at various times for regions, such as the Dallas-Fort Worth, Houston, and San Antonio areas. Although no metrogovernment has ever been implemented in Texas, the Nashville, Tennessee; Portland, Oregon; and Miami, Florida, areas all have implemented metrogovernments in the United States. The basic idea is to collapse the county government, all of the city governments within that county, and at least some of the county's special districts into a single countywide government. Metrogovernment produces economies of scale by eliminating the duplication of services. It also, however, removes many elected officials from office, a prospect that has generated much opposition to the idea from those elected officials. Ethnic and racial minorities who are afraid of losing representation under a metrogovernment also oppose the idea.

Metrogovernment also raises serious questions about how to integrate so many local governments. For instance, would county government retain its status as an administrative unit of the state, or would the new metrogovernment be required to assume both state and local functions? The integration of numerous special districts also poses problems. Recall that special districts are often created to address problems that the county or city viewed as being too local. Would the metrogovernment be required to absorb all special districts, or would it be allowed to choose those it wished to take in? Would the purpose of a metrogovernment be somewhat defeated if several units of local government, such as special districts, still fell outside the metrogovernment's jurisdiction? Of course, even such trivial issues as choosing the color of the police department's cars can also be an obstacle.

Intergovernmental Contracting   One method by which local government can take advantage of the economies of scale without actually adopting a metrogovernment is to encourage the use of intergovernmental contracting. **Intergovernmental contracting** is the practice of one government contracting with another government to provide a service or good. A particular local government may develop expertise in one area, or its size may make it easier to purchase and maintain, for instance, road-grading equipment. Another local government may take advantage of that specialization by contracting for the provision of that good or service. For example, small cities in Texas will sometimes contract with the county sheriff's department to provide police protection, and it has become quite common for many of the entities within a county to contract with the county for the collection of taxes.

Privatization   **Privatization** is another increasingly popular method of coping with an increasing number of urban problems. Privatization is the act of turning over to the private sector—to businesses—functions that either were or are usually considered to be governmental. Privatization can take many forms. For example, a city can contract with a waste-disposal company for the collection of solid waste, and the city pays the private company to perform the service. As with intergovernmental contracting, economies of scale can be achieved. For example, it may be less costly for a city to contract with a janitorial service to clean city facilities than it would be for the city to hire and maintain a staff. Disputes arise, of course, over what kind of services and goods should be privatized. A decision has to be reached as to what kind of services the private sector can best provide by contract, versus what government can best provide directly. This is not just a question of the least costly method, and there are many intangible factors involved in the provision of services.

The privatization of some public services is a controversial issue. Police protection is a prime example of this phenomenon. Police protection has traditionally been thought of as a public function. Increasingly, however, people rely on private security firms for a sense of security and well-being. Indeed, there are gated or walled communities, access to which is controlled by armed guards, security gates, or often both.

Less visible perhaps than privatized police protection is the use of deed restrictions, in place of city ordinances. When housing subdivisions are built, developers often include deed restrictions as a contractual part of the purchase of a home. In other words, the purchase of a home in that subdivision is also an agreement to abide by the terms of the deed restrictions. The restrictions usually govern such things as architectural changes to the home, such as the addition of a room or patio. Deed restrictions can be quite detailed, such as placing limits on the color of paint that may be applied to the outside of the house or even dictating the type of landscaping allowed. Particularly in subdivisions outside a city's limit, deed restrictions are the only form of "city ordinances" that exist.

Subdivisions that have deed restrictions also usually authorize the creation of a homeowners' association. The association is made up of all homeowners in that subdivision and elects officers to run it. The association is responsible for the enforcement of the deed restrictions. Associations are not granted police powers, but they may file civil suits on behalf of the association against individual homeowners for violations. Under Texas law, it is difficult for a homeowner to win in an action brought by a homeowners' association if the homeowners' association can document its actions and has given the homeowner a reasonable opportunity to comply. Deed restrictions may require homeowners to pay dues, which the association may sue to collect. Homeowners' associations are usually involuntary and have some enforcement powers. Indeed, the power of a homeowners' association can be arbitrary, because many deed restrictions contain nuisance clauses that allow the association to restrict almost any type of behavior.

Councils of Government: Solving Problems Together

Councils of government (COGs) have also been created as a partial answer to metropolitan problems.[10] They are also quite novel, acting essentially as regional planning and coordinating bodies for other governments. Although they resemble metrogovernments to some degree and appear to be governments, COGs have no substantive authority or power to enforce resolutions on their constituent government members. Initially established in 1966 as a result of federal requirements, the councils now divide the state into 24 geographic regions. Most members are elected officials from cities and counties within the COG territory that have chosen to be members, though the constituency is somewhat flexible and can be defined, within limits, by the individual COG.

The councils provide technical and managerial assistance to these governments, process applications for federal grants, and run a wide assortment of state and federal programs for the region. Indeed, most COG funding is pass-through money that comes from the state and federal governments. Some funding is also received from dues that constituent governments pay. Perhaps the greatest assets of the COGs are in providing a forum for the disparate local governments to discuss mutual problems, in coordinating various solutions, and in researching and evaluating the impact of the activities of one member on other members. The first rapid transit authority in Texas, the Dallas Area Rapid-Transit Authority (DART), came about from work initially undertaken by the North Texas Council of Governments.

Critical Thinking Exercise: Local governments often overlap in form and function. What reforms would you introduce to bring about greater cooperation and collaboration among local governments?

LOCAL GOVERNMENTS AND POLITICAL CHANGE

Local governments do not often start periods of creedal passion, but they are sometimes the target of creedal passion. Many aspects of local government in Texas are the result of periods of creedal passion in the United States as a whole and in Texas in particular. The 1876 constitution restored and strengthened the role of county government and laid the foundation for the later growth of local governments in Texas.

The progressive movement of the early 1900s brought to the state the council-manager form of city government and at-large-by-place elections. Both were the results of a period of creedal passion at the national level aimed at ending the corruption often associated with city politics. The hurricane disaster in Galveston produced a period of creedal passion at the local level, ushering in another reform, the commission form of city government.

In response to the period of creedal passion at the national level engendered by the Civil Rights movement of the 1960s, many cities (such as Dallas, Houston, and San Antonio) changed their methods of electing city councils. In fits and starts, the cities went from at-large-by-place elections to single-member district systems. A few small cities in Texas have adopted cumulative-voting systems in response to the ongoing struggle over minority voting rights.

Obviously, a period of creedal passion has not occurred in county government. Although criticized by students of government, counties seem to be locked in complacency.

> **Critical Thinking Exercise:**   Home-rule cities in Texas have a considerable amount of autonomy and independence from the state. How might that independence be used to foster change in government?

LOCAL GOVERNMENTS AND DEMOCRACY

The extensive use of local government in Texas is a reflection of the commitment to an ideal of democracy that strives toward having government as close to the people as possible. This is particularly noticeable in the use of home-rule cities and special districts and the perception of the county as a unit of local government, instead of as an administrative unit of the state. How well does this system reflect the conditions for democracy? Is it fundamentally majoritarian or pluralist in nature?

Local government is, indeed, close to the people, but the issue is whether that closeness is meaningful and translates into more opportunities for people to influence governmental policy. One of the paradoxes of United States national government and Texas state government and politics is that the governments that are physically closest to the people also seem to be furthest removed from their awareness. Turnout rates for local elections are generally well below those of state or national elections. Most voters can name the president of the United States, the governor of the state, and a United States senator, but they may not be able to tell you who is the mayor of their city or the president of the local school board. This means that relatively few individuals—those who actually vote in the elections—make the decisions for the majority. While the condition of political equality is well established at the local level, the conditions of nontyranny and deliberation are more problematic.

The condition of nontyranny is satisfied in a formal sense, of course, but the low levels of turnout at the local level raise the issue on a practical level. In many local elections, particularly those for special districts, the turnout is often less than 10 percent. That creates the possibility that a minority will take over and run the district in a manner detrimental to the majority. On the other hand, as long as political equality prevails, the majority can always simply turn out and vote for whomever they choose.

The condition of deliberation is even more problematic. Although local government is the level of government closest to the people, it is in many ways the most obscure. Meeting the condition of deliberation requires that complete information be available. Information on local governments is often rather obscure. Consider the amount of coverage that local governments receive in the typical government class. Most of us who teach the courses spend far more time on state and/or national government. The dearth of information extends to political campaigns. Comparatively little is known about local offices and local candidates. Paradoxically, Jacksonian democracy may have reduced meaningful democracy in Texas. The long ballot gives individuals numerous opportunities for exercising democracy, while making it more difficult to deliberate about the issues and candidates involved in the elections.

> **Critical Thinking Exercise:**   The paradox of local government is that it is the closet to us, yet we seem to know little about it. In terms of the conditions for democracy, how well does local government meet those conditions? Why is that the case?

SUMMARY

This chapter has examined cities, counties, special districts, and the institutions that can join them together. These local governments are among the least-understood and visible parts of government, but they may also be the most important. Cities have grown in importance this century, especially since the 1940s, when the number of Texans living in urban areas surpassed the number living in rural areas. Texas is now a highly urbanized state. There are two types of incorporated areas: general-law and home-rule cities. The ordinance-making abilities of general-law cities are restricted to what the state will allow them to do, and such cities generally provide only basic services. In contrast, home-rule cities are typically larger and, given the increased demands for services with a larger population, are granted by the state a great deal of discretion in what they can regulate. Cities govern themselves using one of three forms of government: mayor-council,

council-manager, and commission. The at-large method of electing city councils has often provoked much controversy since the late 1970s, as it tends to favor majoritarian rather than pluralist democracy. Many cities have reformed their election methods to promote greater minority representation.

Counties are administrative units of the state, keeping numerous types of records and administering state and federal programs. They also bear responsibility for building and maintaining county roads and bridges. Counties tend to be seen as a local government, rather than part of the state government, and most officials are elected at the local level. As their structure has remained essentially unchanged since passage of the 1876 constitution, county governments have many critics.

Special districts number in the thousands in Texas, and they span a wide variety of forms and purposes. They are special-purpose governments, designed to meet one or a few needs that other governments cannot or will not fulfill. Sometimes a need—such as more streetlights in one neighborhood—is too localized, but sometimes a problem—such as pollution, flood control, and electrical generation along a river—crosses many governmental territories. Particularly in unincorporated areas, special districts often provide utility services a city would otherwise normally supply. Although many citizens have contact with independent school districts, hospitals funded through special districts, and rapid transit authorities, few Texans are aware of the role, purpose, powers, or existence of special districts.

Finally, because local governments are local, they often find that they must coordinate their activities with other governmental entities. Metrogovernments represent a new way of understanding local government, to create a new level or type of government for addressing the problems of regional urban areas. Councils of government (COGs), intergovernmental contracting, and the privatization of governmental services are all recent changes in how local governments work together.

KEY TERMS

municipal incorporation	county commissioner
general-law cities	county sheriff
home-rule cities	tax assessor-collector
mayor-council	county clerk
city council	elections administrator
council-manager	district clerk
city manager	county treasurer
commission	county auditor
at-large-by-place system	county manager
single-member district	spoils system
proportional representation	merit system
cumulative voting	unit-road system
annexation	special district
extraterritorial jurisdiction (ETJ)	metrogovernment
general-obligation bonds	intergovernmental contracting
revenue bonds	privatization

commissioners court
county judge

councils of governments (COGs)

SUGGESTED READINGS

Brischetto, Robert R. and Richard L. Engstrom. "Cumulative Voting and Latino Representation: Exit Surveys in Fifteen Texas Communities." *Social Science Quarterly* 78 (December 1997): 973–991.

Foster, Kathryn A. *The Political Economy of Special-Purpose Government.* Washington, D.C.: Georgetown University Press, 1997.

Hajnal, Zoltan and Terry Nichols Clark. "The Local Interest Group System: Who Governs and Why." *Social Science Quarterly* 79 (March 1998): 227–241.

Jones, Lawrence, Nirmal Goswami, and Ralph Warren. "An Assessment of Capital Budgeting in Texas Cities." *Texas Journal of Political Studies* 19, no. 2 (1997): 51–64.

McKenzie, Evan. *Privatopia: Homeowner Associations and the Rise of Residential Private Government.* New Haven, Conn.: Yale University Press, 1994.

Tees, David W., Richard L. Cole, and Jay G. Stanford. *The Interlocal Contract in Texas.* Arlington, Tex.: Institute of Urban Affairs, University of Texas at Arlington, 1990.

Thomas, Robert D. "The Politics of Turf: City Growth through Annexations." In *Perspectives on American and Texas Politics,* 5th ed. eds. Kent L. Tedin, Donald S. Lutz, and Edward P. Fuchs, 193–227. Dubuque, Iowa: Kendall/Hunt Publishing Company, 1998.

NOTES

1. Dave Harmon, "Spurs Get New Home; Rockets Don't," *Austin American-Statesman,* 2 November 1999, A11; also see House Research Organization, *Session Focus,* "On Deck: Financing Sports Facilities in Texas," 12 March 1997, for more background.

2. Delbert A. Taebel, Rod Hissong, and Theresa M. Daniel, "The Public Financing of Professional Sports Arenas—Who Should Pay and Who Benefits?" *Texas Journal of Political Studies* 21 (June 1999): 51–64.

3. See Institute of Public Affairs, *Forms of City Government,* 7th ed. (Austin Tex.: University of Texas, 1968); and Delbert A. Taebel and Joe Clark Humphrey, *Local Governments in Texas* (Manchaca, Tex.: Sterling Swift, 1979), 2–10.

4. Rex C. Peebles, "City Council Elections: A Third Alternative," working papers,1995.

5. Robert R. Brischetto and Richard L. Engstrom, "Cumulative Voting and Latino Representation: Exit Surveys in Fifteen Texas Communities," *Social Science Quarterly* 78 (December 1997): 974.

6. Robert Brischetto, "The Rise of Cumulative Voting," *Texas Observer,* 28 July 1995, 6–10, 18.

7. See Taebel and Humphrey, *Local Governments in Texas,* 27–40, for a discussion of county government.

8. See Ibid., 47–52; and Woodrow G. Thrombley, *Special Districts and Authorities in Texas* (Austin, Tex.: University of Texas, 1959), for further discussions of special districts.

9. The FHA is a government agency that makes it easier for people to buy homes by guaranteeing the loan. If a person who bought the house defaults on the loan, the institution making the loan will be covered against loss by the FHA. In order to be FHA approved, a house must meet certain minimal building standards.

10. See Taebel and Humphrey, *Local Governments in Texas,* 59–67.

13 Civil Liberties and Civil Rights

★ Scenario: The Texas Bill of Rights

Jane Doe, a fictitious person, had faced sexual harassment at work for some time. After her pleas for help seemed to fall on deaf ears at the company she worked for, she decided to seek legal counsel. Her lawyer advised her to sue her supervisor and her company for creating a hostile work environment, one in which employees feel threatened or just uncomfortable about their status. In Jane's case, her supervisor had implied that she would not get a raise or a promotion unless she was willing to have sex with him. He was constantly calling her names, such as "Sweetheart," and putting his arm around her. Even though she tried to tell him that his behavior was unwelcome and inappropriate, he persisted.

Jane Doe went to her supervisor's superior and complained about her supervisor's conduct but was rebuffed. In essence, she was told that it was part of the corporate culture and that if she did not like it, she could look for another job or a transfer to another department. In spite of the fact that she could find no one else willing to complain about her supervisor and knew that taking on company policy, or in this case the lack of company policy, would be a difficult ordeal, she decided to pursue the matter through legal counsel.

Civil suits involving sexual harassment may be filed in a civil court at either the state or the national level. Jane Doe's attorney advised her to file suit in state court. Like many other people, Jane Doe had assumed that the national government provided all the protections of liberties and rights that were necessary or available. She was puzzled by her lawyer's suggestion that she file suit in a Texas state court.

When questioned, Jane Doe's lawyer replied that the national government established the floor for civil liberties and civil rights in the United States; that is, through legislation and United States Supreme Court rulings, the national government has established a minimal level of liberties and rights, below which the states may not go. The states, on the other hand, establish the ceiling, above which civil-rights protection does not extend. While the states may not offer to their citizens fewer civil liberties and rights than the national government affords, they may offer more. The situation of a state government offering more protection than the national government is the direct result of a federal system of government. In a federal system of government, the state may do anything it wishes unless prohibited by the national government. While the national government does prohibit the states from offering less protection of civil liberties and civil rights than it does, it does not prohibit the states from offering more protection.

Jane Doe's lawyer argued that in the case of sexual harassment, the state of Texas's Equal Rights Amendment at least offered the potential for greater protection against sexual harassment than national legislation did. As a result, the lawsuit was filed in state court on grounds that the Equal Rights Amendment to the Texas Constitution's Bill of Rights had been violated. ★

INTRODUCTION

Civil liberties and civil rights are two of the most fundamental features of the American system of government, written into the United States and Texas Constitutions. The terms *civil liberties* and *civil rights* are often used interchangeably, but a distinction can be made between them. Civil liberties and civil rights are both freedoms. **Civil liberties** are those freedoms or privileges that are possessed because government is prohibited from doing something. The Bill of Rights to the United States Constitution begins with "Congress shall make no law. . . . " Thus, the freedom of speech, for example, derived from the First Amendment to the United States Constitution, is based on a prohibition placed on the United States Congress. Civil liberties include the freedom of religion and the rights of those accused of a crime.

Civil rights, on the other hand, can be thought of as those freedoms granted by government. In other words, a person has these freedoms because the government says that he or she does. That does not necessarily mean that civil rights are given or taken at the whim of the government. First, in a democratic society, the government is a reflection of the will of the people. People have the civil rights

Te★asIndex

How States Guarantee Rights

Substantive changes in bills of rights to state constitutions, 1990–1997:

Total proposed: 79

Total ratified: 59

Percentage ratified: 75

Texas: Total proposed, 2

Texas: Total ratified, 2

17 State have gone beyond the United States Constitution to grant additional protections to their citizens:

Texas: Yes

New York: No

California: Yes

Florida: No

14 State constitutions have an equal rights amendment covering gender:

Texas: Yes

New York: No

California: No

Florida: No

that they have given themselves. Second, civil rights may be, and often are, embedded in constitutions, thereby making them somewhat difficult to change. The most common civil right is that of citizenship. Who is or is not a citizen of the United States and of the State of Texas is a matter that government decides. Other civil rights are the right to vote and the right not to be discriminated against for a variety of purposes and reasons.

The two basic models of democracy are majoritarian and pluralist. Pure majoritarian rule would give no veto to minorities because it holds that the majority should always rule. The American tradition is not pure majoritarian but has a pluralist element, which protects minorities from arbitrary rule. Civil liberties and rights afford this protection. Civil liberties and civil rights are often thought of in the United States in individual terms, and the smallest minority is a particular individual. Civil liberties and civil rights have the consequence of protecting the individual, a minority, against the arbitrary rule of the majority. The degree to which individuals possess civil liberties and civil rights is a major indicator of whether the society will be majoritarian or pluralist in nature.

As discussed in Chapter 3, the people of Texas live under two distinct sets of laws, those of the United States and those of the State of Texas. Most discussions of civil liberties and civil rights center around the Bill of Rights and other amendments found in the United States Constitution. The United States Bill of Rights begins with the words, "Congress shall make no law. . . . " As one might suspect from the language used, the Bill of Rights found in the United States Constitution was originally meant to apply to the national government only. The application of the United States Bill of Rights to state governments was not possible until passage of the Fourteenth Amendment to the United States Constitution, and actual enforcement did not take place until much later, through the process of selective incorporation.[1]

Texas, like every other state, also has a Bill of Rights. In this chapter, the focus is on civil liberties that derive from prohibitions on government found in the Texas Constitution and on civil rights as they exist in Texas. One may wonder why the Texas Constitution should even be examined. Does not the United States Constitution's Bill of Rights afford people all the protection they need? There are at least two reasons for examining the state's constitution. First, while it is true that the United States Constitution is the supreme law of the land, that does not mean that state constitutions are meaningless. While the state must grant to its citizens the same level of protection the national government does, it is only bound to that standard as a minimum. In other words, the State of Texas may grant more civil liberties and civil rights than the national government does, but not less.

Second, the Supreme Court of the United States is now perceived as being more judicially restrained than it has been in several decades. As a practical matter, the result of this trend on the court has been to at least slow the rate at which civil liberties and civil rights have been expanded at the national level. Because the states may go beyond the national government, many lawyers and constitutional scholars have come to view state constitutions as a new avenue for expanding civil liberties and civil rights. This phenomenon has been labeled the "new judicial federalism." As a result of the new judicial federalism, increased attention has been given to state constitutions and their bills of rights in recent years. Table 13.1 compares the key features of the Texas Bill of Rights with provisions of the U.S. Constitution.

CIVIL LIBERTIES

Civil liberties accorded the citizens of Texas are found in Article 1 of the Constitution of the State of Texas, which consists of 33 sections. One major difference between the United States Constitution and the Texas Constitution is the way the liberties and rights are stated. The United States Bill of Rights starts with the phrase, "Congress shall pass no law. . . . " Thus, the wording of the civil liberties found in the Bill of Rights to the United States Constitution are essentially negative in character. The Texas Constitution has a more affirmative tone to it, a topic discussed in more detail later in this section.

Speech and Press (Expression)

The First Amendment to the United States Constitution is often said to contain the "preferred" freedoms. They are so called for at least two reasons. First, the freedoms of speech, press, religion, assembly, and petition are listed first, which could indicate that they were meant to be given priority over other freedoms. The

Table 13.1   COMPARISON OF TEXAS BILL OF RIGHTS WITH UNITED STATES CONSTITUTION AND BILL OF RIGHTS

Article I	Nature of right guaranteed	Comparable national constitutional provision	Differences
Section 3	Equal protection	Fourteenth Amendment	Texas confers equal protection; the nation prohibits denial of equal protection
Section 3a	Equal protection	None	Texas specifically prohibits discrimination because of race, color, gender, creed, or national origin
Section 4	Religious freedom	First Amendment	Texas has a more specific ban on religious tests and discrimination
Section 5	Witnesses not disqualified by religious beliefs	First Amendment	Texas grants more specific protection for religious belief and lack of belief
Section 6	Freedom of worship	First Amendment	Texas provision is more expansive and guarantees protection equally of all religions for worship, as well as a right to worship or not to worship
Section 7	Appropriations for sectarian purposes	First Amendment	More specific prohibition on the establishment of religion
Section 8	Freedom of speech and press, libel	First Amendment	Texas affirmatively grants these rights, and defense of truth is given constitutional dimension
Section 9	Searches and seizures	Fourth Amendment	Texas makes grant of right to protection from unlawful searches and seizures and requires a warrant to describe person, place, or thing "as near as may be"; national requires warrant "particularly describing"
Section 10	Rights of accused in criminal prosecutions	Fifth and Sixth Amendments	Texas allows representation by self or attorney or both and requires grand jury indictment for felonies
Section 13	Due course of law	Fifth Amendment	Texas also guarantees due course of law and open courts remedy
Section 19	Due course of law	Fifth and Fourteenth Amendments	Texas also provides due process for those to be "in any manner disenfranchised"
Section 27	Right of assembly; petition for redress of grievances	First Amendment	Texas also has a right of remonstrance
Section 29	Provisions of Bill of Rights excepted from power of government, to forever remain inviolate	None	

Source: Adapted from James C. Harrington, *The Texas Bill of Rights: A Commentary and Litigation Manual.* Austin, Tex.: Butterworth Legal Publishers, 1993.

Supreme Court of the United States has often interpreted the First Amendment as such. Similarly, the freedoms of speech, press, religion, petition, and assembly in the Texas Constitution are found in Article 1. The same argument could be applied to the Texas Constitution.

A second, and more persuasive, argument is that the freedoms of speech, press, religion, assembly, and petition are the preferred, or fundamental, freedoms because they are necessary to a truly free, democratic society. Issues of public policy must be debated openly and completely. Rational decisions can only be made under conditions of complete information. The only way to ensure that an approximation of complete information is available to the citizens of a society is by making sure that the citizens at least have the opportunity to hear all opinions and claims to the truth.[2]

One of the conditions of democracy discussed throughout this text is deliberation. As outlined in Chapter 1, deliberation has two aspects to it. First, the amount of deliberation, or discussion, that is allowed or possible on public policy questions determines in part how democratic a society can be. Second, the quality of that deliberation is also important, changing the effectiveness of deliberation and democracy. Genuine deliberation requires that complete information, or at least as complete as possible, be available. The freedoms of speech, press, and religion are crucial to complete information and, hence, to genuine deliberation. Article 1, Section 8 of the Texas Constitution states:

> That the general, great and essential principle of liberty and free government may be recognized and established, we declare:. . . . Every person shall be at liberty to speak, write, or publish opinions on any subject, being responsible for the abuse of that privilege; and no law shall ever be passed curtailing the liberty of speech or of the press.

In the areas of free speech and press, the Texas Supreme Court has tended to go beyond the United States Supreme Court in granting protection to the citizens of Texas. That trend has been evident in every Texas constitution, beginning with the one of 1836. The 1836 constitution's Declaration of Rights contained 17 articles and an introductory paragraph prohibiting its violation. The declaration provided the model for all the constitutions that followed.[3]

The 1876 constitution contained 29 sections in its Bill of Rights, only one less than the original proposal introduced at the 1875 constitutional convention. The Bill of Rights has been amended only eight times since then, generally strengthening the protections it accords individual citizens. All of the Texas constitutions have placed limits on the government's ability to regulate speech and the press. All of the constitutions have also given the rights of free speech and a free press an affirmative stance. Of the argument that the Texas Constitution guarantees protection beyond that of the United States Constitution, Texas civil rights attorney James Harrington writes:

> In addition to the intent discernible from the overall thrust and structure of the state constitutions, especially the 1876 version, specific historical evidence indicates that the framers of the Texas Constitution sought to protect free expression beyond the guarantees in the federal charter.[4]

Historically, the Texas courts had upheld free-speech and free-press rights long before the United States Supreme Court required the states to apply to their citizens the First Amendment of the United States Constitution.

Protesters at an antigun-control rally oppose all regulations of guns, based on the belief that the right to bear arms, stated in the U.S. Bill of Rights, should prevent any regulation of firearms.

In 1992, two cases before the Texas Supreme Court explicitly enunciated the idea that the Texas Bill of Rights accords a greater degree of protection to its citizens than does the United States Constitution. First, *Davenport v. Garcia,* a free-speech case, dealt with a gag order in the settlement phase of a toxic-chemical exposure suit brought on the behalf of 213 children and many adults. The gag order prohibited the lawyers from discussing or publishing anything about the case with anyone except their clients and their staff. The case provides an interpretive model for the analysis of state constitutions because it looked at the philosophical and historical background of the Texas Bill of Rights. The case also conducted an analysis of the language of Section 8 to discern the proper translation of terms from 1875 (when the section was last debated and written) to the present. *Davenport* also examined the role that the Bill of Rights plays in the constitution and examined earlier Texas cases that had found greater than national protection of expression.

The second case, a civil free-press case, *Star-Telegram, Inc. d/b/a Fort Worth Star-Telegram v. Walker,* involved the Texas Supreme Court overturning an order by a Tarrant County trial judge that forbade the *Fort Worth Star-Telegram* from publishing the name of a rape victim, even though the victim's name had been exposed at the trial. The cases of *Davenport* and *Star-Telegram* both lay out the conditions that must be met to restrain free speech and free press. There are basically two conditions under which **prior restraint** (the prevention of publication) may occur: (1) There must be a real threat of immediate and inescapable harm, and (2) there must not be any alternative to dealing with the threat, which would be less violative of free-speech rights. To prevent the publication of something requires that it can be demonstrated that a threat of swift and irreversible harm be present. Also, there must not exist a way of countering the threat that does not interfere with free speech and press rights. These criteria have never been met.[5]

The right of free speech may often conflict with other rights. For instance, free-speech rights have conflicted with property rights in Texas. The collision of these two rights provides an instructive example of the differences in the ways that free speech is protected at the national and the state levels.[6] The right of individuals to own property is accorded protection under the Fifth and Fourteenth Amendments to the United States Constitution and by Sections 17 and 19 of Article 1 of the Texas Constitution.

The controversy over the rights of free speech and the rights of the use of one's property has led to different interpretations by the United States Supreme Court and state supreme courts. The **controlling law** (a court decision that determines how substantive cases should be decided) at the national level is found in *March v. Alabama* and *Hudgens v. NLRB.*[7] In *March v. Alabama* (1946), the U.S. Supreme Court held that the First Amendment permitted Jehovah's Witnesses to distribute literature in a company-owned town because it was very similar to other towns. The court returned to the doctrine expounded in *March* in *Hudgens v. NLRB*. *Hudgens* dealt with striking workers who wanted to picket in a shopping mall. The court ruled that they did not have the right to picket because the mall did not meet the public-function doctrine enunciated in *March*. The public-function doctrine was further defined by declaring public functions to be those performed exclusively by state governments. The rationale behind this is that the First and Fourteenth Amendments protect free speech and assembly by placing restrictions on state action, not on action by private parties, as long as the acts are nondiscriminatory.[8]

In contrast to national law, the conflict between free speech and private property manifested itself in Texas state law in the case of *Nuclear Weapons Freeze Campaign v. Barton Creek Square Shopping Center*. In 1983, the Nuclear Weapons Freeze Campaign wanted to pass out literature and to gather signatures on petitions at Barton Creek Square Shopping Center in Austin, Texas. The owner of the shopping mall prohibited the group from doing this. The Nuclear Weapons Freeze Campaign asked the state court to prohibit the owner from stopping them.

In deciding the case, the trial court looked at First Amendment cases under the United States Constitution, how other state constitutions have been interpreted on the same subject, the difference in the wording of the national constitution and the state constitution, and the history of Texas's free-speech provisions. The court decided that the Texas Constitution does grant an affirmative right to free speech. As a result, the fact that the Nuclear Weapons Freeze Campaign wanted to carry out activity on private property did not provide an automatic bar to their activity. The court took note of the fact that the proposed activity was not destined for residential property or a small retail establishment. The court also recognized that the granting of permission to exercise the rights of free speech, assembly, and petition on private property would constitute a violation of the owner's property rights. Therefore, the court was required to balance the competing rights of speech, assembly, and petition and the right to private property.

Barton Creek Square Shopping Center is the largest mall in Austin. The common, nonshopping area of the mall consists of 180,000 square feet. The Nuclear Weapons Freeze Campaign sought to use 120 square feet of the area. Barton Creek Square had previously allowed other community groups to use the mall on a limited basis. During one 18-month period, noncommercial groups had used the common area on more than 50 occasions.

The court also determined that although sidewalks partly bordered the mall, they were almost invisible from the mall itself. Cars were not required to stop at the entrance to the mall, and the primary method of access to the mall was by automobile. Consequently, limiting the petitioners' access would have practically prevented the nuclear-freeze advocates from speaking to shoppers or obtaining their signatures on the petitions. The protesters had conducted similar activities at other Austin shopping centers without incident. They had agreed to abide by all conditions set forth by the shopping centers and agreed to pay any costs incurred by the shopping center due to their activities. The protesters argued that for the purpose of engaging others in discourse and obtaining signatures on petitions, any other way would not be as effective.

The court ruled that the protesters would not unduly interfere with the operation of the mall. Therefore, the right of the owner to exclude the Nuclear Weapons Freeze Campaign was not sufficiently injured to justify the denial of their free speech, assembly, and petition rights. The court did grant the property owner the right to adopt reasonable time, place, and manner restrictions on the group. Further, the property owner was allowed to exercise his speech rights by posting disclaimers next to the group, disavowing any connection to Nuclear Weapons Freeze Campaign. The decision of the court was never appealed.

The case of *Right to Life Advocates v. Aaron Women's Clinic* also addressed the clash of the competing rights of speech and property. The Houston Court of Appeals decided the case in favor of property because the facts of the case were different from those described for the *Barton Creek Square* case. "Members of the defendant right-to-life organization picketed, distributed literature, and engaged in 'sidewalk counseling' on the building property, seeking to prevent women entering the clinic from terminating their pregnancies."[9] In this case, the property owner asked for an injunction that would prohibit the protesters from engaging in their activity on the premises of the clinic. The court ruled in favor of the clinic. The court used the same balancing test as the court in the *Barton Creek Square* case but obviously arrived at a different conclusion.

The Houston court of appeals tried to balance the rights of speech, assembly, and petition against the right to property. In *Aaron,* the building was a single-use building with immediately adjacent streets where the protesters' activities could be carried out in full view of the clinic. Perhaps the biggest difference in the two cases lay in the economic impact of the two activities on the private property. While the Nuclear Weapons Freeze Campaign would arguably have virtually no impact on the businesses at Barton Creek Square Shopping Center, the protesters at the abortion clinic could have had a substantial economic impact on the clinic's profits. As a result, the court reasoned that in the Barton Creek case, there was not enough "taking" of private property to outweigh the rights of speech, assembly, and petition; but in the abortion clinic case, there was sufficient "taking."

Remonstrance

One of the rights that Texas citizens enjoy, which is not found at the national level at all, is the right to remonstrance. This is a little-known and little-understood right. The First Amendment to the United States Constitution grants citizens the right to petition government for a redress of their grievances. Article 1, Section 27 of the Texas Constitution gives to the citizens of Texas the right of petition, address, or remonstrance. Remonstrance has sometimes been considered the same as the right to petition, but Robert Hall argues that if you assume that the framers of the constitution were not merely repeating words and had given some consideration to the words they were using, then the right to remonstrance must mean something different from the right either to petition or to address government.[10]

The argument that the right to remonstrance is more than the right to petition is an important one. The right to petition has often been interpreted narrowly as merely the right to a one-sided process of communication by citizens to their government, consisting of an effort to initiate new actions or a new remedy in response to problems. Hall argues that the right to remonstrance is more than this. It is the "right to some kind of dialogue with government."[11] A dialogue implies a two-way process of communication. Petitions are relatively innocuous in the sense that they are presented to government, and then government has the option of acknowledging, addressing, or ignoring them. The process of communication is two-way only if the government makes it so. Remonstrance requires that government respond to the demands of its citizens.

The history of remonstrance in Texas is a long one. Stephen F. Austin evidently delivered a remonstrance to the Mexican government prior to the Texas revolution, and he expected some kind of response to it from Mexican authorities. Each Texas constitution has contained the right to remonstrance. The most recent instances in Texas involving remonstrances came in 1983 and 1986. In 1983, college professors at a state school in El Paso filed a remonstrance to show their disagreement with action by the school's governing board, which would have abolished faculty tenure. The administration ignored the remonstrance. The professors sued to have the remonstrance enforced. The trial judge, evidently perplexed by something that he was not familiar with, as was the administration at the college, ruled that the professors had no cause for action. In other words, they had no grounds for a case.

In 1986, the El Paso Court of Appeals reversed the ruling of the trial court. The appeals court ruled that a remonstrance must be considered, that it could not simply be ignored. However, the court did not rule that the government agency, the college, must respond in a particular way. "The court equated the citizen's right of remonstrance to an enforceable demand that 'those trusted with the powers of government . . . stop, look, and listen.' "[12] At best, this is a somewhat vague ruling. As a result, a motion for a rehearing was filed, which culminated in the court examining various sources, in an attempt to define the term *consider.* The court concluded that the body to which a remonstrance is directed will demonstrate that it has considered a remonstrance by its actions. The court did not actually require a response.

Hall argues that the history of the use of remonstrance in Texas and the intent of the framers of the constitutions of Texas demonstrate that the right of remonstrance is more than the right to consideration; it is the right to a response. The right to remonstrance is the right to a dialogue with government. Many people feel that "you can't fight city hall." Many citizens feel that government is not responsive to their needs and concerns. That has often been advanced as one of the reasons for low voter turnout. The perception that government is not paying attention may lead to feelings of apathy or even alienation.

In the models of democracy explicated in the first chapter, one of the conditions of democracy was that of the degree of deliberation. A fully developed right of remonstrance that required the government to respond to the concerns of its citizens could have the effect of increasing the degree of deliberation at two levels. First, the degree of deliberation between citizens and the government could be increased. If the desired result is a true two-way dialogue, then a remonstrance could increase the quality of thought and care that is given to public policy on the part of those delivering a remonstrance. After all, it would seem that in the interest of obtaining the desired result, the presentation should be thorough and carefully thought out.

Second, a fully developed right of remonstrance could result in a greater degree of deliberation among public officials. If the recipient of a remonstrance is required to give full consideration and craft a response to it, then in the interest of serving the public, as well as the interests of election and reelection, a carefully crafted response would be in order. If the recipient of a remonstrance was a governing body, such as a board of trustees, then a carefully crafted response would call for a heightened degree of deliberation within that governing body.

Religion

The guarantees of freedom of religion in Texas are found in Article 1, Sections 4 and 6 of the Texas Constitution. In general, Texas has a more specific prohibition against the use of religious tests in such things as employment and discrimination based on religious preferences than does the national government. The specific prohibitions exist in spite of the fact that the constitution requires public officials in Texas to acknowledge the existence of a Supreme Being. However, that provision has no force. The state had agreed not to enforce it, under threat of suit by Madalyn Murray O'Hair during Mark White's tenure as attorney general.

Until the 1990s, the United States Supreme Court held that states must demonstrate a compelling interest in taking actions that infringe upon the exercise of religion. In 1990 in *Employment Division v. Smith*,[13] the United States Supreme Court held that religious conduct is subject to generally applicable laws that are neutral on their face to religion. The United States Congress passed the Religious Freedom Restoration Act in 1993 to restore religious freedom to the status it had before *Smith*. In 1997, the United States Supreme Court ruled in *City of Boerne v. Flores*[14] that the national law could not be applied to the states (see Chapter 3). In response, the Texas legislature passed its Religious Freedom Act in 1999. It prohibits a government agency, state or local, from substantively interfering with the free exercise of religion unless the agency can demonstrate that it acted from a compelling interest and had used the least restrictive means of furthering that interest.

Rights of the Accused

The rights of the accused are the protections accorded to those individuals accused of a crime by the state. Perhaps no other area of civil liberties creates as much controversy. Currently, violent crime is of great concern to many people. Prisons are overcrowded, partly in response to increases in prison sentences and a growing rate of violent crime for a number of years. (Perhaps it should be noted that the overall crime rate has actually declined in recent years.) The criminal justice system is accused of being soft on criminals, and the court system is sometimes blamed for this, especially judges who are perceived as being "too liberal," in that they seem to be more concerned about the rights of criminals than they are about the rights of victims.

One must be careful that complaints are being leveled at the correct source, however. A distinction can be made between the rights of those accused of a crime and those convicted of a crime. Texas, like the rest of the United States, has adopted the presumption of innocence until proven guilty. Given that presumption, the distinction between those accused of a crime and those convicted of a crime is a real one that deserves attention. The rights of the convicted are usually covered under the Eighth Amendment to the United States Constitution, which forbids cruel and unusual punishment. The Texas correctional system was under court order to address problems in the penal system for a number of years (see Chapter 11). As a result, Texas has followed the United States Supreme Court in cases dealing with the rights of the convicted. The focus of this section is not on the rights of the convicted, but on the rights of the accused.

Due Course of Law   Due course of law may be compared to the United States Constitution's provision for due process of law. Due course or due process of law is essentially the notion that all the procedural rules will be followed in any given case. Due process of law is guaranteed by the Fourteenth Amendment to the United States Constitution. The notion that the Texas Constitution provides at least the minimum guarantees afforded by the Fourteenth Amendment was established by the Texas Supreme Court in 1887.[15] The Texas guarantee of due course of law is found in Section 19 of Article 1 of the Texas Constitution. It reads as follows:

> No person of this state shall be deprived of life, liberty, property, privileges, or immunities, or in any manner disenfranchised, except by the due course of the law of the land.

It has been argued that Section 19 has two substantial differences from the Fourteenth Amendment, which results in greater protection for the citizens of Texas.

First, Section 19 does not limit itself to restricting state action but grants an affirmative right to people without regard to the state government. Second, the due process clause of the Fourteenth Amendment confines itself to life, liberty, and property; but Section 19 of the Texas Constitution also includes any way by which a citizen may be disenfranchised. **Disenfranchisement** is usually used to refer to the right to vote, but Texas constitutional law considers the taking away of a citizen's rights, privileges, or immunities in general to be instances of disenfranchisement. Harrington argues that the historical evidence supports interpreting Section 19, Article 1, of the Texas Constitution in broader terms than those provided by the Fourteenth Amendment to the United States Constitution.[16] The United States Supreme Court has also given credence to the notion that the states may go farther than the national constitution does.

> It is first noteworthy that the language of the Texas constitutional provision is different from, and arguably significantly broader than, the language of the corresponding federal provisions. As a number of recent Supreme Court decisions demonstrate, a state court is entirely free to read its own constitution more broadly than this Court reads the Federal Constitution, or to reject the mode of analysis used by the Court in favor of a different analysis of its corresponding constitutional guarantee.[17]

The Texas Constitution also contains an open-courts provision that is intimately tied to due course of law. Essentially, it says that access to the judicial system is guaranteed as a method for the redress of grievances or the settling of disputes.

Search and Seizure   Search and seizure (looking for and taking evidence) provisions are found in the Fourth Amendment to the United States Constitution and in Article 1, Section 9 of the Texas Constitution. The language of the two provisions is similar, although the Texas provision seems to require that each warrant be more specific, in that the person or place to be searched must be described "as near as may be." Until 1991, the Texas Court of Criminal Appeals had always argued that the national provisions and the state provisions concerning search and seizure were virtually identical and should be interpreted in the same manner.

That practice was interrupted when the Texas Court of Criminal Appeals remanded to the Dallas Court of Appeals for an independent and separate analysis under the Texas Constitution the case of *Heitman v. State.* The case was returned to the court of appeals for a judgment based solely on the Texas Constitution's provisions dealing with search and seizure. The Texas Court of Criminal Appeals clearly departed from its earlier practice by stating that it would no longer be bound by national precedent and that protection against unlawful search and seizure, as found in the Texas Constitution, had meaning separate from the United States Constitution.[18]

Self-incrimination   The prohibitions against self-incrimination are found in the Fifth Amendment to the United States Constitution and in Section 10 of Article 1 of the Texas Constitution. The relevant part of the Fifth Amendment says that "No person . . . shall be compelled in any criminal case to be a witness against himself." The relevant part of Article 1, Section 10 of the Texas Constitution says that "In all criminal prosecutions the accused . . . shall not be compelled to give evidence against himself." Although the two provisions are obviously worded virtually identically, the Texas Court of Criminal Appeals has gone beyond national protection. The reason for this seems to be that the United States Supreme Court has been backing away from its previous broad interpretation of *Miranda*. The Texas Court of Criminal Appeals has generally not followed the national trend in cutting back on protection against self-incrimination.

In *Sanchez v. State*,[19] the Texas Court of Criminal Appeals ruled that a defendant's silence prior to receiving the ***Miranda* warnings** could not be used against him or her in a court of law. In *Dunn v. State*,[20] the court reversed Dunn's conviction on the grounds that his waiver of his *Miranda* rights was not made with complete information and rationality because he was never allowed to talk to his lawyers until after he had signed the waiver and a confession to the murder of his father. Under controlling national law, the conviction would have probably been upheld. The Supreme Court of the United States would have argued that the denial of access to the accused was irrelevant to the waiver of the right to remain silent.

Exclusionary Rule   The prohibition against the use of illegally obtained evidence in a criminal trial in Texas is the result of a Court of Criminal Appeals ruling in 1923 that the Texas Constitution did not mandate an exclusionary rule similar to that established on the national level. An **exclusionary rule** says that any evidence illegally obtained cannot be used against a person in a court of law. As a result, the legislature passed the Search and Seizure Act in 1925, which made a warrantless search a crime and which required the exclusion of evidence seized by "officers or other persons in violation of the Constitution or laws of the state of Texas or the United States." Including the phrase "other person" would seem to clear up some of the ambiguity of the Fourth Amendment to the United States Constitution. The provision would seem to preclude the admission of evidence seized illegally by private persons, although the courts have not always been consistent in doing so.

Confrontation   The right to confront the witnesses against you and to cross-examine them at trial is a right that has a long history in common law and is covered by both the United States and Texas Constitutions. In the case of *Long v. State*,[21] the Texas Court of Criminal Appeals reversed a conviction on the grounds that the admission of videotaped testimony of children in sexual-abuse cases violated both national and state confrontation clauses, as well as the state due-course-of-law and national due-process provisions. The court held that the right to confront witnesses was a fundamental right and that any infringement of that right would have to serve a compelling state interest.

The right to confront witnesses is found in Article 1, Section 10 of the Texas Constitution. The applicable part reads, "In all criminal prosecutions the accused . . . shall be confronted by witnesses against him." Appropriate case law in Texas has made it clear that the right to confrontation is fundamental. In *Powell v. State*,[22] the Dallas Court of Appeals held that at some point in the trial, a face-to-face confrontation had to take place between the defendant and the witnesses. This case also involved a sex offense against a child. Even though the lawyer for the defendant was allowed to be present at the taping of the testimony, the court argued that the right to confront could not be delegated entirely to the lawyer. An essential element of the right to confront the witnesses against you is the ability to confer with one's lawyer.

The *Long* and *Powell* cases are "hard" cases. They involve the balancing of the rights of the accused against the feelings and psychological states of the children. The courts decided that the rights of the accused would usually take precedence. However, the courts can recognize a compelling state interest in infringing on the right of confrontation. Although the national courts have done so, the Texas Court of Criminal Appeals has been reluctant to do so. The *Long* case provides an excellent example of the reasoning used in the balancing act:

> The legislative activity that produced [the statute] was, as we have recognized, well intended. However, [if] the legislature imposes barriers on an accused's constitutional rights it should do so narrowly and only with great caution and concern. In the instance of child protection statutes the effort is essentially aimed at reconciling opposites: the innocence of youth stained by experience of age. Although it is not an impossible task it is one that is made difficult by the concerns we must by necessity have for the rights of people accused of crimes, no matter how vile and repulsive the alleged offense. This area of the law is dominated by emotions, which is understandable in light of the interests society wants to protect—abused children. But irrespective of the interests to be protected of greater concern should be the adherence to our constitutional rights. We cannot ever permit emotion charged issues to erode our fundamental liberties. To do so would produce emotionally pragmatic deviations from established standards that will inevitably and ultimately result in a complete erosion of the rights that make us a free society.[23]

One of the characteristics of a pluralist democracy, as opposed to a majoritarian democracy, is the extent to which minorities are protected from the whims of the majority. The rights of the accused represent a classic example of the protection of the minority. The rights provided to the accused by the Texas Bill of Rights help to ensure that regardless of the sentiment of the majority, the accused, a singular minority, will be presumed innocent until proven guilty.

> **Critical Thinking Exercise:** Suppose that you have been arrested for a crime that you did not commit. After carefully taking account of the rights of the accused, which one(s) would you be willing to forfeit or weaken in the name of law and order? Which ideology best reflects your position on the rights of the accused?

CIVIL RIGHTS

Civil rights are those rights that come as the result of a grant of government. Although the technical distinction between civil liberties and civil rights can be drawn, both ultimately serve the same function, the protection of the minority. As in the case of civil liberties, part of the focus in this chapter is to examine the differences between the State of Texas and the United States. In some instances though, the focus is on Texas's reaction to and place within national civil rights legislation. Civil rights can be classified under three major categories: citizenship, voting, and equal protection. The first two categories are self-explanatory. The third encompasses a broad spectrum of issues that generally deal with types of discrimination.

Citizenship

Most people take citizenship for granted; indeed, most people do not even think of citizenship as being a civil right. Citizenship does, however, meet the criteria of a civil right. After all, it is government that decides whether a person is a citizen. In a democratic society, the citizens decide what the government will do, so the decision as to who is and who is not a citizen is not an arbitrary one. Nevertheless, not everyone is a citizen. The seemingly innocuous right of citizenship is very important because it is the prerequisite for other rights. For example, one of the necessary qualifications for voting in Texas is United States citizenship.

Citizenship also defines a person's relationship to the state in other ways. On one level, if you are a citizen of the United States, then you are also a citizen of the state of Texas, if you live here. However, it is the definition of "living here" that can determine whether you are a full-fledged citizen of the state of Texas. As students, most of you are familiar with residency requirements for the payment of tuition. If you are in a state-supported institution of higher education, there are different tuition rates charged for in-state, out-of-state, and international students. If you are a student in 1 of the 50 state-supported community colleges in Texas, there are further distinctions made between in-district and out-of-district students.

Residency requirements illustrate one of the ways that citizens of Texas are distinguished from noncitizens for certain purposes. Differential tuition rates revolve around the idea that those who live in the state or in the district for a year prior to enrolling in college have paid taxes to the state or local governments and have thus paid their share of the taxpayer-supported subsidies that go to the schools. Those students who come to a particular state or district for the sole purpose of attending college have not contributed to the subsidies. The differential in tuition is to make up the difference between what a person would pay as a resident in taxes and the tuition charged.

Residency requirements have a further purpose. They are also reflective of the idea that a person should have developed some kind of interest, or stake, in a particular locale before being able to partake fully of the privileges accorded to already existing citizens. Thus, residency requirements are used to establish eligibility for such things as voting and welfare programs directed at the poor. Some residency requirements are stricter than others.

Age requirements also play a role in the designation of citizenship. Typically, a person is accorded full citizenship rights upon reaching the age of 18 years. There is a notable exception to this, however: the drinking age. Running for public office requires the basic qualification of United States citizenship, but age requirements vary for different offices. In Texas, the minimum age for public office varies from 18 to 30 years. Although often overlooked as a civil right, the condition of citizenship and/or residency is necessary for many of the other civil rights.

Voting

The right to vote is essential to a democratic society. The essence of a democratic system is one in which citizens are afforded the opportunity to participate. One definition of democracy is this: a system in which the things most preferred by the greatest number of people are reflected in public policy. The preferences of the citizenry are usually expressed through voting. Indeed, for most people, the only form of political participation in which they actively engage is the act of voting. Chapter 7 discusses voting in terms of who votes and how they vote. This chapter examines the right to vote.

The major focus of this section is on the contemporary right to vote in the wake of the 1965 United States Voting Rights Act, the most important and comprehensive piece of legislation dealing with voting ever passed. As discussed in Chapter 3, one of the more curious features of the 1876 constitution was its prohibition against voter registration. Under the 1869 constitution, ex-Confederates and government officials were disenfranchised, or denied the right to vote, unless they swore loyalty to the Union. The loyalty oath was accomplished at registration. Partly in reaction to that practice and partly as a result of the populist tide that swept through Texas in the 1870s, voter registration was prohibited.

The prohibition of voter registration seems to indicate that anyone can vote. Of course, this was not literally true. Adult women, for example, did not get the right to vote until much later. Generally, however, males of at least 21 years of age were able to vote. Participation was fairly widespread from 1876 until the turn of the century. In the 1890s, the imposition of Jim Crow laws began in other states, and by 1900, Texas also became interested in legalized discrimination in general and in disenfranchisement in particular.

The rise of political discrimination can be at least partially attributed to white property owners' opposition to changes made during a period of creedal passion. A populist movement swept the country in the late 1800s. The populist movement in the South created an alliance between populists and many southern blacks against the white propertied classes.[24] Although most periods of creedal passion end in reforms that close the gap between the ideals and the practices, this particular period had the opposite result. At least in many states in the South, including Texas, the discrepancy between the ideal of democracy through political participation and the practice of voting was actually widened.

ORIGINAL   TO BE USED FROM FEB. 1, 1964 TO JAN. 31, 1965

POLL TAX *Receipt* ★

COUNTY OF **HARRIS**

No. 10120

★ STATE OF **TEXAS**

DATE _Jan 3_ 19 6 4

RECEIVED OF _H. R. RODGERS JR._

the sum of $1.50 in payment of poll tax, the taxpayer says that:

His ☑ Her ☐ HOME address is _1732 Des Jardines_   ZIP CODE

	YEARS
He ☑ She ☐ is age	21+
and has resided in Texas . . .	
in Harris County	19
in City of _Houston_	

Occupation is _Student_

White ☑ Colored ☐ | Native born ☑

Naturalized citizen of the U.S. ☐

Birthplace—State of _____

PRECINCT NUMBER

218

DEMOCRAT

Party Affiliation (TO BE FILLED IN BY PRECINCT CLERK WHEN VOTING)

ALL OF WHICH I CERTIFY,

(SEAL OF OFFICE)

IF PARTIAL EXEMPTION GIVE REASON _____

By _____ (1)

ASSESSOR AND COLLECTOR OF TAXES, HARRIS COUNTY, TEXAS   DEPUTY

Having a poll-tax receipt, such as the one shown here, was once necessary to prove that a citizen had paid the poll tax, which had to be paid in order to cast a vote in any election. By regulating who could pay the poll tax and who could qualify as a voter, white elites were able to significantly control the voting patterns of minority groups from the post–Civil War era through the first half of the twentieth century.

In 1902, Texas adopted a constitutional amendment establishing a **poll tax,** a fee for voting. The poll tax had to be paid in the period from October 1 to January 31 in the year preceding an election. Registration was still prohibited, but the privilege of voting had to be paid for. The state-imposed fee was $1.50, counties were allowed to levy an additional $0.25, and cities could levy an additional $1.00. By the standards of 1902, $1.50 to $2.75 could be considered substantial. Inflation has risen at least 1000 percent since 1900. In today's dollars, it would equal approximately $15.00 to $27.50. By today's standards, that may not actually seem like much. However, the poor of Texas at the turn of the century did not have a lot of cash. The average monthly wage for manufacturing industries in the South was less than $40. Combined with the fact that the tax was collected over the holiday season (Thanksgiving and Christmas), you can begin to understand why the poll tax was so effective in keeping poor people away from the ballot box. Confronted with the choice between spending up to $2.75 on voting nearly a year later or on Christmas now, what is the likelihood that a poor person would choose to spend the money on voting?

The Democratic Party in Texas moved to disenfranchise even more people in 1923 with the imposition of the **white primary.** Although the law creating the white primary went through several permutations in response to legal challenges, the basic notion remained the same. The Democratic Party could establish its qualifications for membership in any manner it saw fit. One of the qualifications for membership was being white. This would obviously disenfranchise African

Americans in Texas. The combination of the white primary, the poll tax, and Texas being a one-party state effectively meant that voting in elections was limited to white, middle- and upper-class Democrats.

The process of assuring African Americans the right to vote has been long and tangled. It had been assumed that the passage of the Thirteenth Amendment in 1865, abolishing slavery, would suffice to guarantee to ex-slaves the full benefits of United States citizenship. However, many states erected barriers against reaching that goal. As a result, the Fourteenth and Fifteenth Amendments were passed in 1868 and 1870, respectively, to fulfill the aims of the Thirteenth Amendment. More is said about the Fourteenth Amendment in the next section. The Fifteenth Amendment says in part that "The right of citizens of the United States to vote shall not be denied or abridged by the United States or by any State on account of race, color, or previous condition of servitude."

The passage of the Fifteenth Amendment to the United States Constitution attempted to secure the right to vote for those otherwise eligible. As noted previously, though, barriers to voting (through the poll tax and the white primary) were erected in the early 1900s. The white primary lasted until 1944, when the Supreme Court of the United States declared it unconstitutional in *Smith v. Allwright*. The Supreme Court ruled that the white primary violated the Fifteenth Amendment on the grounds that because of Texas's status as a one-party state, the Democratic Party was the sole location of electoral competition. Because nonwhites were not allowed to join the Democratic Party, they could not vote in the Democratic primary. Therefore, they were effectively denied the ability to participate in the political process in a meaningful way.

The poll tax proved to be more difficult to remove. It was not eliminated in national elections until ratification of the Twenty-fourth Amendment to the United States Constitution in 1964. The applicable part of it reads:

> The right of Citizens of the United States to vote in any primary or other election for President or Vice President, or for Senator or Representative in Congress, shall not be denied or abridged by the United States or any other State by reason of failure to pay any poll tax or other tax.

The imposition of the poll tax at the state and local level was declared unconstitutional in 1966 by the United States Supreme Court in *U.S. v. Texas*. With that decision, all but one of the legal barriers to voting in Texas was eliminated.

Nonetheless, disenfranchisement may occur both by legal and overt means and by illegal and covert mechanisms. The right to vote may be denied by overly burdensome registration requirements and/or intimidation at the time of registration or at the polling place by, for example, the use of all-white election judges. As a result of this and other factors, voter turnout among minorities was particularly low. The United States Congress responded to that situation by passing the 1965 Voting Rights Act. The act was an attempt to secure the right to vote for formerly disenfranchised persons, especially African Americans. Section 2 of the act prohibited any state from using any voting prerequisite, the purpose of which was to "deny or abridge the right of any citizen of the United States to vote on account of race or color."[25]

Section 4 had the effect of eliminating so-called literacy tests as qualifiers for voting. Sections 6, 7, and 8 were aimed at making sure that African Americans could vote without intimidation at the polling place. Sections 6 and 7 provided for voting examiners to make sure that discriminatory tactics were not used at registration. Section 8 provided for official poll watchers to be posted at polling places to ensure that people were allowed to vote without intimidation or harassment. Enforcement of the act was placed in the hands of the national government.

Sections 4–9 of the 1965 Voting Rights Act contain the **preclearance** (approval of voting requirements) provisions. The act established a triggering formula for determining what states and counties the act applied to. Even if a state as a whole did not meet the triggering formula, counties within a state could. In other words, the act could be applied either to the state as a whole or to particular counties within a state. The triggering formula stated that any county or state in which less than 50 percent of its population either had registered or had actually voted in the 1964 presidential election would be subject to the provisions of the law. States and counties that met the criteria of the triggering formula under Section 4 were placed under the provision of preclearance in Section 5.[26]

Any state or county that met the triggering formula would have its voting laws frozen until gaining approval from the national government for any proposed changes. Any state or county seeking to change its voting laws would have to submit to the attorney general of the United States or to the U.S. District Court for the District of Columbia all proposed changes that dealt with voting qualifications, or prerequisites for voting, or any standard, practice, or procedure that pertained to voting that had not already been in effect by November 1, 1964. The national government would then determine whether the proposed changes would have the effect of or the purpose of denying or abridging the right to vote on account of race or color. The changes would be given preclearance (approval) on a jurisdiction-by-jurisdiction basis. Section 5 gave to the national government unprecedented authority to oversee the election machinery of state and local government. However, the initiative for seeking approval rests with the jurisdiction making the change. The U.S. Justice Department has never bothered to determine whether all proposed changes have actually been submitted for preclearance.[27]

One of the major problems with minority voting rights since the passage of the Voting Rights Act has been that of **vote dilution:**

> Ethnic or racial minority vote dilution may be defined as the process whereby election laws or practices, either singly or in concert, combine with systematic bloc voting among identifiable majority groups to diminish or cancel the voting strength of at least one minority group.[28]

Any process that has the effect of making a person's vote worth less than that of another person's engages in vote dilution. Dilution of minority voting strength, in violation of the Voting Rights Act, can take many forms. Racial **gerrymandering,** the drawing of district lines to diminish the number of minorities in a district, is one such way. Another is to decrease the proportion of the minority population by annexation of majority areas, or the de-annexation of minority areas, or the consolidation of jurisdictions to increase the majority population relative to the minority population. Dilution of minority voting strength may also be accomplished by requiring **majority runoff elections,** allowing the majority to unite behind a single candidate after voting for several in the regular election. Majority runoff elections are required in Texas for primary, nonpartisan, and special elections.

Other forms of vote dilution include at-large elections rather than single-member districts. At-large elections allow a majority to overwhelm a minority, assuming that voters split along majority-minority lines. If the majority only votes for majority candidates and the minority only votes for minority candidates, then the majority can win all of the seats on a city council, for example. (See Chapter 12 for a full discussion of methods of election of city council members.) **Full-slate laws** (at-large elections), numbered-place laws, and staggered terms can prevent the use of single-shot voting, under the condition of polarized voting on the part of the majority and the minority. **Single-shot voting** refers to the practice of the minority vote uniting behind a single candidate. Last, the minority vote can be split by nominating **straw candidates** to take away votes from a strong minority candidate.

The Texas experience has seen several attempts to dilute minority voting strength. Following the 1954 *Brown v. Board of Education* decision by the United States Supreme Court, adoption of the numbered-place system was increasingly used by cities and school boards. When the majority vote as a bloc, the use of a place system can be employed against single-shot voting or a full-slate law. The fact that the numbered-place system or the at-large-by-place system could be used against minorities almost certainly played a part in their adoption. The Supreme Court of the United States ordered Texas to redistrict its badly malapportioned congressional and legislative districts in 1966. The result was the demise of multimember districts, but the creation of gerrymandered districts was designed to dilute African-American voting strength in Harris County, where Houston is located.[29]

The Houston school district adopted a majority runoff requirement after a white liberal and two African Americans were elected to the seven-person board, under the plurality rule (the candidate who receives the greatest number of votes wins). Perhaps the most egregious examples of attempts at continued disenfranchisement were legislated by conservative Democrats led by then Governor John Connally in 1966. The United States Supreme Court had declared the state's poll tax unconstitutional. In response, the legislature passed a highly restrictive registration law. It included a four-month registration period that ended nine months before the election, strangely reminiscent of the poll tax, without the tax. The Connally Democrats also led the movement to limit the holding of state elections to nonpresidential election years. When finally adopted in the 1970s, the result was a one-third reduction in voter turnout in gubernatorial elections, which had been rising for 20 years.[30] Perhaps one of the more curious features of the Texas response to the Voting Rights Act is the fact that the act did not originally apply to Texas because Texas did not have a literacy test in 1965. However, Texas came under the act's provisions in 1975.

The Supreme Court decision in *Allen v. State Board of Elections*[31] gave the notion of vote dilution constitutional importance and made the use of Section 5 a prominent feature of the 1965 Voting Rights Act. The argument of the plaintiffs in the case was that preclearance was required only of those proposed changes in election laws or procedures that would actually disenfranchise minority voters. The defendants argued that because vote dilution could have the same effect as disenfranchisement, the preclearance provision should apply to changes in laws or procedures that would result in vote dilution. The Supreme Court of the United States agreed with the defendants. Writing for the Court, Chief Justice Earl Warren argued that the act gave a rather broad interpretation to the right to vote, including all things necessary to give a person an effective vote. He went on to write that:

> The right to vote can be affected by a dilution of voting power as well as by an absolute prohibition on casting a ballot. . . . Voters who are members of a racial minority might well be in the majority in one district, but in a decided minority in the county as a whole. This type of change could therefore nullify their ability to elect the candidates of their choice just as would prohibiting some of them from voting.[32]

The 1986 case of *Thornburg v. Gingles*[33] established the criteria for determining whether vote dilution exists.

The first criterion established by the Supreme Court of the United States to prove vote dilution is that the minority must be sufficiently large and geographically compact that at least one single-member district could be drawn around them. The second criterion says that the minority must be politically cohesive, tending to vote as a bloc. The third criterion states that the majority must vote as a bloc that is sufficiently large to defeat the minority's preferred candidate. The second and third criteria examine the degree to which the voting between majority and minority is polarized.[34]

In recent years, the major thrust of enforcement of the 1965 Voting Rights Act has been to thwart vote dilution. In order to avoid possible lawsuits aimed at the practice of vote dilution, more and more changes in election laws and procedures are put through the preclearance process. In 1982, the preclearance provision of Section 5 was extended for another 25 years. Section 2 was also amended to prohibit voting practices, regardless of the purpose of those practices, that had the effect of discrimination in voting. The results of the amendment of Section 2 and of the *Thornburg v. Gingles* case have been to focus attention away from disenfranchisement per se and toward vote dilution. The controversy that currently exists in this area is that of **quotas** in voting. The result of the years of litigation and legislation regarding voting rights has been that, where possible, minority voters must be accorded their own districts. Does that also mean that districts must be drawn in such a way that minorities must be represented in legislative bodies in proportion to their overall percentage of the population? If the population of a city, for example, was comprised of 20 percent Asians, would the city council then have to be at least 20 percent Asian?

The notion of quotas in voting suggests that district lines can be drawn only in order to maximize minority voting strength. However, that can lead to districts that seem to be gerrymandered more so than any district ever drawn to dilute minority voting strength. North Carolina had a district that ran the entire length of the state and was no wider in places than the road it took in. Drawing districts in such a severe way could negate the reflection of interests that are based on attributes other than racial or ethnic background. Such interests could include regional concerns and class interests, as well as others.

The district in question, North Carolina's 12th Congressional District, was ruled in *Shaw v. Hunt*[35] to be the product of unconstitutional racial gerrymandering. The North Carolina legislature then drew up a new redistricting plan in 1997. However, that plan was challenged as unconstitutional and a three judge district court ruled that the plan violated the Fourteenth Amendment's Equal Protection Clause. On May 17, 1999, the United States Supreme Court overturned the lower court on the grounds that the issue was not subject to summary judgment. The court cannot settle a case without examining the facts when the evidence is subject to interpretation.

At issue was the motivation of the legislature in drawing the districts. If the motivation was racial, then the district was based on race and, therefore, suspect and subject to strict scrutiny. The evidence used to support claims of race as the predominant factor in drawing district lines is to look for the absence of the use of such traditional criteria as compactness, contiguity, and respect for political subdivisions or communities defined by actual shared interests. Perhaps the most important criteria is compactness, a measure of the distance between points on the outer boundary of the district. Closely related is the notion of contiguity, measuring how close one part of a district is to another. District 12, under either districting plan, is not very compact. In an effort to adhere to the third criteria of redistricting, do not dilute minority voting strength, legislatures have often used race as a factor in redistricting, resulting in ignoring the second criteria, compactness. The United States Supreme Court has said that anytime race is the predominant factor in the drawing of district lines, it will be subject to strict scrutiny.

Voting is the most widely used method of participation employed in the democratic process. If a democracy is a system in which the preferences of the people are reflected in the making of public policy and voting is one of the ways to reflect those preferences, for many the only one that is used, then voting has a high degree of importance. Political equality is one of the features of equality discussed in Chapter 1. The history of voting rights in Texas traces the history of the quest for political equality from the right to vote to the right to representation.

That concern is further reflected in the differences between a majoritarian and a pluralist system. Political equality, in the sense that each person's vote should be worth the same as anybody else's, is supported by all four of the ideologies described in Chapter 2. Eliminating disenfranchisement guarantees political equality, in the sense that individuals are accorded the opportunity to participate in the system. Because single-member districts are required to be roughly equal in population, political equality is satisfied in the "one person, one vote" sense. It is also majoritarian in the sense that each individual's vote will count as one—no more, no less. The votes can then simply be tabulated to determine the majoritarian outcome.

Vote dilution, on the other hand, does not confront the issue of the right to vote of a single person, but the effects of that vote in a group context. Political equality then makes the transition in meaning from equality of opportunity to equality of result, signifying a pluralist conception of democratic government and politics. Pluralism involves the politics of groups rather than of individuals. The controversy over quotas in representation marks the demarcation between a majoritarian society and a fully pluralist one. Establishing voting criteria that would require legislative bodies to reflect the racial and ethnic mix of their jurisdictions would represent equality of results. Thus, while liberals and populists have tended to support equality of results in vote-dilution cases, conservatives and libertarians have been more reluctant to do so.

Equal Protection

Equal protection is often considered synonymous with equal rights. The government grant of equal protection to its citizens means that each citizen has been granted equal rights. Equal protection has generally been conceived in terms of trying to guarantee equality of opportunity in such things as employment and education. The Texas Constitution contains two equal-protection provisions. Both are more detailed and comprehensive than the United States Constitution's Fourteenth Amendment. Article 1, Section 3 of the Texas Constitution provides that "All free men, when they form a social compact, have equal rights, and no man, or set of men, is entitled to exclusive separate public emoluments, or privileges, but in consideration of public services." Article 1, Section 3a provides that "Equality under the law shall not be denied or abridged because of sex, race, color, creed, or national origin. This amendment is self-operative." Like much of the rest of the Texas Constitution's Bill of Rights, Section 3 is cast in affirmative language. All Texas constitutions since 1836 have contained an equal-protection clause of some sort.

Equal protection can be equated with equal rights, but of course, equal rights cannot be granted and are not granted for all persons at all times. There are limitations. The delineation of those limits is accomplished through the establishment of suspect classifications and fundamental rights. The United States Supreme Court uses three levels of scrutiny: strict, intermediate, and the rational-basis test. At the national level, the U.S. Supreme Court has determined that **strict scrutiny** will be applied to the suspect classifications of race and national origin or ancestry or to the fundamental interests of the right to vote, the right to criminal appeal, interstate travel, the right to procreate, rights involving the parent-child relationship, marriage, and the right to confrontation in criminal cases. Any proposed limitation on these rights would require a compelling state interest, such as the protection of minors. The Supreme Court of the United States has rarely found a state interest compelling enough to limit any of the aforementioned rights.

The Supreme Court of the United States uses **intermediate scrutiny** in cases dealing with aliens (noncitizens), illegitimate children, and sex or gender. Intermediate scrutiny implies that a compelling state interest does not have to be demonstrated for a denial of equal protection to occur. However, the state must demonstrate more than a rational basis for what it is doing. The third level of scrutiny used by the United States Supreme Court involves the **rational-basis test.** The test merely requires that the state have a rational basis for treating people differently.

Generally, the State of Texas follows the precedents established by the United States Supreme Court in determining suspect classifications and fundamental rights. However, the explicit nature of the Texas provision of the state constitution has led to some differences. Many states have an equal-protection clause, but few are worded as strongly as Texas's. Three areas illustrate the differences between the protections afforded by the national government and those provided by the State of Texas. They are the Texas equal-rights amendment, equal protection under Section 3, and privacy.

Equal Rights Amendment   Article 1, Section 3a of the Constitution of the State of Texas is often referred to as Texas's equal-rights amendment. The amendment was adopted by a 4 to 1 margin in 1972. Until 1987, however, the amendment was used sparingly by the courts and even at times seemed to be avoided by the courts. In the *Baby McLean* case,[36] however, the Texas Supreme Court finally established a standard of review that could be used to determine whether the amendment had been violated.

The *Baby McLean* case involved a gender-based distinction applicable to the establishment of legitimacy for children born out of wedlock. The applicable statute provided that the father, but not the mother, of the child had to pass a "best interest of the child" test before being established as a parent of the child. The mother was automatically granted status as the child's mother, but the father had to demonstrate that it was in the best interest of the child for him to be the child's legally recognized parent. Obviously, males and females were being treated differently.

In deciding the case, the Texas Supreme Court refused to argue that the Texas equal-rights amendment should be given an interpretation identical to that of the national equal-protection guarantees and the national and Texas due-process clauses. The court pointed out that if there were no distinction drawn between these laws, then the Texas equal-rights amendment would be rendered moot. In other words, there would be no point in having it. The court could have adopted a *per se* standard that would have automatically invalidated gender-based distinctions under all conditions. Instead, the court opted for elevating gender to a suspect classification and subjecting gender-based distinctions to strict scrutiny.[37]

The Texas Supreme Court did not establish a hard-and-fast rule, arguing that the Texas Bill of Rights was not just a series of rules to be applied blindly, but it was to act as a guide to norms and principles to be applied to particular cases by the courts. The court then went on to establish a guiding principle for gender-based distinctions. Gender-based distinctions must meet a two-part test. Parties favoring such distinctions must (1) demonstrate a compelling state interest and (2) show that no other state action that is not discriminatory and that would also protect the state's interest is possible. The court agreed with the intent of the statute, to encourage unwed mothers to care for their children, but the intent could be accomplished without being discriminatory.[38] Thus, the statute failed to meet the second criterion.

Section 3a of Article 1 of the Texas Constitution has been relied on to reach other findings. Texas courts have eliminated gender-based bias in such areas as evaluating the responsibility to support children, based on the ability to pay; awarding attorney's fees in child-custody cases; and allowing the choice of name, upon marriage.[39] In *Texas Woman's University v. Chayklintaste,* the Fort Worth Court of Appeals held that a university rule requiring female students to reside on campus, but allowing male students to reside off campus, was unconstitutional because a right or privilege was denied solely on the basis of gender.[40]

One of the effects of Section 3a of Article 1 of the Texas Constitution has been to subject gender-based distinctions in the law to strict scrutiny. The distinctions are much harder to maintain in Texas than they are at the national level, where gender-based distinctions receive the intermediate level of scrutiny. The Texas equal-rights amendment has also been used to reach decisions based on the classification of national origin. Travis County District Judge Harley Clark relied in part on the equal-rights amendment to find that the exclusion of migrant farmworkers and ranch laborers from the Worker's Compensation Act and the Texas Unemployment Compensation Act was unconstitutional. Judge Clark argued that the workers constituted a unique class of Mexican-origin persons who had been victimized by discrimination. The acts operated against them as a whole and not against other types of workers.[41]

Equal Protection Under Section 3   The Texas equal-rights amendment has received much publicity and has taken gender-based distinctions to a higher level of judicial scrutiny. Before passage of Section 3a of Article 1, however, Section 3 existed as the other equal-protection clause of the Texas Constitution. Courts use the lowest level of scrutiny for cases involving Section 3, the **Texas version of the rational-basis test.** Recall from the preceding discussion that similarly situated individuals must be treated equally under the law unless there is a rational basis for not doing so.[42]

The Texas Education Code, prompted by the educational reforms of 1984, included a "no pass—no play" provision. Essentially, if students participating in extracurricular activities did not pass their classes, then they could not participate in extracurricular activities for a designated period of time. The law was challenged in *Spring Branch I.S.D. v. Stamos.* The Texas Supreme Court ruled that no fundamental interests or rights were involved and that no suspect classes were affected by the rule. As a result, the court determined that strict scrutiny was not required. The Texas version of the rational-basis test was used, and the law was upheld.[43]

The Texas experience with its equal-protection clause, as found in Section 3 of Article 1, reveals that the Texas version of the rational-basis test is stricter than the national version. It is actually closer to the national judiciary's level of intermediate scrutiny. This was demonstrated in the case of *Edgewood Independent School District v. Kirby,* which found the state's financing scheme for public education unconstitutional, using the equal-protection clauses of the Texas Constitution. A similar argument made 20 years earlier at the national level by one of the same plaintiffs, Demetrio Rodriquez, had been rejected by the United States Supreme Court (see Chapter 14). As in many of the civil liberties examined earlier in this chapter, the Texas Constitution provides protections to minorities that go beyond those provided by the national constitution.

Privacy   In 1978, in *Texas State Employees Union v. Texas Department of Mental Health and Mental Retardation,*[44] the Texas Supreme Court declared that the Texas

Constitution guarantees the right to privacy. The precise meaning to attach to that right is difficult to discern, however. Amy Johnson identifies three general areas in which Texas courts have decided cases: "(1) information—the discovery or disclosure of information about an individual's life, (2) physical intrusion—the physical intrusion into or near the property or person of an individual, and (3) behavior—the regulation of an individual's behavior for the purported good of society."[45] The first category of information includes intrusion into a person's body for gathering evidence. Intrusion may take place through polygraph (so-called lie-detector) tests, blood tests, or urinalysis. It also includes the publication of the names of blood donors with AIDS and the publication of information available through the Texas Open Records Act. Furthermore, it includes the publication of untrue or embarrassing information. In general, the Texas courts have held that this information is discoverable and publishable.[46] Therefore, the Texas courts have done little to expand protection in this area.

The second category of physical intrusion includes the interest in protecting private property. The Texas courts have upheld the right of a person to sue another who entered the person's property without permission. Free-speech rights have been curtailed when demonstrators want to demonstrate in residential areas. Remember, the right to private property is a very powerful one in Texas. However, the Texas courts have generally been reluctant to recognize privacy claims for the purpose of shielding illegal activity.[47]

In regard to the third and last category, the Texas courts have rarely protected behavior that the majority of Texans consider to be immoral, regardless of how private it may be. The Texas sodomy law, for example, has been challenged on the grounds that it violates a person's right to privacy. This is an indication of the Texas inclination toward ordered liberty and thus conservatism and populism. The state has not hesitated to make illegal those things that it thought were detrimental to the moral well-being of the citizens of the state.

The Texas right to privacy was established in the case of *Texas State Employees Union v. Texas Department of Mental Health and Mental Retardation*. The department had a policy that mandated a polygraph test of any employee suspected of patient abuse, criminal activity, or doing something that threatened the health and safety of employees. An employee who refused to take the test faced disciplinary measures by the department. The Texas Supreme Court ruled that Sections 6, 8, 9, 10, 19, and 25 of the Texas Bill of Rights, Article 1 of the Texas Constitution, established a zone of privacy. Those sections deal with freedom of religion, freedom of speech and press, searches and seizures, the rights of the accused, due course of law, and the quartering of troops in private homes, respectively. Those sections collectively establish a right to privacy that can only be violated for a compelling reason. The Texas Supreme Court ruled that the zone of privacy protected workers at the Department of Mental Health and Mental Retardation from mandatory polygraph examinations.[48] The full meaning of the right to privacy has yet to be developed in Texas. The zone of privacy established at the national level derives from the "penumbras and emanations" of the United States Constitution. The Texas zone of privacy has been established in much more concrete language, which could lead to a broader right to privacy than that provided at the national level.

Critical Thinking Exercise: Consider the criteria of geographical compactness and not diluting minority voting strength. Which should receive the greater consideration in drawing district lines? Why? What is the connection between your position and the ideal of equality?

CIVIL LIBERTIES AND CIVIL RIGHTS AND POLITICAL CHANGE

Civil liberties and civil rights initially stem from governmental action in the form of either prohibitions or grants. The specific content and full meaning of those actions are often left to the judicial branch to determine. As discussed in Chapter 11, the judiciary usually follows an inherently slow process. Even cases that are generally thought of as landmark and that appear to make dramatic changes usually draw on a line of precedents that lead to the so-called landmark decision. In addition, because the court system can only act when requested to do so by someone affected by the law or rule in question, periods of creedal passion are rare in the courts. However, the court system can and does respond to periods of creedal passion.

The initial impetus for civil liberties and civil rights does come from governmental action in the forms of constitution making, amendments to constitutions, and legislation. Many of the liberties and rights that the citizens of Texas enjoy have their origins in the Texas Bill of Rights, Article 1 of the constitution. As discussed in Chapter 3, the constitution is a result of a period of creedal passion in Texas. The aftermath of the Civil War, in the form of Reconstruction and the populist movement that swept the country in the 1870s, shaped the 1876 constitution. The affirmative nature of the wording of the provisions of the Texas Bill of Rights is a testament to the suspicion of governmental power that pervaded the 1875 constitutional convention.

The passage of the Texas equal-rights amendment in 1972 is a reflection of the period of creedal passion that swept through the country in the mid to late 1960s and the early 1970s. The initial Texas reaction to that period was to adopt restrictive laws in the area of voting, which tried to undo the reforms of the right to vote ensconced in the 1965 Voting Rights Act. In Texas, the period of creedal passion starts with attempts to diminish the discrepancy between the ideals of political equality and reality, and it ends with a constitutional amendment that carries the promise of narrowing the discrepancy. The courts' subsequent treatment of that promise will help determine whether the discrepancy between the ideal and the reality is widened or narrowed.

Critical Thinking Exercise: The treatment of women has undergone tremendous change in the last 40 years. Consider the Texas equal-rights amendment. In your estimation, does it go far enough in defending the rights of women? Defend your position.

CIVIL LIBERTIES AND CIVIL RIGHTS AND DEMOCRACY

Civil liberties and civil rights have the function of securing liberties and rights for individuals and groups. One indication of a pluralist rather than a majoritarian democracy is the degree to which minorities have veto power over the will of the majority. One of the ways to grant a minority veto power is to establish a rule that requires an extraordinary majority to attain passage of a proposed measure, as with the requirement that amendments to the Texas Constitution must be approved by a two-thirds majority vote of both houses of the legislature. Another way to ensure a minority veto over the will of the majority is to build in an automatic veto by constitutional or legislative prohibition on governmental or private action. Recall that the smallest minority is that of the individual citizen. The Texas Constitution reflects a commitment to individualism by building in many protections for the individual, many of which go beyond the protections accorded by the United States.

The 1965 Voting Rights Act reflects a commitment in its origins to political equality for the individual voter. After initial resistance to the notion by the Texas legislature and many citizens, it seems that the state has recognized the principle of "one person, one vote" for the most part. As a baseline of political equality, the equality of the individual voter at the ballot box is recognized by liberals, conservatives, populists, and libertarians alike.

However, the modern emphasis on vote dilution has shifted the argument from guaranteeing equality of opportunity in voting to ensuring equality of results in voting. The former places an emphasis on having a majoritarian system where a vote is counted equally without regard to its particular origins. The latter reflects an emphasis on pluralist democracy, where the attributes of a given individual that reflect membership in a particular group are important for determining outcomes.

> **Critical Thinking Exercise:** Consider the impact that the Voting Rights Act of 1965 and various court cases have had on the ideal of democracy. Has the effect been to make the State of Texas a more majoritarian or a more pluralistic democracy? Explain.

SUMMARY

Recall from the discussion in Chapter 3 that one of the most important purposes of a constitution is to establish limitations on government. The examination of civil liberties and civil rights in Texas has revealed that there are many limitations placed on the state government. Under a federal system, state governments have authority independent from the national government. That independent authority means that state governments may establish civil liberties and civil rights for their citizens that have a life and meaning separate from the national government.

Federalism means that the national government is supreme. As a result, the states must do the minimum that is required by the United States Constitution, national law, and United States Supreme Court interpretation. However, the state governments may also go beyond the national government. In other words, the state may accord more protections from governmental and private power than the national government does. Indeed, in Texas, that has often been the case. As a practical matter, that means that if the Bill of Rights to the United States Constitution were somehow repealed, a citizen of Texas would still be protected by the state constitution. In a federal system, the state governments do matter—as demonstrated by the discussion in this chapter of those areas of civil liberties and civil rights where the State of Texas has exceeded the requirements of the national government.

KEY TERMS

civil liberties

civil rights

prior restraint

controlling law

disenfranchisement

Miranda warning

exclusionary rule

poll tax

white primary

preclearance

vote dilution

gerrymandering

majority runoff election

full-slate laws

single-shot voting

straw candidates

quotas

strict scrutiny

intermediate scrutiny

rational-basis test

rational-basis test, Texas version

SUGGESTED READINGS

Harrington, James C. *The Texas Bill of Rights: A Commentary and Litigation Manual.* Austin, Tex.: Butterworth Legal Publishers, 1993.

Harrington, James C. "Free Speech, Press, and Assembly Liberties Under the Texas Bill of Rights," *Texas Law Review* 68 (June 1990): 1435–1467.

Herasimchuk, Cathleen C. "The New Federalism: Judicial Legislation by the Texas Court of Criminal Appeals?" *Texas Law Review* 68 (June 1990): 1481–1519.

Kilgarlin, William Wayne, and Banks Tarver. "The Equal Rights Amendment: Governmental Action and Individual Liberty," *Texas Law Review* 68 (June 1990): 1545–1572.

Linzer, Peter. "Why Bother with State Bills of Rights?" *Texas Law Review* 68 (June 1990): 1573–1614.

NOTES

1. *Selective incorporation* is the term used to refer to the United States Supreme Court's practice of selectively incorporating the provisions of the United States Constitution's

Bill of Rights as restrictions on the states. In other words, the United States Supreme Court has gradually applied the provisions to the states but has never applied all of the provisions, and those that have been applied have been so over a number of years.

2. See John Stuart Mill's *On Liberty,* ed. Elizabeth Rapaport (Indianapolis, Ind.: Hacket, 1978), for a defense of the proposition that freedom of speech and press is necessary to a free society.

3. James C. Harrington, "Free Speech, Press, and Assembly Liberties Under the Texas Bill of Rights," *Texas Law Review* (June 1990): 1438–1439.

4. Ibid., 1442.

5. James C. Harrington, *The Texas Bill of Rights: A Commentary and Litigation Manual* (Austin, Tex.: Butterworth Legal Publishers, 1993), 3–4. It is updated as needed.

6. See Joseph H. Hart, "Free Speech on Private Property—When Fundamental Rights Collide," *Texas Law Review* 68 (June 1990): 1469–1480.

7. 326 U.S. 501 (1946) and U.S. 507 (1976), respectively.

8. See Hart, "Free Speech on Private Property," 1469–1480.

9. Ibid., 1479.

10. See Robert E. Hall, "Remonstrance—Citizen's Weapon Against Government's Indifference," *Texas Law Review* 68 (June 1990): 1409–1433.

11. Ibid., 1410.

12. Ibid., 1411.

13. *Employment Division v. Smith* 494 U.S. 872 (1990).

14. *City of Boerne v. Flores* 117 S. Ct. 2157 (1997).

15. See James C. Harrington, *The Texas Bill of Rights,* 102.

16. Ibid., 103.

17. *City of Mesquite v. Alladin's Castle, Inc.* 455 U.S. 283, 293 (1982).

18. See Harrington, *The Texas Bill of Rights,* 52–53.

19. *Sanchez v. State* 707 S.W.2d 575 (Tex Crim App 1986)(en banc).

20. *Dunn v. State* 696 S.W.2d 561 (Tex Crim App 1985)(en banc).

21. *Long v. State* No. 867-85 (Tex Crim App, July 1, 1987)(en banc).

22. *Powell v. State* 694 S.W.2d 416 (Tex App—Dallas 1985).

23. *Long v. State,* 46.

24. Chandler Davidson, "The Voting Rights Acts: A Brief History," in *Controversies in Minority Voting: The Voting Rights Act in Perspective,* eds. Bernard Grofman and Chandler Davidson (Washington, D.C.: The Brookings Institution, 1992), 11.

25. Quoted in Davidson, "The Voting Rights Act," 17.

26. Ibid., 18.

27. Ibid., 19.

28. Ibid., 24.

29. Ibid., 26.

30. Ibid.

31. *Allen v. State Board of Elections* 313 U.S. 544.

32. Ibid, 569.

33. *Thornburg v. Gingles* 478 U.S. 30.

34. Ibid., 50–51.

35. *Shaw v. Hunt* 517 U.S. 899.

36. In *re: Unnamed Baby McLean,* 725 S.W.2d 696 (Tex. 1987).

37. William Wayne Kilgarlin and Banks Tarver, "The Equal Rights Amendment: Governmental Action and Individual Liberty," *Texas Law Review,* 68 (June, 1990): 1553.

38. *Baby McLean,* 698.

39. Kilgarlin and Tarver, "The Equal Rights Amendment," 1554.

40. *Texas Woman's University v. Chayklintaste* 521 S.W.2d 949 (Texas Civ. App.—Fort Worth).

41. Harrington, *The Texas Bill of Rights*, 71.

42. Ibid., 78.

43. Ibid., 78–79.

44. *Texas State Employees Union v. Texas Department of Mental Health and Mental Retardation* 746 S.W.2d (Tex. 1987).

45. Amy Johnson, "Abortion, Personhood, and Privacy in Texas," *Texas Law Review* 68 (June 1990): 1533.

46. Ibid., 1533–1534.

47. Ibid., 1535–1536.

48. Ibid., 1539.

CHAPTER

14 Economic and Social Policies

★ Scenario: Texas School Finance Battles, 1968–2000

In 1968, San Antonio resident Demetrio Rodriguez filed a lawsuit, arguing that Texas's school-finance system violated the U.S. Constitution's guarantee of equality. His children attended school in the Edgewood school district, a poor district that had only $5,960 in property value per student. Students who lived just a few miles away, in the Alamo Heights school district, had $49,000 in property value per student[1]—and far superior educational facilities and services. In 1971, the federal district court ruled in **Rodriguez v. San Antonio Independent School District** that the state's school-finance system violated the U.S. Constitution. On appeal, however, the U.S. Supreme Court upheld the system in 1973, agreeing that it was inequitable, but holding that education was not a fundamental right under the U.S. Constitution. School finance, the court declared, was a matter for states to resolve within their own courts.

Pushed by *Rodriguez* and other federal and state court decisions to reexamine their school-finance schemes, many state legislatures adopted innovative solutions

449

San Antonio parent Demetrio Rodriguez, plaintiff in the landmark Texas school finance cases, with his daughter at her graduation from Edgewood High School.

in the 1970s, such as guaranteed equalized tax valuations. When property wealth bases vary drastically within a state, available tax revenues are much higher in wealthier communities than in poorer ones. An effort to equalize taxing and spending capabilities, then, requires state action. Many legislatures increased the states' share of school spending to reduce reliance on the local property tax.

These changes in school-finance policies were controversial because of the redistribution involved: giving more state money to poorer communities than to richer ones, forcing spending limits on richer communities, or even redistributing some resources from richer to poorer communities. Legislators were buffeted by the forces of some wealthy local communities defending their right to determine school spending policies, other poorer local communities demanding equalized or greater educational expenditures, and courts setting deadlines for reforms.

In Texas, the post–*Rodriguez* years were chaotic. Once the U.S. Supreme Court ruled, antireform forces were back in control, and the 1973 Texas legislature failed to pass a school-finance proposal that had been prepared to respond to the charges of inequity. In 1975, the legislature did pass a reform bill, though reform advocates in the legislature voted against it as being far too little. Since 1975, the legislature has tinkered with the school-finance formulas but has left intact the basic system of local property taxes supplemented by state appropriations.

In 1987, the Edgewood school district sued the state in state court, claiming that the school-finance system violated the state constitution's provisions for "an efficient system of public free schools." Edgewood won in district court and in the Texas Supreme Court. In its unanimous 1989 *Edgewood v. Kirby* decision invalidating the school finance system, the court ruled that the state had to achieve substantial equity, meaning a fair and equitable distribution of resources, among school districts.

The Texas Supreme Court's decision created both a flurry of legislative activity and legislative gridlock. Republican Governor Bill Clements vowed to veto any bill that cost too much. Democratic legislators vowed to meet the court's requirement for a substantially equitable system. Clements vetoed the legislature's bill. After several special sessions, the legislature produced a bill that the governor signed, though Democratic lawmakers argued that it was too weak to be accepted by the courts. They were right. In 1991, the Texas Supreme Court invalidated the new plan.

The Supreme Court told the legislature that it must produce an acceptable system in the 1991 session. The legislature and new Governor Ann Richards adopted a plan by the deadline. The district court upheld the plan, but in a 5-to-4 vote, the Supreme Court ruled that the plan had created an unconstitutional statewide property tax (the state property tax having been repealed in 1982) and was thus invalid. The court held, though, that the plan could continue in effect until 1993.

In 1993, Governor Richards and the legislature produced a plan allowing countywide collection of property taxes that would then be distributed to the school districts. The legislature proposed the plan as a constitutional amendment, but voters rejected it. The legislature returned and produced yet another system, described later in this chapter, and the courts accepted it in 1995. New court challenges to it since then have, so far, been turned back. Governor George W. Bush then championed an increase in state funding of education to lower local property taxes.

The constitutional law established in the *Rodriguez* and the *Edgewood* cases clashed with the idea of local control and with the low priority given to equality by many Texans. When those who believed in more equality could not win in the electoral or legislative arenas, they turned to the courts (both federal and state) and continued the battle. For 30 years, school-finance politics has resembled a Ping-Pong™ game, and the primacy of education as a centerpiece of state social and economic policy ensures that it will always be a battleground. ★

INTRODUCTION

State governments in the twentieth century have focused much of their attention on economic and social policies: **Economic policies** are those that affect economic activity or have economic consequences for individuals or groups. **Social policies**

Te★as*Index*

Social and Economic Demographics

Gross state product, 1996:
Texas, $551.8 billion
California, $962.7 billion
New York, $613.3 billion
Florida, $360.5 billion

Four-Person family median income, 1997:
Texas, $48,007 (38th)
California, $55,217 (20th)
New York, $55,911 (18th)
Florida, $49,913 (32nd)

Medicaid expenditures, 1997:
Texas, $7.3 billion (3rd)
California, $11.4 billion (2nd)
New York, $21.3 billion (1st)
Florida, $4.9 billion (6th)

Medicaid cost per recipient, 1997:
Texas, $2,893 (39th)
California, $2,355 (46th)
New York, $6,771 (1st)
Florida, $3,058 (37th)

Per pupil expenditures, 1997:
Texas, $6,041
California, $5,327
New York, $9,628
Florida, $5,988

Total and per capita state government expenditures, 1997:
Texas, $48.9 billion ($2,515)
California, $117.2 billion ($3,632)
New York, $83.2 billion ($4,590)
Florida, $37.5 billion ($2,557)

guide our development as human beings and our relationships to other humans and to our broader environment. Some policies are both social and economic in nature. The state's $50-billion-a-year budget plays a role in stimulating the economy. Just as significantly, it sets economic and social priorities that influence our everyday activities.

Our southern, one-party, conservative and libertarian heritages influence Texas toward having limited government providing minimal social services. Our large, increasingly diverse, and predominantly urban population, however, has created pressures and demands for Texas to provide both *more* social services and a more *equitable* distribution of health services, educational opportunities, and income-support services.

In this chapter, we examine some specific areas of social and economic policy, including public regulation of private enterprises, poverty, subsidies for businesses and for individuals, public finance, education, welfare, and health care. We explore who is involved in the making of social and economic policies, how ideas and institutions affect policy making, and what the outcomes are. We then analyze social and economic policies in the context of political change and democracy.

ECONOMIC POLICY: WHO WINS, WHO LOSES?

Economics involves job availability, product quality, work environment quality, competitiveness of enterprises, productivity, and business profitability, as well as social, labor, and environmental regulations. Combined, these economic forces determine our standard of living. The **political economy** is the whole web of economic, social, governmental, and political institutions and processes. In this chapter, we see that the state plays numerous roles in the political economy.

Whether intentional or not, changes in economic policy redistribute income. A new highway means profits for construction companies and income for their workers. A freeze on welfare benefits, while population continues to increase, means smaller checks for each recipient. An increase in the sales tax means that a larger share of a working-class family's budget goes to the state than is true for an upper-class family. Much of the debate we hear in the media, legislative deliberations, or political campaigns revolves around a core issue of political economy: who wins and who loses with changes in economic policies.[2]

As we saw in Chapter 3, politicians have been reemphasizing the role of state governments in our political system. Political scientist David Osborne argues in *Laboratories of Democracy* that government's primary role is to nourish the elements that make innovation possible, such as skilled workers, investment money, markets, industrial modernization, and a social system that supports innovation and change.[3] A second agenda of government, Osborne argues, is to bring the poor into the growth process. Government cannot do everything for the poor, nor should it be expected to. However, a massive underclass creates social and economic crises for the entire society, so government must constantly grapple with the dilemmas of poverty. Both agendas affect who gets how much of the state's economic resources. Through its taxing and spending policies, its regulatory and economic development policies, and its education and human services policies, the State of Texas plays a significant role in that redistribution.

Subsidizing and Regulating Businesses

Governments both encourage business activity and restrict those activities. Policies to attract labor or business to a state involve efforts to improve the quality of the workforce, regulate workplace conditions, and boost corporate profitability. A **subsidy** is a grant of economic resources. The state subsidizes businesses to encourage certain economic activity. A **regulation** is a government restriction on certain economic activities. The state regulates businesses to achieve social, economic, or political goals. Sometimes, the goal of supporting economic growth can conflict with social goals.

In the nineteenth century, states subsidized railroads with land, and in the twentieth century, they subsidized the automobile industry with highways. Contemporary subsidies by states include tax breaks, location incentives, debt financing, venture capital, higher-education research entities, and trade promotion. In the 1980s and 1990s, Texas created subsidy programs, such as industrial development zones (with tax reductions) and finance authorities (with reduced interest rates for business loans). Some see a modern paradigm "built around new roles for government in the economy and new partnerships between the public and private sectors. . . . [attacking] problems by using the public sector—in partnership with business, academia and labor—to reshape the marketplace."[4]

Governments regulate business to maintain economic efficiency, to redistribute economic resources, to require compensation for social and economic effects caused by business activities, or to respond to the insistence of businesses when the businesses expect the regulation to benefit them economically and competitively. Texas regulates countless activities, including financial institutions, oil and gas production, utility services, insurance policies, labor organizations, deceptive trade practices, monopoly business practices, and businesses emitting pollutants. Still, most business decisions are not publicly controlled and are under the control of the business owners.

Regulation is an outgrowth of late-nineteenth-century shifts in public opinion, then in public policy, from a *laissez faire* approach (where government keeps out of business affairs) and toward limited regulation of business activities. Congress created the Interstate Commerce Commission (ICC) in the 1880s, and state governments followed with state-level regulations. When railroad officials realized that regulation influenced their economic and political equations, they maintained a permanent and powerful voice in the centers of policy decision making. In 1892, the U.S. attorney general, himself a former railroad industry official, wrote to the president of a railroad company about the new ICC, that it "is, or can be made, of great use to the railroads. It satisfies the popular clamor for a government supervision of railroads, at the same time that the supervision is almost entirely nominal. Further, the older such a commission gets to be, the more inclined it will be found to take the business and railroad view of things."[5]

With the creation of the Texas Railroad Commission in 1891 (see Chapter 4), Texas became one of the first states to regulate railroads. Utilities were the next industry to gain the attention of state governments. New York and Wisconsin were the first states to regulate utilities in 1907.[6] The Texas legislature considered such legislation as early as 1915, but utilities blocked passage of such a bill repeatedly until it finally passed in 1975. In 1999, the legislature deregulated much of the regulated activity.

In the late twentieth century, regulation of businesses expanded to include environmental and energy policies. Such policies are both social and economic in nature. To require people or companies to modify their behavior because of their potential impact on other people is a social policy; to require businesses to pay for environmental cleanup or to install and use pollution-preventing, energy-efficient technology is an economic policy.

The adoption of environmental and energy policies is influenced by several variables that we have examined in previous chapters, such as ideology, public opinion, and the relative strength of interest groups. For instance, libertarianism would oppose such policies as antithetical to the creed of limited government. Liberalism, populism, and conservatism might support such policies, but certainly with conflicting rationales. The level of environmental and energy regulation depends on the relative strength of business, environmental, and public-interest groups. In Texas, business has so long dominated environmental policy making that after years of battling against Texas on air quality issues, a scientific review panel for the U.S. Environmental Protection Agency wrote in the 1970s that the state agency was a "special advocacy group for industry."[7] Texas is by far the largest energy-consuming state in the nation.[8] Both the federal and state governments are involved in regulating the oil and natural gas industries based in Texas, and industry lobbyists play a key role in the policymaking. In the 1920s, the Railroad Commission's authority was expanded to include the transport of gas through pipelines, which quickly became the primary job of the agency. Just as quickly, the industry learned to work closely with its regulators and to get the agency to take "the business view of things." Whether regulatory agencies take an adversarial stance or "the business view" is a critical factor in the workings of the political economy, a subject that we address at the end of this chapter.

Wealth and Poverty

Ironically, Texas is both one of the wealthiest states in the nation in terms of absolute level of economic resources and one of the poorest, with a comparatively high level of impoverishment. Texas has a high level of resources, as measured by gross domestic product and by personal income. Nonetheless, the large number and the high rate of Texas citizens who live below the federal poverty level of income, and the below-average ranking of **per capita personal income** in Texas (total personal income divided by population), indicate that resources in Texas are distributed in a more uneven pattern than in most states. Texas has pockets of extreme wealth and extreme poverty.

Incidence of Poverty in Texas   Each year, the federal government sets an official poverty income level, based on the cost of basic necessities and adjusted for family size. In 1999, the official poverty level of income for a family of four was $16,700; for a family of three, $13,880.[9] In the post–World War II era, Texas has often had a greater number of poor people than any other state. In 1998, when the average poverty rate in the nation was 12.7 percent, 15.1 percent of Texans had incomes below the poverty level, which ranked Texas ninth among the states.[10] Texas also ranks high in percentage of the population without a high school diploma and in percentage of dropouts, and Texas has a young population.[11] These characteristics are generally associated with high levels of poverty because education increases a person's employability, and younger people tend to earn less than middle-aged people do.

This impoverishment is not evenly distributed, either geographically or across social groups. In 1998, 26 percent of Hispanics in Texas lived in poverty, 23 percent of African Americans, and only 7 percent of Anglos and others. In 1995, when the statewide poverty rate was 18.5 percent, Starr and Zavala counties in the Lower Rio Grande Valley had poverty rates of 50 percent; Hidalgo had 42 percent; El Paso had 30.9 percent; Bexar had 19.4 percent; and Harris had 19.1 percent.[12]

Influence of the Wealthy and the Poor on Policy Making   Poor people do not usually participate actively and routinely in the political process in Texas or in the rest of the nation, and the wealthy tend to be much more active. Because state policy making affects economic conditions for all of us, it is understandable that the economic elite are the ones with the most resources to lose through policy changes, and they actively protect those interests. Thus, powerful individuals and economic organizations are often effective in influencing economic policy making to their favor.

All of us have an economic agenda—protecting our standard of living. With the rise of the oil and gas industry to economic dominance, we would expect the industry to have a strong presence in political institutions. Indeed, in 1947, the chairman of the Texas Democratic Party stated that the oil industry was in control of state politics and government.[13] The industry continued as a powerful force in the 1950s and 1960s, blocking proposals for business taxes.

Such efforts to protect a standard of living often are also tied to an ideological agenda. For instance, a poll of business officials showed that they overwhelmingly supported conservative candidates for office throughout the 1950s, and that they were antifederal government, anti–U.S. Supreme Court, and antilabor.[14] A survey of the largest political donors in the state in the 1970s showed that about 90 percent of them gave to conservative candidates. With the advent of "presidential Republicanism" in the middle of the century (see Chapter 4), this conservatism became more consistently Republican.[15]

Often, economic leaders in Texas have influenced policy making by either recruiting and funding political candidates or becoming candidates themselves. In the 1940s and 1950s, Houston-area and statewide politics were heavily influenced by a group of millionaire executives. Houston's "8-F Crowd" met in oilman Herman Brown's Suite 8-F of the Lamar Hotel for poker and politics. They recruited and designated candidates for office, and they raised money and business support for those candidates. One of them, George Brown, was a large contributor to Lyndon Johnson and to conservative governors, and he was crucial in the 1950s efforts to successfully pass state laws limiting labor unions.[16]

Dallas billionaire Nelson Hunt was a leader in the right-wing John Birch Society in the 1960s, and in the 1980s, he helped fund the National Conservative Political Action Committee. Future U.S. President George Bush, a Midland and Houston oil millionaire, ran unsuccessfully for the U.S. Senate as a Republican in

Herman and George Brown, brothers who were oilmen and construction company owners and longtime benefactors of Lyndon Johnson, gathered the business leaders of Houston in Suite 8-F of the Lamar Hotel to play poker, talk business, and plan their recruitment and financing of political candidates.

1964. He won a U.S. House of Representatives seat in 1966 and 1968 before losing a U.S. Senate race again in 1970 to Democratic business millionaire Lloyd Bentsen. Bush received financial help from Dallas oil millionaire Bill Clements.[17]

Both Bill Clements and Clayton Williams—the 1978, 1982, 1986, and 1990 Republican nominees for governor—were among the wealthiest Texans. Robert Mosbacher, another of the wealthiest Texans, served as finance chair for Gerald Ford in 1976 and served as President Bush's Secretary of Commerce. Developer Trammell Crow served as a fundraiser for Ronald Reagan. Dallas billionaire H. Ross Perot contributed money to Clements's campaigns then was appointed by Governor

Clements to run his "war on drugs." Perot was also appointed by Governor White to run his school-reform task force, all before Perot ran for President in 1992 (against then-President Bush) and 1996 and founded the Reform Party.

John Connally, former Bush cabinet member James Baker, and former Democratic National Chair Robert Strauss came from some of the state's largest law firms, which typically have large businesses as their clients. Examples of wealthy businessmen making the leap to politics in the 1990s are Governor George W. Bush and Land Commissioner David Dewhurst.

> **Critical Thinking Exercise:**   What would each of the four ideologies say about subsidizing and regulating business in Texas? What effects would each predict that such government action would have on wealth and poverty? What influence would interest groups have in those policy debates?

STATE FINANCE: PUBLIC MONEY AND PUBLIC POLICIES

Increasingly, state government is a significant player in shaping economic behavior. When governments decide whom to tax, whom to spend money on, how much money to spend, where to place subsidies, whom to regulate, some people gain and some people lose economic resources. Political scientists Virginia Gray and Peter Eisinger argue that state governments' policy choices have important economic consequences. If natural resources are squandered, then a resource is depleted and the state loses a source of income. If tourists shy away because of pollution or crime, then the government loses revenues. Also, if roads and schools are in poor shape, high-tech and other industries will leave the state.[18] Any of those decisions create dilemmas for policy makers. Substantive policy decisions often are tied to state finance issues; thus, state finance becomes an integral part of understanding economic and social policies in Texas.

Budgeting and Borrowing

A **budget** is a plan for how much money one expects to take in and how one proposes to spend that money. Individuals, families, organizations—sometimes even college students—use a budget as a tool to manage money, pay bills, and avert crises. Governments do the same thing, on a much larger scale. Texas uses a **biennial budgeting system,** covering a two-year period. The state's **fiscal year (FY),** the period used for accounting, begins September 1 and ends August 31. For instance, the 2002–2003 biennium begins September 1, 2001 and ends August 31, 2003.

Biennial legislative sessions necessitate biennial budgets, and some legislatures with annual sessions also adopt biennial budgets. Thirty states prepare annual budgets, while 20 states have biennial budgets.[19] The budgeting process is complex, largely because many of the numbers used to create the budget are projections and estimates, and constitutional requirements limit what the legislature can do in Texas.

The Legislative Budget Board (LBB) and the Governor's Budget Office prepare budgets for the legislature to consider. They cooperate to create a matching budget format and to prepare instructions for agencies on how to write and submit budget requests. The two offices hold joint hearings for state agencies to present their requests and for the public to comment upon. In the end, however, each prepares a separate budget proposal to submit to the legislature. For instance, for the 2000–2001 biennium, Governor Bush proposed a biennial budget of $96.4 billion, while the LBB proposed a $93.6 billion budget.

In the budgeting process, legislators must adhere to a constitutional requirement for a **balanced budget**—balancing spending with expected revenues and avoiding deficit spending. **Deficit spending** is spending in the current budget cycle (in Texas's case, the biennium) above and beyond incoming revenue, while **debt** is the total outstanding amount owed from past borrowing. Forty states have a balanced-budget requirement.[20]

Texas refers to its requirement, Article 3, Section 49a of the constitution, as a "pay-as-you-go" policy, though that policy has now been compromised by many bond programs enacted as constitutional amendments. Sometimes the legislature decides that there will not be enough money to pay for a large program, and legislators are unwilling to raise taxes to pay for the program; so they turn to borrowing instead. The state can go into debt (i.e., sell bonds to banks or investors) only if specifically authorized to do so by the constitution.

Texas now has numerous constitutional **bond programs,** such as land and housing programs for veterans, which make up about half the indebtedness; construction projects for the University of Texas and the Texas Agricultural and Mechanical (A&M) University; water development; student loans; farm and ranch loans; park development; and construction of prisons and state buildings. Most of these bonds are to be repaid from revenues generated by the programs (revenue bonds, such as the veterans' loan programs), though some programs rely on repayment from general revenues dedicated to repayment (general-obligation bonds, such as construction projects).

These constitutional bond programs allow a legislature to spend money in a way that does not violate the balanced-budget requirement. As a result, Texas now has a sizable debt. In 1997, Texas had a debt of $12.5 billion, or about $644 per capita. This compares to New York's $74 billion debt, $4,080 per capita; California's $45 billion debt, $1,395 per capita; and Florida's $16 billion debt, $1,093 per capita.[21] In the last few decades, Texas has been relying more heavily on general obligation and revenue bonded indebtedness. Indeed, in 1998, the state had an additional $3 billion in bonds authorized but not yet issued.[22] In 1997, however, voters approved a constitutional amendment limiting state debt from general revenue bonds and obligations.

During the Great Depression, Texas found it difficult to balance the budget, and the legislature sometimes by necessity defied the constitution and employed deficit spending. As a result of the deficits and the difficulties of knowing how much revenue was coming in and how much was being spent, the constitution was amended to include a balanced-budget enforcement mechanism.

Under this constitutional provision, the comptroller of public accounts must provide the legislature with an estimate of how much revenue the state will collect in the coming biennium. When the legislature passes appropriations bills, the comptroller must compare the spending levels with the **revenue estimate** and must certify that the budget adopted by the legislature will be within expected revenues. This is called the **comptroller's certification.** Only one time (in 1990) has a comptroller refused to certify an appropriations bill.[23] If the comptroller refuses to certify a spending bill that the legislature passes, the bill goes back to the legislature and does not become law. The legislature may override a revenue estimate with a four-fifths vote, but that has never happened.[24]

The comptroller issues a revenue estimate at the beginning of each regular session, to guide the appropriations process and to indicate what he or she will be inclined to certify. At the beginning of the 1999 session, incoming Comptroller Carole Keeton Rylander estimated 2000–2001 revenues at about $94 billion.[25] Usually the comptroller will issue a revised estimate some time during the session, either because of changed economic conditions or because of political considerations, such as a larger amount being needed for required spending. Just before the end of the 1999 session, Comptroller Rylander increased the revenue estimate by $807 million (see the Chapter 9 Scenario for a discussion of the politics of her revenue estimate).[26]

Even after knowing the amount of money that it has to plug into a budget, the legislature still faces immense difficulties in balancing the budget. Legislators and analysts often charge that "legislators' hands are tied"—that legislators are not free to decide how to spend the money and how much to spend. For example, over the past two decades, courts have ordered Texas to spend money in the areas of prison management and mental health/mental retardation to bring those programs into compliance with constitutional principles of equal protection under the law. Another restriction the legislature faces is the existence and extent of **dedicated funds.** These are monies that are restricted to designated programs, and the legislature may not spend them for anything else. Funds can be dedicated constitutionally, statutorily, or, if federal funds, by federal requirements.

In 1978, Texas added another restriction by adopting a constitutional spending limit. Article VIII, Section 22 of the constitution now imposes a limit on state spending, calculated by a complex formula tied to the state's economic growth. The state is prohibited from spending more state tax revenue (from funds not constitutionally dedicated) than a formula-calculated amount above the previous budget. The state law enacted to implement the provision specifies that the LBB is to determine the spending limit by estimating the rate of growth of the state's economy. This can be a subjective process, subject to much second-guessing and criticism. The LBB established the estimated rate of growth of the Texas economy at 13.44 percent for 2000–2001.[27]

Texas has a separate constitutional limit on spending welfare for children—a result of the rise to power of conservative Democrats (and perhaps due to a change of public opinion) in the 1940s. For years, that limit was $80 million of state money. (Most welfare spending is federal money.) In 1982, voters approved a constitutional amendment changing that limit to 1 percent of the state budget, which now imposes a limit of about $500 million a year. For instance, in the 1998–1999 biennium, the legislature approved spending of $274 million, or about 0.32 percent of the state budget.[28]

Once the legislature passes a budget, the comptroller certifies it, the governor signs it, and the legislature adjourns, what happens in the event of an emergency with a state agency? Until recently, the agency would have to handle it on its own, or the governor would have to call the legislature into special session. In 1985, voters approved a constitutional amendment (Article 16, Section 69) to give the governor authority to move money from program to program or agency to agency in an emergency. Under this **budget execution authority** the legislature authorized the governor and the LBB, during legislative interims, to move money from one program to another or even from one agency to another. Because the lieutenant governor is the chair and the speaker the vice chair of the LBB (and they appoint the members), this budget execution authority, in essence, allows the governor, lieutenant governor, and speaker the flexibility to handle some budget crises without having to call the legislature into special session. A 1991 constitutional amendment puts the LBB and the governor on equal footing in budget execution. If the governor proposes an alteration, the LBB must ratify it, reject it, or require changes; if the LBB proposes an alteration, the governor must ratify it, reject it, or require changes. Budget execution authority has been used sparingly.

Thus, we see that in the budgetary process, Texas legislators must consider the constitutional balanced-budget requirement, the comptroller's revenue estimate and certification, proposed budgets submitted by the governor and the LBB, dedicated funds, constitutional bond programs, and constitutional spending limits. Now we turn directly to the issues of state revenues and spending.

Revenue

The state has numerous sources of revenue. These include state taxes, federal funds, licenses and fees, lottery income, interest, and other sources. The particular mix of sources of revenue is often a matter of political battles. The choices of what sources of revenue to use and what levels of taxes and fees to exact have wide-ranging effects on the political economy, including the distribution of economic resources and incentives or disincentives for economic activity. Figure 14.1 demonstrates the total Texas revenue by source for FY 1999.

Taxes   The federal, state, and local governments rely on some common forms of taxation and some that are unique to one level of government. In the nineteenth and early twentieth centuries, state governments relied heavily on property taxes. During the Great Depression of the 1930s, local governments started monopolizing the property tax, while the federal government grabbed the **income tax.** In 1932, Mississippi became the first state to adopt a sales tax. By the end of World

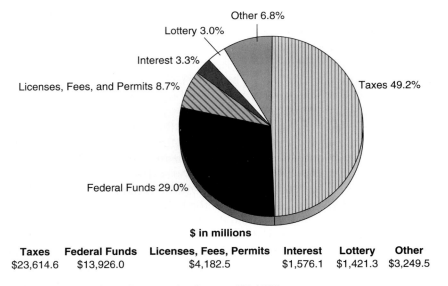

$ in millions

Taxes	Federal Funds	Licenses, Fees, Permits	Interest	Lottery	Other
$23,614.6	$13,926.0	$4,182.5	$1,576.1	$1,421.3	$3,249.5

Figure 14.1   Texas State Revenue by Source, FY 1999
Almost half of the state's revenue comes from state taxes. Grants from the federal
government account for nearly one-third of the state's revenues, with the remainder from
licenses, fees, interest, lottery, and other sources.
Source: Comptroller of Public Accounts, *State of Texas 1999 Annual Cash Report,* p. 24.

War II, the sales tax had become the top tax producer for state governments.
Hawaii began collecting a state income tax in 1901, and other states gradually fol-
lowed, primarily in the 1930s. No states adopted an income tax after 1976 until
Connecticut did so in 1991.[29]

In 1998, the largest producers of tax revenues in the 50 states were sales taxes,
which accounted for 48 percent of state tax revenues; individual income taxes,
34 percent; and corporate income taxes, 7 percent.[30] The tax distribution in Texas
is very different. Figure 14.2 shows the Texas tax revenue spread for FY 1999.

Forty states have both income taxes and sales taxes, relying on different mixes
of those taxes. Forty-three states have an individual income tax. Forty-five states
have a corporate income tax.[31] Texas has neither an individual income tax nor a
corporate income tax. If Texas did have an income tax, how much revenue could it
produce? Table 14.1 compares the 10 largest states and their income tax revenues.
Texas's economic base is closest in size to New York and Pennsylvania. In 1998,
New York received a total of $21.4 billion from income taxes, while Pennsylvania
received $7.6 billion. Other than Texas, the largest states received from 5 percent
to 59 percent of their state tax revenues in income taxes. Thus, Texas could expect
to collect between $2 billion and $15 billion a year in individual and corporate income taxes if it adopted them.

In the absence of income taxes, Texas relies heavily on **consumption taxes**—
i.e., taxes on the consumption of goods. Sales taxes were adopted by more than
half the states in the 1930s, and others in the following decades. Currently, all but

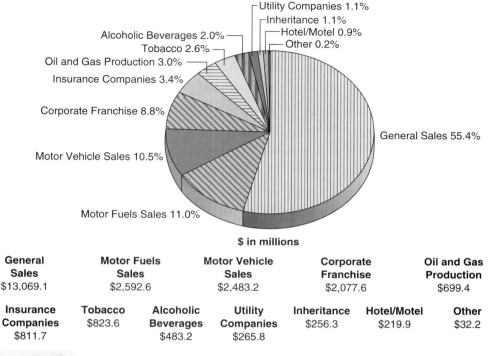

$ in millions

General Sales	Motor Fuels Sales	Motor Vehicle Sales	Corporate Franchise	Oil and Gas Production
$13,069.1	$2,592.6	$2,483.2	$2,077.6	$699.4

Insurance Companies	Tobacco	Alcoholic Beverages	Utility Companies	Inheritance	Hotel/Motel	Other
$811.7	$823.6	$483.2	$265.8	$256.3	$219.9	$32.2

Figure 14.2 Texas Revenue from Taxes, FY 1999

The state has more than a dozen taxes—but no income tax. The general sales tax brings in more than half of all the state's tax revenues. Sales taxes on motor fuels and motor vehicles are the next most productive taxes. The corporate franchise tax is next.

Source: Comptroller of Public Accounts, *State of Texas 1999 Annual Cash Report,* p. 23.

five states have sales taxes. The range of rates for the state general sales tax is from 3 percent to 7 percent.[32] Michigan is the only state with a different kind of sales tax, called a value-added tax or the single-business tax.[33] This tax (used throughout Europe) imposes a tax on a product at each step in its travel through the marketplace, as "value" is added to it. Governor Bush proposed a similar tax in 1997, but the legislature did not adopt it.

Legislative battles were fought repeatedly in Texas over passing a sales tax or an income tax, until sales tax proponents won in 1961, over the objections of both the governor and the speaker. The Texas sales tax started at 2 percent. It has been raised seven times since 1961.[34] The rate is now 6.25 percent, the sixth highest in the nation.[35] In 1999, the legislature narrowed the sales tax by increasing exemptions to it.

Texas has other consumption taxes besides the general sales tax. There are special sales or excise taxes that apply to some products instead of the general sales tax. Texas has a motor fuels tax, currently 20 cents per gallon, which is the nineteenth highest in the nation; the range is from 4 cents to 32 cents. The motor vehicle sales tax is currently 6.25 percent. Tobacco tax amounts vary from product

Table 14.1　INCOME TAX REVENUES IN THE LARGEST STATES, 1998

State	Population (million)	Total state taxes (billions)	Income taxes Individual (billions)	Corporate (billions)	Income taxes as percent of total
California	32.7	$67.7	$27.8	$5.6	49
Texas	19.8	$24.6	$0	$0	0
New York	18.2	$36.2	$18.3	$3.1	59
Florida	14.9	$22.5	$0	$1.3	5
Pennsylvania	12.0	$20.6	$6.0	$1.6	37
Illinois	12.0	$19.8	$7.0	$2.0	45
Ohio	11.2	$17.6	$7.0	$0.8	44
Michigan	9.8	$21.7	$6.8	$2.4	42
New Jersey	8.1	$15.6	$5.6	$1.2	44
North Carolina	7.5	$13.9	$6.1	$1.0	51

Source: U.S. Bureau of the Census, www.census.gov/population/estimates by state, 1998.

to product, and alcoholic beverage tax amounts vary from beverage to beverage. The hotel-motel tax is 6 percent.

Another category of taxes that Texas relies on is **severance taxes.** These are taxes on "severing" natural resources from the ground. Texas has such taxes on cement, sulfur, oil, and gas. Intense, protracted political battles were fought in the early and mid-twentieth century over creating and then raising the rates of these taxes. Severance taxes are often taxes on people outside Texas. Everyone in the United States consumes oil and gas, but most states have to import it from and pay taxes to the few producing states.

From the 1950s through the 1970s, severance taxes provided a growing percentage of state revenues. In 1957, oil and gas severance taxes accounted for 31 percent of all tax revenues.[36] There were particularly sharp increases in revenues from oil and gas in 1970s. Then, oil prices peaked at $39 per barrel in 1982, crashed to $10, then whipped back and forth between $10 and $18 a barrel in the mid-to late 1980s. The state had come to rely on oil and gas revenues so much that the crash caused state budget shortfalls. In 1981, oil and gas severance-tax revenues accounted for 28 percent of all tax revenues. In 1999, they account for only 3 percent of tax revenues. Texas Republican legislators are now proposing abolishing severance taxes.

Texas has several business taxes. The largest is the **corporate franchise tax,** which is paid by corporations, but not by other businesses. Other business taxes, such as insurance-company taxes and utility taxes, produce smaller amounts of revenue. Businesses also pay property taxes to local governments (see Chapter 12). By one calculation, 58 percent of all state and local taxes in Texas are paid by businesses rather than by individuals.[37]

While Texas does not have an explicit corporate income tax, in its corporate franchise tax, it taxes "net earned surplus," which is defined as income plus compensation of officers and directors. Before 1991, the franchise tax was assessed solely on capital, or money value invested. This tended to penalize capital-intensive firms. With the 1991 change, capital or net earned surplus is taxed, whichever is higher. Corporate income is taxed now, even if it is taxed under another name.

Federal Funds   The federal government contributes a considerable amount of money to the Texas economy. Indeed, the amount of federal expenditures in Texas—$86.5 billion in FY 1996[38]—dwarfs the size of the entire state budget. Most of those are direct expenditures for such things as salaries of federal employees. The federal government, however, also grants money to state governments for them to spend. In fact, the most significant nonstate-tax source of revenue for states, including Texas, is **federal funds**.[39] Most federal grants are either categorical grants for designated categories of spending or **block grants** for a general group or block of programs. Today, Texas gets federal funds through several block grants, including the Social Services Block Grant, Child Care and Development Block Grant, Temporary Assistance for Needy Families Block Grant, and others.

Federal funds are made available primarily for welfare, education, and transportation, with smaller amounts for public health, social services, unemployment compensation, law enforcement, and environmental protection. Texas puts so little into welfare that federal funds make up about 60 percent of all health and human service spending by the state. More than two-thirds of federal aid in Texas goes to health and human services (about $9.6 billion in 1999). Significant amounts also go to education ($2 billion) and to transportation ($1.6 billion).

Other Revenue Sources   The state lottery began selling tickets in 1992. The lottery started strong. In 1993, it produced $1.1 billion in net lottery proceeds. In 1995, it produced $1.7 billion, but by 1999, it had slipped to $1.4 billion. Lotteries typically do not produce significant proportions of total state revenue. In its first year, Texas lottery proceeds accounted for 3.3 percent of all state revenues. In 1994 and 1995, it produced 4.3 percent of all state revenues, but by 1999, it was down to 2.9 percent.

The state also receives significant amounts of revenue from licenses and fees, such as the motor vehicle registration fee, and from interest income. In FY 1999, Texas received $4.2 billion from license and fee income and $1.6 billion from interest income.

The newest source of state revenue for Texas is tobacco settlement money. As a result of settlement of a lawsuit by the state against tobacco companies, Texas will receive $15 billion over the next 25 years. In 1999, Texas received the first installment of money, about $1.5 billion.

Level of Taxation   Texans, other Americans, and probably people around the world hate paying taxes and believe that governments take too much of their incomes in taxes. In the United States, total government revenues as a percentage of Texans' personal income averaged 33.9 percent in 1997. On average, the federal government took 23.6 percent, while Texas state and local governments took 10.3 percent.[40] How much is too much is, of course, a matter of personal judgment. What we do know is that Americans pay less in taxes than citizens in most other industrialized countries, and Texans pay considerably less than citizens in most other states. In the United States, taxes take up about 28 percent of the **gross domestic product,** or the economic value of the total amount of goods and services produced. Taxes take up about 50 percent in Sweden, 45 percent in France, 39 percent in Germany, 37 percent in Canada, and 35 percent in Great Britain.[41]

Despite the unpopularity of tax increases, pressure for Texas tax increases grew in the 1970s and 1980s with the state's burgeoning population, increased demands for such services as education, health care, and welfare, and a more diverse legislative membership. Special legislative sessions in the 1980s enacted "temporary" tax increases, many of which were later made permanent. In 1986, Bill Clements campaigned for the governorship on a no-new-tax pledge; in 1987, he signed a $5.7 billion tax increase. These significant tax increases do not always spell political doom for public officials. After her first legislative session, Governor Richards signed a bill increasing state taxes $2.4 billion; her approval rating after the session increased to its highest level to that date.[42]

A **tax capacity** index calculates the amount of revenue that each state *could* raise if it applied a nationally uniform set of tax rates to a common set of tax bases. In 1994, Texas ranked thirtieth among the states in the amount it could raise from state and local taxes (95 percent of the national average), meaning that it has a slightly less than average economic base. However, Texas does not tax at that level. **Tax effort** is the ratio of tax collections to that tax capacity. In 1994, Texas ranked thirty-fifth, taxing at only 89 percent of the average for all states.[43]

No one likes to pay higher taxes. When the legislature considers tax proposals, lobbyists from the businesses that would be taxed are usually strong opponents of the proposals. They are often able to block the tax increases.

Source: Ben Sargent, *Austin American-Statesman.* By permission.

While Texas has high tax rates for many of its taxes, overall, Texas is a low-tax state. Examining state sources of tax revenue only (omitting federal revenues, interest income, etc.), the per capita amount of state taxes Texans paid in FY 1998 was $1,139.[44] Recent cross-state comparisons show that Texas ranked forty-eighth in state taxes per capita (1997 data) and forty-first when state and local taxes are combined (1999 data).[45]

Increases and decreases in taxes have the potential of stimulating or depressing the economy, of attracting businesses or chasing them away. Whether state tax changes actually do have these effects is a matter of intense debate. David Osborne wrote in *Laboratories of Democracy* that "the truth is that tax levels are far less important than most of us assume. Extremely high tax rates obviously scare some investors away, and extremely low taxes just as obviously inhibit government's ability to pay for quality schools, highways, and the like."[46] Political scientist Paul Brace argues that high taxation does hurt economic growth, but high-tax states can lower taxes to stimulate growth, "while a state with low taxes has nowhere to go with its taxes during bad economic times. Furthermore, research by economists has shown that a dollar of expenditure may stimulate more growth than that lost by a dollar of taxation."[47]

Effects of the Texas Tax System on Individuals   The potential effect of the tax system on businesses and on the economy in general is certainly important, but its effect on us as individuals seems more immediate and important to us. Our state tax system, by design or by default, affects individual citizens differently, depending on their economic status and circumstances.

A tax is **progressive** when the percentage of one's income paid for the tax increases as one's income increases. For instance, the federal income tax is designed to be progressive. A tax is **regressive** when the percentage of one's income paid for the tax decreases as one's income increases. A tax is **proportional** (sometimes called a **flat tax**) when everyone pays the same percent of their income for that tax, regardless of level of income.

Everyone acknowledges that Texas's tax system is regressive. In 1995, one study ranked Texas fifth in tax regressivity. The lowest-earning 20 percent of the population paid 13.8 percent of their income in state and local taxes; the middle income group paid 8.5 percent; and the top 1 percent paid 4.0 percent (Figure 14.3). In 1996, another reported that Texas was forty-fourth in progressivity.[48] In 1999, the Comptroller's office suggested that the Texas tax system was "slightly to moderately" regressive.[49]

Why do some states have progressive tax systems and other states regressive tax systems? It depends on the type and mix of taxes that the state chooses. Of course, that depends largely on the strength of private interests and political factors that lead to adoption of those taxes. One study has shown that the more limited the electorate (low voter turnout), the more regressive the tax system.[50] Also, wealthier, growing, and manufacturing-based states tend to have more progressive systems.[51] Income taxes can be designed to be progressive, if policy makers want a progressive system. Other taxes are more difficult to make progressive. Texas relies heavily on a highly regressive tax—the sales tax. On a per capita

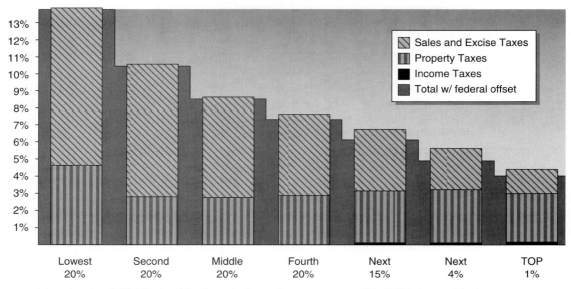

Texas — State and Local Taxes in 1995
(Shares of family income for non-elderly married couples)

	Income Group	Lowest 20%	Second 20%	Middle 20%	Fourth 20%	TOP 20%		
						Next 15%	Next 4%	TOP 1%
	Income Range	Less than $19,000	$19,000–$34,000	$34,000–$50,000	$50,000–$71,000	$71,000–$125,000	$125,000–$395,000	$395,000 or more
	Average Income in Group	$10,900	$26,300	$41,400	$59,200	$89,500	$173,000	$743,000
Sales & Excise Taxes		**9.2%**	**7.7%**	**5.9%**	**4.7%**	**3.5%**	**2.4%**	**1.5%**
General Sales—Individual		4.6%	4.2%	3.3%	2.7%	2.1%	1.5%	1.0%
Other Sales and Excise—Ind.		1.6%	1.0%	0.7%	0.5%	0.4%	0.2%	0.1%
Sales and Excise on Business		3.0%	2.4%	1.8%	1.4%	1.0%	0.7%	0.5%
Property Taxes		**4.5%**	**2.8%**	**2.7%**	**2.8%**	**3.1%**	**3.0%**	**2.7%**
Property Taxes on Families		4.2%	2.4%	2.4%	2.5%	2.6%	2.4%	1.1%
Other Property Taxes		0.3%	0.3%	0.3%	0.3%	0.4%	0.7%	1.6%
Income Taxes		**0.0%**	**0.0%**	**0.0%**	**0.0%**	**0.1%**	**0.1%**	**0.2%**
Personal Income Tax		—	—	—	—	—	—	—
Corporate Income Tax		0.0%	0.0%	0.0%	0.0%	0.1%	0.1%	0.2%
Total Taxes		**13.8%**	**10.4%**	**8.6%**	**7.5%**	**6.6%**	**5.5%**	**4.4%**
Federal Deduction Offset		-0.0%	-0.0%	-0.1%	-0.3%	-0.5%	-0.6%	-0.4%
Total After Offset		**13.8%**	**10.4%**	**8.5%**	**7.3%**	**6.1%**	**4.9%**	**4.0%**

Figure 14.3   A Picture of Regressive Taxation in Texas

In Texas, the poor pay a dramatically higher percentage of their income in state and local taxes, as compared with the wealthy.

Source: Michael P. Ettlinger, Robert McIntyre, Elizabeth Fray, John O'Hare, Julie King, and Neil Miransky, *Who Pays? A Distributional Analysis of the Tax Systems in All 50 States* (Washington, D.C.: Citizens for Tax Justice and the Institute on Taxation and Economic Policy, June 1996), App. I, p. 44. By permission.

basis, the state and local sales tax in Texas in FY 1995 was $1,039—the tenth highest in the nation.[52]

Sales tax regressivity in Texas has been limited by providing an exemption for food and prescription drugs. Recently, its base has been widened to cover more services, but more exemptions have also been added. The issue of regressivity played a prominent role in the 1999 legislative debates over expanding exemptions to the sales tax. Many provisions now modify the regressive nature of the tax, but it is still regressive. Coupled with the absence of a progressive income tax, the result of such heavy reliance on sales taxes is that poor and middle-class Texans pay a higher proportion of their incomes to the state in taxes than do the upper-middle and upper classes.

Spending

In the 1998–1999 biennium, Texas spent $89 billion. The legislature appropriated $98 billion for the 2000–2001 biennium—or about $49 billion a year. In examining how Texas spends its money, we could use any of several categories. We could look at spending by policy area, by state agency, or by object, such as salaries or capital expenditures.[53] Chapter 10 examined the relative size of state agencies, using spending as one basis of comparison (see Table 10.1). Analysis of spending by agencies is not very helpful, though, in comparing Texas to other states, because several agencies may perform similar tasks, and some agencies may perform different tasks in different states. Thus, comparison by policy areas is more useful.

Policy Areas of State Expenditures   For state governments, the largest policy categories of spending are education, public welfare, health and hospitals, and highways. Across the 50 states, 35 percent of the average state dollar is spent for education, 26 percent for public welfare, 8 percent for health and hospitals, and 8 percent for highways.[54] Figure 14.4 shows that Texas spends comparatively more of its dollars for education—38 percent. Corrections, which chiefly means prisons, is the fastest-growing part of state budgets. In Texas, expenditures for public safety and corrections have increased in absolute terms and as a proportion of the budget. In 1988–1989, public safety and corrections accounted for about 5 percent of state expenditures; in 1994–1995, 10 percent; and in 1999, 6 percent.

Texas has a new source of funding for health and human services: tobacco settlement funds. The rationale for the lawsuit was that the state had spent money on health care that it would not have had to spend were it not for tobacco use. In 1999, Texas received the first installment of money. The legislature decided to use the $1.5 billion indirectly, by endowing nine programs. Rather than spending it directly, interest from the endowments of about $150 million will be available annually. For instance, the Tobacco Settlement Permanent Trust Account will yield interest income to reimburse counties and public hospitals for health expenses. However, the bulk of the tobacco money will go

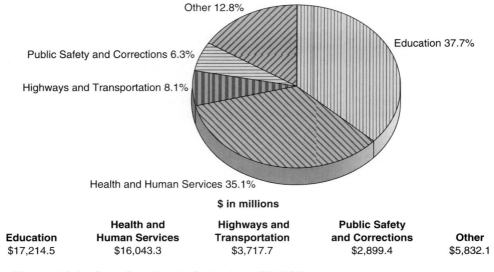

Education	Health and Human Services	Highways and Transportation	Public Safety and Corrections	Other
$17,214.5	$16,043.3	$3,717.7	$2,899.4	$5,832.1

Figure 14.4 State Spending by Policy Area, FY 1999
The state of Texas spends money on a wide variety of policies,—yet more than four-fifths of the state's spending is in four broad policy areas. Education is the policy area that the state spends the most money on, followed closely by health and human services.
Source: Comptroller of Public Accounts, *State of Texas 1999 Annual Cash Report,* p. 34.

to institutions of higher education—primarily to health science and medical programs.[55]

Spending Comparisons Texas's annual budget of about $50 billion seems a huge amount, yet it is dwarfed by state spending in California (about $117 billion) and New York (about $83 billion). When calculated on a spending-per-capita basis, the level of spending in Texas is one of the lowest in the nation. Texas per capita state and local spending combined ranked forty-first in one recent ranking, while state spending ranked fiftieth.[56] The most important determinant of state expenditures is personal income; wealthier states spend more than poorer states.[57] Texas *is* a wealthy state in total personal income, although it is below average in per capita personal income. Per capita spending, however, is the lowest of the states in total and among the lowest in many categories.

Critical Thinking Exercise: Is the level of taxation and spending in Texas too high, too low, or about right? What informs and influences your judgment? What basis of comparison seems appropriate, and why?

EDUCATION POLICY: ENDLESS SKIRMISHES OVER EQUITY AND QUALITY

Texas has a large public school system. We have 3.9 million children in public schools, with 478,000 employees. Of those employees, 254,000 are teachers, which is the highest number in the nation. California has 5.6 million students and 468,000 employees.[58] Until the middle of the nineteenth century, however, education of children was a private or even religious matter in the United States. Texas was forming its political structures and policies at the time that the idea of public education was gaining hold. One of the grievances cited by Texians in 1836 was that the Mexican government had failed to establish a system of public education. The 1836 constitution of the Republic of Texas required the Texas Congress to establish a general system of education, although little was done. In 1854, the legislature made state funds available to local (mostly private) schools,[59] and the public school system slowly became established.

Public education is widely accepted as public policy, indeed, even as a fundamental human right that the political system must provide for. As we saw in the Chapter 10 scenario, however, this long-standing consensus in support of public education is now being challenged by some in the "religious right" communities who question the concept of public education, call for churches to take over the schools, and lobby for public money for private schools in the form of **vouchers.** Even within the context of public education, we experience unending disagreements about the proper roles for the state, local, and federal governments and for parents in administering and paying for public education.

Public Education: Fulfilling Our Constitutional Mandate

Article 7, Section 1 of the Texas Constitution creates a fundamental right to education and an obligation for the legislature to establish and pay for a public education system, declaring that schooling is to be free to all students. The legislature has created a statutory education code to accomplish these goals. State courts have interpreted the broad language of the constitution to mandate legislative support of an equitable public education system. Some legislators in recent years have proposed amending the constitution to ease the requirement.

The constitutional mandate has resulted in the establishment of public schools throughout the state to meet the goal of making education available to all. Texas parents send their children to these public schools at greater rates than parents in most states. Only 5.8 percent of elementary and secondary school students are in private schools in Texas, ranking Texas fortieth among the states. Delaware has the highest percentage of private-school students: 19.1 percent.[60]

Structure of Elementary and Secondary Education   Texas provides public education to its citizens from the time they enter elementary school at age 5 or 6 until they graduate from high school, usually around age 18. Children must be in public, private, or home school from age 6 to 17. The state provides kindergarten, elementary, junior high, high school, and some prekindergarten programs.

Texas has 1043 local school districts, ranking first in the nation.[61] Public school districts are local governments (see Chapter 12). The elected school trustees are unpaid government officials. They set the policies for the districts (within federal and state guidelines and requirements), set the district property tax rate, decide where and when to build new schools, and hire the superintendent to run the schools.

All of Texas is divided among the school districts. There is no uniformity in either geographic size or population size of the districts. Some districts are small—Ramirez Common School District in Duval County had 19 students in 1998—while the largest—Houston Independent School District in Harris County—had 210,988 students.[62]

Texas has 7053 public elementary and secondary schools, second in the nation to California's, and the number grows every year. Almost all of those schools are operated by local school districts. However, in the 1995 revision of the education code, the legislature authorized the creation of **charter schools,** which are public schools operating under a contract granted by the state, with the intention of trying different educational methods. By 1999, there were 145 public charter schools, with 27,000 students, receiving $61 million in state funds. There is both strong support and strong opposition to charter schools. By 1999, a dozen had failed already (some in the middle of the semester), some were experiencing rapid teacher turnover, and some were operating with no school transportation and no school lunches.

Local schools and school districts operate under a shifting degree of state oversight and regulation. In 1928, the constitution was amended to create a State Board of Education. In 1949, the legislature created the Texas Education Agency (TEA), with a commissioner of education selected by the State Board of Education, and provided the first significant state financial aid to local school districts. As a result, the state's portion of school funding jumped to around 80 percent of the total. Opponents feared that increased state participation would lead to loss of local control. Today, the TEA is the largest state agency, based on appropriations, with a budget of $11.4 billion in FY 2000. Almost all of this is pass-through money that the TEA allocates to school districts, however.

In 1995, the Texas legislature enacted an entirely new education code, re-creating the TEA, the State Board of Education, and the commissioner of education but abolishing some state policies and allowing school districts more leeway in deciding policies. The new act also sets out a process for creating home-rule school districts, free from many state requirements and TEA guidance, if local voters so choose. So far, no districts have attempted to convert to home rule.

School Finance: The Clash of Economic and Social Policies   Across the United States, states respond in different ways to demands for educational equity. In Hawaii, the state assumes nearly all costs of education; in New Hampshire, local districts pay for almost all. In the 1998–1999 school year, the State of Texas supplied $17.8 billion for public education, 43 percent of school district budgets; the federal government supplied $3.6 billion, 8 percent, and school districts supplied $20.3 billion, 49 percent.[63] In 1999, the legislature provided $3.8 billion in *new* state money for public education for the 2000–2001 biennium for salaries, property tax replacement, and other uses, the largest increase in public education funding in Texas history.[64]

In addition to the prolonged question of funding equity, much of the school-finance debate has centered on the level of resources that Texas spends. Though the relationship between spending levels and educational quality is a matter of unresolved debate, spending is one variable used to measure adequacy of educational systems. Across the nation in 1998, per-pupil expenditures in public elementary and secondary schools averaged $6,098 per year. Texas ranked twenty-third in expenditures at $5,794. The state spending the most on education was New Jersey at $9,704 per pupil, and Utah spent the least at $3,695. In 1997–1998, the average salary of classroom teachers in Texas was $33,648, which ranked thirty-fourth. Alaska had the highest average at $51,738.[65]

In the late nineteenth century, the legislature allowed towns, cities, and rural school districts to tax for school purposes. The 1876 constitution established a **Permanent School Fund (PSF),** from which the legislature provided funds to school districts. In 1918, the legislature established a state property tax to pay for textbooks, and the state provided its first appropriation from general revenues for local schools. In 1937, the legislature authorized additional payments to low-property-wealth districts.

In the mid-twentieth century, the PSF became the center of the state's contribution to school finance, and in 1982, the state adopted a constitutional amendment repealing the state property tax, which had fallen into disuse. Revenue from thirteen million acres of state-owned lands is dedicated to the PSF, and thus lucrative oil and gas wells provide much of the money for public education. However, this money is an endowment and may not be spent. Only the annual investment income from the fund, the **Available School Fund,** may be spent.

Until the 1950s, the philosophy of local control of schools ensured a minimal state role in financing public education; districts provided for most expenses themselves. Some districts had vast resources to tax for school purposes, while others had little. One consequence of local control—and unequal economic resources among the districts—has been that wealthier districts have repeatedly fought attempts to provide uniform services across the state, fearing that resources in their districts would be siphoned off to poorer districts.

With the 1949 reforms, the state established a minimum level of state support to local schools. However, that level was so low that most districts must raise and spend money—from property taxes—at rates far above the state aid. The property-poor school districts (those with low property values, and thus low tax revenues) cannot enrich at levels near those at which the property-rich school districts (those with high property values, and thus high tax revenues) can. The result has been gross disparities in school-financing capabilities across the state.

With a school-finance system based on district-by-district property taxes, the overall amount of property wealth in a district determines how much money a district can raise at any given tax rate. If the system were completely equitable, each district would have the same wealth, for a 1 to 1 ratio. In 1992–1993, the ratio of property wealth per student, from the richest to the poorest district, was 1035 to 1. In 1994–1995, after the new reforms took place, the ratio was 489 to 1.[66] Tiny districts tend to distort such comparisons, though. Even discounting for the extremes, the system is far from uniform. In 1998, the 35 poorest districts had less than $49,946 in property wealth per student, while the 83 wealthiest districts had $465,535 per student. The state provided 81 percent of the funding for those poorest districts and only 6 percent for those wealthiest districts. Still, those poorest districts received lower total revenues per student ($5,645 versus $7,603) and spent lower amounts than the wealthiest districts ($5,319 versus $6,554 in operating expenses).[67]

A district with a large industrial or oil well base, or even with expensive residences, could set a low to moderate tax rate and reap plenty of money. A district with few industries or oil wells and containing mostly poor to middle-class residential areas, however, would have to set a high tax rate to sustain the school system and often still could not bring in nearly as much money as a property-rich district could. In 1997–1998, tax rates in one-fourth of the districts were set at a rate of more than $1.50 per $100 value while the lowest one-fourth were taxed at less than $1.31 per $100.[68]

It is the persistence of these taxing and spending patterns, and the frustrations felt by parents, students, and teachers in the poorer districts, that led to the *Rodriguez* and the *Edgewood* lawsuits, to 20 years of legislative battles over school finance, and to the 1993 school-finance reform legislation.

The 1993 school-finance reform recaptures and redistributes school tax revenues by limiting district revenues, capping tax rates in districts, and adjusting the state aid formula to guarantee a specified yield per tax effort for districts. The bill capped taxable wealth in a school district at $280,000 per student, though the very wealthiest districts were exempted. In 1999, the legislature raised the threshold to $295,000, but it also increased the guaranteed yield; so there was a net increase in equity. The cap forces richer districts to choose from among five methods to reduce their wealth:

1. Consolidate with another lower-wealth district
2. Detach some property and transfer it to another district
3. Send money directly to the state
4. Pay for the education of some students in another district
5. Consolidate tax bases with another district

In 1997–1998, 86 districts had wealth higher than $280,000 per weighted student. Sixty-six districts chose option 3, while 20 chose option 4; none chose 1, 2, or 5. The state collected $209 million from these districts and redistributed it as state aid.[69] In 1997, the legislature examined alternatives to the 1993 system, and Governor Bush proposed a new consumption tax and higher sales taxes to replace some local property tax revenues. The legislature, however, was not ready for drastic changes to either the school finance system or the tax system. Instead, in 1997 and 1999, because the budget surpluses were so high, the legislature used them to increase state spending for education and to encourage local school districts to lower their property tax rates. Still, after the 1999 session, half the districts planned to raise taxes.[70]

Educational Quality

While national attention focused on the question of school finance in the 1970s, in the 1980s and 1990s, the question of educational quality emerged as a first-priority issue. Do students get the quality of education they should? How do we measure quality? What kinds of policy changes encourage and discourage high quality? What is the relationship between educational quality and the level of school dropouts?

In the 1980s, legislatures and governors increased their role in educational policy making, in an effort to address these questions. Forty-five states increased the number of courses required for graduation; half instituted minimum competency tests; most established minimum grade point averages for participation in sports; 35 required standardized testing for teachers; nearly half provided merit-pay incentives for teachers; and most raised teachers' salaries.[71]

In 1983, Governor Mark White appointed a Select Committee on Public Education, chaired by H. Ross Perot. The legislature adopted much of the Perot committee's recommendations in 1984. The changes increased state equalization aid, increased teacher salaries, established a career ladder for teachers, mandated teacher testing, adopted the no-pass—no play rule for athletes, and established an extensive program of testing for students, including an exit test for high school graduation.

In the late 1990s, educational quality initiatives focused on testing, school safety, and social promotion. The basic test that Texas students must pass is called Texas Assessment of Academic Skills (TAAS). In the most recent years, just two-thirds to three-fourths of students pass all the TAAS tests. The Mexican-American Legal Defense and Education Fund (MALDEF) has sued the state, arguing that TAAS is discriminatory. In 1995, 1997, and 1999, the legislature considered measures to better assure safety in public schools and adopted some of those proposals. In 1999, Governor Bush and others pushed measures to restrict social promotion—the practice by some teachers and schools of promoting students to the next grade whether they had performed well or not, and a compromise version was adopted.

Higher Education: From Community Colleges to Universities

Texas has a vast public higher education system—more than 100 institutions and campuses, loosely regulated by the Coordinating Board of Higher Education. There are 37 general academic teaching institutions, 50 community/junior colleges, 8 medical schools and health science centers, 4 campuses of the Texas state technical colleges, and 9 affiliated agencies, such as the Agriculture Experiment Station. In addition, there are more than 40 private institutions of higher education in Texas. All but 6 of the public universities are organized into 4 senior university systems: the University of Texas System, the Texas A&M University System, the University of Houston System, and the Texas State University System.

THADEUS & WEEZ   by Charlie Fincher

3-10-91

The Texas Supreme Court upheld the constitutionality of Texas's new school-finance system in 1995. However, high property taxes and continued opposition to the system guarantees that Texans—including college students—will continue to study and debate the merits of different financing systems in the coming years. By the way, "gobbledygook" is a term coined by the late Texas Congressman Maury Maverick. *Source:* Reprinted by permission of Charles Pugsley Fincher.

Nearly 1 million of Texas's 20 million citizens are enrolled in public institutions of higher education, with 25,000 faculty. Nearly half of those students attend two-year institutions. Community college freshmen outnumber freshmen at four-year institutions by nearly 4 to 1.[72]

Funding Colleges and Universities   Public colleges and universities get appropriations from the legislature, tuition and fees from students, money from private sources, and funding from the federal government. For the 2000–2001 biennium, the legislature appropriated $11.7 billion for higher education, plus money from the tobacco lawsuit settlement. For institutions affiliated with the University of Texas and Texas A&M University, the legislature appropriates money from the **Available University Fund** investment income, off the endowed **Permanent University Fund (PUF).** Revenue from more than 2 million acres of West Texas land owned by the state is dedicated to the PUF.

The Constitution of 1876 stipulated that the legislature should establish a "university of the first class." Thus, the University of Texas and later the Texas A&M University were created and funded from the proceeds of the PUF. Over the past century, other universities and colleges were created, funded from general revenues and from a much smaller new fund created in the 1940s. In the 1980s, the constitution was amended to replace that fund with a new **Higher Education Fund** and to require the University of Texas System to use the PUF for its campuses that had previously been excluded.[73] Today, the PUF funds 24 institutions, and the Higher Education Fund funds 32 institutions. Of the $11.7 billion in higher education appropriations for 2000–2001, $252 million is from the Available University Fund and $224 million from the Higher Education Fund. In 1999, voters approved a constitutional amendment that, for the first time, will allow some of the PUF investment funds to be used in some circumstances, rather than just the interest income.

The legislature sets tuition rates for state colleges and universities. Tuition has always been low in Texas, compared to public higher education in other states. Tuition for resident undergraduates was $4 per credit hour in 1985, covering only about 3 percent of the costs of education. In the mid-1980s, the legislature began a series of regular increases in tuition. For 2000, tuition was increased $2 per semester hour and for 2001, it was increased $2, so tuition in 2001 was $40 per semester hour. Of course, colleges and universities have instituted a plethora of fees that can outstrip the cost of tuition.

Access to Higher Education   Higher education was formerly available almost exclusively to Anglos, particularly Anglo males, for economic reasons and because of policies that legitimated segregation and discrimination. Today, college education is available to a broader spectrum of people, though African Americans and Mexican Americans still do not make up a percentage of students proportional to their numbers in the Texas population. Of the students enrolled in institutions of higher education in Texas in 1996, 54.3 percent were women, 21.2 percent were Hispanic, 9.9 percent were African Americans, and 4.6 percent were Asian Americans.[74] Indeed, after *Hopwood*, minority enrollment in Texas colleges and universities fell. To counter the effects of *Hopwood*, in 1997, the legislature passed a law stating that all Texas students in the top 10 percent of their graduating class automatically gain admission to a public college or university. It also required the Higher Education Coordinating Board to report on the effects of *Hopwood*. The board noted that minority enrollment was already falling prior to *Hopwood* but that:

> The *Hopwood* decision has had a negative impact on the number of African-Americans and Hispanics applying for, being admitted to, and enrolling in . . . undergraduate and graduate programs at the most selective universities, medical schools, and law schools. . . . As a result of *Hopwood*, both the University of Texas at Austin and Texas A&M University restructured their admissions procedures to eliminate race or ethnicity as a factor and to consider the alternative admissions criteria offered in House Bill 588, which provides automatic admission at public universities to any student in the top 10 percent of his or her high school graduating class. Both institutions also report that they increased their recruitment efforts to help compensate for the effects of *Hopwood*.[75]

College students in Texas can avail themselves of both federal and state financial aid. Texas has long provided the Hinson-Hazlewood student loan program. In addition, 1999 legislation established two new financial aid programs for lower income students: Toward EXcellence, Access, and Success (TEXAS), and Teach for Texas.

Critical Thinking Exercise: Public education began as an idea, and institutions were then created to turn the idea into public policy: public education. How do the ideas and institutions surrounding public education in Texas fit into the framework of the gap between ideals and reality?

HEALTH AND HUMAN SERVICES POLICY: PROVIDING THE NECESSITIES OF LIFE

The rather broad category of health and human services includes health care, housing, food, income, and employment assistance. Sometimes, these policies are referred to as social welfare or socioeconomic policies. Next to education, the State of Texas spends more money on health and human services than on any other policy area. Compared to other states, however, these services in Texas are minimal.

Poverty rates drive social-welfare policies. The greater the number of people who lack the resources to provide for themselves and their families, the greater are the demands placed on the state. As we saw earlier in this chapter, Texas's poverty rate is usually among the highest in the nation. In *Laboratories of Democracy*, David Osborne wrote that "The integration of economic and social programs is particularly important in poor communities."[76] Without such integration, programs designed to improve living conditions for those in poverty are likely to have only a temporary effect.

The Federal–State Partnership

Since the 1930s, the federal government has had antipoverty programs, such as food stamps, that are known as "entitlement" programs. If a person or family meets the criteria, usually being below the official poverty-level income, then the person or family is entitled to the benefits of that particular program. The federal government typically gives the states money for the programs, and the states run the programs. States also put in some money. For some programs, states have leeway in setting entry criteria. For other programs, the federal government imposes requirements on the states for being eligible for federal funds. For some programs, states can choose the level of support they will provide to recipients. Table 14.2 provides snapshots of some of the best-known social-welfare programs. Two federal programs—Social Security and **Temporary Assistance for Needy Families**—demonstrate some of the different arrangements between the federal and state governments in funding and administering social-welfare programs.

The federal Social Security Act incorporates numerous programs. Its best-known program, Social Security, which is also one of the largest entitlement programs, provides benefits for workers no longer employable due to age or disability. These Social Security recipients are also eligible for Medicare, a health-care program. Although Social Security retirement and Medicare are federal programs, the Social Security Act also includes unemployment compensation, which is financed jointly by the federal government, state governments, and employers, and is administered by states. Social Security also includes Supplemental Security Income—federal aid to the aged, disabled, and blind, which can be supplemented by states.

In the 1980s and early 1990s, states began pressing for changes in the federal welfare programs, including instituting "welfare-to-work" programs to try to re-

Table 14.2   SNAPSHOTS OF KEY SOCIAL-WELFARE PROGRAMS

Food Stamps. A federal program providing a monthly allotment to eligible low-income people, which can be used to purchase food.

Head Start. A federal educational, health-care, and social-service program for low-income preschool children, designed to improve their skills so that they do not begin school so far behind other children.

Medicaid. A federal program administered by the states, reimbursing health-care providers for costs of caring for eligible low-income and disabled people.

Medicare. A federal health-care program for the elderly.

Social Security. A federal social-welfare program, including retirement benefits for most American workers; disability benefits; and supplemental income for the aged or disabled. Jointly with the states, it also provides unemployment compensation.

Temporary Assistance for Needy Families. A federal cash-assistance program, enacted in 1996 to replace the longstanding Aid to Families with Dependent Children (AFDC).

Women, Infant and Children Nutrition (WIC). A federal program providing nutrition education and a monthly food grant to low-income women with young children.

---

duce the welfare rolls by placing more of the recipients in jobs. The Texas legislature adopted welfare changes in 1995, including limits on the amount of time that people could collect benefits. In the mid-1990s, Congress joined the welfare reform movement. In 1996, Congress abolished Aid to Families with Dependent Children (AFDC), the long-time joint federal-state program to provide cash assistance to low-income families with children, and replaced it with the new Temporary Assistance for Needy Families (TANF) program. To achieve its goal of removing people from welfare and encouraging them to work, it establishes a five-year lifetime limit for benefits. In 1997 and 1999, the Texas legislature revised its 1995 welfare reform act to implement the new federal program. The Texas TANF caseload declined more than 42 percent from 1995 to 1998.[77]

Assistance for Food, Shelter, and Clothing

When a family or individual is in a crisis situation and needs food, shelter, or clothing, the availability of government assistance depends on the state in which the family or person resides. Typically, large, urban, and politically competitive states provide higher levels of social welfare services. About two-thirds of the states (not including Texas) supply short-term relief programs, but the number is dropping, as several states have abolished their programs.[78] Families in Texas must rely on TANF, food stamps, or Social Security programs.

The federal government has long provided surplus food commodities to the poor and also provides coupons, known as food stamps, which recipients can redeem only for food. The Food Stamp Act is federally funded but is administered by the federal and state governments. In the early 1990s, Texas started using an electronic card, called the Lone Star Card, instead of paper stamps, in an effort to reduce theft, fraud, and administrative costs. A third type of food assistance is the federal Women, Infant, and Children's nutrition program (WIC), which targets funds for food specifically to young children and their mothers.

The Texas Department of Housing and Community Affairs is Texas's lead agency responsible for affordable housing. The federal government provides money for construction of low-income dwellings and for rent supplementation. The U.S. Department of Housing and Urban Development administers the program, but it is implemented through local housing authorities. One provision of the act, Community Development Block Grants, provides money for rehabilitation of housing. A separate Emergency Shelter Grants Program provides limited money for emergency shelters.

Health Care

Skyrocketing costs for doctor and hospital care, increasingly sophisticated medical treatments, the AIDS crisis, the coming-of-age of managed health-care insurance programs, and President Clinton's failed initiative to adopt a national health-insurance program have combined to make health-care policy one of the most salient issues of public opinion. Texas's indicators of public health suggest a continuing need for resources. For instance, the cumulative number of AIDS cases in Texas was nearing 50,000 by 1998, ranking fourth in the nation, and Texas ranks only thirty-eighth in the number of doctors per 100,000 population.[79]

Traditionally, individuals have been responsible for their own health care. For many, coverage under a health-insurance plan is essential to surviving health crises. Many are covered by insurance provided by their employer, but in 1998, 4.9 million Texans were not covered by health insurance, and Texas led the nation in the percentage of its population not covered at 24.5 percent.[80] Because of the gaps in private coverage, there are numerous federal and state programs to assist with health care.

People who do not have health insurance are often unable to afford it. Just as the state constitution requires that education be available for all, it also requires that counties make health care available to all. County hospitals have become responsible for more and more care for impoverished Texans. As other hospitals started turning away people who had no insurance, the legislature stepped in. After the 1985 defeat of a bill requiring hospitals to provide more health care to the indigent (poor people), Governor White called a special legislative session, which enacted a bill that requires hospitals to treat emergency cases, rather than simply sending critically ill patients to county hospitals.[81]

Medicaid is a joint state-federal health-care program that pays doctor and hospital bills for those who qualify for the program. It is available to people with incomes below the poverty level and to medically needy people who have lost their insurance or whose insurance cannot cover long-term care needs. Virtually all states are now enrolling Medicaid recipients in managed care systems.[82] In Texas, State of Texas Access Reform (STAR) has converted Medicaid into a managed care system. About 1.7 million Texans are in Medicaid. Many more are eligible but are not covered.[83] Federal requirements also prohibit states from terminating Medicaid when the state terminates cash assistance. If the agency does not let people know that, however, they sometimes assume that they are also ineligible for Medicaid and do not reapply for it. Since welfare reform, there has been a 14 percent decline in the number of Texas children on Medicaid.[84]

In 1997, the Texas legislature responded to the large number of uninsured children by creating the Texas Healthy Kids Corporation. It contracts with private companies to insure children at lower rates than they could otherwise get. Congress then created a new **Children's Health Insurance Program (CHIP)** as a federal block grant program, with states providing matching revenue. If one qualifies for Medicaid, he or she cannot get CHIP. In 1999, the Texas legislature approved legislation implementing CHIP. There was intense controversy over how broad to make the coverage. Those seeking broad coverage won, and CHIP in Texas now covers children through age 18 who live in families with incomes up to 200 percent of poverty. In 2000, the income cap is $33,400 for a family of four, or $22,120 for a family of two. If one's income is too high for CHIP, then he or she is referred to the Texas Healthy Kids Corporation. Of 1.4 million children uninsured, the state now projects covering 448,000 by 2004.[85]

The Adequacy of Health and Human Service Programs in Texas

Texas spends an enormous amount of money on TANF, though most of it is federal funds. In 2000–2001, Texas received $1.2 billion in federal funds for TANF and spent only $600 million from state funds. Even with that amount of spending, however, there are so many eligible impoverished people in Texas that the amounts per family are miserly. In 1999, the average monthly TANF payment per family in Texas was $188; the amount is scheduled to be $209 for 2001. The 1990s program changes are having an effect. In 1997, Texas had 600,000 TANF recipients.[86] By 1999, there were 339,308 TANF recipients, including 248,168 children and 91,140 adults.[87]

Food stamp enrollment in Texas dropped from its high of 2.7 million participants in 1994 to 1.4 million in August 1999.[88] Texas is more generous with assistance in the form of food stamps than it is with TANF. The average monthly food-stamp benefit per recipient in Texas in 1998 was $79.46, ninth highest in the nation. TANF work and time limit restrictions do not apply to food stamps. Once again, however, there is confusion over eligibility. Since 1994, 1.4 million people have been dropped from Texas's food stamp program. In 1995, two-thirds of those eligible received food stamps; by 1999, only one-third did so. Nearly half of Texas's poor do not receive stamps, yet in 1999, Texas lost about $800 million in federal funds that could have been available for food stamps. In 1999, 56 percent of the poor were not receiving food stamps, although applications dropped less than 7 percent. While the economy has been robust, the demand for food stamps should be lower, but other indicators show continued hunger and poverty problems. For instance, WIC, school lunch programs, and private food bank usage has increased at the same time that food stamp enrollment has dropped.[89]

> **Critical Thinking Exercise:**   Welfare and health-care reforms of the 1990s occurred in the midst of an economic boom. When the next severe recession occurs, what pressures are likely to be felt by the state's health and human service programs? What elements of the Texan Creed will influence those debates?

ECONOMIC AND SOCIAL POLICIES AND POLITICAL CHANGE

Texas is widely known for the low amount of state resources it puts into education and social-welfare programs, compared to other states. Lawmakers, however, are apparently unconvinced that the level of public services is the important factor in debates over changing public policy. What forces are at work that convince policy makers to quickly and dramatically change (increase) spending in such areas as criminal justice or highway construction, but not in areas such as education or social welfare? Surely there are many variables at work: electoral politics, ideology, political culture, the socioeconomic class of policy makers, national forces, courts, the restrictive Texas tax system, and the relative strength of interest groups. Also, a key variable has been the stance of the federal government.

In judging political change, we have to return to the issue of the intensity of public opinion. While Texans seem intently interested in education policy, that interest has not reached a level of creedal passion. The long, convoluted history of school-finance reforms has been driven by court challenges by a few, not by electoral or legislative upheavals by the many. There is some evidence that perhaps passions are now emerging over the issue of religious values and public education, and that passion is beginning to appear in electoral and legislative battles.

A current example of the role of both public opinion and interest groups in political change is the issue of health maintenance organizations (HMOs). The public has become increasingly hostile to HMOs and supportive of their doctors. Doctors, too, have become disenchanted with HMOs, though insurance companies defend them. After an intense legislative battle involving doctors, consumer groups, and insurance companies in 1997, Texas became the first state in the nation to allow HMO members to sue their HMO. This happened despite the legislature's inclination in general to restrict lawsuits. Then, in 1999, doctors persuaded the legislature to pass a bill authorizing collective bargaining by doctors—perhaps the only pro-labor vote by the legislature in years!

When has there been significant public demand for increased state support for social services? There was strong support in Texas for welfare measures in the 1930s, when hundreds of thousands of Texans lost their jobs and fell into poverty. There was a public belief that the ideal of equal citizenship did not square with the reality of wealthy and politically powerful businesses in the midst of poverty and unemployment. The legislature passed welfare programs in step with the federal New Deal.

By the 1940s, public leadership and public opinion had changed, and those supporting a more libertarian posture of no government support for human services were back in power. In 1945, the legislature proposed and the voters approved a constitutional amendment prohibiting the use of any state funds for welfare. Of course, this hands-off attitude at the state level is a large factor in the growth of the federal government in the post–World War II years, as advocates turned away from the states and successfully demanded programs from the federal government.[90]

As the U.S. Congress adopted social-welfare programs from the 1930s through the 1960s, it balanced the demands for government response to poverty with the traditional expectation that such policies be left to state governments. By the 1990s, Congress abolished some federal entitlement programs and let the states decide how to respond to social-welfare problems.

Earlier, we noted that political scientist David Osborne has argued that one agenda of government is to make sure that the poor get some of the benefits of economic growth, such as skills training and good jobs. Will economic growth provide opportunities for the poor who no longer have as secure a safety net as in the past? David Osborne concluded that "even the best economic development system will not do a great deal for the poor. It will help some, but it will also hurt some."[91] In this case, the political changes of the 1980s and 1990s led to changes in economic and social-welfare policies with potentially widespread effects that cannot be evaluated at this time.

When governments decide who to tax, who to spend money on, and how much money to spend, some people gain and some people lose economic resources. The state generally spends money in the same pattern as it did in its near past. Abrupt changes in spending or taxing could trigger political change, or political changes could trigger state finance changes. Significant variables would include the *role of groups* and the *mobilization of latent groups* or of alliances by decisions to give resources to some and to take from others.

Because government spending or taxing initiatives benefit some people and not others, those decisions sometimes trigger political reactions to take back the economic changes. Change can also have broad effects, which can in turn trigger reactions that have nothing to do with the original change. Over the past several years, Texas has raised numerous taxes and has also faced anti-tax sentiment and arguments that tax increases will kill economic growth. So could we expect the antitax political movement, if it is successful in rolling back taxes, to have the effect of stimulating economic growth? Thomas Dye found that increasing the tax burden does retard economic growth, but that this relationship is strongest for high-tax states. When they cut their taxes, their economies responded. For low-tax states, such as Texas and Florida, however, he argued that their economies would not be stimulated much by tax cuts.[92] Thus, a state finance change triggered by a political change may not have the intended effect.

As we have seen throughout this book, fundamental change is rare. Periods of creedal passion can trigger fundamental change. Texans appear to like the idea of low taxes and spending, yet both have increased over the past generation.

Nonetheless, we have seen no significant public reaction to limit the increases. Perhaps that is because the increases have barely kept up with inflation and population growth, so the countervailing sentiment that wants education, highways, and other spending programs balances the antispending, antitax sentiment.

In the absence of creedal passion, the normal political forces prevail in scuffles over state finance. When Lieutenant Governor Bob Bullock proposed an income tax in 1991, he did so partly because he decided that the public was so angry about high property taxes that they would trade lower property taxes for an income tax. There was, however, no groundswell of support for his proposal, so the traditional, and politically connected, foes of income taxation prevailed. We can expect state spending and taxing patterns to remain fairly similar to those now in effect, then, unless one of two things occurs: (1) a political change unrelated to state finance brings in a large number of participants and state officials who are different and who make state finance changes a part of wider changes that they embrace; or (2) a marginal state finance change adversely affects a group that then mobilizes groups to help them win back what they lost, with possible spillover effects into other tax and spending programs.

ECONOMIC AND SOCIAL POLICIES AND DEMOCRACY

Economics is a driving force in the political system. The examination of economic and social policies can offer suggestions for whether political equality, nontyranny, participation, and deliberation were present in the institutions and political processes that led to adoption of those policies. Such an examination can also offer hypotheses for the relationship between the policy outcome and the forms of democracy practiced in those institutions and processes.

Conflict between government and business is unresolvable. They are essentially two competing power systems, one based on economic resources and the other on popular sovereignty and constitutional legitimacy. Political scientist E. E. Schattschneider argued that a key function of democracy has been to provide citizens who have few economic resources with a second power system to counterbalance the economic power embodied in corporations and industry.[93] Thus, we see continual debate over how much democratic control of the economy is legitimate, or how *laissez faire* the economy-government relations should be. Whether regulatory agencies take an adversarial stance or take "the business view" is a critical factor in the workings of the political economy.

In Chapter 7, we demonstrated that socioeconomic inequality is correlated with political participation and, thus, to policy outcomes. If, therefore, the extent of poverty and the minimal level of social-welfare programs in Texas can be presumed to demonstrate social inequality, and greater social equality is necessary for the achievement of political equality, then it would appear that Texas is not increasing political equality (a requirement for democracy)—nor is it experiencing widespread participation.

The decisions that legislators, the governor, and the comptroller make in the state finance process are not made in a vacuum but are very much influenced by economic forces and economic actors. The endless rounds of hearings with the LBB and the Governor's Budget Office, the House Appropriations Committee, and the Senate Finance Committee would seem to demonstrate that deliberative, nontyrannical democracy is alive and well. Because so many people and groups have a lot at stake in the state finance decisions, there are always large numbers of them active in the legislative deliberations, suggesting a pluralist democracy.

Before we conclude that state finance is a model of deliberative and pluralist democracy, however, we still have to examine the question of political equality. Observation of the state finance process demonstrates the central importance of political and economic power in influencing who gets what from state government. When the highway lobby wanted new funding in the 1970s, it mounted a traditional lobbying campaign and won the dedication of monies to its projects, even over the objections of other groups that realized they would be hurt by the shortage of funds for other projects. When poor school districts wanted new funds so that their total funding would equal the funds received by other school districts, they, too, mounted a lobby campaign, in conjunction with allied groups. They did win overall some more state funds, but they did not win equality. So they sued the state and won a partial victory when the courts ordered the legislature to create a "substantially equal" finance system. Thus, the traditional power arrangement in state finance is pluralist in the sense that it does respond to groups. It is not, however, a system of political equality. Groups with little power will not win in the legislative budgeting process, so they must go outside to win change. As former University of Texas Law School Dean Mark Yudof concluded, "the judiciary— nominally the least democratic branch of government—proved to be most responsive to community groups. In contrast, the elected legislature was pressured by a wide variety of forces, including rich school districts, public resistance to increased state taxes, and personal political ambition, so had to bargain its way to a solution that did not necessarily meet the goals of the community groups."[94]

The political equality of the vote does not translate to power equality in the political process and to equal abilities for people or groups to win economic advantage. For one thing, much of the economy is not publicly controlled. It is privately owned and seldom regulated significantly. For another, the political equality of one person–one vote does not necessarily mean that each person has equality in the political process. When businessman Lonnie "Bo" Pilgrim walked around the floor of the Texas Senate in 1989 handing out checks for $10,000 to senators as he was telling them what kind of workers' compensation system he wanted, the message that many heard was that there was a gap between the political ideal of equal influence and the reality of the influence of wealth in economic policy making.

When populists of the late nineteenth century came to a similar conclusion, an era of creedal passion was triggered. Such creedal passion now seems to be lacking; in its place, a strong public cynicism has emerged about the political process and its ability to democratize influence when the wealthy appear to dominate the process. One of the great dilemmas of economic and social policy and democracy is that policy battles affecting the distribution of resources for all Texans are fought and won in skirmishes in which most people are not involved. When coupled with a belief that those with money have greater access to decision makers, the result is cynicism.

SUMMARY

Economic and social policies affect economic activity, have economic consequences for individuals or groups, and guide our development and our relationships with other humans and our environment. Business leaders have long been powerful in state policy making, whether behind the scenes to influence officials and policy making or in the open, as wealthy business owners become government officials themselves. Thus, the economic elite have strong roles in economic and social policy decisions.

Policies adopted by the state government attempt to stimulate the economy, bring the poor into the growth process, and ensure an educated, healthy population. The state's taxing and spending policies both affect economic performance and benefit some groups more than others. When the state stimulates the economy, increases its revenues or benefits particular groups through its spending policies, some groups will win, and some will lose.

The legislature and the governor write the state budget within the confines of a constitutional requirement for spending and revenues to be balanced. They must also adhere to a constitutional spending limit tied to economic growth. Some funds are dedicated to specific spending programs by the constitution, state law, federal order, or court mandate. Between legislative sessions, the governor and the LBB may move money from program to program or agency to agency. Texas borrows money by having the legislature and the voters approve a constitutional amendment for a specific borrowing program.

The state gets money from taxes, federal funds, lottery proceeds, interest, fees, and special revenues. Federal funds are nearly one-third of the budget. Texas's overall tax level is low because we do not pay state income taxes. Nonetheless, the rates for other taxes are high when compared to those of other states. Texas relies very heavily on sales and other consumption taxes. The heavy reliance on sales taxes and the absence of a progressive income tax results in an overall tax system that is extremely regressive—the poor pay a higher proportion of their income to the state than do the wealthy.

The state spends what seems to be a large amount of money, about $50 billion a year. When this is divided among Texans, however, it comes to a small amount per person, compared to what other states spend. Education is the largest area of spending, followed by health and human services. Prison spending has jumped significantly in the past few years.

There are conflicting pressures for Texas to provide more social services and a more equitable distribution of services, as well as demands that Texas keep its public spending low. The vast differences in property wealth from one school district to another triggered decades of battles over the school-finance system. Because of our high level of poverty, Texas has a substantial need for and demand for income support and health programs. Texas, however, has long provided relatively little social-welfare support, with high hurdles of eligibility.

KEY TERMS

Rodriguez v. San Antonio
  Independent School District
Edgewood v. Kirby
economic policy
social policy
political economy
subsidy
regulation
laissez faire
per capital personal income
budget
biennial budgeting system
fiscal year (FY)
balanced budget
deficit spending
debt
bond programs
revenue estimate
comptroller's certification
dedicated funds
budget execution authority
income tax

consumption taxes
severance taxes
corporate franchise tax
federal funds
block grants
gross domestic product
tax capacity
tax effort
progressive tax
regressive tax
proportional tax (flat tax)
vouchers
charter schools
Permanent School Fund (BSF)
Available School Fund
Available University Fund
Permanent University Fund (PUF)
Higher Education Fund
Temporary Assistance for Needy
  Families (TANF)
Medicaid
Children's Health Insurance Program
  (CHIP)

SUGGESTED READINGS

Brunori, David. *The Future of State Taxation.* Washington, D.C.: University Press of America, 1998.

Education Commission of the States. *Governing America's Schools.* Denver, 1999.

Gray, Virginia, and Peter Eisinger. *American States and Cities,* 2d ed. New York: Addison-Wesley-Longman, 1997.

House Research Organization "Writing the State Budget." *State Finance Report,* 19 February 1999, No. 76-1.

Murdock, Steve, Nanbin Zhai, and Rogelio Saenz. "The Effect of Immigration on Poverty in the Southwestern United States." *Social Science Quarterly* 80 (June 1990): 310–324.

Osborne, David. *Laboratories of Democracy.* Cambridge, Mass.: Harvard Business School Press, 1988.

Southern Education Foundation. *Miles to Go: A Report on Black Students and Postsecondary Education in the South.* Atlanta, 1998.

Wilson, Robert, ed. *Public Policy and Community: Activism and Governance in Texas.* Austin, Tex.: University of Texas Press, 1997.

NOTES

1. Richard Lavine, "School Finance Reform in Texas, 1983–1995," in *Public Policy and Community: Activism and Governance in Texas,* ed. Robert Wilson (Austin, Tex.: University of Texas Press, 1997), 121.

2. Lester Thurow develops this argument in *The Zero-Sum Society: Distribution and the Possibilities for Economic Change* (New York: Basic Books, 1980).

3. David Osborne, *Laboratories of Democracy* (Cambridge, Mass.: Harvard Business School Press, 1988), 5. See also Martin Saiz and Susan Clarke, "Economic Development and Infrastructure Policy," in *Politics in the American States: A Comparative Analysis,* 7th ed., eds. Virginia Gray, Russell Hanson, and Herbert Jacob (Washington, D.C.: Congressional Quarterly Press, 1999), 474–505.

4. Osborne, *Laboratories of Democracy,* 14.

5. Grant McConnell, *Private Power and American Democracy* (New York: Alfred A. Knopf, 1966), 284.

6. Virginia Gray and Peter Eisinger, *American States and Cities,* 2d ed. (New York: Addison Wesley Longman, 1997), 358.

7. See House Study Group, "Air Pollution Control in Texas," *Special Legislative Report* No. 65, 3 February 1981, 54.

8. Edith Hornor, ed., *Almanac of the Fifty States, 1999* (Palo Alto, Calif.: Information Publications, 1999), 447.

9. U.S. Department of Commerce, Bureau of the Census, "Annual Update of the HHS Poverty Guidelines." 18 March 1999. Accessed 2 March 2000, http://aspe.hhs.gov/poverty/99poverty.html.

10. U.S. Department of Commerce, Bureau of the Census, *Poverty in the United States, 1998* (Washington, D.C.: U.S. Department of Commerce, 1999); see also "Historical Poverty Tables." Revised 30 September 1999. Accessed 2 March 2000, http://www.census.gov/hhes/poverty/histpov/hstpov21.html.

11. Kathleen O'Leary Morgan and Scott Morgan, eds., *State Rankings 1999* (Lawrence, Kans.: Morgan Quitno Corp., 1999), 130, 469; Kendra Hovey and Harold Hovey, *Congressional Quarterly's State Fact Finder 1999: Rankings across America* (Washington, D.C.: Congressional Quarterly, 1999), 197.

12. U.S. Census Bureau, *Current Population Survey,* March 1998, and "Small Area Income and Poverty Estimates 1995 State and County FTP Files and Description." 12 February 1999. Accessed 2 March 2000, http://www.census.gov/hhes/www/saipe/stcty/sc95ftpdoc.html.

13. Quoted in George Norris Green, *The Establishment in Texas Politics* (Westport, Conn.: Greenwood Press, 1979), 20.

14. James Soukup, Clifton McCleskey, and Harry Holloway, *Party and Factional Division in Texas* (Austin, Tex.: University of Texas Press, 1964), 9–11.

15. Chandler Davidson, *Race and Class in Texas Politics* (Princeton, N.J.: Princeton University Press, 1990), 80–82.

16. Green, *The Establishment in Texas Politics,* 17; Davidson, *Race and Class in Texas Politics,* 105.

17. See Christine Carroll, "The 100 Richest People in Texas," *Texas Monthly,* September 1992, 118–143.

18. Gray and Eisinger, *American States and Cities,* 355.

19. House Research Organization, "Writing the State Budget," *State Finance Report,* 19 February 1999, No. 76-1.

20. Council of State Governments, *Book of the States 1998–99,* vol. 32 (Lexington, Ky.: Council of State Governments 1998), 234–235.

21. U.S. Census Bureau, "1997 State Government Finance Summary Tables, by State." Revised 19 August 1998. Accessed 2 March 2000, http://www.census.gov/govs/www/stsum97.html.
22. Comptroller of Public Accounts, *Texas 1998 Comprehensive Annual Financial Report*, 82.
23. House Research Organization, "Writing the State Budget."
24. Comptroller of Public Accounts, *Breaking the Mold: New Ways to Govern Texas*, vol. 1, (July 1991), 21.
25. Comptroller of Public Accounts, *Biennial Revenue Estimate 2000–2001*, 8 January 1999.
26. By the time she issued the final certification of all appropriations, she certified $96 billion (not including tobacco settlement money, about $2 billion).
27. House Research Organization, "Writing the State Budget."
28. Ibid.
29. Advisory Commission on Intergovernmental Relations (ACIR), *Significant Features of Fiscal Federalism 1993: Budget Processes and Tax Systems*, M-185, vol. 1 (Washington, D.C.: ACIR, 1993), 34.
30. U.S. Department of Commerce, Bureau of the Census, "State Government Tax Collections: 1998." Nd. Accessed 2 March 2000, http://www.census. gov/govs/state-tax/ 98tax.txt.
31. Research Institute of America, *1999 All States Tax Handbook* (New York: Research Institute of America, 1999).
32. Scott Moody, ed. *Facts and Figures on Government Finance*, 33rd ed. (Washington, D.C.: Tax Foundation, 1999), 213.
33. Comptroller of Public Accounts, *Forces of Change: Shaping the Future of Texas*, (March 1994), 168.
34. Comptroller of Public Accounts, *Forces of Change*, 165.
35. These and following tax rates and rankings are from Moody, *Facts and Figures on Government Finance*, 213, and CCH, Inc., *2000 Guidebook to Texas Taxes* (Chicago: CCH, Inc., 1999).
36. Martin Katzman and Patricia Osborn, "Energy Policy," in *Texas at the Crossroads: People, Politics, and Policy*, eds. Anthony Champagne and Edward Harpham (College Station, Tex.: Texas A&M University Press, 1987), 135.
37. Comptroller of Public Accounts, *Forces of Change*, 164.
38. Council of State Governments, *Book of the States 1998–99*, 287.
39. Gray and Eisinger, *American States and Cities*, 304.
40. Tax Foundation, "Total Tax Burden Per Capita and As a Percentage of Income by State, 1999. Nd. Accessed 2 March 2000, http://www.taxfoundation.org/totaltaxburden.html.
41. Moody, *Facts and Figures on Government Finance*, 287.
42. Richard Murray and Gregory Weiher, "Texas: Ann Richards, Taking on the Challenge," in *Governors and Hard Times*, ed. Thad Beyle (Washington, D.C.: Congressional Quarterly Press, 1992), 180.
43. Hovey and Hovey, *Congressional Quarterly's State Fact Finder 1999*, 136–137.
44. Comptroller of Public Accounts, *1998 Texas Annual Financial Report*, 180.
45. Gray, Hanson, and Jacob, *Politics in the American States*, 310; Tax Foundation, Chart 1: Average State/Local and Total Tax Rates by State, 1999. Nd. Accessed 2 March 2000, http://www.taxfoundation.org/prstatelocal99table.html.
46. Osborne, *Laboratories of Democracy*, 255–256.
47. Paul Brace, *State Government and Economic Performance* (Baltimore, Md.: Johns Hopkins University Press, 1993), 114.
48. Hovey and Hovey, *Congressional Quarterly's State Fact Finder 1999*, 157.

49. Office of the Comptroller, *Tax Exemptions and Tax Incidence,* January 1999, p. 44.

51. D. Martinez, "Don't Tax me, Tax the Fella Behind the Tree: Partisan and Turnout Effects on Taxes," *Social Science Quarterly* (December 1997): 895.

52. Gray and Eisinger, *American States and Cities,* 314.

53. Hovey and Hovey, *Congressional Quarterly's State Fact Finder 1999,* 145.

53. Capital budgets include large-cost items with long lives, such as buildings, highways, and bridges. Capital expenditures are not included in the operating budget of many states; rather, the state borrows the money (by selling bonds), and only the annual principal and interest payments on the bonds are included in the operating budget expenses. States spend about 4 percent of annual operating budgets on principal and interest payments on debt. Gray and Eisinger, *American States and Cities,* 325.

54. U.S. Census Bureau, *State Government Finances: 1992* (Washington, D.C.: U.S. Department of Commerce, 1993), xiii.

55. House Research Organization, "Texas Budget Highlights, Fiscal 2000–01," *State Finance Report,* 76-3, 21 October 1999, 25–26.

56. Hovey and Hovey, *Congressional Quarterly's State Fact Finder 1999,* 168, 173.

57. Gray and Eisinger, *American States and Cities,* 325.

58. National Center for Education Statistics, U.S. Department of Education, Tables 40, 66, and 84, "Digest of Education Statistics, 1998." 1 May 1998. Accessed 2 March 2000, http://www.nces.ed.gov/pubs99/digest98.

59. Stephen B. Thomas and Billy Don Walker, "Texas Public School Finance," *Journal of Education Finance* (Fall 1982): 223–226.

60. Hovey and Hovey, *Congressional Quarterly's State Fact Finder 1999,* 196.

61. Texas Education Agency, "Agencies of Public Education." Nd. Accessed 2 March 2000, http://www.tea.state.tx. us/perfreport/snapshot/98/text/agency.html; and National Center for Education Statistics, U.S. Department of Education, Table 92, "Elementary and Secondary Education." 1 May 1999. Accessed 2 March 2000, http://www.nces.ed.gov/pubs99/digest98.

62. Texas Education Agency, "Students." Nd. Accessed 2 March 2000, http://www.tea.state.tx.us/perfreport/snapshot/98/text/students.html.

63. House Research Organization, "The Tax System and Public School Financing in Texas," *Session Focus,* March 24, 1999, 14.

64. Ibid.; Center for Public Policy Priorities, "Senate Bill 4," *CPPP Policy Page,* 16 July 1999, No. 93, p. 1.

65. National Education Association, *1997–98 Estimates of School Statistics,* reported in Hovey and Hovey, *Congressional Quarterly State Fact Finder 1999,* 204–205.

66. Calculated from data in TEA, *Snapshot '94: 1993–94 School District Profiles,* 1995 and *Snapshot '95;* see also Comptroller of Public Accounts, *Fiscal Notes,* Special Public School Issue, March 1991.

67. Texas Education Agency, "Property Wealth Summary Table," *Snapshot '98,* http://www.tea.state.tx.us/perfreport/snapshot/98/text/agency.html.

68. Texas Education Agency, "Property Wealth Summary Table."

69. Texas Education Agency, "Finances," Nd. Accessed 2 March 2000, http://www.tea.state.tx.us/perfreport/snapshot/98/taxeffort. html.

70. House Research Organization, "The Tax System and Public School Financing in Texas," 2; "Texas Budget Highlights," 10.

71. Gray and Eisinger, *American States and Cities,* 465–466.

72. Texas Higher Education Coordinating Board, "Statistical Report 1998. Nd. Accessed 2 March 2000, http://www.thecb.state.tx.us/divisions/grpi/stats98/statmain.htm.

73. Lawrence Redlinger et al. "Funding Higher Education," in *Texas at the Crossroads,* eds. Anthony Champagne and Edward Harpham (College Station, Tex.: Texas A&M University Press, 1987), 187, 188.

74. Hornor, ed., *Almanac of the Fifty States 1999,* 349.

75. Texas Higher Education Coordinating Board, "Report on the Effects of the *Hopwood* Decision on Minority Applications, Offers, and Enrollments at Public Institutions of Higher Education in Texas." Nd. Accessed 2 March 2000, http://www.thecb.state.tx.us/divisions/ane/2146/.

76. Osborne, *Laboratories of Democracy,* 301.

77. Tami Swenson, Steve White, and Steve Murdock, "An Examination of Change in the TANF Caseload and Characteristics of TANF Recipients in Texas, October 1995 through June 1998," Texas A&M Center for Demographic and Socioeconomic Research and Education, August 1998.

78. Gray and Eisinger, *American States and Cities,* 443–445.

79. Daniel Moskowitz, *2000 Health Care Almanac and Yearbook* (New York: Faulkner and Gray, 2000), 98, 206.

80. House Research Organization, "Health Care for Uninsured Texans," *Focus Report,* 4 February 1999, 1; "Texas Budget Highlights," 15.

81. For a history of the 1985 indigent health care bill, see Pat Wong, "The Indigent Health Care Package," in *Public Policy and Community,* ed. Robert Wilson (Austin, Tex.: University of Texas Press, 1997), 95–118.

82. Gray, Hanson, and Jacob, *Politics in the American States,* 372.

83. House Research Organization, "Health Care for Uninsured Texans," 5.

84. Center for Public Policy Priorities (CPPP), "Study: Texas Ranks worst in keeping kids on Medicaid," News Release, 20 October 1999, http://www.CPPP.org/products/media/pressreleases/pr102099.html.

85. CPPP, "Children's Health Insurance Program," *CPPP Policy Page,* 16 June 1999, No. 90.

86. CPPP, "TANF Spending in 2000–01," *CPPP Policy Page* 3 September 1999, No. 95.

87. *Austin American-Statesman,* 27 November 1999, p. A14.

88. CPPP, "Food Stamps Not Reaching Majority of Texas' Poor," *CPPP Policy Page,* 30 September 1999, No. 98.

89. CPPP, "Hunger in a Time of Plenty: Food Stamp Declines in Texas, 1995–1999," 24 November 1999, http://www.CPPP.org/products/reports/fsex.ecsum.html.

90. For a fuller treatment of this argument, see former North Carolina Governor Terry Sanford, *Storm over the States* (New York: McGraw-Hill, 1967).

91. Osborne, *Laboratories of Democracy,* 289.

92. Thomas Dye, *American Federalism: Competition Among Governments* (Lexington, Mass.: Lexington Books, 1990), cited in Gray and Eisinger, *American States and Cities,* 328. See also Brace, *State Government and Economic Performance.*

93. E. E. Schattschneider, *The Semi-sovereign People: A Realist's View of Democracy in America* (New York: Holt, Rinehart, and Winston, 1960), 121.

94. Lavine, "School Finance Reform," 158.

Glossary

accountability in judicial selection (11) a criterion in judicial selection that seeks to hold judges responsible for their actions

administrative law (11) rules and regulations created by executive agencies

administrative procedures act (10) a statute containing the state's rule-making process

African Americans (2) Americans whose ancestors were originally from Africa

agenda-setting hypothesis (6) the theory that the media determine which issues are considered important

agents of socialization (2) families, schools, media, and others that influence a person's political values and beliefs

agriculture commissioner (10) the elected state official in charge of regulating and promoting agriculture

Alamo, the (2) the Spanish mission in San Antonio, which was the site of a major battle between Mexicans and Texians during the Texas Revolution in 1836

amendment (8) a proposed change to a bill in the legislative process

American Creed (1) the five ideas—liberty, equality, democracy, individualism, and constitutionalism—that motivate politics in America

Anglo (2) non-Hispanic whites, whose ancestors were from Europe

annexation (12) the enlargement of a city's corporate limits by taking in surrounding territory

appellate jurisdiction (11) the power of a court to review the decision of a lower court

appointment of judges (11) a method of judicial selection in which positions are assigned by some designated person or group

Asian Americans (2) Americans whose ancestors were originally from Asia

at-large-by-place system (12) an election system in which the positions on a council or board are numerically designated, and voters may vote for one person in each designated position or place

attack spot (7) a short advertisement that attacks the qualities and experience of a candidate's opponent during a political campaign

attorney general (10) the elected official who is chief counsel for the state of Texas

Available School Fund (14) the annual investment income derived from the Permanent School Fund (PSF)

Available University Fund (14) the annual investment income derived from the Permanent University Fund (PUF)

backscratching (8) helping another legislator with a vote, with the expectation that he or she will return the favor

balanced budget (14) a budget in which expenditures and revenues balance out with no deficit

bases of the vote choice (7) the factors that influence a person's choice of candidates in an election (party identification, issues, and candidate characteristics)

benchmark poll (7) a poll used by campaign consultants to assess a candidate's strengths and weaknesses and an opponent's strengths and weaknesses, and to develop campaign themes

benefits of voting (7) the positive, personal effects experienced by a person who participates in an election

bicameral (8) a legislature that has two chambers, such as a House of Representatives and a Senate

biennial budget (14) a budget that covers a two-year period

biennial legislature (8) a legislative body that meets in regular session only once in a two-year period

bill (8) a legislative document intended to create or amend a law

blanket primary (7) a form of primary election in which voters can participate in the selection of all parties' nominees for public office but can only vote for one party's candidate for each office

block grant (14) a federal grant of money to a state for a general purpose or policy area (e.g., education) rather than for a specific program (e.g., Head Start)

boards and commissions (10) the multimember, policy-making bodies that run most state agencies

bond programs (14) specific programs for which the state borrows money by selling bonds to investors

budget (14) a plan indicating how the government expects to take in money (revenues) and how the government expects to spend that money (expenditures)

budget execution authority (14) the authority to move money from one program to another program or from one agency to another agency in an emergency

bureaucracy (10) a large organization organized hierarchically, functionally specialized, and managed by fixed rules

cabinet system (9) a form of executive organization in which the top executive officials are appointed by and responsible to the chief executive

called (or special) legislative session (8) a legislative session that can last for a maximum of 30 days and that is called by the governor

campaigners (7) people whose principal form of political participation is to work in political campaigns

candidate characteristics (7) the personal qualities of a political candidate

captured agency (10) a government regulatory agency that consistently makes decisions favorable to the private interests that it regulates

carrying water (8) sponsoring a bill or an amendment at the request of a lobbyist

charter schools (14) public schools that are chartered by the state, instead of created by local school districts, and that are exempted from many requirements that other public schools must reach, in order to experiment with new or alternative educational approaches

chief budget officer (9) the governmental official who is charged with preparing the state budget proposal for the legislature; the governor

chief executive officer (9) the top official of the executive branch of Texas state government; the governor

chief of state (9) the official head representing the State of Texas in its relationships with the national government, other states, and foreign dignitaries; the governor

Children's Health Insurance Program (CHIP) (14) a new federal-state program to provide health care to children in low- and moderate-income families who have no other insurance

city council (12) the legislative body of a city government

city manager (12) the chief executive officer, hired by the city council, in the council-manager form of city government

civil law (11) the area of law that deals with lawsuits involving the claims of one individual against another individual

civil liberties (13) the protection of individual rights from government infringement

civil rights (13) a government's extension of rights to its citizens

classical democratic theory (1) theory of democracy in which each person participates directly in decisions that affect his or her life

clemency (9) the governor's authority to reduce the length of a person's prison sentence

clientele relationship (10) when a government regulatory agency considers private industry a client to be served

closed primary (7) a form of primary election in which only party members can participate

cognitive dissonance (1) the discomfort that a person feels when his or her behavior is not consonant with his or her beliefs or knowledge

collective benefit (5) a benefit that is provided to all members of a social category

commander-in-chief (9) the executive official who is in charge of the state militia; the governor

commissioners court (12) the legislative body of a county in Texas

commission government (12) a form of city government in which the members of the commission (legislative body) also serve as the heads of the executive departments

committee (8) a subunit of the legislature, appointed to work on designated subjects

common law (11) law derived from the judicial decisions of England; a body of decisions based on judicial precedent; law made by judges

communicators (7) people whose principal form of political participation involves discussing or criticizing government

community activists (7) people whose principal form of political participation involves joining groups to influence public policy

complacency (1) the response that Americans exhibit when they do not clearly perceive the gap between the American ideal and the American reality, and they do not believe strongly in the ideal

complete activists (7) people who engage in all forms of political participation

comptroller (10) the elected state official who is the state's tax collector

comptroller's certification (14) the document signed by the comptroller that states the budget adopted by the legislature will be within expected revenues for the biennium

concurrent resolution (8) a legislative action that expresses the will of both chambers of the legislature, even though it does not possess the authority of a law

conditions of democracy (1) the four conditions—political equality, nontyranny, participation, and deliberation—that are necessary for a government to be considered democratic

confederation (3) a form of government in which the state governments are sovereign, and the national government can only exercise the powers granted to it by the state governments

consent (3) closely connected to the concept of legitimacy, it implies that the citizens of a society have formally granted permission to a political or governmental system to exercise power

conservative (2) a person whose political ideology favors individualism over equality, but social order over individualism

constitutional amendment (3) a change, addition or deletion, to a constitution

constitutionalism (1) the belief that government should be limited through a written document (a constitution)

constitutional revision (3) a complete rewriting of a constitution, which almost always includes major substantive changes

consumption taxes (14) taxes, such as sales taxes or excise taxes, on the consumption of goods

contactors (7) people whose principal form of political participation involves contacting public officials about personal problems related to government

controlling law (13) a decision by a court that determines how subsequent cases should be decided

conventional political participation (7) forms of political participation that are normal, routine, and promoted by government

cooperative federalism (3) a theory of federalism in which the national and state governments work together to formulate and implement public policy

corporate franchise tax (14) a tax on corporations for the right to do business in Texas

costs of voting (7) the personal expenses (time, effort, etc.) that a person must bear to participate in elections

council-manager government (12) a form of city government in which the council is the legislative body, and a professional administrator, hired by the council, is the chief executive

councils of government (COGs) (12) consortiums of local governments that work on mutual problems

county auditor (12) the public official, selected by the district court judges in the county, who is responsible for reviewing expenditures by the county

county chairperson (4) the chairperson of the county party structure

county clerk (12) the chief recordkeeper of a county, also responsible for the records of the county court

county commissioner (12) a member of the commissioners court, who also performs administrative duties

county courts (11) constitutional county courts, county courts of law, and probate courts

county executive committee (4) a political party committee composed of the precinct chairpersons in a county, which assists the county chairperson

county judge (12) the chief executive officer of a county, who is also a member of the county commissioners court and who has judicial duties in some counties

county-manager (12) a form of county government in which the commissioners court would act strictly as a legislative body; the executive functions of the county would be given to a manager (similar to the council-manager form of city government)

county or senatorial district convention (4) a meeting of party delegates elected from precinct conventions within a county or senatorial district

county sheriff (12) the chief law enforcement officer of a county

county treasurer (12) the county official responsible for maintaining county funds and for making payments for the county; the position has been abolished in many counties

court of appeal (11) an intermediate appellate court

court of last resort (11) the final court to which a decision may be appealed

court of record (11) a court in which a transcript, a written record, of each trial is kept

criminal law (11) the area of the law that deals with crimes against the state; the claims of the state against an individual

critical election (4) an election that alters the party allegiance of a significant portion of the electorate, producing a new majority political party

cumulative voting (12) a scheme of voting in which voters are given a number of votes equal to the number of positions open, and voters may use their total number of votes in any combination

cynicism (1) the response that Americans exhibit when they clearly perceive the gap between the American ideal and the American reality, but they do not believe strongly in the ideal

dealignment (4) the abandonment of party allegiance by the electorate

debt (14) the total outstanding amount the government owes as a result of borrowing in the past

dedicated funds (14) funds designated for specific programs

deficit spending (14) government spending in the current budget cycle that exceeds government revenue

deliberation (1) the condition of democracy requiring a meaningful discussion of political issues and candidates so that each person can make an informed and calculated choice

democracy (1) a government in which the people rule

de novo (11) to hear anew; required when a county court exercises its appellate jurisdiction over a case in which there was no transcipt of the original trial

direct lobbying (5) interest-group efforts to influence public officials through personal, direct contacts

Dirty Thirty (8) a group of liberal Democrat and conservative Republican legislators in 1971 who opposed the House leadership and urged legislative reforms

disenfranchisement (13) the taking away of a person's right or ability to vote

district clerk (12) person responsible for the records of the district court

district court (11) state court of general and special jurisdiction

disturbance theory (5) the theory that interest groups form because of a disturbance in society

divided government (9) a government in which one political party controls the governorship and the other political party controls one or both chambers of the legislature

dog-and-pony show (8) committee hearings that last for hours, featuring scores of witnesses telling emotional and personal stories to persuade the legislators to vote a bill out of committee or to kill it

dual federalism (3) a theory of federalism in which the national government and the state governments have separate and distinct areas of responsibility

early voting (7) a voting procedure that allows people to vote over an extended period prior to the actual date of the election

economic policies (14) public policy that affects economic activity or that has economic consequences for individuals or groups

Edgewood v. Kirby **(14)** the state court case that declared that the Texas school finance system violated the state constitution's provisions for "an efficient system of public free schools"

electioneering (5) the involvement of interest groups in political campaigns

elections administrator (12) the public official in heavily populated counties who has primary responsibility for the conduct of elections

elitism (1) the theory which maintains that a small group of privileged people rule

engrossed bill (8) a bill that has been given final approval on third reading in one chamber of the legislature

enrolled bill (8) a bill that has been given final approval in both chambers and is sent to the governor

entrepreneurial theory (5) the theory that interest groups form because of the actions and efforts of leaders or entrepreneurs

episodic frame (6) the media frame that focuses on particular events or concrete examples to illustrate a problem

equality (1) the belief that every person should be treated the same, regardless of physical, social, or economic differences

exclusionary rule (13) the judicial rule requiring that illegally obtained evidence be excluded from a trial

external political efficacy (7) the feeling that government is responsive to a person's demands

extraterritorial jurisdiction (ETJ) (12) the area outside of, but contiguous to, a city's corporate limits, over which the city can exercise some control

federal funds (14) grants of money from the federal government to the state government

federation (3) a form of government in which neither the national government nor the state governments receives its powers from the other government; both governments get their powers from a constitution

filibuster (8) a tactic used by a senator to try to kill a bill by holding the floor for an unlimited amount of time, thus blocking a vote on the bill

first reading (8) the Texas Constitution requires three readings of a bill by the legislature; first reading is when the bill is introduced, its caption is read aloud, and it is referred to committee

fiscal year (FY) (14) the period used for accounting purposes by the government (September 1 to August 31 in Texas)

flat tax (14) a tax method that collects the same percentage of each person's income regardless of income level

focus groups (7) small groups used by campaign consultants to assess the emotional responses of potential voters to candidates, issues, or advertisements

framing (6) the media's ability to alter the statement or presentation of choice problems

free-rider problem (5) the problem that interest groups face when people in a particular social category are able to receive benefits without joining the group that helped to achieve those benefits

full-slate laws (13) laws that facilitate majority bloc voting by the use of at-large-by-place elections

full-time equivalent (FTE) (10) a unit of measurement for number of employees

general election (7) the election held on the first Tuesday after the first Monday of November in even-numbered years, to elect public officials

general-law city (12) a city that may do only what the general laws of the state permit it to do

general-obligation bonds (12) bonds issued for a general purpose; hence, everyone in that taxing authority is generally obligated to pay for them

germane (8) related to the topic

gerrymander (8, 13) drawing voting district lines in a way either to help or to hurt an incumbent or a group of voters such as Democrats, Republicans, Anglos, African Americans, or Mexican Americans

good government (10) a term used for policies that open up agencies to public participation and scrutiny and that minimize conflicts of interest

governing schema (6) the schema held by the public and the politicians, which views politics as a morality play pitting good versus evil

government (1) the institutions that make public policy for a society

government reorganization (10) attempts to change the structure of government agencies, due to the nature of the policy problems, the personalities and political dynamics at work, and the organizational structure in vogue at the time

governor's message (9) message that the governor delivers to the legislature, pronouncing policy goals and budget priorities

gross domestic product (14) the economic value of the total amount of goods and services produced in a country (or a state)

gubernatorial (9) of or by the governor

gutting (8) amending a bill in committee or on the floor in such a way that it severely weakens the bill or changes its original purpose

Higher Education Fund (14) a constitutionally dedicated fund providing money for capital projects for colleges and universities not a part of the University of Texas or Texas A&M University Systems

Hispanics (2) Americans with Spanish surnames (e.g., Mexican Americans, Cuban Americans)

home-rule city (12) a city that may do anything it wishes, unless specifically prohibited by the state or national government

House speaker (8) the leader of the Texas House of Representatives, elected by the representatives, from among the House members

hypocrisy (1) the response that Americans exhibit when they do not clearly perceive the gap between the American ideal and the American reality, but they strongly believe in the ideal

ideal constitution (3) a constitution that outlines the basic functions and structures of government, leaving the detail to another body, usually the legislature (*see also* **statutory constitution**)

ideal-reality gap (1) the discrepancy between the ideal of the American Creed and the reality of American institutions

ideologues (2) people whose political opinions are guided by an ideology

impeach (8) to accuse a person of official wrongdoing

impeachment (8) the process that formally charges a public official with an impeachable offense

implement (10) putting legislatively mandated policy into effect

income tax (14) a tax on either a person's or a corporation's annual income

incumbent (8) current officeholder

independence in judicial selection (11) a criterion of judicial selection that seeks to keep judges free of political pressure

indirect (grassroots) lobbying (5) interest group attempts to influence public officials by mobilizing the group's members to contact their elected representatives or by changing public opinion on an issue

individualism (1) the belief that each person is important and that society is less important than each individual in society

institutions (1) the government bodies, such as the legislature, that make governmental decisions

intellectual qualifications in judicial selection (11) a criterion of judicial selection that requires judges to possess wisdom, knowledge, and common sense

intergovernmental contracting (12) the practice of one government contracting with another for a particular good or service

intermediate scrutiny (13) a lower level of judicial review than that of strict scrutiny, but higher than that of the rational-basis test

internal political efficacy (7) the feeling that a person has the ability and skills to influence public policy

iron triangle (5, 10) a model postulating that public policy making is controlled by private interest groups, regulatory agencies, and legislative committees

issue network (5) a collection of people who share an interest in a policy area but who have different views on government policy regarding that policy area

issues (7) a basis for the vote choice that emphasizes the candidates' positions on public policies

joint resolution (8) a legislative document that either proposes an amendment to the Texas Constitution or ratifies an amendment to the U.S. Constitution

journalistic schema (6) the schema held by journalists, which views politics as a game played by politicians for personal gain, advancement, or power

journalists' creed (6) the values shared by journalists

justice of the peace courts (11) local trial court of limited jurisdiction in criminal and civil cases

keying (8) watching another legislator to see which way he or she is voting (or watching a lobbyist) before deciding how to vote

Killer Bees (8) a group of senators who, in 1979, broke the quorum to defeat a bill and uphold the Senate's two-thirds rule for considering bills

laissez faire **(14)** an economic philosophy maintaining that government should not regulate business and its activities

land commissioner (10) the elected state official responsible for managing and leasing the state's property, including oil, gas, and mineral interests

Legislative Budget Board (LBB) (8) a joint legislative committee that prepares the state budget and conducts evaluations of agencies' programs

Legislative Council (8) a joint legislative committee that provides bill drafting, policy research, and program evaluation services for members of the legislature

legislative leadership (8) the House speaker, Senate president, and committee chairpersons

legislative opposition (8) legislators who either generally oppose the legislative leadership or oppose them on a particular bill

legislative oversight (10) actions by the legislature to oversee agencies and programs that it created and authorized, through such things as audits, sunset review, and review of expenditures, staffing, functions, rules, regulations, and performance

legislative party caucus (4, 8) an organization of legislators who are all of the same party, and which is allied with a political party

legislative process (8) the process the legislature follows in creating and enacting legislation

legitimacy (3) popular acceptance of the political or governmental system

liberal (2) a person whose political ideology favors equality over individualism, but individualism over social order

libertarian (2) a person whose political ideology favors individualism over social order and over equality

liberty (1) the belief that government should not infringe on basic human rights

line-item veto (9) the power of the governor to select one or more lines of an appropriations bill and to veto them, while allowing the rest of the bill to become law

litigation (5) the use of the legal system to advance a group's interests

lobbyist (5, 8) a person who attempts to influence the actions of government officials

local elections (7) elections held by local governments to elect local officials

logrolling (8) the practice of a legislator supporting and voting for another member's bill (especially a local bill affecting only the author's district), with the assumption that he or she

will then support the legislator's bill when it comes before the legislature

majoritarian democracy (1) the form of democracy in which the majority rules

majority runoff election (13) an election in which a candidate must receive a simple majority of the votes to win; if no candidate receives a simple majority initially, then a runoff is held between the two top vote getters

mandates (3) orders from the national government to the state governments to follow certain policies

marketing (7) a component of contemporary campaigns—the techniques used by campaign consultants to sell their candidate to the voters

material benefit (5) a tangible benefit (a job, money, etc.) that results from membership in a group

mayor - council government (12) a form of city government in which the mayor is the chief executive and has authority over city departments

media (2, 7) the print and broadcast sources of information about political events in society; a component of contemporary campaigns—the use of mass media (print and broadcast) to reach voters during a political campaign

Medicaid (14) a joint state-federal health-care program, available to people with incomes below the poverty level and to medically needy people who have lost their insurance

merit system (12) a system for hiring, promoting, and firing government employees, based on their merit or qualifications

metrogovernment (12) the combination of all local governments in a given area, usually a county, into one governing body

Miranda **warning (13)** a warning issued to accused criminals which informs them of their rights during interrogation—to remain silent, to have an attorney, to have one appointed if indigent, and to advise the accused that any voluntary statements can be used against them in court

Missouri Plan (11) a judicial-selection method that incorporates appointment with nomination by a review committee and a retention election to achieve all three criteria of judicial selection: accountability, independence, and quality

money (7) a component of contemporary campaigns—the possession or access to money as a resource for political campaigns

moralism (1) the response that Americans exhibit when they clearly perceive the gap between the American ideal and the American reality, and they strongly believe in the ideal

motor-voter registration system (7) a system that allows eligible voters to register when they obtain or renew their driver's license.

municipal court (11) local trial court of limited jurisdiction that has jurisdiction over some civil suits and violations of municipal ordinances

municipal incorporation (12) a charter from the state that allows a city to operate as a municipality

Native Americans (2) the original inhabitants of what is now Texas (also called American Indians)

new federalism (3) a theory of federalism that advocates shifting power from the national government to the state governments

nonpartisan election (11) an election in which the candidates' party affiliations are not indicated on the ballot

nonparty legislative caucus (8) a group of legislators organized around some attribute other than party affiliation

nontyranny (1) the condition of democracy requiring that government protect the fundamental rights of every member of the society

Office of State–Federal Relations (9) a state agency, the director of which is appointed by the governor, which serves as a liaison between the two levels of government

open primary (7) a form of primary election in which any registered voter can participate

opposition research (7) research on a candidate's opponent used by campaign consultants to develop negative advertisements during a campaign

ordinances (11) laws created by local governments

original jurisdiction (11) the authority of a court to hear a case for the first time

overrepresentation (9) higher numbers than would be expected from a group in a comparison with that group's numbers in the general population

override (9) the ability of the legislature to cancel a governor's veto by a two-thirds vote in each chamber

partisan election (11) an election in which the candidates' party affiliations appear on the ballot

participation (1) the condition of democracy that requires most citizens to be politically active

party identification (7) a psychological attachment to a political party

party in government (4) the people who are elected and appointed to public office under the party label

party in the electorate (4) the people who identify with a given political party

party organization (4) the people who occupy positions in the political party structure

patronage (9) a system in which party members or friends of the officeholder are rewarded with government employment

penultimate office (9) the last office held prior to the current one

per capita personal income (14) the total personal income of a population divided by number of people in the population

per diem (8) legislators' per day allowance, to cover room-and-board expenses while on state business

permanent party organization (4) the political party structure that operates throughout the year, which includes the party's precinct chairpersons, county chairpersons, executive committee members, and party chairperson and vice chairperson

Permanent School Fund (PSF) (14) a state fund consisting of revenue from state-owned lands (primarily lucrative oil and gas royalties), which is dedicated to public education

Permanent University Fund (PUF) (14) a state fund consisting of revenue from state-owned lands in West Texas (primarily lucrative oil and gas royalties) which is dedicated to higher education

petition for review (11) a request for the Texas Supreme Court to review a decision by a lower court

plural executive (9) an executive branch in which power and policy implementation are divided among several executive agencies rather than centralized under one person; the governor does not get to appoint most agency heads

pluralist democracy (1) the form of democracy in which individual preferences are expressed through groups

plurality election (13) an election in which the candidate with the greatest number of votes wins

policy making (10) the creation of public policies

policy process (10) the process that includes policy making, policy implementation, and policy evaluation

political action committee (PAC) (5) a group formed to influence the election of candidates for public office through campaign contributions

political campaigns (7) the efforts by candidates for public office to pursuade voters to support their candidacies

political connectedness (7) the connection that a person feels to politics

political economy (14) the web of economic, social, governmental, and political institutions and processes

political equality (1) the condition of democracy requiring that each person's political preferences receive equal consideration and that each person has an equal opportunity to develop his or her political preferences

political ideology (2) a set of consistent attitudes and values concerning the scope and purpose of government

political participation (7) any attempt to influence or support government and politics

political socialization (2) the process whereby a person learns the important political attitudes and values of his or her society

political trust (7) the feeling that government makes decisions that are in the best interest of most people

politics (1) the authoritative allocation of values for a society

politics of creedal passion (1) periods of moralism in American politics

poll tax (13) a fee for voting, ostensibly collected to pay for the administrative cost of elections; the effect of the tax was to disenfranchise poor people

populist (2) a person whose political ideology favors equality over individualism and social order over individualism

pork barrel (8) appropriations of money to a project in a single legislative district

precinct chairperson (4) the chairperson of the precinct party structure

precinct convention (4) the meeting of all party members in an electoral precinct; the convention is held on the same day as the primary election, after the polls have closed

preclearance (13) the requirement that the United States Justice Department must give prior approval to any changes proposed in election methods in those jurisdictions covered by the Voting Rights Act

primary election (7) electoral contest to choose a political party's candidates for public office

priming (6) the media's ability to establish the criteria for evaluating politicians

prior restraint (13) the government's prevention of the publication of some information; censorship

privatization (12) the act of turning government functions over to private businesses

pro-tempore (pro-tem) (8) a legislator who temporarily serves as legislative leader in the absence of the Senate president or House speaker

processes (1) how decisions are made and how people can influence opinions

progressive tax (14) a tax in which the percentage of a person's income paid in taxes increases as the person's income increases

promotional spot (7) a short advertisement that promotes the positive qualities and experience of a candidate for public office

proportional representation (12) a system that apportions seats in a legislative body according to the percentage of the vote won by a particular political party

proportional tax (14) a tax in which every person pays the same percentage of his or her income in taxes; *see flat tax*

prospective vote (7) a vote for a candidate for public office based on what the candidate promises to do if she or he is elected

protesters (7) people who use unconventional forms of political participation to influence public policy

public opinion (6) the evaluations of a large number of people on an issue of public policy

public opinion change (6) the media's ability to influence public opinion

public policy (1) the decisions or outputs of government, which include not only laws, executive orders, and judicial decisions, but also the implementation of those laws, orders, and decisions

Public Utility Commission (PUC) (10) a full-time, three-member paid commission appointed by the governor to regulate public utilities in Texas

purposive benefit (5) a benefit that comes from group membership when a particular policy or ideology is advanced

quality in judicial selection (11) a criterion of judicial selection that seeks to ensure that judges are competent

quasi-judicial (10) a government commission that receives petitions from companies or individuals, hears evidence in a hearing similar to a judicial proceeding, and rules on the petition

quorum (8) the minimum number required to conduct business (as in a legislative body)

quotas (13) a mandate that the composition of a group be in proportion to the ethnic, racial, or gender composition of the jurisdiction in which it operates

Railroad Commission (10) a full-time, three-member paid commission elected by the people to regulate oil and gas and some transportation entities

random sample (6) a sample in which every member of a group has an equal chance of being selected

rational-basis test (13) discrimination may be justified by establishing a rational basis; in essence, the state must demonstrate that the relationship between the means (discrimination) and the ends (goal) is rational

rational-basis test, Texas version (13) stricter than the national version, closer to the United States Supreme Court's level of intermediate scrutiny

realignment (4) the switch in party affiliations created by a critical election

redistricting (8) the redrawing of election-district boundaries

regressive tax (14) a tax in which the percentage of a person's income paid in taxes decreases as the person's income increases

regular session (8) the biennial 140-day session of the legislature, beginning in January of odd-numbered years

regulation (14) a government restriction on certain economic activities

rehabilitation (11) a philosophy of criminal justice that stresses reforming a person who is convicted of a crime

representation (8) the authorization for a person to act on another person's behalf, usually granted through an election

response to the ideal-reality gap (1) the four ways that Americans react to the cognitive dissonance resulting from the discrepancy between the American ideal and the American reality

retribution (11) a philosophy of criminal justice that stresses the debt owed to society by a person convicted of a crime

retrospective vote (7) a vote for or against a candidate for public office, based on the candidate's or an opponent's past performance

revenue bonds (12) bonds issued for a special purpose, such as a convention center; the activity generates revenue that pays for the bonds

revenue estimate (14) an estimate, made by the comptroller and given to the legislature, of how much revenue the state will collect in a given biennium

revolving door (10) an exchange of personnel between private interests and public regulators

right-to-work law (3) a provision stating that a person does not have to belong to a union to get a job; states with right-to-work laws are also known as open-shop states

Rodriguez v. San Antonio Independent School District **(14)** the 1973 U.S. Supreme Court case that declared the Texas system of funding public schools did not violate the U.S. Constitution's Fourteenth Amendment

rule making (10) the adoption of standards and processes by which agencies operate and make decisions

sample (6) a smaller group of individuals drawn from a larger group, whose opinions are measured

sampling error (6) the difference between the group's actual opinion and the sample group's opinion that occurs due strictly to chance variations

schema (6) a cognitive structure that people create to organize and process information about a subject

second reading (8) the Texas Constitution requires three readings of a bill by the legislature; the second reading is when the real debate occurs

secretary of state (10) the state official appointed by the governor to be the keeper of the state's records, such as state laws, election data and filings, public notifications, and corporate charters

selective benefit (5) a benefit that is only provided to interest-group members

Senate president (8) the Texas Constitution specifies that the lieutenant governor is the Senate president and presides over the Senate

Senate two-thirds rule (8) the rule in the Texas Senate that requires that every bill win a vote of two-thirds of the senators to suspend the Senate's calendaring rules, so that the bill can be considered

senatorial courtesy (9) a Texas Senate practice that requires the governor to preclear a nominee with the senator in whose district the nominee resides

severance taxes (14) taxes on severing natural resources from the ground

Sharpstown scandal (8) the legislative scandal of 1969–1972, which resulted in a bribery conviction of the House speaker and set the stage for the 1973 session, which passed numerous governmental reforms

simple resolution (8) a legislative resolution that goes through only one chamber, such as the resolution to adopt House rules or a resolution commending a citizen

single-member district election (12) an election in which the jurisdiction is divided into geographic zones; voters may elect one person in each zone and may only vote in the zone in which they live

single-member districts (8, 12) each legislator or local official represents a separate, distinct election district

single-shot voting (13) a group of voters who unite behind a single candidate to maximize the group's influence

social connectedness (7) the interpersonal, community, and general social ties that a person feels

socialization of conflict (8) conflict that is broadened to include a wide array of actors in the public arena

social policy (14) public policies guiding our development as human beings and our relationships to other humans and to our broader environment

solidary benefit (5) a social benefit that comes from membership in a group

speaker's lieutenants (8) House members who make up the speaker's team, assisting the speaker in leading the House

speaker's race (8) the campaign to determine who shall be speaker of the Texas House for a given biennium

speaker's team (8) the leadership team in the House, consisting of the speaker and his or her most trusted allies, who are usually appointed as committee chairs

special district (12) a form of local government usually devoted to a single purpose, possessing specified powers; generically used to refer to both special districts and authorities

special elections (7) elections that are held at times other than primary or general elections

special (or called) session (8) a legislative session of up to 30 days, which is called by the governor

split-ticket voting (7) voting for candidates of different political parties (*see also* **straight ticket voting**).

spoils system (12) a system in which government jobs are awarded on the basis of political connections rather than qualification; *see* **patronage**

staggered terms (10) terms of office for members of boards and commissions that begin and end at different times, so that a governor is not usually able to gain control of a majority of the body for a long time; overlapping terms for public officials

state convention (4) the meeting of political party delegates elected from county and senatorial district conventions

state executive committee (4) the party committee, consisting of 62 members, which makes decisions for the state party between state conventions

state party chairperson (4) the state party leader who is elected by the state convention delegates

statutes (11) laws created by a legislature

statutory constitution (3) a constitution that specifies in detail what the government can and cannot do (see also **ideal constitution**)

straight-ticket voting (7) voting for all the candidates of one political party; an election system that allows a person to vote for all of the candidates of a particular political party with one mark on the ballot (*see also* **split-ticket voting**)

straw candidates (13) candidates for public office who do not intend to win but rather intend to take votes away from another candidate or candidates

strict scrutiny (13) the highest level of review given to a discrimination case by the United States Supreme Court; discrimination must be justified by demonstrating a compelling state interest

subsidy (14) a grant of economic resources

succession (9) the constitutional declaration that the lieutenant governor succeeds to the governorship if there is a vacancy

sunset (10) establishment of a date on which particular agencies will cease to exist

symbiotic relationship (6) a mutually beneficial relationship between two entities

tacit consent (3) informal acceptance of a political or governmental system, usually accomplished simply by continuing to reside in an area

taking a walk (8) leaving a committee hearing or the floor to avoid having to take a vote on a controversial bill, if such a vote would hurt the legislator with one group or another

tax assessor-collector (12) the chief tax collector of a county

tax capacity (14) the amount of revenue that each state could raise if it applied a nationally uniform set of tax rates to a common set of economic activities

tax effort (14) the ratio of tax collections to tax capacity, as measured by a tax-capacity index

Temporary Assistance for Needy Families (TANF) (14) the federal-state cash-assistance program adopted in 1996 (as a part of welfare reform) to replace Aid to Families with Dependent Children (AFDC)

temporary party organization (4) a political party structure that includes conventions at the precinct, county or senatorial district, and state levels

term limits (8) statutory or constitutional limits on the number of terms that a public official may serve in the same office

Texan Creed (2) the ideas that motivate Texas politics, resulting from Texas's historical experiences

Texas Court of Criminal Appeals (11) the highest state court for criminal cases

Texas frontier (2) the experience of Texans with Mexicans, Native Americans, and the environment as they expanded their settlement of Texas

Texas Natural Resource Conservation Commission (TNRCC) (10) a full-time, three-member paid commission appointed by the governor to administer the state's environmental programs

Texas Rangers (2) the mounted militia formed in Texas to create and maintain order on the frontier; currently, the investigative unit of the Department of Public Safety

Texas Supreme Court (11) the highest state court for civil cases

that dog won't hunt (8) a debating point suggesting that the legislator does not believe another member's argument

thematic frame (6) the media frame that places issues in a general or abstract context to illustrate a problem

third reading (8) the Texas Constitution requires three readings of a bill by the legislature; third reading is the final reading, unless the bill returns from the other chamber with amendments

three-part party structure (4) the three components of a political party—party organization, party in government, and party in the electorate

torts (11) the area of civil law that involves a private or civil wrong, such as libel, slander, personal injury, and product liability

tracking polls (7) polls used by campaign consultants to track changes in the voters' preferences during a campaign and to assess the effectiveness of campaign commercials

trial de novo (11) a new trial, required when an appeal is made from a court that does not keep a record of the trial

turnover rate (8) the percentage of a legislature that is represented by newly elected members

unconventional political participation (7) forms of political participation that are less common and that challenge the government

underrepresentation (9) lower numbers than would be expected from a group, in comparison with that group's numbers in the general population

unitary government (3) a form of government in which the states are allowed to do only what the national government permits

unitary primary (7) a form of primary election, which combines the selection of candidates and the election of public officials in one election

unit-road system (12) a system under which all county roads and bridges in a single county would be placed under a single authority

veto (8,9) a governor's action to nullify a newly passed bill

vote dilution (13) the practice of making a person's or a group's vote worth less than another person's or group's vote

voters (7) people whose principal form of political participation is voting in elections

voter turnout (7) a calculation that measures the extent of voter participation in elections, usu-ally calculated as a percentage of age-eligible voters (the number of voters in an election, divided by the number of people 18 years of age or older, multiplied by 100)

vouchers (14) appropriations of public money for use in paying tuition and expenses at private schools

white primary (13) a primary election in which African Americans were excluded

writ of *habeas corpus* (11) a court order directing an official holding a person in custody to bring that person before a court to inquire into whether that person is being held legally

writ of mandamus (11) a court order directing a public official to perform a public duty

writs of error (11) Supreme Court review process replaced by **petition for review**

Photo Credits

Index